Contracts

EXAMPLES & EXPLANATIONS

ASPEN PUBLISHERS

EXAMPLES & EXPLANATIONS

Contracts

Fourth Edition

Brian A. Blum
Professor of Law
Lewis & Clark Law School

Wolters Kluwer
Law & Business

AUSTIN   BOSTON   CHICAGO   NEW YORK   THE NETHERLANDS

Aspen Publishers
Attn: Permissions Department
76 Ninth Avenue, 7th Floor
New York, NY 10011-5201

Printed in the United States of America

1 2 3 4 5 6 7 8 9 0

ISBN 978-0-7355-6241-7

Library of Congress Cataloging-in-Publication Data

Blum, Brian A.
    Contracts: examples & explanations / Brian A. Blum. — 4th ed.
        p. cm.
    Includes bibliographical references and index.
    ISBN 978-0-7355-6241-7 (alk. paper)
    1.   Contracts — United States.   I.   Title.

KF801.B58   2007
346.7302 — dc22

                                                        2007006921

About Wolters Kluwer Law & Business

Wolters Kluwer Law & Business is a leading provider of research information and workflow solutions in key specialty areas. The strengths of the individual brands of Aspen Publishers, CCH, Kluwer Law International and Loislaw are aligned within Wolters Kluwer Law & Business to provide comprehensive, in-depth solutions and expert-authored content for the legal, professional and education markets.

CCH was founded in 1913 and has served more than four generations of business professionals and their clients. The CCH products in the Wolters Kluwer Law & Business group are highly regarded electronic and print resources for legal, securities, antitrust and trade regulation, government contracting, banking, pension, payroll, employment and labor, and health-care reimbursement and compliance professionals.

Aspen Publishers is a leading information provider for attorneys, business professionals and law students. Written by preeminent authorities, Aspen products offer analytical and practical information in a range of specialty practice areas from securities law and intellectual property to mergers and acquisitions and pension/benefits. Aspen's trusted legal education resources provide professors and students with high-quality, up-to-date and effective resources for successful instruction and study in all areas of the law.

Kluwer Law International supplies the global business community with comprehensive English-language international legal information. Legal practitioners, corporate counsel and business executives around the world rely on the Kluwer Law International journals, loose-leafs, books and electronic products for authoritative information in many areas of international legal practice.

Loislaw is a premier provider of digitized legal content to small law firm practitioners of various specializations. Loislaw provides attorneys with the ability to quickly and efficiently find the necessary legal information they need, when and where they need it, by facilitating access to primary law as well as state-specific law, records, forms and treatises.

Wolters Kluwer Law & Business, a unit of Wolters Kluwer, is headquartered in New York and Riverwoods, Illinois. Wolters Kluwer is a leading multinational publisher and information services company.

To Helen, Matt, Nicole, Shelley, and Trevor
with love

Summary of Contents

Summary of Contents

Contents

Contents

Chapter 3. The Doctrine of Precedent and a Contract Case Analysis   35

Chapter 4. The Objective Test and Common Law Offer and Acceptance   51

Contents

Chapter 7. Consideration

Chapter 10. Interpretation and Construction: Resolving Meaning and Dealing with Uncertainty in Agreements   267

Chapter 11. The Statute of Frauds   317

Chapter 12.   The Parol Evidence Rule   347

Chapter 13. The Judicial Regulation of Improper Bargaining and of Violations of Law and Public Policy   385

Contents

Chapter 14. Incapacity   453

Chapter 15. Mistake, Impracticability, and Frustration of Purpose   473

Chapter 16. Conditions and Promises   517

Chapter 17. Breach and Repudiation   573

Chapter 18. Remedies for Breach of Contract 627

Contents

Chapter 19. Assignment, Delegation, and Third-Party Beneficiaries   **719**

Contents

Preface

I expect that most readers of this book will be first-year law students who will use it as a resource to assist in learning and understanding the law of contracts — to prepare for class, to unravel and supplement class materials and discussion, and to review and prepare for exams. In deciding on the scope, depth, and approach of the book's coverage, I have aimed at their needs. My focus has been on what is likely to be most appropriate and helpful to a person who approaches contract law as a novice and is trying to assimilate and understand not only the details, but also the larger issues of this complex subject.

In revising this book for its fourth edition, I have renewed my efforts to provide an accessible and helpful treatment of the law of contracts. I have not changed the focus or approach of the prior editions, nor the extent or nature of its coverage. Instead, I have concentrated on matters of detail, altering text and diagrams to the extent necessary to update the materials and to add clarity, providing fresh examples and explanations and cases, and changing or removing those original examples and explanations that called for refinement.

The Treatment of the Sale of Goods in the Fourth Edition: The Revisions of UCC Articles 1 and 2

Article 2 of the Uniform Commercial Code (UCC), which governs contracts for the sale of goods, is an important part of the contracts course. In recent years, there have been two significant changes to the UCC as it relates to sales of goods. Article 1 was revised in 2001 and Article 2 in 2003. At the time of writing this edition, revised Article 1 has been adopted by about half the states. No state has yet adopted revised Article 2. (The nature of the UCC and the process of revising and enacting it are explained in section 2.7.1.) This means there are two forms of each of these Articles. In some states, the older version of one or both is still the law, while others have adopted or may soon adopt the revision. Different contracts courses focus on one or the other or both versions. To ensure that this book will be helpful no matter which version of Articles 1 and 2 you study, this edition accommodates both. Whenever either Article is discussed, both versions are cited and there is an explanation of any differences between them.

The Style, Approach, and Purpose of This Book

Like many other law school courses, contract law is typically taught by means of discussing and debating cases and other materials that have been assigned for reading in advance of the class session. A terrible flood of information is unleashed by this process, and few students can assimilate and appreciate it all by simply studying the casebook and listening in class. Supplementary reading is indispensable to understanding and digesting what is covered in class. To be most useful, such a supplementary text should be written with an awareness of the coverage, depth, and scope of most contracts courses, and with a sense of what students are likely to need by way of additional reading. In writing this book, I have tried to keep that goal in mind. Relying on my own experience as a teacher of contract law, and on the content of casebooks, I have tried to maintain the discussion in this book at the level that may be expected in a typical contracts class.

To achieve this purpose, it is not enough to outline legal rules or to state doctrine. Although it is surely one of the aims of a contracts class to teach the current rules of law governing contracts, a knowledge of current legal rules is only one of the components of an adequate understanding of contract law. Students are also expected to learn the derivation and development of the rules, their historical and contemporary rationale, the public policies that they are meant to serve, and the way in which they coalesce to form a coherent body of law. Because neither rules nor their underlying policies are static, and are often unsettled and the subject of controversy, students must also be exposed to the uncertainties of the law and must learn to develop the ability to evaluate critically and to form judgments. In addition, like so many other courses in law school, a contracts course serves the goal of exposing students to broader issues of legal process, legal analysis, dispute resolution, and lawyering skills such as drafting, advising, and evaluating the strength of a case. This book attempts to encompass this range of learning.

Although this book contains much textual discussion of the rules and policies of contract law and of the themes mentioned above, it is not a traditional treatise. Its purpose is not to provide a highly detailed and comprehensive exposition of the law of contracts, with exhaustive citation of authority. Its principal aim is the clear and accessible explanation of the fundamentals of the law, with a particular concentration on what information is likely to be helpful to a student who approaches the subject for the first time. For this reason, it tries to articulate assumptions and to express doctrine and policy accurately, while avoiding finicky distinctions and qualifications that are more likely to confuse than to elucidate.

As part of the effort to clarify legal principles and the relationships between contracting parties, I have used diagrams extensively. I believe that visual representations can be a great help in clarifying and reinforcing verbal exposition.

The Use of Examples and Explanations

It is difficult to learn the law by studying abstract principle. Concrete examples are needed to place doctrine in context and to show how it operates to affect behavior and to resolve disputes. Examples are therefore used extensively in the text itself to illustrate concepts under discussion. In addition, a distinctive feature of this book is the use of "examples and explanations," which take up a substantial part of each chapter. Their purpose is not only to provide further illustration and discussion of the subject matter of the text, but also to give students a means of self-testing on the topics covered. The examples pose questions based on hypothetical facts, and the explanations analyze and offer a resolution of the problems. As a general rule, the examples and explanations do more than simply provide a means of reviewing what has been stated in the text. To resolve them adequately, one must use reasoned argument and must thoughtfully apply the principles set out in the text. You will therefore benefit the most from them if you do not merely read through them, but rather take the time to formulate your own answer to an example before reading its explanation. This will allow you to test your knowledge and understanding of the material, to practice identifying issues, and to develop skills in composing and organizing answers to the kind of questions commonly found in exams.

The Organization of This Book in Relation to Your Contracts Course

There are a number of different ways to organize a contracts course, and the casebooks reflect quite a diverse approach to the sequence in which material may be covered in class. It is therefore quite possible that your contracts course will not follow the same sequence as the chapters in this book. (For example, some courses begin with remedies for breach of contract, which is not covered here until Chapter 18, and some begin with consideration doctrine, which is not reached until Chapter 7.) This book has been written with an eye on the divergent ways in which the topics of contract law are presented in class, so a student should have no trouble reading chapters out of order. To use this book in the same sequence as your contracts course, simply refer to the table of contents or index to find the part of the book that deals with the subject under discussion in class. Cross-references are included in each chapter to help give you an idea of where to find allied topics or further reference to the subject under discussion.

A Recommendation About Chapters 1 Through 3 and the Glossary

Irrespective of the organization of your class, I do recommend, however, that you read Chapters 1, 2, and 3 as soon as possible. These short chapters are intended as an introduction to some of the root principles of contract law and legal analysis. They contain basic information and guidance on core concepts, terminology, and case analysis that may not be articulated fully or at all in your class materials or discussion. A little time spent in working through these chapters at the beginning of the semester may save you needless puzzlement and confusion. Also, you should refer to the glossary at the end of the book for short definitions of terms that may be unfamiliar to you.

The Use and Citation of Authority in This Book

To make this book as readable and accessible as possible, I have kept citation of authority to a minimum. You will find none of the detailed footnotes and citations that you would expect in a treatise or law review article. However, some sources of authority are such an integral part of the process of learning contract law that to omit them would impede understanding. These sources are referred to constantly throughout the book. They are:

1. The RESTATEMENT (SECOND) OF CONTRACTS (referred to in the book in abbreviated form as Restatement Second), a compendious and highly influential formulation of the rules of contract law.
2. Articles 1 and 2 of the Uniform Commercial Code (UCC). Article 2 governs contracts for the sale of goods and is the principal focus of our study of the UCC. Article 1 is supplementary to Article 2. It has general provisions applicable to all Articles or the UCC, including Article 2.
3. Caselaw. Court opinions are a vital source of law in our system. I discuss cases selectively but regularly in the text and also, to a lesser extent, in the explanations. I do not use cases merely as authority for legal rules, but as factual illustrations and as a means of highlighting legal principles, argument, and reasoning. I selected many of the cases in this book because of their interesting or even entertaining facts. I have tried to use recent cases wherever possible to reflect the law in its contemporary state. However, there are many important or well-known older cases that are taught in almost every contracts course, and I have included those too. I have also kept an eye on the content of casebooks and have made a point of mentioning some of the cases that have been chosen by casebook authors. You should therefore find that at least some of the cases discussed here are familiar from class.

Brian A. Blum
February 2007

Acknowledgments

I owe thanks to many people who have helped me with successive editions of this book. I have had able research assistance from a number of Lewis & Clark law students for each edition of this book. I have also benefitted from the guidance and careful editorial work of several members of the staff of Aspen Publishers. Finally, I am grateful to the many students and professors who have used this book and who have offered comments and suggestions.

CHAPTER 1

The Meaning of "Contract" and the Basic Attributes of the Contractual Relationship

§1.1 INTRODUCTION

Some contracts courses may begin with material that provides students with background information on the law of contracts. Others may launch immediately into the study of substantive principles of contract law. Whatever form your contracts course takes, you may find it helpful to read the first three chapters of this book right at the beginning of your course. They introduce and articulate basic concepts about contract law and our legal system that you will find very helpful as you begin your studies. Many of the principles and concepts introduced in these three initial chapters will appear frequently throughout the book, so this will not be the only time that you read about them. However, this first encounter will set the stage for your studies and will enable you to begin to understand legal analysis and identify themes that run through contract law. You will find immediately that the discussion goes well beyond the exposition of rules of law. Even if one assumes that it is possible to articulate a clear and settled body of rules (an assumption that you will quickly find to be false), the rules are just one component of what needs to be studied in learning the law. Rules do not exist in a vacuum, but must be understood in light of historical perspective, public policy, legal theory, and the legal process.

We begin our introductory survey in this chapter by defining what is meant by a contract. This discussion gives you a brief overview of a number of the central themes of contract law and it broadly sketches the contractual relationship. Chapter 2 describes some of the fundamental concepts and distinctions that are essential to a comprehension of contract law in the context of our legal system as a whole. It explains the importance of historical perspective and legal theory, describes the nature of our common law system, and introduces the crucial distinction between judge-made law and statutory law, with particular reference to the statute that pervades contract law, Article 2 of the Uniform Commercial Code (UCC). Chapter 3 concentrates on the nature and composition of judicial opinions and on the method of analyzing and gleaning legal rules from them. Its primary purpose is to explain the doctrine of precedent as it applies in contract law and in our legal system as a whole. The Examples in Chapter 3 offer a specimen opinion, constructed to provide an exercise in reading, understanding, and applying the precedent of a judicial decision. Because contract law is commonly taught through the study of court decisions, you will become familiar with the methodology of case analysis as you use it throughout the contracts course. However, Chapter 3 provides an early opportunity for you to focus on and to begin to understand how to approach caselaw and case analysis.

§1.2 THE LEGAL MEANING OF "CONTRACT"

By the time they reach law school, most people have a good idea of what a contract is. Nevertheless, lay usage of a legal term such as "contract" is likely to be less exacting than the legal definition, and so we must begin by defining and describing the elements of contract. It is not easy to provide a simple and accurate definition of a legal relationship as complex as contract, and the following definition is necessarily an oversimplification. However, it serves as a starting point for discussion and allows us to focus on the crucial elements of the relationship.

A contract may be defined as an **exchange relationship** created by oral or written **agreement** between **two or more persons**, containing at least one **promise**, and recognized in law as **enforceable**. This definition reflects several essential elements:

1. An oral or written agreement between two or more persons
2. An exchange relationship
3. At least one promise
4. Enforceability

The central concept of each of these elements is introduced below and will be returned to in greater detail later in the book.

§1.2.1 An Oral or Written Agreement Between Two or More Persons

Probably the most important attribute of contract is that it is a voluntary, consensual relationship. There need only be two parties to a contract, but there is no limit on the number of parties that could be involved in the transaction. A contract is created only because the parties, acting with free will and intent to be bound, reach agreement on the essential terms of their relationship. It is the element of agreement that distinguishes contractual obligation from many other kinds of legal duty (such as the obligation to compensate for negligent injury or to pay taxes) that arise by operation of law from some act or event, without the need for assent.

Although voluntary agreement between the parties is essential to the creation of contract, "agreement" in the legal sense is subject to an important qualification. The law does not require that the parties reach true agreement, in a **subjective** sense—that their minds are in accord. It is enough that the words and conduct of a party, evaluated on an **objective** standard, would lead the other party reasonably to understand that agreement was reached. (The reason for using this objective standard is explained in sections 1.4.3 and 4.1.) Also, **volition** should not be taken too literally. We assume that a party may not be acting with completely free will in entering into a contract. He may feel some compulsion to make the contract as a result of market forces, the persuasiveness of the other party, necessity, or the lack of a more attractive alternative. However, volition does at least mean that a party cannot be improperly coerced or tricked into making a contract, and the law has principles and standards (covered in Chapters 13 and 14) to distinguish when pressure to make a contract is no longer acceptable, and has so undermined the party's will as to defeat his volition.

Note that our definition refers to an **oral or written** agreement. In common terminology, people often use the word "contract" to refer to a written document that records the parties' agreement. However, it is important to understand that "contract" describes a relationship that may not be recorded in a document. As a general rule, a contract does not have to be in writing to be a binding and enforceable legal obligation. (Under a legal rule called the **statute of frauds**, there are some types of contract that must be recorded in a signed writing to be enforceable. This is discussed in Chapter 11. However, most contracts are not covered by the statute of frauds, and are binding as soon as oral agreement has been reached.) Of course, it may be harder to prove an oral contract than one that has been recorded in writing, but do not confuse problems of proof with the more fundamental question of enforceability.

§1.2.2 An Exchange Relationship

As mentioned earlier, a contract is a *relationship*. By entering into the agreement, the parties bind themselves to each other for the common purpose of the contract. Some contractual relationships last only a short time and require minimal interaction. For example, a contract for a haircut involves a fairly quick performance by the hairdresser, followed by the fulfillment of the customer's payment obligation. Other contractual relationships, such as leases or long-term employment or supply contracts, could span many years and require constant dealings between the parties, regulated by detailed provisions in the agreement.

The essential purpose of the contract relationship is *exchange*. The trade in property, services, and intangible rights is fundamental to our economy and society, and the primary function of contract is to facilitate and regulate these exchanges. The concept of exchange (discussed more fully in Chapter 7) means that the very essence of contract is a *reciprocal* relationship in which each party gives up something to get something. These "somethings" are as varied as one could imagine: The owner of a car could sell it for cash or barter it for other goods; a celebrity's butler may promise to reveal his employer's dark secrets to a tabloid for cold hard cash; an inventor may trade the rights to her idea for a promise by a manufacturer to develop the idea for mutual profit; a fond uncle may promise his nephew money in exchange for an undertaking not to drink, smoke, and gamble. These situations vary greatly. Some involve tangible things, others intangible rights. Some of the promises have economic value, others do not. Yet their basic format is the same — a bargain has been reached leading to a reciprocal exchange for the betterment (real or perceived) of both parties.

As discussed in Chapters 7, 8, and 9, the modern concept of contract embraces some transactions in which exchange in the traditional sense is tenuous. Nevertheless, exchange continues to be the principal motivation for contracting and the guiding rationale for the rules of contract law.

§1.2.3 Promise

Because a contract is a relationship, the law of contracts is not concerned with passing encounters that do not create relationships. Instantaneous exchanges, although they are consensual and do involve a trade, do not constitute contracts. For a contract to exist, there must be a **promise** — that is, some commitment for the future, some assumption of liability lasting beyond the instant of agreement. This is because if neither party makes a commitment, there is nothing to enforce and no need for the law of contracts to be concerned with the exchange.

The concept of promise or commitment needs explanation and refinement. A promise is an **undertaking to act or refrain from acting** in a specified way at some **future** time. This promise may be made in clear and **express** words, or it could be **implied** — that is, inferred from conduct or from the circumstances of the transaction. Furthermore, as the definition indicates, only one promise needs to be made for a contract to come into existence. It may sound a little odd to say this, having just characterized contract as a reciprocal relationship. However, this does not detract from the principle of reciprocity because one party may exchange an instantaneous performance (and hence make no promise) for a promise of future action by the other.[1]

The following illustration shows the distinction between an instantaneous exchange (also called an executed exchange) and a contract: Rocky Rapids decided to sell his kayak. He placed it on the sidewalk in front of his house with a sign that read "For sale, as is. $400."[2] Eddy Undertow saw the sign and decided to buy the kayak. He handed over $400 in cash to Rocky and took the kayak away. This is an instantaneous exchange and therefore not a contract. Eddy paid cash and made no promise to do anything else. Rocky's legal obligation was completely performed as soon as he let Eddy take the kayak. He also made no promises.

However, the transaction would have been a contract either if Eddy had given a check to Rocky for $400 instead of cash, or if Rocky had not sold the kayak "as is," but had instead assured Eddy that it was in good condition and watertight. In each of these situations, at least one of the parties would have made a promise. Eddy's check would be a promise because a check is not an immediate payment, but a short-term credit transaction in which Eddy, in effect, promises Rocky that his bank will pay Rocky the $400 on presentation of the check. Likewise, had Rocky given a warranty, he would have made a future commitment relating to the kayak.

§1.2.4 Legal Recognition of Enforceability

The previous section made the point that an agreement without a promise is not a contract. However, when a promise does exist, so that contract comes into being, it is the fundamental role of contract law to ensure that the

---

1. Where at the instance of contracting, promises remain outstanding on both sides, the contract is called bilateral. If one of the parties has already fully performed at the instant of contracting, and all that remains is a promise by the other, the contract is called unilateral. Do not worry about this distinction now. It is explored in section 4.12.

2. The words "as is" in a sale transaction mean that the goods are sold without any warranty from the seller as to their condition or quality. The creation and disclaimer of warranties is a complex topic, beyond our scope. Assume for the purposes of this discussion that the "as is" disclaimer eliminated any warranty that might otherwise apply and that Rocky made no other promise.

promise is upheld. The importance of this task cannot be stressed too strongly. In a world in which promises were not taken seriously, only instantaneous exchanges could occur. There could be no building, manufacturing, stable employment, or frequent flyer programs. The resulting wasteland would be far worse than any portrayed in the nastiest post-apocalyptic science fiction movie.

Contracting is often described as an act of **private lawmaking** by which persons create a kind of personalized "statute" to govern their relationship. One can only envisage contract as private legislation if it has the attribute of any law — **recognition and enforcement** through the **compulsive power of the state**, acting through its **courts**. It is therefore a hallmark of contract that it creates law binding on the parties and confers on them rights and obligations cognizable in law.

Of course, this does not mean that a party has to resort to the compulsive power of the law in every contractual relationship. In most cases, parties to contracts perform because they want to. They voluntarily entered the transaction because they desired its benefits, and nothing has happened to change this. Even in cases when the exchange has become less desirable or more burdensome, a party may still make the effort to perform as promised out of a sense of moral duty or because it values its reputation for reliability or the goodwill of the other party. Sometimes the power of legal enforcement has an indirect influence in deterring breach, because a reluctant party knows that failure of performance could result in litigation.

However, in those cases in which the promise is broken, the power of legal enforcement enables the disappointed party to sue. In the first instance, the role of the court is to adjudicate any questions concerning the existence of a valid contract and to resolve any disputes over its terms and their breach. Once it is established that a contract was entered into and breached, the court will enforce it by giving a **remedy** for the breach. This leads us to consider a vital and pervasive issue in contract law — the determination of what remedy is available to the victim of a breach. The most obvious form of remedy may seem to be for the court to force the breacher to do what was promised. For example, say that Eddy did not give immediate possession of the kayak to Rocky but promised to deliver it the next day in exchange for $400 cash. The next day, when Rocky arrived with the $400 in hand, Eddy said he had changed his mind and refused to go through with the sale. This is a breach of the contract. If Rocky sued Eddy, one might assume that the primary mode of legal enforcement of the contract would be a court order compelling Eddy to hand over the kayak against payment of the $400.

However, it is a firm principle of contract law (for reasons explained in Chapter 18) that the primary remedy for breach of contract is not such **specific enforcement** of the promise. An order compelling performance is available in only exceptional situations. Rather, it is a judgment awarding

compensatory damages to the disappointed party. That is, the disappointed party must prove that the breach caused financial loss, and the court will award judgment against the breacher to compensate for that financial loss. Thus, Rocky would have to show that he had lost money as a result of the breach. For example, he may testify that following Eddy's refusal to deliver, he sought to buy another kayak of a similar type and condition, and could not find one of equivalent quality for less than $450. Rocky's damages are $50. The court will award him a money judgment in this amount. If Eddy fails to pay the judgment voluntarily, Rocky will attempt to recover the debt through a process called **execution**. Under this procedure, a court official (usually called a **sheriff**) is commanded by the court (in a document called a **writ**) to try to seize property of Eddy's and to sell it at public auction to raise the money needed to satisfy the judgment. If the sheriff is unable to find any property, the judgment debt remains unsatisfied. There is little further that can be done.

The purpose of sketching this enforcement process here is to make the point that legal enforcement seldom entails judicial compulsion of performance. In most cases, the plaintiff's victory in court is nothing more than a determination that the defendant owes him a stated amount of money. This does not end the matter because the plaintiff now has to collect the debt. If the breacher has no means of paying the judgment, the process of trying to enforce the contract could involve additional cost and inconvenience, and still end in frustration. This is an important perspective to take with you as you begin to study the law of contracts.

§1.3 CONTRACT AS A GENERAL BODY OF LAW APPLICABLE TO DIVERSE TRANSACTIONS

Contract law covers a wide range of very different transactions — leases and sales of real and personal property, employment, credit, insurance, construction, and so on. These many and diverse types of contract each have their own attributes and concerns, so it stands to reason that there cannot be a single and uniform body of legal rules that applies to all of them. With each type of contract, special rules develop to respond to distinct features of the transaction or particular needs or issues in the commercial context. For example, a whole body of law has developed to protect consumers who purchase goods or seek credit and is not applicable when the purchaser or borrower is a commercial entity; employment contracts are subject to rules designed to protect the rights of workers; a construction or procurement contract with the government is subject to regulations not found elsewhere;

insurance and banking contracts are also controlled by specific regulations. This recital could continue for some length. Although each of these categories of contract has its specialized rules, they all share common ground and are based on similar general principles that are encompassed within a general law of contracts.

The law of contracts is the common core of rules and principles applicable to all contracts and it governs except to the extent that it has been varied by laws specific to the transaction. This specific law may have been created by statute or by judicial decision, or both. You will therefore find, as you read through this book and your class materials, that all kinds of different contracts are considered. In most cases, because we are considering this common core of rules and principles, the type of contract involved is not of overwhelming significance. The law discussed is usually relevant to other types of contract. However, this is not always so, and one must always be on the lookout for variations, whether statutory or judge-made, based upon the particular features of the contract in issue.

§1.4 THE FUNDAMENTAL POLICIES AND VALUES OF CONTRACT LAW

Although contract law is not usually at the center of political debate and contracts professors are almost never invited to discuss their work on talk shows, it would be a mistake to think of it as purely technical and bloodless. There are a number of strongly held ideological values at the bottom of contract law and its rules are motivated by conscious and deliberate public policy. Some aspects of the ideology and policy of contract law have already been intimated in section 1.2 and they will be raised throughout the book. An understanding of the law's basic goals and assumptions is essential to a full appreciation of legal rules and so it is useful to identify and articulate significant policy themes from the outset. This section introduces them briefly.

§1.4.1 Freedom of Contract

The consensual and voluntary nature of contract was stressed in section 1.3. The power to enter contracts and to formulate the terms of the contractual relationship is regarded in our legal system as an exercise of **individual autonomy**—an integral part of personal liberty. The converse is also true: Because contracting is an exercise of personal liberty, no one may be bound in contract in the absence of that person's assent. In the United States, the power of contracting has been elevated to a status higher than that accorded it under English common law because it is guaranteed by the Constitution. (The due process clause, U.S. Const. amends. V and XIV, and the contracts clause, U.S. Const. art. 1 §10, provide the constitutional safeguards of liberty of contract.)

Liberty of contract is augmented by another right protected by the due process clause — the right to hold and deal with property. Contracts involve the exchange of economic values, whether in the form of tangible property, services, or intangible rights. These are property rights and the power to use or dispose of them, or to choose not to do so necessarily brings into play their constitutional protection. Furthermore, where the contract involves the rendition of personal services by an individual, that person's right to dispose of her labor or to withhold it unless she wishes to dispose of it is protected by the prohibition on involuntary servitude in the Thirteenth Amendment. The ideological basis of contract freedom is reinforced by the *pragmatic consideration* that economic intercourse is most efficient when its participants desire it and are free to bargain with each other to reach mutually desirable terms.

While freedom of contract is a fundamental value, the exercise of this freedom by one person cannot be untrammelled. Like other liberties, it is **delimited by corresponding rights** held by **other persons**, and by the **state's legitimate interest** in appropriate **regulation**. It stands to reason that the absolute exercise of contract freedom by a dominant party will diminish or defeat the exercise of similar freedom by the weaker party. To avoid this happening, the courts or legislature must provide rules that protect the weaker party from being overwhelmed by the free exercise of contractual power by the stronger. Therefore, for example, a large insurance company or an employer may have its freedom of action curtailed so that it cannot impose harsh or one-sided terms on an insured or an employee. The problem of dealing with the imbalance of contract power and other aspects of unfair imposition is dealt with fully in Chapter 13.

Quite apart from the problem of ensuring a proper balance in the contractual freedom of the parties, the state may have an important interest in reaching an accommodation between freedom of contract and other fundamental values. For example, policies prohibiting criminal enterprise, protecting the environment, or forbidding anticompetitive behavior may require restrictions on the right to make certain contracts or on including certain terms in them. Once again, these issues will be discussed in detail later. For the present it is enough to note that while contract liberty is an important value, it is subject to a variety of limitations that are justified either by the protection of corresponding rights in other persons or by the demands of other public interests.

§1.4.2 The Morality of Promise — *Pacta Sunt Servanda*

The Latin maxim *pacta sunt servanda* (agreements must be kept) comes from Canon law.[3] It reflects a longstanding moral dimension of contract in our law — that there is an **ethical** as well as a legal **obligation** to **keep one's contractual promises**. Contracts should be honored not only because reliability is necessary to foster economic interaction, as discussed in section 1.4.3, but simply because it is morally wrong to break them. The role that this basic moral value plays in contract law is subtle. You will see later that courts and scholars often underplay the moral aspect of keeping promises and deal with breach of contract in purely economic terms. It is often suggested, for example, that breach of contract is an acceptable economic choice, provided that the breacher pays monetary compensation. Nevertheless, it would be a mistake to assume that society or courts are indifferent to the ethical implications of dishonoring contracts. Courts do react with express disfavor to deliberate breaches, particularly if motivated by bad faith, and rules of law have developed to cater at least to the more extreme situations. Even where no moral judgment is articulated, the choice of applicable rules sometimes reflects disapprobation of wrongful conduct. Outside of the realm of litigation, social pressure and business relationships frequently provide disincentives to treat contractual undertakings in a cavalier fashion.

§1.4.3 Accountability for Conduct and Reliance

The objective test of assent was introduced in section 1.2. In determining whether or not a person agreed to a contract or specific contractual terms, the person's manifested conduct by words or action is given more weight than her testimony about her actual intentions. An emphasis on the objective appearance of assent is important not only because of **evidentiary** considerations (that is, it is easier to prove because it is observable) but also because one of the fundamental values of contract law is that a person should be held accountable for words or acts reasonably manifesting intent to contract, and that the other party, acting reasonably, should be entitled to rely on that manifestation of assent. (Note that the perception of the conduct by the other party is also subject to an objective test of reasonableness. One who places an unreasonable and idiosyncratic interpretation on conduct has no right to expect protection of that unreasonable reliance.)

---

3. Canon law is a system of ecclesiastical law developed from Roman law by the medieval Catholic church. Although it is not part of the English common law, it existed as a parallel system in England, governing matters within the Church's jurisdiction, until the English Church broke away from Rome. As a result of their long period of co-existence, many principles of Canon law influenced the common law.

Thus, the principles of accountability and reliance qualify the value of voluntariness — volition is not measured by the true and actual state of mind of a party, but by that state of mind as made apparent to the outside world. Even if a person does not really wish to enter a contract, if she behaves as if the contract is desired and intended, that conduct is binding, and evidence of any mental reservation is likely to be disregarded. (Of course, this rule is not absolute. As we see later, where the manifestation of assent is induced by trickery, coercion, or other illegitimate means, there are grounds for going behind it.)

The value of protecting reasonable reliance is pervasive in contract law. It has both a specific and a general aspect. It is **specific** in that a person who has entered a contract has the right to rely on the undertakings that have been given. If they are breached, the law must enforce them. It is **general** because when parties in numerous specific situations feel secure in relying on promises, the expectation arises in society as a whole that contracts can be relied on, and that legal recourse is available for breach. This general sense of reliance, sometimes called **"security of contracts"** or **"security of transactions,"** is indispensable to economic interaction. If it did not exist, there would be little incentive to make contracts, which would not be worth the paper on which they are written.

In summary, accountability for conduct that induces reasonable reliance is a vital goal of contract law. This is tempered by the consideration that in some cases manifested conduct is induced by illegitimate means, and one who uses such means cannot truly be regarded as having relied on the apparent assent.

§1.4.4 Social Justice and the Protection of the Underdog

It has already been suggested, in connection with both freedom of contract and reliance, that modern contract law is sensitive to the imposition of contractual obligations as a result of coercion, dishonesty, or lack of meaningful choice resulting from power imbalance. Much of the material later in the book deals with the issue of balancing freedom of contract and accountability for manifested conduct against the need to protect vulnerable parties from unfair imposition. Because this is so pervasive a concern, it should at least be acknowledged in this overview of contract policy.

§1.4.5 Fairness

Fairness is such a loose concept that it cannot be discussed in the abstract. The fairness of any result can only be measured in the context of societal standards and expectations. In the contract setting, it must also be evaluated in light of the various goals and policies mentioned in this section. Nevertheless, it would be remiss not to at least draw to your attention that courts do not mechanically apply rules of law. Judges and juries are sensitive to the equities of individual cases and the circumstances of the parties, and where a mechanical application of rules achieves a result that seems to be unjust, there is likely to be some adjustment or even manipulation of the rule to avoid it.

Contract law has some express doctrines that address the question of unfairness, such as the doctrines of unconscionability and good faith. However, even where there is no clear and specific doctrine, you will find many cases in which the court's desire (and duty) to achieve a just result may have the effect of diverting or evading a resolution called for by a doctrinaire approach to the issues.

§1.4.6 The Economic Aspect of Contract Law

Because contracts are concerned with economic exchanges, contract law must inevitably be quintessentially economic in its purpose. Its goal is to facilitate trade and commerce, to regulate the manner in which people deal with each other in the marketplace, and to enforce commercial obligations. It should therefore be no surprise that this body of law, concerned with economic relationships, should respond to and reflect the prevailing economic conditions and philosophy. In the United States, this basic philosophy has always been *capitalist* and geared towards the ideal of a *free market*. Indeed, the political value of freedom of contract is directly related to this economic ideology.

The extent to which market forces should be allowed to reign free, and the degree to which the courts or legislature should regulate them is a source of ongoing debate between so-called "conservative" and "liberal" economists, and the relative influence of one or the other of these schools of thought tends to dominate during particular periods and in particular jurisdictions. Contemporary contract law has tended to move away from the strong laissez-faire approach of the late nineteenth and early twentieth centuries, but there continues to be a lively exchange of views between those who stress economic values such as **efficiency** and those who advocate a greater emphasis on other **social or moral values**. The concept of economic efficiency and its balancing against other values is raised in several parts of this book but is most strongly featured in the discussion of remedies in Chapter 18. The point to be made in this introductory note is that economic considerations are likely to be intertwined with the other goals and aspirations set out here.

Examples

Claire Basement held a garage sale at her home last Saturday. She placed price tags on all the items offered for sale and set them out in her garage and on her driveway. She posted a large sign at the front of her property proclaiming "Mammoth garage sale! All sales are final. All items sold as is." The sign was prominent and was undisputedly seen and understood by all buyers before they made their purchases.

Claire entered into the following transactions. Based on the attributes of contract in section 1.1, which of them appear to qualify as contracts? (Note that with the exception of the first, all the transactions below relate to sales of goods. They would therefore be subject to Article 2 of the Uniform Commercial Code. This statute is introduced in section 2.7 and will be referred to frequently throughout the book. However, you do not need to apply it or to know about it to answer these questions.)

1. On the morning of the sale, Claire realized that she would need some help. She saw her neighbor in his front yard, called him over and offered him $50 if he would assist her at the sale for the day. The neighbor agreed to do so provided that Claire paid him in advance. Claire gave him $50 in cash and he immediately took up position in the garage, waiting for the first customer.

2. Customer 1 picked out a sofa priced at $50. He gave Claire a $50 bill, loaded the sofa onto his pickup, and drove away.

3. Would the answer to Example 2 change if Customer 1 had given Claire a check for $50 rather than cash?

4. Customer 2 bought a large fish tank for $45 and paid cash to Claire. Because the tank was heavy, Customer 2 reversed her pickup onto Claire's driveway so that she would not have to carry it far. In backing the vehicle onto the driveway, she failed to notice a table of glassware, which she knocked over, smashing the table and all the glass. Claire claims that Customer 2 has bought the glass in accordance with the well-known maxim "You break, you take." Does this seem like a fair argument?

5. Customer 3 liked a lamp but wanted his wife to see it before he bought it. He asked Claire to set it aside and not to sell it before he could return with his wife. Claire obliged and placed the lamp in the house. Customer 3 never returned. By removing the lamp from the sale, Claire lost the opportunity of selling it to someone else. Does Customer 3 have a contractual obligation to Claire?

6. Customer 4 expressed interest in buying a stereo for $300. He had no car, and could not take the stereo away. He and Claire therefore agreed that

Claire would deliver it to his home at the end of the day and would collect his payment at the same time.

7. At the end of the day, Claire had a pile of things that had not been sold. She called a charitable thrift store and offered to donate these items. The store agreed to accept them and Claire promised to drop them off at the store on Monday.

Explanations

1. Claire's agreement with her neighbor satisfies all the attributes of contract: The two of them agreed to enter into a relationship in which Claire exchanged money for the neighbor's services. (The example does not make it clear exactly what these services entailed, but the issue of determining the precise terms of the relationship is deferred for now.) Claire's performance was instantaneous — it was complete at the time of contact, and she has no future commitment. However, the neighbor's performance, by its nature, cannot be performed instantaneously but will last the whole day. Therefore, at the time of contracting the neighbor has made a commitment — a promise. For a contract to exist, it is sufficient that only one of the parties has made a promise.

2. Both Customer 1 and Claire have performed instantaneously — delivery of the goods was exchanged for payment of the cash. Because there are no outstanding obligations at the time of agreement, this is not a contract. (Claire would have assumed an obligation if she had warranted the sofa, but she did not. She did not expressly give any warranty, and her sign on the lawn made it clear that all goods were sold as is. This should be enough to preclude any warranty.)[4]

3. The answer would change if Customer 1 had paid by check. Unlike cash, a check is not a completed act of payment but merely an instruction by Customer 1 to his bank to pay Claire upon presentation of the check. In other words, this is a credit transaction in which Customer 1 impliedly promises that funds will be available to pay the check when it is deposited. Customer 1 has therefore made a future commitment, which makes this a contract.

4. The purchase of the fish tank is another instantaneous exchange. With regard to the broken table and glassware, Claire argues, in effect, that custom creates an implied contract to pay for broken goods. It is possible

---

4. The possibility of a warranty and its disclaimer was also raised in the illustration in section 1.2.3 involving Rocky's sale of his kayak to Eddy. Assume here, as you did there, that the disclaimer effectively excluded any warranty.

for a contract to arise by implication from conduct in light of well-accepted custom or usage. If Claire can prove such a custom (which must be done by witnesses who qualify as experts in the field of activity) she may be able to establish an implied contract, even though there is no express exchange agreement. More likely, if Customer 2 has any liability to Claire, it is for negligence in tort, based on her failure to exercise care in reversing her truck.

5. It may sound as if a contract was created between Claire and Customer 3, and this would be so if Claire promised to reserve the lamp in exchange for a promise by Customer 3 to return. Whether or not such binding commitments were made is a matter of interpretation — to be determined in light of what the parties said, and any general usage with which they reasonably should be familiar. On the brief facts given here, it is probably unlikely that Customer 3 did make any binding commitment to return and cannot therefore be liable for any lost opportunity suffered by Claire.

6. The transaction with Customer 4 appears to satisfy all the attributes of contract. Unlike the contracts in Examples 1 and 3, this one contains unperformed promises by both parties at the time of agreement.

7. Even if Claire and the thrift store each made promises respectively to donate and accept the goods, there is no contract here because the element of exchange is missing. The thrift store gave nothing to Claire in exchange for the goods. This is a one-sided transaction — a donation. In technical terms, this transaction is not a contract because it lacks consideration — a concept discussed fully in Chapter 7.

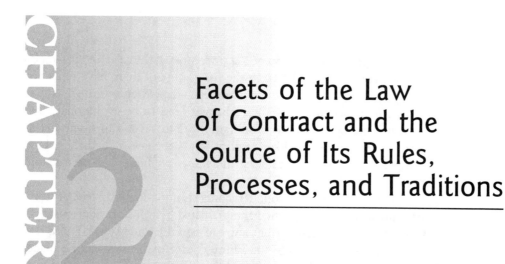

Facets of the Law of Contract and the Source of Its Rules, Processes, and Traditions

§2.1 THE PURPOSE OF THIS CHAPTER

Chapter 1 introduced the legal concept of contract and outlined the policies and ideological values of contract law. This chapter covers some more fundamentals. Although much of what is said here will slowly become apparent as you study contracts, it is very helpful to have these basics explained before you begin to encounter them in cases and other materials. The chapter begins with a little history and theory. It then has a brief discussion of the source of contract law and some of the structural and conceptual aspects of the legal system of which it forms part. It ends with an introduction to two important documents that you will work with throughout the course: a statute called the Uniform Commercial Code (UCC) and a text known as the Restatement, Second, of Contracts.

§2.2 THE HISTORICAL PERSPECTIVE OF CONTRACT LAW

The primary purpose of the contracts course is to teach you the contemporary law of contract. However, you cannot fully appreciate the current law without some sense of its history. Indeed, the very process by which the law is decided involves some degree of historical analysis, as the discussion of precedent in Chapter 3 shows. Most of the rules and principles of contract law were developed in the past. Some of them have remained relatively unchanged while others have been adapted or overruled as they have become superannuated. These changes tend to be evolutionary and incremental, built upon a traditional framework that is still apparent. In this respect, contract law is like a great and ancient cathedral, whose contemporary appearance reflects millennia of building, destruction, rebuilding, and addition.

Therefore, although the contracts course is not a course in legal history, modern doctrine must be studied and evaluated in its historical perspective. It is only in this way that current law can be fully understood, and a reasonably reliable prediction of the future course of the law can be made. Because a lawyer's work often centers on a prediction of how a court may decide an issue that could arise in the transaction, the ability to gauge the direction of the law is invaluable.

Although an understanding of the substantive law is one of the principal purposes of studying cases through the historical spectrum, this is not the only insight to be gained. The historical progression of caselaw is at the very heart of our common law system of jurisprudence. By tracing the development of legal rules over time, the student learns about the process of legal evolution. Familiarity with this process is essential to the analysis of court opinions and other legal materials. The common law and its rulemaking process are examined in section 2.4 and Chapter 3.

§2.3 CLASSICAL AND CONTEMPORARY CONTRACT LAW

§2.3.1 Classical Contract Law

Although the common law of contracts is many centuries old, it did not become a systematic, interwoven body of doctrine until relatively recently. Prior to the eighteenth century the law of contract was seen not so much as a cohesive system of rules, linked by general principles, but as a collection of discrete rules, each specifically applicable to various particular types of transactions. From the eighteenth century, English legal scholars began to think of contract law in more systematic terms. They began to recognize that the specific rules reflected a general approach to contracts that could be identified and formulated as broader doctrine. This trend developed in both England and America during the nineteenth century, at a time when economic and industrial expansion called for a more sophisticated and comprehensive system of contract law. It reached its zenith in what is referred to as the **classical period**. While one could quibble about the exact dates, the classical period can be thought of as spanning the last decades of the nineteenth century and the beginning of the twentieth. The Restatement, Contracts, published in the 1930s (introduced in section 2.8) reflects the mature thinking of the classical school, but by that stage the classical conception had already begun the process of change that leads into the contemporary period.

To find a general doctrine of contract, the classicists examined decided cases, extracting from them a set of coherent and well-defined rules, which they then used as the basis for constructing more abstract general principles. The general principles formed a framework for organizing and linking the rules into a body of doctrine. Some classicists went so far as to conceive of *law as a science* in which certain and consistent results could be achieved in the resolution of cases by the rather mechanical process of selecting the right rule from the body of doctrine and applying it to the facts.

The classical school reflects the priorities of its age, which greatly valued free enterprise, private autonomy, and a laissez-faire approach to economic activity. Classical theory therefore stressed the facilitation of contractual relationships and favored a strictly **objective** approach. If parties manifested contractual intent, the classicists favored enforcement of the transaction. They were not inclined to probe the actual state of understanding of either party. This meant that they were not especially sensitive to the impact that enforcement of an apparent contract might have on a party whose exercise of free will may have been impaired by economic impotence or lack of sophistication.

The classical approach was also heavily influenced by the legal philosophy of **positivism**, which stressed the primacy of legal rules and considered the court's principal role to be finding and applying those rules to the facts of individual cases. Because of its emphasis on clear rules and its belief in a scientific approach to adjudication, classicism tends to be relatively formalistic and rigid.

§2.3.2 Contemporary Contract Law

As the twentieth century wore on, the classical conception of contract law began to erode. Enthusiasm for the free market was tempered by a growing recognition of the need to regulate the freedom of powerful contractors, to safeguard the rights of weaker parties, and to affect social policy concerning matters such as consumer protection, employee rights, and business ethics. The formalism of the classical approach came to be perceived as too rigid and too heavily biased in favor of dominant contracting parties. The idea that law could be treated as a science sounded more and more naive as insight into human interaction grew, and it was realized that the creation and resolution of contract relationships is too complex and variable to admit of "scientific" determination.

Succeeding schools of legal philosophy turned away from heavy reliance on rules, which may create the illusion of certainty, but do not in fact adequately reflect what really occurs in the resolution of cases. Instead, law came to be studied in a multidisciplinary way, taking into account its social context and the actual workings of the legal system. While many different approaches to contract law can be identified during this century, the two most influential schools were the **sociological jurisprudents**, who studied the relationship between law and society, and the **legal realists**, who stressed the dynamics of the legal process, challenged the preeminence of rules, and advocated a looser, more flexible approach to legal analysis.

Today, we have become used to thinking about law in a broader context and to considering not merely what the doctrine says, but also how it actually works in light of such factors as the makeup and philosophy of the judiciary, the use of legal tactics, and the social goals to be achieved. In this, we are indebted to the insights of the legal realists who forever changed our way of thinking about law. Legal realism (sometimes called **neoclassicism**) remains the dominant approach to the law. However, **other schools of thought** continue to evolve as scholars and judges build on or challenge the realist tradition. Some writers advocate a jurisprudence that emphasizes the promissory and consensual aspects of contract law; others criticize legal rules for inadequately reflecting the central importance the relational aspect of contracts; others view contracts from the perspective of groups who have historically been excluded from power, and criticize traditional contract rules as instruments of the dominant economic class. Perhaps the most influential of the post-realist philosophical trends has been the **Law and Economics** movement. Although the movement consists of scholars who have differing views, the common thread of the scholarship is to examine law from the perspective of economic principles, and to be concerned with the economic efficiency of legal rules. Commonly, those who advocate the economic analysis of law urge that laws should be primarily concerned with the facilitation of exchanges on the free market, and should not seek to regulate conduct as a means of social engineering.

In sum, we are left with a contemporary contract law that is a mix of doctrine, policy, and process, at a stage of sophistication that goes beyond that of the classicists. Nevertheless, one must acknowledge the importance of the classical period. The classicists' quest for a comprehensive body of clear and certain rules was a milestone in the evolution of contract law. Many of our current rules and principles were formulated during the classical period and modern developments have proceeded from that base. Our law still reflects the tension between the classicists' desire for *certainty and formality* (an orientation towards clear rules) and the need to *understand the legal process* and to develop flexible rules that accommodate and correctly describe that process.

§2.4 THE MEANING OF "COMMON LAW"

The "common law" is often referred to in legal writing. This term is confusing to the uninitiated because its meaning varies depending on the context in which it is used.

§2.4.1 "Common Law" Used to Designate Our Legal System as a Whole

In early times, much of English law was based on local custom, applied in local courts. As the centralized Royal Courts began to increase in importance, their decisions formed the basis of a national law that gradually overshadowed local law. This national law, common to all of England,[1] came to be called the "common law." When Britain established colonies around the world the settlers transplanted English law into these foreign territories. In most of the ex-colonies, including those that became the United States, the common law of England has remained the basic legal system. Therefore, the term "common law" used in the broadest *international* sense, designates a country whose **legal system** is **based on the common law of England**. These countries share a legal heritage and an approach to legal analysis even though they may have widely different political, economic, and social structures and may have diverged in their rules of substantive law.

Most other countries in the world have legal systems derived from Roman law, as developed in continental Europe. Because the source of Roman law was the *Corpus Juris Civilis* of the emperor Justinian, these systems are called **Civilian**. Cross-pollination and the unifying pressure of international commerce have reduced the differences between the civil law and the common law, but each system continues to have a distinctive approach to legal analysis. In the present context, probably the most striking difference is that Civilian systems have a long tradition of comprehensive *codification* and tend to focus on their codes and scholarly commentary as a source of law. By contrast, common law systems tend to emphasize more strongly the *role of the judge* in the development of the law.

---

1. Note that the text refers to English, not British, common law. The United Kingdom does not have a unitary legal system. English common law applies in England and Wales. Northern Ireland's law is based on English law, but has its own variants. Scots law is quite distinct from English law. It draws its legal tradition from both English and Civil law.

§2.4.2 "Common Law" Used to Denote the Judge-Made Component of Our Legal System

When the focus moves from the international (i.e., characterizing the legal system as a whole) to the domestic (i.e., examining the components of the system), "common law" takes on a different meaning. It refers to those portions of our law based upon *decisions of the courts*, as distinct from those created by legislation. Contracts is described as a common law subject because most of its rules have been developed over the years by judges rather than by legislators. (This process of development is described in Chapter 3.)

This does not mean that there is no statute law governing contracts. Even in early times, the English parliament enacted some law concerning contracts which became part of the received common law. In the modern period, legislative action has increased considerably, and there are many areas of contract law that have been legislated upon. Some of these statutes **codify** the common law. That is, they take rules and principles already developed by judges and put them into statutory form. The purpose of this may be to reinforce or clarify the law or to make it more accessible. A statute may do more than codify, though. It may *reform, alter, or modernize* common law rules, it may intervene to hasten or mold the development of doctrine, or it may be enacted with the express purpose of changing legal rules developed by courts, or it may create new rules designed to deal with a problem not yet addressed by courts. As noted in section 1.3, some statutes are confined to particular contracts while others are of general application. Because contracts are governed by state law, as explained in section 2.6, some states have more extensive statutory treatment of contract than others. Although legislatures have, over the years, enacted many laws that relate to contracts, the field is still regarded as part of the common law, because judge-made rules continue to predominate.

§2.4.3 "Common Law" Used to Denote a Process or Approach to Legal Analysis

The prior two meanings of "common law" are relatively easy to spot, but the term is also used in a more subtle sense. It is sometimes used to describe the mode of legal thinking and the process of judicial development inherent in a common law system.

As mentioned before, the common law develops through the decisions of judges in actual cases. Whether a rule's origin is the common law or statute, it will ultimately be applied by a judge in a specific case. In deciding the case, the judge interprets and may embellish the rule. Over time, as courts apply the rule in more and more cases, it acquires a judicial gloss that becomes part of the law. Therefore, in using *patterns of thinking* and *modes of analysis* molded by the common law tradition, judges continue to develop the law, even if the source of law is statutory. This process is as much part of the common law as the judicial creation of rules. In a civilian jurisdiction, by contrast, the judicial application of statutory rules tends to be more confined to the case under decision, and is less likely to be influential in the development of legal doctrine.

§2.5 THE DISTINCTION BETWEEN LAW AND EQUITY

The distinction between law and equity permeates the common law system, and you will find discussion of it throughtout this book. An early explanation will help you to understand the distinction when you encounter it. In everyday usage, "equity" simply means fairness. In law, it is sometimes used this way as well. However, it also has a more technical meaning.

Sections 2.4.1 and 3.2 briefly discuss the way in which the Royal Courts developed the common law. As practiced in the Royal Courts during its formative period, the common law was a rigid system. It was based on forms of action called **writs**. A litigant seeking a remedy applied to court for a writ (a written order calling on someone to do something) compelling the performance claimed. The writs were narrow, specific, and formalistic. Although new writs were developed as the need arose, it often happened that a person who needed relief could not fit the case into a recognized writ, and could therefore not obtain relief at law. The Monarch had the prerogative to do justice between his or her subjects, and if the court could not give a remedy, the Monarch had the power to intervene. The Monarch did not deal with these matters personally but delegated them to the **chancellor**, the highest royal officer. Over time, the chancellor had more and more of these cases in which relief was given on the basis of fairness (equity in the usual sense) in the **absence of a remedy at law**. This eventually led to the growth of a court of chancery, which had jurisdiction over all those claims for relief that were equitable in nature. The court of chancery developed its own rules and principles and became something of a competitor of the courts of law.

This dual system of jurisdiction lasted for many centuries. Over time, it became a matter of established practice that certain claims and remedies were legal in nature and others were equitable. For example, a claim for damages for breach of contract was within the jurisdiction of the law courts, but law courts had no power to order a party to perform the contract. Therefore, a claim for specific performance of a contract or for an injunction prohibiting breach could only be granted by the equity court. Furthermore, the equity court would not assume jurisdiction unless the plaintiff could show that the legal remedy of damages was not an adequate remedy under all the circumstances of the case. Thus, the common law system, in its broad sense, incorporated a jurisdictional division between the courts of common law (used here in a narrower sense) and equity. This dual system was part of the common law of England adopted by American jurisdictions, and so it entered our legal system. It is even embodied in the U.S. Constitution. For example, Art. III §2 extends the judical power of the United States to all cases in law and equity arising under the Constitution or the laws of the United States. Amendment VII preserves the right to a jury trial in suits at common law, but does not mention equitable suits because courts of equity did not have juries when the Constitution was drafted.

Since the nineteenth century the distinction between law and equity has been eroding both in England and in the United States. Separate courts of equity have been abolished in the federal system and in most states. Courts of general jurisdiction now hear both legal and equitable suits. Also, the substantive distinction between law and equity is fading as many principles of equity gradually become incorporated into the law as legal principles. However, the distinction is not entirely dead, and it has an impact in many areas. For example, the availability of remedies is still influenced by the rule that a party who claims equitable relief must show that the legal remedy is inadequate; the right to a jury trial is confined to actions at law and is not available in equity suits; an appellate court has a much wider scope of review in an equity suit; and some courts still confine equitable defenses and doctrines to suits in equity and do not recognize them in actions at law. Again, it must be stressed that none of these distinctions are applied with the same rigor as they used to be, and there are many cases in which courts have moved away from them. Nevertheless, the tradition is strong and its breakdown is gradual and uneven, so it must be taken into account even in modern cases. We will return to the law-equity distinction periodically as it comes up in different areas of contract law.

§2.6 STATE LAW GOVERNS CONTRACTS

The common law of contract (as well as much of the statutory law governing contract) is state law. Although there is some federal law applicable to contracts, it is limited to federal concerns such as the regulation of interstate commerce or to contracts entered into by the federal government. Because contracts are within the realm of state law, most contracts cases are decided by state courts. However, because federal courts sometimes acquire jurisdiction over cases that involve issues of state contract law (for example, because there is diversity of citizenship, or because the contract dispute may arise in a bankruptcy case under federal law), it is not uncommon to find a federal court deciding a state law contracts issue. Where a federal court hears a state law contracts case, it applies the law of the state whose law governs the transaction, and is bound by state law precedents. (*See* section 3.2.2.)

It is therefore not, strictly speaking, correct to talk of *the* law of contracts. There are in fact 50 different bodies of state contract law in this country, as well as those in U.S. Territories and the District of Columbia. Each one of the states, except Louisiana, has adopted the common law of England as its basic legal system. (Louisiana adopted the civilian system, in the form of the French Code Napoleon during the short period that it was a French possession.) However, although each state has its own contract law, there is a significant degree of similarity in the laws of the states. Not only does the law of every state (except Louisiana) derive from the common law, but also, as the law develops state courts and legislatures are influenced by each other. This makes it possible to study a generalized law of contract in law schools, and to select cases based not on the state from which they emanate, but on the quality of their facts and legal exposition. Therefore, while you should always bear in mind that a particular rule of law may not be followed in every state, you can be confident that you are studying broadly accepted principles and are learning the reasoning and analytical skills that will enable you to find the answer to a legal question wherever you end up practicing.

§2.7 THE UNIFORM COMMERCIAL CODE (UCC)

§2.7.1 The UCC as a Uniform Model Statute and State Legislation

a. The Creation and Purpose of the UCC

As mentioned earlier, contracts are generally governed by common law except to the extent that legislation has been enacted to codify, change, or add to it. The UCC is such a statute. Although all of contract law is, in a sense, commercial, the UCC is not applicable to all contracts. It covers only certain specific types of commercial transactions. Each type of transaction is provided for in a separate article of the UCC. In the contracts course, we are concerned with only one of the types of transactions covered by the UCC — sales of goods, governed by UCC Article 2. We also deal with some of the provisions of UCC Article 1, which contains general provisions that apply to all articles of the UCC, including Article 2. Most contracts courses cover basic principles of the sale of goods because sales of goods are such commonplace contracts, and because there is a close relationship between Article 2 and the development of the common law. The other types of commercial transaction, covered by the remaining articles of the UCC (as well as some of the more specialized and complex principles regarding sales of goods) are left for courses on commercial law.

The provisions of the UCC are not entirely a modern legislative innovation. Many of them are based on earlier statutory enactments, going back to the late nineteenth and early twentieth centuries and on principles and rules developed under common law. One of its goals is to **codify** (record in statutory form) well-established rules, but it is equally concerned with clarifying and modernizing the law. Therefore, while the UCC has built on principles formulated under the common law and its predecessor statutes, it has also sought to reform outdated or unsatisfactory laws and to bring the legal rules into line with contemporary commercial practice.

Apart from codifying and reforming commercial law, the other goal of the UCC is to unify it throughout the country. Like the law of contracts generally, commercial law is state law. There is, therefore, no national legislature that can enact a single commercial statute with nationwide application.[2] The only way to create uniform commercial law among the states is to draft a model statute and to persuade the legislature of each state to enact it. This task was undertaken jointly by two very influential national law reform organizations, the National Conference of Commissioners on Uniform State Laws (NCCUSL) and the American Law Institute (ALI). Their work resulted in the completion of a model code during the 1950s. The aim of having this model code adopted has been fully successful, and it has been enacted in every state except Louisiana. (As noted in section 2.6, Louisiana has a civilian system, and the enactment of the UCC as a whole was not appropriate. Louisiana has enacted some portions of the UCC.) Of course, the law of the states can never be entirely uniform. Some states have made legislative variations from the standard model provisions. Even when states have enacted the same uniform provisions, courts in different states often reach divergent interpretations of the code provisions.

b. Revisions of the UCC

The process of reform and updating did not end with the drafting of the current Code. Shortly after the completion of the model code, a Permanent Editorial Board was set up to review the Code and propose amendments. The process of amendment is slow because the drafters take many years to develop recommendations for change, and after they are promulgated

---

2. Of course, Congress has enacted commercial legislation where it has felt competent to do so under the commerce clause (U.S. Const. art. 1 §8 cl. 3) which gives Congress power over interstate commerce. However, general commercial law is the law of a particular jurisdiction and is reserved to the states under the Constitution.

by NCCUSL and ALI, they still have to be adopted by state legislatures. Nevertheless, since the enactment of the UCC, changes have been proposed by NCCUSL and ALI to various Articles of the UCC, and those revisions have generally been adopted by state legislatures.

Articles 1 and 2 have been reviewed periodically since their original enactment. Most recently, NCCUSL and ALI completed a revision of Article 1 in 2001 and (after more than a decade of effort and debate) a revision of Article 2 in 2003. As noted above, the promulgation of a revised official text of a Code article by NCCUSL and ALI does not make it law. Each state legislature must enact it for the changes to take effect as the law of that state. At the date of writing this edition, 22 states have enacted the **2001 revision of Article 1** and there are bills to adopt it pending in a few other states. No state has yet enacted the **2003 revision of Article 2** and only two state legislatures have reached the stage of considering bills that may lead to its passage. Some of the proposed changes to Article 2 are controversial and the revision has not been received enthusiastically, so it is not clear if and when states will decide to adopt the revised article. Therefore at the present time, the older version of Article 1 is still the law in just over half the states, while just under half have adopted revised Article 1.[3] Pre-revision Article 2 still remains the law everywhere, but that may begin to change. This means professors have to choose whether to focus on either the pre-revision or the post-revision versions of these articles, or to teach both. This edition of the book tries to accommodate whatever approach is taken in your class by addressing both versions. Because pre-revision Article 1 is still widely used and pre-revision Article 2 is currently the law of every state, I have kept the focus of this book on the pre-revision versions of both these articles. However, every discussion of or reference to provisions in Articles 1 and 2 includes (either in the text or in a footnote) a citation to the corresponding provision in the revised version with an explanation of the change and a comment on whether and to what extent the revision has changed the law.

c. Citations to the UCC

When the UCC is cited in this book and in other texts (including your casebook), the citation is to the model code, that is, to the Official Text as promulgated by NCCUSL and ALI. For example, section 102 of Article 2 is cited as §2.102. However, when a UCC section is cited in a case, the court usually cites the state statute in which the Code was enacted in the court's

---

3. As you may realize on reading this, where some, but not all, states adopt the revision of an article, the UCC's goal of uniformity is placed under great strain because there are two versions of the uniform law. NCCUSL and ALI therefore endanger uniformity when they promulgate a new official text. But if they fail to update the law, they run the risk that individual states will make their own amendments, which could be even more destructive of uniformity.

jurisdiction. For example, a Connecticut court would cite section 102 of Article 2 as General Statutes §42a-2-102, and an Oregon court would cite it as ORS §72-1020. As you can see, it is usually not that difficult to identify the model code section because it is incorporated into the statutory citation.

d. The Official Comments to the UCC

When NCCUSL and ALI drafted the original Code (and also when they drafted revisions) they included a commentary after each section to explain and expand upon the provisions of the section. This commentary, called the Official Comments, is typically not part of the statute as enacted by the states. It is therefore not binding law, as the text of the actual section itself is. However, the commentary is very important because it reflects the intentions of the drafters. Courts treat the Official Comments as highly influential and often rely on them in interpreting the Code. You will frequently see them mentioned in the cases.

§2.7.2 The Use and Application of UCC Article 2

As mentioned already, the UCC covers a variety of different types of commercial transactions, and each type of transaction is contained in a separate, self-contained Article. The only articles that concern us in the contracts course are Article 2, governing the sale of goods, and Article 1, which has general provisions applicable in all articles, including Article 2.

UCC §2.102 states that Article 2 applies to "transactions in goods."[4] Although the word "transaction" is broader than the word "sale," you should not be concerned about this. You can assume for all purposes in the contracts course that if the contract is a **sale of goods**, Article 2 governs and *must be applied*. **Goods** are defined in UCC §2.105(1)[5] to include movable things other than money and various intangible rights. A **sale** is stated in

---

4. UCC §2.102 has not been changed in the 2003 revision of Article 2.
5. In the 2003 revision of Article 2, the definition of "goods" is in §2.103(k). The revised definition has some differences from the existing one. It still covers all movable things other than money or various intangible rights. However, its most significant change is that it excludes "information" from the definition of goods. Official Comment 7 to the revised section explains that this exclusion applies to the transfer of information (such as computer software) that is not associated with goods, but that Article 2 will apply if the information is a component of goods. Therefore, for example, Article 2 is not applicable to a sale of software on its own, whether it is delivered in intangible form by downloading it or in tangible form such as a program on a disk. But Article 2 would be applicable if the sale is really of goods themselves, and the software is a component of the goods, designed to make them operate. (For example, a car or household appliance that has some computerized feature.) If revised UCC §2.103(k) becomes law, one can foresee litigation where it is not clear if the information itself or the goods that contain the information is the primary aspect of the sale. It should be mentioned that if transactions in information are not governed by Article 2, they

UCC §2.106(1) to consist of the passing of title from the seller to the buyer for a price.

To the extent that the provisions of Article 2 differ from the general rules of the common law of contract, the statute prevails. It would, therefore, be a serious error to try to resolve an issue arising from the sale of goods by simply applying the common law. Conversely, if the contract is not a sale of goods, Article 2 is not applicable and must not be used directly. (As explained in section 2.7.3, it could nevertheless be of persuasive weight and may be used by analogy in appropriate circumstances.)

In many cases, it is relatively easy to tell whether a contract involves a sale of goods. For example, a customer's purchase of clothing from a department store is obviously a sale of goods. Conversely, a contract with a laundry to clean clothes, while relating to goods, is for the provision of a service. Similarly, the purchase of a house, while a sale transaction, involves real property, not goods. However, some transactions are more complex and include both a sale of goods and a component that is not a sale of goods. For example, a contract to repair a car may include both the supply of parts (a sale of goods) and the provision of labor. When such a hybrid transaction is in issue, most courts use a "predominant purpose" or "predominant factor" test to decide whether to apply Article 2. If the sale of goods is the more significant aspect of the transaction, and the non-sale component is incidental to the sale, Article 2 applies. However, if the sale of goods is ancillary, and the other component is predominant, Article 2 does not apply and the transaction is governed by common law. Some courts favor a different approach, known as the "gravamen" test. Under this test the court does not attempt to classify the contract as a whole one way or the other, but applies Article 2 if the controversy in question relates to the sales component, and applies common law if the issue arises out of the services component. These alternative tests are explored more fully in Example 1(f).

If a contract is for the sale of goods, this *does not mean* that *common law* rules and principles are *irrelevant*. UCC §1.103[6] expressly states that the principles of law and equity supplement the provisions of the code unless displaced by particular code provisions. Therefore, to the extent that Article 2 is consistent with the common law, common law rules and principles are *used in conjunction* with the code provisions. In some areas, the rule of Article 2 may be the same as that of common law, so that cases interpreting the common law rule remain relevant. In addition, Article 2 is not comprehensive — it

---

will be subject to a separate statute applicable to the licensing and use of software. During the same time that NCCUSL was working on the revision of Article 2, it attempted to draft a uniform law on information transactions, which was originally proposed as Article 2B of the UCC. That model statute was highly controversial, and was eventually promulgated separately by NCCUSL as the Uniform Computer Information Transactions Act (UCITA). UCITA has not been successful and few states have adopted it.

6. Section 1.103 is renumbered 1.103(b) in revised Article 1.

does not deal with every aspect of the law governing the sale of goods. In areas where Article 2 is silent, it is intended that the *common law fills the gap.* Therefore, even in a transaction involving the sale of goods, there is a substantial degree of interaction between Article 2 and the common law.

Quite apart from this, Article 2, like other statutes, must be interpreted and applied by courts. Therefore, when a court decides a case interpreting a section of Article 2, this case serves as precedent for later courts. Through this common law process, a judicial gloss has developed that refines the generality of code sections and creates more detailed rules by application to varied factual situations.

This abstract description of the symbiotic relationship between Article 2 and the common law will become more concrete as specific substantive topics are considered. For the present, take the point that Article 2 must be used in any case or problem involving a contract for the sale of goods, but recognize that the statute is not the only source of law. Consistent common law rules and judicial interpretations of the Code section are also applicable.

§2.7.3 The Influence of Article 2 in Cases Involving Contracts Other Than Sales of Goods

Although Article 2 is not directly applicable beyond contracts for the sale of goods, it has exerted considerable influence on the development of the common law. Because the UCC is a modern, reform-minded statute, its changes in the law regarding sales are often found to be attractive by courts dealing with other contracts. The approach of Article 2 is therefore often consulted as a source of guidance when other contracts are involved, and if the court finds the issues and the purpose of the law to be *analogous* to those involved in a sale transaction, the court may decide to generalize the Article 2 resolution. As a result, there has been a trend in modern cases for older rules of common law to develop in the same direction as Article 2. This trend has been reinforced by the RESTATEMENT (SECOND) OF CONTRACTS, which has deliberately adopted many provisions of Article 2 in formulating its rules of the common law of contracts.

§2.8 WHAT IS THE RESTATEMENT (SECOND) OF CONTRACTS?

The Restatement looks like a statute. It has numbered sections that set out rules in statutory style, followed by comments and illustrations. However, unlike the UCC, the Restatement is **not a statute**. It is a **secondary** authority[7] — a textbook setting out the rules of the common law of contract as its drafters find them to be, or sometimes, would like them to be. It is created by the American Law Institute (which, as you may recall from section 2.7.1 is one of the organizations involved in drafting the UCC).

The rules in the Restatement are largely extracted from decided cases, but this does not mean that they actually represent what the majority of courts have held. Despite its name, the Restatement **does not necessarily "restate"** the **settled law**. Indeed, given the number of jurisdictions involved, it is often not possible to find a settled law. Also, because it seeks to offer guidance on the direction that its drafters feel the law should take, it sometimes favors a legal rule that has had only minimal acceptance in decided cases. Therefore, while the Restatement is very influential and is frequently cited and relied on by courts, its "rules" have to be treated with some caution. They may not really reflect what the courts of a particular jurisdiction have actually held.

The current Restatement is the second to be published. The original was produced in the 1930s. It was the first thorough systematization of contract law, and the first comprehensive attempt to give coherent form to American contract doctrine. As such, it was immensely important in the development of the modern common law of contracts. As mentioned in section 2.3.1, it reflected classical thinking and tended towards the formalism and objectivism of the classical school. By the 1960s, the Restatement had become outdated, and a revision was begun, culminating in the Restatement Second, published in final form during the 1980s. The Restatement Second reflects the post-classicist thinking described in section 2.3.2, and is also heavily influenced by the UCC, which had been enacted by the time that work was begun on the Restatement Second. As mentioned before, its adoption of rules and concepts from Article 2 has helped to generalize the innovations of that statute.

The Restatement Second is cited frequently in this book. (Although its full citation form is "RESTATEMENT (SECOND) OF CONTRACTS," this is truncated here to "Restatement Second.")

Examples

1. As mentioned in section 2.7, UCC Article 2 is directly applicable only to sales of goods, even though it may have persuasive influence in cases involving other contracts. Students studying contract law often overlook this and become muddled, forgetting about Article 2 when the contract is

---

7. The term "secondary authority" refers to legal writings like textbooks, law review articles, and commentaries that lack the binding force of official sources of law — such as statutes and court decisions (called "primary authority"). To the extent that a secondary authority is reliable and persuasive, it could be influential, but it never binds a court.

a sale of goods or citing it as the governing law when the contract does not involve a sale of goods. These simple questions on the scope of Article 2 are included early in the book to emphasize the distinction between sales and other contracts. Which of the following contracts would be governed by Article 2?

(a) The sale of a condominium.

(b) A contract to employ someone as a sales clerk in a department store.

(c) The sale of a cow.

(d) The sale of Michelangelo's *David*.

(e) A contract under which a sculptor agrees to make a marble copy of *David* for $10,000.

(f) The sale of food in a restaurant.

Explanations

1(a). Although this is a sale, a condominium is not goods but real property. The concept of movability distinguishes tangible personal property that is capable of being moved (even if machinery is needed to move it) from land and structures on land that are so incorporated into the land as to become united with it. Article 2 does not govern the sale.

1(b). Although the clerk will be selling goods in the course of his employment, the contract to employ him is not a sale of goods but a contract for labor (services).

1(c). Although the cow is a living animal, not an inanimate object, it still qualifies as goods. Livestock and crops (including unborn animals and growing crops) are clearly included within the definition of goods in UCC §2.105.[8]

1(d). Although David is rather big, he is movable with some effort and therefore is goods. The fact that he is a priceless work of art is not relevant to the classification.

1(e). A contract to make a copy of David is also a sale of goods. Because the end product to be delivered under the contract—the completed copy—is the subject matter of the transaction, it is a sale of goods, even though the process of manufacture involves labor as well as materials. Most goods have to be manufactured by someone. It is therefore not enough to exclude a transaction from Article 2 merely because the seller used labor to create the goods. As a rule of thumb, if the seller's labor is entirely employed in the creation of the tangible, movable end product that is sold, the transaction is a sale of goods.

---

8. Revised UCC §2.103(k).

1(f). The sale of food in a supermarket (even if the food sold is a sandwich made on site by an employee in the deli department), like the sale of the replica of David, is a sale of goods subject to Article 2. As noted in Explanation 1(e), where all the labor provided by the seller is devoted to the fabrication of the end product to be delivered to the buyer, this is a pure sale. However, a restaurant meal involves both the sale of the food and the provision of services associated with it, such as serving it and providing a table, silverware, and (in the better class of eatery) even a cute little candle to create the appropriate ambience. This makes the transaction a hybrid that includes a sale of both goods and services.

As noted in section 2.72, courts use one of two alternative tests to decide if Article 2 applies to hybrid transactions. The "predominant purpose" test is more widely followed, but some courts favor the "gravamen" test. The difference between these two approaches, and the reason why it may be important to decide whether the UCC applies, can be illustrated by *Newmark v. Gimbel's Inc.*, 258 A.2d 697 (N.J. 1969). The customer of a beauty parlor suffered severe skin irritation on her scalp and hair loss following the application of a permanent wave solution to her head by the hairdresser. The customer sued the beauty parlor for personal injury, both in tort and under a theory of breach of warranty. The tort cause of action failed because the customer could not establish that the beauty parlor had been negligent in using or applying the solution, so she had to rely on the warranty cause of action to obtain relief. However, a claim of breach of warranty could only be made if the transaction was a sale of goods, because Article 2 contains implied warranties that are not available under common law. The trial court applied the predominant purpose test. It found that the predominant purpose of the transaction was the rendition of beauty services, to which the supply of the solution was incidental. It therefore found Article 2 inapplicable so that no implied warranty existed. The Supreme Court declined to follow this approach. It considered that the policy of protecting consumers from harmful products should apply with equal force, whether those products are supplied in a sale or as part of a service. Because the predominant purpose test precludes relief in cases in which the service component dominates, it undermines this policy. The Court held instead that if it was the goods themselves that caused the injury, Article 2 warranties should apply to the claim arising from that injury.

Courts that prefer the predominant purpose test may recognize that it could provide less protection to a buyer of goods where the goods are supplied incidentally to a service. However, they reject the gravamen test as too awkward and difficult to apply. It is often problematical, and even impossible, to break a contract into separate components to apply a different set of rules to its different parts. In *Pittsley v. Houser*, 125 Idaho 820 (App. Ct. 1994), the court articulated this concern in deciding to apply the predominant purpose test to a contract for the sale and installation of carpeting. The court felt that the gravamen test offended one of the fundamental goals of the UCC—to simplify and clarify the law relating to commercial transactions.

Where a court applies the predominant purpose test, it has to evaluate what the predominant purpose of the contract is. In making this decision, courts look at all the circumstances of the transaction. The relative value of the sale and non-sale aspects of the contract are important, but the court also looks at other factors to decide the purpose of the contract, such as the language used by the parties in the agreement and their reasonable expectations based on the nature of the transaction and the commercial context.

The Doctrine of Precedent and a Contract Case Analysis

§3.1 STUDYING CONTRACT THROUGH APPELLATE CASES — AN INTRODUCTION AND A NOTE ON PERSPECTIVE

This chapter is primarily concerned with case analysis and the doctrine of precedent. Because the analysis of cases is so central to the study of contract law, it is worth spending some time at the outset on the techniques and principles of reading, understanding, and applying caselaw. It is likely that you will receive instruction on this skill in your legal writing and research class, and you will also begin to develop it as you proceed through your contracts course and other substantive law courses. This chapter, which ends with an Example based on a fictional court opinion in a contract dispute, should help you to gain some early insight into the process of working with caselaw.

The study of case reports has been the standard teaching methodology in law schools since the latter part of the nineteenth century. In its initial use, the casebook reflected the classical conception described in section 2.3. It was thought that students could "find" the law in the cases, using the scientific approach to the study of law. While the focus of casebooks has changed to reflect the broader and more flexible post-classical view of law, case analysis is still largely used in teaching contracts. This is appropriate because case analysis is an important skill for lawyers, and the study of cases allows exposure to the common law method described in section 2.4.3. Case reports also serve as illustration of what would otherwise be abstract principles. Some casebook authors love to throw in weird cases or misguided opinions to challenge the students' critical faculties or to provoke debate.

As valuable as this learning process is, it is helpful to approach it with a recognition of some of its shortcomings. First, a collection of cases seldom produces a nice, concise and organized discourse on the law. That is why books like this one are needed. Second, the emphasis on caselaw gives students a rather skewed perspective because they are constantly exposed to transactions that have gone wrong — indeed, so irreconcilably wrong that the parties have felt it necessary to litigate, usually all the way to the appellate level, rather than to compromise. It is important to remember that only a fraction of contracts end up in litigation and fewer still reach the highest courts without being settled along the way. A related problem with the case method is that it focuses too strongly on contractual disputes at the expense of other lawyering skills such as counseling, drafting, and negotiation. Although there is an unavoidable emphasis on litigation when law is studied through cases, this problem can be ameliorated by paying attention to formation and negotiation issues whenever they are raised in the cases.

State court cases in casebooks are mostly decisions of appellate courts. In fact, in most states, trial court opinions do not create precedent and are not published.[1] States typically have two levels of appellate courts. Appeal from the trial court is usually made first to an intermediate court of appeals. Thereafter, there is the possibility of a further appeal to the state's supreme court. Unlike trial courts, which consist of a single judge (with or without a jury), an appellate court sits in panels consisting of several judges. The exact size of the panel varies from one jurisdiction to another. If all the judges on the panel agree on the result and its rationale, the court is able to render a unanimous decision. However, it is common for members of an appellate panel to disagree on the proper disposition of the case. When that happens, the decision of the court is that adopted by the majority of judges on the panel. (The **majority opinion** is written by one of them and joined by the others.) A judge who disagrees with the reasoning of the majority but agrees with the result may write a **concurring opinion** (or, if more than one judge concurs, each may write a separate concurring opinion). A judge who disagrees with both the reasoning and the result may write a **dissenting opinion** (or, if there is more than one dissenting judge, separate dissenting opinions). Sometimes a panel is so badly divided that no majority of its judges sign onto any opinion. In that case, the opinion with the most votes becomes the **plurality opinion** of the court.

---

1. As noted in section 2.6, federal courts do sometimes deal with contracts cases. In the federal system, trial court decisions are published and are often included in casebooks.

§3.2 HOW JUDGES MAKE CONTRACT LAW: JUDICIAL PRECEDENT

§3.2.1 What Is Precedent?

As mentioned in section 2.4.1, the common law developed in the Royal Courts of England. Although the Monarch was the font of justice, he or she could not deal personally with disputes between subjects, so this task was delegated to judges. As these judges decided cases over time, they came to realize that *similar situations* should be resolved in the *same way*. This allows for efficiency in the administration of justice, it enables people to predict case outcomes more accurately, and it serves one of our fundamental conceptions of justice: the equal treatment of people in like situations. As the common law developed, it became established practice for court decisions to be recorded so that they could be used as the basis of resolving later cases. This meant that a decision no longer only settled the dispute between the immediate parties. It formed a rule to be followed in the next case involving similar facts. As the number of recorded decisions grew to cover a greater variety of cases, the collection of legal rules expanded to create a compendious body of law.

The principle that a judicial decision creates a rule of law, binding upon later cases with similar facts, is known as the **doctrine of precedent** or, in Latin, **stare decisis** (roughly translated, "the decision stands"). The doctrine is peculiar to common law. Although civilian systems accord some weight to judicial precedent, they rely primarily on comprehensive codes and scholarly commentary as the source of legal rules. Court decisions are typically regarded as an exercise in applying the law, rather than the process of creating it, and judges more commonly conceive of their role as dispute resolution rather than lawmaking. With the exception of certain high courts and constitutional tribunals, court decisions in civilian countries are short, not very analytical, and fact-based.

§3.2.2 Who Is Bound by Precedent?

Obviously, the parties to a case are bound by the judicial determination of their suit. However, the doctrine of precedent deals with the binding effect of the decision beyond the parties, on later cases between other litigants. The first general rule of the doctrine has already been alluded to: The rule of a case is only binding on later cases with *substantially similar facts*. If there is a material factual difference between the cases, the earlier decision is not on point. Of course, no two cases are likely to have exactly the same facts, so the issue is one of substantial similarity — are the crucial factual elements sufficiently similar that the second case comes within the rule of the first. Even when there are notable factual differences, the later court may find the circumstances of the cases to be analogous, so that the rule may be treated as governing the second case as well.

As you can imagine, there are many instances in which the opposite also occurs. When a court does not favor applying the rule of the earlier case, it may look at the facts very narrowly and find factual differences that distinguish the cases. Often, the decision to analogize or distinguish facts is based on the judge's view on the soundness or error of the ruling in the prior case. As a result, the issue of factual similarity is often hotly contested in argument before the court when counsel for one party wishes to bring the case within the rule but the other does not wish the precedent to govern.

A precedent does not bind every court in the country. It is binding only on the court that *decided the case* and courts of *inferior rank* in the same *judicial hierarchy*. As explained in section 2.6, the judicial hierarchy that usually deals with contract cases is the state court system. Therefore, if the state supreme court decides a case, the rule of that case is binding on the supreme court itself (subject to the qualification stated below), as well as every other court in that state. If the case is not appealed to the state supreme court, the intermediate appellate court makes the final decision in the case. Its decision binds all courts in the state except for the supreme court, which is senior in the judicial hierarchy. If, later on, a different case with substantially similar facts does reach the supreme court, the court may find the earlier decision of the intermediate appellate court persuasive, and may decide to adopt it. However, it is not bound to do so. A case decided, even by the highest court, in one judicial hierarchy (that is, the supreme court of one state) is of no binding force on any court in another judicial hierarchy (another state). Again however, it could be of persuasive weight because courts often look to the cases decided in other states for guidance in resolving issues of first impression in their own jurisdictions.

The relationship between state and federal courts is too complex for discussion in any depth here. As a broad rule, when a *federal court* decides a matter of state law, it must follow precedents established by the courts of that state. If the superior courts of the state have not yet had occasion to decide the particular legal issue, the federal court must try to determine from analogous or related caselaw how the state courts would decide the matter if presented with it.

The statement that a court is bound by its own decisions requires some explanation. The principle of stare decisis imposes an obligation on a court to follow its own precedents. This is true even when the membership of the court changes, so that different judges hear the later case. However, the need for flexibility and development in the law must be weighed against the policies of predictability and fairness that motivate the doctrine of precedent. Therefore, if the court believes that its prior decision was wrong or that it no longer makes sense in light of changes in society, it is at liberty to overrule the prior decision. Most judges do not do this lightly and are very reluctant to depart from precedent unless a strong case is made for doing so. A lower court does not have the same discretion to deviate from the precedent of a more senior court and is bound by it even if the lower court considers it wrong. Of course, as indicated earlier, there may be enough difference in the facts of the cases to allow the court to distinguish the unwelcome precedent. Finally, it should be remembered that (within the limits on legislative power prescribed by the U.S. and state Constitutions) the legislature is always free to overturn a judicial decision, even by the highest court. If the legislature does not like a rule established by a court, it can pass a statute that changes the rule.

§3.2.3 The Drawbacks of the System of Precedent

The advantages of the system of precedent — efficiency, predictability, and fairness — have already been alluded to. The system also has some drawbacks. First, it can **perpetuate unsound or unfair rules** when a later court is bound by a poor or outdated earlier decision. As just mentioned, there are means of avoiding this problem by making factual distinctions when possible, by overruling if the court is of sufficient rank, or by legislation. However, the inertia inherent in both the legislative and judicial processes often allows unsatisfactory rules to remain in force.

Second, rulemaking through court decisions tends to be **sporadic and disorganized**. When a legislature decides to enact a law, it can proceed in an orderly way to address the problem comprehensively. It can hold hearings, order staff research, and engage in debate. A statute can then be fashioned that is designed to deal with all the issues involved and to set out all the applicable rules. Caselaw develops more spasmodically. Courts have no control over the order in which cases arise, and they can respond only to the immediate issue involved in each case. They cannot legislate broadly but must confine themselves to resolving the dispute at hand. The rules that they create are very specifically tied to the facts in the case. As a result, judicial development of doctrine is haphazard. Some areas of law may be covered thoroughly because they are litigated frequently, while others may languish for decades. Some areas of the law may thus be regularly refined and updated while others are neglected. It sometimes happens that a major issue remains unresolved for years, because no party has wished to pursue it to the point of a definitive appellate pronouncement. Again, sometimes these gaps may be filled by legislative action, but they often are not.

Third, it is often **harder to find the legal rule** in a judicial opinion than in a statute. Statutes usually simply state their rules. Judge-made rules are contained in **opinions**, which can be dense, detailed, and lengthy pieces of writing. An opinion sets out the facts of the case, contains an often extended dissertation on the law, and finally reaches a decision or **judgment** resolving the issues between the parties. Somewhere in this body of writing, there are legal rules that serve as precedent. It is not always obvious what these rules are. To find them, the lawyer must study and interpret the case. To make matters worse, if the case has been decided by a divided appellate court, it can be harder still to determine the precedential weight of a majority or plurality opinion, called into question by concurrence or dissent.

§3.3 THE ANATOMY OF A JUDICIAL OPINION

§3.3.1 *Ratio Decidendi* (Rule or Holding) and *Obiter Dictum*

As mentioned before, the opinion states the facts of the case. In the opinion of a trial court, the facts are those as determined by the **factfinder** (the jury, or in non-jury cases, the judge) after weighing the evidence and resolving conflicts in testimony. The factual conclusions reached at trial are not disturbed on appeal unless they are so unreasonable that no support can be found for them in the evidence. Therefore, the recital of facts in an appellate opinion is based on the findings at trial. As the previous discussion indicates, the factual basis of the opinion is very important because the rule of the case can only be determined with reference to it.

Having laid the factual foundation for its decision, the court proceeds to resolve the *legal issues*. The judge could simply state the rule to be applied and give judgment. However, in most cases that involve significant legal issues, the judge justifies and articulates the *rationale* for the rule and its application in the case. The statement of the rule and its reasoning are the portion of the case that constitutes the precedent. This part of the opinion is called the **rule** or the **holding** or, in Latin, the *ratio decidendi* (roughly translated as "reasoning for the decision").

Frequently, the opinion does not confine itself to matter that is directly related to the resolution of the dispute before the court, but ranges beyond this to deal with **ancillary** or **collateral** matters on which the judge considers it necessary to express a view. These collateral discussions may be included, for example, to further explain and qualify the holding or to give guidance in future cases on how this court will view variations of the factual circumstances. This collateral matter is called *obiter dictum* ("said in passing") or simply **dictum**. As stated before, because it is *not necessary to the disposition* of the case, it is not binding precedent and has only persuasive value. A simple exercise in identifying the rule of a case and distinguishing it from dictum can be found in the examples.

§3.3.2 The Process of Inductive and Deductive Reasoning in the Creation and Application of Legal Rules

When a general rule is applied to a particular case, a process of **deductive reasoning** is followed. The general rule, accepted as true, serves as the major premise. The particular facts to which it will be applied are the minor premise. Provided that there is a necessary connection between these two premises, a conclusion is produced that must also be true. For example:

Major premise. (The generally applicable rule of law): The contract of a minor is voidable at the instance of the minor.

Minor premise. (The particular facts): June Nior is a minor who entered a contract and now seeks to avoid it.

Conclusion: June has the right to avoid the contract.

Deductive reasoning, therefore, allows a rule of law to be applied in a particular case.

But where did this major premise, the rule of law, come from? In the common law, it has been created by precedent through a process opposite from deductive reasoning: The ruling in a particular case is generalized to create a rule of law applicable beyond the case. This is called **inductive reasoning**. In an earlier case another minor, Joe Venile, had entered into a contract with May Jore that he sought to avoid. In that case the court ruled that Joe, as a minor, had the power to avoid the contract. This rule then becomes generalized by the doctrine of precedent, so that it declares that not simply Joe, but all minors, may avoid contracts. The next time a minor, such as June, seeks to avoid a contract in a case with substantially similar facts, the general rule is applied by deductive reasoning to resolve it.

It must be stressed that the facts in the subsequent case (the minor premise[2]) must be substantially the same as in the prior case, otherwise there is no connection between the major and minor premise necessary to reach a conclusion. As stated earlier, material rather than absolute similarity is required. But even when there is a notable difference in the facts, the rule could be applied by analogy if the rationale motivating the first decision is equally applicable in the second. For example, say in the next case the issue arises whether a mentally impaired adult has the power to avoid a contract.

---

2. This is not a pun.

41

The rationale for the decision in the first case was that when a person requires protection from bad judgment and exploitation resulting from youth, the values of freedom of contract and the protection of reasonable reliance in the marketplace must be weighed against the need to protect the minor. The court in the second case may find that the rule should be applied to a mentally impaired adult too, because this rationale is equally compelling in this case.

§3.3.3 The Use of Authority and Supporting Rationale in Judicial Opinions

Much has been said already on the use of precedent and legal exposition to justify the court's conclusion. The strength and extent of precedential authority and the force of the court's reasoning must be evaluated critically by one who wishes to interpret the opinion and to evaluate its worth as precedent. It is therefore useful to take a little more time to point out some of the elements that constitute the rationale in an opinion.

When the decision is based on a prior case that serves as precedent, the earlier case is cited with some explanation of why it is controlling. The same is true if a rule of statute law is applicable. In some cases, this citation of authority may be the only justification advanced by the court for the rule. That is, in deciding in a particular way, the court may rely solely on an established rule and advance no explanation of its own. For example: "The contract of a minor is avoidable at the induce of the minor. See *Joe Venile v. May Jore.*"

However, if there is no controlling precedent or statutory provision, the court cannot simply rely on some authoritative source for its rule. It has to develop the rule itself and must explain why it does so. Even when there is authority, the court may consider it useful to bolster that citation to authority by explaining why the rule makes sense. Most policy rationales for a rule fit into one or more of three related but distinct classes:

1. A rule may be justified on the basis of **public policy** goals. The court feels that some particular social, economic, or political policy is served by the rule. For example, the court may discuss how it balanced the countervailing policies of freedom of contract and reliance against the protection of a minor.
2. A rule may be grounded in **ethics or fairness.** For example, the court may justify the minor's power of avoidance by arguing that an adult should not contract with a minor, because this is exploitive. It may also focus on the injustice of holding a person of tender years to a contractual commitment. The unfairness to the minor, combined

3. The Doctrine of Precedent and a Contract Case Analysis

with the unethical conduct of the major party and the likelihood that that party could tell by appearances that the other was under age, justifies the minor's power of avoidance.

3. Courts sometimes rationalize results on the basis of **institutional efficiency**. For example, the court may concede that some minors are more sophisticated than others, so that some may indeed be able to make a mature judgment. However, the court may conclude that a clear rule setting a definite age for contractual capacity is efficient because it is certain and avoids litigation over the question of actual competence.

As you read opinions, take note of their structure. You will find that one or more of these justifications appear in all of them.

Examples

1. This example provides a simple illustration of case analysis and the operation of the doctrine of precedent. It is based on an opinion in a fictitious case involving a minor's contract. Although the substantive law of contractual capacity is not discussed until Chapter 14, the principles of substantive law are not difficult to grasp and the focus is on the analysis in the opinion rather than on the rules of law. Read the opinion and consider the questions that follow it.

Supreme Court of Savannah, 2006
LORNA GREEN, Plaintiff
v.
MO MEADOWS, Defendant

VERDANT, Chief Justice, delivered the opinion of the court.

Plaintiff, Lorna Green, owns a golf practice putting course. On February 1, 2004, she entered into an agreement with defendant, Mo Meadows, doing business under the name "Mo's Mowing Services." In terms of the agreement, defendant agreed to mow the plaintiff's course bi-weekly during the period March 1 to October 31, 2004, for a total price of $20,000, payable in weekly installments. At the time of the agreement, defendant was 17 years old and just two weeks short of his 18th birthday. Plaintiff did not know or even think about his age. He was of mature appearance, operated his own business, and approached plaintiff to solicit the work. Although plaintiff was unaware of defendant's domestic circumstances, he had in fact been living on his own for some time and was financially independent of his parents. Two days after entering into the agreement with plaintiff, defendant accepted a more lucrative business opportunity that precluded him from performing the mowing services for plaintiff. He therefore called plaintiff and told her that he was no longer able to mow her course. At this stage the contract was fully executory — that is, no services had been performed under the contract, and no payments had been made.

After trying in vain to persuade defendant to honor his undertaking, plaintiff made inquiries and found another person to perform the same services for a fee of $30,000. This was the cheapest substitute available. Plaintiff then sued defendant for $10,000, the difference between what the services would have cost her under her contract with defendant and what they cost under the substitute transaction. This is the correct measure of damages because it compensates plaintiff for her disappointed expectation and places her in the position that she would have been in had the contract been performed. However, these damages are only recoverable if defendant's refusal to perform was an actionable breach of contract.

None of the above facts were disputed at trial. Defendant admitted entering into and subsequently refusing to perform the contract. The sole defense that he raised was that he was a minor at the time of contracting and therefore had the right to avoid the contract, which he did a couple of days later. The trial court found in favor of defendant on this issue of law and granted judgment in his favor, dismissing plaintiff's claim. The court of appeals affirmed.

On appeal to this court, plaintiff concedes that defendant was a minor both when entering and terminating the contract. However, plaintiff urges us to hold defendant bound to the contract under the circumstances of the case: Defendant was almost 18, operated his own business, looked mature, lived independently of his parents, and fully understood the nature of the transaction. Plaintiff dealt fairly with defendant and had no knowledge of his age. In effect, while plaintiff acknowledges that a minor's contract is normally avoidable, she contends that the application of that rule in the present case would be highly technical and unfair. While this argument has some appeal, it is contrary to the law and policy of this state and must fail.

At common law, a person attained the age of majority at 21. However, in 1960 the legislature of this state changed the age of majority to 18. The statute expressly states that "until midnight on the day preceding a person's 18th birthday, that person shall be a minor for all purposes in law." Clearly then defendant was a minor both when he contracted and disaffirmed his contract.

The law of this state on minors' contracts was first pronounced on by this court in *Senex v. Youngblood*, 50 Savannah Reports 100 (1908), in which we held that a contract entered into by a minor may be avoided by the minor, either expressly or by implication, at any time before attaining majority or within a reasonable time thereafter. As we explained in *Senex*, this rule is intended to protect minors from improvidence and bad judgment and to prevent advantage-taking by adults. This rationale is as applicable today as it was when first advanced, and the rule has been followed consistently ever since. Plaintiff refers us to *Teenbride v. Groanup*, 150 Savannah Reports 200 (1945), in which we recognized an exception to the rule where a minor had become fully emancipated from her parents as a result of marrying and setting up her own home. However, the marital status of the minor was a material element of that case and distinguishes it from the situation before us today. Given the law's purpose of affording protection to minors, we are not inclined to broaden the rule in *Teenbride*.

It may be true, as plaintiff argues, that it is technical and unfair to allow an independent and mature minor to avoid a contract entered into so close to majority. However, this argument invites the court to abandon a clear and definite rule in favor of a case-by-case investigation into the minor's circumstances. While it may be arbitrary to fix contractual capacity as arising at a precise hour on a person's 18th birthday, this rule is at least predictable and easy to apply. A fact-based analysis of a minor's actual ability to use mature judgment would create uncertainty in the law and would surely encourage litigation. The arbitrary rule does not really impose great hardship on the major party who has the opportunity to demand proof of age whenever dealing with a person of youthful appearance. In any event, even if plaintiff's argument has merit, it is better addressed to the legislature than to the courts, because the legislature has spoken on this matter and we have no authority to disregard a clear statutory provision.

Finally, we note in passing that plaintiff has referred us to several decisions from other states in which it has been held that a minor loses the right to disaffirm a contract where he or she has misrepresented his or her age. The wisdom of such decisions may be called into question, given the policy of protecting minors from improvident and irresponsible behavior. Nevertheless, we need not pass on this question here, because there is no evidence that defendant affirmatively misrepresented his age. It is not enough to constitute a misrepresentation that a minor simply appears to be over 18 and says nothing to counter that impression.

We find, therefore, that the courts below did not err in giving judgment for the defendant and we affirm.

WEED, Justice, dissenting.

In allowing defendant to avoid this contract, the majority adopts an absurdly rigid approach. While it is true that minors need protection from improvident action and exploitation by adults, there is no evidence in this case to suggest that any such factors were present. Rather, defendant unscrupulously and coldbloodedly reneged on his contractual promise purely for the sake of exploiting more profitable economic opportunities. Given the age and independence of defendant, he was in fact emancipated. His situation is really indistinguishable from that of the married minor in *Teenbride*, and the rule in that case should have been followed. By refusing to extend that rule and narrowly confining the *Teenbride* decision, the majority allows defendant to escape his undertaking with impunity and teaches young people a very poor lesson on business ethics. The advantage of legal certainty is greatly outweighed by the need to do justice between the parties in specific cases.

Furthermore, the majority's claim that its hands are tied by statute is misconceived. The statute simply fixes the age of majority. It says nothing of the court's power at common law to recognize appropriate exceptions to the general rule concerning the avoidability of minors' contracts. Indeed, the rule in *Teenbride* was already in existence at the time that the statute was enacted, and no one has suggested that the statute was intended to overrule it.

For the above reason, I dissent from the majority opinion and would reverse the decision of the lower courts, awarding judgment to plaintiff.

Consider the following questions based on this opinion:
(a) What is the holding of the case?
(b) What non-binding dicta can you find in the majority opinion?
(c) What is the precedential effect of the dissenting opinion?
(d) Bearing in mind the discussion of judicial rationale in section 3.3.3, identify the rationales used to support the majority opinion and the dissent.
(e) Consider the differing treatment of the *Teenbride* decision in the majority and dissenting opinions. What does this tell you about the process of following precedent?
(f) What lessons do the majority and dissenting opinions teach on the role of courts and the relationship between judicial and legislative rulemaking?

2. After *Green v. Meadows* was decided, the supreme court of another state had to resolve a case with substantially similar facts. The case is one of first impression in this other jurisdiction (that is, there is no judicial precedent in the state on this issue). What impact will the *Green* decision have in the resolution of this subsequent case?

3. After *Green v. Meadows*, a trial court in Savannah is dealing with a case in which a minor deliberately and expressly misrepresented to the major party that she was 20 years old and bolstered this misrepresentation by producing a forged driver's license. Is *Green* binding authority in this case? If not, does it offer the court any guidance on how to dispose of the case?

4. In another subsequent case before a trial court in Savannah, the facts are almost identical to those in *Green v. Meadows*. The only material difference is that the contract was entered into three days before the minor's 18th birthday. One week after his birthday, before the services had been delivered or paid for, the minor disaffirmed the contract. How does *Green* affect the disposition of this case?

Explanations

1(a). The holding of the case is the legal rule of the case that becomes binding precedent. It is narrowly confined to those pronouncements of law necessary to resolve the factual issues in the case. The rule in this case may be formulated as follows: A person is a minor until midnight of the day before his or her 18th birthday. A wholly executory contract[3] entered into by a minor at any time before reaching majority is avoidable by the minor if expressly disaffirmed by the minor prior to majority. This right of avoidance continues to exist even if the minor lives apart from and is financially independent of his or her parents. A minor has no duty to disclose his or her age, and the minor's physical appearance and the major party's lack of knowledge of the minor's age are not relevant to the right of avoidance.

   Notice that the holding is considerably narrower than the court's discourse on the law. For example, although the court says disaffirmance can occur expressly or by implication, before or within a reasonable time after reaching majority, the facts in the case are that disaffirmance was express and occurred before majority. Therefore, the court's recognition of implied and post-majority disaffirmance are dicta, not part of the holding. Also, it is a significant fact that the contract was wholly executory, so this must be reflected in the formulation of the holding. Although the absolute tone of the opinion suggests that the same rule may apply even if one or both parties had performed wholly or in part, this factor could change the equities of the case and require a different resolution. The holding must be narrowly drawn to show that this issue was not before the court in this case.

1(b). There are a number of dicta in the majority opinion. Remember that a dictum is a statement on the law that is not necessary for the resolution of the case but is pronounced on by the court in passing. A dictum is not binding precedent, but it has persuasive value. It allows the court

---

3. A wholly executory contract is one in which neither party has begun to perform its obligations under the contract.

to expound on legal doctrine and policy and provides guidance on how the court would be likely to deal with a later case having facts that present the issue discussed. Apart from the two dicta mentioned in Explanation 1 (a) concerning implied and post-majority disaffirmance, the majority opinion contains the following dicta:

  (i) The discussion of plaintiff's damages is dictum because plaintiff lost the case on the issue of capacity, making the issue of remedy moot.

 (ii) The court's recognition of the exception regarding emancipation in the *Teenbride* case is dictum because the defendant in this case was not married. Note, however, that the court hints that it is not particularly well-disposed to the precedent, and this may undermine its value, as discussed in 1 (e) below.

(iii) The discussion of misrepresentation of age is holding to the extent that the court states that physical appearance combined with nondisclosure does not constitute misrepresentation. This aspect of the opinion does address facts in issue in the case. The remainder of the court's observations on this question are dicta at best. Their import is discussed in Example 3 below.

1 (c). The dissenting opinion is merely the view of this individual judge. No part of it, whether directly related to the facts or not, is the holding of the case. It is not binding precedent. However, a dissent can be influential, particularly when it is the well-reasoned opinion of a respected jurist. When a court in another jurisdiction seeks persuasive authority, a dissenting opinion may be preferred to the majority approach. Even in this jurisdiction, the dissent may in time persuade the majority of the court to move away from the position adopted in this case. Alternatively, as the court's composition changes, successors to the current majority may be more sympathetic to the dissent's view. Dissents do not always have these beneficial effects. Sometimes the existence of dissent on the court can undermine the force of the majority opinion or cause confusion for lawyers trying to interpret the case.

1 (d). The majority opinion uses all the elements referred to in section 3.3.3. The authoritative basis for the decision is the *Senex* case and the state statute. This recourse to authority is bolstered by rationale based on public policy, fairness, and institutional efficiency: The protection of minors from improvidence and exploitation serves both the ends of public policy and fairness; the preference for the arbitrary but certain rule is justified with reference to the goal of institutional efficiency; and the court's deference to the legislature is based on both policy and institutional grounds.

As the dissent shows, the court is not unanimous in the perception of how these different rationales come into play. The dissenting opinion finds the *Teenbride* case to be applicable authority and the statute not to be on point. It considers that the majority opinion does not serve the goals of public policy and fairness, and finds the goal of institutional efficiency to be outweighed by the policy of fairness.

1(e). The treatment of the *Teenbride* case in the majority and dissenting opinions highlights the point that a precedent is binding only when the facts of the cases are substantially similar. It seldom happens that a later case is identical to an earlier one, and it is often difficult to know whether factual differences between them are material enough to disqualify the earlier case as binding precedent. Sometimes the court's view of this issue is colored by its desire to follow or depart from the earlier decision. The majority apparently does not like the rule in *Teenbride* and does not wish to use it, so it finds the case distinguishable on the ground that the minor in the earlier case was married. The dissent feels that the independence of the minor is a relevant consideration and therefore feels that *Teenbride* should be followed. The dissenting judge therefore refuses to find the fact of marriage to be a material difference between the cases.

1(f). One of the perpetual issues confronting courts is the relationship between the judicial and the legislative role. While judges clearly do make law through the common law process, this function is circumscribed by the predominant lawmaking authority of the elected legislature. Therefore, if a statute deals with an issue, the judge must apply the statute and not disregard it. In this case there is a statute prescribing the age of minority. The difference between the majority and dissenting opinions reflects a different view on the scope and intended meaning of the statute. The majority interprets it as providing authority for a rigid rule on contractual capacity; the dissent sees it merely as altering a common law rule on age, while preserving judicial discretion to deal with the actual effect of minors' contracts. The issue of statutory interpretation can be difficult, and the extent to which the court is willing to defer to perceived legislative intent is often influenced by the judge's broad or narrow view of the court's rulemaking function.

2.   This decision is not binding precedent in another judicial hierarchy. When a court deals with an issue of first impression in its jurisdiction, it is likely to seek guidance by consulting the decisions in other jurisdictions and will be influenced by the persuasiveness of supporting rationales in decided cases which should have been brought to its attention by one or the other party during the course of argument. Because the court of another state is not bound by the majority

opinion, it could find the dissent to be more compelling and may decide to use it as persuasive authority.

3.   As noted in Explanation 1 (b), *Green* is only of binding authority in its holding that physical appearance plus nondisclosure is not misrepresentation. Beyond that, the court's observations on misrepresentation are no more than dictum. In fact, the court does not even provide clear dictum on this question. It merely refers to decisions in other states that recognize an exception for misrepresentation and then calls into question the wisdom of those decisions. Therefore, although the decision does not give clear guidance to the trial court in the later case, it does hint that if the judge recognizes the misrepresentation exception, the decision may be overturned on appeal. This signals to the judge (and to the attorneys in the case) that some careful and thorough argument should be prepared if reliance is to be placed on the misrepresentation.

4.   As noted in Explanations 1 (a) and (b), the holding of *Green* is confined to disaffirmance by the minor before reaching majority. In the later case, disaffirmance occurred after the age of majority, so it is not within the rule of *Green*. However, *Green* has a very clear dictum that post-majority disaffirmance is also effective if within a reasonable time. (The earlier case of *Senex* said the same thing, but we do not know if it was dictum or holding in that case. If it was holding, that case is binding precedent. If it was dictum, the fact that it was reinforced by later dictum in *Green* strengthens its persuasive force.) Therefore the trial court should take the pronouncement in *Green* very seriously. Of course, *Green* does not say what a reasonable time after majority would be, and the trial court will have to resolve that issue.

CHAPTER 4

The Objective Test and Common Law Offer and Acceptance

§4.1 INTERPRETATION AND THE OBJECTIVE TEST

§4.1.1 The Communication of Contractual Intent

The next three chapters are concerned with issues of contract formation. Few aspects of this topic are unaffected by interpretation questions, so it is useful to address principles of interpretation at the outset. This is not the first time that interpretation is discussed, nor will it be the last. As in life generally, interpretation is a pervasive process in contract law.

Mutual assent is the basis of contract. This means that each party must intend to enter the contract and must agree with the other to do so on mutually acceptable terms. In some galaxies beyond our solar system, beings have evolved to the point where they can communicate telepathically. Having not yet developed that faculty, we terrestrials can only make our contractual intentions known by communicating them: by employing outward signals such as words and actions that are observed and given meaning — that is, interpreted — by another. Sometimes this process can be successful. The utterer's intent is accurately conveyed by unambiguous words or actions that are fully understood by the other party. But this is not always so. Communication can be fouled by so many different causes: The utterer's thinking may be fuzzy or confused; a poor choice of words or actions may obscure intent; a manifestation of intent may be perceived differently or misconstrued by the person to whom it is addressed; or secret reservations or deviousness may result in deliberate obfuscation. Therefore, while contracts are consensual relationships and we do like to think of them as a genuine "meeting of the minds," the minds of parties often may not be in true accord, even though their manifestations of assent appear to be congruent.

§4.1.2 Assent and Accountability: Subjective and Objective Tests of Assent

When imperfect communication leads to a dispute about the existence or terms of a contract, two fundamental contract policies must be accommodated. The **assent policy** dictates that contractual obligation should not be imposed on a person who did not in fact agree to be bound. However, if the need for true assent is too heavily stressed, the **policy** of **protecting reliance** is undermined. If no one could rely on words or conduct that indicate assent, it would be difficult for anyone to have confidence in the system of commercial exchange. Therefore, the assent policy must be tempered by the goal of protecting the expectations of one who reasonably relied on the appearance of assent. A person must be held accountable for behavior that signifies assent. Many nineteenth-century courts gave overwhelming weight to the assent policy and would refuse to find a contract unless there had been true mental consensus — a genuine "meeting of the minds." In other words, actual assent, determined **subjectively** by looking at each party's actual understanding, was a prerequisite to contract.

During the classical period (roughly, late nineteenth and early twentieth century, as explained in section 2.3.1) thinking changed. Courts focused more on the need to protect reasonable reliance on the apparent meaning of the manifestation. Classicists felt that a subjective approach was wrong in principle because it made transacting less dependable. It was also not workable because it placed too much store on obviously unreliable (and not easily rebuttable) self-serving testimony of actual intent. Classical contract law therefore moved toward the opposite pole, refusing to see any relevance in the subjective state of mind of the parties and employing a strict **objective** or external test for assent. If agreement was apparent from the manifestations of assent, reasonably interpreted, a contract had been formed on the terms reflected in the manifestation. It was neither necessary nor permissible to receive testimony on what either party actually thought or believed.

A complete disregard of the actual state of mind of the parties gives too little weight to the assent policy and could lead to injustice where subjective evidence could cast some light on the meaning of a manifestation. For example, evidence of a party's subjective understanding could provide an alternative explanation of the meaning of words or actions, or it could indicate justifiable misapprehension induced by the other party's unfair bargaining methods. Recognizing this, modern law has moved away from the strict objectivist approach of the classical period, and is not as absolute in its focus on the manifestation of assent. It is now accepted that evidence of a party's state of mind may sometimes be helpful in interpreting or giving a context to words or conduct, provided that the subjective evidence is credible and compatible with the overt behavior. Although less rigid than it used to be, the objective test is firmly established and a subjective "meeting of the minds" is not required for contract formation. In the absence of compelling contrary indications, assent is legally sufficient if each party, by the deliberate use of words or conduct, manifested agreement to be contractually bound.

The contemporary approach is reflected in several sections of the Restatement Second. In defining a promise, §2 speaks of a manifestation of intent by the promisor that justifies the promisee in understanding that a commitment has been made; §3 describes "agreement" as a manifestation of mutual assent; §§19 and 20 stress the accountability principle by holding a party liable for deliberate manifestations by words or conduct, made with reason to know that they will create a reasonable impression of assent. UCC Article 2 does not specifically address the objective test, which is therefore governed by the general principles of common law by virtue of §1.103.[1]

§4.1.3 The Operation of the Objective Test in Contemporary Law

Having introduced the objective test, we now look more carefully at its operation and implications. The test may be thought of as having both a substantive aspect (that is, it prescribes a legal standard for determining assent) and an evidentiary aspect (that is, it regulates what evidence is admissible to prove intent). Although these aspects are closely interrelated, it aids understanding of the objective test to articulate and describe them separately.

a. The Substantive Aspect: The Legal Standard for Determining Assent Is Objective and External

Manifestations of assent are interpreted, not in light of what the utterer actually meant or the other party actually understood, but from the standpoint of a *reasonable person in the position of the party* to whom the manifestation was made. That is, we ask not what the words or actions *did mean* to either

---

1. Section 1.103 (numbered §1.103(b) in the 2001 revision of Article 1) adopts the general principles of common law to the extent that they are not displaced by the particular provisions of the UCC.

party, but how they *should have been understood* if interpreted reasonably, in the context of the transaction, by a person with the knowledge and attributes of the party to whom they were directed. The reason for this, of course, is that the objective test is aimed at balancing the requirement of assent with the protection of reasonable reliance. It is therefore not concerned with any quirky or misbegotten perception of meaning that may form in the mind of the party to whom the manifestation is directed, but with the rational meaning that should have been placed on it by that party. How do we find this reasonable person? In essence, this is a construct meant to represent the community standard, as identified by the trier of fact.

An example may help to illustrate the way in which the "reasonable person" construct focuses the enquiry: Penny Less borrowed money from Uncle Rich in the past, but never repaid the loan. One day she again asks Uncle Rich to lend her $500. Uncle Rich, tired of Penny's sponging, says sarcastically, "Yes, and you'll repay it like you did last time!" It does not matter that Uncle Rich thought he was saying "No," or that Penny (who is thick-skinned and does not easily recognize sarcasm) thought that he was saying "Yes, and you can take your time about repaying me." The real issue is how a reasonable person of Penny's education, background, and familiarity with Uncle Rich would have understood the response. (Or, stated differently, how Penny, acting reasonably, should have understood it.)

b. The Evidentiary Aspect: Evidence of Observable Action Is of Principal Relevance, and Testimony of a Party's Thoughts Is, at Best, Marginally Useful

It stands to reason that an objective standard must focus on objective evidence — that is, evidence of observable signs of agreement — to establish contractual intent. Objective evidence includes such things as a signature on a writing, spoken words, or behavior pertinent to the transaction. Subjective evidence — that is, testimony by a party as to what he or she thought, intended, or believed when making the manifestation — is of questionable value. Classicists tended to exclude such evidence entirely on the basis that it was absolutely irrelevant because the parties' subjective intention was beside the point. Some modern courts may still take this approach, but the tendency today is to be less rigid. The court may admit subjective testimony as having some role in explaining the meaning of the manifestation but it is not likely to be given weight unless it can be reconciled with the objective indicia of assent or explains why the manifestation should be discounted.[2] The

---

2. As suggested earlier, the manifestation should not be accepted at face value if the subjective evidence suggests that it may have been induced by improper bargaining practices employed by the other party. That is, the discrepancy between thoughts and actions results from fraud, imposition, or other unfair behavior by the other party. For example, a person signed a

dubious reliability and relevance of subjective evidence affects its credibility, even if it is admitted.

c. The Relationship Between Objective and Subjective Elements

The difference between a strict and a relative objectivist approach may be illustrated as follows: A homeowner asks a contractor to give her an estimate on cleaning her roof. The contractor gives her an oral price quote and hands her an order form authorizing the work and promising to pay the price. She manifests contractual intent by signing the order form. She later denies having entered a contract and claims that she thought that her signature merely acknowledged receipt of the estimate. A strongly objectivist court would disallow this testimony as irrelevant because manifested intention is all that counts. A court approaching the objective test with more flexibility may admit the evidence but is likely to give it little weight. There is no indication that her misapprehension was caused by some trickery or unfair pressure on the part of the contractor, and her manifestation of assent was clear. Her subjective evidence so starkly conflicts with the reasonable import of her actions that she must either be lying or was unforgivably careless in signing an unread document. She is appropriately held accountable for giving the impression of assent, even if she did not actually intend to agree. When a writing is signed without having been read and understood, courts often express this accountability principle as a **"duty to read"** the document before signifying agreement with its contents.

In summary, when parties disagree on the meaning of their words and actions, their intent must be decided by the factfinder. The resolution of ambiguity, obscurity, and miscommunication is accomplished by an evaluation of observable, external signals used by the parties to communicate intent. If the dispute centers on whether a contract was formed at all, this enquiry is directed to the fundamental question of whether they manifested intent to enter the relationship. If it is clear that they did make a contract, the focus of the enquiry is on the question of what terms were agreed. The external standard is used because an enquiry into what each party had in mind is neither efficient nor fair. It would place too heavy an emphasis on unreliable evidence and fails to protect reasonable reliance on words or conduct.

d. Lack of Serious Intent: Jokes and Bluffs

The observation was made in section 4.1.1 that miscommunication of intent can result from many different causes. Most commonly, the problem is

---

memorandum of agreement with a gun to his head, or after having been tricked into doing so by a misrepresentation concerning its identity and legal effect. Although this is surely an issue to be noted here, discussion of the doctrines governing improper bargaining is deferred to Chapter 13.

inadvertent failure to express intent clearly. However, there are some cases in which a party who claims lack of contractual intent alleges that he was not serious about making a contract, but was joking or bluffing, and that the other party should have realized it. Although this does not happen very often, there are a few well-loved cases that involve this situation, and that serve as good examples of the application of the objective test.

One of these is *Lucy v. Zehmer*, 84 S.E.2d 516 (Va. 1954). Zehmer, the owner of property, contended that his offer to sell it to Lucy was a bluff. The alleged contract was made under most unbusinesslike circumstances while the parties sat drinking one evening in a restaurant operated by Zehmer. The memorial of the alleged contract was written in very sketchy terms on the reverse side of a restaurant guest check. When Lucy sought to enforce the sale, Zehmer claimed that it was not intended seriously. He testified that he and Lucy had been drinking too much, and he was just calling Lucy's bluff because he did not believe that Lucy had the money to buy the property. Whatever Zehmer's actual intent may have been, the court found that Lucy was in earnest and under the objective test, had no reason to believe that Zehmer was not. (The court also declined to allow Zehmer to avoid the contract on grounds of mental disability caused by intoxication because it did not believe that Zehmer was drunk enough.)

More recently, in the rather wacky case of *Leonard v. PepsiCo, Inc.*, 88 F. Supp. 2d 116 (S.D.N.Y. 1999), the court found that an alleged offer really should have been reasonably understood as a joke. Pepsi conducted a promotional campaign in which buyers of Pepsi products could earn "Pepsi points" which could be redeemed for prizes listed in a catalog. The points did not all have to be earned by consuming soft drinks. As long as 15 actual points were submitted with the redemption form, the remaining points required for the prize could be purchased for ten cents a point. The TV commercial advertising the promotion showed various prizes that could be won (such as t-shirts and sunglasses) and the number of points needed to win them. The commercial ended with a teenager landing a Harrier jet on the grounds of his high school. As he emerged from the jet, the words "Harrier fighter, 7,000,000 points" appeared on the screen. Leonard submitted a redemption form claiming the jet. He included the 15 original Pepsi points and a check for just under $700,000 to buy the balance of the 7 million points needed. Pepsi refused to award the jet to him on a number of theories. One of them was that the jet was used in the commercial merely for humor and entertainment, and could not reasonably have been understood as a real prize. (The other theories are discussed in Example 8(a).) The court agreed. It found that no reasonable person could have understood the commercial to be a serious offer of a jet, but would have realized that the use of the jet was just to add an absurd comic touch and to exaggerate the excitement of the drink. Furthermore, the fact that a Harrier is a fierce war machine unsuitable for consumer use and costing some $23 million would alert the reasonable viewer that it could not possibly be offered in exchange for about $700,000.

---

§4.2 THE OFFER AND ACCEPTANCE MODEL

§4.2.1 Introduction

The formation of the contract is the beginning of the parties' legal relationship, but it is also the culmination of a process of bargaining. This is reflected in the expression that parties "conclude a contract," which means, not that they have finished performing, but that they have completed the interaction leading up to the execution of a contract.

In some cases, a deal may be struck very quickly, with a minimum of bargaining: One party may make a proposal that is accepted without qualification by the other. In other cases the path to contract formation may be long and arduous. Initial proposals may lead to counterproposals, negotiations, and compromise. If the transaction is complex, each step in the process may require consultation with different corporate departments, technical experts, and attorneys. In either event, where this interaction is successful, there comes a time when the parties reach agreement and bind themselves to the relationship — a contract comes into being.

Sometimes the creation of a contract is marked by the signing of a written memorial of the agreement.[3] When this happens, it is relatively easy to fix the time of formation and the exact terms of the contract. However, this helpful indicator of formation is not always present because the parties may have formed a contract without recording it in a formal comprehensive writing. A contract could be contained in a series of correspondence or in some other collection of interrelated documents; it could have been made orally with the intention of later drafting and signing a written memorial or it may be partly written and partly oral or entirely oral.[4] Such circumstances may create uncertainty and disputes over the question of whether a contract was formed at all, and if so, whether certain terms became part of it. The rules of offer and acceptance provide a framework for resolving these questions.

---

3. In colloquial speech, people often talk of "signing a contract." Strictly speaking, this is inaccurate terminology. The contract is the legal relationship between the parties, and the document that is signed is actually the record or memorial of that contract.

4. Under the statute of frauds (see Chapter 11), certain types of contracts are not enforceable unless their essential terms are recorded in a signed writing. However, many contracts are not subject to this rule and are fully valid and enforceable in oral form. This does not mean that it is a good idea to dispense with a written memorial, even where the law does not require writing. It is harder to prove the existence and terms of an oral contract.

The offer and acceptance model has often been criticized as too rudimentary and artificial to cope with many contemporary methods of contract formation. For example, it bears little resemblance to what actually happens in the complex negotiations mentioned above, or where transactions involve the use of standard forms. In the latter case, the UCC has attempted a statutory modification of the rules, discussed in Chapter 6. In other situations, if there has not been legislative intervention, it is left to the courts to develop new rules or to analogize from existing ones to reach a realistic resolution.

§4.2.2 When Are Offer and Acceptance Issues Presented?

Upon learning the rules of offer and acceptance, an inexperienced student may be tempted to waste time and effort in trying to unravel the sequence of offer and acceptance in every case or problem. However, not every contract dispute raises formation issues, because the parties may not be in disagreement over the facts of formation. The rules of offer and acceptance tend to be relevant in three types of dispute:

First, the rules of offer and acceptance may be used to determine if a contract came into existence at all where the parties dispute whether their communications resulted in the formation of a contract. Second, even if it is settled that a contract was formed, a determination of which communication constituted the offer, and which was the acceptance, can resolve a dispute about the content of the contract. Third, the rules of offer and acceptance can be relevant to the determination of which state's law governs the contract or which state's courts have jurisdiction to hear a dispute over the contract. This issue may arise where the parties are located in different jurisdictions and communicate across state lines, so that the point of contract formation becomes relevant to choice of law and jurisdiction. This third situation is merely noted here and is not discussed further. The remainder of this chapter is confined to the application of offer and acceptance rules to resolve questions about the existence and terms of the contract.

§4.2.3 The Basic Model

The rules of offer and acceptance are based on a particular conception of how contracts are formed. In the simplest terms, they envisage that one person (called the **offeror**) makes an offer to another person (the **offeree**) to enter into a contract on specified terms. (Note that the legal meaning of the word "person" includes not only individuals, but also incorporated organizations such as corporations, partnerships, associations, and government bodies. When an organization contracts, it is represented by an authorized officer who acts as its agent.)

The offer creates a **power of acceptance** in the offeree so that she can bring the contract into existence by signifying **acceptance** of the transaction on the proposed terms. If the offeree **rejects** the offer either expressly or simply by not accepting it within a particular time, the offer lapses and no contract arises. If the offeree is interested in forming a contract, but not on the exact terms proposed, the offeree may respond by making a **counter-offer**, which has the effect of terminating the original offer and reversing the process: The original offeror now becomes the offeree with the power of acceptance. This could go on several more times until the parties reach accord or tire of trying. There are some variations and complications that could arise, as the following sections will show.

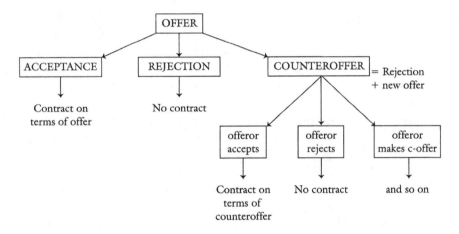

§4.3 THE RULES OF OFFER AND ACCEPTANCE

Possibly more than most other areas of contract law, offer and acceptance has a number of firm-sounding rules that seem quite technical in nature. This creates a sense of certainty and order that can be deceiving. As usual, there is not complete agreement between courts on what the rules are. Even where courts apply the same rule, factual circumstances, considerations of fairness, and issues of interpretation often lead to variations in result. This discussion relies heavily on the rules formulated in the Restatement Second. These rules must be approached with the usual awareness that, while persuasive and generally representative of the caselaw, they do not bind and are not always followed by courts.

The rules of offer and acceptance set out in this chapter are also generally applicable to sales of goods under UCC Article 2. Apart from §2.207 (dealt with at length in Chapter 6) and §2.205 (covered in Chapter 5), Article 2 has only a couple of provisions that deal with offer and acceptance. Sections 2.204 and 2.206 (numbered the same in the 2003 revision of Article 2) are very general, and set out the broad principle that courts should not take a technical approach to contract formation, but should focus on the question of whether the parties' interactions indicate intent to make a contract. These two sections are discussed further in section 6.1.

§4.4 THE NATURE OF AN OFFER, AS DISTINCT FROM A PRELIMINARY PROPOSAL

Restatement Second §24 describes an offer as a ". . . manifestation of willingness to enter into a bargain, so made as to justify another person in understanding that his assent to that bargain is invited and will conclude it." This definition identifies the hallmarks of an offer. The offer must contain these elements either expressly or by implication:

1. Because an offer must be manifested, it must necessarily be **communicated** to the person to whom it is addressed. An offer cannot take effect until it becomes known to the offeree.
2. The offer must **indicate a desire to enter into a contract**. To do this it has to specify the performances to be exchanged and the terms that will govern the relationship. It is important to remember that as the creator of the offer, the offeror has control over what its terms will be. (The traditional maxim is that the offeror is "master of the offer.") In addition to proposing the terms of the exchange, the offer may also prescribe the manner and time for an effective acceptance.
3. The offer must be **directed at some person or group** of persons. Although an offer is usually addressed to a specific person, it is legally possible to make an offer to a defined or undefined group. Where this happens, it is a question of interpretation if it contemplates multiple acceptances or may be accepted only by the first person to reply.
4. The offer must **invite acceptance**. It may or may not indicate how and by what time this acceptance is to be communicated. If a mode and time for acceptance are prescribed, they must be followed. If these are not set out in the offer, the court must decide whether the acceptance was reasonable and timely.
5. The offer must create the reasonable understanding that upon acceptance, a **contract will arise without any further approval** being required from the offeror.

The last hallmark distinguishes an offer from a proposal intended as nothing more than an overture; that is, a tentative expression of interest in transacting, an invitation to make an offer, or a request for information that may lead to an offer. To be an offer, the communication must convey the reasonable understanding (note the objective standard) that the offeror intends a contract to arise and expects to be **committed upon acceptance**. The offeror thus confers on the offeree the power to decide whether or not a contract will come into being. (As mentioned earlier, this is known as the **power of acceptance**.) If the proposal reserves to the proponent the final say on whether to be bound, it is not an offer but merely a preliminary communication.

Of course, it is up to the person initiating contractual negotiations to choose whether the communication is to be an offer or an overture, and the careful choice of language eliminates or at least reduces the risk that the communication may be misunderstood. However, when intent is not clearly expressed, the communication must be interpreted **objectively**. The question is whether, taking into account the entire context of the communication, the addressee was justified in understanding that the proponent intended to be bound on acceptance.

For example, if the owner of property wishes to make an offer to a prospective buyer, she may write:

> I offer to sell you my farm "Bleakacre" for $2 million cash. If you wish to buy this property you must deliver your written acceptance to me by midnight on Friday, October 13, 2006.

The strong wording (including the use of the terms "offer" and "acceptance") leave little doubt that an offer is intended. If, on the other hand, the owner wanted to make it clear that this is not an offer, she may couch the letter something like this:

> I wish to sell my farm "Bleakacre" and will consider an offer of not less than $2 million. I invite you to make an offer if you are interested in purchasing it.

However, if the owner is less precise in her choice of language, she may come up with something like this:

> I am willing to sell my farm "Bleakacre" to you, but will not accept less than $2 million cash. Let me have your reply as soon as possible.

This flabby language does not make the offeror's intention clear. It could lead the addressee to understand the communication to be an offer, whether or not the owner meant it as such. The ambiguity could keep a couple of lawyers happily employed for some time as the parties litigate over its meaning.

One cannot be sure who will win the last "Bleakacre" dispute because I have not provided any contextual information that may clarify the ambiguity in the owner's letter. In trying to resolve disputes like this, one must weigh all the facts of the case. Courts have identified some general indicia that help to distinguish an offer from a preliminary proposal:

1. The **words used in the communication** are always the primary indicators of what was intended. Even where the language of the communication does not make its import absolutely clear, clues to reasonable meaning may be found in what was said. The use of terms of art, such as "offer," "quote," or "proposal," may be helpful but are not conclusive if the context indicates that they were not used in their legal sense. (For example, realtors' lawn signs sometimes announce that a property is "offered for sale," yet no one would seriously argue that the seller thereby makes an offer in the legal sense.)

2. Because an offer is intended to form a contract upon acceptance (and as discussed below, an offeree is not usually permitted to accept in terms that go beyond the offer), a communication that **omits significant terms** is less likely to be an offer. Therefore, the comprehensiveness and specificity of the terms in the communication are an important clue to its intent.

3. The **relationship of the parties**, any previous dealings between them, and any prior communications in this transaction may cast light on how the recipient reasonably should have understood the communication.

4. Where parties are members of the same community or trade, they are or should be aware of any **common practices or trade usages**, so these are taken into account in determining reasonable understanding of a communication.

It must be stressed that these are just factors to be considered. This is not a list of firm rules and it is not exhaustive. The facts of each case must be evaluated to decide on the reasonable meaning of a communication.

In most transactions, a proposal to make a contract is directed to a specific, identified person. This is what happened in all the Bleakacre examples. However, an offeror could communicate a desire to enter a contract with multiple persons. The addressees could be a defined group or the public at large. Most commonly, this occurs where a person places an **advertisement** in a newspaper, catalog, website, or other medium of mass communication. The question of whether an advertisement is an offer or merely an invitation to make an offer must be resolved by the usual process of interpreting its apparent reasonable intent in light of its language in context. If it is an offer, the advertiser is bound to a recipient of the communication as soon as that recipient signifies his assent to its terms. If it is not an offer, but merely a solicitation, a recipient makes an offer by responding and the advertiser has the discretion to accept or reject that offer. Therefore, the question of whether or not an advertisement is an offer can have serious consequences if the advertiser did not expect to be committed to multiple contracts. In most situations, common practice in the marketplace would lead a reasonable person to understand that an advertisement or other generally disseminated proposal is not an offer, but merely a solicitation. However, this is just a general assumption. It can be overturned by the advertiser's choice of language or by proof that commercial practice does support the reasonable understanding that an offer was made.

One of the best-known cases that found an advertisement to be an offer is *Lefkowitz v. Great Minneapolis Surplus store*, 86 N.W.2d 689 (Minn. 1957). The store published a newspaper advertisement that read "Saturday 9 A.M. Sharp 3 Brand New Fur Coats Worth to $100 First Come First Served $1 Each" (lack of punctuation in the original). Although the plaintiff was the first person at the store on Saturday morning and he tendered the $1, the store refused to sell a coat to him on the grounds that it was a "house rule" that the offer was intended for women only. The next week the store placed a similar advertisement in the newspaper in which 3 items were listed for $1 each, "First Come First Served." One of the items was a "Black Lapin Stole Beautiful, worth $139.50." The plaintiff was again the first to show up at the store, but his tender of the $1 was again refused. The plaintiff sued for damages for breach of contract based on the difference between the value of the garments and the $1 price. The store contended that the advertisements were not offers, but merely invitations to the public to make offers to the store. The plaintiff made an offer which it declined. The court agreed that this may often be true, but the legal effect of the advertisement depends on its apparent intent as reasonably understood by the plaintiff. The terms of the advertisements were clear, definite, explicit, and left nothing open for negotiation. They therefore qualified as offers. The store's "house rule" did not restrict the power of acceptance to women because it was not expressed in the offer.[5]

---

5. Of course, the plaintiff had been told of the "house rule" before he accepted the second offer, but the court did not address this. Although the court found that both advertisements led to binding contracts, it only gave the plaintiff damages for the second contract, measured as the difference between the price of $1 and the advertised value of the stole, $139.50. The court said that damages under the first contract were too speculative because the advertisement stated only that the coat was worth "to $100," and it did not state a precise value. This seems unduly strict because the court could have used the maximum value asserted by the store as the best evidence of the coat's worth.

§4.5 THE EXPIRY OF THE OFFER BY PASSAGE OF TIME

§4.5.1 The Specified or Reasonable Duration of the Offer

An offer does not last forever. It has a limited duration and lapses if not accepted in time. As the creator of the offer, the offeror is entitled to specify the time within which the acceptance must be made. If the offeror does not state the duration of the offer, it must be accepted within *a reasonable time*. The offeror takes a risk by not specifying a time for acceptance because the question of what period is reasonable for acceptance may be unclear until settled by litigation. To decide what is a reasonable time, the factfinder must ask what amount of time would be needed to receive, consider, and reply to the offer under all the circumstances of the transaction. As a rough guide, it is usually assumed that if the parties are in each other's presence, the reasonable time for acceptance concludes when they part company, but if they communicate at a distance by mail or similar noninstantaneous means, the time for transmission must be taken into account. Other factors relevant to this question include the nature of the transaction; the relationship of the parties; any course of dealing, custom, or trade usage; the means of communication used; and the stability of the market.

An offeror may not entirely eliminate the risk of uncertainty by stating a time for acceptance, if the time specified is *ambiguous*. For example, if the offer requires acceptance by 5 P.M. Pacific Daylight Time on Friday, October 13, 2003, there can be no doubt as to the exact time that the power of acceptance ends. However, an acceptance required "within five days" is ambiguous because it does not indicate if the five-day period runs from the date of the writing or receipt of the offer, or whether the offer can be accepted after business hours on that final day.

§4.5.2 The Effect of a Late Attempt to Accept

If the offeree attempts to accept the offer after the period for acceptance has expired, the legal effect of this late communication may be difficult to decide and depends on the circumstances and the language used. It could be a *legally meaningless act*. Alternatively, the course of dealings between the parties and the language of the late acceptance could create the reasonable understanding that it is a *new offer* by the former offeree, creating a power of acceptance in the original offeror. In some cases, especially where there is doubt about the exact duration of the offer, the offeror's *failure to object* to a late acceptance may suggest either that it was not late at all, or even if it was late, that the offeror acquiesced in the delay, making the acceptance effective despite its tardiness. There is thus no hard-and-fast rule on the treatment of a late acceptance, and its effect must be determined on the facts of each case.

§4.6 TERMINATION OF THE OFFER BEFORE ITS EXPIRY BY LAPSE OF TIME

The stated or reasonable duration should be thought of as the longest period that an offer could remain open. It may terminate even before that under four circumstances identified in Restatement Second §36:

§4.6.1 Rejection

The offer lapses if the offeree rejects it. Once rejection has been communicated, the offeree cannot recant the rejection and accept, because the offer has come to an end. A purported acceptance after rejection could, of course, qualify as a new offer by the former offeree.

§4.6.2 Counteroffer

As explained in section 4.8, a counteroffer is treated as a rejection of the original offer and the substitution of a new offer by the original offeree. A counteroffer therefore has the same effect as an outright rejection in terminating the offeree's power to accept the original offer.

§4.6.3 The Offeror's Death or Mental Disability

If the offeror dies before the offer is accepted, the offer lapses automatically, even if the offeree did not know about the offeror's death at the time of attempted acceptance. Despite the fact that the rationale for the rule appears to be subjectivist (there can be no "meeting of the minds" if death intervenes before acceptance) the rule is still generally followed. Note that it applies only when the death occurs before acceptance. Once a contract has been formed, the supervening death of a party does not terminate it unless the contract expressly or impliedly contemplates that the death of a party will terminate it. The contractual obligation remains a liability of the estate, which must perform if possible or pay damages for breach.

The mental disability of the offeror is treated by §36 in the same way as death, so that if the offeror becomes mentally incompetent between the time of making the offer and the time of acceptance, the offer lapses. But if the mental disability arises after acceptance, it does not affect the formation of the contract. Note, however, that the offeror's mental incapacity before the time of acceptance could be analyzed on a different basis. Instead of treating it as a lapse of the offer (resulting in no contract), it could be seen as creating a contract by a mentally incompetent person. As will be explained in Chapter 14, the effect of this is to create a voidable contract (one that exists but can be voided by the offeror) rather than to preclude formation at all.

§4.6.4 Revocation

Unless the offer qualifies as an option or as a firm offer under UCC Article 2 (discussed in Chapter 5), an undertaking to keep it open for a particular period is not binding on the offeror. The offeror therefore has the power to revoke the offer at any time before its acceptance, whether or not the offer states that it will be held open for a stated time.

Revocation only *becomes effective* when it is *communicated* to the offeree. This usually means either that the offeree has received notice of revocation from the offeror or that the offeree has learned from other reliable sources that the offer has been withdrawn. The offeror therefore bears the risk that the offeree may have accepted the offer, thereby creating a contract, before receiving notice of revocation. (The mechanics of acceptance are explained later. For now, merely take note that it is possible for an acceptance to take effect even before the offeror hears about it.) The effect of this is that the offeror has the responsibility to withdraw the manifestation of contractual intent created by the offer, and until he does so must assume that it could still be acted upon. The distinction between direct and indirect revocation requires some expansion:

As indicated above, revocation can take effect either where the offeree receives notice of revocation from the offeror (called direct revocation) or where the offeree has learned indirectly of the withdrawal of the offer. For **direct revocation** to be effective, the offeree must receive notice of revocation that clearly indicates on a reasonable interpretation that the offeror is no longer willing to enter the contract. As with other communications, obscure or ambiguous language could give rise to a dispute over meaning and to interpretational difficulties.

The legal concept of **receipt** requires that the **notice becomes available** to the offeree so that if acting reasonably, the offeree would be aware of its contents. The nature of an effective receipt depends on the circumstances of the offer. For example, if a written offer was made to a specific offeree, a written notice of revocation is deemed to be received when the writing is delivered into the possession of the offeree or his authorized representative or it is deposited in an authorized place, even if the offeree fails to handle it physically or to read it. By contrast, if the offer was made to multiple persons in some publication, a revocation published in the same way as the offer is effective, whether or not a particular offeree actually read it.

Although the offeror may have failed to give direct notice of revocation, or something may have gone wrong with the communication, an offer is nevertheless **revoked indirectly** if the offeror takes action clearly inconsistent with the continued intent to enter a contract, and the offeree obtains reliable information of this action. For example, the offeree would be taken to know that the offer to sell "Bleakacre" has been revoked if, while considering the offer, the offeree learns reliably that the property has been sold to someone else. This conclusion would not be reached if the information is uncertain (for example, the offeree had merely heard rumors to this effect), or the action is not clearly inconsistent with the continued existence of the offer (for example, if the offeree was aware that the offeror was negotiating the sale but had not yet committed to sell to someone else).

The classic case establishing the principle of indirect revocation, decided by the Chancery Division of the English Court of Appeal, is *Dickenson v. Dodds* 2 Ch. D. 463 (1876). Dodds made an offer to sell real property to Dickenson. The offer specified that it was open for acceptance until Friday 9 A.M. On Thursday, Dickenson heard from a third party that Dodds had been "offering or agreeing to sell" the property to someone else. Immediately after hearing this, and before the deadline, Dickenson communicated his acceptance to Dodds. Dodds declined it, saying that it was too late because he had already sold the property. The court found that although Dodds had not communicated his revocation, Dickenson had indirectly obtained information that he no longer intended to sell the property to him. The court expressed its opinion in subjectivist terms, saying that as Dodds had changed his mind before Dickenson accepted, there could be no meeting of the parties' minds. However, the case can be reconciled with the objective test because Dickenson reasonably knew that Dodds had changed his mind.[6]

§4.7 THE NATURE AND EFFECT OF ACCEPTANCE

Acceptance is the **offeree's manifestation of assent** to the offer. It is the event that brings the contract into existence because, as noted before, the offer necessarily contemplates that the parties will become bound immediately upon the offeree's exercise of the power of acceptance.

---

6. *Dickenson v. Dodds* also stands for the rule that a promise to hold open an offer for a stated time does not bind the offeror unless consideration is given for that promise. This is dealt with in Chapter 5.

Acceptance must be a volitional act, performed freely, deliberately, and with the **intent** to enter a contract on the terms of the offer. Like the intent to make an offer, intent to accept is determined **objectively**. The question is not whether the offeree actually intended to accept, but whether a reasonable person in the offeror's position would have understood the manifestation as an acceptance. As always, the objective standard is not rigid, so that a manifestation of acceptance does not bind the offeree if coerced or induced by fraud. Similarly, as discussed in section 4.10.2, the offeror cannot structure the offer in a way that traps the offeree into inadvertent acceptance.

Only the offeree may accept the offer. The offeree is, of course, the person whose acceptance is invited by the offer. This is most commonly a single specific person, but an offer could be made to several identified persons or even to a broad or unidentified group. Unless the offer indicates otherwise, or is clearly open to anyone who sees it, it is regarded as personal to, and can only be accepted by, the person or persons to whom it is addressed. An identified offeree cannot transfer the power of acceptance.[7]

As stated earlier, the offeror, as the proponent of the transaction, has the power to set out not only the terms of the proposed contract itself but also the requirements for an effective acceptance. To validly accept the offer, the offeree must acquiesce in the offeror's terms and must manifest this agreement in the manner and within the time prescribed. If either of these two conditions are not satisfied, the attempted acceptance may be ineffective. Time for acceptance has already been discussed. We now examine the content and mode of acceptance.

§4.8 QUALIFIED OR EQUIVOCAL ACCEPTANCE

§4.8.1 The General Rule That an Acceptance Must Correspond to the Offer

Under classical common law, the acceptance must correspond exactly with the offer. This is sometimes called the **"mirror image"** or **"ribbon matching"** rule. A response is not an acceptance if the offeree imposes conditions on the acceptance or seeks to change or qualify the terms of the offer. Some courts, particularly in the older cases, have applied this rule rigidly, so that any variation in the response to an offer disqualifies it as an acceptance. (In section 6.3 we return to the "mirror image" rule and discuss it in more detail in contrast to the UCC's treatment of mismatching acceptance.) The better,

---

7. This rule only applies to offers. Once a contract has been formed, a party is normally allowed to transfer (assign) his or her rights under the contract. Assignment is discussed in Chapter 19.

more contemporary approach is to tolerate minor discrepancies and to apply the rule only where the response makes *material* changes in the transaction proposed in the offer. The "mirror image" rule follows from the principle that the offeror places the final decision on contract formation with the offeree. Therefore, the offeror must be taken to invite assent only to the terms proposed and not to terms unilaterally imposed by the offeree in the course of acceptance. Were this not so, making an offer would be a risky business. The offeror could find herself bound to a contract very different from that proposed. Therefore, the rule is justified in most cases when the parties are making deliberate proposals and counterproposals, provided that the court confines it to significant discrepancies between the offer and the purported acceptance.

The rule is not as defensible where the parties seek to contract by exchanging *preprinted standard forms*, and the conflicts are between the standard terms in the forms. Because people often do not read printed terms on forms, the parties may be unaware of the conflict and may both believe that they have a contract. The application of the "mirror image" rule in such a case could lead to the conclusion that a counteroffer was made where an acceptance was really intended. UCC §2.207 attempts to address this problem, as discussed in Chapter 6, but UCC Article 2 only applies to sales of goods. Where other contracts are involved, the common law "mirror image" rule still applies. However, a court need not be inflexible in using it and most modern courts are likely to adopt an approach that recognizes commercial reality and avoids technical rigidity. Therefore, the impact of the mirror image rule could be softened by the materiality qualification and by the principles of interpretation discussed below.

§4.8.2 The Legal Effect of a Non-Conforming Response

If an acceptance must conform exactly with the offer, what is the legal effect of a response that is not an unequivocal expression of assent? The answer to this question depends on the reasonable interpretation of the response. If, reasonably interpreted, it indicates that the offeree intends to enter a contract only as qualified in the response, it is a **counteroffer**. A counteroffer is defined in Restatement Second §39 as an offer by the offeree to the offeror, relating to the same matter as the original offer and proposing a different substitute bargain. The counteroffer is therefore both a **rejection** of the offer and a **new offer** by the former offeree for a contract on different terms. It thus terminates the original offer and creates a power of acceptance in the original offeror. Because the original offer lapses, the offeree has lost the power to accept it if the offeror rejects the counteroffer.

However, the response may reasonably suggest a different meaning. It may be an **outright rejection with an explanation**, in which case it may not give the former offeror an opportunity to accept. Conversely, it may not be a rejection at all but merely a **request for information** or a **suggestion for changes**, made with the intent of reserving the decision to accept until the offeror reacts to the request.

Some examples will illustrate these distinctions:

Say that the owner of "Bleakacre" writes to a prospective buyer, offering to sell the property to her for $2 million. The offeree replies, "I accept your offer provided you reduce the price to $1.9 million." There can be little doubt that this is a counteroffer. It causes the original offer to lapse and gives the owner the opportunity to accept the buyer's new offer.

If, instead, the offeree had replied, "I am interested in the property, but not at your price," this cannot be a counteroffer because no new proposal is made as to price. It sounds like a rejection with an explanation of the reason for the rejection, apparently encouraging the owner to make a second offer.

As a third possibility, the offeree may reply, "I am considering your offer. Do you propose a cash sale, or will you take a mortgage for the price?" This appears to be a request for elaboration or possibly a proposal for a change of terms, but it is made with the apparent intent of not foreclosing acceptance if the offeror replies in the negative. A similar intent to hold open the possibility of acceptance may be found if the offeree merely suggests a change ("I am considering your offer. Before I decide, let me know if you would be willing to throw in the living room furniture") or makes a grudging acceptance ("As I really need the property, I reluctantly agree to your excessive price").

These examples are relatively unambiguous. Often, of course, the reply may not make it clear exactly what the offeree has in mind. For example, if the reply is "Would you accept $1.9 million?" it is not clear if this is a counteroffer, terminating the buyer's power of acceptance, or merely a request for modification of terms, intended to keep alive the buyer's opportunity to accept the offer if the offeror sticks to the asking price. As with other communications, the ambiguity of the response leads to a greater risk of dispute and litigation.

Sometimes, a response may seem to add terms that are not expressed in the offer but that are *implicit in the offer* or would be incorporated into the offer by law or usage. If so, the response may appear superficially to be a counteroffer, but it is in fact an unqualified acceptance, because it merely articulates what was inherent in the offer.

For example, the owner of "Bleakacre" offers to sell the property to a prospective buyer for $2 million. The offeree responds, "I accept your offer, subject to your proof of clear title, payment to be placed in escrow and made to you against transfer of the deed." The offer is silent on these points. It did not warrant good title and said nothing about payment being concurrent with transfer of the deed. However, common usage and accepted legal practice implies these terms in a contract for the sale of land, so they were part of the offer in the absence of language clearly excluding them. Articulating them in the acceptance does not harm its effectiveness. I have used a fairly clear case to illustrate this distinction. It is not always that easy to decide whether terms in a response merely reflect what was unexpressed in the offer. Resolution of this question may involve legal argument on whether a term should be implied in law, or a factual dispute over the existence and pertinence of an alleged usage.

§4.9 THE MODE OF ACCEPTANCE

An acceptance must be manifested and communicated. The offeror has control over the manner of acceptance, and, in addition to stipulating the terms of the proposed contract, the offeror may specify what the offeree must do to accept. To be an effective acceptance, the offeree's response must be in conformity with these instructions. However, if the offer does not require acceptance to take a particular form, no special formalities are required for effective acceptance.[8] It may be signified in any manner reasonable under the circumstances, including spoken or written words or conduct, and conveyed by any reasonable means of communication. As explained in section 4.12, the acceptance may be a promise to perform the requested exchange or the actual performance of the offeree's consideration.

To avoid confusion, it is important to distinguish the **substantive terms** of the offer (that is, the terms of the proposed contract itself) from the **instructions concerning acceptance** (that is, the **procedure** that must be followed by the offeree to accept). The substantive terms are central — they go to the very heart of the relationship. The instructions for acceptance are simply concerned with the most convenient and efficient way of communicating assent. The offeror's dominant concern is to make the deal, and the method of communicating assent is merely ancillary to the achievement of this purpose.

Although the manner of acceptance is ancillary to the goal of making a contract, this does not mean that the offeror is indifferent to controlling it. If the offeror is concerned about knowing of the acceptance as soon as it takes effect and of having written proof of it, the offer should prescribe an exclusive mode of acceptance that ensures acceptance only takes effect

---

8. Subject to the qualification that if the statute of frauds applies, as discussed in Chapter 11, the acceptance must satisfy the statute's requirement of writing to be effective against the offeree.

upon the offeror's personal receipt of a signed letter of acceptance. If the offeror does not care about the mode of acceptance and is willing to assume any risk of late or undelivered notice of acceptance,[9] the offeror may not specify a mode at all or may indicate a permissible but not exclusive mode. Factors such as the desire to accommodate the offeree's convenience, to encourage acceptance, or to maintain good relations with the offeree, may outweigh the offeror's desire for certainty and may dissuade the offeror from making too fine a point of the procedure for accepting. Taking this into account, the usual assumption of the law is that unless the offer clearly indicates otherwise, the offeror is more interested in attracting the acceptance than in being punctilious about the mode of acceptance.

In summary, the rules governing mode of acceptance are:

1. When the offer clearly manifests the intention that a prescribed mode of acceptance is **mandatory and exclusive**, the offeror's intent must be deferred to, and that particular manner of acceptance must be complied with exactly.

2. If a manner of acceptance is specified, but it does **not reasonably appear intended as exclusive**, any reasonable method of acceptance is effective provided that it is consistent with the prescribed mode and provides protection to the offeror equal to that of the stated mode. As always, the wording and circumstances of the offer must be interpreted to decide if a mode of acceptance is exclusive and, if not, whether the mode used is reasonably consistent with that specified.

   For example, say the offer states, "Please signify your acceptance by mailing your written and signed acceptance. . . ." The offer does not make it clear that mail is the only acceptable medium, so a written, signed acceptance by private courier is probably just as good. However, a faxed acceptance may not be, because the communication would be a copy rather than an original signature and possibly less verifiable as genuine.

3. If the offer does **not specify any mode** of acceptance, the test for the appropriateness of the communication is even less stringent. The offeree may use the same mode as used by the offeror, or any other method of communication that is customary for transactions of that kind or is reasonable under the circumstances.

---

9. For example, under the "mailbox" rule, discussed in section 4.11.2, if it is reasonable to accept through the mail or a similar medium, the acceptance takes effect as soon as properly deposited in the post or introduced by the offeree into whatever other appropriate delivery system is used. It is therefore possible that the offeror will not know of the acceptance until some time after it occurred, and bears the risk of the acceptance never arriving. If the offeror does not wish to take this risk, the offer should exclude this mode of acceptance in favor of one (such as personal delivery by hand) that will ensure instantaneous knowledge of acceptance.

§4.10 INADVERTENT ACCEPTANCE AND SILENCE OR INACTION AS ACCEPTANCE

§4.10.1 Inadvertent Acceptance

Although the objective test is used to determine intent to accept, the offeree must at least know about the offer to accept it. To this narrow extent, the subjective state of mind of the offeree could take precedence over his apparent intention. It does not happen too often that an offeree inadvertently manifests intent to accept an offer that he does not know exists. However, this has come up in cases in which the offer is not communicated to the offeree, but the offeree's subsequent conduct creates the impression of acceptance. The best-known case involving such a situation is *Glover v. Jewish War Veterans of the U.S.* 68 A.2d 233 (D.C. 1949). The association published an offer of reward for information leading to the arrest and conviction of the murderer of one of its members. On being questioned by the police, the mother of the girlfriend of one of the culprits furnished information that led to his apprehension and ultimate conviction of the murder. The act of providing the information would have been the acceptance of the offer of reward.[10] However, when she gave the information to the police, she did not know of the reward, and only found out about it afterwards. The court held that she was not entitled to the reward. She could not have intended to accept an offer of which she was unaware.

The result of the case seems harsh and contrary to the purpose of the rule. The reason for requiring knowledge of the offer is to protect the offeree from being held to an inadvertent manifestation of acceptance, so this rationale does not apply when the offeree desires the acceptance to be effective. However, the result may be justified on a different ground — because the offeree did not know about the offer, she was not induced by it to furnish the information, and the court's refusal to find a contract did not defeat any reliance interest that she might have had. This argument did not persuade the court in *Anderson v. Douglas Lomason Co.*, 540 N.W.2d 277 (Iowa 1995). The Court had to decide whether an employee was protected by a provision in the employees' handbook that required progressive discipline and precluded summary dismissal. When an employer adds provision to a handbook, this is treated as an offer which the employee accepts by continuing in employment. However, the employee in this case had not read the handbook and did not know of the provision. Therefore, if

---

10. As explained in section 4.12, the offer in this case is for a unilateral contract, and so the giving of the information is both the act of acceptance and the performance required under the contract. That is, the only way that the offeree can accept is to render the requested performance.

knowledge of the offer is required for an effective acceptance, this employee would not have been protected by the provision in the handbook barring summary dismissal. The court refused to follow the rule requiring knowledge of the offer for effective acceptance. It reasoned that a strong policy of treating employees evenhandedly would be defeated by distinguishing employees who had read the handbook from those who had not. In a subsequent case in Iowa (the same jurisdiction) involving a handbook that had not been read by the employee, the Iowa Court of Appeals distinguished *Anderson* and refused to find a contract. In *Poekes v. City of Orange City* 707 N.W.2d 336 (Iowa App 2005) the court noted that *Anderson* had created a narrow exception to the usual rule that an offeree must have knowledge of an offer to accept it. However, the court found a significant factual difference in the cases. In *Anderson* the employer actually gave the handbook to the employee, while in this case, the employer, although it never officially rescinded the handbook, had discontinued using and distributing it. The employee had simply found it in her desk drawer. (That is, this seems to be a case in which both the offer and the acceptance were inadvertent.)

§4.10.2 Acceptance by Silence or Inaction

The offeror cannot impose a duty on the offeree to take some affirmative step to reject the offer, making failure to act an acceptance. For example, the offer cannot impose a duty on the offeree to speak by stating ". . . if you do not wish to accept this offer, you must deliver notice of rejection to me by Friday, failing which you are deemed to have accepted."

To illustrate further, in *Pride v. Lewis*, 179 S.W.3d 375 (Mo. App. 2005) a potential buyer of real property made a written offer to purchase it from the owner. The owner signed and returned the offer, signifying intent to accept it, but changed the closing date on the offer from May 15 to June 1. The court, applying the "mirror image" rule, found that the alteration of the closing date made the owner's response into a counteroffer. The buyer did not respond to the counteroffer, did not attend the closing, and never requested the return of his earnest money. The issue in the case was whether the buyer could be taken to have accepted the counteroffer by failing to object to the change in the closing date (of which he was aware) or to claim return of his earnest money. The court held that silence or inaction could not be an acceptance except in narrow circumstances where there is a duty to speak. Although it would have been courteous for the buyer to tell the owner that he rejected the counteroffer, there was nothing in the relationship that required him to notify the owner. Furthermore, there was no explanation on record of the buyer's failure to request the return of his earnest money, and that alone was not enough to signify assent to the counteroffer.

Because the purpose of this rule is to protect the offeree from imposition, it only applies if the offeree does not wish to be bound by her silence. If the offeree intends to accept by remaining silent, she may rely on this mode of acceptance, which was, after all, authorized by the offeror. Therefore, an offeror who invites acceptance by silence assumes a risk of uncertainty. The meaning of the silence depends on the offeree's subjective intent, and the offeror cannot be sure if the failure to reject is an acceptance.

There are two situations in which silence binds the offeree, even in the absence of intent to accept. First, silence operates as acceptance if the offeror proffers property or services with the offer, and the offeree, having a reasonable opportunity to return or refuse them, **exercises ownership rights** over the property or **accepts the benefit** of the service. For example, to promote a new wine, a local wine shop leaves a case of wine on the offeree's doorstep with an offer to sell the wine for $200. The offer ends with the statement, "You may refuse this offer by returning the wine to us within 24 hours of delivery. If you do not return it, you have accepted this offer and must mail your check to us within a week." The offeree is not required to return the wine, or to communicate with the offeror in any way to reject the offer. He can simply ignore the wine. However, if he drinks it or pours it down the sink, he does accept the offer.[11] (If the offeree does not want the wine on his doorstep indefinitely, he can call on the offeror to remove it, and if the offeror fails to do so within a reasonable time, the offeree can dispose of it.)

Second, silence may operate as acceptance if prior dealings between the parties or other circumstances make it **reasonable** for the offeror **to expect** the offeree to give **notice of rejection**. For example, say that the offeree was a longstanding customer of the wine shop, which had regularly delivered cases of wine to the offeree whenever it had a new wine to promote. On receiving wine on previous occasions, the offeree had either returned the cases or paid for them.

§4.11 THE EFFECTIVE DATE OF ACCEPTANCE AND THE "MAILBOX" RULE

The question of when acceptance takes effect is linked to but distinct from the method of acceptance. Where the parties are in **instantaneous communication** — negotiating face-to-face, talking on the telephone, or communicating live by electronic means — they are in a position to hear or observe each

---

11. To protect people from this kind of marketing practice, and to discourage merchants from using it, federal legislation varies this common law rule if the merchandise is sent through the mail. The recipient may keep and use the unsolicited goods without becoming obliged to pay for them. States may have similar laws relating to merchandise delivered otherwise than through the mail.

other's manifestations immediately. There is no temporal separation between the offeror's expression of acceptance and its communication to the offeree. Therefore, the general rule is that the acceptance occurs *as soon as it is manifested*.

However, where the parties are at a distance and the means of communication entail a delay between the manifestation and the offeror's knowledge of it, there are two possible points at which we could treat the acceptance as becoming effective. (It could take effect immediately upon its being uttered, or only upon its coming to the offeror's attention.) As with the mode of acceptance, the offeror has the right to *specify when acceptance becomes effective*. In many situations if a mode of acceptance is prescribed, this also implicitly establishes the effective point of the acceptance. For example, if the offeror requires acceptance to be only by the personal delivery of a signed, written acceptance, this covers both the mode of acceptance and the event (delivery) that brings it into effect. However, the offeror may not have specified a mode of acceptance or, even if having done so, may not fix the point at which the acceptance takes effect. For example, the offer may state that acceptance must be by mail, but may not make it clear if a contract comes into being upon the acceptance being mailed or only upon its being received by the offeror.

In the *absence of specification* in the offer, the acceptance takes effect as soon as it is put out of *the offeree's possession*, provided that the acceptance is made in a manner and via a medium expressly or impliedly *authorized* by the offer. Therefore, if acceptance by mail is permissible, acceptance occurs as soon as the offeree deposits a properly stamped and addressed acceptance in the mailbox. The burden is on the offeree to prove *proper dispatch*, so the offeree should make a good record of the mailing to avoid evidentiary problems. The offeree must also ensure that the letter is correctly addressed, stamped, and otherwise properly prepared for delivery. Provided that the acceptance was properly mailed before lapse of the offer, it does not matter that it was received after the offer terminated or was never received at all. The law allocates the risk of uncertainty and of lost or delayed mail to the offeror. This is often referred to as the **mailbox** or **deposited acceptance** rule. Although the mail was used as an example here, it is not confined to communication through the post office and applies whenever a non-instantaneous medium of communication is used.

Over the years, there has been some discussion of why the transmission rather than receipt of the acceptance brings the contract into effect. Probably the most convincing rationale is that the offeror could have allocated the risk of uncertainty, delay, or non-receipt to the offeree. As this was not done, it is appropriate to leave this risk to the offeror and give the offeree a reliable basis of knowing that acceptance has occurred.

The "mailbox" rule does not apply if the **acceptance follows a counteroffer or rejection** — that is, the offeree initially mails a rejection and then changes her mind and mails an acceptance. To protect the offeror, who might receive the rejection before the acceptance, the acceptance only takes effect on receipt. Therefore, if it arrives before the rejection, the offer is accepted, and if it arrives afterwards, it is ineffective.

Restatement Second §63(b) says that the "mailbox" rule also does not apply, and acceptance is only effective on receipt, if the offer is irrevocable (that is, it is a valid option). Comment f to §63 justifies this on the basis that irrevocability sufficiently protects the offeree, so the "mailbox" rule is not needed to safeguard the offeree's interests or to provide a dependable basis for knowing that the acceptance has occurred. Some courts are unconvinced by this reasoning and see greater merit in having a standard, predictable rule for all acceptances.

If the "mailbox" rule does not apply, acceptance takes effect only on receipt — the writing must come into the possession of the addressee or his authorized representative, or must be deposited in an authorized place. (Provided this has happened, the addressee does not actually have to read it.) It is important to remember that the "mailbox" rule applies only to acceptances. A rejection or counteroffer sent by the offeree, and a revocation sent by the offeror, is effective only on receipt.

§4.12 ACCEPTANCE BY PROMISE OR PERFORMANCE: BILATERAL AND UNILATERAL CONTRACTS

§4.12.1 The Distinction in Perspective

Students find the bilateral-unilateral distinction confusing. To keep it in perspective, bear two things in mind. First, the bilateral-unilateral distinction is nothing more than a particular application of the general principles governing the proper mode of acceptance. Second, the distinction does not come up often because most contracts are clearly bilateral.

§4.12.2 The Offer for a Bilateral Contract

As stressed in sections 4.5, 4.9, and 4.11, the offeror has the power to prescribe the time, effective date, and method of acceptance. Included in this power is not only the ability to authorize or require a particular medium of acceptance (such as the mails, telephone, or personal delivery) but also a particular action to manifest acceptance. The most common action used to signify acceptance is the use of *words*, oral or written, to express assent. When words are used to accept, the acceptance invariably constitutes a promise of future performance. For example, if the owner of "Bleakacre" offers to sell it for $2 million and the offeree replies by expressing acceptance, a contract is created under which both the parties make promises of future performance: The offeror promises to convey the farm and the offeree promises to pay the price. Because, at the point of contract formation, both parties have outstanding promises to be performed in the future, the contract is said to be **bilateral.**

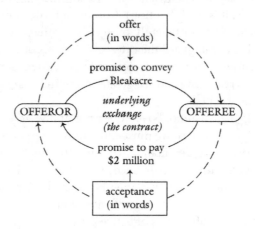

Instead of authorizing acceptance in the form of words, the offeror could demand a *nonverbal signification of acceptance.* The offer could state, for example, "I offer to sell you 'Bleakacre' for $2 million. If you wish to accept this offer, you must stand in your underwear at the corner of Main and Broadway at 2 P.M. today. This is the only way that you may accept this offer." If the offeree complies with this request, the offer is accepted. At that point a contract comes into being under which the offeror promises to convey "Bleakacre" and the offeree promises to pay $2 million. Although this offer required the offeree's assent to be signified by conduct instead of words, this is still a **bilateral** contract. The prescribed act of acceptance has exactly the same legal effect as the delivery of a piece of paper on which the words "I accept" are written. By performing the act, the offeree signifies assent and impliedly promises to perform the consideration (payment of $2 million) demanded in the offer.

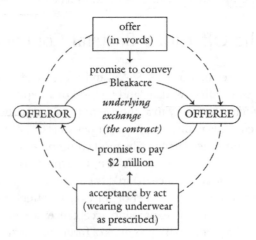

§4.12.3 The Offer for a Unilateral Contract

In the last example, the prescribed act of acceptance was merely intended to *symbolize* assent to the offer. It is nothing more than a mode of acceptance and has nothing to do with the actual performance—the exchange of detriments—called for by the contract. However, the offeror could have structured the offer so that the act of acceptance is *not merely symbolical*, but is at the same time also the performance of the offeree's side of the contract. For example, the offer could have stated: "I offer to sell you 'Bleakacre' for $2 million. To accept this offer you must come to my office today at 2 P.M. and pay me $2 million in cash. This is the only way that you may accept this offer." The **act of acceptance** is also the **complete act of performance.** The offeree's consideration under the contract is furnished in full immediately upon acceptance, and the offeree has no further duty under the contract. All that remains is for the offeror to perform the promise in the offer and to transfer title and possession of "Bleakacre." Because, at the moment of formation, only one of the parties has a promise outstanding, the contract is said to be **unilateral.**

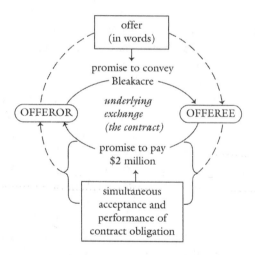

Note, therefore, that "unilateral" does not mean one-sided, in the sense that only one party has given or done something. As explained in Chapter 7, a transaction in which one of the parties has made a promise and the other has given or promised nothing in return lacks consideration and is not a valid and enforceable contract. Rather, the word "unilateral" signifies that although both parties have given consideration, only one of them has made a promise as consideration. The other has furnished consideration by rendering the required exchange performance at the very point of contract formation.

§4.12.4 When the Offer Does Not Clearly Prescribe Performance as the Exclusive Mode of Acceptance

In the last example, the offeror made it clear that acceptance could only be made by performance of the offeree's consideration, so there is no doubt that a unilateral contract was called for. In the occasional case, even in the absence of such clear language, the nature of the offer and the circumstances in which it is made compel the conclusion that nothing but performance of the consideration could qualify as acceptance. Perhaps the best common example is the offer of a reward. If the owner of a lost dog nails a notice to a pole offering $100 to anyone who finds and returns the cherished beast, it is hard to imagine that the offeror reasonably expected to be contractually bound to the first person who calls and promises to find the dog. Rather, the offeror appears to contemplate that the offer of reward is accepted only when a person shows up with darling Fido.

However, while an offeror could make an offer in a way that clearly permits acceptance only by performance, this is fairly uncommon. More likely, where acceptance by performance is feasible, the offer appears ambivalent on the mode of acceptance and does not clearly indicate this to be the exclusive mode. There are some older cases that devoted considerable energy to deciding if the offeror intended a unilateral or bilateral contract. This debate has largely been stilled in modern law as writers and courts have realized that an offeror who did not take the trouble to specify an exclusive mode of acceptance probably doesn't care exactly how the offer is accepted. Therefore, the general approach, as reflected in Restatement Second §32 and UCC §2.206, is to assume that unless the wording of the offer or the circumstances clearly indicates otherwise, the offeror is indifferent to whether acceptance is by promise or performance, so the offeree may choose to accept either way. As section 4.9 indicates, this approach is in keeping with the broader treatment of mode of acceptance.

For example, the offeror delivers an offer to the offeree on Monday stating, "I offer to sell you 'Bleakacre' for $2 million. If you wish to buy it, you must pay me $2 million in cash at my office on Friday at 2 P.M." Clearly, it is a term of the proposed contract that the buyer's performance — the delivery of her consideration under the contract — must take place on Friday at 2 P.M. at the seller's office. However, the offer does not clearly restrict acceptance to the payment of money on Friday at 2 P.M. Therefore, if the offeree is anxious to close the deal immediately and to bind the offeror before Friday at 2 P.M., she could write to the offeror on Monday, stating "I accept." A contract immediately comes into existence on dispatch of the letter. The offeree has accepted by making a promise on Monday to perform as required on Friday, and the offeror's offer immediately becomes a promise to convey the property at some future (unspecified but reasonable) time. The early acceptance by promise creates a bilateral contract that binds both parties. The importance of this is that the offer has now become a contract, so the offeror is bound and has lost the right to revoke the offer.

OR, at offeree's election:

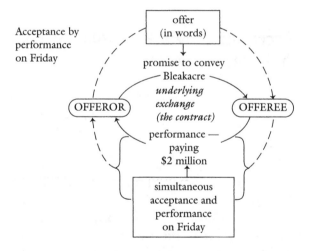

§4.12.5 When the Offer Does Not Clearly Prescribe Promise as the Exclusive Mode of Acceptance

Under the same principle, an offer that contemplates a promissory acceptance could be accepted by performance unless it is clear that acceptance can only be by promise. For example, the owner of "Bleakacre" wishes to clear some dead trees off the property to make it more attractive for sale, so on

October 20 she writes to a tree remover, "I need the two dead firs removed from my property by the end of October and will pay $500 for the job. If you would like to do this work, please accept this offer by October 24." Instead of replying, the offeree went out on October 22 and removed the dead trees. The performance is an effective acceptance, creating a unilateral contract under which the owner has promised to pay $500. Although the offer contemplated a promissory acceptance, we can conclude that the offeror was indifferent to whether acceptance was by act or promise because the offer made it clear that removal at some time before the end of October was desired.

However, a different conclusion would be reached if the offer is for some future performance by the offeree, and it is not reasonable to believe that the offeror intended the offer to remain open for that long a time. For example, if the owner of "Bleakacre" had written in December, requesting the service in February, we can assume that she did not reasonably intend to be kept on a string until February and needs an earlier acceptance by promise.

Note that the conclusions reached here and in section 4.12.4 are really nothing more than an application of the general rules of interpretation used to find the reasonable intent of the offer with regard to the time and manner of acceptance.

§4.12.6 Acceptance by a Performance That Cannot Be Accomplished Instantly

In the examples concerning the offer to sell "Bleakacre," the offeree's contractual performance was cash payment, a single, relatively instantaneous act. Not all performance can be accomplished in one stroke. For example, "Bleakacre" is run-down and overgrown. The owner writes to her nephew, "If you come down and clean up the property for me this summer, I will pay you $2,000 when the work is complete. You need not make a decision now. If you wish to accept my offer, just come down this summer and do the work."

If the nephew did respond early by making a promise, and the aunt thereafter revoked before the summer, we would have to decide if the offer called for acceptance only by performance. We would probably conclude that it did not, because neither the language used nor the circumstances reasonably indicate that performance was intended as the exclusive mode of acceptance. However, assume that the nephew did not make an early promissory reply and that the aunt did not revoke before the summer. The nephew came down in early summer and began the work of clearing the property. Before he completed the task, the Aunt changed her mind about cleaning up the property and revoked her offer.

If acceptance only takes place on completion of performance, the nephew risks revocation while he is in the process of performing. To protect him from this risk, Restatement Second §§62 and 45 give legal effect to the commencement of performance. Section 62 applies where the **offer does not mandate acceptance by performance,** so that it can be accepted either by performance or promise. The commencement or tender[12] of performance constitutes an **implied promise to complete the performance** within the time called for by the offer. Therefore, the commencement or tender of the performance is, in effect, an acceptance by promise creating a bilateral contract. In the present example, as soon as the nephew began work, a bilateral contract came into being under which he was committed to complete the work by the end of summer, and the aunt was committed to pay him $2,000 on completion.

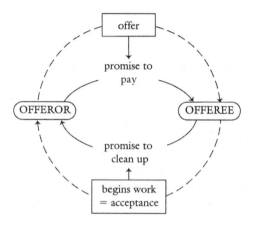

Restatement Second §45 applies where the offer calls for **performance** as the **exclusive mode** of acceptance (that is, it is clearly an offer only for a unilateral contract), so that the commencement of performance cannot be an acceptance by promise, because such an acceptance is not authorized. Restatement Second §45 treats the beginning or tender of performance as creating an **option** in favor of the offeree, so that the offeror loses the right to revoke once performance has been tendered or begun. To exercise the option, the offeree must complete the performance in the required time. If he fails to do so, the option is not taken up and the offer lapses. This means that the offeror is discharged from her own performance under the offer, so the offeree receives no contractual payment[13] for the incomplete work.

---

12. A tender is an offer of performance by a party who is willing and able to begin it.
13. Because the nephew's work may have resulted in an unpaid-for benefit to his aunt, he may be entitled to recover the value of this benefit on the ground that it would unjustly enrich his aunt to allow her to enjoy the benefit of his work without paying for it. That is, he may be entitled to restitutionary relief under the theory of unjust enrichment — a basis of relief distinct from contract. We do not consider this here, but defer discussion of unjust enrichment to Chapter 9.

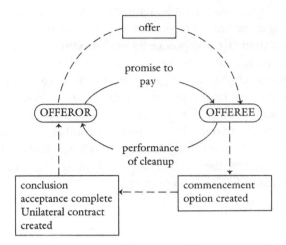

From the offeree's point of view, it is more advantageous to have commencement of performance treated as creating an option instead of an acceptance by implied promise. The latter approach brings the contract into existence as soon as performance begins, so the offeree is bound to complete the work and failure to do so not only precludes his contractual recovery but also makes him liable for damages for breach of contract. This is why the more favorable option approach is confined to the rarer cases where the offeror actually forecloses promissory acceptance.

The comments to Restatement Second §§45 and 62 emphasize that neither the promise nor the option arises merely when *preparation for performance* starts. The actual performance must be begun or tendered. In some situations it may be relatively clear where the dividing line between preparation and performance is to be drawn, but in others the line could be fuzzy. For example, when the nephew packs his belongings in his car and sets off for the property this is probably preparation, but when he buys necessary tools and equipment for the specific task of clearing the property, this may be closely enough linked to his contract obligation to be actual performance.

§4.12.7 Notice When an Offer Is Accepted by Performance

As we have seen, when an offer is accepted by a promise, the offeree must in some way communicate the manifestation of assent to the offeror. If an offer is accepted by performance, the acceptance normally comes to the offeror's attention as a matter of course, because the offeror receives the performance. Unless the offer requires notice of performance, the offeree ordinarily has no duty to take action to notify the offeror of acceptance. However, the offeree does have a duty of notification if the performance in question is **not rendered directly** to or in the presence of the offeror and the offeror has **no reasonably prompt and reliable means of learning** of it.

Say, for example, that the owner of "Bleakacre" does not live on the land but resides in a distant state. She has no contacts in the area and is not likely to visit the property because she is elderly and in poor health. If her nephew responds to her offer not by promise, but by commencing the clearing work, she is not likely to learn of his acceptance unless he tells her. Therefore, although the nephew may accept by performance and need not communicate with the aunt to accept, he is required to notify her within a reasonable time after commencing performance if he knows or should know that she has no means of learning of his acceptance with reasonable speed and certainty. This notice is not itself the acceptance, which occurred as soon as performance began, but if it is not given (and the aunt does not otherwise hear of the performance) within a reasonable time, the acceptance becomes *ineffective* and the aunt's contractual duty is discharged.

§4.12.8 Reverse Unilateral Contracts

A reverse unilateral contract comes about when the offeree **accepts by promise**, but the **offeror's performance** occurs and is **completed** at the **instant of contract formation**. This is also a unilateral contract because only one party — the offeree in this case — has a promise outstanding at the point of contracting. For example, hearing that his friend is in financial difficulty, the offeror approaches the friend and holds out ten crisp $100 bills, saying "Here, I'll lend this to you for a year at 6 percent interest." If the offeree accepts by taking the money, he thereby promises to repay the loan on the offeror's terms. However, the offeror has no outstanding obligation because his performance was completed immediately upon acceptance. This type of contract presents no special offer and acceptance issues, and the offeree's response is subject to all the normal rules for acceptance.

§4.13 STANDARD FORM CONTRACTS AND THE ACCEPTANCE OF UNKNOWN TERMS

It seems reasonable to assume that when an offer is made, it will set out all the terms that the offeror proposes as part of the contract. This is sometimes, but not always true. Section 4.8.2 already alluded to one situation in which the contract has terms that are not actually expressed: a contract may contain terms that are not stated, but that are nevertheless part of the contract because they are implied by law or usage. (Implied terms are covered in sections 10.6. to 10.9). Apart from this, it quite frequently happens that an offeror (typically a large corporation that enters into many standardized contracts) has drafted standard terms that are not made available to the offeree at the time that she accepts the offer and are only revealed to her later. There are many common transactions in which this happens. For example, a person calls an airline or theater box office to book an air ticket or a concert ticket. Conventional offer and acceptance analysis usually treats the offer and acceptance as occurring at the time of booking. In requesting the booking, the buyer invites an offer. The airline or box office offers the buyer an available booking, and the buyer then accepts by agreeing to take it. Some time after the booking, the buyer receives the ticket in the mail. It contains standard terms that were not discussed at the time of booking. A similar situation could occur, for example, where a person calls an insurance agent to buy an insurance policy, or a person buys a product at a store which has standard terms (such as a warranty or a license agreement) printed on a piece of paper in the sealed carton. Where terms are only revealed to the offeree after she has bought the goods or services, there may be a dispute about whether a contract was formed at all, or even if both parties concede that a contract exists, there may be a dispute about whether the standardized terms formed part of the contract.

The traditional rules of offer and acceptance were not formulated with this type of transaction in mind, and they are not a comfortable fit. There are a number of different ways in which transactions of this kind can be approached. Four of these possible approaches are as follows:

1. The court simply applies traditional offer and acceptance rules: The offer and acceptance occurred at the time of booking or buying the goods or service. Terms not divulged to the offeree at that time are not part of the contract because the offeror cannot unilaterally impose terms on the offeree after the contract was formed.

2. As in 1, the court treats the offer and acceptance as having occurred at the time of booking or buying. However, if a transaction of this kind is commonly subject to standard terms, a reasonable buyer should have known that and should have ascertained what they are. If he failed to do that, he did not fulfill his "duty to read." He is therefore taken to have agreed to any of the standard terms that are reasonably expected.

3. The court adjusts the view of when an offer and acceptance occurred: there was no offer and acceptance at the time of booking or buying. Rather, the delivery of the standard terms (which occurs upon delivery of the ticket, policy, or goods that contain notice of the terms) is an offer. The buyer accepts the offer if he does not reject it within a reasonable time by returning or declining the benefit of the contract. This imposes a duty to read at the time of delivery and gives the buyer the opportunity to refuse to contract on the offeror's standard terms.

4. The court does not get too involved in the technicalities of offer and acceptance. Clearly a contract was intended by the parties. It focuses instead on the disputed term itself to decide if the offeree had a reasonable opportunity to become aware of it, and if the term itself is fair and within the range of reasonable expectations.

In *ProCD, Inc. v. Zeidenberg*, 86 F.3d 1447 (7th Cir. 1996) the district court had followed the first approach, but the court of appeals reversed, adopting the third approach. A buyer bought software at a retail store. The box in which the software was packaged contained a license that limited the use of the software to noncommercial purposes. The court held that the license was a term of the contract. It disagreed with the trial court that offer and acceptance occurred at the retail store. Rather, the vendor of the software made an offer by supplying the software with the license, and the buyer accepted by failing to return the software and using it. The facts of the case made it possible for the court to reach this conclusion because the license expressly gave the buyer the right to return the software for a refund if the license terms were unacceptable. It would be hard to justify finding offer and acceptance at this stage if the buyer had no right to decline the goods and services (as is often true, say, with travel bookings). Although the court's analysis is couched in terms of offer and acceptance, the opinion makes it clear that the court's real concern is policy-based. The court felt strongly that mass vendors of goods and services must rely on standard terms to protect their rights. The court reasoned that it would be impractical and would place a great burden on transacting to require them to articulate these terms in detail at the time of sale. Therefore, provided that the terms are fair and should reasonably be expected, the court considered that they must be given effect. A court with less enthusiasm for standard terms, and a greater concern about the imposition of terms on users of goods or services may be less inclined to this approach.

Casavant v. Norwegian Cruise Line Ltd, 829 N.E.2d 1171 (Mass. App. 2005) illustrates the fourth approach. In October 2000, the Casavants booked a roundtrip Boston-to-Bermuda cruise aboard a Norwegian Cruise Lines ship. The cruise was to depart on September 16, 2001. They paid a deposit at the time of booking and paid the balance of the total ticket price by July 2001. It was only upon receiving the tickets at the beginning of September 2001 that the Casavants were given the standard terms of the contract. One of the standard terms placed all risks of travel on the passenger. Another was a forum selection clause that required all disputes under the contract to be commenced and litigated in Florida. As you can see from the dates, the Casavants received the tickets just a few days before the terrorist attacks of September 11, 2001, and the cruise was scheduled to leave a few days afterward. The Casavants were frightened to board a cruise ship (especially one that left from Boston, from which two of the hijacked planes originated) so

87

they sought to postpone or cancel their cruise booking. Norwegian refused to reschedule or to cancel and refund the ticket price on the basis that the contract allocated any risk of travel to the passenger. The Casavants sued Norwegian in Massachusetts, their home state, for refund of the ticket price. The sole issue to be decided was whether the trial court was correct in dismissing their case because they had agreed to litigate any dispute in Florida. The court of appeals reversed the dismissal on the ground that the forum selection clause did not bind the Casavants. The court was vague on exactly when the contract came into being, so it is not clear if it saw the offer and acceptance as having occurred at the time of booking or only when the standard terms were delivered with the ticket. (However, language in the opinion seems to suggest that the court considered contract formation to have been deferred until the latter event.) The court concluded that because the Casavants did not have sufficient time to reject the terms of the contract without sacrificing their payment, the forum selection clause was unfairly imposed and unenforceable. (The issue of unfair imposition of standard terms is taken up more fully in section 13.12 and in Example 6 of Chapter 13.)

Examples

1. Joe Kerr owns and lives in a handsome Victorian house that has been in his family for over 100 years. Every time that his friend Hume Orless has visited him, Hume has said, "Joe, I love your house. Please sell it to me right now." Joe has consistently answered, "Never!" After this had been going on for many years, Joe became irritated with it. As far as he knew, Hume had no money and had never been serious in his request to buy the house. It was simply mindless prattle. Joe decided to put an end to the annoying routine by shaming Hume into silence. He prepared a deed of sale that he placed in a drawer. The deed was on a real legal form that Joe had purchased from a stationer. He fully filled out all the blanks, included a price somewhat exceeding the market value of the house, and signed it. The next time Hume was at the house and urged Joe to sell it to him, Joe whipped the deed out of the drawer and exclaimed, "O.K. Hume. Put up or shut up! Sign this and the house is yours."

   Instead of reacting with embarrassment and confusion, as Joe expected, Hume coolly read the deed, expressed satisfaction, and signed it. At first, Joe thought that Hume was playing along with him, but it is now clear that he did not see the bluff, took the offer seriously, and does have the financial means of buying the house. Hume insists that the transfer proceed. Joe is sick with grief at the prospect of parting with his beloved family homestead. Is he bound?

2. Professor Ivor E. Tower has spent the last three years working on his book entitled *Foolproof Contracting — A Lay Person's Guide to Effective Dealmaking*. On

completing the book, Ivor set about getting it published. On July 1, he sent an identical letter and a copy of the manuscript to several publishers. The letter read: "I submit the enclosed manuscript for your consideration. If you would like to publish it, let me know by July 30. I want the book published as soon as possible, at least within this year. If you are willing to commit to this, I would be willing to give it to you on the customary terms, and expect the usual royalty of 15 percent of sales."

One of the publishers to whom he sent the book was Sel Phelp Publications, Inc. The editors at Sel Phelp read the book, which was a real page-turner. They decided that they would like to publish it. On July 24, Sel Phelp mailed a letter to Ivor, in which it accepted the book for publication, committed to have it published within the year, and enclosed its standard form contract for Ivor to sign. The terms in the form contract are those generally found in publishing contracts, and included a royalty of 15 percent of sales. On July 25, before receiving Sel Phelp's letter, Ivor signed a contract with one of its competitors for the book's publication, and he immediately faxed a letter to Sel Phelp telling them that the book had been given to another publisher and was no longer available for publication by them. Ivor received Sel Phelp's letter later that day. Is Ivor now in the uncomfortable position of having made two contracts for the same book?

3. Kay Nine was going on an overseas trip for the month of July. At the beginning of June, she booked a space in a kennel for her dog, Pettodor. A few days later, she remembered that her cousin, Doug Sitter, a college student, often needed a place to stay during the summer. She thought that it would be a good idea if he could take care of Pettodor and her house while she was away. On June 10, Kay wrote the following letter to Doug:

> Dear Doug,
>
> I am going to be away from July 1 to July 30. I had planned to put Pettodor in a kennel, but it occurs to me that you may be free during July and may enjoy staying at my house for the month. You will just have to take care of Pettodor and keep an eye on things. In return, you will have free accommodation, and also, before I leave on vacation, I will give you $500 for food and other expenses.
>
> I have booked the kennel, so I don't need to hear from you right away. If you would like to spend July here, just come down on June 29. If you are not here by the end of that day, I will assume that you cannot make it, and I will take Pettodor to the kennel on the 30th.
>
> Best wishes,
>
> Kay

Doug received Kay's letter on June 12. He had nothing to do during July and liked the idea of an all-expenses-paid month in Kay's house. He wrote back immediately telling her that he would be down on June 29. Doug mailed the letter on June 13, but he wrote the wrong zip code on the envelope. The post office was able to deliver it anyhow, but it was considerably delayed and Kay received it on June 20. In the interim, she had recalled what a slob Doug was and had changed her mind about having him live in her house. On June 21, she wrote back to him, telling him that she was going to kennel Pettodor after all, and no longer needed him. Doug received the letter on June 23. Doug feels aggrieved because he believes that Kay cannot simply back out of their arrangement. Is he right?

4. Art Walls owns a building whose exterior has been spraypainted by vandals with infuriating regularity. In an attempt to put an end to this expensive nuisance, he placed an advertisement in the newspaper on January 15, offering a reward of $1,000 to ". . . anyone who furnishes information leading to the arrest and conviction of those guilty of defacing the walls . . ." of his building. On January 16, the police arrested Fresco Furtive, a young man who was caught in the act of spraypainting another building in the neighborhood. Under aggressive questioning by the police, Fresco broke down and confessed to having committed several other acts of vandalism, including the spraying of Art's building. He was tried, convicted, and placed on probation.

Although Fresco was not aware of the reward offer at the time of his confession, he found out about it later that day. He claims the reward. Upon hearing this, Art is outraged. He says that he never intended to pay the culprit himself, and in any event, when he said "conviction," Art had a stiff jail term in mind and not some wimpy probationary sentence. Is Fresco entitled to the reward?

5. Assume that the police obtained no confession from Fresco Furtive. However, Fresco's nocturnal artistry had been observed by N. Former and I. Witness, two denizens of Art Wall's neighborhood who happened to be lurking separately in the area that night. Although neither of them are public-spirited enough to expose Fresco for free, they both happened to read Art's reward offer on January 15, and independently contacted Art to tell him who had vandalized his building. N. Former told him on the morning of January 16, and I. Witness told him that afternoon. As a result, Art filed charges and Fresco was arrested and tried. He was convicted of the offense and was sentenced to five years on a chain gang. Being completely delighted with this result, Art is happy to pay the reward. The problem is that both N. Former and I. Witness claim it. Art refuses to pay it twice and does not know who should receive the $1,000. To whom is he liable and for how much?

6. Last August, a country club held a golf tournament to raise funds for an organization called "Youth Golf America" that arranges and funds golf camps for troubled children. To support the charity tournament, the Caddy-Lack Golf Cart Co. donated one of its luxurious electric golf carts to be used as a prize for anyone who hit a hole-in-one during the tournament. Just before the tournament, the cart was displayed in front of the clubhouse with a sign that stated:

HIT A HOLE-IN-ONE
AND WIN THIS FABULOUS GOLF CART

by
CADDY-LACK

Courtesy of Caddy-Lack, "The Cadillac of Golf Carts"
Caddy-Lack is a proud sponsor of Youth Golf America. Thank you for supporting our children.

The charity tournament took place on Sunday, and no one qualified for the prize by hitting a hole-in-one. Caddy-Lack did not get around to removing its display until Monday at 5 P.M. On that Monday afternoon, Jock Awesome passed the display as he set out for his weekly golf game. He read the very obvious large print as he walked by, but did not stop to read the smaller print at the bottom of the sign referring to the sponsorship of the youth organization. He did not know that there had been a tournament on the day before and did not realize that the display was intended to be applicable only during the tournament. As luck would have it, at 5:15 P.M. he hit a hole-in-one at the 17th hole.

As he hurried back to the clubhouse to claim his prize at the pro shop (which was the official Caddy-Lack representative at the club), he was puzzled to notice that the cart and sign had been removed. It was only when he claimed the prize that he discovered that the offer was confined to the tournament. Nevertheless, he says that he is entitled to the cart. Caddy-Lack refuses to give it to him. Who is right?

7. On April 10, Maggie Cumlaude, a bright and enterprising law student, wrote a note to one of her professors, Prof. Minnie Wage, and slipped the note under her door. The note stated: "I would love to be your research assistant this summer. I will be available to work 40 hours per week from June 10 through August 15 and would like to be paid $12 per hour. Please reply by April 16 if you are interested."

On April 13, Minnie replied, stating "I would like to have you work for me this summer, but $12 seems a little steep. I usually pay my research assistants $8 per hour. Tell me as soon as possible how you feel about this." She got Maggie's home address from the registrar and put the letter in the mailbox on her way home from work on April 13. Maggie received it the next day.

When Minnie was sitting in the faculty lounge on the morning of April 16, her insufferable colleague, Prof. Max E. Molument sidled up to her and gloated: "Your cheapness lost you a good research assistant. When Maggie Cumlaude told me a couple of days ago that you would only pay her $8 an hour, I outbid you and hired her for $10."

Minnie rushed to her office and wrote another note to Maggie that read "On thinking about this matter further, I have decided that $12 per hour is a fair rate, so I agree to pay what you ask. I look forward to having you work for me. I will be away at a conference until June 12. Please come to my office on June 13 to get instructions on your assignment."

She mailed the note on April 16, and Maggie received it on April 17. Do Maggie and Minnie have a contract?

8. Flaky Cereal Co. manufactures "Flaky's Frosties" sugar-coated cornflakes. The logo for this product is a cute cartoon leopard named "Frosty Fangs." To promote the sale of its cornflakes, Flaky ran a competition, which it announced on the back of the cereal boxes. The competition was initiated in May 2005. Its simple point was that people could win various prizes by sending in the tops of cereal boxes accompanied by a form printed on the back of the box. The more tops that were collected, the bigger the prize. The box listed four categories of prizes: Four box tops earned a plastic "Frosty Fangs" pin, 10 earned a cuddly "Frosty Fangs" stuffed toy, 20 earned a "Frosty Fangs" watch, and 1,000 earned a real leopard cub. Each of the prizes was illustrated by a color photograph. The back of the cereal box proclaimed: "Boys and Girls, collect your box tops now and send them in by January 1, 2006, to claim your prizes! (Prizes limited to quantities on hand, so don't delay.)"

Manny Eater owns "Carnivore Campground," a safari park. He had been trying to obtain a leopard for some time, but leopards are very expensive (a good specimen can cost up to $500,000) and hard to get. Manny happened to buy a box of "Flaky's Frosties" (his favorite cereal) in early June. When he read the back of the box at breakfast the next day, he had a brilliant idea. He went from one supermarket to another until he had bought 1,000 boxes of "Flaky's Frosties." (At an average of $4 a box, this cost him $4,000.) In mid-June 2005, he mailed the box tops to Flaky with the properly completed form and claimed his prize of a leopard cub.

Flaky refused to deliver a leopard club to Manny on several grounds:

(a) It denied that it had any legal obligation to Manny because the back of the cereal box was merely an invitation to consumers to claim prizes, and not an offer. Therefore, by submitting the box tops and form Manny made the offer, which Flaky rejected.

(b) Even if Flaky did make an offer on its cereal boxes, the offer was open only to "boys and girls," not to grown men. Manny therefore had no power of acceptance.

(c) The leopard club obviously was not intended as a prize but was just a bit of hyperbole to attract attention to the competition. This was obvious to any reasonable person because leopards do not make good pets, no consumer could reasonably be expected to consume 1,000 boxes of cereal in the few months before the expiry date of the competition, and no reasonable person would believe that a rare and expensive animal could be won for the cost of 1,000 boxes of cereal.

(d) Even if Flaky did make an offer, it expressly stated that prizes were limited to quantities on hand, and Flaky never had a leopard cub. Has Flaky committed itself to award this prize to Manny?

9. Spammer's Seaside Resort sent an e-mail to Annette X. Plorer, in which it stated, "Take advantage of our off-season rates! Spend a week at the beach for as little as $1,000! This is a limited-time offer, so visit our website and book now!" Annette visited Spammer's website. After viewing what was available and the prices of various room options, she filled in the appropriate boxes on the website, selecting an arrival and departure date and a seafront room. The website showed that the price of the room for the period was $1,500. Annette clicked on the "book now" button. This brought up another page in which she filled out her name, address, and credit card information. She then clicked on the "submit booking" button. A message came up on her screen that set out the particulars of her booking and stated, "Thanks for your booking. Your confirmation number is 100889456. Please print out this page for your records." The next day Annette changed her mind and no longer wished to spend a week at Spammer's Seaside Resort. Has she committed herself to a contract?

Explanations

1. Under the objective test it is not enough for Joe to assert that he did not actually intend to sell his house. He is accountable for his apparent intent, as reasonably interpreted by Hume from his words and actions. We do not judge Joe's manifestation purely on the basis of Hume's subjective interpretation, nor do we look at it from the perspective of reasonableness in the abstract. The proper test is whether a reasonable person in Hume's position would have understood Joe as manifesting contractual intent. That is, was Hume, under all the circumstances of their relationship, and knowing what he did about Joe, justified in concluding that the offer was serious? Joe apparently took great trouble to make his bluff

credible, and there seems to be nothing that could have reasonably indicated to Hume that Joe was fooling around.

This example is based on *Lucy v. Zehmer*, 84 S.E.2d 516 (Va. 1954), discussed in section 4.1.3d. Like Mr. Zehmer the joke was on Joe.

2. If Ivor's letter of July 1 was an offer, Sel Phelp's reply of July 24 could constitute an effective acceptance, as discussed below. If it was not an offer, but merely an invitation to deal, Sel Phelp's letter of July 24 was itself an offer which was not accepted. A communication is an offer if it manifests the maker's intent to invite acceptance and conveys the reasonable understanding to the addressee that, upon acceptance, the maker expects to be committed to a contract without any opportunity for further approval. The test of intent is objective, focusing on what Ivor apparently intended, as perceived by a reasonable person in Sel Phelp's position. The language of the offer is the most important indication of apparent intent, but the context of the transaction — including any prior dealings between the parties, usages that are or should be familiar to them, or other circumstances relevant to the transaction — can cast light on what must reasonably have been intended. No such contextual evidence is available in this case.

The language of Ivor's letter does not solidly convey his intent one way or the other. There are aspects of it that quite strongly suggest an offer: He provides for a specific date for response, he states that he "would be willing" to give the book to Sel Phelp in exchange for the publication commitment, and he does set out the essential terms on which he would like to contract. The rather vague reference to "customary" terms may suggest that further negotiation is contemplated, but if publication contracts tend to follow a common and well-accepted format, even these terms may be sufficiently certain to be ascertainable. Had the letter indicated that the manuscript had been sent to several publishers, this would have given some indication to Sel Phelp that it may not have been intended as an offer. However, the letter gives no hint that it is a form sent to multiple parties. Where a communication is phrased in the unclear way that Ivor has chosen, it is quite hard to predict how a court will decide what was intended. A person who does not clearly express intent in negotiations runs the risk of being held to an offer when none may actually have been intended.

A couple of cases illustrate the disparate situations in which a communication must be interpreted to decide if it is an offer, and what considerations a court may take into account in deciding whether a communication may reasonably be understood as an offer. In *Bourque v. Federal Deposit Insurance Corp.*, 42 F.3d 704 (5th Cir. 1994) the FDIC was liquidating a failed savings bank and selling its assets, including a piece of real property that Bourque wanted to buy. Bourque made the original offer to buy the property for $105,500, which the FDIC rejected in a letter stating "FDIC's counteroffer is $130,000. All offers are subject to approval by the appropriate FDIC delegated authority. FDIC has the right to accept or reject any and all offers." Bourque replied, agreeing to buy the property at this price but the FDIC sold it to someone else. Bourque claimed that the FDIC made a counteroffer which he accepted. However, the court found that FDIC's letter was not a counteroffer. Even though it used the word "counteroffer" and specified clear terms, it was qualified by the language that made it clear that the FDIC retained the final say in deciding whether to form the contract.

In *Barnum v. Review Board of Indiana Employment Security Division*, 478 N.E.2d. 1243 (Ind. App. 1985) the court had to decide if a laid-off employee was disqualified from unemployment benefits on the grounds that he had refused an offer of suitable employment. When layoffs were imminent, the employer had employees fill out a "recall choice form" which allowed the employee to state if he would prefer to be laid off or employed in a reduced position. The employee indicated a preference for layoff. The Review Board concluded that this was the refusal of an offer of employment which disqualified him from benefits. The court disagreed. It held that the form could not qualify as an offer under Restatement Second §24 because it provided no specifics about what the reduced position would be, and did not commit the employer to re-employ the worker. It did nothing more than indicate the possibility of re-employment and gave the employee an opportunity to express interest.

If Ivor did make an offer, Sel Phelp's response is likely to qualify as an acceptance. By leaving it to Sel Phelp to formulate terms in accordance with custom, Ivor implies into his offer an intent to contract on terms that are standard and usual in the trade. Provided that the terms in the standard form are indeed customary, they would not conflict with or add to his offer. With regard to the other terms regarding the publication date and royalties, the response is entirely in accord with Ivor's proposal. Ivor did not stipulate a mode of acceptance and transmitted his offer by mail. Sel Phelp's response by mail was therefore authorized, and the mailbox rule would apply, making the acceptance effective upon mailing. As a result, the revocation of July 25 was too late.

3. Doug is probably right. Kay's letter is surely an offer. It sets out the terms of the proposed transaction and gives the reasonable impression that Doug's acceptance will create a binding contract. The question is whether the offer was for a unilateral contract prescribing that the rendition of performance was the exclusive mode of acceptance. If it was, Doug's letter was not an effective acceptance, and Kay's revocation was communicated to him before he had a chance to accept. Where an offer is for a unilateral contract, and the act of performance is instantaneous,

acceptance occurs immediately that the act is performed. However, where performance cannot be instantaneous, but will take time — as in this case, where it spans a full month — acceptance is not complete until the performance is finished (on July 30). In the interim, an option is created in law as soon as Doug shows up at Kay's house on June 29, which protects Doug from revocation by Kay during the course of his performance. (As it is an option, Doug would have the right to cease performance at any time, thus terminating his act of acceptance and precluding the formation of a contract.)

In modern law, courts do not readily assume that an offer calls for performance as the exclusive means of acceptance. Therefore, unless an offer clearly prescribes performance as the exclusive mode of acceptance, a promise is permissible. There is no language in Kay's letter to signify that Doug can accept only by showing up at the house on June 29. In fact, the very nature of a unilateral contract is inconsistent with her apparent intent. As she will be paying Doug in advance and relying on him to care for the dog, she could not reasonably have intended that his commencement of performance would merely give him an option, and would create no promise by him to continue to take care of the dog.

Doug's case is a parody of *Davis v. Jacoby*, 34 P.2d 1026 (Cal. 1934). An elderly uncle, in distress over his failing business affairs and his wife's illness, wrote to a favorite niece and her husband, asking them to come down to California from Canada to help him manage his finances and take care of his wife. In return, he promised them that they would be made the heirs of his and his wife's estates. The niece's husband replied, agreeing to come, and this undertaking was confirmed in further correspondence. While the niece and her husband were preparing to leave for California, the uncle committed suicide. They arrived there shortly afterwards and did take care of the aunt until she died. They then discovered that they had not been made heirs under either the uncle's or aunt's will. When they sued the uncle's estate in contract, the trial court held that the uncle's letter called for a unilateral contract, so it could not be accepted by the promise in the nephew's letter. The plaintiffs therefore never accepted the offer, because it was revoked by the uncle's death before they arrived in California. The supreme court reversed. It held that an acceptance by promise is permissible unless a contrary intent is clear. The uncle's letter was ambiguous as to the mode of acceptance, but the words "let me hear from you as soon as possible" suggested that a promise was contemplated. In addition, there was a close relationship of trust from which it could be inferred that the uncle would have been satisfied with a promise, and indeed, a promise would have been necessary to reassure him because he was concerned about the long-term care of his wife.

As Kay's offer did not require performance as the exclusive mode of acceptance, Doug's promise in his letter of June suffices as an acceptance.

Because Kay made the offer through the mail, an acceptance via the same channel of communication is authorized, and the "mailbox" rule would apply, provided that the mailing was proper. However, the mailbox rule presupposes proper mailing and does not apply if the acceptance is improperly mailed. This is illustrated by *Casto v. State Farm Mutual Automobile Insurance Co.*, 594 N.E.2d 1004 (Ohio App. 1991). The insured had two policies with the insurer, covering a Jaguar and a Porsche. At about the beginning of October 1987, the insured received renewal notices for the two policies, showing that the premium was due on October 10. (As the court observed, an insurer's renewal notice constitutes an offer by the insurer to enter a new contract for insurance for the period specified in the policy, and it is subject to the general rules of offer and acceptance.) When the insured did not pay the premiums on time, the insurer sent cancellation notices on October 16, indicating that the policies would be cancelled on October 29. (The insurer conceded that had the premiums been paid by October 29, it would have renewed the policies without interruption of coverage.) On October 20, the insured mailed two checks to the insurer, one for each vehicle, in two separate preaddressed envelopes supplied by the insurer. The payment for the Porsche was delivered before October 29, but the envelope containing the payment for the Jaguar did not have a stamp and was never delivered. The insured had an accident in the Jaguar on November 20. It was only after the accident that the post office returned the unstamped letter to the insured, and she realized that the premium had not been paid. The court held that acceptance of the offer by mail was authorized because the insurer sent its offer by mail and had included a preaddressed envelope for return of the premium (which was the acceptance). Therefore, the mailbox rule would normally apply, and acceptance would be effective on mailing, not on receipt. However, the mailbox rule presupposes proper mailing, which the offeree must prove, and because the insured failed to stamp the letter, and as a result the letter was never received, the mailbox rule was excluded and the renewal offer had not been accepted.

Because Doug misaddressed the letter, the mailing was deficient and receipt was delayed, which deprives Doug of the protection of the "mailbox" rule. However, if a wrongly mailed acceptance does in fact reach the offeror, it is effective upon receipt. Kay received the offer before she communicated her intent to revoke, so the revocation is too late. A contract has been concluded, and Doug is justified in feeling aggrieved.

4. The advertisement clearly appears intended as an offer, so this issue does not require discussion. The most reasonable interpretation of public offers of reward is that they require acceptance, not by promise but by performance of the consideration called for — in this case, the furnishing of the information. If the confession qualified as an acceptance,

it would have created a unilateral contract under which the only outstanding promise is Art's commitment to pay $1,000. As no time for acceptance was stated, the offer had to be accepted within a reasonable time. The next day surely is reasonable under the circumstances. The issue is whether the confession could qualify as an acceptance. There are three arguments against treating it as such.

First, Fresco was not aware of the offer when he provided the information. Even under the objective test, apparent acceptance cannot be treated as acceptance unless deliberate and made with knowledge of the offer. In this respect, Fresco's situation is similar to that of the plaintiff in the *Glover* case discussed in section 4.7. As noted in section 4.7, the rule requiring knowledge of the offer is intended to protect the offeree from being held to an inadvertent manifestation of assent. This rationale does not apply here because, like the plaintiff in *Glover*, Fresco desires the acceptance to be effective. Nevertheless, there may still be a good policy reason for applying the rule because Fresco's ignorance of the offer means that he has no reliance interest to protect.

Second, even if Fresco made the confession with knowledge of the offer and intent to accept it, he has no power of acceptance unless the offer was addressed to him. The offer is addressed to "anyone" and is apparently aimed at the public at large, so on its face it is open for acceptance by any person who reads it and performs the requested act of furnishing the information. However, even though the offer expresses no restriction excluding the culprit as a possible offeree, the context of the offer may lead to the reasonable construction that this restriction was implied. This argument might be bolstered by the public policy of not permitting a criminal to gain from his crime. (But it could be argued that considerations of public interest point in the opposite direction. The reward is for the information, not the crime, and it may encourage confessions.)

Third, Art's argument that "conviction" requires a prison sentence is unconvincing. In the absence of evidence of some special usage, language is interpreted in accordance with its plain meaning. The conviction of a criminal is the determination of guilt in a court proceeding, and is distinct from sentencing.

5. There are three possible resolutions of this issue: Both informants accepted the offer and Art is liable to each of them for $1,000; both informants accepted and must share the reward; or the reward is due to N. Former only, because the offer was no longer open when I. Witness sought to accept. Art's offer is not clear on what happens if more than one person seeks to accept, so its reasonable intent must be ascertained by interpretation.

A person could make an offer in a way that permits multiple acceptances and thus many contracts. However, where it is clear from the offer that a single performance is all that the offeror needs, the more reasonable inference is that the offer is open to the first person who accepts by rendering the performance requested. Once that performance is given, the object of identifying and prosecuting the criminal is achieved, and it is no longer possible for another to give information that accomplishes the stated goal. If the condition of expiry is implicit in the offer, it is not necessary for the offeror to publish notice of revocation. Therefore, the best resolution is that the $1,000 must be paid to N. Former. The possibility of sharing may have been presented if each of the witnesses provided only part of the information needed to identify Fresco, but that did not happen here. Also, it does not matter if the testimony of both witnesses led to Fresco's conviction. The reward was for the information, not for the testimony.

6. Believe it or not, something like this actually happened. This example embellishes the facts in *Cobaugh v. Klick-Lewis, Inc.*, 561 A.2d 1248 (Pa. 1989), in which a car dealer offered the prize of a free car for a hole-in-one hit during a charity tournament. The dealer failed to remove the display after the tournament, and a golfer who hit a hole-in-one demanded the prize. The facts of *Cobaugh* were somewhat more favorable to the golfer than those in this problem because the sign did not in any way suggest that the display related to a tournament, and it had not been removed between the fateful golf stroke and the claim of the prize. The court found that the display was an offer, reasonably understood by a person seeing it as being open for acceptance by anyone who performed by hitting a hole-in-one. Upon accomplishing this feat, the golfer accepted the offer and was entitled to the car. The offer is for a unilateral contract because the dealer does not conceivably contemplate acceptance by promise. (There are a surprising number of hole-in-one cases. For another example, see *Harms v. Northland Ford Dealers*, 602 N.W.2d 58 (S. Dak. 1999) in which the court likewise held that the golfer accepted the car dealer's offer of a car prize by the act of hitting the hole-in-one. Unlike *Cobaugh*, the golfer in *Harms* was playing in the tournament for which the prize had been offered. The problem was that the tournament organizers had failed to inform participants that the rules of the competition required women golfers to hit the ball from the men's tee. Ms. Harms hit the ball from the women's tee, and the dealer disqualified her from the prize. The court held that the dealer was bound by the terms manifested to participants, and could not impose an unexpressed condition on the plaintiff.)

Jock cannot claim that he thought the offer was open for acceptance if the smaller print would have signified to a reasonable reader that the offer had lapsed at the end of the prior day's tournament. The language on the sign is not as clear as it could be. It does not expressly identify the tournament or confine the offer to it, but it does raise the possibility that the offer related to some charity event. A reasonable golfer, knowing the usual custom of offering prizes and promotions in connection with such tournaments, may well understand that the offer was no longer open for acceptance. If so, Jock has no claim.

The removal of the display before Jock claimed the prize is not legally relevant. If, contrary to what I suggest above, the wording of the offer does not reasonably indicate that it had lapsed, it had already been accepted by performance. Therefore, even if removal of the display could be treated as a sufficiently clear signal of revocation, it occurred after acceptance. When an offer is to be accepted by performance, it is the act of performance itself that creates the contract. If the act would not otherwise come to the offeror's attention, the acceptance falls away unless the offeree notifies the offeror of acceptance within a reasonable time. However, this is not a problem here because Jock did give immediate notice to Caddy-Lack's agent. A revocation between performance and reasonable notification is ineffective.

The most convincing resolution is that Jock failed to read the sign properly, and he should not reasonably have understood the offer to have been open for acceptance. He therefore cannot claim the prize.[14]

7. If Maggie's initial note is not an offer, there is clearly no contract because Minnie's responses would themselves be nothing more than unaccepted offers. However, Maggie's letter can reasonably be interpreted as an offer. It contains a specific proposal and appears to contemplate that a positive response by April 16 would conclude a contract.

Minnie's first response could be a counteroffer. If it is, it operates as a rejection, and the offer lapses so that there cannot be a later acceptance. However, the wording used by Minnie suggests that she did not intend an unequivocal rejection and counteroffer, but rather that she wished to explore the possibility of a change in terms. She appears to be negotiating an alternative while holding open the possibility of acceptance if Maggie refuses to budge on her initial demands. This being so, it would have been possible for Minnie to abandon her effort at securing more favorable terms and to accept the offer on April 16. Acceptance by mail would likely have been permissible because Maggie did not prescribe an exclusive medium of acceptance, and acceptance may be by any reasonable means. Also, as Maggie did not specify that acceptance would only

---

14. There were two other issues in *Cobaugh* that are beyond the scope of the present discussion but are worth noting for future reference. One concerned the question of whether hitting a hole-in-one (a fortuitous event, beyond the control of the golfer) could really be treated as a detriment for the purpose of finding consideration for the promise of a prize. If it is not a detriment, the promise of the prize named would likely be treated as an unenforceable promise of a gift. The other issue involved is the question of whether the competition was an illegal gambling contract.

be effective on receipt, the "deposited acceptance" or "mailbox" rule applies. The acceptance would have taken effect on April 16, as soon as Minnie deposited it in the mailbox, correctly addressed and stamped.

However, there are two reasons why Minnie's letter of April 16 does not qualify as an effective acceptance. First, it may not be an acceptance at all because it still does not completely correspond with the offer. It calls for Maggie to begin work two days after the date specified in the offer. Although this may be a minor variation, a strict application of the "mirror image" rule disqualifies it as an acceptance. The variation is less likely to be a problem if the less rigid "materiality" standard is used, because the change in dates may be too insignificant to be a material alteration of the offer's terms.[15] The problem created by the change in dates could also be overcome by interpreting the offer as impliedly authorizing Minnie to make minor adjustments in the dates.

A more serious problem is that the offer had been revoked before Minnie accepted it. Revocation is only effective when communicated to the offeree. However, even if, as happened here, the offeror fails to communicate the revocation to the offeree, the offer may be indirectly revoked when the offeree obtains definite and unambiguous information from a reliable source that the offer is no longer open for acceptance. (See *Dickenson v. Dodds* discussed in section 4.6.4.) Minnie did receive apparently reliable information from Max that Maggie has agreed to work for him and was no longer able to do research for Minnie. (There is no suggestion that Maggie has time to work for both of them.) Therefore, even if Minnie's response to Maggie on April 16 qualified as an acceptance, it was too late because it occurred after the offer had been revoked indirectly.

8. Flaky's arguments should be resolved as follows:

    8(a). The usual assumption is that advertisements (including competitions designed to promote products) are not offers but merely solicitations for offers from the public. When a member of the public responds to the solicitation with an offer, the advertiser may then accept or reject it. Although this is what ordinarily should be understood, it does not mean that an advertisement can never be an offer. Like any other communication, its reasonable intent must be determined by interpretation. Therefore, as the *Lefkowitz* case in section 4.1 shows, an advertisement could qualify as an offer if it is clear, definite, and explicit; leaves nothing open for negotiation; and makes it apparent to a reasonable person that a commitment is intended without further action by the advertiser. (See Restatement, Second §26, Comment *b*.)

---

15. The concept of materiality is introduced more fully in section 6.5.2.

Although *Lefkowitz* is an old case, it continues to be influential. It was used by the court in *Harris v. Time, Inc.*, 191 Cal. App. 3d 449 (1987). Time made the mistake of sending a piece of junk mail to one Joshua Gnaizda, the three-year-old son of an attorney. The letter, inviting Joshua to subscribe to *Fortune* magazine, was contained in a window envelope. The text of the letter viewable through the window declared "JOSHUA A GNAIZDA, I'LL GIVE YOU THIS VERSATILE NEW CALCULATOR WATCH FREE Just for Opening this Envelope Before Feb. 15, 1985." The final portion of the text was below the window and obscured by the envelope, but when opened, it could be seen to continue "AND MAILING THIS CERTIFICATE TODAY." Joshua's dad demanded that Time give Joshua a calculator watch without requiring a subscription, and, when it refused, he initiated a class action lawsuit on various grounds, claiming, inter alia, compensatory damages for the class of plaintiffs for the combined value of all the watches as well as punitive damages of $15 million. In addressing the cause of action based on contract, the court held the text of the mailer, as revealed through the envelope window, did constitute an offer. Like the advertisement in *Lefkowitz*, it was clear in its terms, called for a specific act of acceptance (opening the envelope), and left nothing for further negotiation. The offer was therefore accepted by opening the envelope.

However, although the court found the existence of a contract, and hence potential liability for damages, it stopped short of imposing liability on Time. It upheld the dismissal of the case on the maxim "de minimis non curat lex"—the law is not concerned with trifles. In other words, the court considered that the proper response to junk mail is to throw it away, not to sue over it. It was therefore not anxious to reward the plaintiff. However, its finding that Time's promotion was an offer must surely have made an impression on Time and others who employ advertising of that type. Although cases like *Lefkowitz* and *Harris* are resolved by application of the mechanics of offer and acceptance, the opinions indicate that the courts were really motivated by the concern that advertisers should be held accountable for what they appear to promise.

Lefkowitz was also cited but distinguished by the court in *Leonard v. PepsiCo* (discussed in section 4.1.3 in relation to the objective test). In addition to finding that there was no serious intent to contract for the supply of a Harrier jet, the court dealt with the issue of whether PepsiCo made an offer at all in its promotion. (In fact, the actual disposition of the case was based on the offer and acceptance issue, so the court would have found for PepsiCo even if it had not addressed the joke question.) Leonard contended that the TV commercial was an offer which he accepted by submitting the redemption form. The court found that the commercial could not be an offer because, unlike the advertisement in *Lekfowitz*, it was not detailed or specific enough. The catalog clearly could not have been an offer of the Harrier because it did not even mention the jet. However, the court went on to discuss whether the catalog could be an offer with regard to those items that were listed in it. It found that PepsiCo did not make an offer in the catalog because the catalog lacked words of limitation such as the phrase "first come, first served" used by the store in *Lefkowitz*, and no reasonable customer could have believed that PepsiCo intended to risk exposure to an unlimited number of acceptances. (It is worth stressing that this conclusion is not beyond doubt, and another court may have seen the catalog differently. The prize offerings were specific, and nothing was left for negotiation. The best way for an advertiser to make sure that the advertisement, catalog, or other publication is not an offer is to include specific language stating that it is not.)

How should Flaky's promotion be interpreted in light of these cases? The cases show that in interpreting advertisements courts weigh two factors: On one side is the usual market expectation that few advertisements are intended to give members of the public the power to bind the advertiser simply by responding to the advertisement. However, if an advertiser uses language that reasonably indicates a willingness to give potential customers the last word on forming a contract, it could be bound immediately upon the customer's response. The crucial indicators of such an intent are clarity and completeness in the proposed terms of the transaction, and the absence of any language or circumstances that may suggest a reservation of the right to retain control over the process of contract formation. In addition, courts are mindful of the need to hold advertisers responsible to the public for promises made in their advertisements. Although false advertising is statutorily regulated, contract law can also serve as a means of policing misleading or extravagant assertions and imposing liability on those who make them.

Flaky's promotion is fully set out on the backs of its cereal boxes, which seem to describe the prizes with particularity (including an illustration) and to set out in detail the mode of responding and the performance required in exchange for the prizes. The boxes also specify an expiry date for responses and contain a limitation to protect Flaky from having to award more prizes than it has on hand. There seems to be nothing left for future resolution, so all that is called for is a response in the proper form.

This may indeed be a case in which a court could find that Flaky's choice of language and format belies the normal expectation of a solicitation and creates an offer.

8(b). Flaky asserts that even if the box does create an offer, Manny could not accept it because it was open only to "boys and girls." This is a better argument than the store's claim in *Lefkowitz* because there is at least some basis for claiming that the limitation was expressed in the offer. However, even if "boys and girls" can be interpreted to mean "children," there is no language that restricts the offer to them or clearly excludes adults from claiming the prizes.

8(c). Flaky's next claim is that a reasonable person would understand that the leopard cub was not a prize, but included just a bit of hyperbole to attract attention to the competition. This argument is based on several grounds: the unsuitability of leopards as pets, the high number of box tops needed, and the huge discrepancy between the value of the cub and the cost of 1,000 boxes of cereal. These rationales are similar to those advanced by the court in *Leonard v. PepsiCo* to support the conclusion that the TV commercial could not reasonably have been understood as serious.

Flaky's joke is certainly more apparent than that of Joe or Mr. Zehmer in Example 1, but not quite as obvious as that in the Pepsi commercial. Nevertheless, a reasonable cereal box reader (if such a creature exists) could have been alerted to the likelihood that this was not seriously intended to be part of the offer. There is at least a plausible argument that this was a joke, not a serious offer.

8(d). Flaky's final argument is that even if it did make an offer, it expressly stated that prizes were limited to quantities on hand, and it never had a leopard cub. This interpretation of the qualification gives it an evasive meaning that the advertiser should not be allowed to advance. A more reasonable understanding of the qualification is that Flaky has stocks of all prizes, based on a fair expectation of responses, but that it will be released from supplying prizes once demand for an item exceeds these expectations. To allow Flaky to claim that the language permits it to begin with no prizes of a particular kind would be to condone deceptive advertising. As noted in Example 8(a), courts are mindful of this issue when interpreting advertisements.

9. Section 4.2.1 noted that the offer and acceptance model, based on the concept of active bargaining between parties in person, can be quite remote from the way in which many contracts are actually created in the modern marketplace. Standard form contracting has long been recognized as stretching the model, but transactions through electronic media (particularly when part of the process is automated) strain it

even further. Nevertheless, analogies can be drawn and common patterns exist no matter what process of contracting is used, so the concept of offer and acceptance can still serve as the basic framework for resolving electronic transactions. (It should be noted, however, that electronic commerce may not be left entirely to determination on principles of common law. Legislatures have taken up the issue of providing legal rules that apply to and regulate electronic commerce.)

Spammer's initial e-mail cannot reasonably be interpreted as an offer even though it uses the words "limited-time offer." It proffers the accommodation and its minimum cost ("as little as $1,000") in a general way, without any specific proposal that could be accepted by simple assent to its terms. Such specificity is achieved once Annette has made the selections on the website. It is therefore possible that Spammer makes an offer by showing the selected rooms, prices, and dates as available for booking on the website. (Despite the reference to "as little as $1,000" in the promotional e-mail, the actual offer for the accommodation is $1,500.) If it is an offer, Annette manifests assent to it and accepts by clicking the "submit booking" button. The listing of products or services on a website may not generally be seen as an offer (in this respect they are similar to advertisements or catalogs) but this is just a usual assumption, not a hard-and-fast rule. The listing on the website must be interpreted in context to see if it could reasonably be understood by the customer to be an offer. Marketplace usage and general expectations could play a significant role in deciding if a customer might reasonably understand the website to be making an offer. If there is any question about the legal effect of inviting customers to enter transactions on a website, the owner of the site can avoid uncertainty on this issue by making it clear on the website whether the customer's submission of the order will conclude a contract. We are not told if Spammer did this.

If Spammer's listing of the property on its site is not an offer, Annette's clicking on the "submit booking" button seems to meet all the criteria of an offer to take the accommodation at a price of $1,500. The screen that appeared immediately afterward could be an acceptance. Clearly, the screen was generated automatically, so Spammer had no conscious and deliberate intent to accept at the time that the response was sent. However, a party can set up an electronic response in a way that will allow the law to treat the automatic response as an effective acceptance. Modern law has come to recognize that a party can, in effect, create an "electronic agent" to act on its behalf by accepting an offer that the program identifies as meeting predetermined standards. It therefore seems quite likely that Annette has committed herself to a contract. We look at the question of electronic contracting again in the context of a sale of goods in Example 3 of Chapter 6.

CHAPTER 5

Options and Firm Offers

§5.1 INTRODUCTORY NOTE ON THE APPLICATION OF THE DOCTRINES OF CONSIDERATION AND PROMISSORY ESTOPPEL

It was noted in section 4.6.4 that an offer is revocable, even if it states that it will be held open for a stated term, unless it meets the legal requirements for an option or a firm offer under Uniform Commercial Code (UCC) Article 2. We now look at these legal requirements. Although options and firm offers may logically follow (or even be included in) the discussion of offer and acceptance, they can be difficult to understand without some knowledge of the doctrines of consideration and promissory estoppel. To minimize confusion, many casebooks defer this aspect of offer and acceptance until after those doctrines have been covered. For this reason, they are included in this short, self-contained chapter instead of being treated with offer and acceptance in Chapter 4. If your course is structured so that options are dealt with separately from offer and acceptance, you should return here when you reach this subject in class. For those who must tackle options and firm offers before consideration and promissory estoppel, this chapter has a brief preliminary explanation of those doctrines that should be adequate for present purposes.

§5.2 THE VALIDITY OF OPTIONS AT COMMON LAW AND CONSIDERATION DOCTRINE

An option is a **promise to keep an offer open for a stated period of time.** That is, the offeror undertakes not to revoke the offer for a specified period, so that the offeree is assured of a set time to consider and respond to the proposal without the risk of its being withdrawn before the expiry date. As discussed earlier, an ordinary revocable offer does not bind either party until acceptance, and then binds them simultaneously when acceptance is properly communicated. However, an option binds the offeror to his promise to keep the option open, and in this sense he is committed before the offeree becomes bound. As soon as the option is effectively granted to the offeree, the offeror has no right to withdraw unless the offeree declines to accept in the prescribed time. The offeree is, of course, not bound until acceptance.

We already noted, in connection with the discussion of revocable offers in section 4.6.4, that under common law a promise to keep an offer open for a stated time is not binding on the offeror unless the offeree has given consideration for that promise. Recall that in *Dickenson v. Dodds*, 2 Ch. D. 463 (Court of Appeals, Chancery Division, 1876), the court held that Dodds was legally entitled to revoke his offer before its expiry date because Dickenson had not given consideration for Dodd's promise to keep the offer open. As you will see in Chapter 7, the question of what constitutes consideration is complex. We cannot begin to explore that here. For present purposes it is enough to understand that in exchange for the grant of an option (the offeror's promise to keep the offer open and not revoke it for a designated period of time) the offeree has to give something to the offeror.

The most obvious "something" would be a cash payment or a promise to pay a specific sum of money for the option. But it could be a transfer of property or a promise to transfer or it could be something more abstract like the giving up of a legal right. Whatever form the consideration takes, the basic legal requirement is that the grantee must "pay" for the option by transferring or promising property or sacrificing a legal right in exchange for the promise to keep the option open.

Because an option is a form of offer, it necessarily contemplates that, if accepted, a contract will come into existence involving the exchange of performances contemplated by the offer. For example, if the offeror writes to the offeree offering to sell "Bleakacre" to her for $2 million, and giving her until next Friday to accept, the offeror contemplates an exchange of the farm for $2 million. Upon acceptance of the offer, the offeree promises to pay the $2 million, and that payment is surely consideration given in exchange for the farm. However, this consideration, exchanged under the contract proposed in the offer, is distinct from and does not also support the option itself. To be valid, the option must have its **own separate consideration** — the offeree must, in effect, purchase the option by providing an additional consideration, tied to the promise not to revoke. In the above example, if at the time of receiving the offer the offeree had paid the offeror $100 in exchange for the promise to keep the offer open until Friday, the promise not to revoke would have qualified as a valid and binding option. (This is represented in the next diagram.)

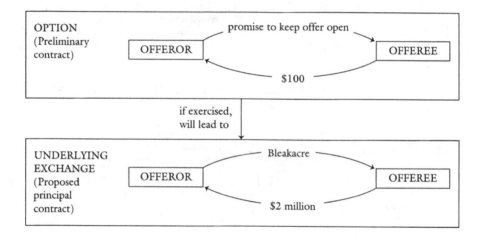

This rule requiring separate consideration for an option only applies in relation to the formation of a new contract — that is, when the option is a promise not to revoke an offer to enter into a contract. If an *option is granted within an existing contract*, it is part of the bundle of rights exchanged in the contract and is supported by the grantee's contractual consideration.

For example, no separate consideration would be required if Buyer is the tenant of "Bleakacre" under an existing lease, and the lease contains a term granting Buyer the option of purchasing the property for $2 million at any time before expiry of the lease. This option is simply one of the rights purchased by the lessee under the lease and is supported by the consideration given by the lessee under the lease (such as the payment of rental). It does not need separate consideration to bind the lessor. This distinction may be shown as follows:

OPTION IN THE FORMATION OF A NEW CONTRACT

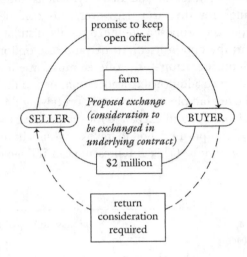

OPTION AS PART OF THE DETRIMENT EXCHANGED
IN AN EXISTING CONTRACT

The rationale of consideration doctrine is explored in Chapter 7 and is not discussed in detail here. However, as Chapter 7 will show, one of the principal aims of the doctrine is to confine legal enforcement to those transactions in which the parties have actually exchanged promises or performances. It refuses legal enforcement of a gratuitous promise — one that is given as a gift without any return benefit. Options are not usually motivated by gratuitous intent. Their common purpose is commercial — by committing to give the offeree an irrevocable opportunity to accept, the offeror hopes to facilitate a desired economic exchange. For this reason, courts usually try to uphold an option if there is any basis for finding consideration for it. As long as the option has been obtained by fair means, its term is not unduly long, and the parties have taken the trouble to formalize the grant in a writing that recites that consideration was given, a court is likely to uphold the option. Therefore, courts often accept **nominal consideration** (that is, a small payment or minimal performance that is patently not equivalent to the actual commercial value of the option) or even **sham consideration** (that is, consideration that is recited in the grant of the option purely for the sake of formality, but not actually given). This approach is reflected in Restatement, Second §87(1)(a), which says that the grant of an option is valid if it is in writing, signed by the grantor, recites a purported consideration for the offer, and proposes an exchange on fair terms within a reasonable time. (Of course, not all courts adopt this flexible attitude, and some may refuse to find an option to be valid if the consideration is nominal or a sham.)

§5.3 RELIANCE ON AN OPTION WITHOUT CONSIDERATION: THE APPLICATION OF PROMISSORY ESTOPPEL TO PROMISES OF IRREVOCABILITY

We have already seen one situation in which reliance on a revocable offer has created an option: Section 4.12.6 explains how the commencement of a non-instantaneous performance creates an option in favor of the offeree when the offer is for a unilateral contract. (That is, the offer requires performance as the exclusive mode of acceptance.) Although no consideration was given for this option (and indeed, there may not even have been an express promise to keep the offer open), an option is created by law to protect the reliance of the offeree in beginning the combined act of acceptance and performance.

Quite apart from this type of case, the doctrine of promissory estoppel has been used to create an enforceable option when *no consideration* was given for the promise of irrevocability. Promissory estoppel, discussed in Chapter 8, has developed as a basis for providing relief to a promisee under circumstances when a promise made does not qualify as contractual (because, for example, it lacks consideration), but the equities of the situation demand that the promise be enforced wholly or in part. To have a promise enforced under this doctrine, the promisee must establish that the **promise** was deliberately made with the **reasonable expectation** of **inducing** her to rely on it, that she did act (or sometimes, refrain from acting) in **justifiable reliance**, and that she suffered some **detriment** as a result. Once this is shown, the court has the discretion to achieve an equitable result by enforcing the promise fully or to the extent necessary to do justice.

When the promise in issue is an undertaking to keep an offer open, the offeree can use promissory estoppel to bind the offeror to honor that commitment only if she can show that despite having not given consideration for the promise of irrevocability, she was justified in relying on it.

For example, Seller writes to Buyer, offering to sell her farm "Bleakacre" to Buyer for $2 million and undertaking to hold the offer open until Friday.

As noted earlier, the promise not to revoke the offer until Friday is not a binding option because Buyer has given no consideration for it. However, assume that Buyer intends to accept the offer by Friday. On Tuesday, believing he still has time to accept, he quits his miserable job in the city so that he can devote full attention to his new farm. On Wednesday, before Buyer has had the chance to communicate his acceptance, Seller revokes the offer. Buyer disregards the revocation and notifies Seller of his acceptance on Thursday morning. He claims that his reliance on the promise of irrevocability caused him to leave his job before accepting the offer, and if it is not enforced, he will suffer unfair detriment. Restatement Second §87(2) recognizes the possibility of applying promissory estoppel in this kind of situation. It sets forth requirements modeled on §90, the section that covers promissory estoppel generally (discussed in section 8.6).

Seller did make a promise to keep the offer open until Friday, and she must reasonably have expected that her promise in clear terms would in some way cause the buyer to rely on being able to delay acceptance until Friday. It also is apparent that Buyer did in fact take detrimental action on the assumption that the offer would remain open — he abandoned his job before securing his contract rights by acceptance. However, it is less clear that Buyer was justified in burning his bridges in reliance on a promise of irrevocability for which he had paid or given nothing. A court that is concerned about preserving the requirement of consideration for a valid option would be likely to require a stronger showing of justifiable reliance before enforcing the promise of irrevocability under the doctrine of promissory estoppel. But a court that questions the value of consideration doctrine in this context may be less exacting once it is convinced that the promise was in fact made with apparent serious intent.[1]

The issue of applying promissory estoppel to create an option has come up periodically in cases involving **subcontractor bids**. Although there is some variation in the facts of these cases, this is their typical pattern: Reliant Contracting Co., a prime contractor plans to bid on contract to build an apartment building for City Housing Corp. Reliant needs subcontractors to perform many aspects of the project, so it calls for subcontractor bids for various parts of the work. One of jobs to be subcontracted is the supply and installation of a central heating system. Several heating companies submit bids for this aspect of the construction. One of them, Lobidder Heating Co., submits a bid for $2.5 million. This is the lowest bid for the heating, and it is $200,000 less than the next lowest bid. Reliant uses Lobidder's bid in formulating its own bid to City Housing. Reliant is awarded the contract to build the building. Shortly thereafter, Lobidder discovers that it made an

---

1. Courts are generally wary of imposing liability for promises made in the period of negotiation before contract formation. This issue is raised in connection with other types of precontractual promises in sections 8.5, 8.6, and 10.10.

error in calculating its bid, which should really have been $2.9 million. Lobidder tells Reliant of the error. It withdraws its bid and refuses to perform the work for less than $2.9 million. Reliant is left in the lurch. It is now committed to its contract price with City Housing, but it has to pay $200,000 more to the next highest bidder for the heating work. Is there a basis for Reliant to claim damages from Lobidder?

Reliant might argue that it has a claim for **breach of contract** because Lobidder's bid was an offer which Reliant accepted by using the bid in making its own bid. The problem with this argument is that even if Lobidder's bid was an offer, Reliant did not communicate acceptance of it before Lobidder revoked it. Communication of acceptance is required unless the offeror dispensed with it, so mere use of the bid is not enough to constitute acceptance. Usage or the other circumstances of the case could give rise to an implied waiver of communication, but such a usage or circumstances would have to be proved. It would be particularly difficult for Reliant to make this argument if it did not itself expect to be bound to Lobidder merely by using its bid.

Reliant might argue that Lobidder's offer was an **option** — that Lobidder impliedly promised that it would not revoke the bid until Reliant had a reasonable time to accept it after the award of the prime contract. The problem with this argument is, first, that there would need to be some factual basis to imply such a promise. Second, even if it could be implied, Reliant would have trouble showing that it gave Lobidder the consideration necessary to validate it. The best argument for consideration is that Reliant made an implied promise that if it used the bid, it would be committed to accept it. However, Reliant probably did not consider itself bound by use of the bid, and unless usage or other circumstances show otherwise, it would be difficult to imply such a promise.

The argument that has been most successful in cases like this is that although there is no contract or option, the promise to hold open the offer should be enforced under the doctrine of **promissory estoppel**. Promissory estoppel, in effect, serves as a substitute for consideration in creating an enforceable option. To enforce the option under promissory estoppel, Reliant must establish that all of its elements are satisfied. These elements are:

1. Lobidder must have made a **promise**. There is no express promise here, but all the circumstances could give rise to an implied promise by Lobidder to keep its bid open for a reasonable time to enable Reliant to accept it expeditiously as soon as it is awarded the construction contract.
2. Lobidder must **reasonably** have **expected** that Reliant **would rely** on its promise. Reasonable expectations are based on the entire context in which the promise was made, including not only the language and apparent firmness of the promise, but also the prevailing practices in

the industry and any prior relationship that the parties may have had. Reliant must establish that, under all these circumstances, a reasonable person in Lobidder's position would have realized that Reliant might rely on its bid in formulating the bid to City Housing.

3. Reliant must have **relied justifiably** on this promise. This requirement examines not only the question of whether there were reasonable grounds for Reliant to believe that a serious promise was made and could be relied upon, but it also requires consideration of the nature and justification of the action taken in reliance. It precludes recovery if Reliance reasonably should have realized, in comparing Lobidder's bid to others, that Lobidder likely made an error.

4. **Enforcement** of the promise must be **necessary to avoid injustice**. This element is usually satisfied if all the other elements are present and the prime contractor suffers the significant detriment of being bound to the owner for a price based on the subcontractor's bid. However, it also takes other equities into account, such as whether Reliant acted in good faith in accepting the bid as soon as possible, and did not try to speculate at Lobidder's expense, say, by bid shopping (that is, using the bid to shop around for a lower bid from competing subcontractors).

5. **The remedy**. Note that it is the promise to keep the offer open that is being enforced by promissory estoppel. It is therefore necessary for Reliant to have a claim for breach of contract, that it did in fact accept the offer within a reasonable time of being awarded the prime contract. If it did so, the parties formed a contract under which Lobidder committed to perform the heating work for $2.5 million. If Lobidder refuses to perform, it has breached that contract. Reliant can therefore employ another subcontractor and hold Lobidder liable for the extra cost reasonably incurred.

Two famous cases, separated in time by about 25 years, are usually used to contrast the differing approaches that courts may take in resolving a situation like this. The facts of the cases were similar to those outlined above, and in both the courts found that there was no basis for finding an accepted offer, and no consideration for a valid option. They differed on the propriety of using promissory estoppel to validate the option. In *James Baird Co. v. Gimbel Bros., Inc.*, 64 F.2d 344 (2d Cir. 1933), the court refused to adopt a promissory estoppel theory to make the subcontractor's bid irrevocable. In part, this approach can be explained by the fact that the promissory estoppel doctrine was much less developed at the time and had been largely confined to situations in which a donee had taken action in reliance on a promise to make a gift. The court was reluctant to extend it to the commercial context. However, even if it was appropriate to use the doctrine in a commercial case, the court felt that the contractor was not justified in relying on an unaccepted offer. If it wanted to bind the offeree to the offer, it should have purchased an option. As it did not do this, it assumed the risk of committing itself before securing its subcontract.

By contrast, in *Drennan v. Star Paving*, 333 P.2d 757 (Cal. 1958), the court did apply promissory estoppel doctrine to hold the subcontractor to an implied promise not to revoke its bid. The court saw no reason to confine the doctrine to donative promises, but recognized the protection of justifiable reliance as a general value of contract law. (This position has since become well accepted.) The court saw the creation of an option in this situation as analogous to the legal recognition of an option to protect an offeree who begins to accept a unilateral offer by commencing a non-instantaneous performance. (*See* section 4.12.6). The court held that in the commercial context, the subcontractor must have understood that the prime contractor might use its bid in calculating the bid for the prime contract. The prime contractor did rely justifiably on the bid. The discrepancy between the bid of this subcontractor and others did not alert the prime contractor to the possibility of a mistake. The court made it clear that the doctrine should be applied carefully and selectively in the precontractual context because promises are not normally made during negotiations prior to making a contract, and a party is not normally justified in acting in reliance until the contract is concluded. The court also stressed that the prime contractor must attempt to accept the bid within a reasonable time of being awarded the prime contract.

There are a number of more recent decisions that have followed the approach in *Drennan*. In *Pavel Enterprises, Inc. v. A.S. Johnson & Co., Inc.*, 674 A.2d 521 (Md. App 1996) the court accepted that where usage creates an expectation that a general contractor will rely on a subcontractor's bid in formulating its own bid, promissory estoppel can be used to validate the option without consideration. The court stressed that the general contractor must behave fairly to merit the protection of promissory estoppel. Any manipulation such as bid shopping will defeat reasonable reliance. In *Deide Construction v. Monterey Mechanical Co.*, 22 Cal. Rptr. 3d 763 (Cal. App. 2005) the court of appeal found the doctrine of promissory estoppel to be applicable where the prime contractor had committed itself to the property owner on the basis of the subcontractor's bid. The trial court had held that when the prime contractor discovered the error in the subcontractor's bid, it should have asked the owner to release it from its contract. The court of appeals disagreed. It would be unjust to require the prime contractor to sacrifice its profit and reputation. However, because the variance between the bids of the subcontractor and its next lowest competitor was $425,000, the court remanded the case for a determination of whether the prime contractor was reasonable in relying on such a low bid. In *I&R Mechanical, Inc. v. Hazelton Mfg.*

Co., 817 N.E.2d 799 (Mass. App. 2004) the court found that the elements of promissory estoppel were not satisfied. Applying offer and acceptance principles, the court found that the subcontractor's bid did not amount to an offer, but merely solicited an offer from the prime contractor. This in itself precluded the use of promissory estoppel because there was no promise. Even if promissory estoppel was applicable, the discrepancy between the subcontractor's price and other bids was so great that it should have alerted the contractor to an error. In addition, the contractor had also engaged in bid shopping, which was both inequitable and indicated that it was not relying on the bid.

§5.4 THE EFFECT OF AN OPTION

As stated already, the principal effect of a valid option is to keep the offer open for the stated period. The offeree's power of acceptance does not expire until the end of that period and is generally not cut short by action that would terminate an ordinary offer. Most importantly, this means that the offeror *cannot lawfully revoke* the option prior to its expiration. It also means, at least in cases when the offeree has given valuable consideration for the option (as opposed to nominal or sham consideration), that the option does not come to an end if the offeree rejects it (or makes a counteroffer, which is effectively the same as a rejection) before the end of the option period. If the offeree changes her mind she is able to *countermand the rejection* by communicating acceptance before the end of the period. This rule is based on the premise that the grantee has paid consideration to acquire the effective option, which is a valid contract in itself. If so, rejection before the end of the option period amounts to a waiver of contract rights by the optionee, and such a waiver is unenforceable if the optionee did not receive new consideration for it. (This principle is expanded on in section 13.9, where modifications to an existing contract are discussed.) This rule is subject to a qualification: Although waiver needs consideration, the doctrine of *estoppel* may protect the offeror who reasonably relied on the rejection to his prejudice. Therefore, if the offeror has taken substantially detrimental action in reliance on a rejection (such as contracting with someone else for the same performance), the offeree may not reverse the rejection by later acceptance.

To accept an irrevocable offer, the offeree must *communicate acceptance* to the offeror within the option period. This usually requires that the offeror actually receives the acceptance because, as noted in section 4.11.12, some courts do not apply the "mailbox" rule to an option.

§5.5 FIRM OFFERS UNDER UCC §2.205

In a sale of goods, §2.205[2] dispenses with the need for consideration to validate an option (called a "firm offer" in the section) under defined circumstances. The section only applies when all of its prerequisites are satisfied, namely:

1. The offer to buy or sell goods must be made by a **merchant.** Under §2.104(1)[3] a merchant is a person who deals in goods of the kind involved in the transaction or who otherwise, by trade or profession, represents that he has skill or knowledge in regard to the goods or the transaction. In essence, a merchant, as distinct from one whose dealings in the goods is casual or inexpert, is a person who trades professionally in goods of that kind, either as seller or buyer. Although Article 2 does not in all cases provide different rules for merchants and casual buyers and sellers, there are some sections — §2.205 being one of them — that are applicable only to merchants or have stricter standards for them. Some of these sections are applicable only in transactions "between merchants," that is, if both parties to the transaction are merchants, but others apply if only one of them is. Section 2.205 fits into the latter category. For the rule validating firm offers to apply, only the offeror need be a merchant. (For further discussion of the merchant status, see section 6.5.2.)
2. Under the existing §2.205, the offer must be in a **signed writing.** The 2003 revision changes this to a signed **record** to include recording by means other than writing. This is likely not a substantive change. Even under current §2.205, a court, taking contemporary commercial practice into account, is likely to treat the term "writing" to include electronic records.
3. It must give an **assurance** to the offeree that it will be held open.
4. If the assurance is contained on a form supplied by the offeree, the offeror must sign the assurance separately. The purpose of this is to ensure that the offeror was aware of the term and is not bound by an assurance of irrevocability hidden in the offeree's boilerplate. The 2003 revision changes "on" a form to "in" a form to encompass forms that are electronic and have no tangible existence.

If all these conditions are satisfied, consideration is not needed to make the offer irrevocable for the *time stated*, or for a *reasonable time* if no expiry date is

---

2. The 2003 revision of §2.205 is the same as the current version, save for a few minor grammatical adjustments and the change mentioned in item 2 below.
3. The 2003 revision of Article 2 makes some small adjustments to §2.104(1), but does not change it substantially.

specified. Section 2.205 limits the period of irrevocability to a maximum of three months, so that neither a stated time nor a reasonable time can exceed that period. Therefore, if the option is intended to last more than three months, the offeree must give consideration to validate it beyond the three-month period.

Examples

1. Shelly Shally had been negotiating with Reva Cation for the purchase of "Blandacre," an old farm now engulfed by suburban sprawl and zoned for housing development. By May 1, 2003, they had reached agreement in principle on the price and the other important terms on which the sale would be made, but Shelly could not decide if she really wanted the property. She said that she needed time to think about it. Reva realized that she would frighten Shelly off if she pushed too hard, but she sensed that given a little time, Shelly would probably decide to buy the property. Reva therefore agreed to give Shelly a short time to make up her mind. On May 1, she wrote out and signed the following document, which she gave to Shelly:

   > It is recorded that Reva Cation is willing to sell her property "Blandacre" to Shelly Shally for $500,000, subject to the following terms . . . (the note then set out the material terms of the sale). If Shelly wishes to buy this property, she must notify Reva in writing by 5 P.M. on May 3, 2003. Reva undertakes not to sell the property to anyone else or to withdraw this offer before that date.

   Shelly spent many sleepless hours agonizing over the purchase during the night of May 1. On the morning of May 2, she was pretty sure that she did want the property. She wrote a note to Reva accepting her offer, but decided that she would wait a little before delivering it to Reva, just in case she had second thoughts. Finally, on the morning of May 3, she decided finally that she would buy "Blandacre." She called Reva, and when Reva answered the phone, Shelly said, "Good news, I've decided to accept your offer. I am coming over right away with a written acceptance." Reva replied, "Sorry, I was offered a better price by someone else, and I've just sold the property."

   Does Shelly have any recourse against Reva?

2. Would it have made a difference to the result of Example 1 if the last sentence of the written offer signed by the parties had instead stated, "In consideration for $1.00 received, Reva undertakes not to sell the property to anyone else or to withdraw this offer before that date"? After signing the offer, Shelley handed a dollar bill to Reva.

3. Assume that Reva had leased the property to Shelley for the period of one year at a monthly rental of $1,000. One of the terms in the lease gave

Shelly the option to purchase the property for $500,000. To exercise the option, Shelly had to ". . . give written notice to Reva, to be received not later than 30 days before the expiry of the lease period."

On the fortieth day before the expiry of the lease, Shelly wrote to Reva informing her that she did not intend to exercise the option. Reva received that letter on the thirty-eighth day and immediately replied, acknowledging receipt and confirming that the option had lapsed. Shelly received the reply on the thirty-sixth day. Later on that same day, Shelly changed her mind and decided that she did want to buy the property. She wrote a second letter, countermanding the first and exercising her right to purchase the property. Reva received the second letter on the thirty-fourth day before expiry of the lease. Has Shelly bought the property?

4. Reva did not make any offer to sell "Blandacre" to Shelly. Instead, she planned to develop it herself. Because she did not intend to farm the land any more, she no longer needed her tractor, and she advertised it for sale. Harv Ester read the ad and came to see the tractor on May 1. He liked it, but wanted some time to decide whether to take it. Reva agreed to give him some time to make up his mind. On that day, she wrote and signed a note that stated, "It is recorded that Reva Cation is willing to sell her tractor [the model and make was described] to Harv Ester for $5,000 cash. If Harv wishes to buy it, he must notify Reva in writing by 5 P.M. on May 3, 2003. Reva undertakes not to sell the property to anyone else or to withdraw this offer before that date."

On May 2, Reva sold the tractor to someone else and notified Harv that she withdrew her offer. Can Harv refuse to recognize the revocation and accept the offer, thereby creating a binding contract?

5. In August, Lois Bidder, a building contractor, was invited by the owner of land to submit a bid for the construction of a new building. Lois was given until September 15 to submit the bid. To produce an accurate bid, Lois needed to know what she would have to pay plumbers, electricians, and other specialists to whom work would be subcontracted. On September 1, she sent the building specifications to a number of potential subcontractors and invited them to submit bids by September 13, explaining that she required the bids by that time to enable her to submit her own bid for the whole project on time.

Esther Pel was one of the electricians invited to bid on the electrical work. After studying the specifications, Esther calculated the amount of material and labor required and submitted a written bid for $100,000. The bid stated: "This bid is open for your acceptance within a reasonable time after you have been awarded the prime contract."

Upon receiving the bid on September 13, Lois compared it to others received and saw that it was $20,000 cheaper than the next lowest bid. She therefore decided to use Esther for the electrical work and included her figure in the bid to the owner. Lois submitted her bid on September 14, and the owner accepted it on September 15.

Lois immediately prepared letters to all the selected subcontractors, notifying them that their bids had been successful and that the project would proceed. Just before the letters were mailed, Lois received a fax from Esther, stating that on checking her calculations after submitting her bid, she had discovered that she had mistakenly omitted the cost of electrical wire. As a result, her costs had been underestimated by $30,000 and she could not profitably perform the work for the bid price. Esther apologized for the error, which resulted from having to get her bid ready in a rush, and regretted that she must withdraw her previous bid. She was willing, however, to perform the work for $130,000.

Lois faxed back, informing Esther that she had already committed herself to the owner on the basis of electrical subcontracting costs of $100,000 and she considered Esther bound by her original bid.

Is Lois justified in taking this position?

Explanations

1. Reva's note is clearly an offer to sell the property to Shelly. It apparently sets out all the material terms on which she intends to enter the contract, and requires nothing more than a proper signification of acceptance to create a binding relationship. The offer contains an unequivocal promise that it will not be revoked. The problem is that Shelly has given no consideration to Reva for the promise to keep the offer open. A promise not to revoke an offer is treated as distinct from the underlying contract that would come into existence upon valid acceptance, so it needs its own separate consideration to qualify as a binding option. Shelly cannot therefore argue that consideration for the promise of irrevocability is furnished by the $500,000 that she would have committed to pay for the property had a contract arisen. *Dickenson v. Dodds*, discussed in sections 5.2 and 4.6.4, establishes both that consideration is needed to validate an option, and that an offer that does not qualify as an option can be revoked indirectly.

   Shelly's case is a little different from *Dickenson*, in which the offeree heard of the revocation before making any communication of the intent to accept. Because she spoke first during the telephone conversation, Shelly did in fact signify her assent to the offer before Reva was able to tell her that the property had been sold. However, the offer clearly called for a written acceptance, and an oral acceptance by telephone does not provide the evidentiary protection of a writing and cannot be regarded as a mode of acceptance reasonably authorized by the offer.

By contrast, the revocation need not be in writing, even though the offer was. As long as the revocation is in fact communicated to the offeree, it is effective and need not necessarily be in the same form as the offer. It is therefore too late for Shelly to rush over to Reva's place with a written acceptance. Finally, as Shelly took no action in reliance on the promise to keep the offer open, she has no basis for relief under the doctrine of promissory estoppel. The mere delay in acceptance on the strength of the promise is not in itself enough to constitute the type of detrimental reliance contemplated by the doctrine. (The type of reliance necessary is explored in Example 5.)

2. In this changed form, the grant of the option now records that consideration was given for it. We have no indication of what the actual economic worth may be of a three-day option to buy a piece of property for $500,000, but it is probably fair to assume that $1.00 does not and is not intended to bear any relationship to the option's actual value. Rather, it is inserted in the grant purely for the sake of formality. The parties know that consideration is required to validate the option, so they provide for it in a nominal amount for the purpose of showing their intent to create a legally binding promise. As a general rule, courts are willing to respect the parties' effort to validate an option by providing for nominal consideration, as long as there is no indication that the parties had the purpose of misleading someone else, or that the grantor was tricked or otherwise taken advantage of by the grantee. (When you deal with consideration doctrine in Chapter 7, you will recognize that this approach accords with the general principle that consideration exchanged by the parties need not be economically equivalent.)

3. Here the option is not a self-standing promise by Reva to keep an offer open. Rather, it is one of the obligations she has assumed under the lease with Shelly in exchange for Shelly's consideration — her promise to pay the monthly rent. It is part of the collection of rights that Shelly has purchased under the lease and is enforceable like any other term of the contract. It needs no separate consideration.

   In terms of the lease, Shelly had until 30 days before the expiry of the lease term to exercise her option. Ten days before this deadline, she sent a letter informing Reva that she did not intend to buy the property — in effect, rejecting the offer to sell. Her letter was received and acknowledged in writing by Reva. Had this been an ordinary offer, it would have been effectively terminated before Shelly changed her mind and decided to accept. However, when a grantee has purchased a valid option by giving consideration for it, a contract exists. As you will see in sections 7.5 and 13.9, an agreement to modify a contract or to give up rights under it is itself a contract and requires consideration to be binding. Therefore, if one of the parties gives up contract rights without receiving any consideration in exchange, the disavowal of rights does not bind her. The effect of this is that even though Reva accepted Shelly's relinquishment of her right to exercise the option, she gave Shelly no consideration in exchange for it. Shelly was therefore not bound by her abandonment of the option, and her subsequent letter was an effective exercise of the option. There is an exception to this rule if the grantor took detrimental action in reliance of the rejection of the option, say by committing herself to sell to someone else. However, that did not happen here. The "mailbox" rule does not apply to the acceptance of an option, but on our facts this creates no problem for Shelly because the letter exercising the option was received by Reva before the end of the option period.

4. As in Example 1, the offeree has given no consideration for the promise to hold the offer open. At common law, Reva's promise not to revoke would not bind her, and her revocation would be effective. However, this is a sale of goods, so if the requirements of UCC §2.205 are satisfied, the promise is binding as a firm offer despite the lack of consideration.

Section 2.205 only applies if the offeror is a merchant. (It is not necessary that the offeree be a merchant as well.) There may be a basis for finding that Reva is a merchant with regard to the tractor sale, but whether she has sufficient work-related expertise in transactions of this kind to qualify as a merchant under §1.104(1) is a question of fact that cannot be finally decided on the scanty information furnished here. She had apparently been farming "Blandacre" until recently, and had used the tractor for that activity. A farmer (even one who is disposing of the farm and its equipment) may qualify as a merchant with regard to farming implements, not necessarily because she deals in goods of that kind with any frequency, but because, by her occupation, she holds herself out as having knowledge or skill in relation to the goods or the transaction. The issue, in essence, is whether she has sufficient sophistication and knowledge of the trade to be subject to Article 2's more exacting rules for "professionals."

If Reva does satisfy the definition of a merchant, the offer is binding on her as a firm offer until its stated expiry time of 5 P.M. on May 3, because it meets the other requirements of §2.205: It is in a writing (a record) signed by her, and it gives assurance that it will be held open for a stated time, not exceeding three months. Harv may therefore ignore the attempted revocation and accept the offer before the time for acceptance lapses. This will create a binding contract. (Although Harv will not necessarily be able to compel Reva to deliver the tractor, he will be able to claim any money damages suffered as a result of the breach.)

5. By soliciting bids, Lois was inviting subcontractors to make offers. The language used by Esther in her bid creates the reasonable understanding that she intended it as an offer with a promise of irrevocability for a

reasonable time after the prime contract was awarded. The undertaking not to revoke does not bind Esther, however, because she received no consideration for it. (There could have been consideration if Lois had bound herself, expressly or impliedly, to use the lowest bid, but there is no indication of such a commitment.) Although Lois used Esther's offer in calculating her own bid, there is no evidence of circumstances that would make this an acceptance of the offer. Esther revoked the offer before Lois had the chance to communicate her acceptance. Because there is no consideration to validate the promise not to revoke, Lois can only hold Esther to her promise of irrevocability if she can validate that promise on grounds of promissory estoppel. As the discussion in section 5.3 indicates, the availability of promissory estoppel in this context is now well established.

The question is therefore whether the facts satisfy the elements of promissory estoppel. Esther made an *express promise* of irrevocability, so the element of promise is easily established. It is likely that this promise was made with *the reasonable understanding that Lois would rely on it* if she used Esther's bid. In *Drennan*, the court emphasized that the expectation of reliance is a factual question, to be decided under all the circumstances, including common practice in the industry. We do not have any information about industry practice. If it is a general practice in the industry for subcontractors to protect contractors who use their bids as the basis of bidding on prime contracts, there is a strong likelihood of a reasonable expectation of reliance. Even in the absence of such a clear practice, the language Esther used in her bid suggests a reasonable expectation of reliance — it recognizes that her bid might be used and that Lois needed time to accept after she was awarded the contract.

There are two factors to be considered in deciding whether Lois's *reliance was justified*. First, was Lois reasonable in understanding that a promise was made on which she could rely? This question parallels the above analysis, now examined from the perspective of a reasonable person in Lois's position, that found a promise and intent to induce reliance. There is no reason to reach a different answer. Second, should Lois have suspected an error when she saw that there was a $20,000 discrepancy between Esther's price and the next lowest bid? Even if she did not know for sure that Esther must have made a mistake, she had a duty to enquire if the low price looked wrong, and she cannot just jump at the bargain. Of course, there could be many explanations for variations in price, so the question is whether, under all the circumstances, she was reasonable in not questioning it.

Promissory estoppel relief must be necessary to *prevent injustice*. This element calls on the court to weigh all the equities of the situation, including the strength of the elements discussed above. A predominant issue here is the degree of detriment that will be suffered by Lois if the promise to hold the offer open is not enforced. As in most of the bid cases, this detriment is an increase in the costs of the job and a corresponding loss of profit. The more dramatic this loss is, and the less the reasonable alternatives for averting it, the stronger the injustice. Other factors also enter the determination of injustice. Several of the cases discussed in section 5.3 examined the conduct of the prime contractor in the way it used the bid. An unreasonable delay in acceptance after the award of the prime contract, or any kind of manipulation such as bid shopping, could tip the balance against the grant of relief. In this case, Lois was not guilty of any such misconduct. She accepted the bid immediately upon being awarded the prime contract and just two days after the bid was submitted.

The appropriate remedy in a case like this is to enforce the promise to keep the bid open so that Lois's acceptance is effective, even though made after attempted revocation. Because the acceptance is effective, a contract was created. If Esther failed to perform it, Lois can claim damages measured by the difference between Esther's price and the higher price that Lois reasonably had to pay to another subcontractor for the work.

Offer and Acceptance Under the UCC, and the "Battle of the Forms"

§6.1 GENERAL PRINCIPLES OF OFFER AND ACCEPTANCE IN THE UCC

Uniform Commercial Code (UCC) §1.103 (revised §1.103(b)) states that unless they are displaced by particular provisions of the Code, the general principles of common law apply to transactions governed by the Code. UCC Article 2 says very little about the process of offer and acceptance, so the formation of a sales contract is largely subject to the common law rules discussed in Chapter 5. While Article 2 defers to the common law on most offer and acceptance issues, it does strongly encourage courts to be realistic and to keep an eye on business practice in resolving formation disputes. As Chapter 5 indicates, this flexibility has spread beyond the UCC and is reflected in the modern common law approach to offer and acceptance generally.

The two Code sections (in both the current and revised version of Article 2) that most directly address general formation issues are §§2.204 and 2.206. Narrower formation topics are covered in §2.207 (discussed in the remainder of this chapter) and §2.205 (discussed in section 5.5). The fundamental point made by §2.204 is that the court should *focus on the existence of agreement* between the parties, whether shown by words or conduct, and if agreement is apparent, the court should *not be concerned about technicalities* but should do what it can to uphold and enforce the contract. Section 2.206 eschews technical rules on the manner and medium of acceptance and emphasizes that an offer should be interpreted as inviting acceptance by any reasonable mode unless the offer or circumstances make it clear that the mode is restricted.

The general approach to formation under §§2.204 and 2.206 is illustrated by *Bio-Tech Pharmacal, Inc. v. International Business Connections, LLC.*, 184 S.W.2d 447 (Ark. App. 2004). The buyer, a manufacturer of nutritional supplements, bought raw products from the seller for several months. There were a number of transactions that followed the same pattern. The seller would locate material of the kind used by the buyer and would then call the buyer to tell it of the material's availability and price. If the buyer wanted the material it would so indicate during this phone call and would then issue a written purchase order which it sent to the seller. The purchase orders described the material, quantity, and price. They also contained standard language that stated "Order/price confirmation w/ship date must be faxed/emailed immediately." The seller never sent any confirmations, but just shipped the goods. The buyer received and paid for the shipments without complaining about the lack of confirmation. After this had been going on for some months, the buyer suddenly canceled orders on the basis that the seller had failed to send the confirmations. When the seller sued the buyer for damages resulting from the buyer's failure to take goods ordered, the buyer argued that the orders never became contracts. It claimed that the purchase orders were offers that prescribed an exclusive means of acceptance — the faxing or emailing of a confirmation. Because the seller had not done that, no contracts came into being. The court acknowledged that an offeror has the right to prescribe an exclusive mode of acceptance. However, §2.206 states that unless otherwise unambiguously indicated, an offer is to be construed as inviting acceptance in any manner reasonable in the circumstances. The language of the offer did not qualify as unambiguous. Even though it required confirmation, it did not make it clear that this was the only means of accepting, or even that confirmation was a mode of acceptance rather than a contractual duty. The court also questioned whether the purchase order was the offer. It could be that offer and acceptance occurred during the phone conversations, and the purchase order was merely a written confirmation.[1]

The provisions of existing §§2.204 and 2.206 have been amended slightly in the 2003 *revision*. The principal change to §2.204 is a recognition that contracts can be formed through electronic means, including the use of an "electronic agent" by one or both parties. Revised §2.103(g) defines an

---

1. The court also discussed the effect of the pattern of conduct in the prior transactions. As explained in section 10.6.2, the conduct of parties in prior similar transactions (course of dealing) or in the performance of the transaction in question (course of performance) could have a bearing on interpreting terms of the contract. The court noted that the buyer's failure to insist on confirmations in the earlier sales is persuasive evidence bolstering the interpretation that confirmation was not intended as an exclusive mode of acceptance. Alternatively, this conduct could constitute a waiver of that requirement. (The distinction between waiver and course of dealing or performance is made in section 10.6.2b.)

"electronic agent" to mean a computer program or other automated means of initiating or responding to a communication without human intervention. The text of existing §2.206 is contained in revised §2.206(1) and (2). Revised §2.206(3) is a new subsection, but its content is not new. It has been moved from existing §2.207(1). Section 2.206(3) provides that a definite and seasonable expression of acceptance in a record[2] operates as an acceptance even if it contains terms additional to or different from the offer. As Comment 3 to revised §2.206 points out, the purpose of this provision is to make it clear that the "mirror image" rule (see section 4.8.1) should not be followed. As long as the intent to accept is clear, definite, and timely (seasonable), the response should not be treated as a counteroffer just because it has terms additional to or different from the offer. As mentioned above, this provision used to be set out in §2.207. (Its meaning in the context of §2.207 is discussed more fully in section 6.5.) Its removal to §2.206 is organizational (as discussed in section 6.7), but it also likely has the effect of making this principle generally applicable, and not confined to cases involving a "battle of the forms."

§6.2 THE SCOPE AND PURPOSE OF UCC §2.207

The current version of §2.207 is awkwardly drafted and has led to considerable interpretational difficulty. The 2003 revision changes the section dramatically in ways that will be explained below.[3] To reduce the confusion of trying to understand the existing and revised versions of this section, the following text deals with them separately. Sections 6.3 through 6.6 discuss the existing law, and section 6.7 explains how the revision will change it. The Examples and Explanations that deal with §2.207 are based on the existing version of the section, but there is a discussion at the end of each Explanation that explains how the revision will be likely to change the answer or the analysis.

In its current form, §2.207 is implicated whenever one or both parties use written communications in the process of forming a contract for the sale of goods. Often, but not always, these writings are on preprinted forms that contain standard terms known as **"boilerplate."** (That is, they are standard provisions commonly employed in contracts of that kind.) As may be expected, the standard terms used by a party are usually designed to protect the interests of that party, so if seller and buyer both use standard terms, a conflict between them is likely. Because standard forms are so common,

---

2. Revised Article 2 uses the term "record" instead of "writing" to encompass means of electronic recording.

3. Recall, as explained in section 2.7.1, that the 2003 revision of Article 2 has not been enacted in any state at the time this edition of the book is being written. Therefore, at this time, the current version of §2.207 is still the law in every state.

many §2.207 cases are concerned with resolving disparities between them — hence the nickname, **battle of the forms.**

§6.3 THE PROBLEM TACKLED BY §2.207: THE COMMON LAW "MIRROR IMAGE" AND "LAST SHOT" RULES

The premise of §2.207 is that common law offer and acceptance rules are based on a model of individualized bargaining that does not fit the reality of most modern sales transactions. Buyers and sellers do not typically haggle over all the terms of the sale but focus on the essentials such as the description, price, and quantity of the goods. The remaining details of the contract may be left to custom or practice or they may be set out in a written order, acknowledgement, or confirmation. The use of preprinted forms is very common today, so these writings are often standardized and, as stated earlier, are designed to protect the interests of the party who produced them. In most cases, standard forms do not create problems. Even if there are conflicts in detail, the buyer and seller focus on the heart of the sale itself and do not even notice the discrepancy. The goods and money change hands, and the sale is completed without any dispute. But every so often something happens in a transaction that causes a party to lay claim to a right tucked away in its document.

For example, Buyer sends Seller a written order for a Louden LeThal Model XZ100 Rivet Gun, for a price of $450, C.O.D. delivery in 30 days. The order is on Buyer's form that contains a preprinted indemnity provision, stating that if anyone suffers injury in operating the gun and successfully sues Buyer, Seller shall indemnify Buyer by paying the judgment and Buyer's legal fees. On receipt of the order, Seller immediately sends an acknowledgement that accords with the order in all respects, except for the indemnity. The seller's acknowledgement has a preprinted indemnity provision that says exactly the opposite, requiring Buyer to indemnify Seller for any such claims that may be made against Seller.

It could happen that no problem ever arises to bring this conflict to light. Delivery and payment occur and the machine is used without incident, so that no one ever has to worry about the opposing indemnities. However, one of two things could go wrong in the transaction, making the discrepancy crucial.

1. One of the parties may wish to escape the transaction prior to delivery. Upon discovering the divergence between offer and acceptance, it may use it as the basis for asserting that no contract came into existence. In other words, the conflict between the writings could provide a **pretext for reneging** on the contract.

2. If this does not happen and the machine is delivered, one of Buyer's workers may be injured in operating it. At this point a dispute arises on the allocation of liability under the contract. The conflict in the writings would have to be resolved to decide **whose term** (if either) **became part of the contract.** This is, of course, not a dispute about the existence of a contract but about its content.

Under strict common law principles,[4] these issues would be decided under the "mirror image" and "last shot" rules. Under the **"mirror image"** rule, Seller's nonconforming response prevents the acknowledgement from being an acceptance and makes it a counteroffer. Even if the parties thought that they had a contract, none came into existence upon sending of the acknowledgement, and if either party wishes to renege before performance, this could be done with impunity.

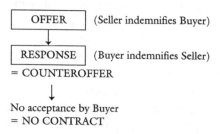

OFFER	(Seller indemnifies Buyer)
RESPONSE	(Buyer indemnifies Seller)

= COUNTEROFFER

No acceptance by Buyer
= NO CONTRACT

If neither seeks to escape the contract and the rivet gun is shipped and accepted by Buyer, Buyer's conduct in accepting it is an implied acceptance of the counteroffer, whether or not Buyer read Seller's reply. As a result, a contract is created subject to Seller's term, purely because Seller's was the **"last shot,"** that is, the last communication before acceptance of the goods.

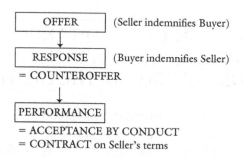

OFFER	(Seller indemnifies Buyer)
RESPONSE	(Buyer indemnifies Seller)

= COUNTEROFFER

PERFORMANCE
= ACCEPTANCE BY CONDUCT
= CONTRACT on Seller's terms

The drafters of the UCC considered this result to be unduly rigid and unrealistic, especially where the conflicting terms are in standard forms. It fails to take into account that the parties really were in agreement over the

---

4. Although Article 2 is not applicable to contracts other than sales of goods, courts are influenced by its provisions in developing common law rules. Therefore, a court may not rigidly apply these strict principles in a common law case.

essential terms of the contract, and the reply was in fact intended as an acceptance. It places too much store on a clash of boilerplate terms that are unlikely to be read. To treat the term as creating a counteroffer therefore ignores commercial reality and produces the wrong result by facilitating dishonor of the agreement up to the time of performance and by imposing an unexpected term on the offeree thereafter.

To rectify this problem, the current version of §2.207 attempts a twofold approach. First, it rejects the "mirror image" rule. If a response can reasonably be interpreted as an acceptance, it is recognized as such despite a variation from the offer. A contract is therefore created and the door is closed on a party who later wishes to renege. Except in narrow circumstances, the conflicting term in the acceptance falls away and does not become part of the contract. Second, it rejects the "last shot" rule. If the response cannot fairly be interpreted as an acceptance and it is a counteroffer, subsequent performance is not deemed an acceptance by conduct. Therefore, although a contract is recognized by virtue of the mutual performance, it is not simply on the terms set out in the last communication. Rather, conflicting terms fall away and are replaced by supplementary terms in the UCC.

While §2.207 does reform these deficiencies in the common law, it has problems of its own. As noted earlier, the existing §2.207 is generally acknowledged to be poorly drafted, difficult to apply, and capable of achieving results just as arbitrary as those under common law. The 2003 revision is intended to simplify the section and to eliminate the often tortured analysis that has to be engaged in under the existing provision. Although it is too early to say what interpretational problems might be encountered under the revised §2.207, it does seem, at first glance, that the section should be much easier to deal with.

§6.4 "EXPRESSION OF ACCEPTANCE" AND "CONFIRMATION," THE TWO DISTINCT SITUATIONS COVERED BY THE EXISTING §2.207

So far, we have considered only the offer and acceptance implications of §2.207, and indeed, most of this chapter focuses on that aspect of the section. However, it is important to recognize that §2.207 has another application. One of the confusing things about §2.207 is that it does an awful job of keeping its two facets separate, and it tries to talk of both in the same breath. It is concerned not only with the question of whether a reply to an offer is an acceptance but also with cases in which, after an oral or informal agreement is reached, one or both parties sends off a written confirmation with terms different from or additional to those orally agreed. These situations present different issues. In the context of offer and acceptance, the section deals with the question of whether the reply to an offer was an acceptance, and if so, what were the terms of the resulting contract. (Offer and acceptance is covered in section 6.5.)

In considering the effect of a confirmatory memorandum following an oral or informal agreement, one is no longer concerned with offer and acceptance because this has already occurred and the contract has come into existence.[5] The issue here is whether a party's post-formation addition or change should be given any effect. The general rule at common law is that neither party can unilaterally modify the contract simply by sending a writing with new terms to the other. Although §2.207 basically follows this rule, it does give effect to such alterations in limited circumstances. (Confirmations are covered in section 6.6.)

§6.5 OFFER AND ACCEPTANCE UNDER EXISTING §2.207

§6.5.1 Existing §2.207(1): Acceptance, Rejection, and Counteroffer

The language of §2.207(1), relating to offer and acceptance, may be charted as follows:

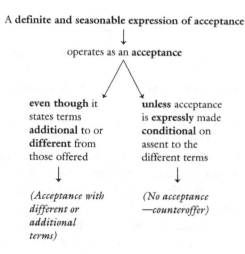

A definite and seasonable expression of acceptance

↓

operates as an **acceptance**

even though it states terms **additional** to or **different** from those offered

unless acceptance is **expressly** made **conditional** on assent to the different terms

↓

(Acceptance with different or additional terms)

↓

(No acceptance —counteroffer)

---

5. In some cases, an oral agreement is not enforceable. As discussed in Chapter 11, a sale of goods for a price of $500 or more ($5,000 or more in the 2003 revision of Article 2) is subject to the statute of frauds provided for in §2.201. That is, the sales agreement must be memorialized in a writing or record signed by the party against whom it is to be enforced. Therefore, when such a contract is made orally, it exists but cannot be enforced. However, once a written confirmation is sent, the contract becomes enforceable, at least against the sender, if the confirmation meets the requirements of the statute of frauds.

a. The Offer

Section 2.207(1) provides no guidance on whether the initial communication qualifies as an offer. This question must be resolved under the *general common law principles* set out in section 4.4. Once an offer is established under common law, §2.207(1) concentrates on the question of whether or not the response is an acceptance. It abolishes the "mirror image" rule, so the response to the offer need not match it exactly to be an acceptance. Instead, a fact-based approach is adopted to distinguish a reply that is clearly not an acceptance (so it can fairly be interpreted at best only as a counteroffer) from a reply that really is an acceptance with terms at variance with the offer. The following diagram illustrates this dichotomy.

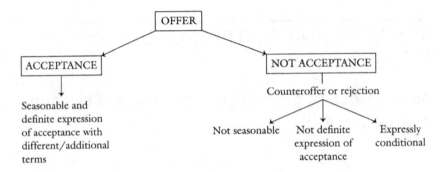

b. Replies That Are Not an Acceptance

If the response is clearly **not a definite expression of acceptance** or if it is sent after the offer has lapsed (that is, it is **not "seasonable"**) or if it **expressly states that acceptance is conditional on assent to its new terms**, then it is a rejection or counteroffer.

For example, Buyer writes to Seller offering to buy a Louden LeThal rivet gun for $450, C.O.D. delivery in 30 days and requiring acceptance by Friday. If Seller sends an acceptance on the following Monday, the acceptance is not seasonable and hence ineffective. Similarly, there is no acceptance, even if Seller responds in time, if the response states "Thank you for your order. Unfortunately we no longer stock Louden LeThal products, but we have a similar rivet gun made by Fierce & Fearsome which you can have on the same terms." The response proposes a sale of goods different from those ordered. This divergence from the transaction-specific terms in the offer cannot fairly be viewed as a definite expression of acceptance.

Even if the variation is not that central to the performance requested in the offer, the response is not an acceptance if it specifies that acceptance is conditional on the offeror's assent to some new or altered term. So Seller makes a counteroffer if it returns a timely acknowledgement in accord with all Buyer's proposed terms, but with the added provision: "Your order is accepted on condition that you agree to indemnify us for any claims of injury arising out of the use of the goods described above." This expressly conditional assent could be contained in preprinted standard language. Even if it is, §2.207(1) apparently gives effect to it. This is ironical because the purpose of §2.207 is to underplay the effect of boilerplate. As mentioned in section 6.5.2, this is not the only instance in which §2.207 can be interpreted as adopting an inconsistent approach to standard terms.

As under the common law, a counteroffer terminates the offeree's power of acceptance and creates a new power of acceptance in the former offeror. If the offeror elects to exercise that power, it can *accept the counteroffer,* creating a contract on the offeree's terms. If not, no contract comes into being unless the parties go ahead and perform. As noted in section 6.3, when such *performance follows a counteroffer,* §2.207 departs from the common law. Unlike the common law, it does not assume that acceptance can be inferred merely because the offeror subsequently proceeds with performance of the transaction. The counteroffer is accepted only if it is clear that the offeror was aware of the alteration in terms and manifested assent to it by unambiguous words or action. If there is no such clear acceptance, a contract is recognized by virtue of the performance, but its terms are resolved under §2.207(3).

This may be represented as follows:

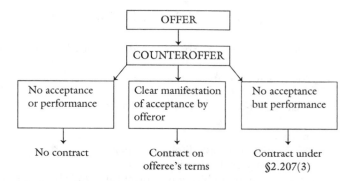

c. A Response That Is an Acceptance with Additional or Different Terms

If the response is a **definite and seasonable expression of acceptance,** and it is not expressly conditional on assent to any new terms, it is an acceptance even though it states terms different from or additional to those in the offer.

For example, say that Seller's response in the last illustration had no language making the acceptance expressly conditional on Buyer's assent to the indemnity but had simply contained preprinted language stating, "The buyer shall indemnify us for any claims of injury arising out of the use of the goods described above." The response is likely to be an acceptance despite the new term. The fact that Seller expressed agreement with all the central terms of the offer and that the indemnity is set out in a printed standard term gives rise to the reasonable interpretation that its primary focus was on making the sale, and its intent was to accept. A contract is therefore formed, and the question of whether the indemnity becomes part of it is dealt with in §2.207(2), discussed below.

Note that §2.207(1) covers both **"additional"** and **"different"** terms—a distinction that creates problems discussed in section 6.5.2c. It is not always easy to decide if a term is "additional" or "different," and this depends on the interpretation of the offer. As a rough guideline, a term is different if it varies or contradicts something provided for in the offer, but it is additional if it adds new matter not covered in the offer.

§6.5.2 Existing §2.207(2): The Treatment of Proposals in an Acceptance

The language of §2.207(2) may be charted as follows:

The **additional** terms are construed as **proposals** for addition to the contract.
↓

Between **merchants**

such terms become **part of the contract**
↓

unless:
(a) the **offer expressly limits** acceptance;
(b) they **materially alter** it; or
(c) notification of **objection** to them has already been given or is given within a reasonable time after notice of them is received.

a. The Scope and Basic Purpose of §2.207(2)

Section 2.207(2) *only applies* if the response to an offer is found to be an *acceptance*. It does not apply to a counteroffer, which only leads to a contract if accepted or if performance occurs as contemplated by §2.207(3). Because §2.207(1) contemplates that a contract exists despite a variance between the terms of the offer and acceptance, §2.207(2) treats any such additional terms as **proposals** that do not become part of the contract unless the conditions in the subsection are satisfied.

b. The Grounds for Excluding Proposals from the Contract

Section 2.207(2) is couched in deceptively positive terms. It says that the additional terms enter the contract *unless* one of the stated exceptions apply, but this is a very big "unless." The exceptions leave the rule applicable only to relatively unimportant terms in a small range of cases. *In most situations, the offeree does not succeed in adding terms in the acceptance,* and the general impact of §2.207(2) is to exclude most proposed additions. We now examine each of the exclusions. Note that they do not all have to be satisfied for the term to be excluded. If any one applies, the term does not enter the contract.

i. Additional Terms Do Not Become Part of the Contract Unless Both Parties Are Merchants

The **definition of "merchant"** in §2.104(1) is much broader than in common usage. It includes not only a person who deals in goods of that kind, but also one who, by following a particular occupation, has or represents having knowledge or skill concerning the goods. Therefore, as Comment 1[6] to §2.104 points out, even a person that does not trade in the goods could be a merchant if that person is a "professional" user of the goods, as opposed to a "casual or inexperienced seller or buyer." Section 2.207(2) requires that the transaction be *between merchants.* They must both be merchants, and if either of them is not a merchant, this ends the matter. The proposals do not become part of the contract, even if none of the other exclusions apply.

ii. The Term Does Not Enter the Contract If It Materially Alters It

Materiality is a complex issue, to be discussed more fully in section 17.3. Simply speaking, a term is material if it provides for an important aspect of the contractual performance. That is, it is a **significant element of the exchange bargained for by a party.** Although some terms are more obviously important than others, one can seldom decide materiality in the abstract. The contract must be *interpreted in context* to decide if the provision in question did occupy this central role in the bargain. This concept is expressed in the context of proposals under §2.207(2) by Comment 4 to §2.207. It says that a proposed alteration in an acceptance is material and

---

6. Section 2.7.1 introduced the role and effect of comments to the UCC. They are the drafter's explanation of the intent and purpose of code sections. They are very influential but are not part of the statute.

does not enter the contract if it would result in "surprise or hardship" to the other party.

"Surprise" is determined with reference to reasonable expectations in light of common practice and usage. If a particular term is widely used, the party has reason to assume that it would be part of the contract, and its inclusion should be no surprise. (Of course if it is that common, it may be implied in the oral agreement or offer in any event.) **"Hardship"** means that the term imposes an unbargained-for burden (financial or otherwise) on, or detracts significantly from, the reasonable expectations of the other party. The concept of hardship does not do much to help resolve the question of whether an alteration is material, because it begs the question of materiality rather than helping to answer it: A material alteration causes hardship, therefore it is material.

The Comment's use of the disjunctive "or" is misleading because the concepts of surprise and hardship are usually both elements of materiality and, in most cases, must both be satisfied to some degree. That is, even an important alteration may not be material if its inclusion should be fully expected, and a trivial alteration should not be treated as material, even if it is unexpected. The basic point of the exclusion is this: Even if the sale is between merchants, a proposed term does not enter the contract if it has more than a minimal impact on the exchange, and it is not sufficiently common to be expected.

iii. The Term Does Not Enter the Contract If the Offer Limits Acceptance to Its Terms

Even if the parties are merchants and the term is not material, it does not become part of the contract if there is *language in the offer expressly limiting acceptance to its terms.* This means that an offeror can simply eliminate the possibility of proposals entering the contract by putting appropriate standard language in the offer. This again raises the issue noted in the discussion of preprinted "expressly conditional" language in a purported acceptance. By giving effect to standardized exclusions or conditions, §2.207 breaks faith with its avowed purpose of disregarding boilerplate.

iv. The Term Does Not Enter the Contract If the Offeror Objects

If the offer did not limit acceptance to its terms, the offeror still has an opportunity to eliminate the proposal by *subsequent objection,* either in anticipation of the proposal or within a reasonable time of acquiring notice of it. This appears to contemplate not only a deliberate objection but also a standard objection issued by the offeror as a matter of course.

This again raises the inconsistency displayed by §2.207 in its reaction to boilerplate.

c. The Omission of "Different" Terms from the Text of §2.207(2)

As noted in section 6.5.1, §2.207(1) refers to "additional" and "different" terms, while §2.207(2) only mentions "additional" terms. This has created two problems. First (as stated in section 6.5.1) it is not always easy to tell if a term is "additional" or "different." Second, it is not clear if the omission of "different" terms in §2.207(2) was really intended or was just an oversight. The failure to include "different" terms in §2.207(2) has led courts to adopt *divergent approaches* to the treatment of terms found to be "different":

Some courts have treated the omission as **inadvertent** and have applied the subsection irrespective of whether the term may be classified as "additional" or "different." This approach has some support in Comment 3, which seems to assume that both fall within §2.207(3). (Although the Comment is apparently talking about confirmations rather than an acceptance.) It also has the obvious advantage of eliminating the problem of struggling to distinguish them.

Other courts have taken §2.207(2) literally and have held that because "different" terms are not covered in the subsection, they must simply be **disregarded.** Once it is held that the response is an acceptance, there is no basis in principle for allowing this unilateral proposal to slip into the contract, and it must be excluded. The fact that "different" terms are not mentioned in §2.207(2) suggests not that they be treated more favorably than "additional" terms, but that it be treated less so. In other words, the "different" term can never become part of the contract, even if it meets all the tests for inclusion in §2.207(2).

A third approach is to **treat the conflicting terms as cancelling each other out.** Some courts have reasoned that if the purpose of §2.207 is to take boilerplate less seriously, it makes no sense to prefer one of the "different" terms over the other, so they should both fall away and be replaced by whatever term the law would supply in the absence of agreement. (This has been called the **"knockout"** rule.) Although this approach seems to accord with the spirit of §2.207, there is no basis for it in the express provisions of the section. It sounds a little like the solution prescribed in §2.207(3), but that provision applies only where the parties perform despite their failure to conclude a contract. It is not directly on point and is at best justified by analogy when the offer has been accepted and the issue is whether a proposed "different" term in the acceptance is included in the contract.

§6.5.3 Existing §2.207(3): The Effect of Mutual Performance When No Contract Is Formed by the Parties' Writings

The language of §2.207(3) may be charted as follows:

Conduct by both parties
that recognizes the existence of a contract
is **sufficient to establish a contract** for sale
$\downarrow$

although
the writings of the parties do not otherwise establish a contract.
$\downarrow$

In such a case
the terms of the particular contract consist of
those terms on which the **writings** of the parties **agree**
together with
any **supplementary terms** incorporated under any other provisions of
this Act

Section 2.207(3) only applies when there is no contract formed by the writings — typically because the offeree's response is not an acceptance with additional or different terms but a counteroffer which has never been deliberately accepted. As noted earlier, the common law "last shot" rule treated the offeror's performance as an acceptance by conduct of the counteroffer, thereby imposing the risk of inadvertent assent to the offeree's variation in terms.

Section 2.207(3) seeks to avoid this unfair imposition. If no contract was formed by the writings of the parties, but their conduct (typically in the form of tendering and accepting performance) shows that they intend a contract, the contract is recognized as existing. However, its terms are not simply those contained in the last communication. The contract includes only those terms on which the parties' writings agree, and all conflicting terms fall away. Any gaps in the contract are filled by supplementary terms recognized in the UCC. If there is any applicable trade usage or course of dealing or performance between the parties, the missing terms can be supplied as a matter of factual implication.[7] Failing that, the UCC itself provides a number of standard terms (known colloquially as **"gap fillers"**) that are implied as a matter of law into all sales of goods unless excluded by the contract. (For example, unless the parties agree otherwise, §2.308 states that

---

7. The role of trade usage, course of dealing, and course of performance in the interpretation of contractual intent is discussed in section 10.6.2. For the present, it is enough to understand in general terms that the context in which the parties made their contract often provides much useful information on what they must have intended their contract terms to be.

delivery must take place at the seller's premises; §2.310 requires payment on delivery; and §§2.314 and 2.315 provide for minimum warranties.[8])

To illustrate the operation of §2.207(3) reconsider the example of Buyer's order for the Louden LeThal rivet gun for $450, C.O.D delivery in 30 days. Seller responds by accepting the order expressly on the condition that Buyer agrees to Seller's indemnity provision. It was noted in section 6.5.1 that the expressly conditional language makes the response a counteroffer. Buyer never communicates assent to this condition. In fact, having not read the reply, Buyer is not even aware of the term. Seller ships the rivet gun and it is accepted and put to use by Buyer. One of Buyer's workers is injured when operating the gun and sues Seller as manufacturer of the machine. Under common law, Buyer's conduct in accepting the delivery would be deemed an acceptance of the counteroffer, making Seller's indemnity provision part of the contract. Under §2.207(3), however, a contract is recognized on the terms on which the writings agree (description, quantity, price, delivery, and payment) and the indemnity falls away. The resulting gap is filled by implication. (Whether a seller has such a right of indemnification against a buyer in the absence of agreement would be resolved by a complex interaction of contract and tort law, beyond our scope.)

§6.6 WRITTEN CONFIRMATION FOLLOWING AN ORAL OR INFORMAL CONTRACT UNDER EXISTING §2.207(1) AND (2)

It is impossible to decipher the provisions of §2.207(1) with regard to written confirmations. The subsection seems to say that ". . . a written confirmation that is sent within a reasonable time operates as an acceptance even though it states terms additional to or different from those . . . agreed upon, unless acceptance is expressly made conditional on assent to the additional or different terms."

However, this makes no sense. The written confirmation apparently follows an agreement. Although §2.207(1) does not say what this agreement might be, Comment 1 indicates that the drafters contemplated a situation in which an oral or informal agreement is followed by written confirmations. Presumably, this means that the parties have actually made a contract already. If so, the subsequent writing cannot be an acceptance, conditional or otherwise. The process of offer and acceptance has already been concluded.[9] If a contract

---

8. Although these citations are to current sections of Article 2, they remain correct under the 2003 revision.
9. As mentioned in footnote 5, the contract is fully enforceable in its oral form unless the price of the goods is $500 or more ($5,000 or more under the 2003 revision) in which case

already exists, the purpose of any confirmations is, of course, to confirm what has been agreed. This may be motivated by a need to satisfy the statute of frauds or simply by a desire to create a written record of the transaction.

Therefore, the references to acceptance in §2.207(1) are inappropriate in the context of confirmations and should be disregarded. This leaves us with just a few snippets of disjointed statutory language to interpret. What it seems to be trying to say is:

1. If an oral or informal contract is formed,
2. and if one or both parties thereafter send written confirmations,
3. and one or both confirmations go beyond or vary what was agreed orally or informally,
4. any terms that add to or differ from the oral contract cannot simply become part of the contract,
5. but must be treated as proposals in the same way as proposals in an acceptance.

This leads to the conclusion that where confirming memoranda are involved, the only issue is whether the new terms in a confirmation become part of the contract. This question is decided using the same analysis, set out in section 6.5.2, as would be used if the additional or different term were contained in an acceptance. The one difference, of course, is that one is not so much concerned with a clash between conflicting writings (in fact, only one party may have sent a confirmation) but between one or more writings and the original oral or informal agreement.

Section 2.207(3) states that it governs where conduct establishes contractual intent but ". . . the writings of the parties do not otherwise establish a contract." If mutual performance occurs after a confirmation, a literal reading of §2.207(3) suggests that it is applicable. The contract arises, not from the writings but from the earlier oral agreement. This is surely not the intent. Section 2.207(3) is meant to deal with situations in which no contract would exist in the absence of performance and not where an oral contract has been concluded. Remember, however, that although §2.207(3) is not directly applicable, some courts have followed its spirit by adopting the "knockout" rule when a confirmation has terms "different" from the oral contract.

§6.7 THE 2003 REVISION OF §2.207

The 2003 revision amends §2.207 dramatically. The new section is much shorter and more succinct. It no longer deals with the issue of whether a

---

it does not become enforceable until reduced to writing sufficient to comply with the statute of frauds.

contract has been formed, so it has no equivalent of the existing §2.207(1). Instead, as mentioned in section 6.1, it moves to §2.206(3) the issue of whether a response with additional or different terms qualifies as an acceptance. In the revision, §2.206(3) sets out the general principle that a definite and seasonable expression of acceptance in a record constitutes an acceptance, even if it has terms additional to or different from the offer. As in current law, the revised Article 2 continues to adopt the principle that an acceptance need not be a mirror image of the offer, and that a contract can result from the parties' exchange of forms or other communications, whether in writing or electronically, even where those writings or records have terms that do not agree.

Section 2.206(3) no longer makes provision for an acceptance that is expressly made conditional on assent to its terms, thereby eliminating the possibility that an offeree, by including this boilerplate language in all its acceptance or acknowledgment forms, will automatically be treated as having made a counteroffer. Therefore, as Official Comment 3 to revised §2.206(3) points out, the question of whether the response is a counteroffer will be decided on the general principles inherent in the concept of a definite expression of acceptance. That is, the language and terms of the offeree's response must be interpreted in context to decide if they sufficiently express assent as to qualify as an acceptance. Of course, even on this more general approach, it is likely to be significant if an offeree makes his acceptance expressly conditional on assent to its terms. Language to that effect will surely be an influential factor in deciding that a counteroffer was intended.

Because formation issues are removed from §2.207, that section is confined to the question of what to do with additional or different terms. To resolve this issue, §2.207 adopts a test that is based on the concept reflected in the current judicially-created "knockout" rule and in the existing §2.207(3). It extends this same general rule to the three situations that are treated differently in the existing provisions of §2.207. That is, the same rule applies where conduct of both parties recognizes a contract, but their records (writings or electronic communications) do not establish a contract (currently dealt with in §2.207(3)); where a contract is established by offer and acceptance through an exchange of records, but the terms do not agree (the acceptance issue currently dealt with in §2.207(1) and (2)); and where a contract is formed in any way (including by oral or informal communication), and a subsequent recorded confirmation contains different or additional terms (currently dealt with in §2.207(1) and (2)). The universal solution in all these cases is for the contract to consist of the terms on which the parties have agreed, whether in the record or otherwise, plus terms supplied or incorporated by Article 2. Simply stated, the revision gets rid of all the agony of trying to decide if the nonconforming terms in the acceptance should become part of the contract, and it eliminates the general orientation toward the terms proposed by the offeror. Instead, once it is clear that a contract was in fact created, it adopts the approach of keeping terms on which the parties agree, and eliminating all conflicting terms. The gaps created by removing those terms are filled by substituting gap fillers, either supplied by the Article 2 default provisions or from another appropriate source, such as trade usage or common law. The Examples and Explanations indicate how the 2003 revisions are likely to change the way in which §2.207 issues will be analyzed and resolved.

Examples

1. Ann Teek is an antique dealer. Two of her customers, Art Deco and Bo Haus, collect tableware from the 1920s and '30s. Whenever Ann manages to find a new item, she calls both of them to give them an opportunity to buy it. Ann recently acquired a richly decorated platter made in 1935. She called both the customers and invited them to come and see it. Art came to the store at 3 P.M. on Monday to inspect the platter, which was marked with a $499 price tag. He said he was interested in buying it and would let Ann know his decision by Tuesday evening. Bo came to the store at 4:30 P.M. on the same day. He liked the platter and asked Ann if he could take it home to show it to his wife. Ann agreed and he took it away.

   Just as Ann was closing the store at 8 P.M. that evening, Art called and told her that he wanted the platter. Ann agreed to sell it to him and arranged for him to collect it on Wednesday. Ann then called Bo intending to tell him that the platter had been sold and to ask him to bring it back on Tuesday. Bo answered the phone. As soon as he heard that it was Ann calling, and before Ann could tell him that she had sold the platter to someone else, Bo said, "Hi Ann. My wife loves the platter. I'll take it." What is Ann's legal position?

2. Carr Buff's hobby is restoring vintage cars. After working on it for many years, he just completed the restoration of a 1957 Ford. On December 15, he parked the car in the parking lot of a shopping mall. When he returned to it, he found a note stuck under the windshield wiper that read: "Dear owner of 1957 Ford: I love this car and would like to buy it from you. I offer to pay you $100,000 for it, which I will pay on delivery of the car and its title papers. If you would like to sell the car to me, please reply to the address below as soon as possible, but not later than December 20. On your acceptance, we will arrange a date to complete this transaction before Christmas." The note was signed by Rod Hott, and contained a street address.

   After thinking about the offer for a couple of days, Carr decided to accept it. On December 18 he mailed a letter to Rod in which he said, "I agree to sell the Ford to you for $100,000. Please note that payment must be in cash or by cashier's check. Call me as soon as you get this letter to arrange the time for delivery. Note, however, that I sell the car to you on condition that you agree to return it to me for one day on February 15 next year, because I have already entered it in an antique car exhibition on that day." Rod received the letter on December 21.

(a) Do Rod and Carr have a contract on December 21?

(b) If so, what are its terms?

(c) Assume that after Rod reveived Carr's letter on December 21, he called Carr and they arranged for delivery on December 24. Carr delivered the Ford and the title to Rod, who handed Carr a cashier's check for $100,000. Neither party said anything about Carr borrowing the Ford for the exhibition on February 15. On February 10, Carr called Rod to arrange to collect the car for the exhibition, but Rod refused to give it to him, claiming that he had no contractual obligation to do so. Is Rod correct?

3. Tutu O'Severn decided to take up dance lessons. She needed shoes, so she searched the Web and found the website of Ballet de la Forms, Inc. (Ballet), a supplier of dance equipment. She selected a pair of shoes for $150, clicked on them to place them in her virtual "shopping cart," and filled out the online order form in which she inserted her name, e-mail address, shipment and billing address, and credit card particulars. In the box called "delivery options," she selected "standard, 1 to 2 weeks delivery." She clicked the "submit" button. A couple of seconds later, an automated response appeared on the screen headed "Order Confirmation." It set out a confirmation number, the details of the order as submitted by Tutu, and instructions on how she could track the progress of the shipment.

Two days later, Tutu received an e-mail from Ballet, which stated, "Thank you for your order. Regrettably we are out of stock of the item that you ordered. We expect new supplies shortly and will ship as soon as possible. Please allow 4 to 6 weeks for delivery." Tutu was disappointed, but resigned herself to wait for the shoes.

Three weeks later, Tutu received another e-mail from Ballet, which said, "We are pleased to inform you that the shoes that you ordered are now in stock. Unfortunately, the manufacturer has increased the price since you placed your order, and the shoes now cost $250. If you would still like to buy the shoes at the new price, please resubmit your order." Tutu insists that she had already bought the shoes at the original price, and that Ballet is obliged to deliver them to her at that price. Is she correct?

4. In addition to shoes, Tutu needed tights for her dance lessons. She called Leo Tard, a specialist in dancing attire, and ordered three pairs of tights for a total of $350. She arranged with Leo that the tights would be delivered C.O.D. within a week. Leo immediately shipped the tights to

Tutu, accompanied by his standard invoice. The invoice stated "For sanitary reasons, we cannot accept the return of clothing delivered to a customer. All sales are final once the clothing leaves our premises." By the time that Tutu received the tights, a week later, she had changed her mind about taking dancing lessons and no longer wants the tights. Leo insists that she has bought them and cannot return them. Is he right?

Explanations

1. This Example is analyzed under the current version of Article 2. However, the section citations, analysis, and result would be the same under the 2003 revision. The facts make it clear that Ann did make an oral sales contract with Art. (The oral contract is binding because the price of the goods is under $500, so the statute of frauds in §2.201 does not apply. As noted before, the price would have to equal or exceed $5,000 under the 2003 revision.) The issue is whether she also has a contract with Bo, leaving her liable for breach of contract to whichever of her customers ends up without the platter. This is a sale of goods governed by UCC Article 2. However, Article 2 has very few specific offer and acceptance rules, and except to the extent that they are displaced by provisions of the Code, general principles of common law are applicable. UCC §2.204(1) and (3) provide a flexible test for deciding whether a contract was formed: It may be made in any manner sufficient to show agreement, including conduct. If the parties intended to contract, missing terms do not cause it to fail for indefiniteness if the court can find a reasonably certain basis for giving a remedy.

   Ann's conduct in allowing Bo to take the platter home is ambiguous. It could be an offer or merely an invitation to Bo to make an offer. It is an offer if Bo would be justified in understanding that his assent would conclude the bargain, without any need for further assent by Ann. It has sufficiently definite terms to qualify as an offer. The subject matter of the sale — the platter — is identified and the price is exhibited on the price tag. Because Bo has possession of the platter, delivery can be accomplished upon acceptance. Although payment terms are not expressed, there have apparently been prior dealings between the parties from which they can be inferred. If not, §2.310 makes payment due on receipt of the goods unless otherwise agreed. The fact that Ann gave Bo the plate suggests her assent to payment within a reasonable time of acceptance. The facts do not indicate that Bo knew or had reason to know that he was not the only person that Ann had approached about buying the platter. If he did know this, he may not have been justified in understanding Ann's words and conduct to be an offer.

If Ann made an offer, §2.206 dispenses with technicality in the mode of acceptance. It presumes that unless a particular manner and medium of acceptance is clearly required, acceptance may be by any means reasonable in the circumstances, and may be either by promise or performance. No mode of acceptance was specified, and given the informal, oral nature of the offer, a telephonic acceptance by promise seems appropriate.

Although Ann called with the intent of revoking, revocation only takes effect when that intent is manifested to the offeree. Bo accepted before Ann could express the revocation. By contrast, in *Greene v. Keener*, 402 S.E.2d 284 (Ga. 1991), the buyer took a piece of furniture home to see if it fit in with his decor. The seller called later and told him that she no longer wished to sell it, thereby effectively revoking the offer before he had a chance to accept.

2(a). *Analysis under current Article 2.* This is a sale of goods, so §2.207 applies. Although it is nicknamed the "battle of the forms," §2.207 is not confined to transactions in which forms are used. Article 2 does not deal with the question of whether a communication qualifies as an offer, so general common law principles apply. Rod's letter appears to qualify as an offer. It sets out the terms on which he proposes to buy the car, and can be reasonably understood to confer a power of acceptance on the offeree. Although Rod does not know who the owner of the car is, he has addressed the offer to the owner, an identifiable person.

Carr intends to accept. Unless the offer clearly prescribes a particular mode of acceptance, §2.206 permits acceptance in any manner and medium reasonable under the circumstances. Rod included his address on the offer, and did not specify a method of acceptance. Therefore, a response by mail is authorized because mail is surely a reasonable mode of acceptance. As Rod invites response by mail, the "mailbox" rule applies. Therefore, assuming that Carr properly stamped and addressed the letter, his acceptance took effect on December 18 before the offer lapsed, even though Rod only received the letter on December 21.

Under §2.207(1), a response qualifies as an acceptance if it is a definite and seasonable expression of acceptance. We have determined that it was seasonable (that is, timely). It is more difficult to decide if Carr's letter was a definite expression of acceptance. His response does not exactly accord with the offer. His statement that the price must be paid in cash or by cashier's check does not deviate from the offer because payment in cash on delivery is implied in the offer. Rod's letter is silent on the method of payment, and in the absence of agreement to the contrary this is the payment term implied by §2.310. Carr's condition about borrowing the Ford on February 15 does go beyond the terms of the offer. He says that he sells the car to Rod "on condition that you agree to return it to me for one day on February 15." This conditional language appears to qualify Carr's assent to the contract, and could be interpreted as making his acceptance expressly conditional on assent to the new term. If so, the statutory qualification in §2.207(1) applies and the section treats the letter as a counteroffer. It is therefore not a definite expression of acceptance. Courts tend to interpret the "expressly conditional" element of §2.207(1) narrowly, so it is conceivable that a court may find that the borrowing of the car is merely a proposal for a term in the contract, and not a condition of acceptance. (To reach this result, a court would have to strain against the rather clear language of Carr's letter.) If Carr's letter is a counteroffer, the parties never reached agreement because Rod did not accept it, and the parties have no contract on December 21. If the term about borrowing the Ford does not make Carr's response expressly conditional, Carr's letter otherwise indicates a desire to accept the offer, so it could qualify as a definite expression of acceptance, which would result in the parties having made a contract on December 21. Question (b) deals with the content of the contract.

Analysis under revised Article 2. The answer to this question might be the same under the 2003 revision of Article 2, but the analysis to reach the answer would be somewhat different. As a matter of organization, the revision removes the question of whether a contract was formed from §2.207, and places it in §2.206(3), which states that "a definite and seasonable expression of acceptance in a record operates as an acceptance even if it contains terms additional to or different from the offer." Under §2.206(3), we would still have to decide if Carr's response was an acceptance or a counteroffer. The revision eliminates the concept of a response that is expressly conditional on assent to the new term, so the test of whether the response is a counteroffer is based on the more generalized test that applies under current law when the response does not use expressly conditional language: Was the response so ambivalent, or so much at odds with the transaction-specific terms of the offer that it cannot reasonably be read as a definite expression of acceptance? On this more general test, Carr's desire to enter into the transaction on Rod's terms would be clear, had it not been for his qualification about being able to borrow the car for a day. This may more easily allow a court to find, not a counteroffer, but an acceptance with an additional term. However, it is not clear what impact the elimination of the "expressly conditional" language will have. Where a party does express acceptance as conditional on assent to an additional or different term in the purported acceptance, this quite strongly suggests a counteroffer, even under the more general standards of §2.206(3).

2(b). *Anaysis under current Article 2.* If we assume that Carr's response was an acceptance rather than a counteroffer, the term becomes a proposal for addition to the contract. A proposal for a new term in the acceptance does not normally become part of the contract, but §2.207(2) creates a narrow exception to this rule. Section 2.207(2) does not apply unless both parties are merchants. The facts do not indicate what Rod does for a living. He may be a dealer in antique cars, or may just be a consumer who liked the Ford and wanted it for personal use. Carr restores old cars as a hobby, but that does not in itself make him a merchant. To qualify as a merchant under §2.104(1), Carr would have to deal in antique cars or hold himself out, by virtue of his occupation, "as having knowledge or skill peculiar to the practices or goods involved in the transaction." This language is not broad enough to cover a hobbyist who may make the occasional, isolated sale of a car that he has restored.

If both parties were merchants, §2.207(2) would apply. (There is an interpretational difficulty relating to the omission of the word "different" in §2.207(2), as explained in section 6.5.2. On our facts, we can probably skirt that difficulty because the proposed term relating to Carr's use of the Ford on February 15 seems to be additional rather than different. As a general rule of thumb, we can consider a term additional if it adds to rather than contradicts the offer.) As the offer did not expressly limit acceptance to its terms, and Rod did not give notification of objection to the term, §2.207(2) will incorporate the term into the contract unless it materially alters it. Materiality is a question of fact, to be decided on interpretation of the parties' reasonable intent in light of the circumstances of the transaction and the parties' reasonable expectations. We cannot answer the question of materiality without a further exploration of these matters, but it may be that an obligation to lend the car to the seller for one day for purposes of exhibition may not constitute a material alteration of the offer. If so, the term would become part of the contract if both parties are merchants. If not, it falls away.

Analysis under revised Article 2. The analysis of this question is different under the 2003 revisions. Once it is determined that Carr did accept the offer under §2.206(3), so that a "contract is formed by an offer and acceptance," we go to a relatively straightforward "knockout" rule in §2.207, under which we have a contract based on the terms on which the parties have agreed, plus gapfillers supplied or incorporated by Article 2. As Carr's proposal to borrow the Ford on February 15 is not agreed to or supplied as a gapfiller, it falls away.

2(c). *Analysis under current Article 2.* The parties have now proceeded with performance of the contract, so there is no longer any question of whether a contract exists. If Carr's response was an acceptance with a proposal for an additional term, the fact that the parties have performed the exchange would not be significant. The analysis to decide if the proposal became part of the contract would be the same as in question (b): If the parties were both merchants and the term was not a material alteration of the offer, it would have entered the contract under §2.207(2) and Rod would be obliged to lend the Ford to Carr on February 15. Otherwise, the term did not become part of the contract, and Carr has no right to borrow the Ford.

However, if Carr's response was not an acceptance but a counteroffer, the parties' subsequent performance is important because it would create a contract under §2.207(3). Section 2.207(3) applies where the conduct of both parties recognizes the existence of a contract, even though their writings do not otherwise do so. The resulting contract is on the terms on which the writings agree, supplemented by Article 2 gapfillers. Because the term relating to Carr's use of the Ford on February 15 is not one on which the writings agree, and there is no default rule under Article 2 that allows a seller to regain temporary possession of the goods for exhibition purposes, Carr has no right to demand the Ford.

Analysis under revised Article 2. The 2003 revision of §2.207 results in a similar "knockout" effect, but the rule is more streamlined and applies both where Carr's response was an acceptance with an additional term ("a contract is formed by offer and acceptance") and where Carr's response was a counteroffer ("conduct by both parties recognizes the existence of a contract although their records do not otherwise establish a contract"). In either event, Carr's term will not become part of the contract.

3. This is our second look at a transaction conducted over the Internet. See Example 9 of Chapter 4 for a discussion of offer and acceptance issues in an electronic transaction that does not involve a sale of goods. This answer is based on current Article 2 but we would reach the same result under the 2003 revision. This is explained in the body of the Explanation.

Unless the language or the circumstances strongly indicate otherwise, the usual assumption is that the proffering of goods on a website, catalog, or advertisement is not an offer, but a solicitation for offers from the public. We are not told exactly what the website said, but we will assume that there was nothing in its language to overturn the usual assumption. Tutu's order was made on an electronic form supplied by Ballet, but this does not detract from the order's qualities as an offer, and it can reasonably be interpreted as such. It sets out the terms of the proposed transaction with particularity and reasonably appears to invite acceptance by shipment or promise to ship the goods. Ballet's immediate automated response might conceivably be seen as an acceptance, but this is not likely. It has no language that signifies assent to the order, and seems to do no more than confirm that the order was received. (The 2003 revision of Article 2 does recognize the possibility that a party might contract through an "electronic agent," as explained in section 6.1, but this question is not implicated if the automated response cannot reasonably be understood as an acceptance.)

Ballet's e-mail a couple of days later could qualify as an acceptance, but it changes one of the terms of the offer — the time of delivery. As in Example 3, we again have to decide if this makes the e-mail a counteroffer or a response with a proposal for a different term. Ballet's e-mail does have some indication of assent to the offer — it seems to accede to the order and undertakes to ship as soon as possible. However, it also makes it clear that it cannot ship by the date specified in the offer. To treat it as an acceptance with a proposal for change would place Ballet in the risky position of simultaneously accepting and repudiating the terms of the offer. It is therefore more reasonable to interpret Ballet's response as a counteroffer, which will not bind it to a contract unless Tutu agrees to the new delivery term. If that is so, Tutu apparently did agree subjectively, even though she did not manifest this agreement expressly. Silence is not normally regarded as effective assent under common law, and this is even more so under §2.207, which operates on the assumption that people do not read forms, and requires an articulated expression of assent to bind a party. Notwithstanding, because Tutu claims that her silence was acquiescence, the need to protect her from inadvertent acceptance of the counteroffer falls away, and a court may hold Ballet to the counteroffer on the grounds that Tutu did assent to it, and Ballet, by saying that it would ship as soon as possible, impliedly dispensed with the need to communicate assent. If we find either that Ballet's response was an acceptance with a proposed different term,[10] or a

---

10. Even if we decided that the response was an acceptance with a different term, we would not have to go through the agony of determining if the later delivery date became part of the contract, because that is not in issue. However, it is worth noting, just for the sake of exercise, that if this had been an issue, the term would not have entered the contract under §2.207(2)

counteroffer that was accepted by Tutu, Ballet is bound to deliver the shoes at the original price.

The approach to this question would not change under the 2003 *revision*. As noted in Example 3, the question of whether a contract was formed has been moved from §2.207(1) to §2.206(3), which now has language to similar effect, except for the exclusion of the concept of an acceptance expressly conditional on assent to its new terms.

4.   *Analysis under current Article 2.* The facts make it clear that Tutu and Leo made an oral contract on the phone. Because an enforceable contract came into existence at the time of the telephone call,[11] there are no offer and acceptance issues implicated in Leo's response. The only question to be decided is if Leo's "no return" term was part of the contract. The garbled language of §2.207(1) muddles the very different situations that occur when the additional or different terms are in a confirmation rather than an acceptance. However, where a post-contractual confirmation is concerned, the purpose of the section is not to raise an offer and acceptance issue, but simply to provide the same rule for confirmations as applies to additional or different terms in an acceptance. That is, they only become part of the contract if both parties are merchants and none of the three other barriers to entry in §2.207(2) apply. Because Tutu is not a merchant, the answer is simple: an additional or different term in the confirmation does not become part of the contract. The twist here is that Leo's term may not actually be additional or different on the facts of the case. It may have been if, for example, the question was whether it precluded the return of defective goods, because it would then have conflicted with the warranty of merchantability that would have been implied in Tutu's offer. However, the issue here is whether Tutu can reject goods that are in conformity with the contract, purely on the ground that she no longer wants them. In the absence of a term in her offer that gives her this right (whether express or implied by clear and accepted usage), she cannot simply change her mind and refuse to accept the goods. Therefore, on these particular facts (and assuming the absence of an established usage), Leo's term does not add anything that would not already be implied as a matter of law in the offer.

Analysis under revised Article 2. The result under the 2003 revisions should not change, but the process for dealing with additional or

---

because Tutu is not a merchant. In any event, as the term is "different" rather than additional, some courts would not apply §2.207(2), even in a sale between merchants.

11. The price of the goods is less than $500, so the sale is not subject to the statute of frauds and the oral agreement is enforceable. Had the price been $500 or more, the oral agreement would not have been enforceable on its own, so the subsequent written confirmation would have had to be a writing sufficient to satisfy the statute of frauds.

different terms in a post-contractual confirmation is clarified and simplified. Because formation questions are taken out of §2.207 and put into §2.206, the revised §2.207 no longer has the language that confuses offer and acceptance and confirmation issues. Instead, it just adopts a blanket rule for contracts formed by offer and acceptance, and for contracts formed in any manner and confirmed by a record with terms different from or additional to those in the contract. In both cases, the "knockout" rule applies, leaving the contract on the terms agreed to by the parties, supplemented by gapfillers.

CHAPTER 7

Consideration

§7.1 CONSIDERATION AS THE BASIS OF CONTRACT OBLIGATION

Consideration can be fun.[1] It has a network of interlocking rules that can be applied to all kinds of silly cases featuring beneficent aunts, sanctimonious uncles, hypothetical tramps, mysteriously illusory promises, and detriments that are actually beneficial. Yet at the same time, consideration doctrine can be a huge pain in the neck. How often have poor students (and poor professors) cursed the quirk of history[2] that left us with so sad a legacy. It is not that the basic rules of consideration are difficult, arcane, or unfathomable. The real problem lies in rationalizing these rules, understanding how courts are likely to use them, and justifying them in light of the policies of contract law.

One thing is clear: Consideration doctrine is in a state of flux. It has evolved away from the more rigid and certain classical form. Courts have long recognized that an inflexible insistence on doctrinaire rules can undermine freedom of contract by precluding the enforcement of serious promises, fairly and voluntarily made. As a result, they have manipulated the rules, created exceptions and legal fictions, and have increasingly

---

1. Obviously, depending on your idea of fun. It does help to be deranged.
2. Apart from the odd historical allusion, I will spare you the history of consideration. It arose from and is peculiar to the common law tradition. It is either unknown or scoffed at by civilian lawyers, who have always managed quite well without it. (If you do not know what is meant by "common law" and "civilian," see section 2.4.1.)

recognized alternative theories for enforcing promises that lack consideration. It is therefore not enough simply to learn the rules of consideration and to attempt to apply them mechanically to a set of facts. Consideration must be studied with an awareness of the purpose of these rules, a focus on their impact in each transaction, and an understanding of the way in which consideration doctrine fits in with the broader principles and policies of contract law. You will not be fully able to appreciate this complex interaction between consideration and other elements of contract law just yet, but it will become more apparent as your study of contract law proceeds. At this stage it may be helpful to alert you to some themes that you will begin to see:

1. Often you will find that although consideration doctrine is the basis of a decision, the court is really concerned with the *legitimacy of the transaction* in issue and is in fact using the doctrine to achieve an appropriate result in the case. Therefore, a court may stretch to find consideration when the promise appears to be seriously intended and fairly obtained, but may more readily apply the doctrine to invalidate a promise that appears to have resulted from advantage-taking or unfair dealing. In this respect, consideration often serves a purpose parallel to other doctrines such as fraud, duress, or unconscionability (discussed in Chapter 13) in the *policing of bargaining behavior.*

2. Consideration is an essential element of contract, and a promise is not recognized or enforced as contractual unless consideration has been given for it. However, an obligation assumed without consideration may be enforceable under an *alternative theory* such as promissory estoppel, restitution, or moral obligation, discussed in Chapters 8 and 9. Therefore, although we may decide in this chapter that a promise or assumption of duty is not a contract because of lack of consideration, this may not mean that the person to whom it is owed is without remedy. Under appropriate circumstances there may be grounds for full or partial relief under one of those other theories, developed to avoid the injustice of turning away an obligee[3] empty-handed where the lack of consideration precludes contractual liability.

§7.2 THE ESSENCE AND SCOPE OF CONSIDERATION

When "consideration" entered the legal lexicon many centuries ago, its usage by lawyers was apparently close to its lay meaning of "reflection,"

---

3. An obligee is a person to whom an obligation is owed.

"contemplation," or "thinking." It was a vague concept that probably did no more than assert the general principle that a promise must be seriously contemplated and deliberately intended to be legally binding. As courts expounded on this principle over the years, they gradually embellished it so that it came to require something more than a serious and deliberate intent to be bound. It demanded, in addition, that some quid pro quo be given for the promise by the **promisee** (that is, the person to whom it was made).[4] In other words, a purely gratuitous promise — one that is not "paid for" in some way — cannot be enforced as a contract. This is the essence of consideration doctrine. From this, we can draw some initial inferences about the scope of our subject:

1. We are concerned with the validity of promises. Consideration is only an issue when there is an outstanding promise to be enforced, and it does not affect the validity of an **executed** performance — that is, one that has already been completed. Therefore, even if a donor gives property or services to another as a gift, once the transfer is completed, it is an executed gift and it is too late to claim that no consideration was received.

2. Although consideration issues may potentially arise in connection with any unexecuted promise, there are two types of cases in which it presents no problems, simply because its absence or presence is so obvious. At the one end of the scale, we have the unquestionable **donative promise**, in which the promisor, motivated by kinship, friendship, or generosity, unconditionally undertakes to make a future gift and asks for and receives nothing in return. There is no point in agonizing over consideration here because it is obviously absent, and the promise is not legally binding. For example, following his 300th nosedive into the snow, Al Pine has become terminally frustrated with the sport of skiing. He decides to give his skis to his friend Buster Legg and promises to drop them off at Buster's home as soon as he gets out of traction. Until the skis are handed over to Buster, this is simply an unexecuted promise. There is no suggestion that Buster gave Al any quid pro quo for the promise, which is purely gratuitous. On these facts, consideration is not in issue because it is so obviously absent. If Al changes his mind and fails

---

4. In discussions of consideration, the person who makes the promise is called the **promisor** and the person to whom it is made, the **promisee**. This terminology is clear where only one party has made a promise, and the issue is whether some immediate performance of the other is consideration. However, in many contracts, both parties make promises and each is therefore both promisee and promisor. In such a case, common usage is that the word "promisor" denotes the person whose promise is sought to be enforced, and "promisee" refers to the recipient of that promise whose return promise is challenged as insufficient to constitute consideration.

to deliver the skis, Buster can sulk or pout or even have a massive tantrum, but he has no legal recourse.

At the other end of the scale, we have the straightforward **commercial exchange** in which the promise is clearly purchased for an economically equivalent price, so that there is no plausible argument that consideration was lacking. For example, instead of promising to donate the skis to Buster, Al agrees to sell them to him for $100, their market value. Buster pays Al $100 in cash immediately, and Al promises to deliver the skis as soon as he leaves the hospital. On these facts, there is no issue that Al's promise was not paid for.

Between these two obvious cases is the happy hunting ground of consideration doctrine, in which apparently commercial promises are made for an unclear or questionable exchange, and apparently gratuitous promises have strings attached to them. Unless you are using very boring class materials, most of the consideration cases that you study will fall within this range.

§7.3 THE ELEMENTS OF CONSIDERATION: DETRIMENT, BENEFIT, AND BARGAINED-FOR EXCHANGE

The broad statement was made above that a promise must be paid for to be contractually binding. As you will soon see, "payment" for the promise is much more complicated than you might first have suspected. In the earlier cases, courts often said that the quid pro quo for the promise could be furnished by anything that was either a **detriment to the promisee** or a **benefit to the promisor**. The promisee suffers a detriment if she is left poorer in some way, because property, money, or some legal right has been given up to the promisor. It follows that from the perspective of the promisor, the receipt of such property, money, or rights from the promisee is a benefit. Therefore, in most situations, the benefit to the promisor is just the mirror image of the promisee's detriment.

Older cases stated that only one of these need be shown for consideration to exist. During the late nineteenth century, courts began to recognize that it was not enough simply to look for detriment or benefit. It also had to be apparent that the promisee's detriment was suffered in **exchange** for the promise: The parties must have **bargained for** (that is, agreed to) an exchange of the promise for the detriment, so that each induces the other. This became known as the **"bargain theory"** of consideration.[5]

---

5. Justice O. W. Holmes is credited with being primarily responsible for articulating the bargain theory, but it has been plausibly argued that he simply recognized what was already happening in the cases, rather than created a new requirement for consideration.

Because benefit to the promisor is simply a natural consequence of having the promisee suffer whatever detriment was sought in the exchange (that is, the benefit is simply getting what was bargained for), the bargain theory obviates any need to focus on benefit to the promisor as a distinct element of consideration. (As explained in section 7.3.2, the fact that some tangible benefit was received may have evidentiary value in showing that an exchange was intended.)

So far, the words "detriment," "benefit," and "bargained-for exchange" have been used in an abstract way. These are terms of art that can easily be misinterpreted. We now explore their scope and meaning.

§7.3.1 What Is a "Detriment"?

A legal detriment is any **relinquishment of a legal right**. In the legal sense, "detriment" does not mean that the person has suffered some horrible harm, loss, or injury. In fact, a detriment could even be something that benefits or advances the interests of the sufferer. The important element is not harm but the yielding of a legal right. It could take the form of an immediate **act** (that is, doing or giving something), a **forbearance** (refraining from something), or the **partial or complete abandonment of an intangible right**.

It could equally be a *promise* to act, forbear, or abandon a right in the future. Provided that an immediate performance is a detriment, a promise of that performance creates a future liability to perform, which is also a detriment. Consideration doctrine does not discriminate between the immediate suffering of detriment and a commitment to suffer that detriment at a later time. To be a promise, and hence a detriment, the undertaking must be a genuine commitment. If it is hedged with qualifications, it may not qualify as a promise. This is discussed in section 7.9.

In the example of the sale of skis by Al to Buster for $100, Buster's payment of $100 was an act constituting his detriment. It would equally have been a detriment if, instead of paying the money, Buster had promised to pay $100 to Al on delivery of the skis. As the act of payment is consideration, the promise to perform that act is also consideration. (Al's detriment is, of course, the promise to deliver the skis. This is a standard bilateral contract, in which the promise by each party is exchanged for and induces the promise by the other.)

If instead of paying or promising to pay $100, Buster had accepted the promise of the skis in settlement of a prior overdue claim of $100 that he had against Al, Buster's detriment would be the abandonment of his right to sue on the claim, or alternatively, his forbearance from exercising that right.

7. Consideration

In these examples, the exchange of Buster's detriment for Al's promise can be shown as follows:

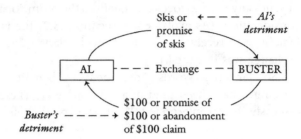

Because both the skis and the money (or the claim for money) have economic value, it is not hard to see that each party suffers a detriment by giving them up. If instead of asking for $100 for the skis, Al had agreed to give them to Buster in exchange for Buster's promise to quit smoking, the detriment to Buster is less obvious. Unanimous medical opinion is that giving up smoking is decidedly not detrimental but is beneficial. Notwithstanding, because Buster has the legal right to smoke, his promise to refrain from doing so (forbearance) is a legal detriment and can qualify as consideration for Al's promise of the skis. Restatement Second §79(a) reflects this principle by stating that if the requirement of consideration is met, there is *no additional requirement of loss or disadvantage* to the promisee.

One of the best-loved cases illustrating the meaning of detriment is *Hamer v. Sidway*, 124 N.Y. 538 (1891), in which sanctimonious Uncle William Story promised $5,000 to his nephew, William II, if the nephew refrained from drinking, using tobacco, swearing, and playing cards or billiards for money until he reached the age of 21. Young Willie complied but had not been paid by the time that his uncle died. The court enforced Willie's claim against the uncle's estate. It rejected the estate's argument that Willie had not given consideration for his uncle's promise. Defining consideration as either a benefit to the promisor or a detriment to the promisee, the court found that Willie's abstention from the stated activities pursuant to the promise was sufficient detriment, because it was the abandonment of his legal right to engage in them. The legal benefit to the uncle did not need to be economic. His benefit lay in having his expressed desire fulfilled. Although the court in *Hamer* used the older definition of consideration, the result is consistent with the bargain theory in that Willie's conduct seems to have been intended as the exchange for the promise.

This concludes our first look at the concept of detriment. Specific applications of this subject are discussed below.

Premisees D ——> E

B—>P

§7.3.2 How Does Benefit to the Promisor Fit In?

Benefit to the promisor is even more prone to misunderstanding than detriment to the promisee. As stated earlier, it used to be one of the alternative tests for consideration, but under the bargain theory, it plays only an *evidentiary* role. In many cases, the promisee's detriment translates easily into a benefit to the promisor. In the exchange of the promise of skis for money, the detriment to Buster (a loss of $100) is obviously a benefit to Al (a gain of $100). By contrast, when Al's promise of skis is exchanged for Buster's promise to quit smoking, it is not as clear that Buster's detriment of giving up the legal right to smoke translates into any benefit to Al. However, in the same way as "detriment" has a very broad meaning, "benefit" is seen as meaning simply that Al *got what he bargained for.* It does not need to be shown that Al received any tangible or economically valuable gain. Restatement Second §79(a) states that a gain or advantage to the promisor is not a requirement for consideration.

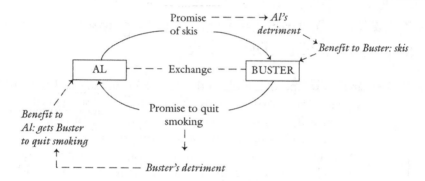

Thus, we need not ask why Al wished for Buster to quit smoking, nor need we speculate what is in it for him. His motive in making the exchange is not of central concern, as long as it is apparent that he intended to exchange his promise of skis for the promise to quit. This does not mean that Al's motive is entirely irrelevant, because it could be evidence of his intent to make the exchange. If a gain or advantage to Al can be identified, this bolsters the argument that he did in fact bargain for the detriment suffered by Buster. This issue is discussed further in the next section.

§7.3.3 The Bargained-For Exchange

As stated in section 7.2, the bargain theory was formulated around the turn of the century and it is now thoroughly well-established in our law. It is reflected in Restatement Second §71, which requires that a performance or return promise must be bargained for to constitute consideration. That is, it must be **sought by the promisor** and **given by the promisee** in **exchange** for the promise. Section 33 reinforces this by defining a **bargain** as an agreement (in turn defined as a manifestation of mutual assent) to exchange promises, performances, or promise for performance. The bargain theory recognizes that contracts are voluntary exchange relationships involving reciprocal promises or performances. It means nothing if a party suffers a legal detriment unless the parties agree that it is the price for the promise.

Be careful not to get too carried away by all this talk of bargain and inducement. "Bargain" simply means "agreement" and does not suggest that the parties have to dicker back and forth or to negotiate at length. If each agrees to a performance desired by the other, the bargain can be struck instantly without any fuss. Also, the **objective test** (discussed in section 4.1) applies to the determination of contractual intent, so "inducement" is gleaned from the manifestation of intent rather than from a probing of the party's actual state of mind. The motive for the transaction is therefore the *apparent motive*, as evidenced by the nature of the exchange in context.

§7.3.4 The Distinction Between Bargained-For and Incidental Detriment

In the example of the sale of the skis for $100, the fact that Al and Buster had agreed to an exchange seems obvious. In most commercial transactions the existence of a bargained-for exchange is not in question. Exchange also seems to be quite clear in the case of the promise of skis for the promise to quit smoking. Even though the motivation is apparently not commercial, we can still understand an incentive for the exchange based on friendship. However, what if Al had said to Buster, "If you walk over to my car, I will give you the skis that I have on my rack." Under the broad concept of legal detriment, Buster's act of walking to the car is a detriment: He gave up his legal right to remain where he was and undertook the perambulation across the parking lot. However, this detriment seems incidental to Al's promise. Common experience suggests that the parties did not see it as the price for the skis but simply as the act needed to take delivery of the gift. That is, it is a condition of the gift. This conclusion is based, not on a probing of Al's innermost thoughts but on the apparent purpose of his request, based on our understanding of human motivation. There is no evidence from which one could reasonably understand that Al was so desirous of having Buster walk across the lot, that he felt it was worth promising him skis to induce him to do it.

The same conclusion would follow if Al had said to Buster, "Put out your hand, and I will place a $10 bill in it." It would be hard to argue with a straight face that the act of extending the hand was bargained for as the exchange for the money. Al's apparent purpose is to give a gift to Buster, and the request to position the hand is merely intended as a means of its efficient delivery — better than cramming it in his ear or casting it on the ground.

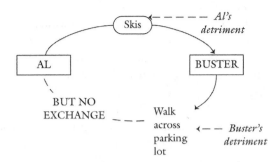

However, there may be some additional evidence that makes this conclusion less obvious, so that under all the circumstances, Buster may reasonably understand from Al's words and conduct that the extension of his hand was a bargained-for detriment. (Note the objective test used here: It is not what Buster in fact understood, but what he has reasonably understood. We measure Buster's interpretation of Al's words and conduct from the perspective of a reasonable person in Buster's position.) Say, for example, that Buster was one of those sidewalk performers who strikes a pose and tries to stand dead-still like a statue. Al's offer of money may well be in exchange for the hand movement, because Buster could reasonably infer that Al is bargaining for the pleasure of seeing Buster abandon his art for filthy lucre. (Is that pleasure worth $10? We do not usually need to inquire. As discussed in section 7.6, once exchange is determined, it is not necessary to evaluate the adequacy of consideration.)

This example again confronts the awkward fit between benefit to the promisor, motive, and the objective test of intent. When no benefit to Al was evident, we concluded that the detriment was not bargained for. When additional facts were supplied that suggested a motive, albeit not an economic one, the conclusion was that the detriment was bargained for. Yet we did not try to seek Al's actual motive for the exchange, but rather his apparent motive. The benefit to the promisor, measured objectively, is purely the satisfaction of having his apparent desire fulfilled. This is sufficient to support a finding of exchange. (As we will see later in this chapter, the exchange requirement has many facets.)

§7.3.5 The Distinction Between a Detriment and a Condition of Gift

One of the most elusive distinctions in consideration doctrine is that between an act or promise that is a legal detriment, and one that merely relates to the manner in which a gift is to be used. For example, Al Umnus promises to donate $10,000 to his alma mater and specifies that the gift is to be allocated to the college's scholarship program. The college accepts the promise and agrees to use the funds as specified by Al. The college has made a promise to Al in return for his promise of $10,000, but is that promise consideration? As a doctrinal matter, the answer is no, because the college's promise is not a legal detriment. At the time of the promise, Al has not handed over the money to the college, and the college has no right to spend Al's money. Therefore when it makes the promise to use Al's prospective payment in a specified way, it does not forbear from any legal right that it has at the time of the promise. This is not a contract, but merely a gift with a condition attached.

The distinction between a contractual undertaking and a commitment to use a gift as specified by the donor is so slippery that a court can easily overlook it, especially if it sees the public interest as best served by enforcing a charitable promise. The court's inclination to enforce such a promise is easier to justify on doctrinal grounds if the court can find in the donee's undertaking any promise that goes beyond the simple promise to use the gift for its intended purpose. This additional promise could be enough to constitute a detriment. Say, for example, Al and the college had agreed not only that the promised funds would be used for the scholarship program, but also that the college would include Al's name on a donor's list published in its alumni magazine. The college's promise to publicize the gift goes beyond the use of the money, so it can constitute a legal detriment. To be sure, it is a small detriment, and the idea that it was exchanged for (that is, induced) the promise is quite artificial, but it is likely enough to qualify as consideration. As discussed in section 7.6, the court does not enquire into the adequacy of consideration.

A few cases illustrate the subtlety of the distinction between a detriment and a promise to use a gift as required by the donor. In *King v. Trustees of Boston University*, 420 Mass. 52 (1995) the estate of Dr. Martin Luther King Jr. sued the university to recover papers that Dr. King had deposited with the university library. The estate claimed that Dr. King gave the university only temporary custody of his papers, but the university asserted that he had transferred ownership of them. At the time of handing over the papers, Dr. King had written a letter to the university reserving ownership of the papers until his death, but stating that they would become the property of the university when he died. The question was whether this promise to transfer ownership of the papers was merely an unenforceable gift, or a contract for which the university had given consideration.[6] The court upheld the jury's finding that the university gave consideration to

---

6. You may be wondering if it could not have been argued that Dr. King's deposit of his papers with the university was an executed gift, making consideration doctrine irrelevant. Although the university had possession of the papers, it held them only as bailee. The promise that required consideration was Dr. King's promise to transfer ownership of the papers to the university.

Dr. King. When accepting the papers, the university had undertaken to index them, to take care of them, and to make them available to researchers. The court found that these duties went beyond a mere promise to use the gift as instructed by the donor. Recognize that the court could easily have reached the opposite conclusion. There is a good argument that these duties were nothing more than conditions imposed by Dr. King on the use of the gift.

In *Massachusetts Eye and Ear Infirmary v. Eugene B. Casey Foundation* 417 F. Supp. 2d 192 (D. Mass. 2006) the foundation pledged to give $2 million to the infirmary to be used for a voice restoration research program. When the foundation terminated its pledge, the infirmary sued it for breach of contract. The foundation moved to dismiss the case on several grounds, one of which was that the infirmary gave no consideration to the foundation for its promise. The court refused to dismiss the case because it considered that there was a colorable argument that the infirmary gave consideration for the pledge by committing to use the funds only for the express purpose of supporting the voice restoration program, and by undertaking to submit biannual reports to the foundation. Again, the decision could have been opposite — the infirmary's undertakings can be seen as no more than conditions of the gift. The court, citing the *King* case, revealed the policy rationale for its decision. It observed, quite obliquely, that the public interest in protecting and supporting charitable subscriptions calls for a different standard to decide on the existence of consideration in relation to charitable pledges.[7]

Sometimes this distinction comes up in cases that do not involve charitable gifts. For example, in *Bono v. McCutcheon*, 824 N.E.2d 1013 (Ohio App. 2005) the parties entered into an agreement under which McCutcheon gave Bono possession of a whippet puppy named Doozie. Bono paid no money for Doozie, but the agreement required her to keep the dog in good condition, to show her, to breed her, to give McCutcheon a puppy from her first litter, and to allow McCutcheon to take and breed her for one litter. At some time later, McCutcheon regained possession of Doozie and refused to return her. Bono sued for conversion and breach of contract. McCutcheon moved to dismiss the suit, claiming that there was no contract because Bono had not paid anything for the dog.[8] The issue was whether Bono's undertakings were consideration for the dog or just conditions of gift. The trial court found no consideration and granted the motion to dismiss but the

---

7. In both *King* and *Massachusetts Eye and Ear Infirmary*, the court also discussed the issue of whether the promise would be enforceable had there been no consideration, but the donee had acted in reliance on the promise. In such a situation, the doctrine of promissory estoppel may provide relief. We will cover this issue in Chapter 8.
8. Contrary to the *King* case, it seems that the argument could have been made here that even if Doozie was a gift, the gift had been executed when McCutcheon originally gave possession of the dog to Bono, so there was no need to find consideration. This issue was not raised in the opinion.

court of appeals took the opposite view and reversed. Again, it is hard to be sure that the court of appeals was right and the trial court was wrong.

§7.4 THE PURPOSE AND FUNCTION OF CONSIDERATION DOCTRINE

So far we have looked at the basic principles of consideration and have identified the grounds of some of its rules but have not sought any comprehensive explanation of the rationale of the doctrine. Such a discussion is vital to an understanding of consideration and to a critical appraisal of its appropriate use in individual cases. This important discussion has been deferred until now because it is difficult to appreciate before an exposition of the doctrine itself.

Some people doubt that consideration has any useful purpose at all. They consider it an historical relic that could disappear unmourned, its functions being more effectively performed by other doctrines of contract law. Yet consideration is still a dominant force in contract law. Unless this can be attributed solely to the inertia of the common law, it must mean that courts still find consideration doctrine to be more useful than harmful. What are the most convincing justifications for the retention of this old common law doctrine? In 1941, Lon Fuller wrote his celebrated article, *Consideration and Form* (41 COLUM. L. REV. 799), which has ever since formed the starting point for all discussion of the modern role of the doctrine. Fuller identified both formal and substantive bases for consideration.

§7.4.1 Formal Functions of Consideration

Fuller recognized that legal formalities serve three interrelated functions: **"Evidentiary"** (i.e., provide evidence of the existence and terms of a contract), **"cautionary"** (i.e., make the parties aware that they have made a serious legal commitment), and **"channelling"** (i.e., provide an objective basis for a court to determine that the promise is contractual, rather than a mere generous impulse or a tentative or informal expression of intent). The functions are interrelated in that a formality that satisfies one of them is likely to satisfy all.

At least up to a point, consideration serves the functions of legal formalities. For example, when Al exchanged his promise to deliver his skis for Buster's payment of $100, the fact that $100 was given for the promise tends to prove that it was made (why else would Al be sitting with $100 of Buster's money?); it forces Al to realize that he has made a binding commitment to part with his skis; and it tells the court that this truly is meant as a legally enforceable exchange transaction.

Recognize that the argument that consideration satisfies formal functions is at best a partial answer. If its role were purely formal, it could easily be dispensed with because these formal functions could be accomplished simply by having a rule that upholds written, signed promises. However, this is not the law. A promise of a gift, even if executed in writing with due formality, is not treated as binding.[9] Even if the parties go to the trouble of reciting a formal or nominal consideration for the sake of trying to validate the gift, this is not usually recognized as sufficient to support the gratuitous promise. (See section 7.8.)

Therefore, parties cannot be assured of avoiding consideration problems by clearly and soberly executing a document that satisfies the functions of legal formalities. If consideration serves only the functions of legal formality, this result makes no sense. To justify it, there must be some substantive basis for requiring consideration.

§7.4.2 The Substantive Basis for Consideration

If legal formalities are thought of as procedural in nature, substantive justifications of consideration are based on the goals and policies of substantive contract law. Because the concerns generated by gift promises are quite different from those arising in gratuitous commercial promises, we should begin by distinguishing the substantive rationale for non-enforcement in these separate contexts. We can then consider more general rationales, applicable to both.

a. The Reasons for Not Enforcing Gift Promises

The substantive basis of consideration is often expressed in market terms: Exchange transactions are enforced as contracts because society has a vital interest in the reliability of commercial exchanges, but gift promises are **"sterile"** and of little commercial utility. This rationale has the ideological

---

9. In this respect, modern law has moved away from older common law which did have a formal device — the **seal** — that could be used to make a promise binding without consideration. The promisor could create a binding gratuitous promise by sealing the document. Originally, the seal was made by dripping sealing wax on the document and impressing the hot wax with a signet ring. In time it became acceptable simply to append the letters "L.S." (locus sigilli — meaning "in place of a seal") to a signature. The seal did not develop as an exception to consideration doctrine but predates the doctrine, which applied only to "informal" (i.e., unsealed) promises. Today, the seal has been abolished or given only residual evidentiary effect in most jurisdictions. In only a few states has the formal device of the seal been replaced by a statutory method of formally validating a gift promise.

undertones of the Victorian work ethic and conjures up images of slothful remittance men, lolling about on some tropical veranda, wasting their lives away in booze, and other unmentionable pursuits. In truth, few gifts are economically sterile. The donee's use, expenditure, or saving of the gift surely has some impact on the marketplace, and a charitable gift has social as well as economic utility.

A more convincing rationale lies in the *equities between donor and donee,* contrasted with those between parties to a commercial transaction. Gifts tend to be motivated by affection, gratitude, or altruism and usually have a stronger emotional impetus than commercial exchanges. There may be some moral obligation to keep the promise, but nothing was given in exchange for it, and the donee has lost nothing except the prospect of a gift.[10] The donor should therefore be able to recant without legal liability. This protects the donor against improvidence and also indirectly protects his or her creditors who did give value for their claims. For example, a person, much inspired by an evangelist, promises a large donation to his ministry. The next day the promisor realizes that the donation would leave her so short of money that she will not be able to pay her bills. If she could not renege on the promise, the evangelist would have the same claim to her assets as any creditor from whom she has purchased goods or services. However, consideration doctrine assures that while the creditors can hold her to the promises for which she received value, the preacher's recourse must be sought in some celestial forum. The terrestrial courts will not enforce the promise.

This rationale is the substantive echo of the formal **cautionary** function. That is, while the presence of consideration cautions the promisor that a legal duty is being assumed, its absence creates the expectation that the promise can be revoked without legal liability. In a circular way, this expectation itself bolsters the need to retain the requirement of consideration: Because gift promises have not been enforced, a donor may make a promise in the reasonable expectation that it will not be binding, and the continued insistence on consideration protects this reasonable expectation. In other words, the fact that the rule has existed for so long, in itself justifies its continuation.

Although it is widely accepted that gift promises should not be enforced, this rule is not applied absolutely. Sometimes the equities of a case call for the enforcement of a gratuitous promise, and courts have the means of finding a basis for enforcement either by a manipulation of the broad concept of bargained-for detriment (as introduced in section 7.3.1) or under the alternative doctrines discussed in Chapters 8 and 9.

---

10. If the donee has suffered some loss in reliance on the promise, the alternative theory of promissory estoppel, discussed in Chapter 8, may provide relief.

b. The Reason for Not Enforcing Commercial Promises Without Consideration

A commercial promise without consideration may sound like a contradiction in terms. After all, one may think that a promise without consideration must by definition be a gift. However, there are many examples in this chapter of promises lacking consideration even though motivated by commercial ends. For example, an apparent promise may in fact be illusory; or the promise may have been made during negotiations, before the other party made a firm return commitment; or the promise may have been made in recognition of some economic benefit that is not given in exchange because it predates the promise or is expected but not actually promised.

In a commercial transaction, in which altruism, affection, or gratitude is not a motivating factor,[11] the rationale relating to the nonenforcement of gifts is inapplicable. Therefore, to refuse enforcement of the promise as a contract, the court must be satisfied that the parties did not intend it to be such. That is, that the promise was in fact an **informal, non-binding expression of intent**, or it was **otherwise not reasonably expected to create a legal duty**. If, on the other hand, the court is persuaded that serious legal commitment was reasonably intended, it is likely to make great effort to give effect to that intention by scouring the transaction to find consideration for it.

c. Consideration as a Means of Policing for Unfair Bargaining

In both donative and commercial settings, consideration continues to be useful to courts as a means of refusing to enforce a promise that was extracted by unfair or illegitimate means. This is hardly a unique function of the doctrine in that there are many other principles of contract law designed to prevent the enforcement of promises induced by fraud, duress, and other unfair bargaining methods. Indeed, as noted earlier, it is often claimed that these other means of policing contract formation are more direct and efficient than consideration doctrine. Nevertheless, the requirement that there must be consideration has historically played an important role in this area of contract law, and it has continuing value as one of the tools available to the court for this purpose.

---

11. Of course, I do not suggest that these impulses are always absent in the commercial setting. There may be situations in which gratitude is the overwhelming or possibly the only motive for an apparently commercial promise, and affection or friendship may play some role in a commercial exchange. To the extent that these motives are strongly present, the transaction may in fact be a gift and hence subject to the policy relating to gratuitous promises, even if the context is commercial.

§7.5 DETRIMENT AND "PRE-EXISTING DUTY"

§7.5.1 The Basic Rule

If a detriment is the relinquishment of a right, it follows that one does not suffer a detriment by doing or promising to do something that one is *already obliged to do* or by forbearing to do something that is *already forbidden*. Therefore, the rule is often stated that the performance of, or promise to perform, a pre-existing duty is not consideration. For example, say that Al and Buster contracted last week for the sale of Al's skis to Buster for $100, C.O.D. delivery to be effected at a specified future time. Before the date due for delivery and payment under the contract, Al discovers that he has under-charged for the skis. He approaches Buster and asks him to agree to change the price to $150. Buster believes that he did underpay and feels that the skis are still a good buy at $150. Not wishing to take advantage of Al's mistake, he agrees to pay the extra amount. This second agreement does not create a binding contract because Al gave Buster no consideration for his promise to pay $50 more. Al already had a duty to deliver the skis under the original contract, and he neither gives nor promises anything new. It cannot be a legal detriment to promise what he is already obliged to do. As a result, Buster's second promise is not binding, and if he later regrets it, he can insist on delivery of the skis for the original price of $100.

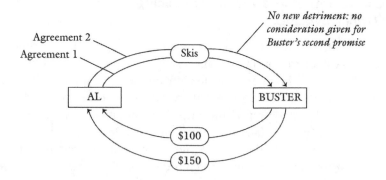

No new detriment: no consideration given for Buster's second promise

The pre-existing duty rule only applies if the performance of the prom-isee is completely encompassed by the pre-existing duty. Therefore, if Al had in any way added to his performance or obligation as an incentive to Buster's agreement to pay more (for example, Al offered to throw in a set of used thermal underwear), this *new increase in his detriment* would be sufficient to constitute consideration for Buster's promise of more money. The fact that the underwear is not worth anywhere near $50 will usually not matter because, as explained in section 7.6, economic equivalence is not normally required in the exchange.

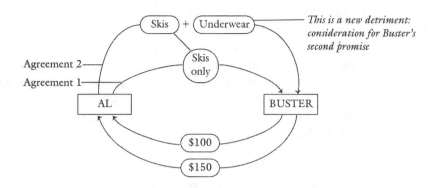

This is a new detriment: consideration for Buster's second promise

§7.5.2 The Justification for the Rule Where the Duty Is Owed to the Promisor: Coerced Modifications

It is quite easy to express the pre-existing duty rule in its basic form, but application of the rule is seldom this simple. In some cases, the problem may be factual. For example, it may be unclear if a pre-existing duty exists or if the detriment in the later agreement really is coextensive with this duty. However, the bigger problem is a conceptual one. Why have the rule at all? True, it is consistent with and simply a specific application of the concept of detriment, so the rule is doctrinally justifiable. But what policy does it serve?

The rule makes most sense when, after a contract has been made, one of the parties takes advantage of the other's dependence on his performance, by threatening to breach the contract unless the other promises to increase her payment or other return performance. When a modification of an existing contract has been coerced in this way, the court can employ the pre-existing duty rule to void the unfair modification. Although we will return to the subject of contract modification in section 13.9 in connection with a broader study of the doctrines governing unfair bargaining, we must deal with it here as well, because it has a significant connection to consideration doctrine. To illustrate, say that a traveller, on arriving at the airport of a large city, contracts with a cab driver to pay him $35 to take her to a hotel on the other side of town. Halfway through the journey, as they are driving through a dark and frightening part of town, the cab driver jams on the brakes, turns to the passenger, and says, "Sorry, but unless you agree to pay me $100 for my fare, I am going to dump you off here." Of course the passenger agrees to this modification of the contract. However, the cab driver had a pre-existing duty to complete the trip. He has therefore given the passenger nothing more than what he originally promised—transport to the hotel. Because he has suffered no further detriment in exchange for the passenger's promise to pay another $65, this promise of

169

additional payment lacks consideration and the passenger can refuse to pay any more than \$35 when they reach the hotel.[12]

Although the justification of the rule is the prevention of this kind of coerced modification, the rule has two serious shortcomings. First, a promisee who knows of the rule can evade it simply by adding some minor new detriment to his side of the exchange (such as a promise to throw in used underwear with the skis). Second, the rule covers all modifications, even those, such as the price increase in the contract between Al and Buster, that are legitimately agreed to. In these circumstances (unless the parties know the rule and provide for some new detriment by the promisee), application of the rule precludes parties from making a binding agreement to modify the obligations of one of them, even when circumstances justify a modification and the promisor genuinely agreed to it without unfair pressure. Such an *unquestioning use* of the rule *undermines freedom of contract* and has led many commentators and courts to believe that the rule is unnecessary and undesirable. Coercion can be more directly dealt with under doctrines such as duress and bad faith, and unless the modification has been induced by illegitimate pressure, there is no reason to refuse its enforcement by a mechanical application of the rule.

In fact, the UCC has abolished the rule and replaced it in §2.209[13] by a **good faith** test. (This is discussed more fully in section 13.9.) In a common law case, some courts may be willing to take a bold approach, adopting the UCC test of good faith, but others consider themselves bound by consideration doctrine. They will therefore only uphold a modification, even though genuinely consensual, if, on examining its terms, the court can find some new detriment suffered by the promisee. Of course, if the court is convinced of the legitimacy of the modification, it will make great effort to find a new detriment, even if slight in relation to the value of the modification. The disparity in value of the exchange can be disregarded under the rule that the court does not inquire into the adequacy of consideration.

Another possibility is that the modification may fit into a well-recognized exception to the rule: If the modification was motivated by supervening difficulties that so affect the basic assumption under which the contract was made, courts have long held modification to be enforceable, even in the absence of consideration. The underlying rationale for this exception is that a modification to take account of an unexpected burden on the promisee is less likely to be coercive. Of course, the exception can only be used where the facts support it. The promisee must be able to show that such an unforeseen difficulty did arise in the course of performance and did motivate the modification.

---

12. Furthermore, she need not tip him, either.
13. Section 2.209 is the same in the 2003 revision of Article 2, except for minor amendments not relevant here.

§7.5.3 Pre-Existing Duty to a Third Party

So far, we have talked only about a pre-existing duty owed by the promisee to the promisor. What if the duty is owed to someone else? For example, Al has contracted with Ava Lanche to sell his skis to her for $200; C.O.D. delivery is to take place next week. Ava has promised her friend Buster that when she gets her new skis, she will give him her old ones. Buster is therefore most anxious for the sale to go through. To give Al an additional incentive to honor his contract with Ava, Buster promises Al that if Al delivers the skis to Ava as arranged, Buster will give Al his almost-new thermal underwear. Al has already made a commitment to Ava to deliver the skis. The pre-existing duty rule would appear to apply, in that he has incurred no new detriment in exchange for Buster's promise.

Note however, that the concern about extorted contract modification is not present in a case like this, so this justification for the pre-existing duty rule is not applicable. Some courts (and Restatement Second §73) simply confine the pre-existing duty rule to cases in which the duty is owed to the promisor. An alternate way of looking at the situation is to say that Al does incur a detriment in that he forbears from the right to negotiate with Ava for the cancellation of the contract. (He also forbears from the power but not the right to breach the contract with Ava, but as detriment is the relinquishment of a legal right, forbearance from breach is not a very kosher detriment.)

A pre-existing duty may be owed, not to the promisor or a third party, but to the state or the public. This type of duty presents slightly different policy concerns because the public interest may demand that external incentives to obey that duty must be discouraged. This is particularly so when the promisee is a public official, and an additional reward for performing the public duty may create the danger of corruption or favoritism. For example, a police officer has a pre-existing duty to apprehend criminals. Therefore, if the owner of a store promises a police officer a reward for catching the robber who robbed the store, the court is likely to invalidate this promise on the basis of the pre-existing duty rule. However, the true basis for refusing to recognize a contract is not some technical approach to consideration doctrine, but the public policy that a member of the public schould not be able to influence the police officer's priorities in performing his duties.

§7.5.4 Pre-Existing Duty and the Compromise of an Existing Claim

Say that On February 1, Lender lent Borrower $5,000, payable with 8 percent interest on August 1. In late July, Borrower told Lender that he was having financial difficulty and could not repay the loan in full by August 1. Borrower offered to pay lender $1,000 on August 1, and to pay the balance in installments over the next five months. Borrower acknowledged that interest would continue to accrue on the outstanding balance at the rate of 8 percent per month. Lender agreed to grant the extension. Consideration doctrine dictates that Lender is not bound by her agreement to accept late payment on this **undisputed claim**. Although she gave consideration by promising to forbear from demanding full payment on due date, Borrower gave her no consideration in return. Borrower was already committed to repay the loan of $5,000 with 8 percent interest, and he undertakes no new detriment by promising this again. (Although interest is now payable over a longer period than originally envisaged, the loan agreement undoubtedly contemplated that 8 percent interest would accrue until the debt was paid.) However, had Borrower agreed to some additional detriment, such as the payment of interest at a higher rate or the payment of a late fee, this would have been sufficient consideration. As you can see, the rule applied in this situation is just a specific application of the rule discussed in section 7.5.2 on contract modifications without consideration. As noted in that section, it is difficult to find a convincing policy justification for applying the rule where Borrower has not coerced the modification or acted in bad faith, and Lender freely acceded to the request for an extension. (This is why UCC §2.209 has replaced the consideration requirement with a good faith test where a sale of goods is involved.)

An agreement to extend or reduce an undisputed debt must be distinguished from the **compromise of a disputed claim**. For example, Lender agreed to lend $100,000 to Borrower at 8 percent interest for a year to enable Borrower to keep operating his struggling business. This was a valid contract. (A promise to advance money was exchanged for a promise to repay it with interest.) Lender breached the contract by refusing to advance the money. Borrower could not borrow the money elsewhere and his business collapsed. Borrower sued Lender for damages of $250,000, which he claims is his loss as a result of the collapse of his business, caused by Lender's failure to honor her loan commitment. Lender defended the suit on the basis that Borrower cannot prove that the business would not have failed anyway, and that Borrower's damages are speculative. Before the case went to trial, the parties negotiated a settlement under which Lender agreed to pay Borrower $20,000 in full settlement of his claim and Borrower agreed to dismiss the lawsuit. Here, each party has given consideration to the other. Borrower forbore from asserting his claim in full, and Lender agreed not to persist in her defense that she owes nothing to Borrower. As a matter of public policy, settlements of litigation are encouraged because the public has an interest in the consensual resolution of lawsuits. However, this public policy is clearly not served unless the dispute is genuine and in good faith. It is not in the public interest to allow a person to coerce payment by making and settling a spurious claim, or to resist payment by advancing a groundless defense. Therefore, when consideration is the forbearance of a claim or defense, courts do, to some extent, enquire into the adequacy of consideration by probing the legitimacy of the dispute. Apart from the policy consideration, there is a doctrinal justification for this approach. A person has no legal right to assert a vexatious claim or defense. Therefore, he does not forbear from a legal right, and he suffers no legal detriment, by compromising it.

Obviously, in any dispute that is litigated, one of the parties loses because the court finds his claim or defense to be without merit. Therefore, legitimacy cannot mean that the party's contentions would ultimately have prevailed had the case gone to trial. Rather, the test for legitimacy is based on the existence of enough doubt about the claim and defense to make the dispute genuine. Restatement Second §74 adopts a test that measures legitimacy on, alternatively, an objective or subjective standard. Either the claim or defense must be **objectively reasonable** (that it is subject to reasonable doubt because of uncertainty in fact or law), or the party asserting the claim or defense must have an honest belief in its merits (that is, he is **subjectively in good faith**). Some courts are stricter and require the claim and defense to satisfy both the objective and subjective standards — that it has a colorable legal basis, and also that it is asserted in good faith. Some courts do not enquire into the objective plausibility of the claim or defense, but require only an examination of the good faith of the party asserting it. In many cases, the outcome of these tests may amount to the same thing because it may be hard to convince a jury that a party had a genuine belief in the validity of a claim or defense that has no objective basis of support. However, the subjective test does allow the court to take account of honest ignorance. Whatever test is used, the legitimacy of the claim must be determined as at the date of the agreement, not in light of later events.

For an example of a case in which the court required only a good faith belief in the merits of the claim, see *Denburg v. Parker, Chapin, Flattau, & Klimpl*, 604 N.Y.S.2d 900 (1993). A law firm's partnership agreement contained a clause that created financial disincentives for a partner to leave the firm and practice in competition with it. Provisions of this kind are void as against public policy because, by discouraging a partner from setting up a competing practice upon leaving the firm, they inhibit his clients' right to maintain access to the attorney of their choice. The firm sought to enforce the provision against a partner who left the firm and the partner challenged its right to do so. The parties then settled the dispute by agreement. Thereafter, the ex-partner claimed that the settlement agreement lacked consideration because it compromised an invalid claim. The court upheld the settlement. Although the partnership's claim was not legally tenable, the firm believed in good faith that it was viable. This was enough to validate the firm's forbearance as consideration.

§7.6 THE MEASUREMENT OF DETRIMENT: ADEQUACY OF CONSIDERATION

When skis are exchanged for money, items of ascertainable economic worth are involved, so it is usually not difficult to determine if there has been equivalence in the exchange. It is a lot harder to value the right given up by Buster in promising to quit smoking. However, this generally does not matter, because consideration doctrine does not require that the performances or promises exchanged be of equal value. As long as a legal detriment has been suffered in exchange for the promise, the court *does not inquire into its value in relation to the promise.* (Restatement Second §79(b).) A related principle is that there does not have to be an *equivalence* in the *number of promises or performances* provided by each party. One party can exchange a single promise or performance for multiple promises and performances by the other. For example, Al could have given Buster the skis in exchange for Buster's payment of $100 plus his promise to stop smoking and his forbearance from asserting a claim that he has against Al. For the purposes of finding consideration, we need not worry that Buster has given up three rights to one of Al's, nor need we fret about whether the promise of the skis is worth more or less than Buster's detriment.

The rule that the court will not inquire into adequacy of consideration is based on the policy of enforcing the voluntary exchange on the terms agreed by the parties. Once consideration has been found to exist, the court should not second-guess the value placed on the exchange by the parties at the time of contracting, even if it now appears that one of them received a great bargain and the other was underpaid. Therefore, if Al's skis are actually worth $500, and he agreed to sell them to Buster for $100, the court should not allow him to escape the contract and disappoint Buster's expectations. This argument has even more force when the economic value of one of the performances is hard to determine (or was so at the time of contracting). For example, one really cannot place an economic value on Buster's promise to stop smoking, so one cannot even be sure that this promise was an inadequate exchange for the skis. (Some may think that $100 is overpayment for taking the sensible action of overcoming a dangerous addiction, while others may think it is a measly reward for the agony of withdrawal.)

This principle makes sense where the agreement is the product of fair bargaining, because the parties bear responsibility for setting the value of the exchange. The disparity in value may be the result of many and varied factors such as poor judgment, inaccurate cost calculations, bad luck in market predictions, or even deliberate underpricing. Whatever the reason, the party who received less than the value of his or her performance has no basis to complain. However, this general rule does not apply in two situations: First, adequacy of consideration does become an issue when the disparity in the exchange results from **oppressive** or **underhand bargaining** or **justifiable mistake.** When assent is negated by such a defect in the bargaining process, doctrines such as fraud, duress, unconscionability, or mistake allow the court to take cognizance of the disparity in exchange and to overturn the transaction or to adjust its terms to equalize it. (These doctrines are dealt with in Chapters 9 and 15.) Second, if the consideration given for a promise has so small a value in relation to the promise that it is obviously **nominal**, it may fail to satisfy the requirement of exchange, and the transaction may be viewed as a gift. This is discussed further in section 7.8.

§7.7 PAST PERFORMANCE

Because exchange is the basis of consideration, each party's detriment must induce and be induced by the other's. Therefore, if the promisee suffered the detriment before the promise was made, it cannot be said that the detriment was exchanged for the promise. Although the detriment may have induced the promise, it was not itself induced by the promise which had not yet been made. This means that if a person makes a promise to compensate another for some prior performance, that prior detriment cannot be consideration for the promise. The promise is seen as gratuitous and non-binding, even if it was seriously and freely made, and even if the prior detriment conferred a valuable benefit on the promisor.

The prior detriment is often referred to as **past consideration**, but this is a misnomer, because it is not consideration at all. For example, say that Al had fallen into a crevice while skiing, and Buster, risking horrendous peril, saved him. After being extracted from the crevice, Al gasped to

Buster, "In consideration for saving my life, I promise to give you my skis." This promise is not supported by consideration because Buster's detriment had already been suffered and was not truly induced by or exchanged for the promise. This result could be justified by the cautionary function of consideration. Buster probably did not act for commercial motives, and Al's promise can reasonably be seen as a gift, impulsively induced by feelings of gratitude. Conversely, it is not hard to see the merit in making Al give poor Buster the measly reward, and some courts have responded to this type of situation by formulating an alternative theory, commonly called "moral obligation," to enforce the promise. This is discussed in Chapter 9.

§7.8 FALSE OR NOMINAL CONSIDERATION

It was stated in section 7.6 that courts do not normally inquire into the adequacy of consideration, but leave it to the parties to decide what their promises or performances are worth. This is an important principle, because it protects the autonomy of the parties and upholds the security of transactions by preventing the evasion of contractual duties by the party who made the wrong economic judgment. However, as mentioned already, this general rule is subject to two exceptions. The first, relating to policing doctrines such as fraud or duress, is discussed in Chapter 13. We turn to the second here.

A person promising a gift may know enough about the law to realize that consideration is needed to validate the promise. To make the gift binding, the promisor may **falsely recite** that consideration has been received (provide for a **sham** consideration) or may provide for some **nominal detriment** to be given by the promisee. Provided that the promisor has not been tricked into this pretense of consideration and it is not designed to defraud some third party, it seems consonant with the policy of contractual autonomy to allow the parties to use this device to validate the promise. However, Restatement Second does not take this approach. While it asserts the general rule that courts should not inquire into adequacy of consideration, it states several times that the *pretense of a bargain* does not satisfy the exchange element, so that a false consideration, which does *not in fact induce* the return promise (or, at least, cannot reasonably be conceived as doing so), should not be treated as sufficient. (*See* §71, Comment *b*; §72, Comment *c*; §79, Comment *d*; and §81, Comment *b*.)

Because the nominal or sham consideration satisfies the formal functions discussed in section 7.4, the rationale of the Restatement's position must lie in the substantive justifications for consideration. We have already disposed of the policing function by excluding situations in which the promisor has been deceived or the parties have some ulterior motive of misleading a third party. This leaves the justifications relating to the nonenforcement of gratuitous promises. Sometimes, the circumstances may suggest that the goal of protecting against generosity may outweigh the policy of upholding private autonomy, but in other situations, despite what the Restatement says, the better approach may be to take the apparent consideration at face value. This is particularly so when the formal functions of consideration are fully satisfied by a clear document and there is no suggestion of advantage taking or underhand conduct by the promisee, and no indication that the promisor acted impulsively and with immediate regret.

Although some cases do refuse to recognize consideration when it is clearly nominal or false, others decline to question the adequacy of nominal consideration, and counter an allegation of sham (falsely recited) consideration by interpreting the recital as an implied promise to provide the stated act or forbearance at some future time, or by estopping[14] the promisor from denying receipt of recited consideration. Many courts do not follow one or the other of these approaches rigidly but may select whichever one seems appropriate on the facts of the particular case. That is, adequacy is not questioned if there is no indication of impropriety or rashness, but nominal or sham consideration may be treated as insufficient if circumstances suggest that the promisor needs protection from generosity, impulsiveness, or unfair imposition.

Both Restatement Second and the courts adopt a more lenient attitude to purely formal consideration in **options.** An option is a promise to keep an offer open (that is, not to revoke it) for a specified period of time. Like other promises, it must have consideration to be binding on the promisor. However, as explained in section 5.2, because an option is granted to induce the grantee to enter a contract desired by the grantor, the common law more readily accepts nominal consideration to validate options. Furthermore, a false recital of consideration may be more readily interpreted as a promise to furnish the consideration or may be more easily found to estop the grantor from asserting that the recital was a sham. UCC Article 2 has gone even further and (as discussed in section 5.5) dispenses with consideration for options (called "firm offers") for the sale of goods under certain circumstances.

---

14. Estoppel is explained in section 8.4. In short, its impact in this context is that because the promisor has participated in setting up the pretense of consideration, he or she cannot now deny that consideration was given. The promisor's earlier conduct induced the promisee reasonably to rely on the validity of the promise and the promisor is therefore held accountable for that conduct and is precluded from asserting that the consideration is a sham.

§7.9 THE QUALITY OF A PROMISE AS CONSIDERATION: "MUTUALITY OF OBLIGATION," ILLUSORY, CONDITIONAL, AND ALTERNATIVE PROMISES

§7.9.1 Mutuality and Illusory Promises

The requirement of mutuality of obligation is expressed in the old maxim "both parties must be bound, or neither is bound." Taken too literally, the concept of mutuality can be confusing and misleading, because it seems to suggest that one could never have a unilateral contract, or a contract in which one of the parties has the legal right to escape liability. Yet, both types of contract are well recognized in law. It has been explained in section 4.12 that a promise can be exchanged for an immediate performance, resulting in a unilateral contract in which only the promisor has an outstanding obligation at the instant of contract formation. Elsewhere in this book many other situations are described in which only one of the parties is bound because the other has the right to end the contractual relationship. This is true, for example, in an option contract (*see* section 5.4) or a contract that is voidable by one party on such grounds as minority (*see* section 14.2.1), incapacity (*see* section 14.3.3), bargaining impropriety (*see* section 13.3), or mistake (*see* section 15.5). It is also quite valid to provide in a contract for a party to have the right to terminate the contract by giving notice.

Therefore, in modern law, "mutuality" does not mean that both parties must make a future commitment or, if they do, that each must be bound with the same degree of firmness. It also does not mean that the parties must have equal and coextensive obligations under the contract. Because there need not be economic equivalence in the exchange, it is permissible and common for one party to incur far more numerous, extensive, or onerous obligations than the other.[15]

---

15. Sometimes the disparity in rights is so severe and the contract is so one-sided, that the court will refuse to enforce the contract as a whole, or will refuse enforcement of the unfair term. Usually, the court uses doctrines such as unconscionability (*see* section 13.11) or public policy (*see* section 13.13) to tackle the problem of unfair imposition. However, there are cases in which the court uses consideration doctrine to achieve this end. This occurred, for example, in *Hooters of America, Inc. v. Phillips*, 39 F. Supp. 2d 582 (D.S.C. 1998). (The decision was affirmed without discussion of the consideration issue at 173 F.3d 933 (4th Cir. 1999).) Hooters moved to dismiss an ex-employee's complaint of sexual harassment and wrongful discharge on the grounds that she had entered an agreement to arbitrate all claims and disputes. However, the agreement was structured so that the employees were absolutely bound to arbitrate, but Hooters had discretion to terminate the agreement on notice and to change the arbitration rules and procedures without notice. The court held that the disparity in the rights of the parties was so significant, and the agreement was so favorable

7. Consideration

If "mutuality" does not carry any of these implications, what does it mean? In modern law, it is nothing more than a specific application of the general principle of consideration: When consideration consists of the exchange of **mutual promises**, the **undertakings** on **both sides** must be **real and meaningful**. If the promise of one party has qualifications or limitations so strong that they negate it, it is really no commitment at all. Because it does not bind that party, this lack of consideration voids the apparent contract, so neither party is bound. For example, Buster promises to buy Al's skis for $100, and Al promises to sell them to Buster unless Al changes his mind. This qualification reserves such unlimited discretion to Al that he has really promised nothing. His apparent promise is said to be **illusory** and hence cannot be consideration.

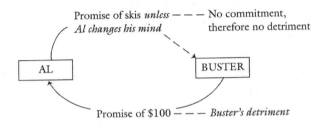

Using the language of mutuality, we could say that because Al is not bound, Buster is not bound either. However, we do not need to formulate it this way. The real problem is that Al has suffered no detriment because he has neither given nor actually promised anything to Buster. Therefore, Buster's return promise lacks consideration and is not binding. (Al may have thought that he was being very clever in getting a promise from Buster while keeping his own options open, but his lack of commitment removes binding force from Buster's promise too, so Al cannot hold Buster to his promise if Al decides to exercise his discretion to go through with the sale.) Because "mutuality" is redundant and misleading, Restatement Second §79(c) and Comment f disavow the concept and stress that it should not be thought of as a separate or additional requirement for consideration.

In the above example, Al's promise was illusory because he retained unlimited discretion to perform. This is possibly the most obvious illustration of an illusory promise. However, a promise could also be illusory for other reasons. For example, it is also an illusion to promise something based on a condition that cannot occur—say that Al gives his skis to Buster in return for Buster's promise to pay $100 for them if, by the end of the week, Elvis is returned to earth by the aliens who stole him.[16]

---

to Hooters, that Hooters had not really made any commitment at all. As a result, the arbitration agreement lacked consideration.

16. Of course, some people do not believe this to be an impossible condition.

§7.9.2 Interpretation and the Use of Implied Terms to Cure an Apparently Illusory Promise

The examples given so far try to provide obvious illustrations of the absence or presence of commitment. It is not always this easy to tell if a qualification so eviscerates a promise as to make it illusory: The promise could be subject to some degree of discretion that may not be broad enough to negate commitment. For example, Al and Buster agree that Buster will buy Al's skis for $100 C.O.D. next Monday on condition that Buster can obtain a loan of $100 by then. Al's promise to sell the skis is firm, but Buster's promise to buy is subject to a condition. It could be argued that Buster has made no real commitment. He can prevent fulfillment of the condition simply by not trying to borrow the money. However, if we **imply** into Buster's undertaking a **promise to use best efforts** to secure a loan, we impose a detriment upon him and cure the lack of commitment. This promise to make best efforts is not the same as a promise to buy the skis, so that Buster has no obligation to consummate the sale if he tries conscientiously but unsuccessfully to secure the loan. But if he makes no effort at all, he is liable for breach of contract.

This brings to mind one of the most cherished cases in the contracts repertoire—*Wood v. Lucy, Lady Duff-Gordon*, 222 N.Y. 88 (1917)—in which Judge Cardozo implied an obligation to use best efforts to validate an exclusive dealing contract between Lucy, a fashion maven of her time, and Wood, her business agent. Wood had agreed to pay Lucy half the profits earned from placing her endorsements and selling her designs, but had not, in so many words, promised to promote her wares. When Lucy breached the exclusive agency by endorsing products on her own and keeping all the profits for herself, Wood sued for his share. Lucy argued that there was no contract: Although Wood had undertaken to pay half the profits to her, he had not actually promised to do anything to earn those profits. In light of the obviously commercial intent of the agreement, the court concluded that Lucy's grant of an exclusive agency necessarily gave rise to the implication that Wood was obliged to use best efforts in generating profits. UCC §2.306(2)[17] follows this approach by implying an obligation of best efforts in exclusive dealing contracts involving goods.

We look more closely at the principles of interpretation — including the implication of terms by a court — in Chapter 10. The point to note here is that in most transactions with a commercial purpose, apparently discretionary promises can fairly be interpreted as subject to some implied limitation. When contracting, the parties usually intend their promises to be meaningful, and a later assertion that one of them is illusory is probably just a pretext to escape a bargain that is no longer desired. The process of implying terms to give content to apparently vacuous language comes up in many types of cases, and you will find many examples of this as you read through this book. However, there are some situations in which absolute discretion is exactly what was intended, because one of the parties takes the gamble that the attractiveness of the product or service will be enough to motivate the other to exercise discretion favorably. In such a case, if a court imposes unintended limitations on that discretion, it creates a contract out of an informal relationship that was not intended to be one.

§7.9.3 "Mutuality" in Requirements and Output Contracts Under UCC §2.306

Most sales contracts involve a single item or a specified quantity of goods. In some situations, however, it may suit the parties to leave the quantity of goods open-ended on the understanding that the quantity to be supplied under the contract will be determined either by the buyer's requirements or by the seller's output. The parties are likely to find a requirements contract most desirable if the seller is confidant that it can produce enough to satisfy the buyer's demands, and the buyer is unsure of its exact needs and wishes to avoid the risk of ordering a specified quantity which may turn out to be short or excessive. An output contract suits the parties when the seller wishes to dispose of its full production in one transaction, and the buyer is confident that it can use all that the seller can supply.

For example, assume that the seller is a vinyard and the buyer is a winery. The buyer is not exactly sure what quantity of grapes it will need next year because it only buys grapes to supplement what it produces on its own vines. The quantity it needs will depend on its own crop yield. The winery therefore does not want to try to predict its needs in advance by

---

17. Section 2.306 is unchanged in the 2003 revision of Article 2.

contracting for a set quantity of grapes because this could lead to waste if its own grapes are plentiful, and a shortfall if they are scarce. The buyer therefore makes a **requirements** contract with the seller under which the buyer promises to buy and the seller to supply the buyer's total demand for grapes during a specific period. By contrast, an **output** contract better suits the parties' needs if the buyer knows that it can use everything that the seller produces — it can never grow enough of its own grapes to satisfy its needs, and it has enough capacity to use all its own grapes plus all the grapes that the seller can produce. The seller is happy to sell its entire crop to the buyer, because this saves the costs of multiple transactions with different buyers. The parties therefore enter an output contract under which the seller promises to sell and the buyer to take all the grapes grown by the seller during a specified period.

Some earlier cases refused to uphold requirements and output contracts because the flexible quantity term was regarded as too vague and also because such contracts lacked "mutuality." That is, the broad discretion given to the party who determined quantity made that party's promise illusory because a requirements buyer could elect to have no requirements and an output seller could decide to produce no goods. In time, it came to be generally accepted that requirements and output contracts served a valuable commercial purpose, and that this approach was untenable. The problems of vagueness and lack of mutuality were solved by recognizing that even if the contract did not say so expressly, the discretion to determine quantity is limited by an implied obligation of good faith or reasonableness, and by an implied obligation of exclusive dealing.

The obligation of **exclusive dealing** is essential for an arrangement to qualify as a requirements or output contract. The promise to buy requirements or to sell output is meaningless if the party with the discretion could simply manipulate the extent of the requirements or output by buying or selling elsewhere.[18] As noted above, even if there is no express promise of exclusive dealing, it is often possible to imply it from the language of the contract in context. See, for example *Esso Geometric v. Harvard Industries*, 46 F.3d 718 (8th Cir. 1995). However, sometimes the language used in the agreement or the context may preclude such an interpretation. For example, in *Brooklyn Bagel Boys v. Earthgrains Refrigerated Dough Products, Inc.*, 212 F.3d 373 (7th Cir. 2000) the court could not find any basis for interpreting the contract to require the buyer to buy all its bagel requirements exclusively from the seller, so it found the arrangement to be merely a "buyer's option"

---

18. The obligation for exclusive dealing need not necessarily relate to the party's entire requirements or output of a product. It is permissible to confine it to a defined portion of the requirements or output, provided that the scope of the exclusive dealing is clear and identifiable. For example, a seller of corn could agree to commit only the output from particular fields, or a buyer of office stationery could commit to take only its requirements of 20 lb. copier paper from the seller.

under which the seller made an ongoing offer to sell bagels at a stated price, accepted by the buyer each time it placed an order. This means that there was no requirements contract, but rather a series of discrete contracts which imposed no ongoing obligation on the buyer to buy bagels.

The relationship between a buyer and seller in a requirements contract is illustrated by the following diagram. (In an output contract, the discretionary performance would be on the seller's side of the exchange.)

This approach forms the basis of UCC §2.306(1) that implicitly recognizes the **exclusive dealing** obligation and imposes both a good faith and a reasonable expectations test on the party who determines quantity. It states that when a contract measures quantity by the seller's output or the buyer's requirements, this means the **actual output or requirements** as may occur in **good faith**. In addition, it provides that the quantity tendered or demanded may not be **disproportionate** to any estimate, or if no estimate was stated, to any **normal** or otherwise **comparable** output or requirements. UCC §2.306(1) is structured so that the good faith test is applicable in all transactions of this kind. Good faith is an elusive standard because the concept is so vague, but courts take much trouble to give it content.[19]

a. The Good Faith Standard

The elements of good faith are different in the current and revised versions of Articles 1 and 2. Under the *current version of Articles 1 and 2*, the general definition of good faith, set out in §1.201(19) is purely subjective — "honesty in fact in the conduct or transaction concerned." However, if a party is a merchant,[20] current §2.103(1)(b) imposes a higher standard which includes both a subjective and objective test — not only honesty in fact, but also "the observance of reasonable commercial standards of fair

---

19. It is discussed further in section 10.8.2.
20. The merchant status is explained in sections 5.5 and 6.5.2.

dealing in the trade." *Revised Articles* 1 *and* 2 abandon the distinction between merchants and non-merchants with regard to good faith. Revised §1.201(20) adopts the test set out in current §2.103(1)(b) as the general definition of good faith. Revised §2.103(j) merely duplicates the definition in §1.201(20). It was noted in section 2.7.1 that at the time of writing this edition of the book, about half the states have adopted revised Article 1 but no state has yet adopted revised Article 2. Some of the states that have adopted revised Article 1 have declined to enact the revised general definition of good faith, and have kept the purely subjective test as the general non-merchant standard. For the present, at least, one therefore needs to be careful of this lack of uniformity in the definition. However, for purposes of output and requirements contracts, the issue of whether to apply a purely subjective standard of good faith or a mixed subjective and objective standard is not usually of concern. Both parties to a requirements or output contract are typically merchants, so under both the current and revised Articles 1 and 2, the mixed subjective-objective standard will apply.

Defining good faith in general terms is all very well, but applying that definition to particular conduct to decide if it is honestly motivated and commercially reasonable is much more difficult and involves an evaluation of all the circumstances. Clearly, the very fact that the parties have made a requirements or output contract means that they must contemplate that the buyer or seller is not bound to fixed quantities, and that it may make a decision that significantly changes its requirements or output. The crucial question is therefore to determine if that decision was made in good faith. *Empire Gas Corp. v. American Bakeries Co.*, 840 F.2d 1333 (7th Cir. 1988) is one of the leading cases on this issue. The court said that it would clearly not be good faith for a buyer to reduce its requirements by buying the goods from another seller, or to reduce orders simply because it has second thoughts about the contract or because the contract is not as advantageous as it had hoped. However, a buyer may be in good faith in reducing its requirements for legitimate and compelling business reasons, such as technological advances that change fundamental needs or dramatic changes in market demand for the buyer's products.

b. The Disproportionality Standard

In addition to the good faith test, §2.306 sets out a test of proportionality. It states that if the parties' expectations of quantity are based on a stated **estimate** or a **normal or otherwise comparable prior** output or requirement, the quantity tendered or demanded cannot be **unreasonably disproportionate** to what has been estimated or customary. Stated simply, this provision means that quite apart from the good faith standard, the terms of the contract or the parties' course of dealings or performance could place a limit on what may be demanded in a requirements contract, or tendered in an output contract. Obviously, because the whole purpose of the contract is not to tie the parties to a specified quantity, an estimate stated in the contract or a prior course of dealing between the parties cannot be intended to bind the parties to a fixed quantity. However, it does set a level of expectation about the approximate quantity to be supplied. Therefore, if the contract states an estimated level of requirement or output, or if prior dealings establish an expectation of what that level will be, the actual requirements demanded or output supplied under the contract cannot be disproportionate to what was expected. For example, if a requirements contract states that the buyer estimates needing 10 tons of steel, it may not be a disproportionate demand for the buyer to order 10.5 or 11 tons, but an order of 20 tons is surely disproportionate. Disproportion is not measured by any fixed formula or percentage. Rather, it is a question of fact, based on the reasonable expectations of the parties, to be decided under all the circumstances of the case.

There is an important limitation to the disproportionality standard. Courts have generally interpreted the language of §2.306 as confining the disproportionality test to **increases** in demand or output, and **not to decreases**. Therefore, if the buyer's requirements or seller's output is less than the estimated or customary level, only the good faith test applies. The *Empire Gas* case, above, is one of the cases that so held. See also, for example, *Wiseco, Inc. v. Johnson Controls, Inc.* 155 Fed. Appx. 815 (6th Cir. 2005). The buyer in Wiseco was a supplier of headrest stays to Daimler-Chrysler for use in Jeeps. It entered into a requirements contract with the seller to supply some of the components to be used in the headrests. The buyer's orders for the parts dropped dramatically when Jeep changed the headrest design, making the particular components supplied under the requirements contract inappropriate. The court adopted the interpretation that the disproportionality test did not cover reductions in demand. It applied the good faith test, and concluded that the buyer had legitimate business reasons for its reduced requirements. It no longer needed the parts because its customer had changed the design of the headrest. The seller bore the burden of proving that the buyer's reduction in requirements was in bad faith, and it had not sustained that burden.

§7.9.4 Conditional Promises

In the example in which Buster promised to pay for the skis if Elvis is returned by the aliens, the promise was illusory because it was conditional on an event that could not occur. However, a promise is not illusory merely because it is conditional. A qualified or conditional promise is good consideration provided that the contingency is genuine. That is, it is an uncertain future event within the realm of possibility and outside the complete and discretionary control of the promisor. If these requirements are satisfied, the conditional promise is a commitment. A legal detriment is suffered, even though the obligation to perform the promise only comes into effect upon fulfillment of the condition. For example, Al promises to give his skis to Buster tomorrow, and the parties agree that Buster need not pay for them unless he wins this week's state lottery, in which he has already bought a ticket. Buster promises that if he does win the lottery, he will pay Al $100 for the skis. Although Al's promise is absolute, and he must deliver the skis as promised, Buster's return promise is conditional. If he wins, he must pay. If not, he gets the skis free. The contingent nature of his promise does not prevent it from being consideration, because he suffers the **detriment** of **binding himself** to pay on the happening of an **uncertain future event outside his control**. This is a real contingency (unlike the return of Elvis) and it is not within Buster's unbridled discretion.

A type of conditional promise that appears to involve very wide discretion is a **condition of satisfaction**. This is a condition that allows one of the parties to reject a performance by the other (and to refuse to perform his own undertaking) if he is not satisfied with it.[21] For example, on February 1, Al and Buster enter an agreement under which Al sells his skis to Buster for $100. The agreement provides that Al will deliver the skis to Buster on February 15 and Buster will pay for them in installments of $10 per month for ten months, beginning on March 1. The agreement authorizes Al to examine Buster's credit record and to cancel the contract by February 14 if the credit report is not satisfactory to him. Such a condition might appear to render Al's promise illusory because he could simply negate his promise to sell the skis by declaring himself dissatisfied with Buster's credit record. However, unless the only plausible interpretation of the agreement is that the parties intended to give unrestrained discretion to the party making the judgment of satisfaction, a court will imply a term that limits the discretion enough to avoid the problem of illusory promise. Therefore, even if the contract does not expressly say so, the party who determines satisfaction is obliged to exercise his judgment either in good faith or reasonably.

To decide whether to apply the subjective good faith standard or the objective reasonableness standard, the court looks at all the circumstances of the transaction. The rule of thumb is that dissatisfaction must be in **good faith** where the performance involves a matter of personal taste, but it must be **reasonable** where the performance is of a technical, mechanical, or commercial nature. Stated differently, a court may conclude that the parties contemplated good faith subjective judgment where the performance involves a matter of personal taste. However, the party whose performance is to be judged would not reasonably expect such an idiosyncratic standard

---

21. Conditions of satisfaction are discussed further in section 16.8.2.

to be applied to a commercial or technical performance. (Of course, parties who want to avoid the uncertainty of allowing the court to decide on the proper standard can simply express in the contract which standard is to be used.)

The evaluation of a person's creditworthiness is a matter of commercial judgment, which means that an objective approach would usually be more appropriate. However, the particular circumstances of this case, involving a consumer-to-consumer sale and a creditor who is not in the business of extending credit, may call for a more subjective test based on good faith satisfaction. Whatever test is used, the point for present purposes is that the implication of a standard to control Al's judgment prevents his promise from being illusory.

§7.9.5 Promises of Alternative Performances

A form of discretionary promise is one involving alternative performances. For example, Al promises to sell his skis to Buster in exchange for Buster's promise, in his discretion, to pay $100 or to mow Al's lawn for two months. Provided that each of the promise, on its own, would be consideration, there is nothing objectionable in permitting a party to select between alternative promises.

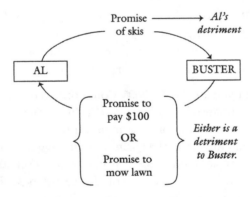

The case is more difficult if *one of the alternatives* imposes so small a burden on the party who has the choice that it *would not likely have induced the promise on its own*. For example, Buster may make the alternative promises either to buy the skis for $100 or to give Al notice of cancellation of the sale. The purpose of this is to give Buster the discretion to escape the contract if he so desires, and he is really no more firmly bound than if he promised to buy the skis if he feels like it. Although the obligation to give notice is a detriment, it is such a slight detriment that it would not on its own be likely to have induced Al to commit himself to sell the skis. Nevertheless, seen as a package with the more burdensome alternative, one can understand that the parties could have been satisfied with the commercial utility of this arrangement, and Al may have bargained for the chance that Buster would exercise his discretion in favor of completing the sale. By refusing to inquire into the adequacy of Buster's alternative detriment of giving notice, a court can uphold the transaction. This may seem like the exultation of form over substance when compared to the invalid purely discretionary promise, but the provision of notice gives the court a basis for validation, if it deems the agreement to have been fairly bargained for.[22]

Examples

1. Penny Less entered college two years ago at the age of 22. At the time, her Uncle Rich, concerned about reports of excessive drinking by college students, promised her that if she did not drink any alcoholic beverages in her first year of college, he would give her $5,000 at the end of that year. Penny thanked Uncle Rich, stating that it would be easy money because she hated the taste of alcohol.

   Penny did not consume any alcohol during her first year of college. When she reported this to Uncle Rich at the end of the year and asked for her reward, he said, "I have changed my mind about giving you the money. Don't be disappointed. Sobriety is its own reward." Was Uncle Rich free to change his mind?

2. Would your answer to Example 1 change if Penny was 19 years old at the time that she made her agreement with Uncle Rich? At that time she was old enough to be a major for the purposes of contracting but below the state's minimum drinking age of 21.

3. In January 2005, Dotty Com borrowed $500,000 from Angel Investor to finance her new startup business. The loan bore 8.5 percent interest and was due for repayment on June 1, 2006. In late May 2006 Dotty told Angel that the business was struggling and she did not have the cash to repay the loan. She believed, however, that if her creditors would give her a break she could save the business, but if they refused to cooperate, she would have to liquidate it. Because the business was presently insolvent, creditors would receive only about 50 percent of their claims on liquidation. Dotty asked Angel to accept 80 percent of the debt in full settlement, and to wait six months for payment. Dotty told Angel that she planned to ask all her other creditors for the same

---

22. For example, in *Johnson Lakes Development, Inc. v. Central Nebraska Pub. Power & Irrigation Dist.* 576 N.W.2d 806 (Neb. 1998) the court held that an obligation to give advance notice of termination was enough to prevent a party's promise from being illusory, provided that the party was irrevocably bound for an appreciable period of time or otherwise rendered some performance that would qualify as consideration.

concession. Angel agreed and the parties executed a written agreement reflecting that Dotty would pay Angel $400,000 in full settlement of the debt, with interest at 8.5 percent, by no later than December 1, 2006. Did Angel receive consideration for this agreement?

4. When Chevy K. Marro was 29 years old, his Aunt Charity expressed the intention of buying him a new car for his 30th birthday. Chevy knew that Aunt Charity always talked big but never did what she promised, so he suggested that if Charity really meant what she said, she would write out the promise and sign it. Charity agreed, and Chevy (known for his shrewd business sense) drew up the document. It stated that Charity, "in consideration for value received" from Chevy, undertook to deliver the car (which was specifically described by make, model, and year) to Chevy on his 30th birthday. Charity and Chevy signed the writing. True to form, Aunt Charity gave Chevy a sweater for his 30th birthday and did not deliver the car.

   (a) Is Aunt Charity obligated by her promise of the car?

   (b) Change the facts to the following extent: The writing stated that Charity undertook to deliver the car "in consideration for Chevy's calculator watch, which he acquired as a reward for subscribing to *Fortune* magazine. The parties record that Chevy delivered the watch to Charity upon signing this agreement." Chevy did in fact deliver the watch to Charity. Is she obligated by her promise of the car?

   (c) When Chevy threatened to sue her for the car, Aunt Charity became very annoyed. She would like to take back the sweater on the basis that Chevy gave her no consideration for it. Does she have the right to reclaim it?

5. Hunter Fortune used to work as a gardener on the country estate of Buck Plentiful, a billionaire. After Hunter was discharged by the grounds-keeper for incompetence, he sued Buck for $1 million, alleging that he was sexually harassed and emotionally abused by the groundskeeper while in Buck's employ. Buck believed that the claim was without substance but did not want any scandal in his household, so he offered to settle the claim out of court for $10,000. Hunter accepted, and a settlement agreement was executed. After the agreement, Buck had second thoughts and refused to pay Hunter. Does Hunter have a valid claim arising from the agreement?

6. Ivor E. Keyes is a gifted pianist. On hearing him play, his beloved Aunt Charity determined to do something to help him advance his career. Ivor told her that he needed to get some training from a really fine pianist to improve his interpretation and style. He had contacted the celebrated Maestro Molto Bravissimo but had not engaged him as a teacher because he could not afford his fee of $150 an hour. Aunt

Charity declared: "You shall have him as your teacher. I will send you a check for $15,000 tomorrow. That should cover 100 lessons." Ivor thanked her and said, "Auntie, if I ever make it to Carnegie Hall, I will get you the best seat in the house." She replied, "Yes, that will be nice, dear. I'll hold you to it." Do Ivor and Aunt Charity have a contract?

7. Save Our Slugs (SOS) is a citizens' organization formed to advance the interests of common garden slugs and to lobby for legislation to prevent assault on their natural habitat. One evening an articulate and persuasive fund raiser for the organization called on E. Z. Tutch to solicit a contribution. The fund raiser's impassioned and heart-rending plea for support convinced E. Z. Tutch that the poor creatures were under siege, and that urgent action was needed to save them from extinction. He therefore signed the following pledge card:

In consideration of my love for my ancient and venerable mother, the earth, and all her little creatures,

And in consideration for the promise of SOS to use my contribution in its tireless struggle to advance the noble cause for which it was constituted,

And in consideration of others subscribing with me to support this worthy endeavor,

E. Z. Tutch *hereby pledges the sum of* $ 500 00/100 *to SOS, payable in* 10 *equal monthly installments, beginning on* Dec 1, 1997

Signed: E.Z-Tutch

Date: Nov. 30, 1997

The next day, E. Z. Tutch realized that he had been overcome by his emotions the prior evening and had acted thoughtlessly. He has had many large expenses lately and really cannot afford the amount pledged.

He regrets his decision to make the pledge and wishes to cancel it. May he do so without incurring legal liability?

8. Gutter Press, Inc. is a publisher of paperback books. Bonzo Steele, a famous bodybuilder and action-movie hero, was recently indicted for the gruesome murder of his agent, and the case has attracted enthusiastic public attention. Gutter Press plans to publish a book on Bonzo's seamy past and his present predicament. It wishes to produce the book as quickly as possible so that it hits the stands at supermarket checkouts before the inevitable lapse of the public attention span.

   Gutter Press engaged Tabb Lloyd, a journalist, to write the book. The parties signed a written agreement which included the following terms:
   (a) Tabb promised to submit a completed manuscript within four weeks.
   (b) Gutter Press promised to publish the manuscript provided that it found it to be satisfactory.
   (c) If the manuscript was published, Gutter Press would pay Tabb a royalty of 15 percent of gross receipts.
   (d) During the first week following execution of the agreement, Gutter Press had the right, for any reason, to cancel it by delivering written notice of termination to Tabb. After the first week, Gutter Press could cancel at any time before completion of the manuscript by delivering the notice to Tabb and paying him a fee of $1,000 for all work done up to that time.

   The day after signing the agreement, Tabb told his friends about it. They were disgusted and accused him of selling out and perverting his art for the sake of a quick and dirty buck. This so shamed Tabb that he no longer wishes to write the book. Can he escape his commitment to Gutter Press?

9. Constance De Votion decided to retire after working for the Turn Coat Corporation for 40 years. On her last day of work, the president of the company called her into his office and presented her with the following letter, signed by all the members of the Board of Directors:

   > In recognition of your long and faithful service to this company, we are honored to give you an all-expenses-paid, two-week vacation at the hotel of your choice anywhere on the North American continent. When you have decided on your destination, please call the company's travel agent to make the arrangements. We hope that this vacation will be a joyful beginning to your richly-deserved retirement.

   Constance spent a happy couple of weeks planning her vacation and settled on a lavish coastal resort. When she called the travel agent, he denied any knowledge of this arrangement and said that he had not been authorized by Turn Coat to book a trip for her. Constance called the president of Turn Coat, who told her with obvious discomfort that, a few days after she left, the Board had to meet in emergency session to approve drastic cutbacks because of a downturn in profits. One of the savings approved was the withdrawal of its promise to her.

Can Constance hold Turn Coat to its promise?

10. Gerry Atrick, another employee of the Turn Coat Corporation, had worked for it for 35 years. Although he used to be a superb worker, he had recently become absentminded and slow. His work was incompetent and had to be redone by others. Gerry was an employee at will, which meant that he could be summarily dismissed. The president was going to fire him, but the president's secretary dissuaded her from doing so by pointing out that the dismissal of such an old and loyal employee would be cruel and would upset and demoralize his co-workers. The president therefore offered Gerry a year's pay if he would retire. Gerry accepted and submitted his resignation. That night, as the president was thinking about the events of her day, she suddenly realized that she did not really care if the staff was upset and she would now have to justify this decision to the tightfisted Board. The next day, she called Gerry into her office, revoked the promise, and dismissed him. Is Turn Coat's promise binding?

11. Peters Pickled Peppers manufactures pickled peppers. Last fall it made an agreement with Hal Apeno, a farmer, under which Hal undertook to supply all the peppers it would need for its bottling operations next season. During negotiations preceding the agreement, Peters told Hal that its average needs in the last five years had been between seven and ten tons of peppers. Hal was satisfied that he could grow sufficient quantities to meet this range of demand. This range of expected requirements was recorded as an estimate in the written contract.

A short time later, Peters' Board met to discuss disappointing sales in the prior year. Studies showed that new and aggressive competitors had gained the lion's share of the pickled pepper market, and all indications were that next year would be even worse. The Board decided to switch from peppers to persimmons, for which there was very little competition. Peters' existing plant was suitable for the processing of persimmons, so the conversion could be achieved at small cost.

Because of this decision, Peters had no need for peppers, and it wrote to Hal telling him so. Hal sued Peters for breach of contract and Peters defended the suit on the basis that it had the right under the contract to order no pickles if it had no requirements. The trial court granted summary judgment to Peters on the theory that there was no contract because the transaction lacks mutuality of obligation. Is the judge right?

Explanations

1. This example pays homage to those great Victorian cases in which a well-to-do family member promises some reward for specified behavior. The facts here are inspired by *Hamer v. Sidway*, discussed in section 7.3.1. Like Willie, the nephew in *Hamer*, Penny's detriment is not "detrimental" in the usual sense because it is really in her best interests. In fact (apparently unlike Willie) she does not even "suffer" in the usual sense because she has no desire to engage in the activity. Notwithstanding, she suffers a legal detriment simply by forgoing something that she is entitled to do. She exchanges this for Uncle Rich's promise of payment, providing him with a non-economic but identifiable benefit.

    Because the benefit to Uncle Rich has no commercial purpose and is apparently motivated by his concern for Penny's well-being, one may be tempted to see his promise as the promise of a conditional gift. However, Penny's promise is not related to the manner in which the gift is to be used nor is it a means of taking delivery of the gift. Even a non-commercial promise may be bargained for if it reasonably appears intended to induce particular action desired by the promisor.

    Another factor that may make Uncle Rich's promise appear to be a conditional gift is that it is hard to imagine that he could sue Penny to enforce her obligation not to drink. However, this can be explained if we recognize that Uncle Rich's offer proposed a unilateral contract, in which Penny gave no undertaking but accepted Uncle Rich's offer by rendering the performance, which was not complete until the end of the semester.[23]

2. As Penny's state of residence prohibits consumption of alcohol by people under the age of 21, she does not have a legal right to drink, so her forbearance is not the relinquishment of a legal right and hence no legal detriment. (The law distinguishes the power to do something from the legal right to do it.) Stated alternatively, she had a pre-existing legal duty to the state not to drink.[24]

    However, the pre-existing duty rule should not be applied here. The rule is best confined to cases in which the duty is owed to the

---

23. The acceptance of an offer for a unilateral contract is explained in section 4.12. In short, if Uncle Rich's offer could be accepted only by the completion of Penny's performance (forbearing from drinking for the entire semester), no contract comes into existence until completion of Penny's performance. Once the performance is complete, a unilateral contract arises in which only Uncle Rich's obligation remains outstanding. If Penny does not perform, she never accepts the offer, and Uncle Rich has no contractual right to enforce. To protect Penny from having the offer revoked after she has begun her performance in reliance on it, the law deems the offer irrevocable as soon as Penny begins her performance.
24. This issue did not come up in the *Hamer* case.

promisor. When the duty is owed to society or to a third party, the principal rationale of the rule — protection from coerced modification — is not implicated. Therefore, unless there is some other justification for it, the rule should not be used to invalidate Uncle Rich's voluntary promise. It could be argued that a public duty should be obeyed of its own force, and a promise given as an incentive to obedience should not be enforced as a matter of public policy. This is justified when the promise is made to a public official as an incentive to the performance of his or her duty, because this leads to danger of corruption or favoritism. However, when the promise is merely an incentive to a private person to obey the law, the corruption problem is absent. Provided that the purpose of the contract is not extortionate (such as the payment of protection money to a mobster), there seems to be no public interest in refusing enforcement of the promise.

3.   The principal focus of this example is the pre-existing duty rule and its application in contract modification. This is just a first look at modification, which is dealt with again in section 13.9.

    The general rule is that a creditor's promise to accept less than the amount owing on an admitted debt or to extend the due date of the debt is not binding, because the debtor incurs no legal detriment in exchange for that promise. (*See* Restatement Second §73.) The debtor had a pre-existing duty to pay the debt now, and his promise to pay it over time adds nothing to that duty.[25] As noted in sections 7.5.2 and 7.5.4, if the agreement to reduce and extend the debt was fairly bargained, it is hard to justify the policy of invalidating the agreement under the pre-existing duty rule. However, a strict application of doctrine will invalidate it unless the court can find that Dotty incurred some new detriment in exchange for Angel's promise to reduce and extend the debt.

    It is not easy to find any new detriment on Dotty's part. Her undertaking to pay interest at 8.5 percent is not a new detriment because she was already obliged to pay interest at that rate under the original contract. Dotty's statement that she intended to approach other creditors with the same proposal could be a detriment if she made a promise to do that. However, as described in the facts, this seems more a statement of intent than a commitment. Finally, a promise not to liquidate a business could be consideration provided that the business is truly in financial trouble and Dotty had the legal right to liquidate it. The liquidation must be a legitimate solution to the financial problems, and not suggested in bad faith as a form of

---

25. Had the debt been disputed, an agreement to compromise the dispute would likely be supported by consideration, as discussed in section 7.5.4 and Example 5.

blackmail. However, again, Dotty's vague reference to the possibility of liquidation does not seem to rise to the level of a promise.

The common law recognizes a narrow exception to the requirement that a modification must be supported by consideration: It dispenses with the need for consideration if the modification is in response to unforeseen difficulties that have imposed an unexpected burden on the promisee. However, financial adversity is usually not unforeseen in a new business venture unless Dotty can establish some significant and unexpected external cause for the difficulty.

4(a). Chevy has given no consideration to Aunt Charity for her promise, which is clearly intended as a gift, not an exchange. The parties have attempted to validate the transaction by reciting that an unspecified consideration has been given. Restatement Second §71, comment b, regards such a false recital as ineffective. Some courts may be more sympathetic to this kind of effort at satisfying the formal function of consideration, but other courts will only uphold a formal recitation of consideration if a promise to furnish the recited consideration can be implied (which cannot be done when the recital does not specify what the purported consideration is), or the promisee's reliance on the promise creates grounds for estopping the promisor from denying the receipt of consideration.

This example is inspired by *Dougherty v. Salt*, 227 N.Y. 200 (1919), in which an aunt gave a promissory note for $3,000 to her eight-year-old nephew at the suggestion of the nephew's mother. The note was on a printed form that stated that it was given "for value received." Despite this language, it was clear that no consideration had been given for the note. The court refused to enforce it merely on the basis of the false recital.

4(b). There is obviously a huge disparity in value between a new car and a cheap giveaway watch. However, the watch could qualify as consideration if the court adopts the approach of refusing to enquire into the adequacy of consideration. The court applied this principle in *Harris v. Time, Inc.* 191 Cal. App. 3d 449 (1987). Recall that this case was discussed in Explanation 8(a) in relation to the question of whether an advertisement could constitute an offer. The court decided that Time did make an offer by stating on the mailer envelope that it would give the recipient a calculator watch "just for opening this envelope." In addition to the offer and acceptance issue, the court considered whether the recipient of the mailer had given consideration for the promise of the calculator watch. Time argued that the mere act of opening an envelope was too slight and valueless to constitute a bargained-for detriment. The court disagreed — Time obviously attached some value to enticing the recipient to open the envelope and, in any event, the court would not enquire into the adequacy of consideration.

If we assume that the calculator watch in *Harris* was a cheap trinket, the disparity between the value of the detriment of opening an envelope and the value of a promise of the watch may not be that great. By contrast, the value difference between the watch and the new car is monumental. In the absence of evidence that Aunt Charity had some special reason for craving the watch, we have to assume that it was exchanged simply as a formality, in an attempt to validate her promise of a gift. Some courts respect the parties' use of this formal device and decline to enquire into the adequacy of the exchange. Others refuse to employ the rule against measuring the adequacy of consideration where the consideration is so slight as to be nominal.

4(c). The gift of the sweater has already been given, and there is no longer a promise to be enforced. Although the absence of consideration precludes enforcement of a promise, it is not grounds for recovering an executed gift. (We need not concern ourselves with any grounds outside of contract law for reclaiming a gift.)

5. Unlike the agreement between Dotty and Angel in Example 3, this settlement agreement compromises a claim disputed on the merits and unliquidated in amount.[26] An agreement to settle a disputed claim is supported by consideration because each party forbears from persisting in the full claim and defense. However, as discussed in section 7.5.4, for consideration to exist the dispute must be genuine. A person has no legal right to assert a bogus claim or defense, so forbearing from that right is not a legal detriment. This technical explanation accords with a more compelling public policy concern: A person should not be allowed to assert a vexatious claim or defense and then to argue that he gave consideration by settling it. Restatement, Second §74 applies an alternative objective or subjective test to decide if a dispute is genuine. Either the claim or defense must be reasonably tenable because of uncertainty in law or fact, or the party asserting it must have a good faith belief in its merits. Some courts require both these standards to be met, and some focus only on subjective good faith.

The Example is deliberately ambiguous on Hunter's claim. The claim appears to be based on alleged sexual harassment, the intentional infliction of emotional distress, and possibly wrongful

---

26. A claim is unliquidated where its amount is uncertain and cannot be determined by simple arithmetic means. The only way that the amount of Hunter's damages can be determined is by a trial.

discharge. If the wrongful acts were committed by Buck's agent, he could be liable for damages. There is, doubtless, a plausible basis in law to make the claim for damages. The crucial question is whether there is a genuine dispute on the facts. If Hunter was in fact discharged for incompetence and his claim is fabricated for revenge or to extort a nuisance payment from his wealthy ex-employer, his forbearance from asserting this bogus claim cannot furnish consideration for the settlement on either a good faith or a reasonableness test.

6.   Aunt Charity clearly has suffered a detriment in promising to pay $15,000 to Ivor. However, this is nothing more than a gratuitous promise, like her promise to Chevy in Example 4, unless Ivor has given consideration in exchange for it. The only undertaking that could conceivably qualify as consideration is his assertion that he will get her the best seat in the house if he ever makes it to Carnegie Hall. (His implicit undertaking to use the money for piano instruction is merely a condition of the gift and cannot qualify as consideration.)

    It is not clear that this really is a serious promise at all. The context in which it was made and its tone suggest that it may have been nothing more than an expression of gratitude and hope for spectacular success. Even if it is a real promise, it has several problems. First, it is very vague. It does not make it clear what is meant by the "best seat," nor does it specify the concert or concerts for which it will be obtained. Second, it is contingent on a very uncertain future event. A conditional promise could qualify as consideration provided that the fulfillment of the condition is not entirely at the will of the promisor, and the contingency is not so remote as to make it unlikely that the event would occur. (A promise subject to such a remote contingency would be nothing more than a sham.) Third, unless Ivor can be interpreted to have promised a large number of free concerts, the value of his apparent consideration is disproportionately small in relation to Aunt Charity's promise. (It is worth even less than the face amount of a ticket because its value must be discounted to take account of the uncertainty of the condition occurring.) Courts normally do not evaluate the adequacy of consideration, and a court may decline to do so in this case. However, sometimes (especially when there are other indications of gratuitous intent) a court could take a significant discrepancy in values into account, and may find that the transaction is really not an exchange but a gift formalized by a nominal return.

    Finally, even if Ivor did make a promise and Aunt Charity accepted it by her response, it does not seem that his promise was in exchange for Aunt Charity's promise. He made it after she had already told him she would give him $15,000, so it cannot be said to have induced her promise.

The basis for holding that Ivor gave consideration for Aunt Charity's promise is therefore quite thin, and the transaction really seems to be nothing more than a promise of a gift. An argument for consideration is not inconceivable, but it is shaky.

7. The pledge recites three forms of purported consideration, but none of them likely qualifies as consideration.

First, E. Z. Tutch's love of nature may have motivated him to make the pledge (and even this is suspect, given that it is a standard recitation on the pledge form), but motive must be distinguished from consideration that must consist of a legal detriment suffered by SOS in exchange for his promise.

Second, even if the commitment by SOS is a promise, given in exchange for E.Z. Tutch's promise to donate money, SOS's promise may not qualify as a detriment to it. To suffer a detriment, SOS must have had the legal right not to use the funds for the promised purpose. However, at the time of making the promise, and until E.Z. Tutch actually gives the funds to SOS, it has no legal right to use them at all. Therefore, its undertaking to use them for the purpose specified by E.Z. Tutch seems more in the nature of an undertaking to use a gift for the purpose designated by the donor. As noted in section 7.3.5, it can be very tricky to distinguish a promise that is a legal detriment from one that is merely a condition of gift. A court may underplay this distinction so that it can validate a charitable promise. The task of finding consideration for a rather obvious gift is made easier if the donee makes a commitment that extends even slightly beyond the mere promise to use the gift as specified. That small additional detriment could qualify as consideration, even if it is implausible that it really induced the promise. In this case, no such additional detriment is apparent.

Third, the fact that others have subscribed or will do so is not consideration because the legal detriment is suffered by those parties and not by SOS. SOS may have provided consideration by promising to seek other subscribers, but no such promise is expressed or implied. Similarly, if a group of donors get together and all pledge to make a donation to an organization, the multilateral commitment of the donors could be sufficient to constitute consideration even if the organization has itself suffered no detriment. However, this did not happen here. The pledge form merely refers to other subscribers.

It would be a stretch to find that SOS gave consideration for E.Z. Tutch's pledge. If the pledge is not supported by consideration, he can cancel it without liability. Consideration doctrine has fulfilled its cautionary function by enabling the donor to escape his generous impulse and allocate his income to the payment of his creditors.

8.   Gutter Press and Tabb have exchanged promises. The issue is whether Gutter Press's discretion to escape its commitment to publish the book and to pay royalties is so wide as to make its promise illusory. The agreement gives Gutter Press two grounds for escaping its commitment. First, it can refuse to publish the manuscript if it finds it unsatisfactory. Second, it has the absolute right to terminate the agreement by giving notice in the first week, and thereafter by giving notice and paying Buck $1,000.

The condition of satisfaction. Conditions of satisfaction were explained in section 7.9.4. Unless the contract made it clear that Gutter Press would have unbridled discretion to be dissatisfied (which it does not) the satisfaction clause obliges Gutter Press to exercise its discretion either in good faith or reasonably. Even if this commitment is not expressed in the agreement, it is readily implied. If the agreement does not specify the standard (as this agreement does not), the court determines whether it is subjective or objective. The rule of thumb is that a subjective standard is used if the purpose of the contract is to serve the party's personal taste, but an objective test is used if the satisfaction clause relates to matters of technical or commercial utility. Subjective satisfaction might be appropriate if Tabb's contract was with an individual who planned to use the manuscript for his personal enjoyment. However, this is a commercial venture, and Tabb surely would not reasonably expect that the publisher could reject the manuscript on the basis for purely subjective reasons. The proper enquiry is whether a reasonable publisher would find the book up to standard and capable of gainful exploitation. Undoubtedly, the writing of literature is not a purely technical matter, so some element of taste must come in to the evaluation, but the focus is on generally acceptable standards in the trade, rather than the idiosyncratic tastes of this publisher. Of course, the question of whether to imply an objective or subjective standard would become important if Gutter Press had rejected the manuscript and we had to decide if it was justified in doing so. However, at this stage, we are concerned only with the question of whether the satisfaction clause gives it such wide discretion as to make its promise illusory. The implication of either a good faith or a reasonableness standard cures that problem.

The termination provisions. An unfettered termination right removes all commitment and makes the promise illusory. However, if Gutter Press undertakes to incur any detriment in terminating, consideration is present. The agreement may be viewed as giving Gutter Press the right to choose between alternative performances, and as long as each one would be consideration on its own, this right to select between alternatives does not negate consideration.

Is each consideration on its own? There can be little doubt that the promise to publish and pay royalties and the promise to pay $1,000 are detriments. The termination on notice in the first week may seem to be an unbridled right to escape the contract, but courts usually uphold agreements subject to such termination provisions provided that notice of termination must be given. The provision of notice is essential and the right to terminate without notice makes the promise illusory. (Even where there is no express requirement of notice, a court may have the basis to imply a promise of reasonable notice if the implication is consistent with the express language of the agreement and supported by the context in which the agreement was made.) The giving of the notice is regarded as a detriment because it is a new duty assumed under the agreement. This may sound a little flimsy and Tabb surely would not have bargained for this as the exclusive consideration for his promise. However, courts are disinclined to inquire into adequacy of consideration unless it clearly appears to be sham or there is some indication that the disparity resulted from deceit or coercion.

In this contract, only Gutter Press has the right to terminate and Tabb has no equivalent right. As a general rule, this does not cause a consideration problem because the parties' obligations do not have to be coextensive. "Mutuality" in that sense is not required, and as long as each party has given consideration in some form, it does not matter that one of them has greater rights under the contract.

In short, neither the satisfaction clause nor the termination provisions should invalidate the contract and Tabb cannot escape his commitment to Gutter Press.

9. The relationship between Constance and Turn Coat is commercial, and Turn Coat's promise is in recognition of valuable work. However, Constance's services were rendered prior to the promise, and not in exchange for it. Her work preceding the promise is "past consideration," and she suffers no new detriment to support the promise.

Because Turn Coat has breached its faith to Constance, the court may make great effort to find some new detriment on her part, however slight, to validate the promise. However, this would be a real strain on the present facts. Her assent to call the agent is some detriment, but it is obviously a condition of receiving the gift rather than bargained for as the price of the promise. If Constance had taken any action in reliance on the promise, the doctrine of promissory estoppel could afford a remedy, as discussed in Chapter 8, but no such action is suggested here. (In *Feinberg v. Pfeiffer*, 322 S.W.2d 163

(Mo. 1959), the court found no consideration for the promise of a pension made by the employer after years of service. However, it did apply promissory estoppel to enforce the promise because the employee had relied on the promise to her detriment. This aspect of the case is discussed in Example 3 of Chapter 8.)

10. The fact that Turn Coat contemplated some benefit — worker morale — from the resignation is not in itself consideration. This is merely the motive for the promise. However, the fact that some benefit would be gained by the company does serve as evidence that the resignation was bargained for in exchange for the promise. The issue in this case is whether the resignation was a legal detriment to Gerry. If Turn Coat could fire him at will, it could be argued that Gerry gave up no legal right by retiring because he had no right to continued employment. However, he did have the right to stay on the job until dismissed. Although this is not a very valuable right, equivalence in consideration is not required, and his sacrifice of the right should be sufficient to support the promise. As noted already, there is a reasonable basis for finding that the company did bargain for the advantage of not having to exercise its power to dismiss him.

In *Katz v. Danny Dare, Inc.*, 610 S.W.2d 121 (Mo. 1980), a longstanding employee suffered a head injury in trying to stop a thief who had stolen money from his employer. The injury impaired his ability to work competently, and the president of the employer (who also happened to be the employee's brother-in-law) tried to persuade the employee to retire by offering him a pension. The employee eventually agreed and left the company with the Board's promise of a life pension. Like Gerry, the employee could have been dismissed at will. A dispute later developed over the employer's obligation to continue paying the pension. Contrary to the resolution that I suggest above, the court held that an employee-at-will gives up no legal right by retiring. This seems to be an unduly narrow view, especially given the obvious desire of the employer to avoid the embarrassment of firing an old employee, injured in the line of duty, and related to the president. Nevertheless, the case turned out satisfactorily, because the court found that the employee had relied on the promise, and it enforced the promise under the doctrine of promissory estoppel. Again, his aspect of the case is taken up in Example 3 of Chapter 8.

11. Shame on the judge for using that naughty phrase that has little meaning in modern law. What the court means, of course, is that it considers Peters' promise to be illusory because Peters has the discretion to have no requirements for peppers. In this too, the judge betrays a sadly old-fashioned state of mind. Many years ago, some courts did take this approach to requirements and output contracts,

but this view died out as it became accepted that contracts for flexible quantities have commercial utility and should not be found to lack consideration. Today, UCC §2.306 places this matter beyond doubt by limiting the discretion of the buyer in a requirements contract and the seller in an output contract. Peters' requirements must be its actual requirements as may occur in good faith. Furthermore, as there is a stated estimate, this sets the range of permissible variation. (Even had there not been an estimate, any normal or prior comparable requirements that Peters may have had would set the range.)

For §2.306 to apply, the contract must in fact be intended by the parties to be a requirements contract. If the buyer does not agree to buy its requirements only from the seller, leaving the buyer free to buy from other parties, there is no restriction on the buyer's discretion and its promise is illusory. That is, although §2.306(1) does not say so expressly, one of the hallmarks of a requirements contract is that the buyer must commit to fill those requirements exclusively from the seller. The description of the transaction in the facts does not indicate if Peters did make this commitment of exclusive dealing in the contract. However, even if it did not do so expressly, the intent to deal exclusively with Hal could be implied from the language of the contract and the context.

Assuming that a promise of exclusive dealing can be implied, the next question is whether Peters breached the requirements contract by deciding to eliminate its requirement for Peppers. The fact that an estimate has been made may suggest that this case can simply be resolved on the disproportionality test. However, most courts have said that the disproportionality test applies only to increases in demand and not to decreases.

Therefore, Peters' elimination of its requirements must be measured on the good faith standard. Because Peters deals in peppers and has knowledge and skill relating to them, it is a merchant under UCC §2.104 and is subject to the definition of good faith in UCC §2.103(1)(b).[27] It is held not only to actual honesty but must also observe standards of fair dealing in the trade. Is Peters' decision, based on a business judgment to discontinue production of pickled peppers, in good faith? Comment 2 to UCC §2.306[28] indicates that the good faith standard permits an honest discontinuance of requirements resulting from lack of demand. It draws a distinction between the justifiable shutdown of the buyer's plant for lack of orders, and an

---

27. As mentioned in section 7.9.3, under revised Article 1 and the 2003 revision of Article 2, the standard of both honesty and the observance of reasonable commercial standards of fair dealing will apply to everyone, not just merchants.
28. The comment is the same in the current and revised versions.

impermissible shutdown merely to curtail losses. This suggests that the good faith standard is not satisfied merely because Peters has made a sensible business judgment based on profitability. There must be hardship serious enough to overcome Peters' duty to honor Hal's reasonable expectations. This seems to be a matter of degree, and it is not clear from the facts whether the threat of competition is so severe as to necessitate the change in product line as a matter of survival.

Promissory Estoppel as the Basis for Enforcing Promises

§8.1 INTRODUCTION

As Chapter 7 shows, consideration is a prerequisite to a valid contract. A promise that has not been bargained for in exchange for some detriment cannot be enforced as a contract. Of course, as we have seen, consideration doctrine has a degree of flexibility that enables courts to stretch the concept of bargained-for exchange to accommodate some deserving cases. But this only works up to a point. Sometimes the facts are such that no manipulation of consideration doctrine could produce a realistic argument that consideration was given for a promise. In many cases the resulting nonenforcement of the promise is an appropriate consequence, but this result can be unfair when the promisee incurred some loss in relying justifiably on the promise. Promissory estoppel has developed to provide relief in such cases. When all its elements are satisfied, a promisor may be held accountable for a promise without consideration, and the court may enforce it either to the same extent as if a contract was made, or to the extent necessary to remedy the unfair result of reliance on it.

Promissory estoppel was first articulated as a distinct basis of liability in §90 of the First Restatement. The original formulation, with subtle revisions, survives in §90 of Restatement Second. Although the Restatement section does not itself call the doctrine promissory estoppel, this name is firmly established by long usage.

Several factors must be considered in deciding whether promissory estoppel relief is appropriate, as will be discussed shortly. However, its essential elements can be stated simply: A **promise** coupled with **detrimental reliance** on that promise. Although these two prerequisites do not always receive the same emphasis, a combination of them must be present for relief to be granted.

§8.2 THE NATURE OF PROMISSORY ESTOPPEL AS AN INDEPENDENT BASIS OF RELIEF OR AS A CONSIDERATION SUBSTITUTE

Although some writers argue that promissory estoppel is growing in importance and that it may one day eclipse consideration as the ground for contractual liability, it remains an *ancillary basis for relief*. If a promise is supported by consideration and there are no other problems disqualifying the promise as contractual, promissory estoppel is not needed. When analyzing a problem, it is therefore logical to first consider if a contract has been formed and to turn to promissory estoppel only if that question is answered negatively.

Because it allows for the enforcement of a promise without consideration, promissory estoppel is sometimes called a **substitute for consideration.** One must approach this phrase carefully, because there is disagreement among both courts and commentators over the categorization of promissory estoppel and its relationship to contract. This debate is partly philosophical, reflecting contrasting opinions on the way that the law should be conceived, and partly empirical, based on different interpretations of how the courts actually treat promissory estoppel. One's view of the nature of promissory estoppel can have significant practical consequences because it has an impact on the approach to relief, as discussed below, and could also affect questions such as the appropriate statute of limitations[1] or matters of procedure.

Those who argue that promissory estoppel is truly a consideration substitute take the view that if the elements of promissory estoppel are satisfied the promise must be treated as a contractual undertaking. That is, when consideration is lacking, promissory estoppel is an alternative basis for finding contractual liability. Comment d to Restatement, Second §90 indicates that the drafters favor this approach. The comment states that a promise binding under §90 is a contract.

---

1. Statutes of limitation specify the period within which a person must commence action on a claim. If suit is not brought within the specified period, it is barred. Different types of claim have different limitation periods. For example, in most states a suit on contract must be commenced within six years of the claim arising but the limitation period for tort is only two years. Therefore, if promissory estoppel is regarded as a contract-based doctrine, its limitation period should correspond to the longer period for contract, but if it is seen as derived from tort, the shorter period may apply.

The opposing view is that promissory estoppel does not result in enforcement of the promise as a contract but is an alternative and independent basis for enforcing the promises — a separate theory of obligation, based not on bargain but on accountability for conduct that induces reliance. This conception of promissory estoppel emphasizes its affinity to tort and sees it more as a redress for injury suffered in reliance than as a consensual relationship.

Probably the best approach is to recognize that the truth lies somewhere in the middle of these positions. The existence of a voluntary promise surely provides some link between promissory estoppel and contract. Yet, the need for demonstrated injurious reliance and the approach to relief makes promissory estoppel quite distinct from contract. It is therefore more coherent to conceive of promissory estoppel as a basis for relief related to contract, yet at the same time separate and distinct from contract.

§8.3 THE DIFFERENCE IN REMEDIAL EMPHASIS BETWEEN CONTRACT AND PROMISSORY ESTOPPEL

The way in which promissory estoppel is characterized — as a contract-based doctrine or an independent tort-like theory — has a bearing on the question of its most appropriate remedial goal. As discussed more fully in section 8.7, if promissory estoppel creates contractual liability, the normal relief for promissory estoppel should be the *full enforcement* of the promise, and it is only appropriate to limit relief under special circumstances. Conversely, if one focuses on the protection of reliance, the remedy should usually be confined to *reimbursement of actual xloss*, with fuller enforcement reserved for cases when justice so demands. This could make a substantial difference in recovery: Contract damages look toward the future and try to place the promisee in the position he or she would have been in had the contract been honored. They aim at giving the promisee the benefit of the bargain by awarding the money equivalent of what the promisee would have gained as a result of the contract. On the other hand, tort-like damages look toward the past and merely try to restore the status quo by reimbursement of expenses and losses.

§8.4 AN INTRODUCTION TO EQUITABLE ESTOPPEL AND ITS LINK TO PROMISSORY ESTOPPEL

As intimated above, the essential function of promissory estoppel is to provide relief for justifiable reliance on a promise given without consideration. Promissory estoppel, articulated in coherent form relatively recently, derives from the much older principle of **equitable estoppel**, also known as **estoppel in pais.** It is therefore helpful to understand the basic idea of equitable estoppel. Equity was introduced in section 2.5. Because a court of equity exercises its discretion to do justice between the parties, it is a general principle of equity that the litigants must themselves behave equitably in seeking the court's assistance. Relief that may otherwise be available is barred by the claimant's unworthy conduct.

Equitable estoppel reflects this principle. Its basic purpose is to **preclude** (i.e., "estop") a person from asserting a right when, by **deliberate words or conduct,** he or she has **misled** the other party into the justifiable belief that the right does not exist or would not be asserted. Like many equitable doctrines, estoppel involves a *balancing of the equities* between the parties and a comparative evaluation of the fault and responsibility of the parties. Therefore, it generally only bars relief when the party asserting the rights deliberately engaged in the misleading behavior with *knowledge or reason to know* it was misleading and would likely induce reliance by the other. In addition, the other, unaware of the true facts, must have *relied* on the misrepresentation in a way that would result in some *loss or prejudice* if the claimant is permitted to assert the right.

For example, Jack Black had just won $2,000 at cards, an activity that his wife, Prudence, firmly forbids. To conceal his ill-gotten gains, he hid the cash in an unused cookie jar. One day, while their niece, Penny Less, was visiting, she dipped her hand into the jar, thinking that it contained cookies. When, instead, she pulled out the wad of bills, Aunt Prudence's suspicious nature was aroused. She demanded to know of Uncle Jack where the money came from. Always a cool customer, Uncle Jack had little trouble coming up with a plausible story to get Aunt Prudence off his back: "Oh . . . well . . . Penny's dad sent the money to me as a surprise gift for Penny. I specially hid it in the jar because I knew that she would find it when she felt in the jar for cookies, which she always does." Although this explanation satisfied Aunt Prudence, it turned out not to have been a clever tactic because Penny scooped up the cash with a squeal of joy, exclaiming, "Now I can take that vacation that I dreamed of and couldn't afford!" Before Uncle Jack could take Penny aside to explain where the money really came from, she left and went directly to a travel agent, from whom she bought a non-refundable air and hotel excursion package. A short while later, Uncle Jack arrived in a breathless frenzy at Penny's door, told her the truth, and asked for the money back.

If Penny refuses to repay Uncle Jack and he is foolish enough to publicize his nefarious activity to Aunt Prudence by suing for it, he would likely be estopped from asserting that it was his own money. He deliberately misinformed Penny that it was hers. Upon realizing that she believed him, he did not reveal the truth to her before she had acted in reliance on his statement. She apparently had no reason to doubt the truth of what he said, and incurred an irreversible commitment on the strength of the belief that she was $2,000 richer. She cannot easily find the money to reimburse him. It does not matter that Uncle Jack made the statement without intent to cheat Penny. Estoppel is not based on fraud but on accountability for deliberate words or conduct that induce reliance and consequent injury. A person who is estopped from asserting a fact is treated as if that fact does not exist, so the falsehood becomes true in the eyes of the law.

This is a case of **equitable**, not promissory, **estoppel** because Uncle Jack made an incorrect **factual assertion** and not a promise. Indeed, estoppel was originally held not to be applicable to promises. During the nineteenth century (and possibly even before that) some courts began to recognize that reliance on a *promise* was just as worthy of protection as reliance on a factual assertion, and they began to apply equitable estoppel to promises. (The theory of these cases was that the promisor was *estopped from asserting a lack of consideration* for the promise, hence consideration was deemed to be present. Therefore the early cases did treat estoppel as a consideration substitute.) Not all courts followed this approach. Some refused relief despite reliance if consideration was absent, and others sought to protect reliance indirectly by bending over backwards to find consideration in the most tenuous of detriments.

By the time of the drafting of the First Restatement, there was enough caselaw to support the inclusion of a new doctrine that came to be called promissory estoppel. The Restatement's formulation (in §90) did not treat the promise as estopping the denial of consideration, but simply recognized **detrimental reliance** on the promise as a basis of enforcing it. Therefore, while the drafters of the Restatement did not necessarily conceive of promissory estoppel as a theory of liability separate from contract, they planted the seeds of this idea. Following publication of the Restatement, the judicial recognition of promissory estoppel grew, and the doctrine has become well-established, even though courts differ on its scope and range. Its formulation in Restatement Second §90 follows that of the original Restatement quite closely but makes changes to reflect its development over the intervening years.

§8.5 THE RANGE OF PROMISSORY ESTOPPEL: GIFTS AND COMMERCIAL TRANSACTIONS

When promissory estoppel first developed, it was primarily used to validate **gratuitous promises** such as family gifts and charitable donations. It was not thought to be applicable to promises made during the course of commercial interaction. It continues to have application to donative promises, but the tendency has been to expand it. Promissory estoppel is now commonly invoked as a basis for enforcing a commercial promise in appropriate circumstances. Of course, promissory estoppel has no role in most commercial transactions. No gift is intended and once agreement is reached, consideration is present. However, we have already seen that consideration problems do sometimes arise in the commercial setting, or other factors may prevent a promise from being enforceable as a contract.

There are at least three broad types of situation in which promissory estoppel may be applicable to a **commercial promise.** Although these situations technically involve a lack of consideration, the real reason for the absence of contractual liability is usually something else, and the real issue is whether it is appropriate to enforce the noncontractual promises.

1. A promise made for good consideration is not enforceable because of *noncompliance with legal formality* such as the statute of frauds. Promissory estoppel may permit the enforcement of the informal promise when fairness demands that the promisor not be allowed to escape liability. Discussion of this ground is deferred to section 11.4 where it is treated in conjunction with the statute of frauds. (Although it could technically be argued that consideration is absent here because an unenforceable informal promise is not a legal detriment, the real issue is whether a promise should be enforced despite the failure to comply with required formalities.)

2. Promissory estoppel may be used to hold a party to a *promise made during negotiations* for an abortive contract. When parties negotiate, they may make tentative commitments, not intended to bind unless and until final agreement is reached. Therefore, as a general rule, statements of intent made during negotiations are not treated as promises, and a party who incurs expense or relinquishes an opportunity on the strength of such a statement usually assumes the risk of loss if no contract comes about. Sometimes, however, a precontractual statement may reasonably be intended as a binding commitment, justifying reliance and attracting liability if not honored. The situations in which this might happen are discussed in section 8.9.

3. Promissory estoppel may afford relief for reliance on a promise that falls short of becoming contractual because of some *defect or omission in the agreement formed by the parties.* For example, there may be a fatal vagueness in the terms of the putative contract, or it may have an escape clause that negates commitment, yet there is enough of a commitment to justify reliance. One could say that this is also a consideration issue, and that the vague or discretionary promise is not consideration. However, the real issue is whether fairness demands accountability even in the absence of a binding contract.

In short, the role of promissory estoppel goes beyond the enforcement of gift promises and covers a variety of promises that do not qualify as contractual, either because they lack consideration or because of some other deficiency or missing element in the process of contract formation.

§8.6 THE ELEMENTS OF PROMISSORY ESTOPPEL

§8.6.1 Introduction and Overview of the Elements

Assume that Uncle Rich says to his niece, Penny Less, "If you enroll in college, I will pay your first year's tuition." On the strength of this promise, Penny enrolls in college, committing herself to the payment of tuition, but Uncle Rich fails to honor his promise to her. It is plausible to argue that the parties have entered into a contract. Penny's enrollment in college appears to have been bargained for in exchange for the promise and, as she had no legal obligation to enroll, this is a legal detriment. Penny could therefore seek enforcement of the promise as a contractual obligation. However, she may not succeed on that ground. As we have seen, in family transactions it is sometimes difficult to distinguish a bargained-for exchange from a gift given subject to conditions as to its use. A court could conclude that Uncle Rich merely promised a gift of money to be used for a specified purpose. On these facts, while Penny may ultimately be found not to have given consideration, she does at least have some basis for arguing that she did. However, in many family transactions, there is no basis at all for finding consideration. For example, if Uncle Rich simply promised to give Penny an unconditional gift of $20,000, and if she decided, on the strength of the promise, to enroll in college, she would have no grounds for asserting that Uncle Rich had bargained for anything in return.

Once consideration is lacking, the promise cannot be enforced as a contract, yet in both these examples Penny has relied on it by assuming a (no doubt horrendous) debt to the college. Promissory estoppel developed as a response to situations like this and affords relief to the promisee when the equities favor holding the promisor accountable for the promise.

The elements for promissory estoppel, set out in Restatement Second §90, center around the promise and detrimental reliance on it. In short, §90 calls for the following factors to be taken into account in deciding whether and to what extent a promise without consideration should be binding:

1. A **promise** was made by the promisor with the **reasonable expectation that the promisee would rely on it**. (This element focuses on the *promisor's conduct* and evaluates his *intent* objectively.)

2. The promise did in fact **induce** the promisee's **action or forbearance**. Although §90 does not say so expressly, this reliance must be **justified**. (This element focuses on the *promisee's reaction* and evaluates his reliance objectively.)
3. The **enforcement** of the promise is **necessary to avoid injustice**. (This element focuses on the *consequence* of reliance. Although §90 does not refer expressly to the **detriment** — that is, **harm or loss** — suffered by the promise as a result of reliance, this is a crucial factor.)
4. The **remedy** may be **limited as justice requires**. (This focuses on the *appropriate form of relief*. The nature and extent of the promisee's **detriment** is relevant here too.)

As this suggests, the decision to enforce a promise involves an evaluation of the conduct and reasonable understanding of each party and the fairness of holding the promisor accountable for a promise that would not otherwise be binding in contract law. While separate elements can be identified, their nature is such that they flow into and affect each other. Thus, for example, if the promise is clear and express, it is easier to infer intent to induce reliance and to justify reliance, and enforcement is more likely to be needed to avert injustice. Conversely, if there is doubt about the apparent promise, it is harder to show these other elements convincingly. We now survey each of the factors outlined above.

§8.6.2 A Promise Must Have Been Made

Section 1.2.3 introduced the meaning of promise and pointed out that not every assertion or statement of intent qualifies as a promise. Unless clear language of commitment is used, it can be difficult to decide if a promise has been made. Words and conduct must be interpreted in all the relevant circumstances of the case to determine if the alleged promisor *manifested an intent to commit* to a particular performance or course of action. *Norton v. McOsker,* 407 F.3d 501 (5th Cir. 2005) illustrates some of the issues that can arise in deciding if a promise was made. A woman had been involved in a 23-year adulterous relationship with a married man. When he ended the relationship, she sued him under various theories. Her promissory estoppel claim was based on the grounds that he had frequently promised during the relationship to divorce his wife and marry her, and also that, both during and at the end of the relationship, he had promised to support her for life. The court of appeals upheld the trial court's grant of summary judgment against the woman. Neither of the alleged undertakings established an enforceable promise. The man's promise to divorce his wife and marry the woman was void as against public policy. His undertaking of lifetime support was too general and nonspecific to qualify as an enforceable promise.

Note that it is manifested, rather than actual, intent that is determinative. As in contract, intent for the purpose of promissory estoppel is gauged by an *objective* test. The question is not what the promisor actually intended, but what the promisee was justified in understanding that intent to be, based on the promisor's utterances and conduct. This could not be otherwise because promissory estoppel aims to protect reliance that necessarily is based on a reasonable perception of exhibited intent rather than on the undisclosed thoughts and beliefs of the promisor. The objective evaluation of whether a promise was intended can sometimes trap a party into a promise that was never actually meant to be a commitment. In *East Providence Credit Union v. Geremia*, 239 A.2d 725 (R.I. 1968) the credit union financed a car purchase and took a security interest in the car to secure the debt. The credit agreement obliged the borrower to keep the car insured and provided that if he failed to do so, the credit union could pay the insurance premium and add the payment and interest to the balance of the loan. When the borrower failed to pay the insurance premium, the credit union notified him that it would exercise its right to pay it and add the cost of the insurance to the debt. The borrower did not respond to the notice. Notwithstanding its notice, the credit union did not pay the premium and the policy lapsed. The car was later stolen. The court found that the credit union's notice constituted a promise to pay the premium. The case was resolved on the basis of consideration doctrine because the court held that the borrower's undertaking to pay interest was consideration for the promise. As a result the credit union was liable for the loss of the car.[2] The court went on to discuss promissory estoppel in dictum as an alternative basis for enforcement and found that all its elements were satisfied, which would have permitted enforcement of the promise under this theory as well. The credit union surely did not think that it was making a promise when it provided in the contract for the right to pay the premium and when it sent the notice. The credit union's contractual right to pay the insurance premium was not for the borrower's benefit, but was designed to protect the credit union's interest in its collateral, and the notice was more in the nature of a threat than a promise.

The objective determination of intent in this context is subject to the same qualification that applies in deciding upon contractual intent — the promise must have been voluntarily and deliberately made. Therefore, as in contract, doctrines such as fraud, duress, and mistake (covered in Chapters 13 and 15) may be used to go behind the objective appearance of a promise. (In addition to affecting the quality of the promise, any improper conduct by the promisee would also, of course, impact his justifiable reliance.)

---

2. The value of the car was not actually paid to the borrower, but was used to offset the balance due to the credit union, thereby eliminating its claim against the borrower.

Also bear in mind the evidentiary, cautionary, and channelling functions served by consideration doctrine. The fact that consideration was not given for the promise means that these functions are not fulfilled by any act of exchange. Therefore, a court must exercise particular care before finding a promise when there is little or no formality in its execution or the circumstances suggest that the promisor may have acted on impulse or with rash generosity.

§8.6.3 The Promisor Should Reasonably Have Expected the Promise to Induce Action or Forbearance by the Promisee

This element is so closely connected to the inquiry into promise that it is a little artificial to treat it separately. However, it is helpful to split the evaluation of promisor accountability into two issues for the purpose of building a framework for analysis. Because the promisor is accountable only for a deliberate and voluntary promise, one must go beyond simply interpreting the meaning of the manifestation and must also evaluate the promisor's *justifiable understanding* of the likely impact of the promise. The circumstances must be such as to warrant holding the promisor accountable for creating the situation leading to reliance and the resulting loss.

This means that the promisor knew or reasonably should have realized that the promisee would likely understand that a promise had been made and would thereby be induced to take or refrain from action of the kind that occurred. (Thus, not only the likelihood of reliance but also the general nature and extent of the response must have been reasonably foreseeable by the promisor.) Again, an objective standard is used, so the promisor is held to a standard of reasonableness, whether or not he actually intended the promise to be relied on.

§8.6.4 The Promise Must Have Induced Justifiable Action or Forbearance by the Promisee

We now move from the promisor's accountability to the promisee's reliance. In dealing with inducement, the text of §90 does not expressly require the reliance to be justifiable, but this principle is referred to in the comments and is inherent in the purpose of promissory estoppel. To decide if the promisee justifiably relied on the promise, we must ask two questions. First, we must ask if the promise did in fact **induce** the promisee's action or forbearance. There must have been a cause and effect between the promise and the conduct, so there is no inducement if the promisee would have incurred the loss or expense even had the promise not been made, or incurred it before the promise was made.

Second, even if the promise did induce the promisee's conduct, he should not be given relief unless his particular response was a **justifiable** reaction to the promise. Justification is evaluated under a largely objective standard with some subjective aspects. It allows weight to be given to the personal attributes and situation of the promisee. The essential question is whether a reasonable person in the promisee's position would have so acted or refrained from acting as a result of the promise. Because the promissor's liability under promissory estoppel is based on a noncontractual promise, the justifiability standard is an essential safeguard. It protects the promisor from being held accountable for consequences caused by a promisee's reaction that could not have been anticipated fairly because it was rash, quirky, or unreasonable. If the promisee behaves in this way, he should bear the risk of having made the judgment to incur loss or expense in the absence of a contract.

As you can see, the inquiry into the nature and strength of the promise, the promisor's reasonable expectation of reliance on it, and the promisee's justification in relying on it tend to meld together. They are frequently just different aspects of the same overall pattern: The stronger the sense of commitment, the greater the likelihood of a reasonable expectation of inducement and, consequently, of justifiable reliance. For example, in the *Norton* case, discussed in section 8.6.2, the court found that the man had made no enforceable promise to marry or to support the woman during or at the end of their 23-year affair. The court also noted that even had his undertakings qualified as promises, the woman would not have been justified in relying on them. His promise of lifelong support was too vague to induce reliance. She could not have had any reliance on his promises to leave his wife and marry her because he had made and broken that promise countless times over the 23 years of their relationship.

Section 90 dispenses with proof of reliance for **charitable pledges** and **marriage settlements.** Leaving marriage settlements aside as beyond our scope, if courts adopted this rule for charitable pledges, a promise to make a charitable contribution could be enforced simply by showing that a promise was made and injustice would result from its non-enforcement. This would essentially dispense with both consideration and promissory estoppel as the basis for enforcing promises to make a charitable donation. However, courts have tended not to take the bold approach of following this rule, and still require a showing of justifiable reliance in the absence of consideration. This serves as a reminder that the Restatement, Second, although highly influential, is just secondary authority that may sometimes reflect what the drafters feel the law should be, rather than what it is. (See section 7.4.2 for a discussion of the policy arguments for and against enforcing charitable promises without consideration.) Of course, courts sometimes reach the result contemplated by the rule by stretching the facts to find justifiable reliance.

§8.6.5 The Promise is Binding if Injustice Can Be Avoided Only by Its Enforcement

This element reflects the total balance that the court must draw after evaluating the equities, so that its decision achieves a fair result in all the circumstances. (This balancing is an aspect of the equitable roots of promissory estoppel.) It takes into account not only the issues of promise and reliance discussed above, but also any other factors that bear upon the appropriateness of enforcing the promise.

The most significant of these is the **detriment or harm** suffered by the promisee in relying on the promise. If one accepts the protection of reliance as the fundamental purpose of promissory estoppel,[3] it is not enough that the promisee had merely a generalized expectation of gain which has been disappointed. The promisee must have suffered some **specific** and **measurable loss** by relying on the promise. Therefore, "detriment" in this context is usually not used in the attenuated sense associated with consideration doctrine but describes a real economic loss such as an expenditure, a sacrificed opportunity, a commitment or some other prejudice of a substantial kind. While some courts may accept less, especially if the other equities strongly favor enforcement, the need to avert injustice by enforcement of the promise is not very strong if there is no loss that needs redress and the only effect of nonenforcement is the failure to receive the promised benefit.

Another important factor that weighs in the balance was mentioned earlier in connection with the promise in section 8.6.2, but should be reemphasized here in dealing with the general equities of enforcement. Comment *b* to §90 stresses that the promisor needs protection from an **ill-considered promise** or a **bogus claim of promise.** Because consideration is absent, its safeguards — the channelling, cautionary, and evidentiary functions — are missing. The court should therefore weigh the lack or presence of formality and the apparent deliberateness of the commitment in deciding whether the equities favor enforcement, and if so, to what extent.

§8.7 THE REMEDY WHEN PROMISSORY ESTOPPEL IS APPLIED

Restatement Second §90 states that the remedy for breach of the promise may be limited as justice requires. Although Comment *d* to that section says that a promise binding under the section is a contract, this limitation of

---

3. It was noted in section 8.2 that some writers argue that the enforcement of a deliberate promise is the true basis of promissory estoppel. On this view, the protection of reliance has a less central role, and the proof of actual loss is less important.

remedy means that the promisee is not necessarily entitled to **full contractual relief.** While the court may grant the promisee full expectation damages to compensate for the loss of bargain resulting from the breach, it has the discretion to provide a lesser remedy. Typically, this lesser remedy would be focused on the **reimbursement** of the **actual loss or expense** incurred in reliance on the promise.

Although §90 suggests a range of damages and makes it clear that the balance of the equities affects the extent of relief, there is some debate on the correct emphasis to be placed on the choice of remedy. Those who see promissory estoppel as a contractual doctrine (a consideration substitute) believe that full contractual relief should be the normal measure of relief and a lesser remedy is appropriate only in exceptional cases. Those who argue that promissory estoppel is an independent tort-like theory of liability consider that reimbursement of actual loss should be the normal relief, with full enforcement confined to cases in which the lesser remedy is clearly inadequate. Some studies suggest that courts do in fact incline to full enforcement except when there is some problem in proving expectation damages. In short, it is difficult to say for sure where the primary focus is, given the spectrum of damages available to courts. It is important to recognize, however, that courts have a discretionary range of relief. This gives a court the flexibility to avoid an "all or nothing" resolution. The court need not confine itself to the question of whether the promise should be enforced at all. It may also consider the possibility of a lesser level of enforcement, and in a close case, it can reach a median position by granting partial relief. Because the court has the flexibility to grant less than full expectation relief, it may be more inclined to find that the other elements of promissory estoppel are satisfied, even if they are not strongly shown.

To illustrate the possible range of remedies and the distinction between full contractual damages and reliance recovery, consider Penny's enrollment in college on the strength of Uncle Rich's promise to give her $20,000: Penny's expectation is $20,000, and full contractual enforcement would give her this amount. By contrast, reliance damages would depend on the extent of her actual loss or prejudice. Therefore, if the year's tuition is $20,000, injustice might be averted only by full enforcement of the promise because she has committed herself for that amount. However, if annual tuition is only $5,000 and Penny is committed for only one year's tuition, enforcement to the extent of $5,000 (or may be $5,000 plus living expenses) may be enough to prevent injustice. Although Penny, in a sense, may have relied on having tuition for more than one year, the broken promise of future funding disappoints her expectation but does not constitute an actual out-of-pocket loss. The facts become more complicated if, in addition to committing herself for $5,000 tuition, she gave up a job to attend college, because her sacrificed earnings are also a reliance loss and should be taken into account in deciding her recovery.

The examples at the end of this chapter focus on general principles of promissory estoppel but do not end our study of this topic. It is also covered in Chapter 8 (promissory estoppel as an alternative to restitutionary recovery); section 5.3 (promissory estoppel in the context of options); section 11.4 (the application of promissory estoppel to the statute of frauds); and section 13.9 (promissory estoppel in relation to contract modification).

§8.8 CHARITABLE PLEDGES AND PROMISSORY ESTOPPEL

When we dealt with consideration doctrine in Chapter 7, we struggled with the distinction between situations in which a charitable pledge (or any other gift promise) is arguably supported by consideration, and those in which a promise made by the recipient is merely an undertaking to use the gift for the purposes for which it was given. Where this ambiguity is resolved by concluding that no consideration has been given, the pledge or promise of a gift may still be enforced under the doctrine of promissory estoppel, provided that the donee can establish that the elements of promissory estoppel are satisfied. (Recall that section 8.6.4 refers to the provision in Restatement, Second §90(2), which seeks to make a charitable pledge binding even in the absence of reliance. Most courts have not adopted this approach and require a showing of all the elements of promissory estoppel, including justifiable reliance, even where a charitable organization is the promisee.)

Allegheny College v. National Chautauqua County Bank, 159 N.E. 173 (N.Y. 1927) illustrates well the interplay between consideration doctrine and promissory estoppel where a donee gives undertakings in return for a pledge. Mary Yates Johnston pledged $5,000 to be paid to the college on her death. The pledge required the money to be used to educate students preparing for the ministry. It also stipulated that the fund would be known as the "Mary Yates Johnston Memorial Fund." She paid $1,000 of this amount while she was alive and the college set it aside for a scholarship fund as stipulated, but did nothing further in reliance on the pledge. The donor repudiated the pledge before her death. After she died, the college sued her estate for the balance of the pledged amount. Justice Cardozo found that the college had given consideration for the pledge because the college, by accepting the $1,000, impliedly promised to memorialize the donor's name. (He did not rely on the college's implied promise to use the fund for the purpose stipulated, possibly because that seems too clearly to be a condition of the gift.) Because he found consideration for the promise, Justice Cardozo did not have to deal with promissory estoppel. However, he suggested in dictum that promissory estoppel could have been used as an alternative basis for enforcing the gift. It is clear from the opinion that the underlying motivation for the court's conclusion was its belief that the charitable pledge should be upheld as a matter of public policy. To get this result, the court strained to fit the facts into a theory of recovery, but those facts do not provide much support for either basis of relief. The legal detriment found by the court is quite flimsy, and it is difficult to see grounds for promissory estoppel. There is no indication that the donor reasonably intended to induce reliance until the money was paid out on her death, or that the college took any action in reliance on the pledge. The mere banking of the money cannot really be seen as the kind of detrimental reliance that would support a claim of promissory estoppel.

King v. Trustees of Boston University, 420 Mass. 52 (1995) similarly found that a promise could be enforced under both consideration and promissory estoppel theories where the circumstances were ambiguous enough to support the contrary conclusion that the donor had promised a gift subject to conditions. This case was discussed in connection with consideration doctrine in section 7.3.5. It was noted there that the court found that by undertaking to index and care for Dr. King's papers and to make them available to researchers, the university had given consideration for Dr. King's promise to transfer ownership of his papers. Although the court disposed of the case on consideration grounds, it also addressed the university's alternative claim based on promissory estoppel. The court stressed that despite Restatement, Second, §90(2), it did require a charitable organization to show justifiable reliance for promissory estoppel relief. However, that reliance was apparent in the actions that the university took (indexing and taking care of the papers and making them available for research) beyond just retaining custody of the papers.

By contrast, in Congregation Kadimah Toras-Moshe v. DeLeo, 540 N.E.2d 691 (Mass. 1989) the court adopted a purely doctrinal approach. The donor had promised $25,000 to the synagogue. The synagogue planned to use the money to convert a storage room into a library to be named for the donor. However, there was no indication that the donor had attached any conditions to his promise, or that the synagogue had promised to use the money for this purpose or to name the library for the donor. The donor died without paying and the synagogue sued his estate. The court found no consideration because the synagogue had not made any promise or suffered any other detriment in exchange for the promise. It also found no basis for enforcing the donor's promise under the doctrine of promissory estoppel because the synagogue had not yet begun the renovation or taken any other action in reliance on the promise. It had merely allocated the fund to the library renovation in its budget, which was nothing more than an accounting entry with no prejudicial effect.

Because *Allegheny College* and *King* both found consideration, they fully enforced the promises as contracts. Had they not found consideration, but had given relief on the basis of promissory estoppel, the remedy may have been the same if the court decided that nothing short of full enforcement would prevent injustice. However, the court would have had the option of awarding the lesser relief of reimbursing reliance costs. For many courts, the lesser remedy is more appropriate unless the detriment to the promisee cannot be undone except by full enforcement. *Estate Timco v. Oral Roberts Evangelical Ass'n.*, 215 N.W.2d 750 (Mi. 1974) is an example of a case in which the court found full enforcement of the promise to be necessary to avert injustice. The court awarded judgment to the promisee for the balance of the price of a building where the promisor, as a member of the association's board, proposed and collaborated in the purchase and induced the association to buy the building by undertaking to pay the balance of the price.

§8.9 PROMISSORY ESTOPPEL AS A MEANS OF ENFORCING PROMISES MADE IN NEGOTIATIONS

§8.9.1 Introduction

Section 8.5 introduced the idea that promissory estoppel may sometimes provide relief for promises made during negotiations. It must be stressed that it is rarely appropriate to apply promissory estoppel to any statement made while the parties are working towards the formation of a contract. In most situations, negotiating parties reasonably understand that nothing said in negotiations is to be taken as a promise, and no commitment is made until a contract is formed. Even though a statement made during negotiations may sound like a promise, a reasonable party should normally realize that it is nothing more than an expression of intention or a proposal for a term that will become an undertaking in the contract if the negotiations culminate in final agreement. Therefore, if a party takes action on an apparent promise made during negotiations, he is likely jumping the gun and assumes the risk of acting prematurely. Notwithstanding this general understanding, there are some situations in which a party truly does make a precontractual commitment, and the circumstances make it reasonable for the other party to act in reliance on it. We have already seen an example of this in section 5.3 on options, where courts used promissory estoppel to enforce a subcontractor's express or implied promise to keep a bid irrevocable where the prime contractor relied on it in formulating its own bid.

§8.9.2 Promissory Estoppel and the Duty to Negotiate in Good Faith

Hoffman v. Red Owl Stores, Inc. 133 N.W.2d 267 (Wisc. 1965) is a classic case that recognized promissory estoppel relief in another type of precontractual situation — where the promise and reliance is founded on a particular **relationship of trust** that arises in negotiations. Hoffman approached Red Owl to set him up with a Red Owl grocery store franchise. After reviewing and approving his proposed financial arrangements, Red Owl encouraged Hoffman to take a series of actions to prepare to open a store. Hoffman conscientiously followed Red Owl's guidance, incurring expenses in the process. After some considerable time, negotiations eventually collapsed, primarily because Red Owl had not been entirely straight with Hoffman about the financing of the business. The parties had not yet made a contract, and Red Owl had never expressly promised Hoffman that he would receive a franchise. Nevertheless, the court awarded Hoffman his wasted reliance expenses on the basis of promissory estoppel. (The court made it clear that relief was confined to the recovery of wasted expenses, and could not include any claim for lost profits.) The court found that Hoffman had placed faith in Red Owl's expertise and good faith, and it had been careless of his interests. Red Owl's indifference to Hoffman's welfare outweighed his naiveté in unquestioningly following its advice. *Hoffman* is distinguishable from the usual negotiation situation because Red Owl so strongly influenced Hoffman's actions that a relationship of trust was created that is not normally present where parties approach each other as adversaries in negotiations. Indeed, the underlying rationale of *Hoffman* and the more recent cases discussed below is that the promisor had violated a duty to bargain in good faith. These cases have an affinity with other cases on this principle that you will encounter in section 10.10.5.

Pop's Cones, Inc. v. Resorts International Hotel, Inc., 307 N.J. Super. 461 (1998), and *Carey v. FedEx Ground Package System, Inc.*, 321 F. Supp. 902 (S.D. Ohio 2004) are more recent cases in which the dominant negotiating party was able to induce the other party's detrimental reliance on its precontractual promises. In both cases, the court was concerned with the alleged promisor's motion for summary judgment. The court refused to grant the motion and permitted the case to go to trial on the promissory estoppel cause of action. *Pop's Cones* involved negotiations for a lease. Pop's operated a frozen yogurt store in a town near Atlantic City. It entered into negotiations with Resorts International (RI) to move the store into RI's casino in Atlantic City. Pop's told RI on several occasions during their protracted negotiations that the time for it to renew the lease on its current premises was approaching. RI assured Pop's that it would obtain a lease in the casino and that completion of the transaction was no more than a formality. On the strength of that, Pop's gave up its current lease. In the end, RI failed to follow through with the transaction and negotiations terminated. Pop's sued RI for damages, and the court refused to grant RI's request for summary judgment on the basis that Pop's allegations made out a case for relief on grounds of promissory estoppel.

Carey is a mind-boggling example of a runaround that makes Red Owl's conduct seem mild by comparison. Carey had approached FedEx in January 2001 in the hope of acquiring a FedEx delivery route. For a period of almost two years, FedEx led him on with assurances that he would receive the route. Carey was in constant contact with FedEx. He followed its many suggestions and directions to qualify as a carrier, and was repeatedly told that he would get a route when it became available. During this period, FedEx induced Carey to buy a truck (which was ultimately repossessed because Carey could not afford payments on it without the income from a delivery route). In addition, to the knowledge of FedEx, Carey's wife gave up her job in reliance on the prospective extra income that Carey would earn once he had the route. When routes did become available, FedEx gave them to other drivers, while reassuring Carey that he was in line for the next route to become available. In the end, Carey never received the route and he sued FedEx on several theories[4] including promissory estoppel. The court denied summary judgment to FedEx on these claims. As to promissory estoppel, the court said that on the facts alleged, a jury could find that Carey had justifiably relied on the FedEx's precontractual promise that he would get a route. The court stressed that relief would be confined to reimbursement for Carey's reasonable reliance losses, and would not cover any profits he might have lost as a result of not obtaining the route. Lost profits are contractual expectation damages, not appropriately awarded under a theory of promissory estoppel.

§8.9.3 Promissory Estoppel and At-Will Employment Agreements

Employment is at will if either party can terminate the employment at any time for any reason. The default rule under common law is that employment is at will unless the parties agree to employment for a definite term, or agree that employment cannot be terminated except for cause or following a

---

4. It is worth mentioning the other causes of action because they add to the sense of bad faith dealing and show why this case, like *Hoffman*, is concerned with the duty to bargain in good faith. One of the causes of action was race discrimination. Carey was African-American and the facts suggested that FedEx's actions in giving other drivers routes before Carey could have been racially motivated. The other was fraud. There were indications that FedEx may have led Carey on because he was doing temporary driving work while he waited for his route and FedEx found it convenient to keep him on hand as long as possible as a temporary driver.

specified period of notice.[5] At-will employment agreements present particular problems of both consideration and promissory estoppel during the period after the employment agreement has been made, but before the employee begins work. Even where employment has been offered and accepted, courts commonly hold that before the employment actually begins, there is no contract because consideration is absent.[6] They reason that since both parties have complete discretion to terminate an at-will employment agreement, neither party makes any future commitment.

In addition, many courts hold that the at-will nature of the prospective employment precludes promissory estoppel relief for the reimbursement of loss for actions taken in reliance on the promise to employ. Although it is readily apparent that an employee is likely to incur some detriment in reliance on a promise of at-will employment, such as leaving an existing job, moving to the location of the new job, or forgoing other opportunities, these courts hold that the employee must bear the risk of this reliance because he has no assurance of job security. *Leonardi v. City of Hollywood*, 715 So. 2d 1007 (Fla. App. 1998) and *May v. Harris Management Corp.*, 2005 WL 3489544 (La. App. 2005) are two examples of cases in which the court held that the disappointed employee could not recover on a contract theory or on the basis of promissory estoppel.

Other courts, for example, *Grouse v. Group Health Plan, Inc.*, 306 N.W.2d 114 (Minn. 1981) find this approach unduly harsh and have been more sympathetic to the disappointed employee. In *Grouse*, a pharmacist gave notice to his current employer and declined another offer of employment on the strength of the health plan's promise of employment. Before he began work, the health plan withdrew its commitment to hire him. Although the court found that the pharmacist had no contractual cause of action because the employment could be terminated at will, the health plan had at least committed itself to allow the pharmacist an opportunity to begin, which induced him to take the detrimental action. He was therefore entitled to promissory estoppel relief.

Even where a court applies promissory estoppel in this context, the relief is likely to be modest. The employee cannot get damages based on his expected salary because he could be terminated at will. Damages such as

---

5. Many employment agreements do eliminate the default rule of employment at will, either by the express terms of the contract itself, or by virtue of rules in an employee handbook published by the employer, or by collective bargaining agreements, or by implication from usage or conduct. Statutes have also made inroads into the at-will doctrine.

6. This discussion is confined to the period before employment has begun and does not deal with the issue of whether it is easier to find consideration or reliance once the employment has commenced. The problem is that even after the employee starts work, both parties continue to have the discretion to terminate at-will employment, and the employee has no promise of continued employment on which he can rely. In *May* (cited in the text, below) the court followed those cases that hold that the same principles apply before and after the employment has begun. Other courts do distinguish between promises made before and after the employee has started working, and may find consideration or reliance as a result of conduct or promises made during the course of employment.

opportunity losses are usually difficult to prove, and damages for giving up the prior employment may be nonexistent if it was also at will. Therefore, relief is likely to be confined to actual out-of-pocket losses such as wasted moving expenses.

Examples

1. Aunt Jenny Rouse was very fond of her nephew, Sponger Scrounger III. She had often given him expensive gifts and had even helped pay his college tuition. After Sponger graduated from college, he took a job as a sales representative. He earned well, but did not think of this as a permanent career. He really wanted to become a lawyer. Sponger told Aunt Jenny that he wanted to quit his job and go to law school, but he was worried about the huge debt that he would have to incur to pay tuition and living expenses for the three years. During this conversation, Aunt Jenny was very sympathetic and told Sponger that she wanted to think about what she could do to help. About a week later, Aunt Jenny wrote a letter to Sponger in which she said, "I have been thinking about your ambition to become a lawyer and would love to see you achieve what you want. I realize what a financial sacrifice it would be for you to stop working and have to borrow so much money, and I would like to help. After considering this problem carefully over the last week, I have decided that you should not have to shoulder such a burden on your own. If you do decide to go to law school, I will give you $20,000 toward your tuition and living expenses, which I will pay to you when you begin law school. I hope that this makes it easier for you to decide what to do."

    After receiving this letter, Sponger immediately applied for admission to law school, paying the required non-refundable $100 application fee. In April he was offered admission for the next academic year, beginning at the end of August. Sponger told Aunt Jenny about the offer and said he was going to accept it. She was delighted and reaffirmed her intention to pay him $20,000 when he began school. A week later, Sponger accepted the law school's offer and paid a non-refundable $500 deposit. He planned to work until the end of July, and did not yet resign from his job. In May, Aunt Jenny died. In June, Sponger showed Aunt Jenny's letter to her executor. The executor told Sponger that Aunt Jenny's letter merely promised him a gift. It was not binding on the estate, which would not honor it. Notwithstanding, Sponger quit his job in July and entered law school at the end of August. He then sued the estate to enforce the promise. Will he likely succeed?

2(a). Tina Terrible owned a large motorbike that she persisted in dumping against the front door of the family home. One day, her father, having grown tired of nagging her to park the bike neatly in the driveway, issued an ultimatum: He told Tina that the next time he found the bike obstructing the front door, he would take it away and lock it in the basement for a month. True to form, Tina ignored this threat and left her bike at the door the next day. When her father returned from work, he saw the bike and resolved to take it to the basement after dinner. Unluckily, while he was eating his dinner, the bike was stolen.

Tina has no comprehensive insurance on the bike. She blames her father for her loss because had he locked up the bike as threatened, it would not have been stolen. Is she entitled to claim the value of the bike from her father?

2(b). Assume facts different from those stated in Example 2(a): Tina, a sweet and conscientious daughter, dutifully parks her motorbike in the driveway every night. She has always had comprehensive insurance on the bike, but she has a lowpaying job and it has been a real struggle to find the money for the very high premiums. When she received the current renewal notice, she thought of terminating her comprehensive coverage, but worried that if she did so, she would be unable to replace the bike if stolen.

One evening, a few days before the premium was due, she told her father of her difficulties. He generously offered to pay the premium for her and took the policy renewal notice from her, promising to pay it the next day. Sadly, Tina's father talks big, but he almost never does what he promises. True to form, he did not pay the premium. A few days later, Tina received a warning of cancellation from the insurer and asked her father if he had paid. He apologized for the delay, but assured her that the check would be mailed to the insurer the next morning. Hearing nothing further from the insurer, Tina assumed that matters had been taken care of. A couple of weeks later, the bike was stolen. She then discovered that her father had never paid the premium.

Can Tina recover from him? If so, what can she claim?

3. Examples 9 and 10 of Chapter 7 identified a consideration problem in which promises of reward for long service were made to retirees at the point of retirement. Under the "past consideration" rule, prior service is not consideration because it has already occurred and is not therefore bargained for in exchange for the promise. Both cases involved the fickle and ungrateful company, Turn Coat Corporation. In summary, the facts were:

In Example 9, when **Constance De Votion** retired after working for Turn Coat for 40 years, the company promised her an all-expenses-paid vacation in recognition of her faithful service. She planned the vacation, but when she tried to book it, she discovered that the company had revoked its promise as part of an economy drive. She could not enforce the promise under consideration doctrine because she had suffered no new detriment in exchange for it.

In Example 10, **Gerry Atrick** was a longstanding employee who had become incompetent. Although he could have been summarily dismissed as an employee at will, the company decided that worker morale would best be served if he could be persuaded to retire. The company offered and he accepted the promise of a year's wages in exchange for his voluntary retirement. The company then changed its mind and fired him. It is arguable that his agreement to retire is sufficient legal detriment to be consideration for the promise of a year's wages. However, the contrary argument could be made that an employee at will gives up no legal right in agreeing to resign because the company can dismiss him summarily.

Assuming that the court finds no consideration for the company's promises to these employees, do these facts support recovery under promissory estoppel?

4.   Since graduating from the Elmo Mater College a few years ago, Al Lumnis has been very successful in business. Toward the end of the financial year, he decided to share a little of his wealth with his old college. As he thought back to his days on campus, he remembered how difficult it had been to find a good cup of coffee. The bilge in the cafeteria was undrinkable, and the closest source of espresso was ten blocks away. He therefore decided that his gift to the college would be a fully equipped espresso bar. He wrote a letter to the president in which he stated: "In consideration of my desire to enhance and enno-ble the quality of campus life at the Elmo Mater College, I hereby pledge to the College the sum of $20,000 to be paid as soon as the College submits plans to me for the construction of a fully equipped espresso bar in the Student Union building. The bar shall be known as the 'Al Lumnis Mochamorial.' "

The president of the college wrote back, thanking Al for the pledge and undertaking to begin work immediately on planning the coffee bar. The president appointed a joint faculty student committee to consult with architects. She also instructed the editor of the alumni magazine to prepare a flattering article on Al and his gift for the next edition of the magazine.

It is now a couple of weeks later. The committee has met a couple of times and has had one consultation with an architect. Copy has been written for the magazine which has not yet been published. The president has just received another letter from Al which states: "My offer to fund an espresso bar was a bad idea. The trouble with kids today is that life is too easy. My character was built by trudging through the snow to get my cappuccino. This hardship gave me the resilience to succeed in business. Please disregard my last letter. I withdraw my pledge."

Can the College hold Al to his pledge?

5. Chilly Winters lived in a cold and congested northern city. Sonny Climes, his college roommate, moved south a few years ago and lives in Tropicana, a balmy southwestern metropolis. Sonny had established a flourishing high-tech business and often told Chilly that if he ever decided to escape the snow and smog, a job would be waiting for him at Sonny's company. After suffering through a particularly harsh winter, Chilly decided that it was time to move south. He called Sonny and asked if a job was still available. Sonny responded, "You bet! Get down here as soon as you can and I'll put you to work. I can start you off as a trainee at a salary of $40,000 a year. Your salary will increase as you become more experienced and assume more responsibility." Chilly agreed and told Sonny that he would give notice to his present employer and would be in Tropicana in a month.

    Chilly immediately gave notice to his employer and his landlord and bought a one-way air ticket to Tropicana. When he called Sonny a week later to tell him his exact time of arrival, he received an unpleasant surprise. Sonny told him that he had just received an offer for the sale of his business that was too good to resist. He had accepted it and planned to retire. He was sorry, but he could no longer employ Chilly.

    Chilly tried to retract his notice to his employer and his landlord, but his employer had already hired a replacement and his apartment had been relet. Chilly found a new apartment at a higher rental. After two months searching, he found a new job that paid the same salary as the old one. He cannot obtain a refund of his airfare, but airline policy allows him to cancel his booking and to use the ticket for travel within the U.S.A. at any time within the next year.

    What recourse, if any, does Chilly have against Sonny?

Explanations

1. Aunt Jenny undoubtedly made a promise to Sponger. The promise is expressed clearly and definitely in a writing after Aunt Charity had time to think about it carefully, and it therefore satisfies the evidentiary and cautionary functions of consideration doctrine. However, Sponger would be hard-pressed to argue that he entered a contract with Aunt Jenny because Sponger gave no consideration for the promise. Quitting a job and enrolling in law school could qualify

as a detriment for consideration purposes, but this does not seem to have been bargained for in exchange for Aunt Jenny's promise. Although Aunt Jenny's promised performance was conditional on Sponger going to law school, this is more properly interpreted as a condition of his gift. As mentioned before, it can be difficult to distinguish a bargained-for exchange from a conditional gift, but the tone of Aunt Jenny's letter and the absence of any requirement that Sponger go to law school, or any promise on his part to do so, more strongly indicates gratuitous intent.

If Aunt Jenny's promise was gratuitous, Sponger's only basis for relief is promissory estoppel. As mentioned earlier, Aunt Jenny's promise is clear. Judged on an objective standard, she was apparently sincere in making the promise, and must reasonably have expected that it would induce Sponger's reliance. The language of her letter itself indicates this expectation by stating, "I hope that this makes it easier for you to decide what to do," and reinforced by her reaffirmation of the promise when Sponger told her of the offer. The more difficult question is whether Sponger's conduct was induced by the promise and was justifiable. The fact of inducement and the justification for inducement tend to flow together on these facts. In deciding on whether these elements are satisfied, we have to consider separately each action taken by Sponger after the promise, because he may have taken some, but not others in justifiable reliance on the promise. Sponger's actions before Aunt Jenny's death — his application to law school, his acceptance of the law school's offer of admission, and his payment of the non-refundable fee and deposit — are causally linked to the promise and are justifiable. Aunt Jenny's promise was clear, carefully considered, consistent with her past generosity, and reaffirmed at the time that Sponger accepted the offer. Sponger had no reason to doubt that he could take the action that the letter encouraged.

Sponger's further action — resigning from his job at the end of July and entering law school at the end of August — were taken after Aunt Jenny had died and her executor had made it clear that the estate would not recognize or perform her promise. If Aunt Jenny's promise was not binding because it was gratuitous, the estate had the legal right to revoke it. This may both break the causal link between the promise and Sponger's actions, and remove his justification for relying on the promise.

This being so, his claim for promissory estoppel should be confined to the detriment incurred before Aunt Jenny died. At that stage, he had done nothing more than complete the law school application process and pay the fee and deposit. Nothing in the facts indicates that he was committed to the law school beyond the forfeiture of the nonrefundable fee and deposit.[7] True, he lost the hope and expectation of receiving help toward his tuition, but this is in the nature of an expectation interest, more properly confined to a case in which a contract is established. Given that Sponger incurred only a modest financial expense and could have avoided any further economic detriment, this does not seem to be a case in which injustice can be averted only by enforcing the promise to its full extent. (It is conceivable that a court that treats promissory estoppel as a consideration substitute may take a different view. That is, it could be argued that once Sponger had accepted the law school's offer on the strength of Aunt Jenny's firm promise, the relationship became enforceable as a contract. If so, Sponger could disregard the estate's effort to back out of the promise and continue to rely on it.)

This Example is inspired by *Alden v. Presley*, 637 S.W.2d. 862 (Tenn. 1982). The Presley in this case was none other than the King and the plaintiff was his fiancée's mother. When the plaintiff decided to divorce her husband, Elvis undertook to pay the expenses of her divorce, to pay out her husband's share of their house, and to pay off the mortgage so she would own the house free and clear. Elvis died after the divorce proceedings had begun, but before the divorce settlement had become legally binding. His estate notified the plaintiff that it would not honor Elvis's promise to pay off the mortgage. Notwithstanding, the plaintiff committed herself to the divorce settlement that released her husband from the mortgage. The court refused to enforce the promise to pay off the mortgage. It was gratuitous, so it was not a contract. It was also not enforceable on grounds of promissory estoppel because the plaintiff was no longer justified in finalizing the settlement in reliance on the promise once she knew that the estate would not honor it.

2(a). The facts of Tina's case are a parody of *East Providence Credit Union v. Geremia*, discussed in section 8.6.2. In that case, the court found that a creditor's threat to pay insurance premiums on a car and to charge them to the borrower constituted a promise to pay the premium, which the borrower justifiably relied on to his detriment. The case is very sympathetic to the borrower despite the fact that he had breached the contract by failing to pay the premium himself and had made no effort to pay in response to the notice or to check if the lender had paid. Tina's claim seems even more outrageous.

---

7. If seen as a basis of relief independent of contract, promissory estoppel is often confined to the recovery of out-of-pocket losses, that is, wasted expenses. If this view is strictly followed, maybe Sponger cannot even recover his fee and deposit from the estate because he did not in fact waste these expenditures if he did ultimately enroll in law school.

Tina clearly has no contractual basis for recovery. Even if her father did promise to remove her bike, there is no hint that she gave any consideration to her father for that promise. Her claim for relief under promissory estoppel is also unconvincing. Even more clearly than the credit union in *Geremia*, the father's apparent intent was to deliver an ultimatum and to threaten punishment, not to make a promise. It is unlikely that he could reasonably have seen his words as likely to induce reliance by taking the very action he proscribed. This is enough to eliminate a claim based on promissory estoppel. However, for the sake of completeness, we can also note that even if her father had made a promise, there is no indication that Tina relied on it and was induced to leave her bike in the driveway because of it. Her action was motivated by simple indolence and carelessness.

2(b). Tina gave no consideration for father's undertaking to pay the premium. It was simply a gift promise motivated by family relationship and cannot be enforced as a contract. Promissory estoppel was developed to provide a basis for enforcing this kind of gratuitous promise, relied on by the promisee to her detriment.

Are the elements of promissory estoppel satisfied? Whether or not Tina's father subjectively intended to honor his undertaking, his words, interpreted objectively, convey a clear commitment to pay the premium. There can be little doubt that he did or reasonably should have expected Tina to rely on it. It was an unequivocal response to her need for financial assistance, made with knowledge of her circumstances and reiterated when the cancellation warning was received.

The promise apparently induced forbearance on Tina's part. There is a suggestion that financial difficulty may have compelled Tina to let the comprehensive coverage lapse had father not undertaken to help. This suggests the argument that she did not really forbear from renewing that coverage on the strength of the promise — she would have let it lapse anyhow. However, she may not have adopted this course. Her concern about the consequences of possible theft could have motivated her to make the sacrifices necessary to find the money for the premium. The mere possibility that she may have forborne even without the promise may not be strong enough to break the causal link between the promise and her forbearance.

Tina's reliance must have been justified. A daughter would usually be justified in relying on her father's clear and unequivocal promise, made with apparently seriously intent. However, she knew that her father, unlike Aunt Jenny in Example 1, had a record of breaking his promises. This could mean that Tina may not have been entirely justified in relying unquestioningly on his word without checking to see if he had made the payment. This point was made in the *Norton* case mentioned in section 8.6.4. While blind faith on the promise of a person known to be unreliable may weaken the promisee's case, it may not be fatal. After all, the promisor is not likely to motivate a court to balance the equities in his favor by arguing, in effect, that although he made a promise, he should not be held to it because he is untrustworthy.

Although Tina may have difficulty establishing the elements of promissory estoppel, if they are satisfied the remaining task is to select the proper remedy. There are no wasted out-of-pocket costs in this case, so reimbursement of reliance expenses is not a meaningful alternative. Even full enforcement of the promise would not cover Tina's loss because that would simply be an award of the cost of the unpaid premium, which is much less than Tina's loss of the entire value of the bike. To decide if the full recovery of the value of the bike is appropriate, the court must weigh all the equities. It must consider the extent to which the elements of promissory estoppel have been established (here, a strong and unequivocal promise, but a possibly unjustified reliance). It must also balance the harm Tina will suffer if it refuses enforcement against the hardship to her father if it enforces the promise. The policies motivating consideration doctrine are also relevant — this oral gratuitous promise satisfies neither the cautionary nor the evidentiary function of consideration doctrine. It is difficult to predict how a court may strike this balance. The balance of equities seems to tilt in Tina's favor, so the court could well hold Tina's father liable for the value of the bike. (In the *Geremia* case discussed in section 8.6.2, the court indicated that had it not found consideration for the credit union's promise to pay the borrower's insurance premium, it would have considered an award of the value of the car appropriate relief under a theory of promissory estoppel.)

3.　There have been a number of cases in which courts have used promissory estoppel to validate a promise of retirement benefits when the promise was found to lack consideration under the "past consideration" rule. This happened in both cases cited in Examples 9 and 10 of Chapter 7, *Feinberg v. Pfeiffer Co.*, 322 S.W.2d 163 (Mo. 1959), and *Katz v. Danny Dare Inc.*, 610 S.W.2d 121 (Mo. 1980). In each of those cases, the court found that a promise had been made with the intention of inducing reliance, that the promisee acted detrimentally in reliance, and that full enforcement of the promise was necessary to prevent injustice.

In *Feinberg*, the employer promised the employee a life pension when she retired. This promise was made about 18 months before her retirement, as a reward for 37 years of service. The employer paid the pension for a few years, but its management then changed and it sought to reduce the amount of the pension. Although the court found that the employee had given no consideration for the promise of the pension, it enforced the promise on the basis of promissory estoppel. The court found that the employer had made the promise with intent to induce reliance, and that the employee had suffered irreversible detriment by retiring on the strength of it. She was too old (and at that stage had become too ill) to find other employment. The court treated promissory estoppel as a consideration substitute and fully enforced the promise as if it was a contract. Similarly, in *Katz* the court found no consideration for the promise of a pension because the employment was at will and the employee could have been summarily dismissed. Because he had no right to continued employment, he suffered no legal detriment by retiring. However, the court fully enforced the promise on the basis of promissory estoppel. This seems inconsistent because, as an at-will employee, Katz did not suffer much of a detriment in retiring in reliance on the promise, since the employer could simply have dismissed him at any time. Nevertheless, the result is fair, and shows that sometimes a court can use the doctrine of promissory estoppel to do justice where it feels constrained to apply consideration doctrine strictly.

Employees do not invariably succeed in enforcing pension promises under the doctrine of promissory estoppel. For example, in *Hayes v. Plantation Steele Co.*, 438 A.2d 1091 (R.I. 1982) an ex-employee was promised that the company "would take care of him" when he retired following 51 years of service. The company paid the employee $5,000 per year for several years and then ceased payments. The court refused to enforce the promise because the undertaking was too vague to be a promise, and also because the undertaking was given after the employee's retirement so he did not retire in reliance on it.

Under these principles **Constance** probably cannot recover. She retired before the promise, so it did not induce that decision. Her only other action was planning her vacation and communicating with the travel agent. Apart from wasting some of her free time, she incurred no loss or expense. Unquestionably, her expectation of a vacation has been dashed by her ingrate ex-employer, but if promissory estoppel is aimed at protecting reliance, the enforcement of this expectation interest is beyond the scope of the doctrine. A gratuitous promise was made, and in the absence of detrimental reliance, it simply fails because consideration is lacking. This unpleasant result could be avoided by underplaying the element of detriment in promissory estoppel. However, the real policy question is whether the "past consideration" rule has any justification at all in a case like this.

Turn Coat Corporation did make a definite promise to **Gerry** with the clear intent to induce action. Gerry relied on it, suffering the detriment of giving up his job. His actual loss is very small because he had no right to long-term employment. Because substantial actual loss is a significant factor in weighing the justice of enforcement, the lack of detriment for consideration purposes could also make the harm too trivial to support promissory estoppel. Nevertheless, as the **Katz** case shows, a court that is literal-minded in applying consideration doctrine may take a more equitable view in relation to promissory estoppel.

4.   Again, this problem treads that uncertain line between a promise with consideration and a gift made subject to instructions on its use, but it more likely falls on the latter side of the line. The recited "consideration" is not consideration at all but merely expresses Al's purpose in giving the donation. Although the president replies by promising to use the fund for this purpose, as a matter of strict doctrine, the college suffers no legal detriment in undertaking to use a gift for its designated purpose. It had no right to the money in the absence of the gift, and hence gives up no legal right by promising to use it in a particular way.

This example raises the different approaches to these ambiguous transactions raised in section 8.8, where *Allegheny College* and *King* found a basis of enforcement either under consideration doctrine or on grounds of promissory estoppel, while *DeLeo* did not. The facts here seem more strongly to point to some degree of reliance than those in *DeLeo* or even *Allegheny College*. Al stipulated that the planning must occur before payment, and the college did begin the planning process in reliance on the promise. However, the reliance had not extended beyond this by the time that Al revoked his promise. This leads to the question of remedy.

Although the court could fully enforce Al's promise to pay the $20,000 under promissory estoppel, it also has the option of providing lesser relief aimed at reimbursing the college's reliance costs. The college should at least be able to recover the fee paid to the architect. It could possibly also receive reimbursement for the value of the time spent by committee members in planning (to the extent that the time of faculty and students has any value at all).[8] If it was reasonably foreseeable that the donation would generate an article in the alumni magazine, the cost of the wasted production effort may also be claimable. Even if all these expenses are awarded, this recovery cannot be more than a fraction of the $20,000 promised.

---

8. Just kidding, of course.

5.   Although the parties were friends at the time of contracting, this is a purely commercial transaction. Sonny appears to have made an offer to Chilly which he accepted. The offer could have been fuller and more precise in setting out the terms of the employment, but there is probably enough specificity to avoid problems of indefiniteness. The agreement does not provide otherwise, so the employment is deemed to be at will, as explained in section 8.9. As noted there, courts commonly do not find consideration for a promise of at-will employment, even after offer and acceptance has occurred, because consideration is lacking as a result of the parties' discretion to terminate at will. Therefore, if Chilly is to get relief, it will have to be on the basis of promissory estoppel.

Sonny did promise Chilly a job. His intent was clearly expressed, and because Chilly told him that he was going to quit his job and move, he must have realized that Chilly planned to act in reliance on the promise. Chilly did rely on the promise, but the difficult question is whether this reliance was justified. As discussed in section 8.9, some courts hold that while a promisee may be reasonable in taking detrimental action in reliance on a promise of at-will employment, this action is not justified for promissory estoppel purposes. That is, the employee cannot shift the risk of his reliance to the employer, because he should understand that he is incurring loss or expense without any promise of job security. Other courts consider this approach too harsh, and are willing to give relief, especially where the promise and intent to induce reliance is clear and there are no specific facts that would make the reliance unreasonable.

However, even if the court grants relief, it is likely to be limited. Chilly could possibly recover the two months' lost salary, but only if he had some security of employment at his old job. If he was an at-will employee in that job, he may not be able to show that loss with reasonable certainty. In addition, Chilly's delay in finding a replacement job would have to be reasonable. If he did not make a reasonably diligent effort in seeking new employment, he cannot hold Sonny accountable for loss that he could have prevented. (This is the principle of mitigation of damages, discussed in section 18.6.3.) Chilly may also be able to claim any increase in rent as a result of having ended his apartment lease in reliance on the promise. Again, he would have to show that he would have had a right to retain his old apartment and that the substitute was reasonable. Chilly might have been able to claim the wasted expense of the air ticket, but because the ticket is salvageable, he has probably not suffered a loss unless he can show that it would not be possible for him to use it within the year or to sell it.

Restitution: Unjust Enrichment and "Moral Obligation"

§9.1 INTRODUCTION

Chapter 8 explained how promissory estoppel can sometimes be used to ameliorate the harsh consequences of consideration doctrine by enforcing a promise that induced justifiable reliance. Although the remedy of restitution is available in a variety of different situations, both within the bounds of contract law and beyond them, in one of its aspects it serves a purpose similar to promissory estoppel by allowing for the enforcement of obligations that do not qualify as contractual. Having drawn this general parallel, it must be stressed that restitution and promissory estoppel have very different conceptual bases. Restitution is not predicated on accountability for promise. In fact, its usefulness is greatest when no promise has been made. Its purpose is the restoration of an unfair gain. Its focus is on cases in which one party has obtained a benefit at the expense of another under circumstances that make it unfair for the recipient to retain the benefit without paying for it.

§9.2 UNJUST ENRICHMENT, THE BASIS FOR RESTITUTION

It is common to confuse restitution, a **remedy**, with unjust enrichment, the **cause of action** that gives rise to the remedy. **Restitution is the act of restoring something or its value.** When a court grants restitution, it adjudges that the recipient of a benefit is obliged to give back that benefit or to pay its value to the person who conferred it. The basis of this judgment is that the recipient has been **unjustly enriched** at the expense of grantor. That is, there is **no legal justification for retention of the benefit without pay.** In short, when the elements of the cause of action, unjust enrichment, are satisfied, the remedy of restitution is the relief awarded. Some writings and court opinions are not punctilious about correct terminology and use the word "restitution" in reference to both the cause of action and the remedy.

Unjust enrichment is not a subcategory of contract law. It is a distinct and *independent basis of obligation*, occupying a place alongside contract, promissory estoppel,[1] and tort. The following illustration attempts to emphasize this relationship between different causes of action and remedies.

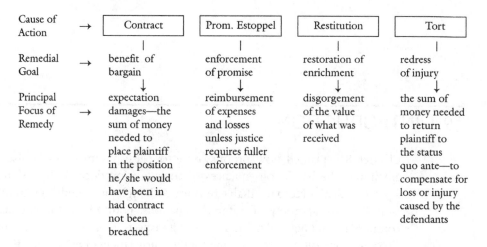

Cause of Action →	Contract	Prom. Estoppel	Restitution	Tort
Remedial Goal →	benefit of bargain	enforcement of promise	restoration of enrichment	redress of injury
	↓	↓	↓	↓
Principal Focus of Remedy →	expectation damages—the sum of money needed to place plaintiff in the position he/she would have been in had contract not been breached	reimbursement of expenses and losses unless justice requires fuller enforcement	disgorgement of the value of what was received	the sum of money needed to return plaintiff to the status quo ante—to compensate for loss or injury caused by the defendants

§9.3 THE RELATIONSHIP BETWEEN UNJUST ENRICHMENT AND CONTRACT

Unjust enrichment is a complex field, covering many situations that have nothing to do with contract. It falls within our scope in two broad areas. These two different roles of unjust enrichment in the contractual context must be distinguished to prevent confusion. The diagram and brief general description is followed by explanatory illustrations:

---

1. But remember that one view of promissory estoppel is that it is not an independent theory of liability but a subcategory of contract law. *See* section 8.2.

9. Restitution: Unjust Enrichment and "Moral Obligation"

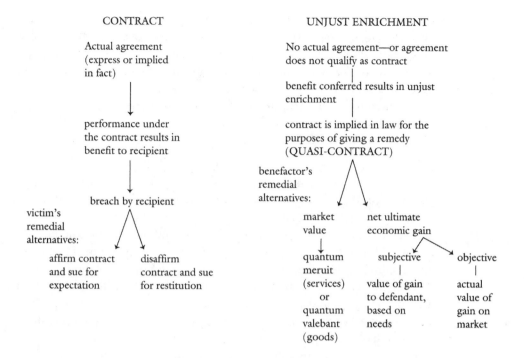

CONTRACT

Actual agreement
(express or implied
in fact)

↓

performance under
the contract results in
benefit to recipient

↓

breach by recipient

victim's
remedial
alternatives:

affirm contract
and sue for
expectation

disaffirm
contract and sue
for restitution

UNJUST ENRICHMENT

No actual agreement—or agreement
does not qualify as contract

|

benefit conferred results in unjust
enrichment

|

contract is implied in law for the
purposes of giving a remedy
(QUASI-CONTRACT)

benefactor's
remedial
alternatives:

market
value

↓

quantum
meruit
(services)
or
quantum
valebant
(goods)

net ultimate
economic gain

subjective

|

value of gain
to defendant,
based on
needs

objective

|

actual
value of
gain on
market

Unjust enrichment serves as an independent theory of liability in cases when *no contract* has come into existence, either because something went wrong or failed to happen in the process of formation, or because the parties simply did not attempt to make a contract. Yet they had some interaction that resulted in the one party obtaining a gain from the other. In situations like this, there is no basis for contractual relief, but unjust enrichment permits restitutionary recovery. The link to contract could be close here because there could be strong contractual elements in the interaction. However, some of these situations have only a marginal relationship to contract, based on the legal fiction called "quasi-contract" explained in section 9.4. This chapter is concerned with cases like these, when no contract exists and unjust enrichment is the basis of obligation.

Unjust enrichment also plays an important role when a *valid contract* does exist but has been *breached.* One of the parties may have conferred a benefit on the other in the course of performing the contract before its breach, and restitution of that benefit may be a better option than enforcement of the contract. (In some cases it may be the only option because, for example, contractual expectation damages cannot be proved.) Even though there is a valid contract, the plaintiff may elect to forego contractual relief in favor of restitution. This role of restitution is an issue of damages for breach of contract. Apart from this brief mention of it and the illustration below, this question is deferred to the discussion of remedies for breach in section 18.9.

The following examples illustrate the range of the restitutionary remedy by showing its application in a number of situations. The first involves restitution when a valid contract exists, the next two show the use of restitution when the parties aimed to enter a contract but their dealings did not result in a valid contract, and the fourth demonstrates the use of restitution when there has been no contractual interaction between the parties.

Illustration 1. *Restitution as an alternative remedy when a valid contract has been breached*

Buyer and Seller make a contract for the sale of Seller's house. Buyer pays a deposit of $5,000 to Seller. Seller later reneges on the contract and refuses to close. Because a valid contract exists, Buyer has the right to claim expectation damages for breach of contract that would place her in the position she would have been in had the contract been performed. If the price under this contract is less than the cost of buying an equivalent house on the market, Buyer's expectation damages would be the difference between the contract price and what she would have to pay for a substitute.[2] However, assume that Seller's house was overpriced, and it turns out that Buyer can purchase an equivalent house for less on the market. Expectation damages are zero because Buyer would have paid more had Seller not breached. Enforcement of the contract does not help her. However, Buyer has enriched Seller by the $5,000 down payment that Seller no longer has any right to keep. His enrichment is unjust and if he fails to repay, the remedy of restitution is available to Buyer to recover the down payment.

Illustration 2. *Restitution when a benefit is conferred pursuant to an invalid or unenforceable contract*

Assume that the parties in the above illustration had made an oral agreement for the sale of the house. Under the statute of frauds, a sale of real property must be in writing and the oral agreement is unenforceable as a contract.[3] Therefore, if Seller reneges, Buyer does not have the option of suing for enforcement of the contract. But because Seller no longer has any right to keep the money, Buyer can, nevertheless, obtain restitution of the down payment on the theory of unjust enrichment.

Illustration 3. *Restitution when a benefit is conferred on the strength of a promise without consideration*

The principle of Illustration 2 applies in other situations when no valid contract came into existence. For example, say that Owner made a written promise to donate the house to Charity, a non-profit organization that

---

2. The measure of expectation damages is fully discussed in section 18.3.
3. *See* section 11.2.

provides shelter for victims of abuse. Before taking transfer of the house, Charity obtains Owner's permission to install a security system on the premises and to build a wall around it. After Charity has done this work, Owner reneges on the promise and refuses to transfer the house. Charity's enhancement of the property was obviously not intended as consideration for the promise of the house and was not bargained for by or owed to Owner. It was simply done to enable Charity to make proper use of the gift. Because the promise is not supported by consideration, Charity cannot enforce it as a contract. But it has improved the house that now remains Owner's property. This unjustly enriches Owner, so Charity can obtain restitution for the value of the wall and security systems.

This illustration raises a number of points that will be discussed later:

1. Unlike the prior illustrations, it involves not the restoration of a fixed sum of money but the value of labor and materials. This is common. When the value of a benefit is not fixed and certain, evidence of value is required as discussed in section 9.6.

2. Owner may not particularly want a security system and wall on the property, but because he changed his mind about giving the house to Charity, he is stuck with paying for them. Under the circumstances, this result is justifiable because Owner authorized the work. However, principles of unjust enrichment ensure that this will not happen when a benefit is imposed on a recipient.

3. These facts appear to support recovery under promissory estoppel: Acting in reliance on the promised donation, Charity incurred a loss in installing the security system and wall on the property. Injustice may be averted only by enforcing the promise, if not in full, at least to the extent of the costs incurred in supplying the materials and doing the work. Although it does not always happen that the same circumstances support relief either in restitution or in promissory estoppel, this is not an uncommon situation. When the claimant has a choice of remedies, the selection between them is based on factors such as ease of proof and extent of recovery. The elements of one may be easier to establish than the other. In addition, the relief for each may be quite different, because restitution focuses on the restoration of the value of the benefit conferred, while promissory estoppel is more concerned with the costs incurred by the claimant.

Illustration 4.   *Restitution in cases when no contractual interaction occurred*

Victim slips on a banana peel and falls down a flight of stairs. Doctor, a stranger who happened to be walking by, administers emergency treatment to unconscious Victim. Doctor has never entered into a contract with Victim who could not consent to treatment because he was unconscious. The only basis on which Doctor could recover a fee for her services is unjust enrichment, on the theory that Victim would have had to pay for them in the marketplace, and it is unjust that he should receive them for free. (The merits of this argument will shortly be explored in more detail.) Although this is not a contract case, it is historically linked to contract law through a quaint legal fiction known as "quasi-contract."

§9.4 THE MEANING OF "QUASI-CONTRACT"

§9.4.1 Quasi-Contract — A Contract "Implied in Law"

Although the claims of Buyer, Charity, and Doctor in Illustrations 2, 3, and 4 are not based on contract, and recovery is premised solely on the policy of preventing unjust enrichment, our legal tradition has created a peculiar fiction that makes the cases sound as if they have something to do with contract. In early common law, courts were bound by a rigid set of writs called **"forms of action."** To obtain relief, the plaintiff had to fit his or her claim into one of these recognized categories of suit. There was no writ for unjust enrichment, so the court needed to fit enrichment claims into some other writ. It chose the contract writ of assumpsit, and squeezed enrichment into a contractual form by pretending that the benefit was conferred on the recipient pursuant to a contract with the grantor. Thus, to use Illustration 4 as an example, the court would act as if Victim had asked Doctor to treat his injuries, so that Doctor could recover the value of her services under the writ of assumpsit. Claims for unjust enrichment based on this fictional contract were said to arise **quasi ex contractu**, and the restitutionary remedy based on this fiction has come to be called **quasi-contract, or contract implied in law.** It is easy to be confused by this terminology, so it is important to remember that a quasi-contract or a contract implied in law is not a real contract. Legal implication is a fiction created for remedial purposes. It must be distinguished from a contract **implied in fact**, which is explained in section 9.4.2.

To put all this terminology together, we can describe the general principle of unjust enrichment as follows: When a benefit has been conferred on a recipient under circumstances in which it is unfair to permit him to retain it without payment, the **cause of action of unjust enrichment** is available to the person who conferred the benefit. Using this cause of action, the conferrer can claim the **remedy of restitution**, under which the court will restore the benefit or its value to her. In order to fit this newly recognized cause of action into existing legal forms, earlier common law courts used various **fictions.** The one that we are concerned with here (there are others that are beyond the scope of a contracts course, but are commonly covered in upperclass Remedies courses) was based on the fiction that the benefit had been contracted for. That is, the court **implied a contract in law**, even though no contractual relationship actually existed between the conferrer and the beneficiary. Restitutionary recovery based on unjust enrichment was therefore described as "quasi ex contractu," and the term **"quasicontract"** has come down to us as an alternative name for this form of relief.

When it comes to enforcement of the obligation, **relief** for unjust enrichment (quasi-contractual relief) can be very different from that for contract. For example, if Doctor had made a real contract with Victim, she could enforce its actual terms and could recover whatever fee was agreed on for the treatment. As no contract was made and the cause of action is a quasi-contract, there cannot be an agreed fee, so recovery is based on the value of the benefit, typically determined by market value as discussed in section 9.6. Sometimes there may be no difference between market value and contract price, but the difference could be significant.

§9.4.2 Quasi-Contract Distinguished From a Contract Implied in Fact

As noted in section 9.4.1, a quasi-contract (or contract implied in law) is not a contract at all, but merely a legal fiction. By contrast, a **contract implied in fact is an actual contract.** There is no difference in the legal nature or effect of an express contract and a contract implied in fact. The only difference is in the manner and evidence of contract formation. The parties create an express contract by articulating their agreement in written or oral words. A contract is implied in fact where the parties do not express agreement in words, but it is apparent from a **reasonable interpretation of their conduct**, viewed in context, that they intended to make a contract.[4] *Yarde Metals, Inc. v. New England Patriots L.P.*, 834 N.E.2d 1233 (Mass. App. 2005) illustrates some of the considerations taken into account in deciding whether conduct gives rise to a contract implied in fact. The Patriots terminated the season ticket privileges of a subscriber after one of the subscriber's guests was removed from the stadium for disorderly conduct. (Although there was some dispute over what the conduct was, it seems that the subscriber's male guest had used the women's restroom.) The subscriber argued that over the last 20 years the

---

4. The distinction between implication in law and in fact is also made where the issue is not whether a contract was formed, but whether it contains a particular disputed term. A term might be implied into a contract in fact, based on evidence that the parties intended it to be part of the contract even though they did not express it. Sometimes, even in the absence of such evidence of agreement on the term, the court might imply the term as a matter of law because the term should be in the contract. This is discussed in section 10.4.

Patriots had routinely and consistently offered it the opportunity to renew the tickets. It claimed that this gave rise to an implied contractual right to renew the season tickets annually. The court disagreed and affirmed the lower court's dismissal of the case. It reasoned that to imply such a contract would contradict the terms printed on the ticket, which stated that the ticket was a revocable license that gave the purchaser no renewal rights for a subsequent year. The court also found that implication of a contract would be inconsistent with common practice and would confer a right on the ticket holder far more valuable than the price paid for the tickets.

The **distinction between quasi-contract and a contract implied in fact** may be shown by adjusting the facts of Illustration 4. Say that Victim slipped and fell down the stairs. Although he was hurt, he was not knocked out. He was fully conscious, mentally alert, and not so shocked or disoriented by his fall as to be incapable of making a contract. Doctor began to administer treatment and Victim did not object. Even though no words of agreement passed between Doctor and Victim, Victim's acquiescence in the treatment, with reason to know that doctors charge for their services, is evidence from which the factual conclusion can be reached that the parties made a tacit contract for medical services. Because the parties did not discuss Doctor's fee, there is no agreed price for the service. Where parties make an actual contract (whether express or implied in fact) but do not specify the price, they are commonly taken to have agreed to the market price unless there is evidence to the contrary. That is, **quantum meruit** is not always confined to quasi-contract. It is sometimes used where there is an actual contract in which the price has not been fixed expressly.

It is not always clear if the conduct of the parties led to a contract implied in fact or gave rise to enrichment to be remedied by the device of quasi-contract. For example, in *Contship Containerlines, Inc. v. Howard Industries, Inc.,* 309 F.3d 910 (6th Cir. 2002) a shipper contracted with a freight forwarder to book its cargo onto a ship. The shipper paid the freight forwarder for the entire cost of the shipping. The shipper then delivered the cargo to the ship, and it was shipped to its destination. The freight forwarder never transmitted payment for the freight charges to the carrier (that is, the ship owner). The carrier sought to obtain payment from the shipper on the basis of contract implied in fact, alternatively, unjust enrichment. In response to the carrier's motion for summary judgment, the court held that there was a genuine dispute of fact on the question of a contract implied in fact, so the issue must go to trial. The shipper had delivered the cargo to the carrier, knowing that the carrier was not performing the service for free. This could provide a basis for implying an actual contract. However, the contrary argument could be made that a contract implied in fact must be based on agreement and the shipper did not reasonably intend to make a contract with the carrier. It had contracted with and had paid the freight forwarder and had never had any contact with the carrier except for the delivery of the cargo. Although the shipper overcame summary judgment on the contract claim, the court did grant summary judgment to the carrier on the unjust enrichment claim. This may seem surprising because the shipper had not been enriched at all — it had in fact paid the shipping costs to the freight forwarder. The court found that this was no defense to the carrier's restitution claim because the shipper, by paying a third-party intermediary, assumed the risk that payment would not be transmitted to the carrier. That is, the court was faced with the task of allocating the loss between two innocent parties — the shipper who had already paid someone else for the service and was not actually enriched, and the carrier who had not been paid for the service. The court allocated the risk to the shipper because it had been the one to cause this problem by entrusting the funds to the third party.

§9.5 THE ELEMENTS OF UNJUST ENRICHMENT

As stated earlier, the remedy of restitution is aimed at restoring money, property, or the value of property or services when it would be unjust to permit the recipient to retain what was received without paying for it. As its name suggests, unjust enrichment is predicated on two elements: The recipient must have been enriched at the expense of the claimant, and the circumstances must be such as to make this enrichment unjust.

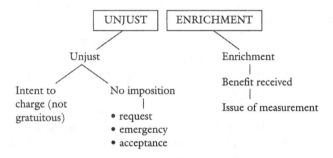

§9.5.1 Enrichment

Enrichment is an **economic benefit.** When a person receives and retains money or property, it is easy to see that the recipient has been enriched to the extent of the payment or the value of the property because the recipient's net worth has been increased by that amount. However, a person could also be enriched by consuming goods or receiving intangible services that result in no long-term financial advantage. One is not obviously made wealthier by consuming a free bag of pretzels or getting a free haircut, but one has saved the cost of buying these items in the marketplace. Naturally, the existence or absence of lasting economic advantage and its extent are factors taken into account in deciding on relief, as discussed in section 9.6. However, it is necessary to recognize the general principle that enrichment occurs whenever something of value is received, even if it does not directly enlarge the recipient's net worth.

§9.5.2 When Is Enrichment Unjust?

To receive restitution, it is not enough that the claimant has conferred an uncompensated benefit on the recipient, because it is not always unjust for a person to receive a benefit without paying for it. Justice is only offended if the conferral of the enrichment meets two criteria: The claimant must have intended to charge for it, and must not have imposed it on the recipient.

a. Intent to Charge

Enrichment is not unjust if the benefit was conferred with gratuitous intent. It is not unfair to allow a donee to keep a gift.[5] Quite the contrary, it would unfairly disrupt the donee's reasonable expectations by allowing the donor to demand payment for something originally given for free. A person who confers a benefit gratuitously is sometimes called a **volunteer.** In the context of unjust enrichment, this word carries more than its common meaning. It connotes not only that something was done or given by free choice, but also with the intent not to seek compensation.

As usual, intent is not measured subjectively but is based upon apparent intent, as manifested by the conduct of the person conferring the benefit in light of all the circumstances. An objective test is used, not only because it is difficult to divine a person's true state of mind, but also because the recipient's reasonable expectations should be protected. Therefore, if a reasonable person in the recipient's position would perceive the grantor as not expecting compensation, the intent is gratuitous, no matter what the grantor claims to have been thinking.

Benefits are sometimes conferred in an emergency when it is unlikely that the benefactor was thinking about compensation at all when taking the beneficial action, so it is sometimes artificial to talk of intent. Therefore,

---

5. Of course, there is no consideration issue once the donation has been given. Consideration doctrine only applies to the enforcement of unexecuted promises.

intent is likely to be determined by inference from the circumstances. One of the significant considerations in deciding whether or not the benefit was conferred with gratuitous intent is the relationship of the benefit to the trade or profession of the conferrer. For example, unless she is particularly crass and cold-blooded, a doctor probably does not think of her fee as she is administering emergency aid to a victim. Nevertheless, if the general expectation is that a doctor would charge for services in these circumstances, intent to charge is attributed to her. Because the doctor rendered professional services, it is conceivable that she had a reasonable expectation of payment. The reasonableness of this expectation would have been even stronger if the doctor was not a passer-by but attended to the victim after he was rushed, unconscious, into her consulting rooms for emergency treatment.

By contrast, if the aid was provided by a lay person, the general expectation is likely to be that there was no intent to charge. We normally think of amateur emergency intervention as public spirited and gratuitous. There is a difficult policy question to be considered when deciding whether services rendered by a nonprofessional should be presumed as gratuitous: We should expect people to respond to crises altruistically without expectation of reward. But a strict presumption of voluntarism could be unfair and could discourage intervention in emergencies, especially if loss or injury was suffered in the course of conferring the benefit.

Sometimes, although there was an intent to charge for the benefit, the intent may not have been to charge the recipient. If so, from the recipient's perspective, the benefit is gratuitous. For example, say a suitor orders flowers on credit for his paramour. If the suitor fails to pay after the florist has delivered them, the florist cannot claim that the recipient was unjustly enriched. Although it had intended to charge for the flowers, it had never intended to charge her.

b. Imposition

If restitution was available for any benefit conferred with intent to charge, this would open the way for all kinds of imposition from busybodies and sleazy operators. Imagine how a homeowner would feel if, upon returning from work one day, she found that her overgrown yard had been weeded and trimmed without her knowledge. On the front door was a note that read:

> Your yard was a mess, so we cleaned it up for you. Our charge is $300. Please send a check right away.
>
> Your friendly neighbors,
>
> O. Fishus
> N. Termeddler

Alternatively, it may not be the neighbors who did the yard work, but some roving landscaper who makes a living by seeking out unkempt yards, beautifying them without permission, and then demanding payment. In either case, the law treats these claimants as **officious intermeddlers.** Even though they did not intend to confer the benefit gratuitously, they were not justified in imposing a benefit on someone without asking first, so they are not entitled to restitution.

Although the above examples are obvious, it is not always so easy to decide if a benefit was conferred officiously. In the clearest case, a benefit is not officious if it was **requested** by the recipient.[6] When the benefit has not been requested by the recipient, it is likely to be officious unless there was some good reason to confer the unasked-for benefit. This is usually satisfied only when an **emergency** has arisen and three conditions are satisfied: First, immediate action is required; second, advance assent is impracticable; and third, the claimant has no reason to believe that the recipient would not wish for the action to be taken.

The greater the urgency and the more at stake, the more likely that unrequested action will be justified. **Threats** to **life or health** are generally regarded as giving greater cause for unsolicited action than threats to property. Thus, the doctor in the earlier example is likely to obtain restitution. Not only was she not a volunteer, she was also not an officious intermeddler. Although the protection of the person of the beneficiary is the strongest justification for unrequested emergency action, an emergency response to avert **harm to property** is also of value to the property owner and to society. Therefore, if a person, in response to an immediate threat, takes lawful and appropriate action to save or preserve the property, he is not likely to be treated as an officious intermeddler.

Even if a benefit is imposed on the recipient, restitution may still be appropriate if, being able to reject it and return the benefit, the *recipient accepts* it. In the yardwork example, the owner of the unkempt yard cannot return the benefit, even if undesired, because it is incorporated into the land. To deem acceptance would eviscerate the rule against intermeddling because there is no means of rejection. However, some benefits can be easily returned. For example, if instead of weeding and trimming, the neighbors beautified the yard by installing a garden gnome, it would be a simple matter for the homeowner to reject the gnome and to allow the neighbor to remove it. If the owner chooses to keep the gnome, acceptance of the unrequested benefit justifies compensation.

---

6. Where the benefit was requested, an actual contract may have been created (so that restitution serves the role as an alternative remedy) but if the request falls short of a contractual commitment, unjust enrichment is the basis of obligation.

§9.6 MEASUREMENT OF BENEFIT

§9.6.1 The Remedial Aim of Restitution

As noted in section 9.2, the remedial focus of restitution is different from contract. Contractual damages are based on the breach victim's expected gains under the contract and are calculated to approximate the monetary value of the benefit that he or she would have realized had the contract not been breached. By contrast, the primary focus of restitutionary damages is not the grantor's loss of expectation, but the *recipient's gain*. They are calculated to approximate the monetary value of what has been given to the recipient. Damages for breach of contract and the distinction between contractual expectation damages and restitution are dealt with in some detail in Chapter 18. However, because restitutionary relief is so tied into the subject matter of this chapter, it seems convenient and logical to deal with the nature and measurement of restitution here.

§9.6.2 Alternative Methods for Measuring Enrichment

The following illustration suggests the two principal ways in which enrichment can be measured:

Maggie Zine owns a newsstand in an office lobby. As she was opening the booth early one morning, she fainted and was rushed to the hospital. She spent the day there for observation and tests and was discharged that evening. Sam Aratan, Maggie's friend, happened to be in the lobby coffee bar when he heard that Maggie had been taken away in the ambulance. As he had the day off, he decided to help Maggie by keeping her booth open. He ran the booth the whole day, making $600 in sales, of which $200 is profit. The going wage for a kiosk clerk is $7 per hour. Sam ran the newsstand for ten hours.

Assume that Sam is neither a volunteer nor an intermeddler, so that he should receive restitution for his services. There are two alternative means of calculating Maggie's enrichment:

1. The market value of Sam's service, represented by the going wage of kiosk clerks, $70, or
2. Maggie's net economic gain — her profit for the day, $200. (Not her net sales, of course, because she had to buy $400 worth of goods to generate the $600 income.)

Market value of the benefit and the recipient's ultimate net fiscal gain are the two alternative choices for measuring enrichment. Market value tends to be the standard measure, but net gain is used when the circumstances make recovery of market value either excessive or inadequate. If net gain is the basis of measurement, the gain could be valued differently depending on whether it is measured objectively — that is, in the abstract (what it is reasonably worth in general) or subjectively — with regard to the beneficiary's particular circumstances. This breakdown may be represented as follows:

We will now look more closely at each of these means of measurement.

§9.6.3 Market Value

When the benefit is the payment of money, value is readily apparent, but if the benefit consists of their receipt of property or services, their value must be established by evidence of their price on the market. If services are involved, the term **quantum meruit** ("as much as deserved") is used to express market value. The term used to describe the market value of goods is **quantum valebant** ("as much as they are worth").[7] Market value is most reliably determined by testimony of an expert who is familiar with the market and can provide objective information about customary pricing. However, if such evidence is not available, the plaintiff may be able to make a prima facie showing of value by providing evidence of his own usual price. This is not the most convincing evidence, but if the defendant offers nothing to rebut it, and the plaintiff's basis for calculating it appears reasonable, it may be sufficient. If there is no evidence of either the objective market value or the plaintiff's usual price, evidence of the plaintiff's costs in providing the property or services may be accepted as the best evidence of value, provided that it appears that the plaintiff acted efficiently and that costs were not higher than they should be. (Of course, the reimbursement of

---

7. This terminology is not confined to restitution, but is also used in connection with contracts in which the parties have left the price open. In fact, the terms derive from contract law and enter the language of restitution through the fiction of quasi-contract.

cost is likely to be a less attractive basis of recovery for the plaintiff, because market price usually consists of cost plus profit.)

§9.6.4 The Recipient's Net Gain

The net actual enrichment of the recipient — that is, the actual amount by which the recipient's wealth is increased — could be more or less than the market value of the services. For example, although the market value of hiring Sam was $70, Maggie actually gained $200 from his services. Conversely, had it been a slow day, her takings from the booth could have been less than $70.

In this example, net gain is relatively easy to determine. This is not always true. Net gain could be speculative or difficult to quantify. Consider the example of the doctor who came to the aid of the victim in an emergency. Say that the customary fee for the doctor's services is $200. If, as a result of her prompt efforts, the victim was saved from death or crippling injury, this is surely worth more than $200 but it is difficult to value the gain. If restitution were to be based on the victim's net gain, testimony would have to be given on the monetary value of his life and health. Conversely, if despite the doctor's valiant effort the victim died soon after the fall, he received no ultimate benefit and has no net gain. In this particular case, the victim's benefit would not be measured on the basis of his net gain, for reasons explained in section 9.6.5, but the illustration does make the point that valuation can be a tough issue.

A further problem with net enrichment is that it can be perceived in two different ways. If it is determined *subjectively*, it is measured with reference to the actual recipient, taking into account the recipient's needs, circumstances, and intentions. *Objective* valuation is based on the worth of the benefit in market terms. (This is not the same as market value of the service, because it is the ultimate gain that is measured by the market standard.) For example, Contractor builds a patio on Owner's property without authorization, but under circumstances that make contractor neither an intermeddler nor a volunteer. The market value of the work is $1,000. The patio enhances the value of the house by $400. However, Owner has no intention of selling the house, and she hates sitting outside, so she has no use for the patio. Owner has received labor and materials worth $1,000 on the market, but her objective net gain is $400 and her subjective net gain is zero.

§9.6.5 Choosing Among Market Value, Objective, or Subjective Net Gain

As the above illustrations show, the means of measuring the benefit can make quite a difference to recovery. The selection of the most appropriate measure is within the court's discretion, exercised to achieve a result that is fair under all the circumstances. The goal is to reach a figure that neither over-nor under-compensates the claimant while imposing liability on the recipient that is realistic and not excessive. While one cannot state hard-and-fast rules in an area involving discretion, there are some guidelines that are commonly followed:

1. **Market value** tends to be the **preferred** measure of recovery because it is likely to be the fairest and most balanced basis of compensating the conferrer at a rate that could reasonably be expected by the beneficiary. Also, because quantum meruit (or quantum valebant) approximates what the contract price would have been, had the parties made a contract for the services or property, it is conceptually most consistent with the underlying theory of quasi-contractual recovery, which is based on a fictional contract. This basis of calculation is therefore particularly appropriate when the benefit had been requested (even though there is no contract), or circumstances indicate that it likely would have been had the beneficiary had the opportunity to do so.

   Maggie would thus be liable to Sam for the $70 reasonable wage, rather than the $200 profit, and the victim would have to pay the doctor $200 for the successful treatment, rather than the value of life and health.

2. If there is some other fault or impropriety in the conduct of the conferrer that is not serious enough to preclude relief, the court may award the lowest measure of relief. For example, when a party materially breaches a contract after having partially performed, the breacher cannot recover under the contract but can obtain restitution for what has been given. Because the breacher is at fault for breaking the contract, restitutionary recovery is limited to the smaller of the market value of what was done or the portion of the price allocated to the performance under the contract. For example, say that a builder wrongfully abandons work after erecting part of a building. The market value of what has been done before abandonment is $5,000, but because the builder underbid, the amount of the contract price attributable to that work is only $4,000. The builder cannot recover more than $4,000, and that amount may be further reduced if the owner has suffered damages as a result of the breach. (This is discussed more fully in connection with material breach in section 17.6.2.)

3. Even in the absence of imposition or fault, if one measure is disproportionately large or small, fairness or reasonable community expectations may require that it not be selected. For example, irrespective of the concern for imposition, there would never be any basis for awarding the doctor the value of the victim's life. Not only could this be a gargantuan recovery, imposing great hardship on the victim and grossly overcompensating the doctor for her work, but it is not customary for doctors to be rewarded for services in this way.

4. If the recipient has been guilty of dishonest or improper conduct, the highest measure is likely to be used. To illustrate, recall the example in which Sam managed Maggie's kiosk after she fainted. Instead of paying over the $600 proceeds to Maggie, Sam used it to buy lottery tickets and won $100,000. Sam is now the recipient of enrichment by using Maggie's property without authority, and his wrongful act in misappropriating it justifies holding him liable for the full extent of his gain. That is, he is treated in law as having won the $100,000 on Maggie's behalf so that he has to disgorge the full amount of his winnings. If he won nothing in the lottery, so that he has no ultimate gain, the value of what he took, $600, is the higher measure and the most appropriate one to be used.

5. If the benefit was *requested* (that is, when there is a contract, but the conferrer elects restitution, or the request does not qualify as a contract), any price agreed to by the parties is probitive *evidence of value* and may be used in preference over other measures.

6. In some cases, none of the more common bases of measurement work at all, and the court may have to use its discretion to make an award more in keeping with the circumstances. For example, say that a climber is stranded on a cliff. A passerby sees this and climbs the cliff and rescues the climber. In doing so, the rescuer falls and is injured. She does not claim a fee for the rescue (which she most likely will not get for reasons stated in section 9.5.2), but she does claim reimbursement of her medical expenses on the theory that it would unjustly enrich the climber if he did not pay them. Although it is possible that the rescuer would be held to have been performed with gratuitous intent, a court may feel that it would be unjust to deny relief altogether. However, the medical expenses do not fit into any of the categories mentioned — they are not the market value of the service, nor the net enrichment of the climber, objectively or subjectively determined. To give relief, the court would have to use its discretion to create a remedy based on plaintiff's post-benefit medical expenditure. This resolution may be fair if the medical expenses are not too high, but if they are substantial, the concern is raised about imposing massive liability on the climber.

§9.7 "MORAL OBLIGATION": RESTITUTION WHEN A PROMISE IS BASED ON A PRIOR BENEFIT

§9.7.1 Introduction

As we have seen, restitution is not dependent on the obligor having made any promise. It is predicated on unjust enrichment rather than commitment.

The doctrine traditionally known as "moral obligation" is something of a hybrid, in that it covers situations in which the facts do not fully support restitutionary recovery, but the justification for giving relief is bolstered by a promise made after receipt of the benefit. In other words, it blends restitutionary concepts and promise.

To illustrate, add a fact to the example of the busybody neighbors, O. Fishus and N. Termeddler, who cleaned up the unkempt yard while the owner was at work and left a bill for $300. As officious intermeddlers, they are not entitled to restitution. However, instead of tossing the bill in the garbage, the homeowner wrote back to them thanking them for their effort and promising to pay the $300 at the end of the month. This promise is not contractual because the neighbors' detriment was "past consideration." It was not exchanged for, but preceded, the promise. Similarly, the sequence of action followed by promise precludes promissory estoppel relief because the neighbors' action was not induced by the homeowner's promise.

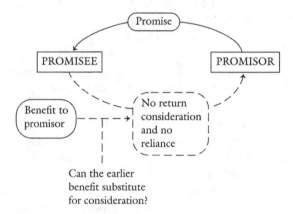

Can the earlier
benefit substitute
for consideration?

The question addressed in this section is whether the *prior benefit plus the later promise* should create a ground for enforcing the promise independent of consideration, restitution, and promissory estoppel.

§9.7.2 Terminology

Under the influence of Lord Mansfield, the great English jurist, a movement grew in eighteenth-century English courts to enforce promises without consideration, purely on the basis that they were morally binding. As Chapter 8 amply demonstrates, this trend did not take root. In the absence of consideration, an obligation cannot be enforced as a contract even if it is morally binding. Relief under promissory estoppel and restitution likewise require more than moral obligation. Indeed, when people say that an obligation is morally binding, they usually mean that the obligor should honor it despite the lack of legal duty to do so.

Notwithstanding this general sense in which "moral obligation" is understood, it has also come to be used as a term of art to describe a particular doctrine under which a promise without consideration may be enforced in a narrow range of circumstances. It is important not to confuse this technical use of "moral obligation" with its wider and more general meaning. Although promises are not enforced simply because they are morally binding, a promise that satisfies the prerequisites of the doctrine of "moral obligation" is enforceable despite the absence of consideration. Because the name of this doctrine is so easily confused with the general meaning of moral obligation, many courts and commentators prefer to use a different label for it. The most common is the **material benefit rule**, or, following the wording of Restatement Second, **promise for benefit received.**

§9.7.3 The Traditional Scope of "Moral Obligation"

Although Lord Mansfield's efforts did not lead to the general substitution of moral obligation for consideration as the basis of contract, some vestiges of this idea remain in our law in the form of narrow exceptions to consideration doctrine. These exceptions apply only to a small number of specific situations in which a debtor makes a promise to pay an earlier unenforceable debt. Although the later promise lacks consideration, the moral obligation to pay the pre-existing unenforceable debt is treated as sufficient to make the promise enforceable.

This is best explained by an illustration using one of the specific situations: the barring of a debt by the **statute of limitations.** Because witnesses disappear and memories fade over time, and because claims should not be allowed to fester indefinitely, all claims are subject to a time bar called a statute of limitations. The claimant must initiate suit before the expiration of a specified period after it arises, failing which the right to sue is lost. The legal effect of expiry of the limitation period is not elimination of the claim, but only of the right to sue on it. For most purposes, this distinction does not mean much, but the vestigial obligation is enough to support a later promise by the obligor to pay the debt.

Say, for example, that Debtor borrowed $5,000 from Creditor seven years ago. The loan should have been repaid six months later, but Debtor never paid and Creditor never got around to suing for recovery of the money. The statute of limitations for contractual claims is typically six years, so the claim is now barred. Upon realizing that the limitation period had run, Debtor was at first jubilant, but then his conscience troubled him. He therefore wrote to Creditor and promised to pay the old loan. Although there was no new consideration given by Creditor for this promise, the pre-existing valid but barred debt is recognized as furnishing a moral obligation sufficient to dispense with the need for new consideration. The new promise is therefore binding on the debtor and can be enforced if he declines to perform it.

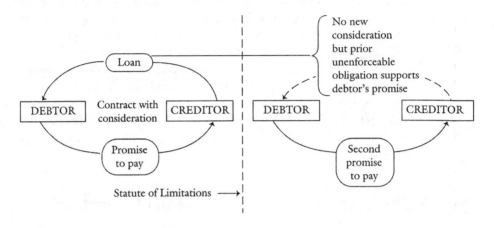

In addition to obligations barred by the statute of limitations, courts have applied this concept of moral obligation in a few other specific situations involving a subsequent promise to honor a pre-existing but unenforceable legal obligation. The two most familiar are prior debts discharged in bankruptcy and prior voidable debts. When a debtor becomes **bankrupt**, his or her prebankruptcy debts are usually paid only in part by a distribution from the bankrupt estate. The balance is discharged and creditors are forbidden by law to take any steps to try to collect it. However, the doctrine of "moral obligation" validates a later promise by the debtor to pay the discharged debt. (This common law rule is now heavily regulated by statute. To prevent creditors from undermining the discharge, the Bankruptcy Code imposes a strict procedure for reaffirmation of discharged debts that includes a variety of safeguards to protect the debtor from agreeing to a reaffirmation that is not in his interests.)

A **voidable** debt is one that can be avoided by the debtor because of some defect in formation or contractual capacity such as fraud, mistake, or minority. A voidable obligation must be **distinguished from** a **void** one. When a putative contract is void (as happens when consideration is lacking), it is a legal nullity and neither party can enforce it. However, if a contract is voidable by one of the parties, that party has the choice of treating the contract as fully valid and enforceable, or relying on the defect to escape the contractual relationship.[8] Under the doctrine of "moral obligation," if the party with the right of avoidance ratifies the contract by a second

---

8. We return to the distinctions between void and voidable obligations in section 13.3.

promise after becoming aware of the defect or after the basis for contractual incapacity has ended, the later promise is binding despite the lack of new consideration.

These discrete situations form the core of the traditional doctrine of "moral obligation," and have become well-accepted exceptions to the "past consideration" rule. The difficult question is whether the doctrine should be broadened beyond this narrow range to create a more general basis for enforcing promises motivated by prior benefits.

§9.7.4 The Broad "Material Benefit" Rule

In *Webb v. McGowan*, 168 So.196 (Ala. 1935) the court, by manipulating consideration doctrine, took the bold step of extending the moral obligation doctrine beyond its well-accepted confines. Webb, working on the upper floor of a mill, was in the process of dropping a large wooden block to the ground when he noticed that McGowan was in the path of its fall. To divert the block from crushing McGowan, Webb held onto it and fell with it. He thereby saved McGowan from death or severe injury at the cost of serious and disabling injury to himself. In gratitude, McGowan promised a life pension to Webb which he paid for several years until his death. His estate discontinued payment. The "past consideration" rule precluded enforcement of the promise as a contract because Webb's detriment preceded and was not exchanged for the promise. However, the court avoided the "past consideration" rule by using a legal fiction — it deemed the detriment to have been contemporaneous with the promise. In justifying this resolution, the court drew analogies to restitution cases and to established situations in which courts had enforced promises to pay prior unenforceable legal obligations. The court considered that McGowan's moral obligation to honor his promise justified expanding those principles.

Webb's broader moral obligation doctrine has not been widely accepted by other courts. However, Restatement, Second §86 does adopt it. Section 86 does not employ the legal fiction used in *Webb*. Instead, it formulates the doctrine as a distinct cause of action under which a promise to pay for a previous benefit may be enforced despite the lack of consideration. Section 86 sets forth the following requirements:

1. The promisor has been **unjustly enriched** by a **benefit previously received** from the promisee.
2. The benefit was **not given as a gift.** (However, according to Comment d, the later promise shifts the **burden of showing gratuitous intent** to the recipient. The effect of this is to allow relief, even if the benefit was gratuitous, unless the recipient (promisor) can prove that the benefit was intended as a gift.)

3. The promisor subsequently makes a **promise in recognition** of the benefit.

If these requirements are satisfied, the promise is binding to the *extent necessary to prevent injustice.* One of the factors to be taken into account in exercising this discretion is the relationship between the value of the benefit and the amount promised. This factor is expressly identified by §86, which specifically requires enforcement to be limited to an amount proportional to the value of the benefit. Beyond this, the general discretion to prevent injustice allows the court to weigh whatever other factors bear upon the appropriate extent of relief.

To illustrate how this doctrine may work, return to the example of the neighbors' claim for the yardwork in which the homeowner made a subsequent promise to pay the $300 bill: The making of the subsequent promise could remove the objection that the neighbors were officious inter-meddlers. The comments to Restatement Second §86 say that a clear, well-considered, and uncoerced subsequent promise to make restitution lessens the concern about imposition by demonstrating the utility of the benefit. Thus, clear and voluntary ratification of the benefit acts as a counterweight to the meddling and changes the equities in favor of enforcement. The facts indicate that the other prerequisites for relief, a prior benefit, enrichment, and an intent to charge are satisfied, so we turn to the question of relief.

The market value of the yardwork is not stated, so we do not know if $300 is disproportionate to the value of the benefit. If it is, the court may reduce recovery. Therefore, although a valuation issue arises here, as it does in a restitutionary claim based on unjust enrichment, the existence of a promise changes the dynamics of the valuation issue. The promise is at least evidence of what the promisor considered the worth of the benefit to be, and evidence of market value is relegated to a subsidiary role of policing the promise to ensure that it is not too generous. Proportionality is a rough equivalence between the amount promised and the value of the benefit, and does not require an exact match. The proportionality require-ment is congruent with the goal of restoring only the enrichment gained by the promisor. It is also related to the cautionary function of consideration doctrine, in that it protects the promisor from a promise that is too generous or rash.

In addition to ensuring proportionality, the court exercises a broad discretion (similar to the overall balancing employed in promissory estoppel cases) to evaluate all the circumstances of the case to decide what must be done to achieve justice. The nature and circumstances of the enrichment and the quality of the promise must both be taken into account. In a case like this one, in which the original imposition was outrageous, the promise must be looked at carefully to ensure that it was a voluntary commitment, unaffected by the manipulations of the intermeddler. The degree to which the promise satisfies the evidentiary and cautionary functions of legal formality is relevant here. In addition, the court must take into account the danger of reinforcing meddlesome behavior and may conclude that even a subsequent promise should not validate the actions of the neighbors.

Although a broad principle of restitution based on a subsequent promise is advocated by Restatement Second, the courts of many states have refused to follow this lead and have not extended "moral obligation" beyond the few narrow situations involving prior unenforceable legal obligations.

Examples

1. Consider whether the following transactions gave rise to a contract implied in fact, and if not, whether they create grounds for finding a contract implied in law (that, is, they establish grounds for relief on the basis of unjust enrichment):

   (a) Sara Nade is a violinist who makes her living as a street musician. One evening she noticed a man sitting at a sidewalk table outside a restaurant. She approached him and began to play. He obviously enjoyed her music and applauded when she finished the piece. Sara asked the man if he would like to hear more, and he requested his favorite tune, which Sara played. At the end of her performance, Sara said to the man, "That will be $20 please."

   (b) Kwazi Contracting Co. entered into a contract with Flyby Nightwatch, Inc. under which Flyby agreed to provide nighttime security services for Kwazi's office premises for a monthly price of $5,000. Flyby had undertaken too many contracts and did not have the staff to perform all of them. It therefore made a contract with one of its competitors, Beneficial Security, Inc. under which Beneficial provided the security officers to patrol Kwazi's offices. Beneficial charged Flyby a monthly fee of $2,000 for this service. The arrangement worked for two months, but ended when Flyby became insolvent and went out of business. At that time, Kwazi had paid Flyby the full $10,000 due for two months' services, but Flyby had not made any payments to Beneficial. During the two months that the services were performed, Kwazi's executives had noticed that the premises were being patrolled by security guards who wore Beneficial arm patches. They thought nothing of this and assumed that Flyby and Beneficial were associated. Because it cannot recover anything from Flyby, Beneficial claims that Kwazi owes it $4,000.

   (c) Quantum Merriment Co., Inc. was planning to build a theme park. It needed to develop some preliminary plans for the park so that its board of directors could make a decision on the feasibility and rough cost of the resort. The president of Quantum approached Ben E. Factor, a designer of amusement parks, and asked him to draw

257

some preliminary plans. Quantum's president made it clear to Ben that he would be doing the work "on spec," which meant that he would only be paid for it if the board decided to go ahead with the development of the park. Ben drew the plans and the board reviewed them. It ultimately decided not to proceed with the development.

2. Benny Fishery has been involved in a longstanding feud with his neighbor, Sam Aratin, arising out of the alleged excretory habits of Sam's dog. Matters have become so bad that Benny has purchased a shotgun and vows to use it on Sam or his dog if either sets foot on his property.

Last Saturday, Benny locked up his house and left on a two-week camping trip in the wilderness. On Saturday evening a faulty appliance caused a fire to break out in his kitchen. Sam saw the fire through the kitchen window. Having seen Benny set off that morning with his camping gear, Sam realized that immediate action was called for. He grabbed his disposable fire extinguisher, smashed the window, and discharged its contents into the flames, dousing the fire. Afterwards he made inquiries and ascertained that Benny was incommunicado for the next two weeks. Sam was concerned that a burglar could easily enter the vacant house through the broken window, so he hired a contractor to replace it for $200. Sam had to pay the contractor because he insisted on cash and refused to wait for his money until Benny returned.

Sam left a note on Benny's charred kitchen counter, telling him what had happened and asking for payment of $300, made up as follows:
(a) Cost of the disposable fire extinguisher, $30.
(b) $200 paid for the window.
(c) Sam's fee for services rendered, $70.

On his return from vacation, Benny sent back Sam's note, having scrawled on it some unpleasant suggestions on what Sam should do with it. Should Sam follow these suggestions, or does he have a right to payment?

3. Change the facts in Example 2 as follows: The fire was so fierce that the extinguisher did not douse it. Sam entered the kitchen through the broken window and tried valiantly to stamp out the flames. He eventually succeeded, but burned his legs badly in the process. As a result, he incurred $4,000 in medical expenses and had to take three weeks unpaid sick leave, losing an additional $2,000. He has no medical or disability insurance. Apart from the financial loss, he has suffered excruciating pain.

When Benny returned from vacation and heard of Sam's sacrifice, he was overcome with gratitude and felt deep remorse for his hostile attitude to Sam's dog. He visited Sam in the hospital and tearfully promised to pay Sam $200 per month for the next three years to compensate Sam for the medical expenses, loss of earnings, and pain. Sam accepted this offer in an emotional display of reconciliation.

Benny paid installments for two months until, looking out of his window one morning, he saw Sam's dog busy decorating his lawn. This rekindled the old feud, and Benny refuses to pay another cent to Sam. Is his promise enforceable?

4. Rhoda Hogg began hearing noises from her car when she accelerated beyond 85 m.p.h. on the freeway. She took the car to Mark Price, a mechanic, to have the trouble determined and repaired. She told Mark that he was to call her for authorization if the repair would cost more than $200. Mark neglected to communicate this instruction to his assistant, who completed an expensive repair without checking with Rhoda. When Rhoda was presented with a bill for $650, she refused to pay it, and insists that she is liable for no more than $200. Mark admits his mistake, but argues that the repair was necessary and $650 is a fair charge for the parts and labor. This is in fact true.

Is Rhoda obligated to pay the $650?

5. Val N. Teer and Justin Richmond entered into a contract of sale under which Val purchased Justin's house. The contract was conditional on Val obtaining a mortgage loan to finance the purchase. Justin knew that Val had a poor credit record and did not qualify for a loan, so he encouraged her to apply to a particular lender that had a reputation for lenience in evaluating borrower qualifications.

Val applied for the loan. While she was waiting to hear the decision on her application, she began to plan her move. One of the items that had to be moved to her new house was a hot tub. As the house had no suitable firm area on which to place it, Val realized that a concrete slab would have to be built on which to install it. She had ascertained from the moving company that she would save considerable costs if the tub could be moved and installed in one operation, because this would eliminate moving the tub to storage and then transporting it and setting it up on site. Because she was anxious to have the slab in place by closing, Val felt that she could not wait for the decision on the loan application. She discussed the matter with Justin, who expressed confidence that Val would get the loan and told her that he would have no objection if she laid the slab immediately. The parties did not discuss what would happen if the loan was refused.

Val's cousin is a contractor and he agreed to build the slab for her for the special price of $1,000. (His normal charge would be $2,000.) A few days after the slab was completed, Val was notified by the loan company that her application had been rejected. As there were no other prospects for financing, the sale fell through.

Justin now has a slab on his property at Val's expense. He has no use for it and it does not enhance the value of his house. Val would like to be reimbursed for the slab. Can she recover? If so, how much?

Explanations

1. (a) Sara made no express contract with the man because no words of agreement were uttered or articulated. They may have entered into a contract implied in fact if, despite the absence of actual words of agreement, their behavior in context, reasonably interpreted, indicates an intent to be bound to each other. A factually implied contract is an actual contract. Once it is established, it has the same legal effect as an express contract. For a contract to be implied in fact, the deliberate conduct of each party, viewed reasonably from the perspective of the other under all the circumstances of the case, must manifest an intent to enter into an exchange relationship under which each delivers or promises a performance to the other. (Restatement, Second §19.) In the present case, there was deliberate overt conduct: Sara played her violin for the man who accepted her performance by listening and requesting an encore. (Of course, if the man just sat at his table and did not interact with Sara in a way that reasonably indicated intent to contract, we could not infer from that passive inaction that he intended to contract with her.) If it is common practice for street musicians to charge for their services and the man knew or should have known this, his conduct in acquiescing in the service could create the inference that he intended to pay the customary fee for the service. However, if no such common practice exists, the man's conduct in listening to the music and requesting another tune would not create an implication of a contract to pay for the service.

   If no actual contact was made, Sara's only basis for recovery would be unjust enrichment. (As explained in section 9.4, this cause of action is still commonly described in the language of the ancient legal fiction, and is referred to as contract "implied in law" or "quasi contract.") To qualify for relief for unjust enrichment, Sara must not have been a "volunteer" or an "officious intermeddler." A volunteer is one who confers a benefit without intent to charge for it. This intent is usually determined objectively, based on apparent intent as perceived by a reasonable person in the position of the recipient. The question of whether it is customary for street musicians to render services gratuitously, which we considered in relation to the question of actual contract, is relevant here as well. If Sara performed the services without reasonable intent to charge, she is not entitled to recover. However, even if she was not a volunteer, she still cannot recover if she was an officious intermeddler — she imposed her services on the man without being asked. Under some circumstances, where an imminent threat to life or property creates an emergency and it is not possible to get authorization to act, a person who provides unrequested services may not be an intermeddler. However, that is not the case here. Even where a benefit is conferred officiously, enrichment may still be unjust if the recipient, having the easy option of rejecting it, accepts it in the reasonable realization that compensation is expected. The man was a captive audience and had little chance of avoiding the benefit. Therefore, he cannot be said to have accepted the benefit just by passively listening to her playing. However, he requested an encore, and this active response may suggest that he accepted the benefit. If so, the problem of imposition may be cured and Sara would be entitled to the value of her services if she can establish that there is a general understanding that street musicians do not perform for free.

If Sara can establish an actual contract implied in fact, she can recover the contract price. In this case, no contract price was settled (her demand for $20 came after the contract was performed), so if an actual contract exists, her fee will be based on a the market value of her services (quantum meruit). This is, of course, the same measure normally used to determine recovery for unjust enrichment. This shows that quantum meruit, although closely associated with restitutionary claims, is not confined to unjust enrichment. It is also used to fix the contract price where parties expressly or impliedly agree to contract for a reasonable price. The $20 that Sara demands may or may not be the market value of her services. This would have to be established by testimony of a witness with expertise in the trade.

1. (b) Beneficial should not be able to recover from Kwazi either on grounds of contract or unjust enrichment. The parties never dealt with each other at all, and certainly never made an express contract. The facts do not support the factual implication of a contract either. A party can be held to an implied contract if it voluntarily accepts services without objection on the reasonable understanding that the services are not rendered gratuitously. However, there is nothing in these facts to indicate such assent or reasonable expectation on Kwazi's part. A contract can only be implied in fact if there is some conduct from which agreement can be inferred. Kwazi's conduct does not give rise to this inference. As far it was concerned, its contract was with Flyby. Nothing alerted it to the possibility that Beneficial might look to it for payment, and it had no involvement or interest in any

arrangements that Flyby might make to find the staff to perform its obligations under the contract.

Beneficial's claim also does not satisfy any of the elements of unjust enrichment. As against Kwazi, Beneficial should be treated as a volunteer. True, it did not intend to render its services gratuitously, but it expected compensation from Flyby, not Kwazi. Beneficial should also be treated as an officious intermeddler as far as Kwazi is concerned. "Officious intermeddler" is used here in its technical legal sense, not in its ordinary sense. Beneficial is not literally an intermeddler because it did not impose its services unasked, but was acting pursuant to its contract with Flyby. However, from Kwazi's perspective, Beneficial can be seen as an intermeddler if it performed the services with intent to hold Kwazi liable for them. Although there was no emergency and Beneficial had ample opportunity to forewarn Kwazi that acceptance of its services could result in liability, it never asked Kwazi to guarantee payment for the work. Finally, Kwazi paid Flyby for the services and was not enriched by anything that Beneficial did. Like *Contship Containerlines* described in section 9.4.2, this case involves the allocation of loss between two innocent parties. However, unlike the carrier in *Contship Containerlines* the loss here should rest with Beneficial. The shipper in *Contship Containerlines* was saddled with the loss because it bore the risk of paying a third-party intermediary who failed to transmit the funds to the carrier. The situation here is quite different. Only Beneficial dealt with Flyby and gave it credit. Flyby was not an intermediary for Kwazi, which did not even have reason to know of the transaction between Flyby and Beneficial.

1. (c) Ben has no right to payment in contract. Normally, where a person requests another to perform a service in the course of business, we would readily find a contract. Even if payment is not discussed, there would be a reasonable expectation that the services are not to be rendered gratuitously, and must be paid for at the customary or market rate (quantum meruit). However, the parties here expressly agreed that Ben's services would be "on spec." Although the parties may have had a contract in which Ben's services were exchanged for the commitment to make a good faith decision about developing the park, this contract contained a contingent payment term, and the condition of payment was not satisfied. The agreement that Ben would not be entitled to a fee unless the board decided to proceed with the development also means that he has no claim for unjust enrichment. In the absence of fulfillment of the condition, he agreed to perform the services gratuitously. (See *Forrest Associates v. Passama-quoddy Tribe*, 760 A.2d 1041 (Me. 2000). The plaintiff conducted a

market assessment for the tribe's possible development of a high-stakes bingo operation. His work was done "on spec," subject to the understanding that he would not be paid unless the tribe went ahead with the development. The tribe did not proceed with the project, and the court held that the plaintiff was not entitled to recover for the value of its work, either in contract or in unjust enrichment.)

2. Unlike Example 1, there is no question here that Sam and Benny have a contract implied in fact. Any relief awarded to Sam would have to be on the basis of unjust enrichment. If Sam did not intend to charge for his efforts, he is a volunteer and cannot receive restitution. His intent is objectively determined based on his reasonable expectations, and it does not matter whether or not he was actually thinking of compensation as he rushed out to fight the fire. It is reasonable to attribute to Sam the intent to claim reimbursement for the extinguisher. However, his claim for the services is another matter. A professional person who renders services for which he customarily charges, usually has a reasonable expectation of compensation, but a neighbor's emergency intervention is more likely intended as altruistic and gratuitous. As to the window — Sam clearly intended to seek reimbursement for the replacement costs and did not do this with gratuitous intent.

To receive restitution, Sam must also not have been an **officious intermeddler**. As noted in section 9.5.2, this means he must satisfy three requirements. Sam's emergency intervention seems to satisfy all three. First, Sam must not reasonably have been able to get Benny's authorization in advance, which he clearly could not. Second, Sam must have had no reason to believe that Benny would object to his actions. Although Benny had made it clear that he did not want Sam on his property, Sam could have assumed reasonably that this ban did not apply in the emergency situation. Third, Sam must have conferred a benefit on Benny. Clearly, his successful action conferred a significant benefit on Benny by extinguishing the fire and saving his property.

Sam is therefore neither a volunteer nor an officious intermeddler as far as the fire extinguisher is concerned, so he should be reimbursed for the market value of the extinguisher. As noted earlier, he is also not a volunteer as regards the window replacement, but he has a more difficult case to show that this action was not officious intermeddling.[9] There was no great urgency to replace the window. Sam could have secured the house by boarding up the window until Benny's return. Benny apparently did accept the benefit of the new

---

9. Assume that Sam was justified in breaking the window in the first place to extinguish the fire. If he was not, he would be liable for improper damage to Benny's property, and he would certainly not be able to make a claim for reimbursement.

window. (The facts do not indicate that he demanded its removal.) This may cure the problem of officious intermeddling. A person is not taken to have accepted a benefit if he cannot return it and has no option to keep it, but a window is capable of removal. Benny is benefited by the new window which he would have had to install himself had Sam not done it. Therefore, the equities favor restitution for this disbursement as well. This being so, the market value of the window repair is the appropriate measure of the benefit. The cost to Sam is probative but not conclusive evidence of market value.

3. This example is inspired by *Webb v. McGowan*, discussed in section 9.7.4. This case is distinguishable from *Webb* in that Sam was injured saving Benny's property, not his person. Although rescue from personal injury or death provides the strongest equities in favor of enforcing the beneficiary's later promise, there is also moral value in upholding a promise in recognition of property preservation.

    Sam would have trouble enforcing Benny's promise as a contract because of the "past consideration" rule. Although it is conceivable that a court would award relief on a theory of unjust enrichment, Sam's claim is an awkward fit for restitutionary recovery. He probably did act with gratuitous intent in performing the service, as explained in Example 2. In addition, restitution focuses on the benefit to Benny, which does not bear a relationship to Sam's loss.

    However, because Benny made the promise in recognition of Sam's prior service, the material benefit rule of Restatement, Second §86 provides a much more satisfactory basis for relief.[10] The premise of §86 is that Benny's subsequent ratifying promise shifts the equities in Sam's favor by recognizing and placing a value on the benefit and creating the presumption that it was not conferred with gratuitous intent. The disproportionality principle assures that the promise is not too generous in relation to the value of the benefit. However, where the focus is not on the value of the benefit, but on the relationship between the promise and the injury, it seems fair to measure proportionality in reference to the injury, not the benefit.

    A court that applies §86 must also take care that the promise was made under fair circumstances, and that it was not induced by coercion or motivated by impulsive generosity. There is no hint that Sam put any pressure on Benny to make the promise. The fact that he made it tearfully in Sam's hospital room soon after the incident could give pause. (The cautionary function of consideration doctrine plays a role here.) However, this concern is alleviated by the fact that

---

10. As noted in section 9.7.4, not all courts have been willing to recognize the broad material benefit rule advocated by §86.

Benny continued to make payments for some time after this emotionally charged moment.

4. In contrast to the previous examples, there is a contract in this case under which services were requested by Rhoda. The problem is that Mark negligently exceeded his authority under the contract. As the repair was necessary and reasonably priced, refusal to award its value enriches Rhoda by giving her a $650 repair for $200.

    If asked, Rhoda may have authorized the repair, but she was given no opportunity to exercise this choice and had the repair imposed on her. She cannot return it because it is incorporated into her property. This imposition makes Mark an intermeddler as much as if he had made the repair without any request. Rhoda's enrichment is not unjust, and Mark is not entitled to quantum meruit relief. He is bound by the maximum price settled by the contract, $200.

    In *Deck v. Jim Harris Chevrolet-Buick*, 386 N.E.2d 714 (Ind. 1979), the case on which this example is based, the court reached this conclusion. Although the mistake may have been honest, the repairer was in a better position than the customer to prevent it and must take responsibility for the negligence that led to the customer's enrichment.

5. The principal purpose of this example is to emphasize the point, made in section 9.3, that some facts may give rise to alternative theories of liability. This case invites consideration of possible recovery under contract, promissory estoppel, or restitution, and a comparison of the remedies under each theory. Unfortunately for Val, her prospects for relief are not good under any of them.

    The claim for **contractual relief is** tenuous at best. The parties had a contract for the sale of the house, but made no express contract concerning the slab. Val clearly intended it for her own benefit and made no commitment to Justin to build it. If she had changed her mind and had not laid the slab, Justin could not have claimed that he had breached any obligation to him. Because the parties apparently did not contemplate failure of the sale, they made no agreement on what would happen in that event. There is no evidence from which to infer a commitment by Justin to pay for the slab if the property remained his.

    Val's claim for relief on the basis of **promissory estoppel** runs into difficulty on the issues of both promise and justifiable reliance. Justin's only express promise, to transfer title to the house, was discharged because Val could not satisfy the condition of financing. While there is some hint that Val relied on Justin's recommendation of a lender and his permission to build the slab, there is not enough here to support a finding that Justin promised that Val would be able to make use of the slab or that he reasonably intended to induce her to build it. By laying the slab in anticipation of a successful loan application, without resolving liability if the sale fell through, Val assumed the risk of wasting her money. In the absence of a clear promise of reimbursement or of circumstances that impose some special duty of care on Justin, Val must take responsibility for poor judgment in the precontractual period.

Restitution is not available, for related reasons. Although Justin has been enriched by the building of a slab on his property, his grant of permission to build was not a request for this benefit. Had he been told that he would have to pay for the slab if the sale fell through, he may well have refused permission. To treat his permission as a request would unfairly impose on him a useless concrete slab that adds no value to his property. Val's failure to resolve his liability in the event of the sale's failure makes her a volunteer. She assumed the risk that if the sale collapsed, she would have conferred a gratuitous benefit on Justin.

Although Val has had no luck under any theory of liability, it is a useful exercise to consider briefly the **different forms of relief** that would have been available to her under each theory: If a contract had been established, she would have been entitled to enforce it and to recover the agreed price of the slab. If no price had been agreed, she would be entitled to a reasonable price based on quantum meruit. If dthe contractor's normal price reflects market value, the market price is $2,000, and the fact that Val obtained the work for $1,000 because of family connections does not detract from the market value. She is entitled to retain this profit unless it could also be implied that she undertook to furnish the slab at her cost. Promissory estoppel would aim primarily at reimbursing Val for her expenditure in reliance, the actual cost of $1,000. Restitution is based on Justin's enrichment, which is normally measured on the basis of quantum meruit in the same way as it would be under a contract with an open price term. It could be as high as $2,000 if that is the true market value of the construction work. But if the slab did not add a full $2,000 value to the property, the award may be reduced to the extent of Justin's actual economic gain. Because he had no use for the slab and it added no value to his property, his ultimate gain is zero, whether measured subjectively or objectively.

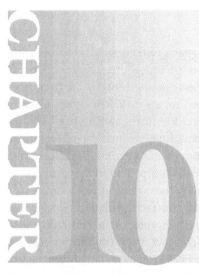

Interpretation and Construction: Resolving Meaning and Dealing with Uncertainty in Agreements

§10.1 THE PROBLEM OF INDEFINITENESS IN AN AGREEMENT

If the terms of an agreement are expressed clearly and comprehensively, the fact of contract formation and the extent of each party's commitment can be ascertained with relative ease by the interpretation of their language in context. However, parties sometimes fail to express their assent adequately because they have left a material aspect of their agreement vague or ambiguous, or they have failed to resolve it or to provide for it at all. When the agreement suffers from this kind of uncertainty, it is said to be **indefinite.**

There could be many different causes of indefiniteness. For example, the parties may not take the trouble of discussing all aspects of the proposed relationship, they may not give enough attention to detail, they may be unclear in their thinking or articulation of what is expected, or they may avoid confronting thorny issues that threaten to collapse the deal. Sometimes it is clear that the parties genuinely intended a contract despite the indefiniteness, but in other cases the lack of resolution means that they had not yet achieved consensus.

The general rule is that no contract comes into being if a material aspect of the agreement is left indefinite by the parties and the uncertainty cannot be resolved by the process of interpretation or construction. The existence of such an irresoluble key aspect of the relationship means that the parties never reached sufficient consensus to conclude an enforceable contract.

This statement of the general rule suggests two central issues that must be confronted in dealing with problems of indefiniteness: First, for an apparent contract to fail for indefiniteness, there must be an **incurable uncertainty** about what the parties agreed to, so that their intent to enter a contract is in doubt, or the court is at a loss in establishing a basis for enforcing what was agreed. This first issue involves many considerations that form the basis of the remainder of this chapter. Second, the uncertainty must relate to a **material aspect** of the relationship. Although an indefinite non-material term does need to be settled by the court if it is relevant to the dispute, the uncertainty does not preclude contract formation.

A term is material if it is an important component of the contract. It is so central to the values exchanged under the contract that it is a *fundamental basis of the bargain*. Although materiality is sometimes obvious, it is not always easy to decide because the significance of a term in any particular relationship can only be gauged by interpreting the facts of the case to uncover the reasonable expectations of the parties. (This broad definition of materiality is enough for present purposes. The question of when a term is important enough to be material is considered in greater detail in sections 6.5.2 and 17.3.)

§10.2 THE APPROPRIATE JUDICIAL RESPONSE TO PROBLEMS OF INDEFINITENESS

If the unclear or unresolved terms do indicate that the parties never reached final, coherent consensus, a court should not try to concoct a contract for them. This would overstep the proper bounds of judicial power. It is the court's job to enforce contracts, not to make them up simply because the parties have engaged in negotiation. However, this does not mean that the court should refuse contractual enforcement unless every material term of the agreement has been expressed with piercing clarity. Such a rigorous standard would err in the opposite direction by failing to recognize a contract when the evidence suggests that the parties reasonably expected to be bound, did intend to enter a contract despite the indefiniteness, and had relied on the existence of a contract.

The balance between these poles results in a general principle that tolerates some degree of indefiniteness provided that the evidence indicates that the parties did intend a contract, and there is some means of resolving the uncertainty, so that a breach can be identified and a remedy provided. Both UCC §2.204(3)[1] and the Restatement Second §33(2) adopt this approach by emphasizing that a contract should be treated as reasonably certain if the language of agreement, interpreted in context and in light of

---

1. Section 2.204(3) is unchanged in the 2003 revision.

applicable legal rules, provides enough content to establish an intent to contract, a basis for finding breach, and a means of providing a remedy.

Although remedies are not discussed until Chapter 18, it is useful to focus on the *relationship between definiteness and remedy* suggested by the UCC and Restatement Second. Definiteness is not absolute but relative, and the degree of certainty required may be different depending on the nature of the controversy and the relief claimed. For example, if the plaintiff claims enforcement of a clear obligation due by the defendant, and the defendant contends that the contract is too indefinite because of vagueness in the plaintiff's obligation, the court does not have to establish the plaintiff's obligation with as much certainty as it would have to do if that was the obligation in issue. Similarly, if the plaintiff is claiming damages for the breach of an unclear obligation of the defendant, the court needs just enough information to determine a monetary award. However, if the plaintiff was seeking specific performance of the obligation (that is, a court order compelling the defendant to perform the contract), the court would need a greater degree of certainty to grant the order because the court must be able to define the obligation clearly if it is going to order its performance.

Although it is relatively easy to identify the general range of appropriate judicial intervention to cure indefiniteness, it is much more difficult to know if an individual case falls within that range: Whether the indefiniteness is properly remediable or should preclude contractual enforcement. As in so many other situations, the answer can only be reached by finding the mutual intent of the parties through the process of interpretation (evaluating the facts) and construction (applying appropriate legal rules that are used to determine presumed intent). Interpretation and construction are explained in section 10.4. Before we examine them in detail, it is useful to further define indefiniteness by looking at the different ways in which it may be manifested.

§10.3 DIFFERENT FORMS OF INDEFINITENESS

Indefiniteness in an agreement could be caused by vagueness, ambiguity, omission, or irresolution. These different shortcomings have much in common, but they may raise different concerns that call for separate treatment. It is therefore useful to begin by articulating this distinction.

§10.3.1 Unclear Terms: Vagueness and Ambiguity

a. Vague Terms

A term is vague (or uncertain) if it is stated so obscurely or in such general language that one cannot reasonably determine what it means. For example,

Lessor agrees to let certain business premises to Lessee for one year in exchange for "a periodic rental payment based on a fair percentage of Lessee's earnings." One cannot determine on the face of this language the amount and the due date of the rent. The wording fails to convey a certain and concrete meaning. *Baer v. Chase*, 392 F.3d 609 (3d Cir. 2004) provides another illustration of incurable vagueness. Baer, an ex-prosecutor and would-be screenwriter, assisted Chase, the creator of the hugely successful series, *The Sopranos*, by helping him with background information on the New Jersey mob and by reading and commenting on his draft script. Baer asserted that Chase had agreed orally that if the show became a success, he would "take care" of him and would reward him "in a manner commensurate with the true value" of his services. The court of appeals affirmed the trial court's grant of summary judgment against Baer on the basis that even if such a promise was made, these terms were too indefinite to enable the court to ascertain with reasonable certainty what performance was to be rendered by Chase. The court acknowledged that indefiniteness can sometimes be resolved by the implication of a term, such as a reasonable price. However, the vagueness in this undertaking was beyond cure.

By contrast, the court did not find indefiniteness to be fatal in B. *Lewis Productions, Inc. v. Angelou*, 2005 WL 1138474 (S.D.N.Y. 2005. Not reported in F. Supp.). The poet Maya Angelou entered into a written agreement with Lewis under which she granted him the exclusive right to represent her in placing her work in greeting cards, calendars, and other stationery items. Lewis agreed to contribute "all the capital necessary" and Angelou agreed to contribute "original literary works." The agreement did not particularize Lewis's duties, but it did provide that the parties would share the net profits of the venture after revenue had been applied to the repayment of Lewis's capital contribution and expenses. Lewis began work immediately. Just over two years after the agreement was entered, and when Lewis was close to executing a licensing agreement with Hallmark cards, Angelou terminated the relationship.[2] Shortly thereafter, she entered into a licensing agreement with Hallmark on her own. Protracted litigation followed in which Lewis sued Angelou for breach of contract.[3] Angelou moved for summary judgment on the ground that the agreement was too indefinite to be enforced as a contract. The court denied her motion. It noted that the court's role was not to make a contract for the parties, and it would not enforce an agreement whose terms are so indefinite that the parties' intentions cannot be

---

2. Although it may not be appropriate to mention this in a family-oriented law book, one of the reasons why the relationship between Lewis and Angelou collapsed was that Angelou was repelled when she saw Lewis grab his crotch while engaged in a conversation at a Las Vegas event.

3. He also sued Hallmark for tortuous interference with contract on the grounds that it induced Angelou's breach by contracting directly with her knowing that Lewis had been negotiating with Hallmark on her behalf.

ascertained with reasonable certainty. However, it observed that courts are reluctant to strike down contracts for indefiniteness and cautioned that courts should not turn the search for certainty into a "fetish." Some degree of indefiniteness can be found in most contracts. The court recognized that the parties did intend to form a business relationship, and it felt that all of the open-ended terms could be given adequate content by supplying a standard of reasonableness and good faith to the parties' undertakings.

b. Ambiguity

A term is ambiguous if it is capable of more than one meaning. Ambiguity can lie in a word itself or in the structure of a sentence. Ambiguity in a word may be illustrated by a term in a lease that confines the use of the premises to "the purpose of conducting a bookmaking business." The word "bookmaking" could refer either to the manufacture of books or to the making and placing of bets on horses and sporting events. Ambiguity can also result from inept sentence construction. For example, although the lease makes it clear that "bookmaking" is used in the latter sense, it goes on to provide that Lessor "shall be entitled to ten percent of Lessee's profits from all gambling activities that shall be lawfully conducted on the premises." The clumsy sentence construction may mean that Lessor is entitled to ten percent of all profits earned by Lessee from gambling, and that Lessee is obliged to conduct only lawful activity on the premises, or it may mean that Lessor is entitled to ten percent of the profits from lawful gambling but gets no share of illegal gambling proceeds.

c. Curing Ambiguity with Contextual Evidence

A term that is not readily comprehensible on its face may not be incurably vague or ambiguous, because it may become clear if interpreted in context. Evidence of what the parties said or did in negotiations, correspondence, or dealings prior to the agreement or during the period following it may help to clarify what they meant by the language used. In addition, clarity may be supplied by a custom or usage in the commercial environment in which the parties made the agreement, or by standardized terms recognized by law. We will shortly turn to these matters in detail. For the present, simply note that language that seems vague or ambiguous in isolation may become more certain if interpreted in the wider environment of the transaction. In the first example above, the vague rental provision may not be as unclear as it sounds if its meaning is embellished by facts in the context. Say, for example, that these clauses are regularly used in the commercial real property market, in which "fair rental" is widely understood to be based on an index published by an association of landlords, and rent is customarily paid monthly in advance. Similarly, the ambiguous word "bookmaking," while unclear in isolation, may become more definite if other provisions in the lease, discussions during negotiations, or other facts are available to show what the parties meant.

But contextual evidence cannot always save a vague or ambiguous term. Sometimes unclear language defies interpretation, even in context, because the circumstances of the transaction are devoid of helpful indicators of meaning. If a central component of an apparent agreement suffers from this degree of incurable indefiniteness, one can only conclude either that no contract was intended or, if it was, that the parties failed to form a clear intent or failed to communicate it well enough to create an enforceable relationship.

d. Establishing Ambiguity by Contextual Evidence

The preceding discussion assumes that the term is unclear on its face, but could be made clear by contextual evidence. The opposite can also be true — although a term may appear to be clear on its face, contextual evidence may show that it is less clear or more ambiguous than a face-value reading may reveal. Some courts insist (especially in older cases, but sometimes in modern cases, too) that if words are clear on their face, interpretation is not a question of fact, but of law, and that the words should be given their **plain meaning**, without recourse to contextual evidence. (This is called a "**four corners**" approach because the court looks for meaning within the four corners of the document.)

However, many courts find this approach too restrictive. If **extrinsic evidence** of meaning (that is, evidence beyond the actual words used by the parties) is available, they are reluctant to make a judgment on the clarity of language based purely on the apparent plain meaning of the words used in the contract. They recognize that even where words seem completely clear, they may not have a single, fixed meaning, and contextual evidence could show that the parties intended their language to mean something other than what the court may think. For this reason, the court will **admit and evaluate contextual evidence relating to meaning**, even though the language appears clear on its face. Of course, the clearer the plain meaning of the language, the more resistant a court may be to crediting extrinsic evidence, and the more convincing the contextual evidence must be to demonstrate that a different meaning was intended.

Pacific Gas and Electric Co. v. G. W. Thomas Drayage & Rigging Co., 442 P.2d 641 (Cal. 1968) is a landmark in the development of the principle that the words used by the parties must be interpreted, not at face value, but within the entire context of the transaction. A provision in a contract to repair machinery provided that the repairer would "indemnify" the owner "against all loss, damage, expense, and liability resulting from . . . injury to property" arising in the performance of the contract. The repairer damaged property belonging to the owner. The owner claimed that the indemnity made the contractor liable for this damage, but the contractor argued that the provision was intended to apply only to damage to property of third parties. The trial court interpreted the language of the provision solely at its face value and concluded that its plain meaning did not restrict the repairer's liability to damage to the property of third parties. The Supreme Court reversed the trial court's decision because the trial court had refused to admit extrinsic evidence offered by the repairer (such as evidence of admissions by the owner and prior practices of the parties) that allegedly showed that the parties intended the indemnity clause to apply only to damage to the property of third parties. The court emphasized that the purpose of interpretation is to determine the intent of the parties, which cannot be done if the court refuses to look beyond the meaning of the words as the judge understands them. Words are just symbols of thought, and the context in which they are used can affect their meaning.

The court applied the principles set out in *Pacific Gas* in *Wolf v. Superior Court of Los Angeles County*, 8 Cal. Rptr.3d 649 (Cal. App. 2004). The author of the book on which the movie "Who Framed Roger Rabbit" was based sued Walt Disney Pictures and Television for royalties that he claimed were due for the commercial exploitation of characters in the book and movie. The agreement under which Disney had bought the rights to the book provided that the author would receive a royalty of 5 percent of "gross receipts." Disney argued that the term "gross receipts" included only cash receipts, but the author contended it also included the value of any other consideration received by Disney from licenses granted for use of the characters. There was no evidence that the parties ever discussed the meaning of "gross receipts," but the author sought to admit the testimony of an expert that trade usage in the movie industry supported his interpretation. The trial court found the term (interpreted in light of the writing as a whole) to be clear on its face and refused to consider the testimony. It granted Disney's motion for summary judgment. Citing *Pacific Gas*, the court of appeals reversed the summary judgment. The court of appeals conceded that, as read in the contract, the meaning of the term might appear to be unambiguous. However, the trial court erred in refusing to consider extrinsic evidence that could show that the parties reasonably intended a different meaning.

§10.3.2 Omitted Terms

If a term is omitted, it simply is not there. The **agreement has a gap** regarding that particular aspect of the relationship. Say that Lessor and Lessee discussed and wrote out most of the terms of the lease, but did not address the amount of the rent orally or in writing. This could mean that they failed to reach agreement on this crucial term, so that no lease came into being. However, it could also mean that the parties did not consider it necessary to articulate the amount of the rent, because they assumed that the rent would be reasonable, based on the fair market rental for commercial property of this kind. In other words, the apparent gap in their agreement indicates not a lack of consensus, but an intent to adhere to some "off-the-shelf" market or legal standard that they thought of as too obvious to need articulation. To decide which of these two possibilities is the right one, their intent must be determined by looking at the language of the agreement as a whole in light of all the circumstances of the transaction.

§10.3.3 Unresolved Terms

An unresolved term differs from a vague or omitted term in that the parties have **raised the issue** in their agreement but have **not yet settled it,** leaving it to be resolved by agreement at some later time. For example, when Lessor and Lessee negotiated the lease, they reached agreement on all the terms of a ten-year lease, including the rent to be paid for the first year. However, neither of them wished to commit to a fixed rental figure for the remaining years of the lease, and they could not agree on the method for calculating the annual rent increases. They became tired of arguing about this issue and were anxious to get the lease signed. They therefore executed a written lease setting out all the agreed terms, including the first year's rent, and providing that the rent for the remaining period of the lease would be negotiated further in the week before Lessee took occupation of the premises.

In this situation, the indefiniteness results from the deliberate postponement of agreement on the amount of consideration to be paid by Lessee for the bulk of the lease period — certainly a material aspect of the lease. Therefore, at this point there is no lease in existence despite the consensus on most of its provisions. A material term is left unresolved, and the parties clearly do not intend it to be supplied by some external standard. They have simply not yet reached final agreement. It could be that their undertaking to negotiate further imposes some obligation on them to try to reach consensus, but such an "agreement to agree" is not regarded as definite enough to create a firm and final contract. (As discussed in section 10.11, it could, however, create an ancillary commitment to bargain in good faith.)

---

§10.4 ASCERTAINING THE MEANING OF AN AGREEMENT: INTERPRETATION DISTINGUISHED FROM CONSTRUCTION

§10.4.1 Introduction to the Distinction

The processes of interpretation (inferring meaning from facts) and construction (inferring meaning as a matter of law) have been alluded to in earlier chapters.[4] If you have read them already, the basic point of the present discussion will not be entirely unfamiliar. This section more closely examines and differentiates the methods and uses of the related but separate functions of interpretation and construction. To begin, a broad distinction may be drawn:

Restatement Second §200 describes **interpretation** as the ascertainment of the meaning of a promise or agreement. It is an **evaluation of facts** (that is, evidence of what the parties said and did and the circumstances surrounding their communications) for the purpose of deciding their mutual intent.

Construction, also called **implication in law**, is likewise concerned with the ascertainment of meaning, but it goes beyond available facts to find, not necessarily what the parties did mean, but what they **probably would (or should) have meant** in making the manifestations that were made. In other words, although the facts do not go far enough to establish the meaning of an indefinite term, the court uses a legal rule to create a meaning for it.

Although this point is expanded upon in section 10.4.2, it must be stressed at the outset that the distinction between interpretation and construction can be subtle and is often not of great practical significance. Nevertheless, it is worth understanding. When possible, it is preferable for a court to find the intended meaning of terms in actual evidence, rather than to construe it, because the courts' preliminary role is to enforce what the parties actually agreed. However, there are two situations in which a court is justified in inferring meaning as a matter of law:

1. As a general matter, construction is appropriate only when the existing evidence supports the reasonable conclusion (based on objective manifestations of assent) that the parties did intend to make a contract, but there is little or no evidence from which a factual inference can be drawn on their intent regarding a particular aspect of that contract. In seeking to effectuate the parties' intent, the court builds on what it knows of the transaction to provide a meaning that seems most reasonable in the circumstances and tries to simulate what the *parties probably would have agreed, had they focused on the issue.* This is preferable to an approach that would defeat contractual expectations by demanding clear proof of intent for every gap and uncertainty. It must be emphasized again that implication of meaning in law is based on the premise that the evidence at least points to an intent

---

4. For example, section 7.9.2 discusses the implication of a promise to use best efforts or to exercise reasonable judgment as a means of giving content to an apparently illusory promise, and section 4.1 discusses the interpretation of objective manifestations of assent in the context of offer and acceptance. This is not a definitive list. The issue of interpretation comes up often.

to be bound. If not, the court should not construe agreement as a matter of law.[5]

2. In addition to this general scope of construction, there is a narrower and more aggressive use of the process. In certain limited situations, a term may be implied in law even though it *overrides or conflicts with the evidence of what was agreed.* (But even here, the court will not construe a term to give effect to a contractual relationship unless the evidence reasonably supports the conclusion that the parties manifested intent to contract.)

This stronger form of construction is appropriate when the term must be implied to effect some public policy, or is so fundamental to fair dealing that the law insists that it be incorporated into the contract despite the parties' actual intent. In effect, legally implied terms of this kind are *mandatory* and cannot be varied by contract. Construction of this kind is more a matter of regulation than interpretation. It is discussed further in section 10.9.

§10.4.2 The Distinction in Perspective

The distinction between interpretation and construction is much easier to draw in theory than in practice. Sometimes it is fairly clear that the court is engaging in one or the other, but in many cases the line between them is fuzzy because they lie on a spectrum. At one end of the spectrum, evidence of intent is clear enough to require nothing beyond factual implication to determine the meaning or existence of a term. At the other end, there is no evidence at all from which to derive meaning for a term or to establish its

---

5. There is potential for confusion between what has just been said — that a court should not construe an agreement as a matter of law — and the concept of quasicontract discussed in section 9.4. Chapter 9 is concerned with unjust enrichment, a cause of action distinct from contract, in which relief is based on the fact that the defendant has been enriched at the plaintiff's expense as a result of receiving some benefit from the plaintiff, and justice requires that the benefit should be returned or paid for. The remedy for unjust enrichment is restitution — the restoration to the plaintiff of the benefit or its value. Because early common law courts were bound by rigid forms of action, they could not simply recognize unjust enrichment as a new basis for relief, so they fit it into the form of action for contract. To do this, they used a legal fiction under which they deemed the benefit to have been contracted for. As a result, restitutionary relief based on this legal fiction has come to be known as arising out of quasi-contract, or contract implied in law. This was purely a procedural form devised for the purpose of remedying unjust enrichment and had nothing to do with actual contract. Although courts are no longer constrained by this formalism, the terms "quasi-contract" or "contract implied in law" are still commonly used in connection with restitution. However, the purpose of quasi-contract is the remediation of unjust enrichment. The creation of a legal fiction to remedy unjust enrichment is, of course, very different from what is being discussed here — the inference that the parties did in fact make a contract. It would be improper for a court to draw that inference as a matter of law — to construe it — in the absence of some factual basis for believing that this comports with what the parties must have intended.

existence, so the parties' intent is necessarily determined via implication in law. However, many cases lie somewhere in the middle of the spectrum, so that the resolution of contractual meaning is based partly on interpretation of and partly on extrapolation from evidence. It may be hard to tell where factual inference ends and legal implication begins. Although this may sound very abstract now, it will become clearer as you read on.

Luckily, it is not necessary for most purposes that this distinction be identified precisely because the end result — the establishment of meaning — is the same. However, it is important for courts and attorneys to understand the distinction. A judge who does not bear it in mind may move too far from established intent and impose obligations that were not reasonably expected or intended. An attorney who is unclear on the difference will have difficulty assessing the strength of an argument concerning meaning and predicting the court's likely response.

§10.5 WHO ASCERTAINS MEANING: JUDGE OR JURY?

There is some confusion over the proper roles of the judge and jury in deciding the meaning of agreements, and cases offer conflicting views on whether the ascertainment of meaning is a matter of fact or law. Because **interpretation** is a **factual process,** the general approach should be that the factfinder (the jury, unless the case is being tried without one) must ascertain meaning after evaluating all pertinent evidence. Conversely, as **construction** is the process of supplying meaning as a **matter of law**, this is a legal question for the judge.

This simple theoretical dichotomy has become blurred. In part, this is because of a longstanding judicial mistrust of juries, which has motivated judges to retain many interpretational issues by characterizing them as matters of law. However, the problem goes beyond this historical lack of faith in juries. Confusion is inherent in the very subtlety of the distinction between interpretation and construction, which often makes it difficult to tell where factual inference ends and legal implication begins. As a result, there are no watertight rules, but there are some general guidelines that are helpful in deciding on the likely roles of judge and jury in the ascertainment of meaning:

1. When there is **no factual dispute** requiring an assessment of **credibility**, but interpretation involves nothing more than establishing the **ordinary grammatical meaning of words**, interpretation is the function of the **judge**. Therefore, when an agreement is written, and all that is required is the determination of meaning by consulting a dictionary or grammar book, it is the judge, and not the jury who pulls the book off the shelf.
2. If meaning has to be decided by the **evaluation of oral testimony** concerning what the parties expressed, or relating to the context from which meaning must be derived, this is more appropriately left to the **factfinder**. This is particularly so if disputes in meaning must be resolved by deciding on the credibility of witnesses.
3. If there is **no pertinent evidence of meaning**, and it can only be divined by legal implication, this is clearly the **judge**'s function.

Of course, as indicated earlier, meaning is often based on a combination of the grammatical meaning of words, contextual evidence, and legal implication. In such cases, it can be very difficult to unravel the proper roles of judge and jury, and concern about control over decisionmaking tends to push in the direction of entrusting the judge to balance the relative probity of these different elements.

Apart from the question of who decides meaning, the fact-law distinction has significance beyond the trial phase of the case. If meaning is determined as a matter of law, it can be reversed on appeal on the **standard of review** for legal questions: that the judge erred in the application of the law. However, if the determination is a question of fact, it can only be reversed if it satisfies a much stricter standard: The evidence must provide no reasonable basis for supporting the factfinder's conclusions. Also, a legal determination has weight as precedent, but a factual one does not.

§10.6 INTERPRETATION: DERIVING MEANING FROM EVIDENCE

§10.6.1 The Meaning of "Interpretation"

This section looks more closely at the process of interpretation and examines the type of evidence that may be available to cast light on the meaning of manifestations of apparent intent. As stated earlier, interpretation first focuses on the normal, accepted meaning of the words used by the parties, but it involves more than an evaluation of language in isolation. The words are used in a context that often provides useful evidence of what the words meant.

The process of interpretation was introduced in section 4.1 on offer and acceptance, where it was noted that agreement is manifested by the use of outward signals: words — whether written or spoken; actions; and, even in appropriate situations, a failure to speak or act. As the parties move towards developing consensus in the process of contract formation, intent thus communicated by each party is necessarily interpreted by the other. If a dispute later arises about whether consensus was reached or about what was agreed, the communications of the parties must again be interpreted — this time in court — to determine which party's interpretation is correct. Under the **objective** test, meaning is based on how words and actions would be reasonably perceived by the party to whom they were manifested. The **subjective** understanding of the parties may have some relevance to the inquiry to the extent that it is consistent with and may help to explain the meaning of the manifestation.

§10.6.2 The Sources of Evidence Used in Interpretation

Manifestations of intent are never made in a vacuum, so there is always some context to the words used by parties in expressing agreement. In some cases, there is **no evidence of context available**. Neither party has any contextual evidence to offer which might be relevant to interpreting the meaning of the words. Where the court has no evidence of meaning extrinsic to the bare language of the agreement it is necessarily confined to interpreting that language to ascertain its meaning. However, where a party **does seek to prove contextual evidence** pertinent to meaning, the court must decide if that evidence should be heard.

As noted in section 10.3.1, where the contract expresses the disputed term in apparently clear and unambiguous language, extrinsic evidence as to its meaning is treated with caution.[6] Some courts are quite strongly resistant to going beyond the apparent plain meaning of the language used in the contract. (This strict "four corners" approach is more common in older cases.) Other courts are more receptive to extrinsic evidence because they recognize that words do not have a constant and immutable meaning and can be colored by context. Because interpretation aims at ascertaining the intended meaning of words, it is important to hear available contextual evidence in trying to decide what meaning the parties intended.

---

6. Where the agreement is recorded in writing, a party's ability to offer evidence of context is much more heavily restricted because of the parol evidence rule, discussed in Chapter 12. In this chapter, we focus on the sources of evidence available to interpret language in agreement, and are not concerned with the parol evidence rule. In Chapter 12 we will examine barriers to admissibility of contextual evidence created by the rule.

Where contextual evidence is available and pertinent, the interpretation of a contract involves five principal areas of factual inquiry. At the center of the inquiry are the actual words used by the parties in the agreement. Even where there is contextual evidence, the language of the agreement is the starting point and the primary source of meaning. The wording of the very term in dispute is the central focus of the interpretation effort, but it cannot be read in isolation from the rest of the agreement and must be interpreted in light of the document (or oral agreement) as a whole. Beyond the language of the agreement, the inquiry spreads to its context. This context includes the discussions and conduct of the parties when they negotiated the contract, their conduct in performing the contract after it was formed (course of performance), their conduct in prior comparable transactions with each other (course of dealing), and the customs and usages of the market in which they are dealing with each other (trade usage). Notice that in each of these four areas we are concerned with objective evidence, in the form of words or conduct manifested by the parties, or verifiable facts in the contractual environment. The evidence of one party concerning what she may have thought or believed is only marginally helpful or relevant. Obviously, not all of these components are present in every transaction. However, the more that exist in a transaction, the richer the background from which meaning can be ascertained. In a fortunate case, all the evidence drawn from these different aspects of the context will point to the same meaning. If they conflict, the general rule (reflected in both current UCC §§1.205(4) and 2.208(2)[7] and in Restatement Second §203(b)) is to give greatest weight to the express terms of the parties, followed in order by any course of performance, course of dealing, and usage.

The Environment for Contractual Interpretation

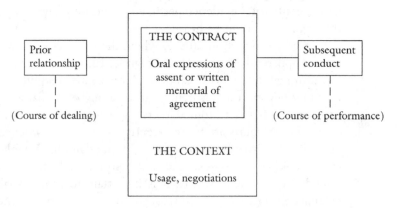

---

7. In the current version of the UCC, course of performance is dealt with in §2.208 and course of dealing and trade usage are dealt with in §1.205. Revised Article 1 combines these three aspects of the interpretational context into a new section, §1.303. The revision does not change the relative weight given to them, and §1.303(e) sets out the same hierarchy as the current §§2.208 and 1.205.

We will look more closely at these indicators of intent in the rest of this section. Before doing so, it is enlightening to see how they were used by the court in one of the best illustrative cases on this subject, *Frigaliment Importing Co. v. B.N.S. International Sales Corp.*, 109 F.Supp. 116 (S.D.N.Y. 1960). The buyer, a Swiss importer, ordered a large quantity of chicken from the seller. The contract called for "U.S. fresh frozen chicken, grade A" of two different sizes. The agreement reflected a lower price per pound for the larger chickens than the smaller ones. When the seller delivered the chickens, the buyer protested that the larger, cheaper ones were not in accordance with the contract because they were stewing chickens, not suitable for frying. The buyer claimed that the word "chicken" used in the contract meant frying chicken so that all chicken delivered had to be of this quality. The seller denied that it had breached the contract by delivering stewing chickens. It contended that the word "chicken" was a generic term for both frying and stewing chickens and that the price difference in the contract made it clear that the cheaper birds would be stewing chickens. The subsequent litigation centered on the meaning of the word "chicken" as used in the contract. The definition of "chicken" in dictionaries and U.S.D.A regulations did not exclude either party's meaning. The court's examination of the terms of the contract document as a whole was somewhat more helpful in casting light on the meaning of "chicken." The price term supported the seller's contention that two different types of chicken were contemplated because the price of the larger birds was below the market price for fryers.

The court moved beyond the written agreement to explore the entire context of the transaction in an attempt to decide if "chicken" should be understood in the narrower or wider sense. Several experts testified as to the meaning of "chicken" in the trade, but the expert testimony was in conflict and did not clearly support the position of either party. Finally, the court considered evidence of the parties' course of performance to see if it cast any light on what they may have meant. The course of performance did not show a common intention because the buyer protested about the stewing chickens immediately on delivery. In the end, despite these efforts, the court was not able to establish what the parties meant by the use of the word "chicken" in the contract, so the case was resolved on the basis of the burden of proof. The buyer lost because it failed to prove that the word was used in the narrow sense that it alleged.

We now move to a more detailed consideration of each of the indicators of intent sketched above.

a. The Express Words used by the Parties

The ordinary meaning of words used by the parties in formulating their rights and obligations is always the primary indicator of what they intended.

Restatement, Second §203(b) and current UCC §§1.205(4) and 2.208[8] give greatest weight to express terms. These express terms might be oral or written (or otherwise recorded) — this does not affect the primacy of the express language.[9] As noted above, although the language of the disputed term is at the center of the court's examination of the express terms, the court does not look at that language in isolation, but reads it in light of the agreement as a whole — it reads all the terms of the written agreement or considers the entire oral contract. Often (as illustrated by *Frigaliment*, above), terms in one part of a contract cast light on terms in another.

Of course, interpretation of the ordinary meaning of the parties' language is not always a simple and mechanical matter, and different judges could find different meanings in the same words. For example, in *Breeding v. Kye's Inc.*, 831 N.E.2d 188 (Ind. App. 2005) Breeding reserved Kye's hall for her wedding. The written agreement stated that $600 of the fee for the facility was for the services of a disc jockey. The agreement also made it clear that the client had no choice of disc jockey because Kye had granted an exclusive license to Sounds Unlimited Productions to provide disc jockey services for all events at the hall. (This suited Breeding well because the owners of Sounds Unlimited were friends of her family and she wanted Sounds Unlimited as the disc jockey at her wedding. In fact this was apparently why she selected Kye's venue.) About three months before the wedding, Kye notified Breeding that its license arrangement with Sounds Unlimited had terminated, and it would not permit Sounds Unlimited to work in its hall. Kye would not budge in its refusal to allow Sounds Unlimited onto its premises, even though Breeding was willing to hire Sounds Unlimited herself. Breeding sued Kye for breach of contract and return of her deposit on the basis that Kye had broken its undertaking to provide disc jockey services by Sounds Unlimited. Kye defended the suit on the basis that the contract was merely for the hire of the hall, and contained no promise to use Sounds Unlimited. The majority of the court of appeals found that the provisions in the contract relating to disc jockey services clearly and unambiguously constituted a commitment by Kye to provide the services of Sounds Unlimited. Despite the majority's confidence in this clarity, the dissent read the contract terms differently and reached the opposite conclusion. It disagreed that the provisions relating to the disc jockey were a promise to Breeding that Sounds Unlimited would provide the services. Rather, they merely limited the client's choice of disc jockey. (The dissent noted that under the objective test, the express terms of the contract were

---

8. As explained in footnote 7, Revised Article 1 provides for this in §1.303(e).

9. An oral agreement is legally binding and enforceable unless the statute of frauds, discussed in Chapter 11, requires it to be written (or recorded). However, even if valid, an oral agreement presents problems of proof that are obviated or reduced by recording the agreement. If there is a dispute over the exact language used by the parties in an oral agreement, the actual words used must be proved as a fact before they can be interpreted.

not affected by Breeding's subjective motivation in selecting the hall because of the disc jockey.)

b. Discussions and Conduct of the Parties During Negotiations

Apart from the actual words spoken or written to express agreement, there may be a history of communication and negotiation leading up to the execution of the contract. Evidence of what was expressed by the parties during the period leading up to contract formation could be useful and relevant to establish the meaning of what was ultimately provided for in the agreement.[10]

c. Any Conduct by the Parties in the Course of Performing Under the Agreement

If the uncertainty to be resolved by interpretation only becomes an issue after the parties have begun performing the contract, their conduct in proffering and accepting, or otherwise reacting to performance may provide evidence of what was intended by an indefinite term. This post-formation behavior is called the **"course of performance"** and its relevance to interpretation is based on the assumption that the actual performance tendered and accepted without objection is a strong indicator of what must have been intended. The evidentiary value of the course of performance is recognized by current UCC §2.208,[11] mimicked by Restatement Second §202(4).

For example, a lease provides that "dogs, cats, and other animals may not be kept on the premises." Lessee owns a pet duck that he thinks of as a bird, not an animal. He has kept it on the premises for several months. Lessor has seen it on several occasions and has never complained. The mutual conduct of the parties creates the fair inference that they were in agreement that "animals" does not include ducks.

Not all post-formation conduct necessarily reflects what the parties intended at the time of contracting. The conduct may simply not be pertinent to the meaning of the term in issue, or, even if it is, it may reflect a subsequent change of mind or a disinclination to enforce rights under the contract.[12] Therefore it is possible to draw the wrong inference from

---

10. Again, the parol evidence rule may restrict the admission of this evidence. See chapter 12.
11. Section 1.303(a) in revised Article 1.
12. It can be difficult to distinguish a course of performance, which casts light on what the parties meant at the time of contracting, from post-formation conduct that is either a waiver of rights or a modification of the contract. For example, the lessor's failure to complain about the duck could indicate that the parties did not include it in the definition. However, it could mean instead that the lessor has simply chosen not to enforce the ban on ducks, or that the parties have implicitly agreed by conduct to eliminate the restriction on animals. If it is not a course of performance but a waiver or modification, it is subject to different rules, which are discussed in sections 13.9 and 16.11.2.

behavior that is ambiguous or does not really have a bearing on the term in issue. There are several guidelines that help to avoid misconstruing conduct as a course of performance:

1. For a course of performance to be valid as a source of interpretation, it must be *pertinent to the meaning* of the term in controversy. For example, if the term in dispute concerned the date on which the rent payments were due, lessor's tolerance of the duck does nothing to clarify the uncertainty.

2. The conduct must show that the party performed or accepted performance *without a protest or reservation of rights*. Therefore, if on each occasion that Lessor saw the duck, she protested that it was not allowed, Lessor's failure to take stronger action does not clarify the meaning of "animals."

3. Conduct by only one of the parties, *not known and acquiesced in* by the other (for example, if Lessee kept the duck inside and Lessor never saw it or knew about it), may show what the performing party understood the agreement to be, but does not prove that the other party shared this view.

4. The more *extensive or repetitious* the conduct, the stronger the inference that it does reflect what was intended by the parties. By contrast, isolated or single instances of conduct are more ambiguous and could simply be a waiver of or disinclination to enforce rights on a particular occasion. For example, merely because Lessor sees the duck on one occasion and does nothing about it, does not necessarily show that she shares Lessee's view of the meaning of "animals."

d. Any Prior Course of Dealing Between the Parties in Similar or Analogous Contractual Relationships

While "course of performance" means the parties' post-contractual relationship, the term **"course of dealings"** refers to any relationship they may have had in the **period before the transaction** in question. The parties may have dealt with each other on prior occasions, and the current transaction may be the latest in a series of similar ones that have taken place over a period of time. If so, the parties' conduct in prior dealings may provide information that helps to interpret a term that has generated a dispute in the present transaction. This is recognized by current UCC §1.205(1)[13] and Restatement Second §§202 and 203.

For example, Lessee previously rented premises from Lessor under a lease that had the identical clause forbidding animals. During the prior lease

---

13. Section 1.303(b) in revised Article 1.

term, Lessor discovered the duck and told Lessee to get rid of it or face eviction. He sadly obeyed and boarded it with his mother. When the parties enter into a new lease with the same term, it is reasonable to infer that they intend its wording to have the meaning established under the prior relationship. If they intend otherwise, they must make this clear in the new lease. If they do not, Lessee cannot claim that "animals," as used in the new lease, does not include ducks.

A course of dealings is only pertinent if the earlier relationship is *comparable or analogous*. The transactions must be substantially similar, the term in controversy must have been present in the earlier dealings, and past conduct must be relevant to the meaning in issue. As with course of performance, *repetition strengthens the inference*, so multiple transactions with consistent, pertinent behavior more clearly establish intended meaning.

e. Any Trade Usage, Common Usage, or Custom That is Reasonably Applicable to the Parties' Dealings

Although the ordinary or general sense of words must be the starting point in any exercise of interpretation, both current UCC §1.205[14] and Restatement Second §202(5) emphasize the significant impact of trade usage on the meaning of language. Parties usually deal with each other in the context of a larger community. This may be a **particular market** (whether international, national, or more local), or it may be a **specialized trade or industry**. If the market has a well-accepted custom or practice that explains language or supplements an omission in an agreement, this customary usage is of value in ascertaining the parties' intent. The *Wolf* case in section 10.3.1 is a good illustration of the role that evidence of trade usage could play in interpreting an agreement. Recall that the dispute in that case was whether Disney was obliged to pay royalties to a book author on value, other than cash, that it had received from licensing characters in the movie "Who Framed Roger Rabbit." Because the agreement provided for the payment of the royalty on "gross receipts," the answer to this question depended on the meaning of that term. None of the parties to the negotiations had any recollection of ever discussing the meaning of the term. The plain meaning of the words, read in relation to other language in the written contract, suggested that royalties might be confined to cash receipts. However, the most compelling evidence of what "gross receipts" might mean was the testimony of a movie industry expert that the term was generally understood to include noncash consideration. The court held that the trial court erred in refusing to receive

---

14. Section 1.303(c) in revised Article 1.

this expert testimony and in granting summary judgment based on its interpretation of the plain meaning of the contract.

The UCC and Restatement Second use the term "usage of trade," which may give the impression that custom or usage is only pertinent where the parties are members of a particular vocation, industry, or profession. However, usages exist even in the general marketplace, and "usage of trade" should be taken to encompass any applicable commercial custom, whether it derives from a specific trade or from a broader market in which the parties are involved. (UCC §1.205 and revised §1.303 recognize this by defining "usage of trade" to include any regular practice or method of dealing in a place, vocation, or trade.)

Older common law did not recognize any practice as a usage unless it was so firmly established as to be notorious, universal, and ancient. The modern approach is more flexible. UCC §1.205, Comment 5[15] explicitly rejects any requirement of great longevity and universality and admits of the possibility of new usages. The UCC test is simply whether the usage is **currently observed by the great majority of decent dealers**. In common law transactions, while some courts may still apply the stricter test, modern common law tends to follow the broader recognition of usage advanced by the UCC.

A party who alleges that a usage explains or supplements an agreement must establish four things.

First, he must **define the trade or market** with which the transaction is associated and must show that **both parties** are **sufficiently connected** to that trade to make the usage fairly attributable to the contract. The determination of the market is sometimes but not always straightforward. For example, say the dispute arises from a transaction between a manufacturer of television sets and one of its distributors. Is the relevant market confined to the distribution market for televisions, or is it broader, say the distribution market for home electronics, or for all electronics, or is the appropriate market wider still, covering the electronics industry as a whole? The choice of the market could be crucial because the existence and nature of usage could be different, or relatively stronger or weaker, if the market is defined more broadly or narrowly.

One of the key factors in defining the trade or market is the parties' relationship to it. If both parties are active participants in the market or trade, usages in that market or trade are readily attributable to their contract except to the extent that the contract clearly excludes a usage. However, if one of the parties is not involved in the market or trade, its usages should not be relevant to the contract unless the non-member party knew of the usage and the circumstances show that the parties reasonably expected it to apply to the

---

15. Section 1.303, comment 4 in revised Article 1.

transaction. As usual, the objective standard is used to decide if a party should be subject to a usage. We are not concerned about whether the party actually knew of and expected the usage to apply, but whether he reasonably should have done so.[16]

Nanakuli Paving and Rock Co. v. Shell Oil Co., 664 F.2d 772 (9th Cir. 1991) illustrates the inquiry into the appropriate market.[17] The case involved a contract between Shell and Nanakuli under which Shell supplied asphalt for Nanakuli's use in paving projects on the island of Oahu. The contract did not have a fixed price term, but provided that the price would be Shell's "posted price at time of delivery." Despite this, Nanakuli claimed that usage in the Oahu paving trade required Shell to "price protect" Nanakuli. That is, where Nanakuli had committed itself to the customer based on a lower posted price at the time of its bid, Shell would charge Nanakuli that price, even if the posted price at the time of delivery was higher. The court defined the scope of the trade broadly to include asphalt suppliers because they had a close relationship with the pavers and had reason to know of the usage.

Second, the party claiming the usage must show that it is **pertinent** to the disputed term. The usage must be relevant to the contract and must relate to the very matter on which the parties disagree.

Third, the party claiming the usage must prove as a question of fact that the **usage actually exists** in the applicable trade or market. This factual question requires both proof of the scope and terms of the usage and of its wide acceptance in the trade or market. Proof of usage is normally established by expert testimony from witnesses who are familiar with the customs and practices in the trade or market.

Fourth, the usage must **not be inconsistent with the express terms** of the agreement. Where the parties make it clear in their contract that they do not intend to be subject to a usage, the expressed intention of the parties overrides the usage. Because established and applicable usage is such a strong indication of intent, courts usually require the term excluding usage to be very clear and unequivocal. For example, in *Nanakuli*, the court did not find the price protection usage to be inconsistent with the contract's express term that the price was to be Shell's posted price at the time of delivery. Although it is difficult to reconcile these terms, the court found no clear indication that the parties did not intend price protection to qualify the express language of the contract.

---

16. Note that the focus is on presumed knowledge rather than actual knowledge of usage. The effect of this is that usage sometimes enters a contract as a matter of construction, not interpretation. This reinforces the point made in section 10.4 that the dividing line between these processes is often blurred.

17. This case is discussed further in relation to the parol evidence rule in Example 4 of Chapter 12.

§10.7 GENERAL RULES OF INTERPRETATION (OR CONSTRUCTION)

When a term is omitted or its meaning is uncertain, this indefiniteness can often be resolved by having recourse to one of a variety of general principles that have been developed by courts as guidelines in the ascertainment of reasonable but unexpressed intent. Many of these rules are based on commonsensical inferences, but some are dictated by policy or a perception of fairness. Some of the rules are old enough to be in the form of Latin maxims and are still commonly known by their Latin names noted below.

These rules are sometimes called rules of interpretation, and sometimes rules of construction — again reflecting the subtle distinction mentioned so frequently before. The important point, from a practical standpoint, is that they are guides to enable the court to draw the proper inferences of meaning from whatever facts may be available. Typically, they are used only when there is some uncertainty in the intent of the agreement. They should not be applied mechanically and must take into account the reasonable expectations of the parties and the underlying purpose of the agreement.

There are many rules of interpretation. They are not all of equal strength, and some are more compelling than others. Obviously, they are not all relevant to every case. Although most of the common ones are included here, no attempt is made to catalog them all. These examples sufficiently illustrate the range and kind of rules covered under this category:

1. If possible, the court should try to interpret an agreement in a way that gives effect to all its terms.
2. Unless the context indicates otherwise, words used in a contract should be given their ordinary general or lay meaning rather than a specialized or technical meaning. For example, in E.M.M.I., Inc. v. Zurich American Insurance Co., 9 Cal. Rptr.3d 701 (2004) a jeweler's insurance policy excluded coverage where jewelry was stolen from a vehicle unless the jeweler's representative was "in or upon the vehicle" at the time of the theft. The jewelry was stolen from the car while the salesman was checking the car's tailpipe. The insurer argued that the term "in or upon" was used in a technical sense to mean that the insured must actually be in the vehicle, not just next to it. The court disagreed. If the insurer intended to use a term in a technical sense, it should so indicate, say by defining the term in the policy. Because the term "upon" was ambiguous, it should be interpreted in a sense that accords with the insured's reasonable expectation that the exclusion only applies where the car is unattended. Meridian Leasing, Inc. v. Associated Aviation Underwriters, 409 F.3d 342

(6th Cir. 2005) followed the same approach in finding that an insurance policy on an aircraft covered damage to the engine when it caught fire upon being started. The insurance policy excluded damage caused by "wear and tear" and the insurer argued that the exclusion for "wear and tear" should be broadly understood to restrict coverage to damage from an accident and to exclude damage resulting from a mechanical problem. The court disagreed. The policy had no technical definition of "wear and tear." In ordinary usage, a fire caused by mechanical fault is not "wear and tear," which means deterioration resulting from the ongoing operation of the plane.

3. *Ut res magis valeat quam pereat*, "The thing should rather have effect than be destroyed." If one interpretation would make the contract invalid and another would validate it, the court should *favor the meaning that validates the contract*. In the same spirit, there are allied rules that prefer an interpretation that would make a term reasonable and lawful over one that would have the opposite effect, and an interpretation that positively rather than negatively impacts public policy or the public interest. For example, recall the lease that was ambiguous because it provided for the lessee to conduct a bookmaking business on the premises. If there is no factual basis for interpreting the word "bookmaking," and gambling is illegal, the preferred interpretation would be that it means the manufacture of books.

4. Specific or precise provisions should be given greater weight than general provisions. For example, one clause in a lease says that "ducks shall be kept on leashes at all times" and another clause says "no dogs, cats, or other animals may be kept on the premises." The specific provision concerning ducks makes it clear that the general rule on animals does not apply to them.

5. Where an agreement consists of both standardized and negotiated terms (or printed and handwritten or typed terms), any conflict between them should be resolved in favor of the *negotiated or handwritten terms*.

6. *Ejusdem generis*, "of the same kind." When specific and general words are connected, the **general word is limited by the specific one**, so that it is deemed to refer to things of the same kind. For example, a lease states that "skateboards, rollerskates, rollerblades, and other means of locomotion are prohibited in common areas and hallways." The common denominator here is that all these items make use of wheels under the feet. On this reasoning, the general words "other means of locomotion" do not include wheelchairs or motorbikes. However, if the common denominator is taken to be wheels, these two items would be included in the general language, but a camel would not be.

7. *Noscitur a sociis,* "known from its associates." This rule is similar to *ejusdem generis,* but is not confined to linked general and specific words. Whenever a series of words is used together, the **meaning of each word in the series affects the meaning of others.** For example, if a term in a lease provides that "no dogs, cats, or primates may be kept on the premises," the meaning of "primates" is qualified by the others. It would therefore cover only primates in the sense of apes and monkeys, and would not forbid the lessee from having his uncle, a bishop, move in with him.

8. *Expressio unius est exclusio alterius,* "The expression of one thing excludes another." This is in some sense the opposite of the *ejusdem generis* rule. When a **thing or list** of things is specifically mentioned **without being followed by a general term**, the implication is that **other things of the same kind are excluded.** For example, a term that prohibits "dogs, cats, and primates" impliedly does not prohibit ducks.

9. *Contra proferentum* (or stated in full, *omnia praesumuntur contra proferentum*), "All things are presumed against the proponent." When **one party has drafted or selected the language** of an unclear provision, the **meaning is preferred that favors the other party.** This rule is often said to be a tie breaker, in that it should be used as a last resort when no more direct and pertinent guide to meaning is applicable. It is not always used as a last resort, however, and tends to be much favored when the proponent of the terms is a party with relatively strong bargaining power who has produced a preprinted standard form for the other's signature. The *E.M.M.I* and *Meridian Leasing* cases in item 2 above both demonstrate this approach to the interpretation of an insurance policy. Insurance policies are prime examples of standard form contracts that are fertile ground for application of the *contra proferentum* rule.

§10.8 GAP FILLERS — IMPLICATION BY LAW TO EFFECTUATE THE PARTIES' REASONABLE INTENT

§10.8.1 Introduction

It was stressed in section 10.1 that construction is an extension of interpretation, employed to reach the reasonable intent of the parties. Normally (subject to the exceptions discussed in section 10.9), a court does not use construction to establish a contract when the evidence indicates that none was intended, nor does it construe a meaning inconsistent with the apparent intent of the parties. Therefore, gap fillers are used to supplement contracts, not to override the parties' probable intent. This means that the parties can "contract out" of a legally implied standard term (that is, they can avoid its application) by expressing a contrary intent.[18]

A gap filler is a provision **legally implied** into a contract to **supplement** or **clarify** its **express language.** As its name suggests, the principal purpose of a gap filler is to supply a logically inferable contract term when it is clear that the parties intended a contract, but have failed to provide adequately or at all for the question in issue. Of course, some apparent gaps in an express agreement could be filled by contextual evidence, so a legally implied gap filler is usually only used when no pertinent contextual evidence is available to establish the existence of a term as a matter of fact.

Gap fillers are thus **standard terms supplied by law.** Some have been developed by courts and others are provided by legislation. Courts and legislatures do not pick them out of the air but base them on common expectations, commercial practice, and public policy. For this reason, the standardized term supplied by law should not usually take the parties by surprise and should genuinely reflect what they likely would have agreed had they discussed the issue. The contract was entered into in the very milieu from which the law developed the standardized term, and so the reasonable (and possibly even the actual) expectations of the parties are likely to be congruent with it.

For example, Buyer agrees to buy Seller's house, subject to Buyer being able to secure the necessary financing. Nothing is said in the written agreement or in the negotiations about Buyer having the duty to make a conscientious effort to obtain the financing. If Buyer does nothing to seek financing, he will likely be held to have breached a legally implied promise to make reasonable efforts to apply for and secure the financing. The implication of such a promise is a logical extension of the express provisions of the agreement and gives effect to the presumed intent of the parties. It recognizes that they probably did not contemplate that Buyer could slip out of his obligations simply by not bothering to apply for a loan. In this way, the implied term *constructs what the parties must have intended*, had they been *acting fairly* and *reasonably*, and it gives effect to their reasonable expectations and to the underlying purpose of the agreement. Note the affinity between legally implied terms and usage, because legally implied terms typically do (or should) reflect the custom of the marketplace. Therefore, this same term requiring best efforts in seeking a loan could probably have been established by evidence of the customary practices pertaining to the sale of a home subject to the contingency of financing. However, the difference is that if a usage is so well-established that it has reached the point of being recognized as a legal standard term, it becomes part of the contract as a matter of law, not of fact. It is therefore not necessary to establish it by evidence.

---

18. The exception to this general rule is discussed in section 10.9.

Some gap fillers are well established and others have been recognized more recently. Additional ones will continue to develop in the future as new legal implications are drawn from changing market expectations. Of course, there cannot be standardized terms for every conceivable gap, so there are some omissions that cannot be cured by legal implication. Some gap fillers supply generalized obligations that are likely to be implied in all kinds of contracts, and some are very specific, relating to particular types of term in specialized contracts. The following samples of general and specific gap fillers illustrate their range and nature.

§10.8.2 Gap Fillers That Supply General Obligations

When a contract does not clearly specify a level of performance but it is clear that the parties' purpose can only be achieved if the obligor puts some energy and dedication into the performance, the law implies an obligation to make **best efforts (reasonable efforts)** [19] to affect the contract's purpose. The above example of the house sale subject to financing illustrates this. Another illustration is provided by *Wood v. Lucy, Lady Duff-Gordon*, 222 N.Y. 88 (1917), discussed in section 7.9.2, in which the court found that an exclusive distributorship contract impliedly required the distributor to make best efforts to sell the product. This general principle is likely to apply in any type of contract under which the grantor of a license, distributorship, or dealership relies on the conscientiousness of the grantee to market a product effectively. The facts and resolution of *B. Lewis Productions v. Angelou*, discussed in section 10.3.1a, are strikingly similar to *Wood*. The court, quoting from *Wood* at length, noted that like Wood and Duff-Gordon, Lewis and Angelou unquestionably intended to form a business relationship in which each party assumed obligations. Rather than defeat this intent by declaring the contract to be too indefinite to enforce, the court followed the approach of *Wood* and supplied an obligation of good faith and fair dealing to give content to the vaguely expressed undertakings of the parties.

The problem with the legal implication of broad, generalized obligations is that they are vague in themselves. Therefore, although they may go part of the way in curing a vagueness or omission in the agreement, they do not settle the scope and content of the obligation. That is, a concept such as "best efforts" is mushy and non-specific, so that it is not enough simply to imply the obligation. The further step must be taken to determine with some

---

19. There may be a difference between "reasonable efforts," which appears strongly objective, and "best efforts," which suggests some blend of subjective and objective standards. However, the distinction is probably not substantial. Whichever term is used, the decision on what constitutes an acceptable effort should take into account both the objective market standards and the subjective honesty and particular circumstances of the party who is to exert the effort.

precision what degree of effort is required by the obligation. It may be easy to find a breach when no effort is made at all, but more clarity is needed to decide if some greater degree of effort is an adequate performance. To define the obligation more acutely, a further inquiry must be made into the underlying purpose of the contract and the reasonable expectations of the parties.

§10.8.3 Gap Fillers That Supply More Specific Rights and Duties

Both the UCC and the common law supply gap fillers that relate to specific aspects of particular kinds of contracts. Some of these are concrete and precise, but others include generalized concepts, such as reasonableness, that present interpretational problems similar to those discussed above. The following selection illustrates the kind of supplementary terms available to fill gaps left by the parties. These are merely random examples. No attempt is made to be comprehensive. Remember, they are only used if the contract has a gap or uncertainty that has not been resolved by contextual evidence.

The **common law** has developed many gap fillers through the process of judicial decision. Three examples, discussed elsewhere in this book, are enough to illustrate this point. First, if the parties to an employment contract do not specify its duration, it is deemed to be terminable at will. (See section 8.9.3.) Second, if the parties do not state that rights under a contract are personal to the obligee, the obligee may transfer (assign) those rights to another person. (See section 10.8.3.) Third, if the contract does not provide for the sequence of performance, it is presumed that when both performances are a single instantaneous act, they must be made concurrently. But if one performance is instantaneous and the other needs time to perform, it is presumed that the longer performance must take place first. Therefore, in the sale of a house, unless otherwise stated in the contract, it is implied that transfer of title and payment occur at the same time, but in a contract to build a house, the builder must complete the construction before the owner has to pay. (See section 16.8.)

UCC Article 2 also has a number of gap fillers. Because they are set out in the statute, they are easier to find than those provided by common law. For example: unless the agreement expresses otherwise, §§2.312, 2.314, and 2.315[20] imply certain minimum warranties that a seller makes under defined circumstances regarding the title to and quality of the goods; if the parties do not specify the price of the goods, §2.305 infers that they agreed to a reasonable price unless the apparent intent of the agreement is

---

20. These sections, as well as the other sections cited as examples below, are not renumbered or significantly altered in the 2003 revision of Article 2.

otherwise; if payment terms are not expressed, §§2.307 and 2.310 assume a C.O.D. sale; §§2.307, 2.308, and 2.309 require that the goods be delivered in a single lot at the seller's place of business within a reasonable time; in a requirements or output contract,[21] §2.306(1) implies both a good faith and a reasonableness obligation on the party who is to determine the quantity of goods ordered or supplied; §2.306(2) implies an obligation of best efforts on both parties when the contract imposes an obligation on one of them to deal exclusively with the other.

§10.9 IMPLICATION IN LAW IRRESPECTIVE OF THE INTENT OF THE PARTIES

§10.9.1 Supplementary Terms That Cannot Be Excluded by Agreement

There is an exception to the general rule, stated in section 10.8, that terms supplied by law are intended to bring out the perceived reasonable intent of the parties and will not be included in the contract unless consistent with that intent. Some legally implied obligations are so fundamental to fair dealing or so strongly demanded by public policy, that they are mandatory and are part of the contract irrespective of the parties' actual intent. Even if they wish to, the parties cannot effectively agree to exclude such a term.

Construed terms of this kind are not properly called gap fillers. They are not default rules, but enter the contract whether or not there is a gap or uncertainty about the parties' intent. Although such strongly construed terms are raised here as part of the discussion of the process of finding meaning in agreement, they are more a *matter of regulation than of seeking intent*. The law's true purpose in such a firm imposition of standard terms is not so much to ascertain what the parties reasonably must have intended, but to limit contractual autonomy in the interest of public policy. Sometimes the policy in question is not directly related to contract law, but is concerned with the undesirable effect of particular contract terms on some other field, such as tort, antitrust, or criminal law. Often, however, the underlying public policy is that of protecting a weaker party from one-sided and unfair terms. In this respect, mandatory construed terms are part of the broader subject of regulating the formation and content of contracts, discussed in Chapter 13.

One of the most important and pervasive mandatory construed terms is the general obligation of both parties to perform the contract reasonably and

---

21. *See* section 7.9.3 for an explanation of this type of contract.

in good faith. Whether or not the agreement expressly articulates this obligation, and even if it expressly excludes it, the law implies it into every contract.[22] This duty is recognized in both current UCC §1.203[23] and Restatement Second §205.

§10.9.2 Construed Terms That Can Be Excluded Only by Express or Specific Language

Below this level of absolute legal implication, there is another category of construed terms that are important enough to be more strongly implied than other gap fillers. Although public policy does not preclude the parties from contracting out of them, it requires the intent to exclude them to be clearly expressed. Stated differently, while most gap fillers enter the contract only when necessary to resolve an uncertainty or omission, there are some that are so strongly implied as a matter of policy that they *become part of the contract unless its express terms clearly exclude them.* In some cases, even a clear exclusion is not good enough unless it complies with specified rules that may prescribe the use of particular language or format.

For example, UCC Article 2 has a policy in favor of providing warranties in certain types of sales of goods. Therefore, although current §2.316(2) allows the seller to contract out of them, it only recognizes a warranty disclaimer as effective if it satisfies certain formalities. To disclaim the merchant[24] seller's warranty of merchantability (that is, that the goods meet minimum trade standards), the sales contract must mention "merchantability" and, if in writing, the disclaimer must be conspicuous. When goods are sold for a particular purpose, the seller gives an implied warranty of fitness for that purpose unless it is disclaimed conspicuously in writing.[25] The goal of these rules is to make it more likely that the buyer notices the disclaimer, and to prevent the seller from hiding it in a mass of boilerplate.

---

22. There is a link between this principle and the second rule of construction mentioned in section 10.7, which favors a reasonable, effective, and lawful interpretation of unclear provisions. However, it goes even further than that rule by imposing a duty of fair dealing on the parties.

23. Renumbered §1.304 in revised Article 1.

24. *See* sections 5.5 and 6.5.2 for the definition of "merchant."

25. The 2003 revision of Article 2 adds language to §2.316 that must be included in a disclaimer of either merchantability or fitness for a particular purpose in a consumer contract. A "consumer contract" is defined in revised §2.103(d) to mean a contract between a merchant seller and a consumer. "Consumer" is defined in §2.103(c) to mean an individual who buys goods primarily for personal, family, or household purposes. Also, revised §2.316 follows the overall pattern of the 2003 revision by substituting the word "record" for "writing" to make it clear that a written disclaimer could be in electronic form.

§10.10 TERMS LEFT FOR FUTURE DETERMINATION

Say, for example, that Owner has completed the plan for a new commercial building and construction is about to begin. Owner has been negotiating with Lessee for a lease of space in the building upon its completion. The parties have reached agreement on the period of the lease, the location and size of the premises, and all other terms except for the rent to be paid. They wish to enter the lease agreement now, even though the premises will not be ready for occupation for two years. However, neither wishes to agree to a set figure because they do not know what the rental market will be like when the building is completed. If they cannot agree on a firm figure, they have a number of alternatives:

§10.10.1 Determination by an Objective Standard

The parties could decide on a formula or an external source or standard, so that the rent will be fixed at a specified future time by some objective criterion. For example, they could provide for the rent to be calculated by applying a published economic indicator to a base figure, or they could base the rent on a market standard derived from average rent charged for comparable buildings in the area at the time of occupation, or they could provide for binding arbitration by an independent arbitrator. In this way they are able to make a valid and effective contract now, but avoid the hazards of trying to predict an appropriate rent figure for the future.

Provided that the formula or standard is properly drafted to furnish a clear and workable method of ascertainment, the term for the future ascertainment of rent is valid and enforceable. At the time selected, the criterion is applied, and the rent figure determined. But if the formula or standard is poorly drafted, so that method of calculating the rent is vague or ambiguous and incapable of clarification by interpretation or construction, no contract has been made because a central term of the contract is unresolved.

For example, in *Walker v. Keith*, 382 S.W.2d 198 (Ky. 1964) a renewal option in a lease expressed the rent payable for the renewal period in the following exquisite prose: "rental will be fixed in such amount as shall actually be agreed upon by the lessors and the lessee with the monthly rental fixed on the comparative basis of rental values as of the date of the renewal with rental values at this time reflected by the comparative business conditions of the two periods." When, at the time for renewal, the parties (surprisingly) had a dispute over the meaning of this language, the lessee asked the court to rule that the parties had agreed to a reasonable rent. Although the trial court granted this relief and fixed rent at a reasonable figure, the supreme court reversed. The court said that the incoherent language did not set out any kind of workable formula or objective standard for calculating the rent, and there was no basis to assume that the parties meant to contract for a reasonable rent. The renewal provision was nothing more than an unenforceable "agreement to agree."

The opposite responses to the incomprehensible term by the trial court and supreme court in *Walker* reflect a dilemma that courts face in deciding when it is appropriate to imply a term to repair the parties' mess. Although a court may be willing to cure a deficiency in the agreement where it believes that the parties truly did intend to make a contract, it will draw the line at some point and will conclude that the deficiency is too great for judicial repair. Different courts may have different views of where the line should be drawn. Restatement, Second leans in favor of a liberal approach. Section 33 recognizes terms of a contract as reasonably certain if they provide a basis for determining breach and giving an appropriate remedy, and §204 encourages the court to supply a reasonable term where it is apparent that the parties intended a contract.

§10.10.2 Determination Within the Discretion of One of the Parties

The parties may decide to leave the determination of the rent to the discretion of one of them. Although such a provision is quite risky for the party who defers discretion to the other, a provision like this is not necessarily too indefinite or lacking mutuality. As we have seen, the discretion can be limited and subjected to acceptable market standards by construing an obligation of good faith and fair dealing.

This was the approach that the court followed in *Arbitron, Inc. v. Tralyn Broadcasting, Inc.*, 400 F.3d 130 (2d Cir. 2005). Arbitron provided listener demographics data used by radio stations to attract advertisers. It entered into an agreement with Tralyn, the owner of a radio station, under which Arbitron granted a five-year license to Tralyn to use these reports. The agreement provided that if Tralyn acquired additional radio stations or assigned the license to a successor that owned additional stations, Arbitron had the right to increase the license fee. It did not specify the amount of the increase or provide a standard for determining it. About two years later, Tralyn was bought by a corporation that owned four other stations and it assigned the license to the buyer. Arbitron increased the license fee. When neither Tralyn nor its buyer paid the increased fee, Arbitron sued. The district court granted summary judgment to Tralyn on the grounds that the agreement was unenforceably vague because it contained no basis for determining the amount of the increase in the license fee. The court of appeals reversed the summary judgment. The contract was not too indefinite because it allowed Arbitron to determine the increase, which it must do in good faith.

§10.10.3 Omission of a Term

If the parties fail to include a central term in their agreement, the court could conclude that they had not reached final agreement on all the material terms of the contract, so no contract has yet been formed. However, the court may find a contract if it is apparent that the parties did intend to be bound and it is possible to fill the gap with a standard term. It is important to recognize that a court will not unquestioningly fill the gaps in an agreement to make a contract. It will only do this if the evidence clearly demonstrates that the parties reasonably intended a contract and it is possible to supply the missing term by reasonable inference. (Where a gap in the agreement shows that the parties had not yet reached final agreement on all the terms, it is possible, depending on the circumstances, that they may have committed to continue bargaining in good faith. This possibility is discussed in section 10.10.5.)

§10.10.4 Deliberate Deferral of Agreement: "Agreement to Agree"

If the parties have purposely left the term unresolved, this presents a different issue. As noted in section 10.3.3, parties may reach the stage of settling most of the terms of a proposed contract, but may not be able to achieve consensus on some aspect of their relationship. They may therefore acknowledge their commitment to the settled terms and undertake to reach agreement on the unresolved term at a later time. The general approach of the common law is that an "agreement to agree" is legally meaningless. No contract comes into existence until all its material terms have been settled. It would be premature to find a contract before negotiations are complete, merely because the parties have settled some or even most of the terms.

For example, in *Joseph Martin Jr. Delicatessen, Inc. v. Schumacher*, 417 N.E.2d 541 (N.Y. 1981) a renewal option in a lease gave the tenant the right to renew the lease for an additional five-year period at "annual rental to be agreed upon." The court found this to be an unenforceable "agreement to agree" because the parties provided no standard for fixing the rent. A dissent in the case argued that because it was clear that the parties intended to create a binding renewal option, the court should fix a reasonable rent rather than refuse to enforce the contract. Restatement, Second §33, illustration 8 expresses these contrasting approaches. It states that a provision for future agreement on price strongly indicates a lack of intent to be bound, but if the parties manifest intent to be bound, the court should determine a reasonable price. (In *Arbitron, Inc. v. Tralyn Broadcasting, Inc.*, above, the court distinguished *Joseph Martin* and reached the opposite result on the grounds that the contract in *Arbitron* did not require future agreement on the fee, but left it to one of the parties to determine the fee in its good faith discretion.)

§10.10.5 Agreement to Negotiate in Good Faith

In most cases, parties who are negotiating understand that no promises are made unless and until they reach final agreement and make a contract. Up to that final stage when the bargain is struck, either party can break off negotiations at will for any reason. Neither has any duty to persist in negotiations or to pursue consensus. Both are free to lose interest, make unreasonable demands, or refuse reasonable offers. The only sanction for uncooperative behavior is the possible loss of the deal. However, in a narrow range of circumstances, some courts have recognized that one or both of the parties may have made a commitment to continue to negotiate in good faith. That is, although the parties have not yet reached final agreement, one or both of them has assumed a duty to make an **honest effort to work towards agreement**. If the parties expressly make this commitment, it may be easier to bind them to it. However, more difficult cases involve situations where there is no express promise to negotiate in good faith, but one of the parties claims that the promise arose by implication from the circumstances of the negotiation. The recognition of an implied obligation to negotiate in good faith is controversial. While some courts have been receptive to it in proper circumstances, others have declined to imply any such undertaking. They consider that even the possibility of being held to an obligation to keep negotiating could inhibit commercial interaction by making parties wary of becoming trapped by engaging in bargaining. It could also give rise to specious claims if negotiations collapse. Bearing this in mind, we will consider the obligation to bargain in good faith as it has been developed by courts that have recognized the possibility that such a duty might arise.

If both parties commit to negotiate in good faith, their reciprocal promises to do so are **consideration** for each other. Their relationship therefore qualifies as a **preliminary contract** to negotiate in good faith. However, it is sometimes clear that only one of the parties has made this commitment and the other is free to walk away from the negotiations at will. A preliminary contract can only be found in this situation if the party not bound to continue negotiations has given consideration for the other's promise by doing or promising something else in exchange for it. If there is no consideration for a one-sided commitment to negotiate in good faith, the proper basis for enforcing that promise **is promissory estoppel.** This means, of course, that the elements of promissory estoppel, including justifiable detrimental reliance on the promise, must be satisfied.

One of the situations in which courts have recognized a duty to bargain in good faith is described in section 8.9.2 in connection with promissory estoppel. That section refers to three cases, beginning with *Hoffman v. Red Owl Stores*, 133 N.W.2d 267 (Wisc. 1965), in which the court applied the doctrine of promissory estoppel to provide relief for what was, in effect, an implied promise to negotiate in good faith. The crucial circumstance common to those cases was that one of the negotiating parties had placed trust in the other to guide him in taking action necessitated by the prospective contract.

All the cases in section 8.9.2 involve a breach of faith by a party with dominant influence in the negotiations. In the absence of influence of this degree, the court is less likely to find an implied obligation to negotiate in good faith. However, even between sophisticated businesses, the implication can arise if the circumstances strongly indicate that there was such a commitment. For example, in *Channel Home Centers v. Grossman*, 795 F.2d 291 (3d Cir. 1986) the parties had been negotiating a lease of premises to be purchased by the lessor. The lessee executed a letter of intent[26] setting out the proposed terms of the lease and the lessor used the letter to obtain financing for the purchase of the building. The lessee also spent $25,000 in preparations for leasing the premises, based on the lessor's assurance that agreement would be reached. The lessor then let the premises to a third party for a higher rent. The court found that the lessor had assumed and breached a duty to continue good faith bargaining. The parties had worked closely towards concluding the contract, its terms had been largely settled, the lessor had undertaken not to negotiate with others, and it had taken the benefit of using the letter of intent to secure financing.

It is one thing to recognize a duty to negotiate in good faith, but quite another to determine, once negotiations have broken down, **what conduct constitutes a lack of good faith** and whether the failure of agreement is **attributable to a breach** of the duty. In *Apothekernes Laboratorium for*

---

26. A letter of intent is a document executed by the parties in which they record their preliminary agreement. In *Burbach Broadcasting Co. of Delaware v. Elkins Radio Corp.*, 278 F.3d 401 (4th Cir. 2002) the court noted that a letter of intent is normally understood to be nothing more than a non-binding expression of intent to work towards a contract. However, if the circumstances so indicate, it could constitute an agreement to negotiate in good faith. In *Norkunas v. Cochran*, 895 A.2d 1101 (Md. App. 2006) the court found that a letter of intent created no obligation. The owner of real property and the prospective buyers signed a letter of intent to sell the property. The letter made it clear a formal offer would follow. When the seller received the formal offer, she signed it but she then decided not to sell the property and did not return the signed offer to the buyer. The court interpreted the language of the letter of intent to be nothing more than a non-binding statement of interest in making a contract — an agreement to agree. The seller's signature on the formal offer did not bind her either because acceptance must be communicated to the offeror to become effective.

Specialpraeparater v. IMC Chemical Group, Inc., 873 F.2d 155 (7th Cir. 1989)[27] the court provided some guidance on the general standard imposed by the duty to negotiate in good faith. It said that a party is not required to abandon its interests or to make undesired concessions. Rather the standard contemplates that the party makes a genuine and sincere effort to build on what has been settled and to attempt to resolve differences. In some situations, it is easy to see that a party made no good faith attempt to negotiate. For example, in *Channel Home Centers*, it was clear that the lessor had breached the duty because it leased the premises to another and terminated negotiations. Lack of good faith may also be clear where a party does not abandon negotiations, but behaves obstructively, for example, by raising new objections to settled terms or remaining inexplicably obstinate. Bad faith is much harder to establish if the party is sneaky enough to pretend sincere negotiations with the ulterior resolve not to reach agreement.

Even if a breach of faith can be proved, the victim may have trouble showing the fact and extent of loss. If the obligation to negotiate in good faith is contractual, the victim of the breach could claim **expectation damages** — a monetary award designed to place him in the economic position he would have been in, had the other party not breached. A plaintiff must establish these damages with reasonable certainty. The problem here is that a promise to negotiate in good faith is not a promise that agreement will be reached, but merely a commitment to make honest efforts to reach agreement. The plaintiff therefore has no guarantee, and probably is unable to prove, that good faith negotiations would have led to a contract. Even if he can prove that, he may find it difficult to show what the ultimate contract terms would have been or what gain he would have made from the contract. As a result, in many cases, the plaintiff cannot recover expectation damages because his alleged loss caused by the breach of the duty is too speculative. However, if the plaintiff has incurred loss or expense acting in reliance on the promise, the court is able to award **reliance damages** to reimburse those losses and expenses. This could be done on a contract theory (reliance damages are an alternative measure of relief for breach of contract), or, as we saw in section 8.9.2, on a theory of promissory estoppel.

§10.11 AGREEMENTS TO RECORD IN WRITING

Say that representatives of a corporation and an advertising agency meet to negotiate a contract for the production of a promotional video. By the end of the meeting they have reached consensus on all the broad terms of the

---

27. If you can say the name of this case ten times while standing on one leg you are not too drunk to operate a vehicle.

relationship. This consensus may be entirely oral, or it may be recorded in a written memorandum or letter of intent. They agree that the corporation's attorney will draw up a written contract reflecting the agreed terms and providing for matters of detail not fully addressed in the negotiations. Upon completion of the document, it will be presented to both parties for approval and signature. A couple of days later, before the writing has been prepared, the corporation changes its mind and no longer wishes to use the agency's services. Can the corporation cancel without legal liability?

If the parties had clearly stated the intended effect of their oral understanding, this question would be easy to answer. However, if they failed to express its intended legal significance, their purpose is unclear. They could have **intended to be bound immediately** upon concluding the oral or informal agreement, so the reduction of this agreement to a final **writing is just a formality**, and they are obliged to execute it provided that it properly reflects what they agreed. Conversely, they may **not have intended to be bound by the oral or informal agreement**, and did not expect any contract to come into existence **until the final, formal writing has been executed and signed.** (In this latter case, the parties may or may not have bound themselves to continue to negotiate any unresolved terms in good faith, as discussed in section 10.10.5.)

The uncertainty of the parties' intention is resolved by the process of interpretation under all the circumstances of the case. *Texaco v. Pennzoil*, 729 S.W.2d 768 (Tex. 1987) is an example of a case in which the overall circumstances led to the conclusion that the parties intended to be bound before executing the formal writing, even though the transaction was complex and the negotiations had not yet resolved all issues. Pennzoil had been negotiating to purchase stock in the Getty Oil Company and reached an agreement in principle with certain Getty stockholders for the creation of joint ownership of the company. A press release was issued by Getty stating that there was an agreement in principle for acquisition of its stock, subject to execution of a definitive agreement and the approval of other Getty shareholders. Following this, but before the writing was executed, the sellers continued negotiations with Texaco, a competing buyer. Texaco ultimately offered them a better deal, and they contracted to sell the stock to it. The case involved a suit by Pennzoil against Texaco for the tort of interference with Pennzoil's contract rights. To decide that issue, the court had to determine if Pennzoil had in fact acquired any contract rights upon conclusion of the negotiations. At trial, the jury found that a contract had been made at the close of negotiations, despite the absence of a final writing. This was upheld on appeal. The court said that although the press release referred to an agreement in principle, subject to execution of a writing, and the transaction was complex enough to necessitate writing, the general tone of the negotiations and public statements could lead a jury reasonably to conclude that the parties considered themselves bound immediately, and that the writing was intended merely to memorialize their contract.

§10.12 MISUNDERSTANDING: TOTAL AMBIGUITY

As discussed in section 10.6, interpretation is based on the objective meaning of the language of an agreement, viewed in its context. We do not seek to ascertain what each party thought or believed, but what they reasonably appeared to intend. Therefore, when the parties have different understandings of their agreement, the party with the more reasonable understanding prevails.

However, it sometimes happens that while the parties have diametrically opposite understandings of a term, each of their interpretations is entirely reasonable, and there is no basis for preferring one over the other. In such cases, interpretation and construction cannot resolve the uncertainty in the apparent agreement. If the uncertainty relates to a material aspect of the agreement, the only conclusion to be reached is that no contract came into being.

The classic illustration of this problem is provided by a mid-nineteenth century English case, *Raffles v. Wichelhaus*, 159 Eng. Rep. 375 (Ex. 1864). A buyer and seller agreed to the sale of cotton on board the ship *Peerless* sailing from Bombay. It so happened that there were two ships named *Peerless* due to leave Bombay with a cargo of cotton in October and December, respectively. The seller had the later ship in mind and the buyer the earlier. Neither of them knew of the existence of the second ship. The ship contemplated by the buyer arrived in England first, but the seller did not tender delivery from that ship. In fact, he apparently did not even own that cotton. When the second ship arrived and the seller tendered delivery, the buyer refused to accept the goods, contending that he had bought the cotton on the earlier ship. The seller sued for breach of contract, but the court granted judgment in favor of the buyer on the ground that the misunderstanding prevented a contract from arising.

The doctrinal basis of the opinion is obscure, so it can be (and has been) interpreted simply as an outmoded subjectivist case, in which the court refused to find a contract in the absence of an actual meeting of the parties' minds. However, the case is now widely accepted as illustrating the kind of situation in which even an objective approach cannot resolve the misunderstanding. As each party was reasonable in believing that the agreement referred to a particular ship, and neither had any reason to know of the other's contrary understanding, there is no way to decide whose meaning should be preferred. That is, there is *no objective criterion* for deciding which ship must have been intended, and a contract on reasonable terms cannot be established. Hence, assuming that the date of delivery is a material term, no contract came into being.

Restatement Second §§20 and 201 seek to convey this principle in language so convoluted that it boggles the mind. In essence, the

Restatement's rule boils down to this: A material misunderstanding precludes contract formation when the parties were *equally innocent* in not reasonably realizing the misunderstanding *or equally guilty* in realizing it but saying nothing. However, if on balancing the degree of fault of the parties, it appears that *one is more accountable than the other* for knowing of the misunderstanding, a contract must be found to exist on the terms understood by the more innocent party.

The *Peerless* principle may be illustrated by a more modern case involving computer accessories rather than ships sailing from Bombay. In *Konic International Corp. v. Spokane Computer Services, Inc.*, 708 P.2d 932 (Idaho 1985), a Spokane employee was instructed to investigate the purchase of a surge suppressor. After making inquiries of several sellers, in which he was quoted prices ranging from $50 to $200, he had a telephone conversation with a Konic representative, who had a product suitable for the purpose. When asked the price of the suppressor, the Konic salesman said, "fifty-six twenty," by which he meant $5,620. However, the Spokane employee, having been used to hearing prices in the $50 to $200 range, assumed he meant $56.20. The suppressor was ordered and installed before this misunderstanding was discovered. Upon realizing what had happened, Spokane tried to return the suppressor, but Konic refused to take it back. Applying "Peerless" and Restatement Second §20, the court held that no contract had been concluded because there had been a complete failure of communication. Each party attached a materially different but reasonable meaning to the manifestation, and neither knew or had reason to know the meaning attached by the other.

Examples

1. Claire Cutter decided to remove a large oak tree in her front yard. She hired Jack Lumber, a tree remover, to cut it down. Jack has no liability insurance, so he requires his customers to sign a simple one-page written contract that includes the following standard term, drafted by his attorney:

   "By signing this contract, the customer assumes sole responsibility for any loss, damage, or injury caused by the performance of work under this contract and indemnifies Jack Lumber for any such claims."

   Claire read and signed the contract. Jack began work a few days later. He negligently failed to take proper precautions to ensure that the tree would fall safely. As a result, it crashed down onto Claire's driveway, pulverizing Jack's truck that was parked there. Jack says that the indemnity clause in the contract makes Claire liable to him for the cost of replacing his truck. Is he right?

2. Fairest Fowls, Inc., is a poultry supplier. Gordon Bleu is a trained chef who owns and operates a restaurant. Gordon had often ordered duck and

chicken from Fairest Fowls before. Although he had always ordered the cheaper quality "regular" birds, rather than the more expensive "gourmet" quality, he had always been well satisfied.

Gordon decided to begin serving more exotic game birds at his restaurant. He found a recipe for pheasant and checked Fairest Fowls' price list to see what it cost. The list showed "regular" pheasant for $5.00 per pound, and "plump deluxe" pheasant for $12.50 per pound. Gordon ordered and received 50 pounds of the "regular" quality.[28] He prepared the birds according to his recipe. When they were cooked, he tasted them and discovered that they were tough and uneatable. He called Fairest Fowls to complain. Fairest Fowls' representative expressed surprise that Gordon did not know what was "common knowledge" in the trade — that "regular" pheasants were old, scrawny birds, sold only for making soup. The more expensive "plump deluxe" variety were intended for eating.

After being told this, Gordon asked some other chefs and wholesale poultry suppliers (eight people in all) if they knew about the distinction between "regular" and "plump deluxe" pheasants. Five of them were fully aware of it and used the same terminology in their businesses. Two did not know the terminology, but they knew that you could not buy eatable pheasant for $5.00 per pound. One had never heard the terminology and would have assumed that you could eat regular pheasant.

In light of this, did Fairest Fowls breach the contract by delivering uneatable birds to Gordon?

3. Beau Teek operates a clothing store in a shopping mall under a five-year lease. One of the terms of the lease gives Beau the option to renew the lease for a further period of five years "at a rental to be agreed at the time of renewal in light of the prevailing economic conditions."

Beau properly exercised his option to renew within the time specified in the lease. Although the parties tried to agree on rent for the renewal period, they were unable to reach consensus. The lessor called on Beau to vacate the premises, but he refused to leave and commenced suit for specific performance, requesting that the court order the lessor to extend the lease for a five-year period at a rent determined by the court to be reasonable.

Should the court grant the order and determine a reasonable rent?

4. Jill Loppy agreed to sell her old car to Carr Less. They wrote out the following on a piece of paper and both signed it: "Jill Loppy agrees to

---

28. The order was oral, but as the total price of the birds was $250, the statute of frauds is not applicable. Also, because there is no written memorial of agreement, the parol evidence rule does not apply to complicate matters. This same contract, in written form, is used in Example 4 of Chapter 12 to illustrate the impact that the parol evidence rule would have on the resolution of this interpretational issue.

sell her 1984 Chev to Carr Less for 90 percent of its retail bluebook value."

The next day, Jill changed her mind and no longer wished to sell her car. She claims that she does not have a binding contract with Carr, and points out that the piece of writing is too skimpy to be a contract because it does not fully describe the car, has an indefinite price term, and omits many essential terms. In particular, it makes no mention of the delivery and payment obligations and warranties. Furthermore, these issues were not discussed by the parties.

Is this a good argument?

5. Chic A. LaMode is a budding fashion designer. She entered into an agreement with Deadwood Enterprises, Inc., under which Chic granted Deadwood the exclusive right for two years to sell her fashion designs. In consideration, Deadwood promised to pay Chic half of all profits and revenues that it earned from any such sales. Chic delivered all her latest designs to Deadwood, representing well over a thousand different garments.

Hearing nothing from Deadwood for a month, Chic called to find out how sales were going. She was told that sales were slow, but she should be patient because things would pick up soon. After waiting another month, Chic received a check for $300 from Deadwood, representing 50 percent of earnings for the sale of two designs for small garments. In a note accompanying the check, Deadwood apologized for the small return, saying that it hoped to do better in the future.

About two weeks later Chic ran into one of her classmates from design school. The classmate told Chic that he had been approaching manufacturers directly, and had sold over $2,000 worth of designs in the last six weeks. Chic would like to dump Deadwood. Can she do so without breaking the contract?

6. Empire Building Products Co., wished to buy a sawmill. A few months ago, it heard that Woody Cutter, a lumberman, was in severe financial distress and had to sell off one of his two sawmills to pay his debts and remain in business. Empire approached Woody and negotiations for the purchase began. After several weeks of meetings, involving attorneys, accountants, and technical advisors, the parties had reached agreement on all the terms of the sale except price. They were deadlocked on this issue. Empire had refused to pay more than $2.5 million. However, Woody refused to take less than $4 million for it. The parties therefore felt that a cooling-off period would be useful, and they agreed to meet two weeks later to see if they could resolve their differences on price. They signed a joint memorandum drafted by their attorneys, setting out the terms on which they agreed so far, and recording simply that they would meet on a stated day to continue discussions on price.

Empire's board met just before negotiations were to resume. Realizing that Woody was under pressure to sell and that he had no other prospective buyer, the board decided not to budge on the $2.5 million price. They knew that this would be a bargain because they had reliably appraised the mill at a value of $3.5 million. At about this same time, Woody, reviewing his precarious financial position, decided not to hold out for his asking price but to come down as low as $3 million (which he realized was below the mill's true value).

When the meeting took place as arranged, Woody made great efforts to persuade Empire to close the gap between the price proposals, but Empire refused to consider anything above $2.5 million. As a result, the negotiations terminated in failure.

Woody had run out of time. Before he could look for another buyer, his creditors petitioned to put him in bankruptcy so that his assets could be liquidated to pay his debts. As a result, he lost both his sawmills as well as most of his other property. He blames Empire for this calamity because its stubbornness prevented the sale of the one mill that would have allowed him to keep his creditors happy while he tried to make his other mill profitable and to turn his business around. Does Woody have any basis for holding Empire liable for his loss?

7. Molly Fido owned a profitable and successful restaurant. She decided to sell the business and she solicited inquiries by placing an advertisement in a trade journal. Faith Fullness responded and they met to discuss the possible sale. At their initial meeting, Faith examined the premises, equipment, and financial records and the parties had extensive but inconclusive discussions about price. Faith expressed strong interest in buying the business and they agreed to meet again in a week. During that week, Faith visited the restaurant several times to observe the operations, service, and customer traffic. She visited her bank to discuss financing and spoke to a couple of potential investors to see if she could raise some capital. Everything looked promising, and she became enthusiastic about buying the business.

At their next meeting, Faith and Molly discussed the sale in earnest. After some hours they had reached agreement in principle on the basic terms of the sale, which Faith wrote down on a yellow legal paid: Faith would pay Molly $300,000 for the equipment, name, goodwill, lease rights, and transferrable licenses. A third of the price would be paid upon the signing of a written agreement, and the balance would be paid in installments over two years. Faith would take over the business and receive transfer of its assets as soon as possible after the agreement was signed, and Molly would remain on as an employee of the business for six months at a salary to be mutually decided. Faith would immediately instruct her attorney to draw a written contract reflecting these terms and dealing with any necessary matters of detail that the parties had not thought of. Later that day, Faith consulted her attorney and gave her the pad with the notes of the meeting. The attorney promised to set to work as soon as possible on drafting the memorandum of agreement.

The next day, Molly received a call from Ruth Less who had also read the advertisement. Molly told Ruth that she had almost certainly sold the business already, but agreed to meet with Ruth anyhow. After a whole day's negotiations, during which Molly disclosed to Ruth the terms of the understanding with Faith, Ruth made a very attractive offer. She is willing to buy the business for $350,000 cash. Molly would like to accept the offer but is unsure if she has legally committed herself to Faith. Has she?

8. Pierre Less saw the following homemade poster on a lamppost near his home: "Lost Dog — Reward $100. If anyone sees a black poodle with the name tag "Raffles" on his collar, please bring him to 1864 Bombay St. to receive this reward." The next day Pierre came across a black poodle which was scurrying about the neighborhood in a state of distress. He looked at the poodle's collar and saw that he had a name tag showing his name as "Raffles." Pierre took Raffles to the address on the poster but the owner would not accept the dog, claiming that it was not his Raffles. It turned out, by strange coincidence unknown to both parties, that another black poodle named Raffles had wandered from his home and had become lost in the neighborhood. The poodle that Pierre found was the wrong one. Nevertheless, Pierre feels that he went to a lot of trouble on the faith of the poster and he wants his reward. Is he entitled to it?

Explanations

1. The question here is whether the indemnity clause is broad enough to impose liability on Claire for loss suffered by Jack as a result of damage he negligently inflicted on his own property in the course of his performance. Do not be too quick to scoff at Jack's claim — remember that he is handy with a chainsaw.

This example invokes *Pacific Gas and Electric Co.*, discussed in section 10.6.2a. As noted there, a repairer of machinery agreed to indemnify the owner against loss for damage to property arising out of the performance of the contract. The dispute was whether the indemnity covered damage to machinery belonging to the owner or applied only to claims of third parties. The trial court, confining its examination to the face meaning of the indemnity provision, held that its plain meaning did not restrict liability to third-party claims. The supreme court reversed the trial court's decision because the trial court refused to look beyond the plain meaning of the words used in the written contract and to admit extrinsic evidence that may have shown that the parties had intended to confine the repairer's liability to third-party property. In Jack's case, there is no similar concern about admitting extrinsic evidence of meaning because neither party offers any such evidence. Where there is no contextual evidence that bears on the meaning of contractual language, the court is necessarily confined to finding meaning within the four corners of the document.

The argument could be made that the language used in this contract is wide enough to cover damage to Jack's truck. It places on Claire "sole responsibility for . . . damage . . . caused by the performance of work under this contract . . ." This may suggest that she is responsible for any damage that may occur during the course of performance, whatever its kind, and whoever its victim may be. However, this interpretation is overborne by other indications of reasonable intent in the contract.

The words "indemnifies . . . Jack . . . for any such claims" suggests that the contract contemplates that Claire is responsible only to protect Jack from third-party claims. This meaning makes sense in light of the purpose of the clause: work is being done on Claire's property, and she therefore assumes responsibility for any loss suffered by a third party as a result of the work. The trial court in *Pacific Gas* did make the point that "indemnifies" is capable of a broader meaning. However, that case was concerned with damage to the owner's property, not the repairer's. Even if the language can be taken to extend beyond third-party liability, it surely cannot mean that Claire should be responsible for damage caused by Jack to his own property as a result of his own negligence. Such an interpretation seems absurd, and it is most unlikely that Claire reasonably expected a generally worded indemnity provision to impose liability on her for Jack's self-inflicted injury.

In addition to being beyond Claire's reasonable expectations, such a provision is not in the public interest. Courts usually require a very specific disclaimer of liability to exclude damage caused by a party's negligence. (See Example 6 of Chapter 13.) A fortiori, a generally worded provision like this cannot give Jack the right to seek compensation from Claire for damage caused by his own negligence. Recall that one of the canons of interpretation is that where the meaning of language is in doubt, a court should choose an interpretation that is reasonable and in accord with public policy.

Finally, if doubt still remains over the proper interpretation of the clause, the contra proferentum rule may be used to resolve the doubt against Jack, who is the proponent of the indemnity.

2. This is a sale of goods under the UCC, but interpretation of the agreement is based on principles not significantly different from those applied in

modern common law. UCC §1.205[29] recognizes the primacy of express terms but also articulates the importance of trade usage and course of dealing in the ascertainment of meaning.

This example is loosely based on the famous chicken case, *Frigaliment Importing*, discussed in section 10.6.2. The principles set out in that case are helpful in resolving this dispute. The ordinary meaning of language is the point of departure, but "regular" has many meanings. Possibly Gordon's prior dealings would support his interpretation that a "regular" bird is eatable, but the prior contracts are not very helpful as a course of dealing because they involved different birds and distinguished "regular" quality from "gourmet," not "plump deluxe." We therefore need to go beyond the bare surface meaning of "regular" to ascribe a meaning to the word. The entire context in which it was used indicates that Fairest Fowls's meaning should prevail.

Sometimes other terms in a contract can cast light on the meaning of the term in dispute, so courts interpret language in the context of the agreement as a whole. For example, in *Frigaliment Importing*, the contract's price term was of some help in supporting the seller's argument that "chicken" was used generically, rather than more narrowly to refer only to fryers. It reflected a different price per pound for the larger and smaller chickens, and the price of the larger chickens was below the market price of fryers. We are not told of any terms in this contract that could explain what the parties meant by "regular," but price could similarly be a helpful indicator of intent.

More significantly, our preliminary information on trade usage strongly supports the meaning claimed by Fairest Fowls. (Of course, if the dispute goes to litigation, trade usage would have to be established by sworn expert testimony, but Gordon's informal survey is good enough for present purposes.) Gordon asked chefs and suppliers what they understood "regular" pheasants to mean. Although they were not unanimous in their response, there seems to be widespread recognition in the trade (defined here as the wholesale poultry market) that the word "regular" refers to pheasants that can be used only to make soup. To prove a trade usage, a party needs only establish it on the preponderance of the evidence. A severe clash of the experts could result in failure to discharge this burden, but there does not need to be unanimity to make a credible showing. As a professional chef who buys poultry from suppliers, Gordon is surely a member of this trade. Even if he did not actually know what "regular" meant, he had reason to know the usage and is bound by it.

---

29. Section 1.303 in revised Article 1.

3. The term relating to the rental for the renewal period is unquestionably vague. It suggests an "agreement to agree" but it does seek to limit the parties' discretion in negotiating by stating a standard: the economic conditions prevailing at the time of renewal. Although the rent provision in this lease is not as tortured and nonsensical as the one in *Walker v. Keith* described in section 10.10.1, it may not be any more workable, and a court may refuse to give effect to the renewal agreement. However, there is a plausible argument for upholding it. After all, the rental provision was not simply an "agreement to agree," and it does refer to what could be seen as a market-based standard, albeit poorly expressed. It is not a great leap beyond their expressed intent for a court to determine and apply a reasonable market standard if they cannot reach agreement. In so doing it upholds an apparent serious intent to be bound, and conforms to the rule of interpretation that favors an effective meaning over one that renders the term ineffective.

4. No. This is a sale of goods, and the UCC is very clear on the question of omitted terms. Section 2.204(3)[30] states that a contract for sale does not fail for indefiniteness, even though terms are left open, provided that the parties intended to make a contract and there is a reasonably certain basis for giving a remedy. In addition, Article 2 contains a number of gap fillers that apply to any agreement of sale in the absence of contrary provisions expressed by the parties. As a result, this skimpy-looking contract is much fuller than Jill suggests.

The goods sold need not be fully described in the writing. Because Jill owned only one 1984 Chev, the identity of the car is not uncertain, and it can be established by oral testimony. The parties need not fix a specific price, as long as they have indicated an objective market standard or some other reasonably certain means of determining it. In fact, the UCC's approach to open price terms is more flexible than reflected in the *Walker* case, discussed in section 10.10.1 and Example 3. Section 2.306 validates express agreement for a reasonable price and implies such agreement unless it is apparent that the parties did not intend to contract for a reasonable price. In this case, there is no need to have recourse to a reasonable price, because the parties have expressed a workable market standard. (Even if they cannot agree on adjustments to base value provided for in the book, an appraiser could make this determination.)

If any of the remaining terms had been settled orally by the parties and just not stated in the writing, oral evidence of their actual agreement would establish these terms. In the absence of any such agreement (and

---

30. The numbering and substantive content of this provision, as well as all the others cited in this Explanation, are unchanged in the 2003 revision of Article 2.

any applicable usage and course of dealing or performance), the UCC provides the following supplementary terms:

(a) The seller is obliged to transfer and deliver the goods, and the buyer must accept and pay for them (§2.301).

(b) The seller accomplishes her tender of delivery by holding the car available for collection by the buyer at her home at a reasonable hour and for a reasonable period (§§2.308 and 2.503). In addition, because the state requires registration of transfer of title for motor vehicles, the certificate of title must be tendered with proper endorsement.

(c) The delivery must take place within a reasonable time (§2.309).

(d) The buyer must pay for the goods (in cash) on receiving them (§2.310).

(e) The seller warrants that she has good title to the goods (§2.312). (A full discussion of UCC warranties is beyond our scope. It is enough to note that no other warranties are implied in law. The two other implied warranties, set out in §§2.314 and 2.315, are not applicable on the facts of this case.)

5. As you may have suspected, this is a cleverly disguised ripoff of *Wood v. Lucy, Lady Duff-Gordon*, discussed in section 10.8.2. As in *Wood*, we can easily infer from the underlying commercial purpose of the contract that Deadwood impliedly promised to make best efforts to place Chic's designs. However, it is a harder case because it requires us to give content to the obligation to use best efforts. The court did not have to do that in *Wood* because it was not Wood's duty to Lucy that had to be enforced, but Lucy's duty to Wood. (She had sold designs herself in violation of the agreement, and Wood sued her for his share of the profits.) Because the court needed to imply the obligation of best efforts only for the purpose of finding that Wood gave consideration for Lucy's promise, it did not have to decide what would have constituted best efforts. Since Chic asserts that Deadwood has fallen short of best efforts, we need to tackle the question of what level of effort would satisfy Deadwood's obligation.

To decide what constitutes best efforts, we must examine both the reasonable expectation in the trade and the scope and resources of Deadwood's operation. The standard seems to be a blend of reasonable efforts (evaluated objectively) and honest efforts (measured subjectively). We do not have enough information to make a decision on whether Deadwood's efforts would qualify. Deadwood apparently had very little success, and Chic's classmate did better without representation. But that, on its own, is not enough to prove that Deadwood breached its obligation of best efforts. The test is not one of result but of endeavor.

6. The parties clearly did not have a final contract at the end of their first set of negotiations. The price term was unresolved and there is no indication that they intended to be bound unless it was settled. This is not a case in which it would be justifiable to infer that they agreed to a sale at a reasonable or market price.

Therefore, the only basis of liability is that Empire had a duty to continue negotiating in good faith, and that it breached it by standing firm and refusing to negotiate further on the price. Negotiations are normally precursors to legal commitment, and they do not in themselves usually give rise to any legal obligations. In most cases, until the parties actually reach agreement and conclude a contract, neither assumes the legal duty to keep negotiating or to try to reach consensus. This has to be the general rule otherwise it would become difficult to distinguish negotiation from agreement, and entering into negotiations would carry too high a risk of liability. As stated in section 10.10.5, some courts are concerned enough about hampering negotiations that they will not countenance a legally binding implied obligation to negotiate in good faith. Even courts that do recognize the duty in principle are cautious about implying it except in the most compelling cases.

In this case, there are strong equities favoring the implication of a duty to negotiate in good faith. It would not have been enough merely that the parties had proceeded quite far in their negotiations and had agreed to meet further to try to resolve their differences over the purchase price. However, Empire knew that Woody was in trouble, he needed to sell, and his options for preserving his business were running out as time passed. It deliberately used his distress to obtain bargaining leverage. A great deal of energy had gone into negotiations already, and substantial consensus had been reached. Given Empire's apparent interest in the transaction and its willingness to meet again, Woody could reasonably have expected Empire to return to the bargaining table in a spirit of honest compromise.

If an obligation to bargain in good faith is implied in this case, what must Empire have done to satisfy it? Bad faith is easy to identify in situations where there has been outright crookery, but it is much more difficult to define in close cases where there is a thin dividing line between bad faith and acceptable commercial hardball. It would not in itself have been bad faith for Empire to make a business decision to stick to its price limit. A party should not be compelled to pay more than it desires. However, when Empire's knowledge of Woody's circumstances and its motive for the refusal to budge are taken into account, its insistence on the low price looks decidedly less wholesome. This is particularly so given Woody's concessions that considerably narrowed the price gap between them.

If Empire did breach its duty to bargain in good faith, what is Woody's remedy? If Woody gave consideration to Empire for its promise to negotiate in good faith (say by making a reciprocal commitment or by suffering some other detriment in exchange for it), the obligation to bargain in good faith is contractual and can be enforced as a contract. However, if there is no consideration for the promise, Woody's cause of action is promissory estoppel, provided that he suffered a detriment in reasonable reliance on the promise. Whichever theory of recovery is used, any damages Woody might recover are likely to be based on whatever reliance loss he can prove. A breach of contract would entitle Woody to expectation damages, but Woody is not likely to be able to prove his expectation interest. Woody would have to make a convincing showing of two uncertain facts to establish a link between Empire's breach and his harm: He must prove not only that a contract probably would have resulted had Empire bargained in good faith, but also that the sale of the mill would likely have enabled him to prevent the loss of his business. In addition, Woody must show the amount of the alleged loss, which is difficult where the present value of the business is in doubt and any value it may have would depend on future management and economic conditions. If such expectation damages cannot be proved, a court is able to award Woody any loss incurred in reliance on the contract to bargain in good faith. These damages would be the same as reliance damages under the theory of promissory estoppel. No reliance expenses are indicated in the facts, so Woody does not appear to be entitled to any compensation.

7. When parties have agreed in principle to the essential terms of a contract, but they contemplate executing a formal, signed writing, the legal effect of their oral or informal[31] agreement may be unclear if they do not specifically express the intended effect of the oral or informal understanding. They may have intended no commitment whatever until the writing is signed. Conversely, they may have concluded a contract already, subject merely to the formality of writing. As a third possibility, even if they have not yet made a final commitment, they may at least have undertaken to bargain over the unresolved issues in good faith. Their purpose must be determined from all the circumstances of their interaction.

All the usual avenues should be explored for helpful indications of intent: the language of agreement itself, statements or actions during

---

31. The term "oral or informal" indicates that the preliminary understanding could either be oral or in some written form short of a final contract. In this Example, the parties' agreement was oral, but it was noted down in an unsigned writing on a yellow pad. An agreement in principle could be even more formal, and could be written up as a signed "letter of intent," which memorializes what has been agreed and provides a framework for further negotiation.

negotiations, trade usage, and course of dealings or performance. No facts are given to suggest that there is any specific trade usage, and there is no indication of prior dealing or subsequent performance, so the only source of information is the circumstances of the transaction itself, evaluated in light of usual commercial standards. Comment c to Restatement Second §27 suggests some of the factors that may help in deciding if a contract was concluded orally or informally. They include considerations such as the extent of the express agreement; the nature and extent of unresolved issues; whether it is normal practice — or, stronger still, legally required — to put a contract of this kind in writing; and the value and complexity of the transaction.

There are some indications that suggest that the parties did not yet intend to be fully bound in contract. The sale of a business is a commercial exchange of a relatively complex and valuable nature, and it seems reasonable to assume that parties would normally expect to sign a written memorandum before being bound. This assumption is strengthened by the fact that a number of known or possible issues were left unresolved. Not only did they deliberately leave open the salary to be paid to Molly for her work in the six months following the sale, but they also anticipated further unidentified issues to emerge when Faith's attorney drafted a comprehensive writing. Some of these may be trivial, but some could be significant and contentious. Of course, these are merely indications. They are not conclusive, and an argument can be made for the opposite result.

It is therefore conceivable that Molly and Faith had entered a binding contract of sale at the conclusion of negotiations. If so, Molly risks legal liability if she reneges. Because this is a close question, let us consider what would happen if there was no final commitment at that stage. Would this mean that there is simply no contract, or do the circumstances suggest that the parties at least agreed to bargain in good faith on unresolved issues, promising to sign unless they encounter a genuine deal-breaker? The circumstances are ambiguous and may not be strong enough to deprive Molly of her normal right to abandon these negotiations in favor of a better deal. The facts do not indicate the level of trust, commitment, or reliance discussed in section 10.10.5 and Example 6. Nevertheless, Faith's dealings with Molly are quite far advanced, oral agreement has been reached on all apparently material terms, and Molly has at least given some implicit assurance that there are no obstacles to the completion of the transaction. It is therefore possible that a court may find that they had reached a stage that precluded Molly from walking away from the deal.

If this is so, it does not invariably mean that Faith is entitled to relief, because she has to prove economic loss. As stated in Example 6, this means that she will have to prove both that the contract probably would have resulted but for Molly's refusal to proceed further, and that following the purchase of the business, she would have been reasonably likely to have made profits in a reasonably certain amount. In the absence of this proof, she may be awarded reliance damages if any reliance loss was suffered. She may have incurred some expenses relating to her inquiries before the second meeting, but no such losses are indicated following the implied promise to bargain in good faith.

8. By placing the poster on the lamppost, Raffles' owner made an offer for a unilateral contract. Pierre accepted it by the act of returning a dog called Raffles to him. (*See* section 4.12.3.) Your initial response to this example may be that although Pierre intended to accept, he did not in fact do so because return of the wrong dog was not performance of the act required for acceptance. However, the wording of the poster simply offers the reward to anyone who "brings" to the stated address a lost black poodle with the name tag "Raffles" on his collar. Pierre performed that act exactly as specified. Of course, Raffles' owner intended to refer to his own dog, but his subjective intent is not determinative. (Maybe it could be argued that the reasonable implication from the poster is that the offer called for the return of the dog owned by the offeror. This is a plausible argument, but the literal wording of the poster does not say that.)

   However, even if Pierre prevails on the offer and acceptance issue, he is not likely to get his reward. While the objective test holds the owner to the reasonable meaning of his words, it presupposes that it is possible to determine the reasonable meaning of the disputed language. If the parties have different understandings of a word and the court cannot say which of them is more reasonable, the objective test cannot resolve the dispute and the conclusion must be that the agreement is subject to a fatal and irresoluble ambiguity. By a further strange coincidence, the problem in this case is quite similar to another, in which one of the parties was named Raffles. (*See* section 10.12.) On the principle of that case, as embodied in Restatement, Second §20, there can be no contract, even under the objective test, if the double meaning of the name cannot be settled by recourse to its most reasonable meaning and the parties are equally blameless for the misunderstanding. Maybe Raffles' owner can be faulted for the way that he worded his poster, but can he be held accountable for not taking into account the possibility that there could be two black poodles called Raffles in the area?

The Statute of Frauds

§11.1 INTRODUCTION

As a general rule, the law gives effect to oral contracts. Although it is almost always a good idea to record a contract in writing to facilitate proof of the fact and terms of agreement, for many contracts this written record is not a prerequisite to validity or enforceability. However, certain types of contract fall outside this general rule and must be written and signed to be enforceable. The requirement of a written record for specified types of contracts[1] entered the law of England just over 300 years ago, through a statutory enactment during the reign of King Charles II.

The original motivation for the rule was a concern over fraudulent testimony, hence the original name of the statute, "An Act for Prevention of Fraud and Perjuries," which came to be shortened to "the statute of frauds." Its principal function was to ensure that a person could not seek to enforce an obligation of the kind covered by the statute purely on the basis of unreliable and possibly perjured oral testimony, but would have to produce some adequate written record of the contract. American jurisdictions have adopted statutes modeled on the original statute of frauds, covering much the same types of contracts. Over the years, many states have enacted additional statutes requiring writing for further types of contracts. (For example, a writing is required for a contract granting a security interest

---

1. The statute covered many types of transactions besides contracts. We are concerned only with its relationship to contracts.

in personal property under Uniform Commercial Code (UCC) Article 9. Often, consumer protection statutes require a written and signed contract for particular sales of goods and services, and may even specify that the writing must set out the terms governing certain aspects of the transaction.) Therefore, although one usually refers to "the statute of frauds" in the singular, there could be a number of statutes in existence in a jurisdiction, each prescribing writing for a different kind of contract. In this discussion, we are concerned only with the general common law statute of frauds and with that prescribed by UCC Article 2.

The *basic rule* of the statute of frauds (referred to from now on as "the statute") is that a contract within its scope **may not be enforced** unless a **memorandum** of it is **written and signed by the party to be charged.** This gives rise to a few initial observations: First, the statute does not require the entire contract to be written, but only a memorandum of it. The degree to which a writing must set out the detail and content of the contract to qualify as a sufficient memorandum is discussed below. Second, only the party who is to be charged, that is, against whom enforcement is sought, needs to have signed it. The signature of the other party is not needed. The question of what constitutes a signature is discussed below. Third, the consequence of non-compliance is usually unenforceability, not invalidity. This distinction is explained more fully in section 11.5. Fourth, as originally conceived and as applied for many subsequent centuries, the statute contemplated that writing and signature would take the form of words or symbols on paper. In recent times, the rapid advance of communications technology has required the adaptation of "writing" and "signature" to take account of communication by other, particularly electronic, media. This change is reflected in state and federal statutes that make electronic signatures effective, and by changes in the 2003 revision of Article 2 that substitute the word "record" for "writing throughout the Article. (This is discussed further below.) Even in the absence of legislation, modern courts take account of technology by drawing analogies between writing and other forms of communication, so as to find that electronic recording in proper form satisfies the writing and signature requirements of the statute.

The statute is intended to prevent a person from enforcing a falsely alleged contract through perjured testimony. However, when a contract was really made orally, the statute can equally be used by the party seeking to evade it. For this reason, there is some concern that the benefits of the statute are outweighed by its potential for abuse. It may be better policy to have no requirement of writing and to allow the factfinder to evaluate the credibility of the oral evidence. These considerations led to its repeal in England some time ago, but it continues to survive in U.S. jurisdictions. The principal focus of the courts has been on making it more flexible to better ensure that it efficiently achieves its purpose while cutting down on the opportunities for abuse. Sometimes this has been done by legislation, as happened by the enactment of a reformed version of the statute relating to the sale of goods in UCC §2.201, but more often, reforms develop in the process of judicial application of the original statutory provisions. Restatement Second §§110-137 seek to reflect contemporary judicial thinking on the statute.

To determine whether problems of enforcement exist under the statute, it is useful to ask three questions in the order represented by the following flow chart:

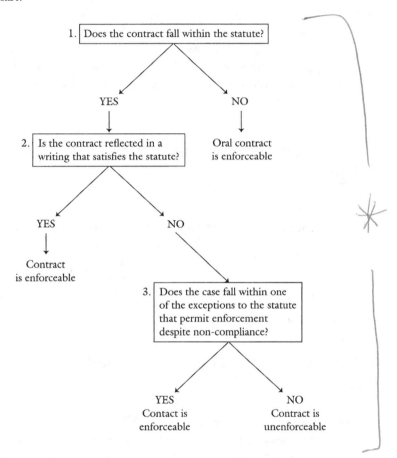

§11.2 THE FIRST INQUIRY: IS THE CONTRACT OF A TYPE THAT FALLS WITHIN THE STATUTE?

The original statute covered six types of contract. Although others have been added in different jurisdictions, these six largely continue to make up the core of modern versions of the statute. This shows remarkable durability, since they are more reflective of the commercial priorities of seventeenth-century Englishmen than of today's economy. The following subsections of this section describe the six categories of contracts that were included in the original statute and continue to be subject to the statute of frauds. (The categories are listed in Restatement, Second, §110, and expanded upon in subsequent sections.) The first three — contracts for the sale of land or an interest in land, contracts that cannot be performed in a year, and sales of goods — cover more common types of transactions. They are the dominant categories and are more likely to be encountered. The last three — suretyships, executors' contracts to answer for a duty of the decedent, and contracts made upon consideration of marriage, relate to a narrower range of more specialized contracts. For this reason, the discussion in the sections following this one and the Examples and Explanations center on the first three categories.

§11.2.1 Contracts for the Sale of Land or an Interest in Land

Like many rules derived from older English law, this rule reflects the importance of land as the principal means of wealth in English society at the time. The statute applies not only to a contract to sell land, but also to any other contract under which land is disposed of, as well as a transfer of an interest in land short of full ownership, such as the grant or transfer of an easement or mortgage. A lease is also an interest in land and must be in writing, but the statute commonly exempts short-term leases from its purview.

§11.2.2 Contracts That Cannot Be Performed Within a Year

Any contract, irrespective of its subject matter, must comply with the statute if it cannot be performed within a year of its execution. Note that the rule is not confined to contracts in which the performance itself will take over a year, but includes any contract — however short the period of performance may be — in which the performance will not be completed within a year of contracting. Therefore, if on July 1, 2003, a customer makes a contract with a popular resort to rent a room for the July 4 long weekend in 2004, the contract falls within the statute, even though the performance will last only three days.

The idea behind the one-year rule is probably to ensure that longer-term contracts are recorded. In part, this reflects the concern that parties cannot be expected to remember unrecorded terms as time passes, but it could also be motivated by the expectation that a long-term contract may involve greater economic value. Commentators have pointed out that if the rule is motivated by this goal, it does not achieve it very effectively because the one-year period does not relate to the length of performance but the period between the making of the contract and the end of performance. Therefore, the rule just as much governs a short, inexpensive transaction (such as the hotel booking used in this illustration) as a long, expensive one. Whatever the thinking behind the rule, it is obviously arbitrary and if rigidly applied, could result in absurd distinctions. For example, if an employment contract is entered into on Monday, for a year's employment beginning that day, the statute is not implicated. However, if the employment period is to begin on Tuesday, the statute applies. Courts try to avoid this kind of absurdity when the evidence strongly suggests that a contract really was made orally, and the court does not wish to refuse enforcement by technical application of the rule.

Because the one-year rule does not seem very rational, courts are generally reluctant to apply it unless it is absolutely clear that the contract cannot be performed within a year of its making — that is, that it would be a breach of the contract for the party to render performance before the one-year date. In some cases, the only possible interpretation of the contract is that it cannot, by its terms, be performed within a year of its making, and the court has no choice but to find that it is subject to the statute of frauds. The hotel booking for July 4 is such a contract. The contract specifies performance on July 4 and the performance date is a material term. The hotel would breach its obligation by tendering the room, not on July 4, but on some earlier date.

However, where the contract does not clearly preclude completion of performance within a year, a court that disfavors the one-year rule will not apply the statute, even if the nature and extent of performance is such that it is unlikely, or even impossible to complete it in a year. This approach is illustrated by *C. R. Klewin, Inc. v. Flagship Properties, Inc.*, 600 A.2d 772 (Conn. 1991). The developer of a major construction project (consisting of a hotel, a convention center, and a large number of commercial and residential buildings) contracted with a general contractor to manage the construction. A written contract was executed for the first phase of the construction, but the contract for the second phase was oral. The developer dismissed the contractor at the end of the first phase. When the contractor sued for breach of contract, the developer applied for summary judgment on the basis that, given the scale of the project, the contract clearly could not be performed in a year. (The contractor conceded that the project would take between three to ten years to complete.) The trial court found that the statute of frauds barred enforcement of the oral contract and granted summary judgment to the contractor. The Supreme Court reversed. It observed that the one-year rule was difficult to justify and should therefore be confined as narrowly as possible to apply only where the contract expressly specifies that performance is required to extend more than a year beyond its execution.

However, when the contract does not contain such a clear obligation, it should be treated as legally performable within a year, even if, as a matter of fact, performance cannot be completed within that period and the parties did not expect it to be.

Contracts that provide for a performance of indefinite duration could be subject to the one-year rule. For example, in *Tucker v. Roman Catholic Diocese of Lafayette-In-Indiana*, 837 N.E.2d 596 (Ind. App. 2005) the court applied the rule to a contract in which the performance had no time limit. A lay religious teacher employed by the diocese sexually abused the plaintiff when she was ten years old. Many years later, when she was an adult, the plaintiff told church officials of the abuse. In exchange for the plaintiff's agreement not to pursue legal recourse, the church officials orally promised that they would strip the abuser of his duties and would ensure that he had no contact with children at the parish. They failed to do so, and the plaintiff sued for emotional distress damages for breach of contract. The court of appeals upheld the trial court's dismissal of the complaint. The diocese could have fired the abuser within the year, but its promise to ensure that he would not have contact with parish children had no time frame. It was an ongoing obligation that could not be performed in a year.[2]

A contract that is to continue for the lifetime of one of the parties is of indefinite term and is treated by some courts as subject to the statute. Other courts reason that provided the contract clearly is intended to terminate on the death of one of the parties, the possibility of the party's death within a year of executing the contract makes it potentially performable within a year. In a few states, the statute of frauds specifically provides that a lifetime contract is subject to the statute.

As discussed in section 11.2.3, UCC Article 2 has its own statute of frauds in §2.201 which applies where the price of the goods sold is $500 or more. (This figure has been increased to $5,000 or more in the 2003 revision.) The current version of §2.201 does not refer to the one-year rule, so it is not clear if a contract for the sale of goods that cannot be performed within a year of its making would be subject to the common law statute as well. (Recall that under UCC §1.103,[3] general principles of common law apply to sales of goods unless displaced by the provisions of the Code.) If the one-year rule applies to sales of goods, a sale for a price under the minimum set by §2.201 would be subject to the one-year statute, and a sale for a price over that limit would be subject to the requirements of

---

2. It turned out that the plaintiff's case had other problems apart from noncompliance with the statute of frauds. The contract was invalid for lack of consideration because the statute of limitations had run on the plaintiff's claim, so she suffered no legal detriment in forbearing from suit. In addition, the court held that emotional distress damages are not available for breach of contract. (*See* section 18.13.) This may explain why the court was readily willing to find that the one-year rule applied.

3. Renumbered §1.103(b) in revised Article 1.

both §2.201 and the common law. This could be significant if the common law statute has more stringent standards. The 2003 revision of Article 2 adds a new subsection (4) to §2.201 which eliminates this issue by making it clear that the one-year rule does not apply to a sale of goods.

§11.2.3 Contracts for the Sale of Goods

As mentioned above, contracts for the sale of goods are no longer covered by the traditional statute of frauds but are provided for in UCC §2.201. Section 2.201(1) requires compliance with the statute where the price of the goods under the sale contract is $500 or more ($5,000 or more in the 2003 revision). Note that the dollar figure refers to the total price under the contract, so the price of all items sold under the contract must be added together to determine if it is subject to the statute. If the price consists of property other than cash, the property must be valued to establish the price.

The scope of Article 2 was discussed in section 2.7.2. In many cases a contract obviously is or is not a sale of goods. However, sometimes the nature of the contract is not so clear. This could be because it is not certain if the item sold qualifies as goods (as opposed to intangible rights or real property), or it is not certain that the transaction is a sale (as opposed to, say, a lease). It could also be because the transaction is a hybrid — it consists of both a sale of goods and the rendition of services related to them. In this situation (as discussed in section 2.7.2), most courts apply a predominant purpose test to decide if the contract is subject to UCC Article 2. Article 2 applies if the sales component is dominant, but it does not apply if the central purpose of the contract is the supply of services, with goods furnished incidentally to the service.

National Historic Shrines Foundation v. Dali, 4 UCC Rep. Serv. 71 (N.Y. 1967) is a good example of how a statute of frauds argument can hang on the question of scope. Salvador Dali, the famously eccentric surrealist painter, made an oral contract with the foundation to execute a painting of the Statue of Liberty on a television show. The painting would then be sold to raise funds for a museum. Dali reneged and defended a suit for breach of contract on the basis that the oral contract was unenforceable under §2.201. He argued that the contract was for the sale of his painting which was worth considerably more than $500. The court rejected this argument. It found that the contract was for Dali's services in performing on TV. The fact that a painting would be created in the course of this performance was merely incidental to this purpose. The rather surreal facts of this case make it different from the normal contract to sell manufactured goods, which is unquestionably a sale. Where the labor of the seller is devoted to the creation of goods as the end product of the work, it is the end product — the goods — that are sold, not the service of making them.

§11.2.4 Contracts to Answer for the Debt or Obligation of Another

This provision covers suretyship contracts. A surety is a person who promises the creditor to pay another person's debt, so that if the other person fails to pay the debt, the surety is obliged to pay it. For example, Borrower asks Lender for a loan. As a condition of lending money to Borrower, Lender requires someone else to agree to pay back the loan if Borrower defaults. Borrower persuades Mom, his mother, to promise Lender to pay Lender if Borrower fails to do so. Borrower is primarily liable on the loan, and is called the principal debtor. Mom, as surety, is secondarily liable. She is, in effect, a backup debtor who assumes the duty to pay a debt that she would not otherwise owe. The secondary nature of the surety's obligation is important to application of the statute. If the promisor is primarily liable on the debt (for example, she is a joint debtor) she is not a surety and the statute does not apply. (Sometimes the term "guaranty" is used synonymously with "suretyship." These two types of transactions both involve a commitment by a person to pay the debt of another, and they are very similar. The subtle differences between them need not concern us here. They both constitute contracts to answer for the debt of another and are subject to the statute.)

There are two justifications for subjecting a suretyship agreement to the statute of frauds. First, the formality of writing serves a cautionary function by alerting the surety that she is undertaking a serious, legally enforceable commitment. Second, it serves the usual evidentiary function of the statute of frauds by preventing the assertion of a possibly bogus claim that a person agreed to pay the debt of another.

The statute relating to suretyship has some difficult qualifications and nuances which we will not get into here. However, one of them is noted briefly: The statute presupposes that the surety undertakes the suretyship for the primary purpose of accommodating and benefiting the principal debtor. Therefore, if the main purpose of the suretyship is to serve the surety's own financial interest—that is, the surety receives a direct economic benefit—the statute does not apply and an oral undertaking is enforceable. This principle only applies if the economic interest of the surety is the main purpose of the suretyship. It is not enough that the surety has some personal stake or self-interest in undertaking liability for the debt.

§11.2.5 Contracts of Executors or Administrators to Answer for the Duty of Their Decedents

The type of contract covered here is one in which the executor or administrator of an estate assumes personal liability to a creditor of the decedent for a debt or obligation incurred by the decedent before his death. That is, the executor promises the creditor that if the estate does not have the funds to pay the debt, he will pay it himself. The statute only applies to debts that the decedent incurred, not to new debts incurred by the estate itself. This provision is really just a specialized version of the suretyship provision discussed in section 11.2.4, because the executor undertakes to answer for the debt of the decedent.

§11.2.6 Contracts upon Consideration of Marriage

This category does not cover a promise of marriage, which can be and usually is oral. (It is sometimes performed by the ritual of one of the parties going down on one knee and proffering a glittery bauble to the other, but that formality is not required by law.) Rather, it relates to a contract in consideration of marriage in which the prospective spouses agree to a marriage settlement or to financial arrangements relating to the marriage. It also covers a promise by a third person (say, a parent of one of the spouses) to settle property or money upon the spouses in consideration of their marriage. The requirement that the contract is in consideration of marriage means that the statute applies only to prenuptial contracts motivated by the impending marriage.

---

§11.3 THE SECOND INQUIRY: IF THE STATUTE APPLIES, IS THE CONTRACT REFLECTED IN A WRITING THAT SATISFIES ITS REQUIREMENTS?

To satisfy the general statute, the written memorial of agreement must satisfy a number of requirements. The requirements of UCC §2.201 are similar, and any significant differences are noted below. The requirements are:

§11.3.1 A Written Memorandum

As mentioned in section 11.1, writing is traditionally thought of as the inscription of words on a tangible surface, such as paper. Because so much modern commerce is conducted by electronic communication, it would be absurd for the law to disregard the recording of contract terms in **electronic form**. By substituting the word "record" for "writing" throughout Article 2, the 2003 revision of Article 2 specifically recognizes that electronically recorded information is equivalent to writing for all purposes under Article 2, including the statute of frauds. "Record" is defined in revised §2-103(m) to mean "information that is inscribed on a tangible medium or that is stored in an electronic or other medium and retrievable in perceivable form."[4] In contracts other than sales of goods, a state may have enacted a statutory basis for recognizing electronic recording. Even if not, courts are receptive to treating electronic recordings as writings for statute of frauds purposes. Where the word "writing" is used in the rest of this chapter, it is meant to include electronic recording.

There is **no particular formality** needed for the writing as long as it contains the statute's minimum required content and signature. For example, you may recall that the land sale contract in Lucy v. Zehmer (the joke case discussed in connection with the objective test in section 4.1.3d) was written on the back of a restaurant guest check. The writing need not be executed with the deliberate purpose of evidencing the contract. It need not be the joint product of the parties or even delivered to the other party. It could be an internal memorandum or a document written for some other purpose than to satisfy the statute. It need not be written at the time of contracting. (Of course, the fact that it was not a purposeful contemporaneous attempt to record the agreement could affect its credibility, but this is a different issue.) Note, however, as discussed in section 11.3.3, a memorandum written and signed by just one of the parties only satisfies the statute to the extent that enforcement is sought against the party who signed it.

The written memorandum of the contract need not be in a single document, so it is possible to satisfy the statute by a **series of correspondence or other linked writings**. It must be clear from the face of the writings that they all refer to the same transaction and, taken together, they must contain all the content required by the statute, including a signature on at least one of them. Some courts require the signed document to refer to the others so that the signature can be attributed to the unsigned document without extrinsic evidence. Other courts are not as strict and require only that it is apparent from the writings that they refer to the same transaction. Oral testimony can then be used to prove that the signature was intended to authenticate the content of the unsigned writings. For example, in Crabtree v. Elizabeth Arden Sales Corp., 110 N.E.2d 551 (N.Y. 1953) the court found that a two-year employment contract satisfied the statute of frauds where the terms of employment were summarized in an unsigned note made by a secretary when the agreement was negotiated, and the employer's signature appeared on two payroll cards that clearly related to the same transaction but did not contain all the essential terms of the contract.

---

4. Just a reminder that no state has exacted revised Article 2 at the time that this edition of the book is being written.

Provided that the writing was made, the statute is satisfied even if it has been **lost by the time of litigation**. Its prior existence and its contents can be proved by oral testimony. This may sound like a strange rule, given that the principal purpose of the statute is to require a written record to prevent a false allegation of contract. It could be just as difficult to detect perjured evidence of a lost writing as it is to expose a bogus claim that a contract was made. Nevertheless, when there is convincing evidence that a writing did exist at one time, this is one further safety valve that prevents abuse of the statute by a party who seeks to escape a genuine contract.

§11.3.2 The Content of the Memorandum

Evidentiary adequacy for the purpose of satisfying the statute is set quite low. All that is needed is enough writing to sufficiently show the existence of a contract. Therefore, the writing does not have to contain every term of the contract, nor need it be completely clear and unambiguous in all respects. The common law and UCC have different standards for sufficiency of the memorandum, but, as usual, the looser UCC test tends to influence courts even in common law cases. Therefore, in some jurisdictions, the difference is fading.

At common law, it is generally required that the writing must at least *identify the parties* and *the nature of the exchange*, and it must set out all or at least most of the *material terms*. Provided that there is enough substance to show a contract, missing or unclear terms can be proved by oral evidence or otherwise resolved by the process of interpretation and construction discussed in Chapter 10.

UCC §2.201(1) provides for a less stringent standard. The only term that must be stated in the writing is the *quantity* of goods sold, so that the contract is not enforceable beyond the stated quantity. Beyond that, §2.201 demands only that "there is some writing sufficient to indicate that a contract for sale has been made between the parties." It expressly states that a writing is not insufficient merely because it omits any term other than quantity, or incorrectly states any term.[5]

Because the level of writing needed to satisfy the statute is quite minimal, it is important to recognize that a writing sufficient for the purposes of the statute may not be clear and full enough to ultimately convince the factfinder that a contract was made on the terms alleged. Compliance with the statute is a *different issue from adequate proof of the contract for the purpose of relief*. If the writing is skimpy or uncertain, the statute of frauds may be only the first hurdle to be jumped by the party seeking enforcement. Thereafter,

---

5. There is no difference between the current and revised versions of §2.201(2) in this respect.

327

the gaps or indefiniteness in the writing will have to be supplemented or cured by interpretation and persuasive extrinsic evidence.

§11.3.3 Signature

a. The Basic Rule of Signature

It is not necessary that the enforcing party signed the writing, because the evidentiary role of the statute is satisfied as long as the *party disputing the existence of the contract* has signed it in person or through an agent. A signature is any **mark or symbol** placed by the party on the paper with the **intention of authenticating it**, so a full and formal signature is not needed. Initials, a logo, or even an "x" is enough. The signature does not have to be placed on the paper after the terms are written down, so if a party's symbol (such as a logo at the top of the page) is already on the paper, that party can adopt the symbol by writing the terms of the contract on the page. Current UCC §1.201(39) codifies this principle by defining "signed" to include "any symbol executed or adopted by a party with present intention to authenticate a writing."[6] Restatement Second §134 is to the same effect.

When the writing consists of *several pieces of paper or other records* (such as a series of notes, letters, or e-mails), it is not necessary that every piece has been signed, provided that it appears from the writings themselves that they all refer to the same transaction. Some courts require that the signed writing actually makes some reference to unsigned ones, but other courts require only that the writings, on their face, relate to the same transaction.

b. Electronic Signatures

Where the writing is not in tangible form, but is recorded in an electronic or other medium, the concept of signature must be adapted to include other means of verifying authorship and adopting the recorded information. Both Congress and state legislatures have responded to this need by enacting statues that give effect to electronic signatures. The federal statute, the Electronic Signatures in Global and National Commerce Act, 15 USC §§7001 to 7031 (called "E-Sign") applies to any transaction involving interstate or foreign commerce. States have enacted equivalent statutes, either by drafting their own statutes or by adopting a uniform statute, the Uniform Electronic Transaction Act ("UETA"). The principal focus of the federal and state statutes is to give legal effect to electronic signatures, and they declare that a signature or other record relating to a transaction may not be denied legal effect solely because it is in electronic form (15 USC §7001(a);

---

6. "Signed" is defined in revised Article 1, §1.201(37) in similar terms to include using "any symbol executed or adopted with present intention to adopt or a accept a writing."

UETA §7). This language indicates the limited scope of the statutes. They provide that to the extent that the law requires a signature, it may not deny effect to a signature in electronic form. The statutes do not purport to deal with the question of whether the signature could be denied effect for some other reason.

"Electronic signature" is defined as "an electronic sound, symbol, or process, attached to or logically associated with a contract or other record and executed or adopted by a person with the intent to sign the record" (15 USC §7006(5); The definition in UETA §2(8) is almost identical). The important point to note about this definition is that it allows a distinction to be made between an identifying symbol that is automatically generated by a computer (such as the "from" line on an e-mail or the sender's identification printed at the top of a fax message) and a deliberate placing of a signature on the communication.

While the sender's **deliberate typing of his name** on the e-mail is quite clearly a signature, his automatically generated name (such as in the message header) is less obviously so. However, an **automatically generated name** can qualify as his signature if he **adopts** it with intent to sign the record. If the name and message are genuine, this adoption should usually occur as a matter of course, even if the sender has no specific subjective awareness that he is "signing" the communication. For example, in *International Casings Group, Inc. v. Premium Standard Farms, Inc.*, 358 F.Supp. 863 (W.D. Mo. 2005) the court, applying UETA, found that the statute of frauds was satisfied by e-mail correspondence. The sender of the e-mails did not challenge their authenticity, and there was no question that they were forged. The court held that the sender's name in the e-mail header was its signature. The court held that when the sender hit the "send" button, it intended to adopt the name in the header to authenticate the e-mail. Although the automatic generation of a name may be more commonplace in electronic communications than it is in writing on paper, this concept is not new. Recall that the definition of signature on paper also contemplates that signature can come about if, by writing the terms of the contract on a piece of paper with his preprinted name or identifying symbol, the writer apparently intended to adopt it to authenticate the record.

With electronic signatures, as with handwritten or printed signatures on paper, a party may deny that the symbol is his signature. He may challenge the **genuineness of his signature**, claiming that it was forged or placed on the record by someone else without authority, or he may assert that his name or symbol on the record was not placed there with the reasonable intent to adopt or accept it. (As mentioned above, this is a particular problem where a name is automatically generated by a computer program.) In the field of electronic communications, problems of forgery and automated identification require special considerations and technological solutions. However, it is important to remember that the evidentiary issue of proving

329

the signature exists with tangible documents as well as electronic records, and to recognize that this involves a problem of proof rather than the legal question or recognizing the validity of an electronic signature. In *International Casings* the court, in accepting an e-mail header as a signature, recognized the possibility that an e-mail message can be fraudulently generated in the name of a person who did not send it. However, the court noted that forgery is not confined to electronic communications, and this possibility should not make an e-mail header insufficient as a matter of law where the alleged sender does not successfully impugn its genuineness.

c. The Exception to the Signature Rule Where Both Parties are Merchants

Section 2.201(2)[7] recognizes one situation in which a writing can be enforced against the party who did not sign it. All the following requirements must be met: Both parties are **merchants**; within a **reasonable time** of the oral contract, one of the parties sends a written confirmation to the other, which is **signed by the sender** and otherwise **satisfies the statute as against the sender**; the recipient has **reason to know** its contents; and the recipient does not give written notice of **objection** to it within ten days of receipt.

In other words, although the contract could normally be enforced only against the sender, as signatory, when both parties are merchants, the non-signing recipient is also bound by the conduct of failing to protest after receiving a writing that should have been read. *Bazak International Corp. v. Tarrant Apparel Group*, 378 F. Supp.2d 377 (S.D.N.Y. 2005) illustrates the operation of the merchant rule where the party seeking enforcement of the contract sends the confirmation by e-mail. The parties made an oral contract for the sale of a large number of pairs of jeans. When the seller failed to deliver the jeans, the buyer sued. The seller moved for summary judgment on the grounds that the oral contract did not comply with §2.201. The buyer successfully invoked the merchant exception in §2.201(2). The buyer had sent an e-mail to the seller setting out the terms of the sale and containing the buyer's typed name. The parties were clearly merchants, and the buyer's e-mail was sent within a reasonable time. The e-mail was a written confirmation containing the essential terms of the contract, signed by and sufficient against the sender. The focus of the opinion was whether §2.201(2) could be satisfied by an e-mail. The court (applying the current version of Article 2 which does not expressly recognize electronic recording as writing) found that it could be. Although an e-mail is an intangible form of communication, it is stored on the computer, is objectively observable, and can be rendered tangible. The court also found that the (pre-revision) UCC

---

7. This provision is the same in current and revised §2.201(2).

definition of "signed" is broad enough to include the typed
e-mail. Finally, the court found that the buyer had shown su
purpose of overcoming the seller's application for summar
the seller had received and had reason to know of the conte
and had not objected to it.

---

§11.4 THE THIRD INQUIRY: IF THE STATUTE APPLIES AND IS NOT COMPLIED WITH, DOES THE ORAL CONTRACT FALL WITHIN ANY OF ITS EXCEPTIONS?

When a contract falls within the statute and fails to comply with it, the
contract is unenforceable as discussed in section 11.5. However, there are
a few exceptions that permit enforcement despite the lack of a sufficient
signed writing. The exceptions are justified on one or both of two broad
grounds. The one (which is a predominant basis for the first exception and
the sole basis for the second) is that circumstances following contract formation provide evidence that a contract was indeed made, so that it is
unduly technical to insist on compliance with the statute. The other
(which strongly motivates the third exception, but may play some role in
the first one as well). is the protection of the interests of a party who suffered
a detriment in justifiable reliance on the oral contract.

§11.4.1 The Part Performance Exception

Following an oral contract, the parties may begin performance, which may
provide *reliable evidence that a contract was made*. Even if the statute applies to the
transaction, the performance satisfies its function, so that refusal of enforcement would be too rigid and would allow a party to renege on an established
contract through a technical application of the statute. Despite the logic of
this reasoning, courts do not wholeheartedly embrace this exception in
common law cases. It is not applied to all contracts subject to the statute.
For example, in *Coca Cola Co. v. Bayback's International, Inc.*, 841 N.E.2d 557 (Ind.
2006) the court, stating that this reflected the majority approach, refused to
apply the exception to a contract that could not be performed within a year
of its making.

Even when it is used, courts usually require a very clear showing that the
conduct does in fact refer to and demonstrate the existence of a contract. In
addition, they often require some degree of prejudice to have been suffered in
reliance on the agreement by the party seeking enforcement, and impose other

limitations that are too detailed to discuss here. Because the part performance doctrine is equitable in derivation, some courts apply it only where the plaintiff seeks the equitable remedy of specific performance, and not where the claim is for the legal remedy of damages. Some courts recognize an exception only if the party seeking enforcement has fully performed. The broad point is that at common law, part performance may allow enforcement of a contract that does not satisfy the statute, but you should not assume that this principle will be readily applied without qualification.

Two subsections of §2.201 give limited recognition to the part performance exception when the contract is for the sale of goods.[8] The two exceptions are narrow and apply only in specific circumstances. The first, in §2.201(3)(a), covers cases in which the seller has begun the manufacture of **goods that are specially made for the buyer** and not otherwise easily saleable. The second, in §2.201(3)(c), allows enforcement of the contract **only to the extent payment** for the goods has been **made and accepted**, or **goods** have been **delivered and accepted**. This means that if one party has performed and the other has accepted that performance, the party who performed can enforce the contract to recover the consideration due for the performance rendered. If only part performance has been made (that is, only part of the goods have been received, or only part of the price has been paid), the contract is only enforceable with respect to what has been done, but cannot be enforced with regard to the balance.

§11.4.2 The Judicial Admission Exception

As the statute is intended to guard against a fraudulent assertion of contract, it would seem logical that a party who admits the contract in pleadings or testimony should not be allowed to raise the statute as a defense. Nevertheless, the *common law* has been loath to embrace such a rule because of a *concern of its impact on litigation.* First, it has been perceived as creating an incentive for perjury because a party may choose to deny the contract to avoid losing the defense by an admission in litigation. Second, because a party can be compelled to disclose information in litigation, the admission may not be truly voluntary. These arguments have been criticized as inadequate to overcome the obvious relevance of admissions in litigation. The UCC has not followed them, and it does recognize an exception for judicial admissions under certain conditions. Under the UCC's influence, the exception is gaining wider recognition in common law too.

The exception is specific and narrow. Section 2.201(3)(b) permits enforcement of a contract against a party, despite non-compliance with the statute if that party **admits in "pleading, testimony or otherwise in**

---

8. These subsections are the same in current and revised Article 2.

court" that a contract was made.[9] The contract is enforceable only to the extent of the quantity of goods admitted. Note that the admission must be made in connection with litigation, and the exception does not extend to admissions in other circumstances. (Of course, a written admission outside of litigation may itself be a memorandum satisfying the statute, but an oral admission in those circumstances has no effect.)

One of the more difficult issues that has arisen in connection with this exception is what constitutes an admission. Clearly, if the party breaks down under cross-examination and concedes the contract, an admission has been made. However, it could also be taken as an admission if a party's pleadings raise a defense on the merits (such as claiming that the other party breached by failure to deliver), rather than clearly denying the existence of a contract. There are also a number of procedural complexities, not addressed here, raised by the question of whether a party can be compelled to admit or deny the contract.

§11.4.3 The Protection of Reliance: Estoppel and Promissory Estoppel

Under some circumstances, **equitable estoppel** may be used to protect reliance on a **false factual assertion**. For example, if one of the parties represents to the other that she has made a signed written note of the contract, and the other reasonably relies on this assertion. However, as equitable estoppel is traditionally confined to an assertion of fact, it is generally only helpful in a narrow range of situations.[10] **Promissory estoppel** is more useful when there is no factual representation inducing reliance, but one of the parties justifiably relies on the oral contract as a promise, thereby suffering some detriment.[11]

Restatement Second §139, a modified version of §90, recognizes promissory estoppel in this context. The elements of promissory estoppel in this situation are similar to those in §90: **A promise reasonably expected to induce reliance**, the inducement of **justifiable reliance** on the promise by the other party, and the need to enforce the promise to **prevent injustice**.[12] Section 139, by its express language, appears to be stricter than §90 because

---

9. The 2003 revision of §2.201(3)(b) substitutes the words "under oath" for "in court."
10. The elements and purpose of equitable estoppel are explained in section 8.4.
11. Promissory estoppel is discussed fully in Chapter 8, and section 8.5 discusses the use of the doctrine in the negotiating setting.
12. In *Tucker v. Roman Catholic Diocese of Lafayette-In-Indiana*, discussed in relation to the one-year rule in section 11.2.2, the plaintiff also asserted the promissory estoppel exception to the statute of frauds. The court of appeals upheld the trial court's dismissal of the claim on this ground as well. Because the statute of limitations had run on the plaintiff's claim, she suffered no detriment in forbearing from suit and there was no need to enforce the promise to prevent injustice.

it specifically stresses the need for reliance of a substantial character, reasonableness by the promisee, and foreseeability of the reliance by the promisor. Despite the articulation of these requirements, §139 is not really that different from §90 in this respect, because, as the discussion in Chapter 8 shows, these elements are implicit in §90 as well.

However, §139 does have one additional element that is unique because it relates to the evidentiary purpose of the statute. One of the factors that the court should take into account in deciding to grant promissory estoppel relief is whether the promisee's conduct in reliance or other available evidence corroborates the existence of a contract. This suggests that even where part performance does not on its own create an exception to the statute, it could be a relevant factor in deciding on whether to grant promissory estoppel relief.

Section 139 does not advocate a routine application of promissory estoppel to circumvent the statute. In most cases, a party is simply not justified in relying on an oral contract which he should reasonably have known must be in writing. Even if the reliance was justified, the detriment that he suffered in reliance may not be substantial enough to merit enforcement of the contract. The remedy of restitution can be used to restore any benefit of performance rendered under the unenforceable contract, so full enforcement of the contract usually exceeds what is needed to avert any injustice resulting from reliance on the oral contract. Some cases suggest that it may be almost impossible for a party to use promissory estoppel as the basis for enforcing an oral contract. For example, in the *Coca Cola* case cited in section 11.4.1 the court followed a line of cases that declined to apply promissory estoppel to enforce the oral contract itself, and confined relief to substantial independent detriment. It is not clear from the opinion what that independent detriment might be, because the court found that the plaintiff was seeking to enforce the very bargain that was rendered unenforceable by the statute and refused relief. Similarly in *Brown v. Branch*, 758 N.E.2d 48 (Ind. 2001) the court refused to apply promissory estoppel to enforce an oral contract to convey land. The court said it was not enough for the plaintiff to show that breach of the oral promise resulted in a denial of her rights under the contract. She must show a substantial and independent injury for which justice demands relief. As in the *Coca Cola* case, because the plaintiff's claim was for enforcement of the benefit of the bargain, the court did not have occasion to explain what this other independent reliance might be.

It is not clear if promissory estoppel can be used to enforce a **contract for the sale of goods** that fails to comply with §2.201. As a doctrine of common law, promissory estoppel could supplement the provisions of §2.201 by virtue of §1.103 (numbered §1.103(b) in revised Article 1) which recognizes general principles of common law unless they are displaced by the Code's particular provisions. There is no provision in §2.201 that specifically excludes promissory estoppel as a basis for excepting the sale from the statute. However, some courts have reasoned that an intent to exclude promissory estoppel can be inferred from the first words of §2.201, "[e]xcept as otherwise provided in this section," followed by the listing of a defined set of specific exceptions in §2.201(3). The 2003 revision of §2.201 eliminates the section's initial words "[e]xcept as otherwise provided in this section." According to Official Comment 2 to revised §2.201 the purpose of this is to make it clear that promissory estoppel is available as a possible means of excepting the sale from the statute.

§11.5 THE IMPACT OF NON-COMPLIANCE WITH THE STATUTE

There is some variation in the statutes of different states and some confusion in the caselaw about the effect of failure to satisfy the statute. The noncompliant contract is sometimes said to be **invalid** or **void** — that is, a legal nullity, of no force or effect. Sometimes it is called **unenforceable** — that is, a contract that is valid, but cannot be sued on and enforced in court. Some cases use these words interchangeably. It is more generally accepted that noncompliance with the statute does not void the contract, but merely makes it unenforceable. Although there are instances in which consequences follow from characterizing a contract as void rather than unenforceable, the distinction is not practically significant for our purposes. In either case, the plaintiff is unable to sue on the contract.

If the contract is unenforceable for non-compliance with the statute, the party seeking to rely on the statute as a defense cannot raise it by a general denial. It must be specifically pleaded as an **affirmative defense**, otherwise it is waived. If the defense is raised and succeeds, the contract cannot be enforced. If neither party has given or done anything under the contract, the practical effect of non-enforcement for most purposes is to put an end to any obligations that the parties might otherwise have had under the contract. However, sometimes a party may have rendered some performance before the contract was declared unenforceable. (Obviously, this partial performance could not have been sufficient to except the contract from the statute as discussed above.) Once the contract is unenforceable, the party who received the performance no longer has a right to keep it. It must therefore be returned under principles of **restitution**. If it was a money payment or the delivery of property still in the hands of the beneficiary, the money or the property itself must be restored. If it was services or property that has been consumed, restitution is usually measured based on its market value, but the court has the discretion to value it differently if fairness so dictates.[13]

---

13. The measurement of restitutionary benefits is discussed more fully in section 9.6.

§11.6 THE EFFECT OF THE STATUTE OF FRAUDS ON MODIFICATIONS OF A CONTRACT

Obviously, neither party can unilaterally change the terms of a contract after it has been made, but a contract can always be modified by agreement between the parties. A modification is a contract in itself, distinct from the original contract that it changes. As a separate contract, it is subject to most of the usual requirements of contract law for formation and validity.[14] As a general rule (unless the statute of a particular state provides otherwise), this means that *the statute of frauds applies to modifications*. Therefore, whether or not the original contract was subject to the statute, if the contract as modified falls within the statute, the modification must be recorded in a writing sufficient to satisfy it.[15] For example, under an original contract, entered into on July 1, 2005, a customer booked a room at a resort for the July 4 weekend in 2006. As the contract cannot be performed in a year, it is subject to the statute. Two weeks after making the contract, the customer called the resort and the parties agreed to change the booking to the Christmas holiday in 2005. The statute no longer applies to the modified contract. The opposite would occur if the original booking was for Christmas 2005, and was changed to Thanksgiving 2006, a date more than a year after the modification. The statute did not apply to the original contract, but it does apply to the modification.

Examples

1. On May 15, Viva Voce, the president of Ritten Records, Inc., interviewed Juan Annum for the position of sales manager. The parties reached agreement on a one-year period of employment, beginning on June 1 at an annual salary of $75,000. At the end of the interview, Viva tore a piece of paper from a blank pad and wrote "Call pers. dept. to enroll Juan Annum as a sales mgr. — 1-yr contract starting 6/1. Pay $75,000 p.a." She told Juan that the purpose of the note was to remind her to call the personnel department so that they would put him on the payroll from June.

---

14. This principle is reflected in the common law rule that a modification needs consideration to be binding. However, that rule has changed under the UCC and is probably in decline at common law too. *See* sections 7.5 and 13.9.

15. Even if the modification would not otherwise be subject to the statute, the contract may provide that all modifications must be in writing and signed. Such a provision can be effective as a kind of contractually created statute of frauds which prevents the enforcement of an oral modification. However, courts sometimes uphold oral modifications notwithstanding the provision. This is discussed in section 12.12.

After the meeting, Juan resigned from his current employment by giving the required two weeks' notice. On May 17, he received a memo in the mail from the personnel department of Ritten Records, Inc. It was written on the company's letterhead and said simply, "We understand that you will be joining us on June 1. Please come in as soon as convenient to fill out the necessary tax forms."

On May 23, before he had a chance to go to the personnel office, Juan received a letter in the mail from Viva on the company's letterhead. It read:

> Dear Juan,
>
> I was happy to be able to extend an offer of employment to you last week. I regret, however, that since then we have reevaluated our earnings for the last quarter and find them disappointing. We have therefore decided not to hire any new employees at this time. I am sorry that we cannot use your services. I am sure that a person of your talents will have no difficulty in finding a suitable position elsewhere.
>
> Sincerely,
>
> Viva Voce
>
> President

Can Ritten Records, Inc. get away with this?

2. Change the facts of Example 1 as follows: Viva did not send the letter of May 23 and Ritten Records still wished to employ Juan. However, on May 23 Juan received a better job offer and is no longer interested in working for Ritten Records. Apart from this, all the facts are the same as in Example 1. Can the company enforce the contract against him?

3. Clay Potter owns a pottery in which he manufactures ceramic ovenware and crockery. Terry Cotta sells such items in his retail store. On June 1, Terry called Clay and spoke to his assistant who accepted his order of 1,000 ceramic mugs of various designs at $5.10 each, for immediate delivery. Later that day, Terry mailed the following printed form to Clay, with the blanks filled out by hand (the handwriting is denoted here by italics):

TERRY'S HOUSEWARES. Terry Cotta, Proprietor.
PURCHASE ORDER
Date *June* 1, 2006
To: *Clay Potter.*
Please ship the following goods immediately: 1,000 *assorted mugs as discussed by phone at* $5.10 *each*

On June 6, Terry received the following letter from Clay:

Dear Mr. Cotta,

I have received your order of June 1. I am sorry that I am out of mugs at present and cannot supply them right now. I am in the process of making a new batch and should have them in stock next month. Due to increased costs, I am going to have to raise the price to $5.50 each. If you would like me to hold your order until that time let me know. Also, tell me which designs you want. Your order refers to an assortment as discussed by phone, but no one here remembers talking to you and we have no record of your call.

Yours truly,

Clay Potter

Terry claims that he already has a contract for immediate delivery at the old price. Can he enforce it against Clay?

4(a). Fresco Fantastico is a famous, top-selling artist. Ore Alloys, Inc. (ORAL) was in the final stages of completing the construction of a new headquarters building. On March 1, 2006, it entered into an oral contract with Fresco under which it commissioned him to paint a mural of its ore smelter on the wall of the building's lobby. The parties agreed that Fresco would begin the mural on May 1 (the date on which the lobby would be ready for decorative work) and would complete it by not later than June 1, 2007. ORAL would pay Fresco $100,000 on completion of the mural. On March 25, 2006, before Fresco had done any work or preparation under the contract, the president of ORAL called and told him that the corporation had changed its mind and no longer desired the mural. Does the statute of frauds preclude Fresco from enforcing his contract with ORAL?

4(b). Change the facts of Example 4(a) as follows: The oral contract between Fresco and ORAL on March 1, 2006 was not for a mural, but for a painting of the ore smelter on canvas for $100,000. Fresco would complete the painting in his studio and deliver it to ORAL by not later than June 1, 2007. On March 15, 2006, Fresco had a large canvas made to fit the space in the lobby and he began to rough in the outlines of the painting. On March 25, the president of ORAL called and told him that the corporation had changed its mind and no longer desired the painting. Does the statute of frauds preclude Fresco from enforcing his contract with ORAL?

5. Annette X. Plorer visited the Web site of Big Browser Megastore.com and selected a Rolex watch for $10,000. She ordered it by clicking on various links; keying in her name, address, and credit card particulars;

and finally clicking a "confirm order" button to confirm her order. After she did this, a message appeared on her screen thanking her for her order and stating that the goods would be shipped in 10 to 20 days. Assuming that a contract was formed through this process, does it satisfy the statute of frauds?

Explanations

1. Although the letter of May 23 suggests that the company is revoking an unaccepted offer, it is clear that an oral contract was made between Juan and the company, represented by its president, on May 15.

    The first question to answer is **whether** the contract is **subject to the statute of frauds**. The only applicable provision of the statute is that covering contracts not to be performed within a year. Although the performance itself will take exactly one year, it is not the length of actual performance that is crucial, but the time between making the contract and the end of performance. This period is approximately two weeks longer than a year. When there is some flexibility in the length of performance, the contract is not treated as falling within the statute if performance could conceivably be completed within the year, but this is not the case here because this is a fixed-term contract. Could it be argued that the performance could end before a year because the employee might die before that time? Although a court is more likely to accept this reasoning when the contract contemplates termination by death (for example, a lifetime employment term), it may be more hesitant to do so if death would merely be a discharge of the duty to perform. However, given the resistance to the one-year rule, it is possible that a court would be willing to entertain an argument that the mere possibility of death makes the contract performable within a year. Of course, such an interpretation would go a long way towards gutting the rule.

    If the contract is subject to the statute, the next question is whether there is a **writing to satisfy it**. To comply with the statute, there must, at a minimum, be a written record, signed by the party against whom enforcement is sought, identifying the parties, setting out the nature of the exchange, and containing most, if not all, of the material terms. The writing need not be contained in a single document, but can be made up of a set of linked documents. Three documents are referred to in the question: Viva's note to herself, the memo from the personnel department, and the letter from Viva. None of these documents on its own is sufficient to satisfy the statute:

    Viva's note to herself probably has enough content to show that a contract was made for a year's employment, and it seems to contain the central terms that were agreed. However, it lacks two elements needed to satisfy the statute: It identifies Juan, but not Ritten Records. Worse still, the absence of any identification of Ritten Records means that even on a liberal definition of signature, there is no symbol placed on the paper to authenticate the document on its behalf. Had Viva written its name on the note, or had the notepad had a company logo on it, an argument for signature could have been made, but nothing like this exists.

Therefore, the absence of Ritten Records' signature prevents the note from being an adequate memorial of agreement. Had the note been signed, it would not have mattered that the note was intended as an internal document. The writing need not be addressed or given to the other party. The facts do not state if the note is still in existence, so it is possible that Viva may have crumpled it up and thrown it away after calling the personnel department. However, this would not necessarily be fatal to Juan's case because as long as he can prove the existence and contents of the note at an earlier time, it need not still be extant at the time of suit. (Of course, if Viva denies writing the note or disputes what it said, Juan's success in his suit will be heavily dependent on his credibility. This is not a happy situation for a plaintiff, who could easily fail to discharge his burden of proof.)

The memo from the personnel department was written on company stationery and exhibits its logo. Although we normally think of a signature as a symbol made on the document at the time of writing, a pre-existing printed name or logo should qualify as a signature because the party adopts it when using the preprinted stationery. Therefore the logo probably qualifies as a signature. The memo also identifies Juan and suggests the existence of a contract. However, the memo does not set out the terms of the contract. Although some degree of omission is tolerated, an indication of the central terms is usually required. In particular, there is no way to tell that this was not a contract for employment at will because of the lack of reference to the period of employment.

Viva's letter of May 23 is signed, but it is of little help to Juan because it does not in any way evidence a contract. In fact, it is written to suggest just the opposite because it is phrased like the revocation of an unaccepted offer.

Although no single document sufficiently complies with the statute, taken together two of the three writings may contain all the content needed to satisfy it. As discussed in section 11.3.1, a set of writings in combination can satisfy the statute if, on their face, they refer to the same transaction and together they include all the required content. (Some courts insist that the signed document actually refers to the unsigned ones, but other courts find that test too rigorous and require only that it is apparent from the writings that they refer to the same transaction.) If Viva's note exists or can be convincingly shown to have existed, and the logo on the personnel department's memo is accepted as a signature, these two writings should be viewed in combination because they both refer to the same transaction. (Although Viva's letter of May 23 has a stronger form of signature, it does not help Juan. Its implicit denial of a contract disqualifies it as referring to the transaction in a probative way.)

If the statute applies and Juan does not succeed in establishing compliance with it, he cannot enforce the contract unless he can fit it into one of the recognized **exceptions** to the statute. The only exception that might apply is promissory estoppel, based on the argument that Ritten Record made a promise in the oral contract, reasonably expecting to induce Juan's reliance, he did justifiably rely on the promise and suffered a substantial detriment in resigning from his existing job.[16] The problem with this argument is that Juan is responsible for knowing the law, and there is no apparent justification for his reliance on an oral contract. If ignorance of the need for a writing is enough to invoke promissory estoppel, the statute would be routinely circumvented.

2.   Although Juan may be able to enforce the contract against Ritten Records either on the basis of the combined writings or under promissory estoppel, the company has no corresponding right. When the writing has been signed by just one of the parties, the statute makes the contract enforceable against that party only. If the rule were otherwise, the statute would have little purpose because it would be too easy for one of the parties to write and sign a bogus document and to claim a contract binding on the other. (The UCC has a limited exception to this rule, discussed in section 11.3.4 and the next Example.) Juan has not signed anything, and Ritten Records has taken no action in reliance on his oral promise. It cannot enforce the contract.

This means, of course, that Juan might be able to enforce a contract against Ritten, but Ritten has no basis to enforce a contract against him.[17]

---

16. You may recall that section 8.9.3 discussed the problem of showing justifiable detrimental reliance on a promise of at-will employment. That issue does not arise here because the contract was for a one-year term. The issue here must be distinguished — it is whether promissory estoppel can be used as a means of enforcing an oral contract that is subject to the statute.

17. Recall that this result does not give rise to a problem of "mutuality of obligation." As discussed in section 7.9.1, provided that both promises are genuine and not illusory, there is no general rule of "mutuality" that prevents one party from being bound because the other has no right of enforcement.

3. Although the price of each item of goods is only $5.10, they are sold together in a single contract, so the price of the sale is their total price of $5,100. The contract is therefore subject to the statute of frauds in UCC §2.201.[18] Terry's order form does not satisfy §2.201(1) as against Clay because it must be signed by the party against whom enforcement is sought. Clay's letter does have his signature ("signed" is defined in §1.201(39)[19] as "any symbol executed or adopted by a party with present intention to authenticate a writing"), but it fails to satisfy §2.201(1) because it does not indicate that a contract has been made. In fact, phrased as a counteroffer, it suggests just the opposite.

    We saw in Example 2 that under the general statute, a writing sufficient to satisfy the statute against one party does not bind the other in the absence of the other's signature. The same rule applies in many cases under the UCC, but §2.201(2) provides an exception to it. If one of the parties sends a confirmation of the oral contract to the other, the statute is satisfied as against the recipient if all the following conditions are satisfied: both parties are merchants; the writing is sufficient under §2.201(1) to satisfy the statute as against the sender; it was sent within a reasonable time; it was received by the other party who has reason to know its contents; and the recipient does not give written notice of objection to it within ten days of receipt.

    Both parties are merchants under §2.104(1) because they both deal in goods of that kind. For the writing to be sufficient against Terry, the sender, it must indicate that a contract of sale has been made between the parties and must be signed by Terry. Beyond this, it need not accurately or fully state all the terms agreed, but it is not enforceable beyond the quantity stated. The order form does set out the essential terms of the contract, including the quantity of the goods. Terry's printed name at the top should qualify as his signature because it was adopted by him to authenticate the form when he filled out the blanks. The only problem is that the form is described as an order, which suggests not a contract, but an offer. It would have been clearer if the form had been headed "order confirmation." Nevertheless, this difficulty can be overcome by the reference to the telephone call that, on a reasonable interpretation, suggests a prior oral order accepted by or on behalf of Clay. This was the approach taken by the court in *Harry Rubin & Sons v. Consolidated Pipe Co.*, 153 A.2d 472 (Pa. 1959) to a form similarly headed "order" that referred to a prior telephone call.

---

18. It would be subject to the statute under both the $500 figure used in current §2.201 and the amount $5,000 used in the revision.
19. Section 1.201(37) in revised Article 1.

The form was sent on the same day as the telephone call, surely within a reasonable time, and Clay's response shows that it was received and its contents read. All is well for Terry so far, but Clay's letter could constitute a written notice of objection. To be an effective objection to the contents of the writing, the response must challenge the existence of a contract. Although the letter from Clay does not say in so many words that it denies Terry's claim of a contract, its import is clearly to that effect. It treats the order as an offer and claims no knowledge of the telephone call. It is in writing and is given within ten days of receipt of Terry's form.

4(a). The contract to paint the mural on the lobby wall is a hybrid transaction involving the supply of goods (paint) and services (applying the paint). As discussed in section 2.7.2, where a contract contains both a sale of goods and the performance of services, most courts apply a predominant purpose test to decide if the contract is subject to UCC Article 2. If the sale of goods is the more significant aspect of the transaction, Article 2 applies, but if services predominate, it does not. There can be no doubt that the parties did not intend to contract for the supply of paint, but for the skills that Fresco would employ in painting the mural. Undoubtedly, Fresco's labor predominates over the materials, both in value and scope. Because the service element is predominant, Article 2 does not apply and the contract is not subject to the statute of frauds in §2.201.

The only category of the common law statute that could apply to this contract is the one-year rule. Fresco was given 15 months from the date of the contract to complete the painting. However, there is no contractual bar to his finishing it earlier. It does not matter that the scope of the work is so large that he may not be able to get it done within a year of the contract. As shown by C.R. *Klewin, Inc. v. Flagship Properties, Inc.*, discussed in section 11.2.2, courts generally interpret the one-year rule restrictively, and do not find it applicable to a contract unless by its terms, it clearly requires the performance to continue for more than a year. The statute of frauds does not preclude Fresco from enforcing his contract with ORAL.

4(b). While it may seem that Fresco has contracted to perform a service by painting the picture, all his work goes into the creation of a tangible, movable end product. Where the delivery of the end product of labor is the subject matter of the contract, it is a sale of goods, whether or not the seller manufactured them. Fresco's contract in this Example is therefore quite different from the contract to paint a mural in Example 4(a) and is also distinguishable from that of his colleague, Salvador Dali, whose undertaking to paint a picture on a TV show was characterized as a contract for services. (*See* section 11.2.3.)

The sale price of the painting is $100,000 so the contract is subject to the statute under both current and revised §2.201. There is no writing at all, so the statute is not satisfied unless one of the exceptions in §2.201(3) applies. The only exception that has any possible relevance is the version of the part performance exception set out in §2.201(3)(a). To invoke this exception, Fresco must show that the goods are to be specially manufactured for the buyer; they are not suitable for sale to others in the ordinary course of the seller's business; before receiving notice of the buyer's repudiation, the seller made a substantial beginning on their manufacture or commitments for their procurement; and the circumstances reasonably indicate that the goods are for the buyer.

Very clearly, the exception has its basis in the principle, recognized to some extent at common law too, that the statute should not be applied to defeat relief to a party when post-formation conduct both indicates detrimental reliance on the oral contract and provides evidence of the contract's existence. By commencing performance or procurement of goods that are specific to the buyer's needs and not readily resalable, the seller incurs prejudice and her actions demonstrate the existence of a contract.

In Fresco's case, the painting is especially commissioned by and reflects a theme of particular interest to the buyer which strongly indicates that the painting is for the buyer. Fresco may be able to sell the painting to someone else in the ordinary course of business. His work is sought after, and many people might find beauty in a smelter.

Fresco bought the canvas and began the painting before the repudiation. Is this a substantial enough beginning? This requirement, combined with that of difficulty of resale, is intended to confine the exception to cases in which non-enforcement would cause hardship to the seller. It is difficult to draw a definite line at which the commitment of time and materials passes from insubstantial to substantial, but Fresco could make a respectable argument that the purchase of the canvas, a major component of the materials to be used, the time spent in conceiving the painting, and the preliminary blocking work is enough to be substantial. However, as the canvas has not been consumed and could be used for another painting, this is not an overwhelming argument.

In short, the performance seems to serve the evidentiary function well, but is less compelling on the question of detriment. Fresco has a chance of success, but this is not an easy case to predict.

5.   This is a sale of goods for a price of $10,000 so it falls within both the current and revised versions of UCC §2.201 and there must be a written memorandum of agreement, signed by the party against

whom enforcement is sought, sufficient to show that a contract has been formed.

Under the 2003 revision of Article 2, there would be no doubt that the electronic records generated in the computers of both parties would satisfy the requirement of §2.201 that there be a record sufficient to indicate a contract of sale. Annette's order, with particulars of the parties, the goods, the price, and the quantity term, accepted by Big Browser with the delivery information, surely evidences the existence of a contract. Under the current version of §2.201, we cannot as readily reach this answer because a court would have to interpret the word "writing" to include electronic records. It is likely that a court would readily do so. If the court has any hesitation on the question, recall that the language of E-Sign, 15 USC §7001(a)(1) speaks not only of signatures, but also of contracts, and provides that "a . . . contract . . . may not be denied legal effect, validity, or enforceability solely because it is in electronic form. As this Internet transaction more than likely involves interstate commerce, the court cannot refuse to enforce the contract merely because it is not in hard copy. (Of course, if either party printed out the order, the court would not even have to bother about applying E-Sign or interpreting §2.201 because a traditional written record would exist.)

The question of the effectiveness of the parties' signatures is settled by E-Sign and UETA, which both require the court to give effect to the electronic signatures of the parties, provided that such electronic signatures exist and they are genuine and otherwise in conformity with the law. The facts present no question of forgery or unauthorized use of equipment, so the sole issue is whether the parties did execute or adopt a symbol associated with the contract. The facts indicate that Annette deliberately entered her name in the appropriate space on the electronic order form. Undoubtedly this qualifies as her signature.

Although the facts do not specify, Big Browser's name or symbol surely appears in its response. If an employee handled the response and typed Big Browser's name or symbol, this qualifies as its signature. Even if the employee did not actually type the name or symbol, the employee's act of sending the message under an automatically generated name or symbol likely constitutes the adoption of that name or symbol with the intent to authenticate the record. Big Browser's response may not have been made by a human at all, but could have been automatically generated by a computer program used by Big Browser. This should not make a difference to the conclusion that its name or symbol should qualify as a signature. Section 6.1 mentioned that the 2003 revision of Article 2 recognizes the possibility that a party can contract through an "electronic agent" — a computer program that is set up to initiate action or respond automatically to a communication. UETA likewise recognizes this possibility in §14, and comment 1 to §14 points out that intention to enter into a transaction can be attributed to a party who sets up a machine to act as his agent. Therefore, attribution of signature to a party should be possible where the automatic signature is by a machine programmed to be an electronic agent, both under the current and he revised definitions of signature.

CHAPTER 12

The Parol Evidence Rule

§12.1 THE APPLICATION AND BASIC PURPOSE OF THE PAROL EVIDENCE RULE

§12.1.1 A Written or Recorded Agreement

The parol evidence rule applies where an agreement is recorded in writing and one of the parties proffers evidence to prove a term that is not contained in the writing or to explain or expand on a term in the writing. As noted several times before, particularly in Chapter 11, contemporary law must include in the concept of writing not just words written on paper, but also forms of recording by electronic or other means. The 2003 revision of Article 2 expresses this in statutory form by substituting the word "recording" for "writing" throughout Article 2. A "record" is defined in revised §2.103(m) to include not only information inscribed in a tangible medium, but also information stored electronically or otherwise retrievable in perceivable form. No state has enacted revised Article 2 at the time of this writing, and even when enacted, it will not apply to contracts other than sales of goods. Nevertheless, the trend of the law is clear, and we should expect that, even in the absence of statutory authority, courts will readily recognize that the rules of common law have to be adapted to take account of electronic records. Therefore, although I use the word "writing" in discussing the parol evidence rule, I assume that this covers not only recording in tangible form, but also in electronic form.

§12.1.2 The Relationship Between the Parol Evidence Rule and Interpretation

The parol evidence rule is closely intertwined with the process of interpretation. As you read this chapter, you will see many links to the discussion of interpretation in Chapter 10. The following general observations on the relationship between the parol evidence rule and interpretation should help to keep things straight.

Although there are some passing references to the parol evidence rule in Chapter 10, that chapter was concerned purely with the rules and principles governing the interpretation or construction of contracts to determine the parties' reasonable meaning. The central point of Chapter 10 is that unless there is no evidence of context available, the meaning of language used in the contract is determined not purely by reference to the dictionary meaning of the words, but by reading the words in the entire context of the transaction. This context may include the discussions between the parties in forming the contract, their previous course of dealing in prior contracts of the same kind, trade usage, and their post-formation course of performing the contract. Where the agreement has been recorded in writing, the parol evidence qualifies what was discussed in Chapter 10 by placing controls on recourse to this extrinsic evidence. In short, it restricts the extent to which some contextual evidence may be considered in deciding what the parties intended in entering the contract.

The impact of the parol evidence rule on the contextual evidence used to interpret the contract depends both on the completeness and clarity of the written record of agreement and on the quality of the contextual evidence. The clearer and more comprehensive the writing, the higher the barrier to the admission of extrinsic evidence. On the other hand, the more compelling the extrinsic evidence, the greater the prospect of persuading the court that it should be admitted. Of course, to decide whether the writing is clear and comprehensive, the court must interpret the writing itself. The effect of this is to create a circular process that can be confounding: the parol evidence rule impacts interpretation by restricting evidence extrinsic to the written contract, but interpretation, often in the light of that very extrinsic evidence, must be used to decide whether and to what extent the writing should have the effect of excluding the extrinsic evidence. One of the most difficult tasks in understanding the parol evidence rule is to appreciate how courts navigate this circular route. As you read this chapter you will find a central theme emerging: courts try to strike a balance between the parties' reasonable expectations that arise from the language of the written contract and their reasonable expectations that arise from the context in which that written contract was formed.

§12.2 A BASIC STATEMENT OF THE RATIONALE AND CONTENT OF THE RULE

The parol evidence rule is based on the principle that when the parties reduce their agreement to writing, they often intend the written record to be the final version of what was agreed. This being so, the final written expression of agreement must have been intended to supercede anything that might have been agreed but was not ultimately recorded in the writing. Accordingly, the fact finder should not hear evidence of terms that were allegedly agreed to but are not reflected in the writing. This evidence is suspect, unreliable, and irrelevant, and is more likely to mislead and confuse than to inform the fact finder. (This rationale is taken up again and illustrated in section 12.3.)

Restatement Second §213 sets out the common law parol evidence rule, as it is applied by many contemporary courts. The UCC rule, in §2.202,[1] is worded somewhat differently, but is largely similar in effect. In essence, both versions of the rule provide that to the extent that the parties execute a **writing that is and is intended to be a final expression** of their **agreement**, no parol evidence may be admitted to **supplement, explain, or contradict** it. However, to the extent that the writing is **not a final and complete expression** of agreement, **consistent, but not contradictory** parol evidence may be admitted to supplement or explain those parts of it that have not been finally expressed.

§12.3 WHAT IS PAROL EVIDENCE?

§12.3.1 The Meaning of "Parol"

"Parol" is derived from the French *parole*, meaning "a word" — more particularly a spoken or oral word. It has the same etymological root as the more familiar modern English word "parole," which has now developed the specialized meaning of a prisoner's early release from jail subject to conditions. Because contract lawyers do not like in any way to be associated with criminal activity, it is a grave breach of etiquette to use that final "e" when referring to parol evidence.

Although the derivation of "parol" suggests that it refers only to oral terms, it extends to written terms as well under some circumstances.

---

1. Section 2.202 is not changed substantively in the 2003 revision of Article 2. It follows the general theme of the revision by substituting the word "record" for "writing." It also has a subtle change with regard to evidence of usage, course of performance, and course of dealing, which is noted in footnote 5 below.

In short, the rule covers both oral and written terms allegedly agreed to prior to execution of the written contract, but not incorporated into the final written contract. It also covers terms allegedly agreed to orally at the time of the written contract, but not incorporated into the written contract.

§12.3.2 Terms Allegedly Agreed to Prior to the Written Contract

The parol evidence rule covers evidence of an alleged term not incorporated into the final written agreement, but claimed by one of the parties to have been agreed to, either in writing or orally, at some time before the execution of the written agreement. For example, Seller and Buyer sign a written agreement under which Seller sells her car to Buyer for $5,000 cash, to be paid on delivery of the car. When Seller thereafter tenders delivery of the car, Buyer refuses to pay the $5,000, claiming that on the day before the agreement was signed, Seller had orally agreed to give him 30 days' credit. If this matter should eventually be litigated, Buyer's testimony about the **prior oral agreement** would be parol evidence. (As we will shortly see, it most likely satisfies all the elements of the parol evidence rule, and the court would therefore refuse to allow Buyer to testify about the prior oral agreement.) The rationale for filtering such evidence through the parol evidence rule is that an allegation of prior consensus on an oral term is suspect when the oral term is not incorporated into the writing executed for the purpose of recording the agreement. Its absence from the writing suggests either that it is a complete fabrication by Buyer, or even if it was agreed to, that the parties intended to supersede it by the written term. Therefore, the evidence should be evaluated with special care by the judge before it is admitted for the fact finder's consideration.

Say that the parties had not negotiated orally, but by correspondence. Their correspondence shows agreement on a 30-day credit term, but their final written contract of sale reflects the C.O.D. term. The **written** evidence of **prior agreement** is also parol evidence. Although the presence of objectively verifiable written evidence of prior agreement reduces concern that Buyer made up the claimed agreement on the credit term, its absence from the final writing still suggests that the parties must have intended to supersede it by the cash term.

§12.3.3 Terms Allegedly Agreed Contemporaneously With the Written Contract

Although the parol evidence rule applies to both oral and written evidence of agreement allegedly made prior to the execution of the final writing, it covers only evidence of **oral agreement** made **contemporaneously** with the final writing. The bar on evidence of contemporaneous oral agreement does not extend to evidence of **contemporaneous written agreement**. There are two reasons for this. First, the existence of a writing is more reliable evidence of agreement than oral testimony. Second, a contract need not be contained in a single document, so that where there are contemporaneous writings, it may not be clear that one of them was intended to supercede the other. They may simply be supplementary to each other. As a result, the parol evidence rule allows any contemporaneous writings to be admitted. (As explained more fully in section 12.6, admission of the written evidence is just a preliminary matter. It allows the evidence to be placed before the fact finder. It does not mean that the fact finder will ultimately conclude that the final agreement is reflected in both writings. It may find that one supercedes the other.)

The type of evidence of contemporaneous oral agreement that is subject to the rule can be illustrated by changing the above example involving the sale of the car. Say that Buyer wishes to testify that when the parties got together to sign the sales contract, he raised the issue of credit and Seller agreed to give him 30 days to pay for the car. However, this agreement is not reflected in the writing. Buyer's assertion is as or more suspect as his claim of a prior oral agreement and is equally subject to the rule.

§12.3.4 Evidence of Subsequent Agreement

The parol evidence rule does not affect evidence of either **oral** or **written** agreements claimed to have been made **after the execution** of the **writing**. The theory behind the parol evidence rule is that the writing is likely to have subsumed all prior understandings, and this presumption cannot have any relevance to an agreement entered into subsequent to the writing. This is in fact a modification, which is subject to its own particular rules but it is not affected by the parol evidence rule.[2]

It is usually easy to tell if an oral agreement was made after the writing because they are separated by some distance in time. However, in some situations it may not be clear if the oral agreement is contemporaneous with or subsequent to the writing. For example, in *Kehr Packages, Inc. v. Fidelity Bank*, 710 A.2d 1169 (Pa. 1998) the bank had agreed to finance the purchase of shares in a corporation. The closing of the transaction took all day. The parties signed a written loan agreement during the course of the day.

---

2. Modifications are dealt with in sections 7.5.2 and 13.9. The written memorial of agreement may itself seek to prevent future oral modifications by requiring that all modifications must be in writing and signed by the parties. The effectiveness of such a provision is discussed in section 12.12.

After the agreement was signed, but before the closing was over, the borrowers asked the lender to increase the amount of the loan. The borrowers claimed that the lender agreed to this increase orally, but the written agreement was not changed to reflect this. The trial court admitted evidence of the oral agreement on the basis that it was subsequent to the writing and not subject to the parol evidence rule. The supreme court reversed and held that the evidence was barred by the rule. The closing was a single, continuous transaction and it was artificial to focus on the exact sequence of the signing and the alleged oral agreement. The crucial point is whether they are both within the same process of formation, and if they are, the parties (especially sophisticated parties, as in this case) should ensure that the writing is changed to include any oral understandings. Because the court found the oral agreement to be contemporaneous and irreconcilable with the writing, evidence of it was excluded.

§12.3.5 Summary of the Scope of the Parol Evidence Rule

The following diagram summarizes the range of the parol evidence rule as discussed in the preceding subsections:

§12.4 A CLOSER LOOK AT THE PURPOSE AND PREMISE OF THE PAROL EVIDENCE RULE

The basic concept of the parol evidence rule is quite simple and its premise is grounded in common sense. Sadly, however, this basic simplicity is completely overwhelmed by the considerable difficulties that emerge when one tries to define the scope of the rule and to apply it to inconclusive facts. The complexity and confusion generated by the rule result largely from the dilemma it presents to courts: The rule serves **a useful role** in permitting the **exclusion of evidence** that is probably **unreliable or dishonest**, but it also has the **potential of producing injustice** by **preventing a party** from **proving what was actually agreed**. A firm rule is more efficient at keeping out undesirable evidence, but is also more likely to exclude legitimate evidence. A more flexible rule allows the court greater discretion in evaluating and determining the reliability of evidence, but it weakens the protection against undesirable evidence and detracts from the certainty and clarity of the law. If you think of the rule as a door to the witness box, its ideal design would keep out the perjurer and irrelevant waffler, but would admit the honest and pertinent witness. The current state of the rule aspires to that design but has not achieved it and probably cannot.

The following illustration indicates the premise of the rule: The Four Crooners is a popular troupe of tenors who sing light opera and ballads. The Four Crooners entered into a written recording contract with Integrated Recording Co., Inc. The contract provided that Integrated Recording would produce and distribute a CD of the Four Crooners' music. The Four Crooners would receive a royalty of 15 percent of gross receipts from sales of the CD. The CD was made and it did very well. One hundred fifty thousand copies were sold in the first month. This resulted in a dispute between the parties and a suit by The Four Crooners for larger royalties. As the basis of the suit, The Four Crooners claim that before they signed the written contract they told Integrated Recording that they were willing to accept a 15 percent royalty on the first 100,000 CDs sold, but if sales exceeded that volume, they wanted a royalty of 18 percent on all sales beyond 100,000 copies. They allege that Integrated Recording agreed to this orally. This change does not appear in the written contract and Integrated Recording denies agreeing to it.

Because the written contract does not mention this alleged term, The Four Crooners have no case unless they are allowed to testify to the oral promise. The rule of law could simply be to admit the evidence of both parties and to leave it to the fact finder (usually the jury) to decide if such an oral agreement was reached. However, the common law has not taken this approach. Instead, it has developed the parol evidence rule, which acts as a gatekeeper by allowing the judge to determine if the jury should be allowed to hear the evidence of the oral agreement.

The primary purpose of the parol evidence rule is to control the jury's decision making. It allows the judge to restrict the information given to the jury, thereby shielding it from evidence the judge finds to be suspect and unreliable. A secondary justification for the rule is that it promotes efficiency in the conduct of litigation. By excluding suspect evidence at the outset (often at the stage of a motion for summary judgment or dismissal), the judge saves the time that would otherwise be wasted in presenting the evidence to the jury and cross-examining the witnesses. Finally, the existence of the rule may help to promote transactional efficiency. Because it exists, parties are more likely to make an effort to record their agreement fully.

As the parol evidence rule relates to the admissibility of evidence, one might be forgiven for assuming that it is a rule of **evidence**. However, it is generally thought of as a rule of **substantive law**. The distinction is subtle: If it were evidentiary, it would be an exclusionary rule based on a presumption that the writing is the best evidence of agreement. Seen as a rule of substantive contract law, it nullifies parol agreements when a writing is executed as a final expression of agreement. This rule of law then leads to the exclusion of the evidence as irrelevant. Happily, one does not usually have to worry about this distinction, because it makes no difference for most purposes. Its principal impact is on matters of procedure. For example, if a federal court deals with a contract case, it follows its own rules of evidence but is bound by the state's parol evidence rule because it is a matter of state substantive law. Similarly, if it were a rule of evidence, a party would waive it by failing to object to the evidence at trial. As a rule of substantive law, it can be raised on appeal despite the failure to object at trial.

Based on these general principles, how is the court likely to react to the Four Crooners' attempt to testify to the alleged oral term? It is quite easy to see why the parol evidence rule might be useful in a case like this. The parties went to the trouble of recording their contract in writing and the royalty provision seems definitive and clear. Surely, had the parties agreed to an 18 percent royalty on sales over 100,000 copies, this would have been in the writing. The absence of the term in the writing suggests either that The Four Crooners are mistaken in thinking that Integrated Recording agreed to it, or they were very sloppy in not making sure that the writing reflected what was actually agreed, or worse, they are making it up. Whatever the reason, the testimony is suspect and maybe it is best that the jury never gets to hear it. Because The Four Crooners' case is entirely based on the alleged oral term, the lawsuit can be dismissed summarily.

Say that the facts of the dispute were different. The written contract is as stated above, but the Four Crooners do not claim an agreement for increased royalties. Instead, they claim that Integrated Recording made an oral promise at the time of signing the contract that it would arrange a ten-city concert tour to promote the CD. It failed to do this and denies agreeing to it. The written agreement is completely silent on the question of promotional tours and concerts. If the parol evidence rule simply barred all testimony of oral agreement, it would be too blunt an instrument. Therefore, the rule is more nuanced. As this testimony does not directly contradict the writing, it may be less presumptively suspect and there may be a greater justification for admitting it. In the following sections we will explore these nuances. Before we look at the rule more closely, it is useful to articulate some of the features of the rule that have been suggested by the preceding discussion:

1. The rule only applies when a *written agreement* (including an agreement recorded by electronic or other means as explained in section 12.1.1) has been executed. The rule applies whether the writing is a comprehensive or incomplete record of the agreement. However, the more complete the written memorandum, the more rigorous the application of the rule.

2. The writing must have been *adopted by both parties*. It need not be signed by them as long as it is shown to be a mutual document. Naturally, the presence of signatures more strongly proves that it is a joint memorandum, but a letter written by one party and received by the other without objection qualifies. A memorandum written by only one of the parties and not disseminated to the other does not bring the rule into effect. To invoke the parol evidence rule, a writing must therefore have qualities beyond those needed to satisfy the statute of frauds. This is because the statute is concerned with the minimal amount of writing needed to establish the existence of a contract, while the parol evidence rule is concerned with the degree to which the writing should be used to exclude extrinsic evidence of what was agreed.

3. Remember that the word "parol" suggests that the rule is *primarily concerned with oral communications* between the parties before or at the time of execution of the writing. However, the rule is not confined to oral communications, and it also covers *prior written communications*.

4. The rule *does not absolutely bar all parol evidence*. If it did, our job would be much easier, but the results of the rule would be bizarre. The purpose of the rule is to exclude presumptively irrelevant or concocted testimony, but not honest and pertinent evidence of what was actually agreed. The rule must therefore be sufficiently fine-tuned to allow the court to make this distinction. Herein lies the greatest complexity and difficulty in devising and applying a rational rule.

5. The rule contemplates a *two-stage process*. When the parol evidence is proffered, the judge must make an initial finding of admissibility. If the judge finds that the evidence is admissible, it is presented to the fact finder (the jury unless the trial is before a judge alone) that hears the testimony and makes the ultimate finding on credibility. The judge's initial determination is characterized as a *question of law*, but it is not necessarily devoid of factual evaluation. This is one of the confusing aspects of the rule. Although the fact finder may eventually have to decide if the evidence is believable, the judge,

in making the initial decision on admissibility, is also concerned with the plausibility of the proffered evidence, a preliminary issue of credibility.

§12.5 THE DEGREE OF FINALITY OF THE WRITING: TOTAL AND PARTIAL INTEGRATION

We begin our discussion of integration on the assumption that the written agreement is clear and unambiguous. Obviously, in many cases, this assumption is false. We saw in Chapter 10 that there are all kinds of reasons why the language chosen by the parties might be indefinite. Where the parties dispute the meaning of the writing and its terms cannot be readily ascertained, this indefiniteness or ambiguity has an impact on the way that the parol evidence rule operates. We will discuss this below in section 12.8. The first task, though, is to focus on the rule itself, which is best done if we put aside the problem of indefiniteness and ambiguity for the time being.

The impact of the parol evidence rule depends on the degree to which the writing executed by the parties constitutes a comprehensive and final written memorandum of their agreement. In short, if the writing is full, complete, unambiguous, and clear, the rule excludes all parol evidence. But to the extent that the written memorandum does not fully and unequivocally cover all of the agreed terms, parol evidence is admissible to supplement it. Even here, however, the parol evidence cannot contradict what has been written or add to those aspects of the agreement that have been fully dealt with in the writing. As discussed in section 12.6, it can be a difficult question of interpretation to determine whether and to what extent the memorandum is comprehensive and final.

If the written memorandum is a complete and final and certain record of the parties' agreement (that is, it unambiguously and clearly expresses every term in the agreement, and it is intended to be the exclusive statement of everything that was agreed), it is said to be **totally (or completely) integrated**. If the writing is truly a total integration, then, by definition, no terms can exist beyond those set out in the writing. It follows that neither party should be allowed to offer parol evidence tending to prove terms extrinsic to the writing, because such evidence is irrelevant or incredible.

If the writing is not a complete and final record of the agreement, it is said to be **partially integrated** or **unintegrated**. The written agreement may fully and finally express some but not all of the terms, or it may not fully and finally express any term. If so, the parol evidence rule completely excludes parol evidence relating to any term that is integrated in the writing, but it permits parol evidence to be admitted to **supplement** or **explain** the writing to the extent that it is not integrated. However, the parol evidence must be

consistent with, and **cannot contradict or vary** terms that have been recorded in the writing.

---

§12.6 THE PROCESS OF DEALING WITH PAROL EVIDENCE

The issue of the admissibility of parol evidence could arise early in the suit if one of the parties applies for summary judgment in response to a claim or defense based on an alleged parol term. Because the admissibility of parol evidence is a legal question, a dispute on admissibility is often appropriate for summary adjudication. If the case is not disposed of on the pleadings and it goes to trial, the admissibility of the evidence may be challenged when an attempt is made to introduce it. As noted before, the evaluation of parol evidence at trial involves two stages. In the first, the judge decides admissibility as a legal matter. If the evidence is admitted, the fact finder evaluates its credibility. We now look more closely at the process involved in each of these two stages, which may be charted as shown in the diagram on page 358.

Stage 1: The judge's determination
In making the finding of admissibility, the judge conducts an inquiry that may itself be split into two sequential components:

1. The first issue to be resolved by the judge is the question of *integration*. Is the writing a full and final, record of the agreement as a whole (that is, a complete integration) or of the particular term in issue (a partial integration). If so, we do not get beyond the first inquiry, because the parol evidence may not be admitted.
2. If the writing is neither a complete integration nor a partial integration covering the term in issue, consistent supplementary parol evidence is admissible. The judge's inquiry then turns to whether the proffered parol evidence is in fact *consistent* with and not contradictory to what has been written. If it contradicts the writing, it may not be admitted, and it still never reaches the jury.

Having drawn this distinction between the judge's two inquiries, it is useful to express a word of caution: It is easy enough to separate the issue of integration from the issue of consistency for the purpose of theoretical analysis, and it is logical that the first must be resolved before the second is reached. However, as a practical matter, the inquiry into integration is often influenced by the question of whether the alleged parol term is consistent with the writing, and these two stages often meld into one

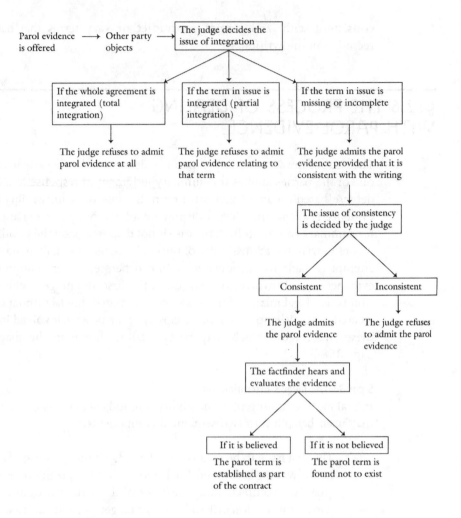

another. That is, unless the intent to integrate is so clear that there can be no doubt on the matter, the extent to which the alleged parol term is reconcilable with the writing may affect the court's decision on whether an integration was reasonably intended by the parties.

Stage 2: The fact finder's determination

If the judge's preliminary inquiry into the evidence leads to the determination that the subject matter covered by the alleged term has not been integrated into the writing and that the proffered parol evidence is consistent with what has been written, the judge rules the evidence admissible. It may then be presented to the fact finder, which is responsible for the ultimate decision on whether the term was agreed to. If the case is to be tried by a jury, the dichotomy between judge and fact finder is clear. However, if the parties have agreed not to try the case before a jury, the judge is the fact finder, and the dichotomy becomes quite artificial. The judge, in the role of legal arbiter, makes the initial finding as a matter of law. If she rules the evidence inadmissible, she must then exercise the professional objectivity of not being influenced by it in her role as fact finder. This is probably not as difficult as it sounds — the fact that the judge excluded it as a matter of law means that she could not have found it very convincing to begin with — as explained further below.

§12.7 DETERMINING THE QUESTION OF INTEGRATION

Integration is a question of intent — truly a factual question, although characterized as one of law for the reasons of judicial control, as discussed above. Therefore, to decide if the parties intended the writing to be a full and final expression of their agreement, the court must interpret it. During the classical period of contract law, courts tended to emphasize the objective test of assent and to place great importance on the reasonable meaning of language. This heavy emphasis on *objectivity* made the question of determining integration relatively easy: If the writing, interpreted as a whole in accordance with the plain meaning of the language used, appeared to be a full and final expression of the agreement, it was deemed to be integrated. Thus, the judge decided the parties' intent to integrate their agreement in the writing purely on the basis of the **"four corners"** of the written document, without recourse to any extrinsic evidence. If the document *appeared* complete this intent was established and no parol evidence was admissible to add to or alter its reasonable meaning. (This earlier emphasis on the "four corners" test explains why courts felt justified in thinking of integration as a legal question. A purely grammatical evaluation of meaning involves no assessment of the credibility of extrinsic evidence.)

The trend has been to move away from a strong "four corners" approach. Most modern courts recognize that even when a writing appears at face value to be comprehensive, inquiry into the **context** in which it was written may dispel this impression. Therefore, in deciding the question of integration, a contemporary court is likely to go beyond the face value of the writing, and to entertain *extrinsic evidence* that may be helpful in revealing that an *apparently integrated writing* was in fact *not intended as such*. The judge's evaluation of this extrinsic evidence is preliminary, and treated as a legal exercise despite the obvious factual and credibility issues involved. If the judge concludes that the evidence is admissible as a matter of law, the fact finder (whether a jury or the judge herself in that role) will be the final arbiter of its factual truth.

When an apparently integrated agreement does not contain the term that was allegedly agreed to, one of the key questions in determining integration under the contextual approach is to ask whether the circumstances offer an explanation of why the term may not have been included in the writing. Restatement Second §216(2)(b) expresses this concept by asking whether the term is such as *might naturally be omitted* from the writing. UCC §2.202, Comment 3,[3] suggests a similar inquiry: Would the term *certainly have been included* in the document had it been agreed to? The UCC test sounds more favorable to admission because it excludes the evidence only if it clearly would have been part of the writing if the parties had agreed to it. However, in most cases, this test would not likely give a different result than the Restatement's inquiry into whether the term might naturally have been agreed separately.

Masterson v. Sine, 436 P.2d 561 (Cal 1968) is one of the best-known cases to apply a contextual approach and to inquire whether a term absent from the agreement might naturally be omitted from the writing. Masterson and his wife sold a ranch to the Sines, his sister and her husband. The contract granted the Mastersons an option to repurchase the ranch at a price to be fixed by a formula. Masterson later became bankrupt and his trustee attempted to exercise the repurchase option to bring the property into Masterson's estate for the benefit of his creditors. The Sines claimed that the trustee could not exercise the option because the parties had orally agreed at the time of the sale that the option was personal to the Mastersons and could not be transferred to or exercised by anyone else. The majority found that such an agreement might naturally be made outside of the writing in a family transaction. The dissent disagreed with the majority's approach and resolution. It found the writing to be integrated on its face and criticized the "might naturally be omitted" test as too uncertain and open-ended. Even if that test was appropriate, the dissent did not find that this oral term would have satisfied it. A restriction on transfer of the option would not naturally be excluded from the writing if the parties had agreed to it. The option itself was granted in the writing, so surely any restriction on its exercise would be set out there too had the parties agreed to it. The dissent also commented on the credibility of the Sines' assertion: it was particularly suspicious because it was aimed at keeping the property out of Masterson's bankruptcy estate.

Myskina v. Conde Nast Publications, Inc., 386 F. Supp.2d 409 (S.D.N.Y. 2005) is a good contrast to *Masterson*. Myskina, a Russian tennis champion, agreed with Conde Nast to pose nude for photographs to be published in a "sports" issue of *GQ* magazine. Immediately before the photographs were taken, Myskina signed a written release in which she irrevocably and unqualifiedly consented to the use of the photographs by Conde Nast. The first photos

---

3. This comment is preserved in the 2003 revision of §2.202.

taken during the photo shoot portrayed Myskina as Lady Godiva. She was not entirely nude in these photos, but wore flesh-colored pants and, had long hair covering her breasts. The photos taken after that were more revealing. Myskina alleged that she had expressed discomfort over posing for them but the photographer assured her that only the Lady Godiva photos would be published.[4] When Conde Nast published not only the Lady Godiva photos, but also some of the nude photographs, Myskina sued it for damages and an injunction on the grounds that the nude photos were published without her authorization. Her suit did not survive summary judgment. She sought to testify to the oral undertaking to publish only the Lady Godiva photos, but the court refused to admit that evidence. The court found that the release, interpreted in its plain meaning within the context of the transaction, was an integrated document that clearly and comprehensively expressed unrestricted consent to publication. The alleged oral term imposed a fundamental condition of consent that would not have been omitted from the writing had it been agreed to by the parties.

The movement away from the plain meaning of the writing should not be exaggerated. Even under the contextual test, if the document does appear to be clear, unambiguous and complete, the court is likely to assume that it is integrated unless the extrinsic evidence is reconcilable with the apparent intent and plausibly demonstrates a justification for going beyond the writing. Also, one should not simplistically relegate the "four corners" approach to history. It still has some sway, and courts have not moved beyond it at a uniform pace. You still find today a range of approaches to the issue of integration that are based both on the strength of the evidence of integration and on the conservatism of the court.

It is common to find a provision in a written contract to the effect that the written contract is the entire agreement between the parties, and that no representations or promises have been made save for those set out in the writing. This is called a **merger clause** because it signifies that all the terms of the agreement have been merged into the writing. Where the written contract appears to be complete, the inclusion of a merger clause is strong evidence of integration. Of course, a court that is inclined to a four corners approach is more likely to defer to a merger clause than a court that stresses interpretation in context. However, even a court that is receptive to contextual evidence gives the merger clause great weight. As a result, a merger clause can be effective in disposing of the issue of integration and insulating the writing from parol evidence. However, a merger clause is not always

---

4. Myskina did not argue (and the court did not consider) that the alleged oral agreement was not subject to the parol evidence rule because it was made subsequent to the written release. This probably would not have been a good argument. Even though the oral agreement followed the writing, which was executed at the beginning of the photo shoot, they did occur during the same period of interaction and should be viewed as contemporaneous. (*See* the *Kehr Packages* case discussed in section 12.3.2.)

conclusive. Sometimes courts will go behind a merger clause and admit parol evidence, where, under all the circumstances of the transaction, one of the parties makes a plausible argument that, despite appearances, the writing is not really integrated, and the alleged parol term can be reconciled with it. A court may be more amenable to such an argument where the merger clause is a standard term in a form contract.

To illustrate some of the difficulties in deciding the question of integration, let us return to the example of the recording contract between The Four Crooners and Integrated Recordings, introduced in section 12.4. Assume that the parties' agreement is recorded in a written contract, five pages long. The contract specifies the songs to be recorded, the date of recording, the date of release, and the royalty of 15 percent to be paid on gross receipts. It has numerous provisions setting out the duties of The Four Crooners in the production of the recording as well as detailed provisions relating to the distribution of the CD and the accounting for and payment of royalties. It ends with a merger clause. The writing appears to be full and comprehensive. Consider the two alternative allegations of parol agreement made by the Four Crooners. One was that the parties agreed orally to a royalty of 18 percent on sales over 100,000 copies. The other was that Integrated Recording undertook to arrange a ten-city concert tour to promote the CD. On a four corners approach, the writing is unquestionably integrated, and no evidence would be admitted of either of these alleged parol terms. The Four Crooners are not likely to do any better on a contextual approach. Even a court that stresses the need to examine context takes account of the fact that the writing is detailed and has a merger clause. The written contract specifies the royalty percentage, so it is not natural that the parties might agree to part of that term separately. It is hard to reconcile the parol augmentation of the royalty term with the unequivocal written term. The term relating to the concert tour is not as badly at odds with the writing, but it does not seem natural that this single term would have been omitted from an otherwise detailed written agreement. In addition, the only contextual evidence tendered is the disputed, self-serving testimony of The Four Crooners themselves about what was said at the time that the writing was signed. (As you can see, credibility issues cannot be entirely divorced from this legal inquiry, and the issues of integration and consistency, while doctrinally distinct, often intermingle in the decision on integration.)

However, say that the written contract was not as detailed as described above. It is a simple, one-page document that sets out the songs to be recorded, the date of recording, the date of release, and the royalty of 15 percent to be paid on gross receipts. It has none of the detailed provisions relating to the parties' performance set out above and no merger clause. Parol evidence on the increase in royalties is still not likely to be admissible because the royalty clause appears to be fully integrated and not easily reconcilable with the alleged parol agreement. However, evidence of the undertaking of a concert tour stands a better chance of admission. The absence of details about the obligations of the parties in performing the contract and the lack of a merger clause could make it more natural that an agreement about a promotional tour might be made separately from the writing.

§12.8 AMBIGUITY OR INDEFINITENESS IN AN INTEGRATED WRITING

As noted at the beginning of section 12.5, the discussion of integration up to now has assumed that the terms of the writing are clear and unambiguous. Where that is not so, a further complication arises: no matter how firmly the parties may have intended the writing to be a full and final expression of their agreement, if a term of the writing is unclear or ambiguous, the writing cannot be treated as an integration of that term. If extrinsic evidence is available to clarify the indefiniteness, that is the best means of ascertaining the parties' intended meaning. Parol evidence is therefore admissible to clarify the uncertainty or ambiguity. This does not mean that uncertainty or ambiguity opens the floodgates to the admission of parol evidence. The evidence must be pertinent to the meaning of the unclear term, and it must be reconcilable with what has been written.

Like the determination of integration, the decision on whether a term is uncertain or ambiguous could be made either on the basis of the four corners of the document, or in context. Under a four corners approach, the court examines the ordinary plain meaning of the term to decide if it is clear. A court that uses the contextual approach assumes that written words do not have a constant, immutable meaning, but that the context in which the words were used could color their meaning. If the court is to establish the parties' true intent, it must go beyond its own perception of meaning and consider evidence of this context.

For example, recall that the written contract between The Four Crooners and Integrated Recording provided that The Four Crooners would receive a royalty of "15 percent of gross receipts from CD sales." Say that The Four Crooners do not make any allegation that the parties agreed to a higher royalty for sales over 100,000 copies. Rather, the dispute centers on the meaning of "gross receipts from CD sales." The Four Crooners say that the phrase is intended to include all income derived from sales of the recording, whether in the form of actual physical CDs, or in intangible forms, such as music files that are downloaded from Web sites. Integrated Recording argues that the clear language of the written contract intends to confine the royalties to receipts from CD sales. The Four Crooners seek to testify that this point was discussed by the parties at the time of signing the

363

contract, and they orally agreed that "gross receipts from CD sales" meant all income from sales of the recording in any form. A literal-minded court, applying a four corners approach may consider the written language to be clear in confining royalties to receipts from CD sales. However, a court that sees context as important is likely to be less confident of the face-value meaning of the writing. Provided that the written language is reasonably susceptible of the meaning alleged by The Four Crooners, it would consider this evidence as a preliminary matter to decide the question of whether the writing is unclear. The court may ultimately decide that it is not. The point though, is that the court would be reluctant to exclude the parol evidence without having the opportunity to think about the word's meaning in light of it. (It is also worth stressing again that even if the court decided to admit the evidence, the Four Crooners must still persuade the jury that the oral agreement was made.)

Pacific Gas & Electric Co. v. G.W. Thomas Drayage & Rigging Co., 442 P.2d 641 (Cal 1968), discussed previously in relation to interpretation in section 10.3.1d, is one of the best-known examples of a broad approach to ambiguity. The repairer of machinery undertook to indemnify the owner for any damage caused during the course of the repair work. The repairer damaged the owner's property. When the owner claimed compensation for the damage, the repairer contended that the indemnity provision was intended to cover only damage to property owned by third parties. The trial court refused to admit contextual evidence offered by the repairer to prove this on the grounds that the language in the written contract was clear and contained no such restriction. The supreme court criticized this approach, saying that words do not have an inherent meaning. What appears plain in the abstract may become ambiguous when viewed in the light of contextual evidence that indicates a meaning to which to words may be reasonably susceptible.

§12.9 DISTINGUISHING CONSISTENCY FROM CONTRADICTION

If the judge decides that the writing is a full and final expression of the parties agreement (that is, it is totally integrated) the inquiry ends and the parol evidence is excluded. However, if the judge determines that the writing is not totally integrated, parol evidence is admissible to **supplement** or **explain** the writing, **but not to contradict** it. Stated differently, even where the agreement is not fully integrated, parol evidence cannot be admitted if it is inconsistent with and cannot be reconciled with what has been written.

Although it is possible, as a doctrinal matter, to separate the enquiry into integration from the question of consistency, the cases show that in practice these two concepts are often interrelated. That is, if the court considers the parol term to be at odds with the writing, this factor may influence the court in deciding whether the writing is integrated. In fact, Restatement, Second's "might naturally be omitted" test and Article 2's "would certainly have been included" test speak as much to consistency as they do to finality of the writing. These two inquiries melded into each other in both the *Masterson* and *Myskina* cases discussed in section 12.7. In *Masterson* the majority's conclusion that the limitation on the option might naturally be made as a separate agreement was motivated in part by its perception that the limitation did not directly contradict any express language in the written grant of the option. The dissent saw the limitation as contradictory because the usual implication of law is that an option is transferable unless the agreement clearly states otherwise. In *Myskina*, the court's conclusion that the release was integrated was based in its view that the limitation on the release would certainly have been included in the writing had the parties agreed to it. The court went on to say that, in any event, a parol term qualifying the extent of the release was inconsistent with the absolute release in the writing.

Masterson and *Myskina* provide insight into another aspect of consistency. A parol term is obviously inconsistent with the writing if it directly contradicts something that is expressed in the writing. For example, if a contract for the sale of a house states that the price is $500,000, evidence of a contemporaneous oral agreement that the parties agreed to a price of $475,000 cannot be reconciled with the writing. However, in *Masterson* and *Myskina* the question of contradiction was more subtle. The alleged parol term did not directly clash with a written term, but it departed from the normal legal or factual implications of the language. That is, there was no language in the written contract in *Masterson* stating that the option was assignable, and there was no language in the release in *Myskina* that expressly authorized the publication of the nude photos. However, the absence of any stated limitations on transfer or on authority to publish created the implied understanding that they did not exist. Courts do not approach the issue of conflict with implied terms uniformly. However, in considering consistency it is important to go beyond the obvious clash with an express term, and to ask more broadly whether the alleged parol term can be reconciled with the legal import of the writing.

§12.10 THE EFFECT OF THE RULE ON EVIDENCE OF COURSE OF PERFORMANCE, COURSE OF DEALING, AND TRADE USAGE

In dealing with interpretation in context, section 10.6.2 explained the meaning of and the role played by course of performance, course of dealing, and trade usage. We now focus on what impact the parol evidence rule might have on the admissibility of this type of contextual evidence. In most cases **course of performance** can be disposed of easily because it is typically not parol evidence. Although it is conceivable that there could be a course of performance between the oral agreement and the execution of the writing, in most situations any course of performance only takes place after the written contract has been executed. However, course of dealing is, by definition, something that occurs prior to the contract and trade usage exists prior and contemporaneously with it. Therefore, a court could treat evidence of **course of dealing** or **trade usage** as a form of parol evidence and could exclude it if the agreement is integrated or, even if not, if it cannot be reconciled with the written terms. However, course of dealing and trade usage differ in an important respect from the evidence of a party on the discussions that led to the alleged parol agreement — a course of dealing or trade usage can be established by more reliable objective evidence of mutual conduct or accepted custom. Courts are therefore more likely to admit evidence of course of dealing and trade usage.

Restatement, Second §213 provides no guidance on how a court should approach this kind of contextual evidence. It refers only to parol terms that were allegedly agreed to between the parties during their interaction leading up to the execution of the writing. By contrast, UCC §2.202(a) specifically permits an otherwise integrated agreement to be supplemented by evidence of course of dealing and trade usage. (Section 2.202(a) also specifically mentions evidence of course of performance which, as noted above, typically does not even qualify as parol evidence.)

Where the written memorial of the contract is not a full and complete expression of the terms of the contract, it is easy to see why a court would be receptive to course of dealing or trade usage evidence to supplement or explain the contract's terms. For example, *Grace Label, Inc. v. Kliff*, 355 F. Supp.2d 965 (S.D. Iowa 2005) involved a contract to supply trading cards bearing the likeness of Britney Spears, to be placed in packets of snack food. Sadly (and I am sure this is no reflection on Britney) the cards smelled bad and were unfit for inclusion in food packages. The seller sought to admit evidence of a course of dealing to establish that it had not breached the contract by supplying smelly cards. The seller offered this evidence of prior transactions to establish the parties' expectation that the seller would use the same materials in printing the cards as it had used in similar prior transactions. The seller had done so, and was therefore not responsible for the problem with the cards. The court overruled the buyer's objection to the admission of this evidence, which it held merely explained and supplemented, but did not contradict the written contract term.

However, UCC §2.202 goes beyond merely allowing evidence of course of dealing, trade usage or course of performance where the agreement is not integrated. It makes it clear that this type of contextual evidence should be admitted even where the writing is intended as a final expression of agreement.[5] That is, §2.202 presumes very strongly that the parties intend to contract in light of their own and the market's customary practices. This means that the parties could reasonably take for granted that the contract includes terms arising from these sources, and may not mention them in the writing, even where that writing is otherwise fully integrated. This strong recognition of course of dealing and trade usage compels parties to use very clear and specific language in the writing if they truly do intend to exclude a course of dealing or a trade usage from their contract.

The strength of trade usage and the likelihood that it will be found consistent with the writing in all but the most overwhelming cases of direct conflict is illustrated by *Nanakuli Paving & Rock Co. v. Shell Oil Co.*, 664 F.2d 772 (9th Cir. 1981). We first encountered this case in section 10.6.2e in connection with the role of trade usage in interpretation. Recall that the written contract under which Shell supplied asphalt to Nanakuli provided that the price of the asphalt was Shell's posted price at the time of delivery. The court held that this clear language was qualified by a trade usage under which the seller would "price protect" the buyer by charging the lower posted price prevailing at the time that the buyer committed itself under a paving contract with its customer. Because the contract was in writing, the court had to decide whether the evidence of trade usage was admissible. Although the price term was clear and seemed quite absolute, the court found no inconsistency between the price term and the price protection usage. *Nanakuli* may go further than other courts in its notion of consistency, but it does show that, at least where a sale of goods is involved, parties should not lightly assume that trade usage or course of dealing evidence will be barred by an apparently integrated writing that does not specifically negate the usage or course of dealing.

§12.11 THE COLLATERAL AGREEMENT RULE

The collateral agreement rule is sometimes referred to as an exception to the parol evidence rule, but it is not really an exception at all. Rather, it follows from an application of the general principles of the parol evidence rule.

---

5. Comment 1(c) to §2.202 states further that the court does not need to find that the writing is ambiguous as a precondition to admissibility of this type of evidence. The 2003 revision of §2.202 elevates this comment into a provision of the section itself. It redrafts §2.202(1)(a) to cover only such evidence offered to supplement the record. It then creates a new subsection 2.202(2), which states, "Terms in a record may be explained by evidence of course of performance, course of dealing, or usage of trade without a preliminary determination by the court that the language is ambiguous."

The collateral agreement rule developed as a means of softening a firm four corners approach to parol evidence at a time when courts were more inclined to determine integration by looking no further than the four corners of the writing. A court that adopts a broader contextual approach to parol evidence and uses the Restatement, Second's "might naturally be omitted" test or Article 2's "would certainly have been included" test does not need the collateral agreement rule because those tests cover the same type of situation and are less rigorous. However, the rule still features in some modern cases.

The gist of the rule is that even where a contract is integrated, if the parol agreement is sufficiently distinct from the scope of the writing, it can be seen as a different contract, **related to but separate from** the integrated written agreement. If so, evidence of this collateral agreement is not barred by the parol evidence rule. Stated differently, even if the alleged parol agreement relates to the same transaction as the writing, if it is self-contained and distinct enough to be seen as a collateral agreement, the parties may **not** have **intended it to be covered by the integrated writing**. Evidence of the collateral agreement may therefore be admitted. The requirement of **consistency** applies even where the parol agreement is found to be collateral, so evidence of a collateral agreement that contradicts the writing may not be admitted. The determination of whether an agreement is collateral can be slippery, and different courts have different views on the relationship between the writing and the parol agreement. A requirement that is regularly expressed is that both the **subject matter** of and the **consideration** for the parol agreement must be distinct and capable of being **separately identified**.

Mitchell v. Lath, 160 N.E. 646 (N.Y. 1928) is one of the best-known cases to deal with the collateral agreement rule. The seller of real property agreed orally to remove an unsightly ice house on land adjacent to the property sold to the buyer. This undertaking was not included in the written contract for the sale of the property. The written contract appeared comprehensive and included a number of other terms ancillary to the sale. The majority of the court refused to find that the agreement to remove the ice house was a collateral agreement — it was related closely enough to the sale of the property that one would expect to find it in the writing if it had been agreed to. The dissent felt that the oral undertaking was distinct enough that the parties could have made it as a separate ancillary contract, not intended to be integrated into the writing. The collateral agreement rule was also considered in *Myskina v. Conde Nast Publications, Inc.*, discussed in section 12.7. The court held that the oral agreement limiting the magazine's right to publish the nude photos was not collateral to, but an integral part of the release, and that it contradicted it. (The close conceptual connection between the collateral agreement rule and the Restatement, Second and UCC tests should be apparent from the account of these cases.)

§12.12 EXCEPTIONS TO THE PAROL EVIDENCE RULE: EVIDENCE TO ESTABLISH GROUNDS FOR AVOIDANCE OR INVALIDITY, OR TO SHOW A CONDITION PRECEDENT

The primary purpose of the parol evidence rule is to keep spurious or irrelevant evidence from the fact finder, but there is always a danger that it may be used to exclude truthful evidence of genuine agreement that was, for some reason, not encompassed within the writing. If the parol evidence relates to an alleged term that was in fact agreed to but is not reflected in a completely integrated writing or is not consistent with what was written, the party seeking to present the evidence is out of luck. By failing to ensure the accuracy of the writing, that party exposed itself to the risk of not being able to prove the term.

However, in some situations, this result may be too harsh, and may play into the hands of an unscrupulous operator who has deliberately taken advantage of the other party. To cater for such situations, there is a well recognized exception to the rule that permits the introduction of parol evidence to show **fraud, duress, mistake, and other bases for invalidating or avoiding the contract**. For example, in *America's Directories, Inc. v. Stellhorn One Hour Photo, Inc.*, 833 N.E.2d 1059 (Ind. App. 2005) the president of America's Directories, a corporation that sold advertising in a telephone directory, used persistent hard-selling techniques to persuade Stellhorn to sign three standard form contracts under which it purchased three years' advertising in the directory. Stellhorn was reluctant to buy the ads, and only did so after being assured orally that he could cancel after one year. The standard form contracts stated unequivocally that they could not be cancelled, and they contained a merger clause excluding all verbal agreements and representations not contained in the writing. Despite that, the court admitted evidence of the oral agreement because the evidence indicated that America's Directories never intended to allow Stellhorn to cancel and it made several other false representations to induce him to enter the contracts. We will deal with the elements of fraud more fully in section 13.6. For the present, it is enough to note that relief is available for fraud if a party makes a fraudulent misrepresentation which justifiably induces the victim to enter the contract. Fraud usually involves a misrepresentation of fact. However, a misrepresentation of intent can also constitute fraud if, at the time of entering the contract, the party making the misrepresentation intends to renege on his promise.

The exception for mistake and improper bargaining creates the risk that the parol evidence tendered to show mistake or misconduct may itself be perjured, thereby defeating the rule's purpose of protecting the integrity of a final writing. However, this risk is seen as necessary to ensure that the rule is not used as a means of defeating a party's right to avoidance.

Along similar lines, parol evidence is also admissible to show that **a fact recited in a writing is false**. For example, say that a contract between Archie, an architect, and Homer, a homeowner, provides, "In consideration for $1,500 paid by Homer, Archie agrees to draw plans . . . ," Archie would be permitted to introduce evidence that the money was never in fact paid. The purpose of this, of course, is to prevent Homer from evading his payment obligation and to allow Archie to recover what is due. The parol evidence turns the recital of consideration into an implied promise to pay. You may remember from section 7.8 that parties sometimes use a false recital of consideration in an attempt to validate gifts. That is, Archie may have agreed to draw the plans for free, and the parties merely recited the fact of payment to make it appear as if Archie received consideration for his promise. In this situation, although the parol evidence does not exclude evidence of nonpayment, the circumstances may make it appropriate to estop Archie from denying receipt of the payment.

Another exception to the rule permits parol evidence to be admitted to show that the **agreement was subject to a condition**. Conditions are explained more fully in Chapter 16. For the present, it is sufficient to understand that the parties may reach agreement on an exchange of performances, but provide that one or both parties' performance obligation will take effect only if a future uncertain event occurs (or does not occur). For example, say that when Archie and Homer were negotiating their contract, Archie told Homer that he was waiting to hear if he had secured a contract to supervise the construction of an office building in another city, and if he got that contract he would have to leave town for a year and could not take on Homer's project. The parties therefore signed the memorandum subject to the oral understanding that their contract was contingent on Archie not being awarded the other contract. Archie is then awarded the other contract and seeks to escape his obligation to Homer by testifying to the oral condition.

If the court finds the writing to be an integration, the parol evidence rule would normally exclude this testimony. However, because the testimony relates to a condition precedent to Archie's performance, the rule does not apply. This exception has long been recognized by courts and is reflected in Restatement Second §217. Comment b to §217 seeks to rationalize it on the basis that if a condition exists, the writing cannot be said to be integrated. This is rather flimsy reasoning, which could just as well be applied to any other alleged term. A point of distinction could be that if a contract is subject to a condition, no obligations come into existence unless the condition is met. However, this is not a convincing rationale either, because a contract subject to a condition precedent is a contract nevertheless. There is no reason to treat the allegation of a parol condition with any less suspicion than some other term claimed to have been left out of the writing. Nevertheless, the exception is well-established.

§12.13 RESTRICTIONS ON ORAL MODIFICATION

As stated before, the parol evidence rule does not exclude testimony relating to agreements made after the writing. These are not part of the environment in which the writing was executed, and they cannot be superseded by it. However, the parties may wish to avoid disputes over possible future allegations of oral modification, and may therefore insert a **"no oral modification" clause** in the writing, stating that no modification will be binding unless written and signed by both parties. Such clauses are difficult to enforce because courts do not usually consider that the parties can effectively restrict in advance their right to modify orally. The parties' power to modify the contract must include the power to modify the "no oral modification" clause, and the fact that they made an oral modification in itself indicates that they did so. Therefore, courts are generally willing to admit evidence of an alleged oral modification despite the existence of the restriction in the writing, and to leave it to the jury to decide whether the modification was in fact made.

UCC §2.209(2)[6] appears to change this approach by expressly recognizing the effectiveness of "no oral modification" clauses. However, the recognition is half-hearted because §2.209(4) provides that even if the later oral modification is ineffective because the original contract requires written modification, the attempt at oral modification may still operate as a waiver of rights under the original contract. Under §2.209(5) the waiver is generally effective. It can only be retracted in relation to future performance if it has not been detrimentally relied upon by the other party, and it cannot be retracted to the extent that it covers performance that has already been rendered.

Examples

1. Ann Cestral owned a house on a large central city lot that had been in her family for four generations. When she decided to move to a smaller condo, she agreed to sell the house to her cousin, Ava Rice. They settled on the price and Ann arranged for her attorney to draw up a contract of sale. When the document was ready for signature, Ann and Ava drove together to the attorney's office. On the way Ann said to Ava, "Our family has owned this house for a long time, and I sold it to you because I want it

---

6. Section 2.209 has not been significantly changed in the 2003 revision of Article 2.

to remain in the family. Promise me that if you ever decide to sell the house, you will give members of our family the right of first refusal to buy it before you sell it to a stranger." Ava agreed. When Ann and Ava arrived at the attorney's office they were given a standard sales agreement which they both signed. The agreement was several pages long and had lots of details. Neither Ann nor Ava told the attorney about their discussion on the way over, so their agreement on the family's right of first refusal was not incorporated into the written contract.

Ava took transfer of the house and moved in. Over the next couple of years, large lots in the neighborhood became very valuable because of their central location. Developers were buying houses and demolishing them so the properties could be used for high-rise condominiums. Two years after she bought the house from Ann, Ava accepted a developer's offer to buy the house for an extraordinarily good price. When Ann found out that Ava had sold the property, she confronted Ava angrily. In response, Ava waved their written contract in Ann's face and yelled, "Show me where this says I can't sell the property to anyone that I please!" Does Ava have a point?

2. Klaus Merger owned two adjoining quarter-acre lots. One had a house on it and the other, overgrown and neglected, had been used by Klaus as a dumping ground for assorted bits of junk, including a couple of broken-down cars. A few months ago Klaus placed the quarter-acre with the house on the market. Andy Gration expressed interest in buying it and negotiations ensued. Andy eventually agreed to buy it for the asking price on condition that Klaus cleared up the adjacent lot and removed all the junk. Klaus agreed to do this.

Klaus then produced a standard-form agreement of sale that he had procured from a legal stationer. The form had the usual provisions found in transactions of this kind, with blank spaces for details such as the property description and price. One of its standard terms was a merger clause, stating "This is the entire agreement between the parties. No agreements or representations have been made save for those stated herein." There was also a large blank space at the end of the form headed "Additional Terms." Klaus filled out all the other blanks in the form but wrote nothing in the space provided for additional terms. The form therefore did not mention the clearing of the adjacent lot. Both parties signed the form.

Klaus never cleared the lot and denies ever agreeing to do so. What are Andy's chances of proving and enforcing the oral agreement?

3. Di Aquiri owns a tavern. Margie Rita runs a small, exclusive distillery that makes a variety of health-conscious, socially responsible, non-alcoholic versions of popular liquors. Di entered into a written contract with Margie under which Di bought 100 bottles of Margie's "fat-free,

sugar-free, sodium-free,[7] non-alcoholic, non-animal-tested, all natural faux tequila." In addition to this description of the goods, the writing stated the names and addresses of the parties, the price of "$10 per bottle, subject to discount for cash," payment terms (30 days after delivery) and delivery date. It also contained a merger clause stating that the writing was intended to be "the complete, exclusive and final expression of all terms agreed to by the parties." Both parties signed the writing and Margie delivered the liquor on due date.

Consider how the parol evidence rule would affect the following different disputes that arose after delivery.

(a) Upon delivery, Di gave Margie's driver a check for $900, this being the stated contract price of $1,000 less a ten percent discount for early payment. Margie refuses to allow Di a ten percent discount. She says that the parties discussed the amount of the discount orally, and she told Di that it was five percent. Di claims that they agreed to a ten percent discount.

(b) Di did not pay the driver. Five days later she sent a check for $900 in payment, less a ten percent discount. Margie's problem is not with the amount of the discount, but with Di's right to it at all. She says that "cash payment" means cash on delivery, so Di is not entitled to any discount. Di says that Margie told her orally that payment within a week of delivery qualifies as cash. Margie denies ever discussing the question.

(c) After delivery Di, who is very fussy about the quality of what she serves to her customers, conducted her usual chemical analysis of the faux tequila. She found that it has traces of fat and sugar (about 0.5 percent of each). Di's tests also revealed that the faux tequila contains about 0.08 percent alcohol. She wishes to reject the goods as nonconforming to the contract and to get her money back. Margie claims that she is not entitled to do this for two reasons. First, Margie has sold liquor to Di in the past with similar small traces of fat, sugar, and alcohol, and Di has never objected before. Second, it is widely accepted in the make-believe-liquor industry that one can never completely remove the good stuff, and beverages described as free of a substance may acceptably contain up to one percent of it.

4. Gordon Bleu, a chef who owns and operates a restaurant, decided to begin serving game birds to his customers. He found a recipe for pheasant and checked the catalog of his regular supplier, Fairest Fowls, Inc., to see what it cost. The catalog showed "regular" pheasant for $5.00 per pound, and "plump deluxe" pheasant for $12.50 per

---

7. It is also taste-free, but the agreement did not specify that.

pound. Gordon decided that "regular" pheasant would be fine, and he called Fairest Fowls and placed an order for 50 birds.

A couple of days later Fairest Fowls delivered the birds, accompanied by its written delivery invoice. The invoice contained the parties' names and addresses, the date, and the statement "Delivered as per order, 50 regular pheasants @ $5.00 per pound. Cash on delivery." The invoice was signed by a representative of Fairest Fowls. Gordon signed the form as requested and paid the driver.[8]

Gordon prepared the birds exactly in accordance with his recipe, but they were tough and uneatable. Gordon complained to Fairest Fowls, which explained that it used the word "regular" in its catalog to denote scrawny birds useful only for soup, and that the more expensive "plump deluxe" variety had to be used if the flesh was to be eaten. Fairest Fowls said that "everyone knew this about pheasants," and it was surprised that Gordon, as a trained chef, was unaware of the distinction.

Gordon insists that there is no reason why he should have understood "regular" in the sense used by Fairest Fowls and he points out that the dictionary meaning of "regular" is "usual, normal or customary." Fairest Fowls claims that it can produce several experts in the restaurant trade who would attest to the fact that "regular" pheasants are commonly understood to be suitable only for soup.

If Gordon and Fairest Fowls cannot settle their dispute and Gordon decides to sue Fairest Fowls for the return of his money, would Fairest Fowls be able to introduce the testimony of its expert witnesses over Gordon's objection?

5. Beverly Hill, a movie producer, offered a leading role in a new movie to Holly Wood, an actress. The parties met with their lawyers and agents and spent the full morning negotiating the terms of the contract. By noon they had reached agreement. Their attorneys spent the rest of the day drafting the written agreement.

The parties met again on the following morning and signed the agreement. After signing, they remained in Beverly's office to celebrate making the deal. As she was sipping her champagne, Holly said, "You know, I am really unhappy about that advance of $2 million that you agreed to pay me next week. I think that it should be higher, say $2.5 million. After all, I have to live until the box office receipts come in." Beverly replied,

---

8. If this example sounds familiar, it is because it is based on Example 2 of Chapter 10. That example involved the interpretation of an oral contract. In the present example, the contract is recorded in the invoice, which is a written memorial of agreement for parol evidence purposes. The goal of this example is to allow you to consider the parol evidence issue that was absent from Example 2 of Chapter 10. After working through this example, you may find it helpful to review Example 2 of Chapter 10 to compare interpretational issues in the absence of the parol evidence rule. (Note that some of the facts concerning the evidence have been changed or simplified in this example.)

"No problem, I'll send you a check for $2.5 million instead." The parties did not amend the figure of $2 million in the written contract, and this agreement was not otherwise recorded in writing. The next week, Beverly sent a check of $2 million to Holly as specified in the written agreement. She denies ever agreeing to pay more. The written agreement does not have a "no oral modification" clause.

Holly immediately sued for the additional $500,000. Beverly applied for summary judgment on the ground that the written contract clearly calls for a payment of $2 million, and no parol evidence can be tendered by Holly to support her claim for more money. Should Beverly be granted summary judgment?

6. Dick Contra is a famous football star. He was approached by Buffy Beefcake who asked him if he would pose for a nude photograph to be used in a "Superjocks 2007" calendar that Buffy was producing. Buffy told Dick that the calendar would feature one naked sports hero per month. Dick would receive a modest fee of $5,000 (really just an honorarium) for posing and allowing the use of his photo, and all profits from the sales of the calendars would go to a hospital that conducted research on the prevention of sports injuries. Dick was a bit bashful and did not like the idea of being photographed in the nude, but he felt that it was for a good cause, so he agreed. Buffy produced a five-page standard form contract which Dick signed without reading it. Had he read it, he would have seen that it said nothing at all about the donation of the profits to the hospital. Instead, it provided that apart from the payment of the $5,000 fee, Dick had no rights or claims whatsoever, and that all profits from the sale of the calendars would be solely the property of Buffy. The writing also contained a merger clause.

Just before the photo shoot, Dick did read the contract and became aware of its terms. When he asked Buffy why there was no mention of the donation in the writing, Buffy denied ever suggesting that anyone except him would receive any of the profits. Dick would like to terminate the contract. If he does so, what are his chances of avoiding liability for breach?

Explanations

1. Yes, faithless Ava does have a point, because if Ann decides to sue on the basis of Ava's undertaking, she is confronted with two hurdles. She must first convince the judge to admit her evidence of the oral term that qualified the writing, and if she succeeds, she must then convince the jury that such a term was in fact agreed to. A written memorandum of agreement was executed, and Ann seeks to testify about a prior oral agreement Ava may object to admission of the evidence under the parol evidence rule, and the judge must determine

as a question of law whether the evidence is admissible. If not, it is excluded and the jury does not hear it, leaving Ann with no case. If Ann can jump this hurdle by satisfying the judge that the evidence is not barred by the rule and is admissible, she may then testify about the conversation before the jury. The next hurdle is to convince the jury that the conversation occurred. If Ava denies it, Ann will only win if the jury believes her over Ava.

In the first stage of this process, the judge considers two questions. The first concerns the issue of integration and involves two possibilities: First, the writing may have been intended as the full and final expression of the parties' agreement (that is, a total or complete integration). If it is, parol evidence is inadmissible. Even if the writing is not a total integration, the alleged parol term may concern a subject that is itself fully and unambiguously dealt with in the agreement, so that it is intended as a complete expression on this issue (that is, the agreement is a partial integration that fully and finally sets out this term). If so, the evidence is likewise excluded.

If the writing is neither a complete integration, nor a partial integration concerning the subject of the alleged parol term, the judge goes to the next level of the preliminary inquiry to decide the issue of consistency. The parol evidence may be admitted to the extent that it is consistent with what has been recorded in the writing. Thus, the evidence may explain an ambiguity or vagueness, or it may fill a gap, but it may not contradict the writing.

The parties' agreement is **integrated** if they intended the writing to fully express everything that they agreed, so that no additional undertakings were made. Under the strictly objectivist "four corners" test, integration is found if the writing appears complete and unambiguous, and there is no obvious gap or inadequacy. Although the facts do not set out the terms of the contract, they were apparently detailed. At face value, it seems final and complete and would be perceived as integrated under this test.

The contextual approach to integration, more favored by modern courts, goes beyond the face of the writing and evaluates contextual evidence to decide the question of integration. The only contextual evidence here apart from the parol evidence itself (Ann's testimony of the conversation) is the fact that the parties were members of the family that had owned the farm for generations. This has a bearing on the question of integration. If the parties were strangers, dealing at arms length, one would expect a term of this importance to be stated in the apparently complete writing. However, the trust and perceived mutual sentiment engendered by the family relationship might plausibly explain why the parties in this case would be happy to allow the writing to reflect only the routine legal formalities and to omit this more personal aspect of their agreement. The point, as expressed in Restatement Second §216(b) is whether the circumstances are such that the term might naturally be omitted from the writing.

In *Masterson v. Sine*, discussed in section 12.7, the parties' family relationship persuaded the majority that an oral agreement prohibiting the assignment of a repurchase option might naturally be made separately from the writing that granted the option. The dissent rejected the majority's test of integration and went on to say that even if that test was used, the oral agreement did not satisfy it. An agreement directly qualifying an absolute right in the written contract would not naturally be omitted from the writing. These contrary approaches show that the resolution of the question of integration largely depends on how liberal a view the court takes on this issue. It is conceivable but not assured that a court could find that the writing executed by Ann and Ava was not intended as a complete expression of the parties' agreement.

If the judge finds that the writing is not fully integrated, Ann's evidence is admissible provided that it **does not contradict** the writing. The oral agreement does not directly contradict an express term, but a restriction on Ava's right to transfer her property freely does contradict the normal legal assumption that an owner has the right to dispose of her property as she sees fit. This is a more subtle contradiction. A court that distrusts evidence of alleged prior oral agreement can make a good argument that this is a contradiction, but a court that is more amenable to the admission of parol evidence can make an equally good contrary argument. Again, this difference of view appears in the majority and dissenting opinions in *Masterson*. The narrower test of inconsistency would allow Ann to go to trial and to attempt to convince the jury that the oral agreement was made. A wider view would enable the court to dispose of Ann's case summarily.

2. The analysis of this problem is the same as that in Example 1, but Andy's problem is worse than Ann's. To begin with, there is a merger clause in the writing, and an unfilled blank suitable for inserting a term like this. Courts tend to be wary of standard-form merger clauses, because they may not have been conspicuous or understood, but this does not mean that such clauses are invariably treated as ineffective. A signatory has a **duty to read** the document before signing it, and one who fails to exercise that duty cannot expect relief unless the bargaining circumstances compel the conclusion of unfair imposition. (More on this in section 13.12.) There is nothing in the facts of this case to indicate that Andy could not be expected to read

and understand the writing or that Klaus had a bargaining advantage that allowed him to impose unfairly one-sided terms.

On a **four corners** test the apparent completeness of the document, the unfilled blank space, and the merger clause will surely lead to the conclusion of integration. Even on a **contextual** approach, the terms of the writing, including the merger clause, are taken seriously. However, the contextual approach at least gives Andy a shot at explaining why the apparent integration was not intended as such. In other words, Andy is given the opportunity to persuade the court that despite the existence of an apparently complete and final writing, this term might naturally have been agreed to separately. On these facts, this does not seem like an easy task. One basis for making this argument is that a standard form was used which does not admit the addition of special terms tailored to the transaction. However, that will not work here because there was space for its insertion on the form. Family connection or some other relationship may explain an informal approach to some special term of a contract, as discussed in Example 1, but Andy had no prior connection with Klaus.

Section 12.11 discusses the **collateral agreement** rule. As you probably noticed, the facts of this Example are reminiscent of *Mitchell v. Lath* which found the rule to be inapplicable to an oral promise to remove an ice house from property adjacent to the property sold. The underlying rationale of the collateral agreement rule is similar to that of the Restatement Second test. In fact, the tests are really just alternative formulations of the same principle. However, the collateral agreement rule is more difficult to satisfy because it requires the parol agreement to be distinct enough from the writing to qualify as a separate but related agreement. To satisfy this standard, the subject matter of the oral and written agreements must cover different performances with identifiably separate consideration. It is hard to imagine that an oral agreement could qualify as separate if it might not naturally be agreed to separately. In addition, Andy made no promise of additional consideration for the oral promise, and there is no indication that the parties intended to allocate any portion of the property's purchase price to the clearing of the adjacent land.

3.   This example involves a sale of goods, so UCC §2.202, the Article 2 version of the parol evidence rule, applies. In general principle, it is substantially similar to the contemporary common law rule, so many courts would not answer these questions differently had this not been a sale of goods. The writing in this case is apparently intended as a complete integration. It contains all the terms essential to a sales

contract and it has a merger clause. Notwithstanding, it is not a watertight final and complete memorial of agreement, so most of the parol evidence suggested by the questions should be admissible.

3(a). Despite the attempt at integration, the parties did not fully express their agreement. They provided for a discount but failed to specify its amount. With regard to this term, the writing cannot be a complete and final expression of their agreement, so evidence of what they agreed orally is admissible to supplement it. Note that neither denies making an oral agreement, but they argue about what was agreed. Neither party's evidence is inconsistent with the writing, so it will all be admitted and the fact finder will have to decide whose version of the discussion is correct.

3(b). Although the amount of the discount was omitted, the existence of that gap does not give Di license to produce parol evidence on other terms on which the writing is the full and final expression. On a "four corners" test, the agreement is apparently integrated on this issue, and Di would probably prevail on the plain meaning of the word "cash." However, Comment 1 to §2.202 makes it clear that the "four corners" approach is not to be used and that meaning must be determined in the commercial context in which the words were used.[9] This does not mean that we abandon all restrictions on admissibility merely because one of the parties is willing to testify as to a meaning different from the obvious ordinary meaning of the writing. The contextual evidence must point to a meaning of which the writing is reasonably susceptible — it must persuade the court that there is some basis for going beyond the apparent clarity of the writing. If not, the evidence should not be admitted because the party offering it has not shown that the apparently integrated writing suffers from an ambiguity or vagueness that requires explanation. (Alternatively, even if there is no integration, the contended meaning does not explain, but contradicts, the writing.)

The only contextual evidence of the meaning of "cash" is the disputed parol evidence itself: Di's allegation about what was said during negotiations. This self-serving testimony is apparently not corroborated by more objective evidence, such as usage or course of dealing. In the absence of some indication that there is a common understanding or a practice between the parties that "cash" means credit of up to a week, it is difficult to reconcile Di's evidence with the word's normal meaning. Even under the more liberal rule of the UCC (and Restatement Second), the evidence should be excluded.

---

9. The official comments to §2.202 have been redrafted in the 2003 revision of Article 2, and they omit express recognition of this point. However, Article 2 still places strong emphasis on interpretation in the commercial context, and this principle still applies.

3(c). Margie is trying to establish both a course of dealing and a trade usage to show that her faux tequila conforms to the contract even though it has traces of fat, sugar, and alcohol. Section 2.202(a) makes it clear that even if a writing appears fully integrated and has a merger clause, evidence of usage and dealing should always be allowed to supplement or explain the writing.[10] However, they may not contradict it. The rationale for this more liberal rule is twofold. First, parties normally take it for granted that this transaction is subject to well-established custom or their own prior practices, so they are unlikely to trouble spelling them out in the writing. Second, the evidence to establish these facts is objective and harder to make up than an account of what was said in negotiations. Therefore, unless the parties negate usages or prior understandings by clear wording (in which case the evidence would contradict the writing), they are assumed to apply despite the silence of an apparently complete agreement.

There is nothing in the writing to indicate that the parties deliberately excluded the usage or practice claimed by Margie, so the general merger clause does not keep out the evidence, and it is admissible unless it is inconsistent with the writing. The writing unqualifiedly describes the tequila is free of fat, sugar, and alcohol, so it could be argued that the writing is contradicted by testimony that small quantities of these substances are acceptable. This again raises the difficult question of deciding whether a qualification to an absolute undertaking is a supplementation or a contradiction. There is no sure dividing line, but courts tend to favor admission of this kind of objective evidence in cases of doubt, requiring quite strong wording of negation to exclude it. A classic example is *Columbia Nitrogen Corp. v. Royster Co.*, 451 F.2d 3 (4th Cir. 1971), in which the written contract provided for the purchase of a specific minimum tonnage of phosphate. The buyer failed to take the minimum and claimed that because of market uncertainties in the industry it was accepted in the trade that quantity specifications were mere projections. Prior transactions between the parties were also alleged to support that reading of the quantity term. The court of appeals held the evidence admissible, reversing the trial court's determination that it contradicted the writing. Do not forget that the decision to admit the evidence is just the first step in the process. Margie must then convince the fact finder that the course of dealing and trade usage did exist and that they support her position.

4. The issue here is the meaning of the word "regular." Gordon contends that its plain meaning is self-evident, but Fairest Fowls argues that it is

---

10. In the 2003 revision of Article 2, this principle is provided for in §202(1)(a) and (2).

ambiguous if understood in light of trade usage. If Fairest Fowls is right, we need not be concerned about whether the parties expected the writing to be an integration. The ambiguity of the word means that, at least insofar as the quality of the pheasant is concerned, the writing is not a complete and final expression of what the parties agreed. Evidence may therefore be admitted to explain the meaning of "regular" provided that the evidence supports a meaning reconcilable with the writing.

A court adopting a "four corners" approach may be inclined to find that there is no ambiguity about "regular" in the context of the writing as a whole, and that it can only have the meaning contended by Gordon. However, such an approach is clearly not appropriate in a sale of goods, because UCC §2.202, Comment I[11] rejects it and calls for consideration of the commercial context in establishing meaning. The evidence of trade usage will be admitted provided that it is consistent with the writing. As nothing else in the writing even remotely pertains to the quality of the pheasant, the only language that must be reconciled with the proffered evidence is the word "regular" itself. If looked at from the patterns of normal speech, it is hard to think of "regular" as meaning "old and scrawny." However, from the perspective of the trade in which the parties are engaged,[12] the evidence suggests that there is no inconsistency. That is, having decided that trade usage may support such an esoteric meaning, rendering the word ambiguous, we must necessarily conclude that the meaning is not inconsistent with the word.

Section 2.202 gives very strong credence to trade usage, which is presumed to enter the contract unless the parties clearly indicate a contrary intent. Therefore, §2.202 makes it unlikely that the parol evidence rule will preclude admission of a trade usage unless the intent to exclude the usage is unequivocally expressed.

5. The alleged oral term for the payment of $2.5 million directly contradicts the clear and unambiguous provision in the writing for payment of $2 million. Whether or not the agreement is fully integrated, it does definitively express the amount of the advance, and there is no way in which the written and alleged oral terms can be reconciled by interpretation. Therefore, if the oral agreement is contemporaneous with the writing, evidence of it would be barred by the parol evidence rule. However, if the oral agreement was made subsequent to the writing, the parol evidence rule does not apply, and there is no

---

11. See footnote 9, above.
12. In Example 2 of Chapter 10, the issue of defining the trade and holding Gordon accountable for the usage was discussed. This issue is not duplicated here, and the facts indicate that the expert evidence covers the restaurant business, of which Gordon is a member.

provision in the agreement barring oral modifications. This example focuses on what is meant by a subsequent agreement for the purposes of the parol evidence rule. If we take a literal approach, the oral agreement was unquestionably made after the writing, and the evidence is admissible. However, such a technical distinction may lead to an absurd result that places too much emphasis on the sequence of events in a single interaction. The alleged amendment was made almost immediately after the execution of the writing, while the parties were still together following the meeting at which it was signed. If the parties really did agree to change the amount of the advance, it would have been easy and natural for them to alter the writing to reflect the change. The fact that the writing was not amended casts suspicion on the claim that the parties agreed to the change. (This argument would be even stronger if the parties' lawyers and agents were still present when the alleged oral agreement was made.)

A timing issue similar to this arose in *Kehr Packages, Inc. v. Fidelity Bank*, discussed in section 12.3.4. The borrowers alleged that after the written agreement was signed, they made an oral agreement with the lender to increase the amount of the loan. The court found the alleged oral agreement to be contemporaneous with the writing because it was made in the course of the closing process in which the writing had been executed.

6. Dick can only cancel the contract without breaching it if he can prove that Buffy's undertaking to donate the profits to the hospital was a term of the contract. His problem is that this term was agreed orally before the writing was executed and it is absent from the writing. Dick cannot claim that he did not realize at the time of signing the written contract that it failed to reflect the oral understanding. He had a duty to read it and is bound by its terms. (In *Myskina v. Conde Nast Publications, Inc.*, discussed in section 12.7, the court invoked the duty to read and firmly rejected Myskina's argument that she did not read the release because she was not fluent in English.) Although we do not have the full terms of the writing, it is compendious and is likely a fully integrated agreement. The fact that it has a merger clause adds weight to this conclusion. Even if the agreement is found not to be integrated, a prior oral promise to donate the profits to a hospital likely contradicts the express term that the profits belong to Buffy alone.

Although there is not much chance that the parol agreement would be admitted under the normal operation of the parol evidence rule, the facts make out a case for application of the fraud exception. As a matter of public policy, courts do not allow a party to use the parol evidence rule to mask a fraud, so parol evidence is admissible to the extent that it is offered to establish fraud. (See *America's Directories, Inc. v. Stellhorn One Hour Photo, Inc.,* discussed in section 12.12.) We will leave a detailed discussion of the elements of fraud to section 13.6. For now, it is enough to note that a victim of fraud can avoid a contract if he can show that the other party made a fraudulent misrepresentation which justifiably induced him to enter the contract. Although fraud usually involves a misrepresentation of fact, it can also arise where a person makes a contractual promise with the deliberate intention of breaking it.

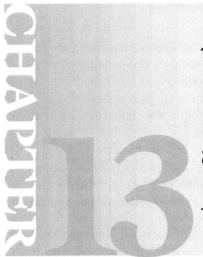

The Judicial Regulation of Improper Bargaining and of Violations of Law and Public Policy

§13.1 INTRODUCTION

This chapter and Chapter 14 deal with several related but distinct doctrines. Sections 13.2 through 13.12 cover a group of doctrines that are designed to regulate improper bargaining: misrepresentation, duress, undue influence, and unconscionability. The theme that connects these doctrines is the balance between the policy of protecting **reliance** that underlies the **objective test** of contract and the policy of **freedom of contract** that dictates not only that parties should have the freedom to enter contracts, but also that they should not be held to contracts to which they did not voluntarily **assent**. Although the objective test focuses on the manifested intent of the parties rather than on their subjective states of mind, a rigid adherence to objectivity could mask the fact that the apparent assent was not genuine, but was obtained by deceit or improper bargaining tactics. The doctrines mentioned above allow the court to go behind the manifestation of intent to decide if a party's apparent agreement is based on an acceptable degree of volition. They are regulatory in that they allow the court to regulate improper bargaining behavior. They are sometimes called policing doctrines.

Section 13.13 deals with a different kind of regulation—the policing of contracts for **compliance with law and public policy**. Although this form of regulation has some affinity to the improper bargaining doctrines, it is distinct. Its focus is not on whether one of the parties induced the other's manifestation of assent by deceit or improper tactics, but whether the contract violates a statute, a rule of common law, or an important public policy.

If it does, the court will not enforce it, even though the parties acted with full knowledge and deliberate intent in entering it. The possibility that a court might refuse to enforce a genuinely consensual contract creates tension between the contractual policies of freedom of contract and assent and the other public policy that is implicated in the transaction. Section 13.3 discusses how courts resolve that tension.

Chapter 14 deals with the problem of lack of contractual capacity, either as a result of minority or of mental illness. Although capacity to contract is a subject distinct from those discussed in this chapter, you will see that there are close connections because it also involves fundamental questions of reliance, assent, and public policy.

§13.2 THE OBJECTIVE TEST AND THE VIABILITY OF APPARENT ASSENT

The discussion of the objective test of assent in section 4.1 stressed that although contract is based on consensus, the law does not require a genuine subjective "meeting of the minds." The focus is on apparent assent, as it would reasonably be perceived by one party from the manifested words and actions of the other. This has to be the general rule, otherwise no one could ever rely on overt indications of assent, and the one party's reasonable expectation of agreement could be defeated by a showing that the other really did not mean what those indications reasonably conveyed.

The principal purpose of the objective test is therefore the protection of reasonable expectations. Although a consistent and unbending application of the test would have the merit of certainty, it could lead to great injustice. For example, Lilly Livered signed a memorandum of agreement to sell her casino to Attila "The Animal" Axehacker. She agreed to the sale because Attila shoved the muzzle of his revolver up her left nostril and indicated his intent to pull the trigger if a signature was not immediately forthcoming. No doubt the signature is a first-class manifestation of assent, but no judge (except for Judge "Greasy" Palmer, who was seen taking a brown paper bag from Attila the other day) would hold Lilly accountable for the reasonable import of her conduct. Not only should she not be held accountable for a manifestation of assent forced out of her, but Atilla was responsible for undermining her free will and cannot legitimately claim that he relied on her assent being volitional. That is, a rigid focus on Lilly's manifested assent — her signature — would serve neither justice nor the goals of contract law. Policing doctrines allow the court to go behind the appearance of assent in cases like this. The policing doctrine applicable in this particular example is duress because Attila induced Lilly's apparent assent by illegitimate threat. Other facts may satisfy the elements of one of the other doctrines discussed below. As a general observation, it can be said that all the doctrines are safety valves for the objective test, so that it cannot be used as a tool of oppression, deceit or advantage-taking.

The evil at which these doctrines aim is *improper behavior in the bargaining process*: trickery, pressure, or unfair persuasion that undermines the victim's free will. For this reason, the principal focus of the doctrines is on the *process of formation* rather than on the unfairness of the resulting terms, and even if the terms of the contract are reasonable, improper bargaining may render it unenforceable. For example, because the means used by Attila to induce assent are wrongful, it would not much matter that he had purchased the casino for a fair price and otherwise on fair terms. However, the *unfairness of the resulting exchange* can be a significant factor in the determination of enforceability. In a case where impropriety is not clearly established, the unfairness of the terms serves as evidence to bolster the claim of wrongful bargaining. Indeed, if the terms are outrageous enough, a court may require only a minimal showing of procedural impropriety as a basis for refusing enforcement.

---

§13.3 GENERAL NOTE ON REMEDY: AVOIDANCE AND RESTITUTION OR ADJUSTMENT OF THE CONTRACT

The remedies available under the improper bargaining doctrines discussed in sections 13.2 through 13.12 form another general thread that runs through this chapter.[1] While there is some variation between them (noted in the discussion of each doctrine), the effect of a successful claim under any of these doctrines tends to be the same.

§13.3.1 Avoidance and Restitution

The usual effect of improper bargaining is to make the resulting contract **voidable** at the instance of the aggrieved party. A voidable contract must be distinguished from a **void** contract. If a contract is void (as it would be, for example, if one party failed to give consideration), it is a legal nullity — in fact it is not a contract at all, so the phrase "void contract" is anomalous. Therefore, neither party can sue to enforce the relationship. By contrast, a voidable contract is a valid contract that remains fully effective unless the

---

1. This discussion is confined to the improper bargaining doctrines. Section 13.13 has its own explanation of remedial issues relating to a contract that is illegal or contrary to public policy.

aggrieved party elects to exercise the right to terminate it. ("Avoidance" is a term of art in contract law, and it is usually confined to situations in which a voidable contract is terminated by the aggrieved party.) In the above example, Lilly, as the victim of duress, has the right to avoid the contract. However, if despite her initial reluctance she now thinks that the transaction is attractive, she may choose not to avoid it. If she desires to keep it in force, Attila is bound. He cannot claim the contract's avoidability as a defense. That power belongs solely to Lilly. However, if the contract had been void, either party would have been able to seek relief on that basis.

The aggrieved party may use the right of avoidance affirmatively, for example, by suing for a declaratory judgment terminating the contract, or defensively, by raising it as a defense when sued on the contract. When a contract is avoided, the general rule is that both parties are entitled to **restitution**. Any benefit received before avoidance by one party from the other must be returned. As the benefit was conferred under a contract that has been brought to an end, retention of the benefit would unjustly enrich the recipient, who no longer has any right to retain it. However, as discussed below, restitution may not be required from an aggrieved party if the benefit received provided no lasting enrichment.

§13.3.2 Excision or Modification of the Offending Term

Although avoidance of the entire contract is usually the remedy sought, in some cases the aggrieved party may prefer to keep the contract but to have its terms adjusted to remove the effects of the other party's improper bargaining. This alternative may not be possible when the problem affects the very basis of the contract, and it is not available in all situations. In other cases, it may be the only remedy available because the problem is not serious enough to merit avoidance. However, in many situations the aggrieved party has a choice between asking the court to avoid the contract or to alter or eliminate the improperly imposed terms.

§13.3.3 The Availability of Damages

Avoidance of the contract or the adjustment of its offending terms are the more conventional remedies for improper bargaining, but in some cases the victim has the alternative of leaving the contract fully in force but claiming damages to compensate for any economic loss caused by wrongful bargaining. This alternative is not available in all cases, but courts do have remedial discretion to award such relief where appropriate. This relief may be aimed at compensating for some loss in consequence of the improper bargaining, or it could compensate for tortious injury where the wrongful act is a tort as well as a bargaining impropriety. Thus, if Lilly afterwards decides to keep the contract in force, she could still sue Attila (if she dares) for the tort of battery. Similarly, as fraud is a tort, the victim of a fraudulent misrepresentation may decide not to avoid the contract, but instead to claim damages in tort for the difference in value between the performance represented and that actually received.

§13.4 THE NATURE AND RELATIONSHIP OF THE DOCTRINES REGULATING BARGAINING

The doctrines considered here are **regulatory** in nature and are often described as **policing** mechanisms. When there is an allegation of unfair bargaining, they allow the court to go behind objective indications of assent to determine if apparent agreement was cajoled by trickery or unfair pressure. This power of regulation must be used with restraint so as to intrude as little as possible on normal and legitimate commercial activity. It is important to recognize that it is not the point of these doctrines to eliminate the advantages of forceful bargaining, savvy decision making or favorable market position. They operate in a free market economy in which contracting parties are expected to try to serve their own interests and to use their available information and resources to obtain the best deal possible. There is nothing inherently wrong in the resourceful use of superior information, clever sales techniques, and the exploitation of advantage. Furthermore, it is to be expected that transactions routinely occur between parties having great disparity in power, sophistication and resources. Regulation aims, not at "leveling the playing field" by cutting down economic advantage, but rather at allowing the court to step in when behavior crosses the line from hard bargaining to unacceptable exploitation. In obvious cases, such as Attila's gun up Lilly's nostril, it is clear that the line has been crossed. But in more equivocal cases opinions differ on the appropriateness of intervention. Some courts and commentators favor policing for only the more extreme cases and see judicial regulation as leading to inefficiency and market interference. Others advocate a more aggressive role for courts as protector of the underdog.

In classical contract law the policing doctrines were very clearly distinguishable and each had relatively firm and specific elements, making it applicable to a narrow range of situations. As they have developed in more recent times (some courts having moved further away than others from the categorizations of classical law), the doctrines have become more fluid so that they have a greater tendency to meld into each other. While they still retain many of their characteristic elements, their points of connection have become more obvious. This means that although the facts of some cases may support the invocation of only one of the doctrines, others may permit alternative analyses under more than one of them. Together, the doctrines form a network of rules that permit courts to deal with a variety of sins that might be committed during the formation of a contract. As we examine the doctrines individually, we will keep an eye on their common ground and interconnections.

§13.5 MISREPRESENTATION GENERALLY: THE MEANING OF "MISREPRESENTATION" AND THE DISTINCTION BETWEEN FRAUDULENT AND NON-FRAUDULENT MISREPRESENTATIONS

§13.5.1 The Distinction Between Fraudulent, Negligent, and Innocent Misrepresentations

A "misrepresentation" is defined in Restatement Second §159 as an **assertion not in accord with the facts**. It is a factually incorrect representation made by one of the parties at the time of contracting. Misrepresentations fall into one of three categories, each of which has different rules. If the assertion is made with knowledge that it is false (that is, a deliberate lie) and with the intention of inducing the other party's agreement, it is **fraudulent**. If the misrepresentation is not a deliberate lie, but reflects a genuine, albeit erroneous, belief by the party making the assertion, it is either **negligent** (the misinformation results from that party's failure to check facts that he had a duty to ascertain) or **innocent**.

The severity and consequences of a misrepresentation depend on the state of mind of the party making the assertion. A fraudulent misrepresentation is the most serious deviation from legal and ethical obligations, which not only violates the contractual obligation of fair dealing, but is also tortious and could have criminal sanctions, too. In addition, a party guilty of fraud cannot be said to have justifiably relied on the other's manifestation of assent. The elements of fraudulent misrepresentation reflect the law's disapprobation of deliberate falsehood: If a fraudulent assertion is proved to have been made, the remaining prerequisites for relief are comparatively lenient. The court may evaluate the consequent inducement on a more subjective standard and the perpetrator's accountability for purposeful deceit usually outweighs any culpability the victim may have for gullibility or carelessness. A negligent or innocent misrepresentation is not as morally reprehensible and may not entirely defeat the perpetrator's reliance interest. Therefore, the decision on whether or not to grant relief involves a closer balancing of the relative culpability of the parties, and a stronger focus on the objective importance (materiality) of the misrepresentation and the victim's duty to verify the facts. Obviously, a negligent misrepresentation weighs more heavily against the perpetrator than an innocent one, and negligence may give rise to tort liability, too.

§13.5.2 The Application of the Parol Evidence Rule to Misrepresentations Made Outside a Written Contract

When a contract is recorded in writing, the misrepresentation may be in the writing itself. If so, the victim of the misrepresentation must prove the falsity of the representation by adducing evidence of facts extrinsic to the writing. The parol evidence rule does not bar this extrinsic evidence because it is not parol evidence. It is not offered to prove a term allegedly agreed to outside the writing, but rather to prove that a fact represented in the writing is wrong.

However, the parol evidence rule does apply where the misrepresentation is not included in the writing, but was allegedly made orally before or at the time of execution of the written contract, or was made in a prior written document. The effect of the parol evidence rule differs depending on whether or not the misrepresentation was fraudulent.

We saw in section 12.12 that even where a written agreement is fully integrated, a party may not invoke the parol evidence rule to exclude proof of a **fraudulent** misrepresentation. The policy of shielding the fact finder from suspect and unreliable parol evidence is outweighed by the policy of protecting a party from dishonesty. Although the parol evidence is admitted, it may not ultimately help the victim of the fraud. As discussed in

391

section 13.6.6, the victim's justifiable reliance on the misrepresentation is one of the elements of fraud, so if the alleged oral misrepresentation directly contradicts an express term in the writing, the victim may not be able to show that she was justified in relying on it.

A **negligent** or **innocent** misrepresentation is not as morally indefensible as a fraudulent one, and is not covered by the exception to the parol evidence rule. Therefore, the rule applies as usual. It bars evidence of a parol misrepresentation where the written contract is fully integrated (and particularly if it contains not only detailed terms but also a merger clause). If the writing is not fully integrated, evidence of a parol misrepresentation that contradicts the written terms is also inadmissible.

§13.6 FRAUDULENT MISREPRESENTATION

§13.6.1 Introduction

To qualify as fraudulent, a misrepresentation must be made with deliberate dishonest intent. The person making it must know it is false and must intend to induce the other party to enter the contract. The most common type of fraud, called **fraud in the inducement**, is a fraudulent misrepresentation concerning a fact that forms the basis of the contract, giving the party to whom it is made a false incentive to enter it. A less common type of fraud, **fraud in the factum**, is a misrepresentation relating to the nature or effect of a document to be signed (for example, persuading someone to sign an order for goods by asserting that it is merely a request for a catalog). The principal difference between them is that fraud in the inducement is generally treated as rendering the contract voidable, but fraud in the factum voids it completely. The discussion and examples in this section are concerned only with the more common fraud in the inducement.

For fraudulent misrepresentation to arise, a party must have made a false representation of fact with knowledge of its falsity and with intent to induce the other party to enter the contract. The other party must have relied on it justifiably to his injury. The materiality of the misrepresentation is expressed as an element by some, but not all courts. We now examine each of these elements.

§13.6.2 What is a "Fact"? Fact, Opinion, Prediction, and Promise

We usually think of a **fact** as something that has existence — an **objectively ascertainable reality**. For example, the seller of a sofa clearly makes a representation of fact if he says "this sofa is made of leather" or "this sofa was made in the U.S.A." If the sofa is actually vinyl or it was made in China, the asserted facts are false. Fact can be distinguished from **opinion** ("I think this is a very beautiful sofa"), a **future prediction** ("this sofa will be the envy of your friends and neighbors"), or a **promise** of future action ("if the sofa does not look good when you put it in your living room, you can return it"). The general rule is that only a misrepresentation of fact constitutes fraud. An opinion or a prediction should be understood as nothing more than an expression of personal belief, taste, or preference, so even if it is not honest, it should not give grounds for relief for fraud. This is particularly true if the expression of opinion or the prediction should be reasonably understood as seller's hype. Similarly, a promise of future action is not a representation of fact, but an undertaking. If it is breached, the proper remedy is a suit for breach of contract, not an action for fraud. However, the distinction between fact, opinion, and promise is not hard and fast. In some circumstances a dishonest opinion or a false promise can constitute a fraudulent misrepresentation.

Contemporary courts recognize that it is not always possible to make a clear distinction between fact and opinion because most **opinions** have a **factual basis**. This is not always true, of course. A seller's claim that a sofa's green and orange plaid fabric is a "fun color" is clearly just opinion. However, if the seller says "this sofa is fashionable," this suggests some familiarity with facts concerning current market trends. The fact-based opinion constitutes a misrepresentation if the party expressing it knows that it is not supported by the facts on which it is based, or if he recklessly makes the statement knowing that he has no clue about the facts on which it is based. Where the opinion of one of the parties is a decisive factor in inducing the other to enter the transaction, the misrepresentation of that opinion goes to the heart of the contract. This is particularly true where the party expressing the opinion has expertise and the other party relies on his recommendation. For example, an attorney who believes that a prospective client has a weak case on the facts makes a fraudulent misrepresentation if he expresses a contrary opinion to the prospective client with the goal of inducing him to hire the attorney to litigate the case.

Rodi v. Southern New England School of Law, 389 F.3d 5 (1st Cir. 2004) is a good illustration of fraudulent opinion. The plaintiff was a law student who was induced to enroll in the law school on the basis of representations that the school was "highly confident" that it would receive American Bar Association accreditation. The school knew that accreditation was important to the plaintiff because he could not be admitted to practice in his state of residence if his degree was not from an accredited school. When the school failed to receive the accreditation in the plaintiff's first year of study, the dean again assured the plaintiff that "there was no cause for pessimism" that the school would be accredited before he graduated. It was not, and the plaintiff sued. The district court dismissed his claim, but the court of appeals reversed and permitted the case to go to trial on a theory of fraudulent misrepresentation. The school knew that it had substantial problems in obtaining accreditation, and the plaintiff had made a credible preliminary showing that the opinions expressed by school officials were not honest, given their knowledge of the A.B.A.'s criteria and the school's prospects of satisfying them.

A **future prediction** is not a misrepresentation of an existing fact but an opinion about what might come to pass after the contract has been executed. It is really no different conceptually than an opinion, and should be approached in the same way. (In the above example involving the attorney, his assessment of his client's case is both an opinion and a prediction.) If the prediction is based on facts that are known at the time of contracting, it must be an honest assessment of how those facts will lead to the predicted result.

A **promise of future performance** is not a representation of fact, but an expression of intent. However, it relates to the present state of mind of the party making it and if it dishonestly represents that state of mind, it could qualify as a fraudulent misrepresentation. It can be very difficult to distinguish a mere breach of contract from a fraudulent misrepresentation of intent. To assert fraud it is not enough for the victim to show that the promise was broken. He must prove that at the time the contract was made, the party making the promise intended not to keep it. Although fraud can be proved by circumstantial evidence, so it is not necessary to have direct evidence of the promisor's state of mind in the form of an admission, it can be very difficult to establish that the promisor had already made up his mind to breach, especially if the promisor was careful to keep its intent hidden.

We saw an example of a fraudulent promise in *American Directories, Inc. v. Stellhorn One Hour Photo*, 833 N.E.2d 1059 (Ind. App. 2005), discussed in relation to the fraud exception to the parol evidence rule in section 12.12. The court held that it could qualify as fraud where a seller of advertising in a phone directory made a promise that the buyer could cancel the contract after a year, intending at the time of making the promise not to honor it. *Carey. v. FedEx Ground Package System, Inc.*, 321 F. Supp. 2d 902 (S.D. Ohio 2004), discussed in section 8.9.2 in relation to promissory estoppel, is another example. Recall that FedEx had kept Carey waiting for a delivery route for almost two years. During this period, it induced Carey to incur economic detriment by reiterating the assurance that he would receive the route while it took advantage of his services as a temporary driver. The court denied FedEx's motion for summary judgment and allowed Carey to proceed to trial on the basis of promissory estoppel. In addition, the court held that Carey had made out a cause of action for fraud. The court noted that although fraud is not usually predicated on a promise of future action, such a promise can qualify as fraudulent if the promisor has no intention of keeping the promise.

Sometimes it is not easy to decide if a misrepresentation related to a fact or to a promise — a representation of future intent. *Kaloti Enterprises, Inc. v. Kellogg Sales Co.*, 699 N.W.2d 205 (Wis. 2005) is a case with such an ambiguity. Kaloti and Kellogg had a long-standing arrangement under which Kaloti bought Kellogg products which it resold to large stores. Kellogg then decided to change its marketing procedures by selling some of its products directly to the same large stores that were Kaloti's customers. As a result, Kellogg would become Kaloti's competitor in that wholesale market. After it had made this decision, Kellogg accepted an order from Kaloti without telling it that Kellogg was about to devour its market. Kaloti only discovered this upon hearing from its customers that they would be buying directly from Kellogg. Kaloti sued Kellogg when it refused Kaloti's demand for cancellation of the sale and refund of the price. The issue in the case was whether Kellogg's failure to tell Kaloti about its impending change in marketing strategy constituted a fraudulent misrepresentation. The court held that Kaloti had made a sufficient case of fraud to overcome an application for dismissal. We will discuss the nondisclosure aspect of the opinion in section 13.6.2b. For present purposes, it is worth noting that the court, without any discussion, simply treated Kellogg's decision to sell its products directly to stores as a fact. However, the fact in issue is Kellogg's intent. If so, the question to be asked is whether Kellogg made a promise, implied from the parties' course of dealing or from a general obligation of good faith and fair dealing, that it would not undercut Kaloti's market. If there was such a promise, did Kellogg intend to break it when making it? The outcome might be the same, but the route to it is different.

§13.6.3 Types of Fraudulent Misrepresentation: Affirmative Statements, Concealment, and Nondisclosure

a. Affirmative False Statement

An affirmative false statement (such as the seller's assertion, mentioned in section 13.6.2, that a vinyl sofa is made of leather) is the most direct and easily identifiable type of fraudulent misrepresentation. *Rozen v. Greenberg*, 886 A.2d 924 (Md. App. 2005) illustrates fraud by affirmative misrepresentation. Greenberg was a tax preparer who specialized in preparing returns for Israeli clients. She received an e-mail from Rozen, whom she did not know, suggesting that as they were in the same business, they should enter into a cooperative arrangement. In the e-mail he represented that he had "headed" a tax preparation service for Israelis for "the last few years." He referred her to his organization's "powerful" Web site. On visiting the Web site, Greenberg read that the organization had a team of account and tax professionals headed by Rozen, who was an experienced CPA. In a subsequent phone conversation, Rozen again told Greenberg that he was very experienced and had many people working for him. Greenberg then met with Rozen who took her to show her what he claimed to be his office, which was very impressive. As a result of these representations, Greenberg agreed to sell her client list to Rozen in exchange for a share of the income that he generated from preparing her clients' returns. It turned out that at the time that he contacted Greenberg, Rozen had no business and no clients and had prepared no tax returns. He had only been a CPA for a few weeks and the office that he showed Greenberg belonged to a tax preparation company at which he was employed. The court of appeals affirmed the trial court's decision that these misrepresentations were fraudulent. (We will return to this case shortly in relation to the other elements of fraud.)

Willen v. Hewson, 622 S.E.2d 187 (N.C. App. 2005) is another example of affirmative fraud. The seller of a large house on an estate advertised it as "peaceful" and "serene." When the buyer inspected the estate, he met the seller's niece who mentioned that there had been problems with "kids coming onto the property after high school football games around Halloween." This caused the buyer some concern and he called the seller to ask her if there had been trespass problems on the property. She assured him that such incidents occurred only once or twice and that her niece was prone to exaggeration. After the buyers bought and moved into the house they found that there was a serious and constant problem with trespass and vandalism which they could not eliminate even by installing a security system and fence. The court of appeals upheld the trial court's determination that the seller was aware of the trespass problem and had made a fraudulent misrepresentation by advertising the property as "peaceful" and "serene" and by answering the buyer's inquiry dishonestly.

b. Concealment

Deliberate conduct to hide a fact is also an affirmative act. Although it may not involve any verbal lie, it is just as dishonest and morally reprehensible. *Jablonski v. Rapalje,* 14 A.D.3d 484 (N.Y. 2005) is a good example. In contrast to *Willen,* which involved human pests, *Jablonski* was concerned with trespassing bats which inhabited the attic of the house bought by the plaintiff. The bat infestation was serious and ongoing. Over the 36 years that the sellers had lived in the house, they had tried to get rid of the bats, but they always returned. During the time that the buyer inspected the house preparatory to buying it, the sellers went to considerable trouble to conceal the bat infestation by using mothballs (which bats apparently dislike) and floodlights to keep them away and by cleaning up the telltale signs of bat presence such as bat droppings and urine. (The case also involved an affirmative misrepresentation. On one occasion the sellers did not do the best job in disposing of droppings, which the buyer noticed. The sellers asserted that they were bird droppings.) The court refused the seller's motion for summary judgment and permitted the buyer to proceed to trial on the basis of fraudulent concealment. *Weintraub v. Krobatsch,* 317 A.2d 68 (N.J. 1974) is an equally delightful case involving a cockroach infestation of nightmarish proportions. The court declined the seller's application for summary judgment and permitted the buyer of a house to proceed to trial on the theory that the seller actively concealed the presence of cockroaches by leaving all the lights on.

c. Nondisclosure (Silence)

Affirmative dishonesty, whether in the form of a false statement or active concealment of the truth, is the clearest case of fraud. However, under some circumstances, a person can commit fraud by keeping silent and failing to disclose a fact. Nondisclosure is the most difficult basis for claiming fraud because it is only fraudulent if the circumstances impose a duty on the party to disclose information. The usual assumption is that where parties contract, each is a free agent in the market, entitled to act out of self-interest. A party may use the advantage of superior information, and owes no duty to the other to reveal facts that motivate her to enter the transaction or that make it particularly attractive to her. Therefore, a buyer of property, having studied the market carefully, is not obliged to tell the seller that the property is underpriced, and the buyer of a commodity does not have to tell the seller that its research on crop yield indicates that the price will soar after the sale. Notwithstanding, a party does not have the absolute and invariable right to keep information secret. Under some circumstances honesty and fair dealing require disclosure. The difficult question is to know when the line is crossed between facts that may fairly be kept private and those that must be revealed.

Restatement, Second, §161 provides guidelines to answer this question. It says that nondisclosure amounts to an assertion that a fact does not exist where the party knows that disclosure of that fact is necessary to correct a previous assertion, or when there is a relationship of trust between the parties. It also requires disclosure where the party knows that it is necessary to correct the other party's mistake as to a basic assumption of the contract, and nondisclosure would violate the duty of good faith and fair dealing. The concept of good faith and fair dealing is quite open-ended and fact-based, so it depends on the circumstances of each case. Two signifcant factors that may be relevant are whether the information should be treated as the property of the party who possesses it (for example, because that party has incurred cost and effort in conducting research or inquiry to obtain it) and whether the information is readily available on diligent inquiry.

A good illustration of the duty to disclose is provided, regrettably, by another creepy-crawly case, this time involving termites. In *Hill v. Jones,* 725 P.2d 1115 (Ariz. 1986) the sellers of a house did not tell the buyers that it had been infested with termites in the past. (The termites had been eradicated, so the problem related to damage that they had caused.) Having gone to the trouble of keeping this quiet, the sellers made the unfortunate mistake of leaving telltale brochures in the kitchen drawer which the buyers discovered after they moved in. The court refused summary judgment for the sellers and allowed the buyers to proceed to trial on the question of whether the duty of fair dealing required the seller to reveal the termite damage.[2]

Just for the sake of getting away from bugs and dealing with a more serious hidden defect in a house, it is worth mentioning everyone's favorite nondisclosure case, *Stambovsky v. Ackley*, 572 N.Y.S.2d 672 (A.D. 1991) in which the court allowed the buyer of a house to proceed to trial on the grounds that the seller failed to disclose that the house was reputed to be haunted. (Unlike the buyers in *Willen* and *Jablonski* who actually encountered the trespassers and bats, the buyer here did not allege that he met the ghosts. It was the reputation of the house that bothered him.) The fact that the seller had widely publicized the haunting, but the buyer was not aware of it and could not ascertain it by reasonable inspection, persuaded the court that fair dealing imposed a disclosure duty on the seller.

Kellogg, discussed in section 13.6.2, also involves nondisclosure. The court considered whether Kellogg had the duty to disclose to Kaloti that it had decided to change its marketing strategy by selling its products directly to Kaloti's customers. It noted that as a general rule, parties transacting on the free market are not normally expected to share knowledge relating to the transaction. However, commercial mores play a significant role in deciding when fair dealing imposes a duty to disclose. Those mores pointed in the direction of disclosure where Kellogg planned by its own action to render Kaloti's purchase unprofitable. In addition, it was significant that the information was possessed exclusively by Kellogg, and Kaloti had no means of discovering it by diligent inquiry.

§13.6.4 Knowledge of Falsity and Intent to Induce the Contract

A guilty state of mind is essential to fraud. This state of mind has two components — **knowledge of falsity** (called **"scienter"**) and an **intent to mislead**. Although it may be possible for one but not the other to exist, in most cases they go hand-in-hand. In defining knowledge of falsity, Restatement Second §162 covers not only an assertion made with the actual

---

2. There were some strategically placed boxes and a potted plant that covered some holes in the floor, so there was also a possibility of active concealment. In addition, the buyers had noticed rippling in the parquet floor which was consistent with termite damage and had asked the sellers about it. They had replied that it was water damage, which may or may not have been true. Accordingly, the buyers may have been able to establish a fraudulent assertion as well.

knowledge that it is not in accord with the facts, but also an assertion made without confidence in its truth or without a known basis in fact. This means that there is some blurring of the line between fraudulent and negligent misrepresentation, because reckless disregard for the truth or an extreme degree of negligence in ascertaining information before making an assertion may qualify as fraud.

§13.6.5 Materiality

It seems logical to assume that relief for fraud should only be available if the misrepresentation was material — that it affected the basis of the bargain in a significant way. It does not make much sense to allow a party to avoid a contract for fraud if the misrepresentation concerned an unimportant aspect of the transaction. However, there is some confusion as to whether materiality is an element of fraud. Restatement, Second §162, comment c and §164 do not require the victim of fraud to prove materiality. It confines the need to establish materiality to negligent or innocent misrepresentations. Some courts follow this approach, but others specifically list materiality as one of the elements of fraud. (For example, most of the cases mentioned above, *Kellogg, Stambovsky, Hill, Jablonski, Willen,* and *Rozen* all assert that the misrepresentation must be material.) Some cases adopt an approach between these two by requiring materiality where fraud is based on nondisclosure, but not where it is by affirmative statement or conduct.

This divergence does not seem to have a significant impact on the result of the cases and it is more subtle than might appear. It is best understood as a matter of perspective rather than of clear doctrinal conflict. Under all formulations of the test for fraud, the victim must establish justifiable reliance, so a fraudulent misrepresentation of a trivial fact is not likely to lead to relief. By not emphasizing the materiality of the fraudulent misrepresentation, Restatement, Second and courts that follow its formulation focus more strongly on subjective inducement. That is, they do not ask whether the misrepresentation is objectively important, but look at whether it induced this particular victim. By contrast, courts that require materiality as an element incline to a somewhat more objective evaluation of the impact of the misrepresentation. Notwithstanding, it is difficult to draw a bright line between these approaches, because even courts that include materiality as an element of fraud tend to take the subjective attributes of the victim into account, as discussed in section 13.6.6.

§13.6.6 Justifiable Inducement

There must be a causal link between the fraud and the contract — that is, the fraud must have motivated the victim to enter the contract, or to enter it on the terms that were agreed. If the victim would have entered the contract on those terms anyway had she known the truth, or if the victim was not justified in relying on the misrepresentation, she is not entitled to relief. As you can see, part of this inquiry is directly linked to the question of the materiality of the misrepresentation but it goes beyond that. In addition, the court must evaluate the impact of the false fact on the victim's state of mind. The difficult question here is whether this impact should be measured objectively (was the victim reasonable in relying on the misrepresentation) or subjectively (even if a reasonable person may not have been hoodwinked, was this victim in fact induced to enter the contract). Although, as we have seen frequently, the law tends to favor an objective test in most situations, public policy dictates a less objective standard where fraud is involved. When a court balances the fault of the perpetrator, who has deliberately lied, against the fault of the victim, who may have been unduly gullible or even careless in believing the misrepresentation, the balance usually weighs in favor of the victim. The result in most cases is a blend of objective and subjective considerations. That is, the court asks whether the victim was in fact induced, but also tests this inducement against the question of whether she would have been induced had she acted reasonably. Often, these inquiries point in the same direction because if a reasonable person would not have relied on the false fact, the victim may have trouble showing, in the absence of some special individual circumstances or attributes, that she in fact relied on it. One can also detect that courts apply a different degree of objective assessment depending on whether the misrepresentation was active (a statement or concealment) or by nondisclosure. Courts are more likely to impose a tougher standard of reasonable inquiry on the victim where the fraud lies in failure to disclose facts.

The cases discussed in section 13.6.3 illustrate the element of justifiable reliance and the blend of subjective and objective considerations that go into determining justification. *Stambovsky* considered that the buyer could justifiably have been mislead by the nondisclosure because he was not local, had no reason to know of the house's reputation, and could not have discovered the ghosts by reasonable inspection of the house. In *Rozen*, the court recognized that Greenberg was not experienced in the sale of a business and was rather gullible. However, the court focused on Greenberg's subjective attributes and rejected the argument that she reasonably could and should have investigated Rozen, should have called for references, and should have noticed that the office that she was taken to did not belong to him. In *Willen*, the court approached the buyers' reliance from a reasonableness perspective but rejected the seller's argument that the buyers' reliance on her assertions was unreasonable because her niece's mention of the trespassing problem should have caused them to conduct an independent investigation. The court noted that there were no visible indicia of trespass and vandalism to place the buyers on inquiry and, in any event, even if the buyers were unreasonable, the seller cannot seek to avoid the consequences of her false representation by arguing that the buyers should not have trusted her. In *Jablonski*, the buyer visited the house many times and had it professionally inspected. The buyer observed the bat droppings on one occasion, noticed the floodlights in the attic, and also smelled the mothballs and bat urine.[3] The court disagreed with the sellers' contention that the buyer's reliance was not justifiable because he had ample opportunity to discover the bats. Applying a reasonable diligence standard, the court found that there was enough evidence to suggest that the sellers had thwarted the buyer's ability to discover the infestation.

§13.6.7 Injury and Remedy

Courts commonly include as a final element of fraud that the victim must have been injured. Injury is easy to see if misrepresentation caused the victim to overpay for the contractual performance — that is, that the performance is valueless or less valuable than it would have been had the representation been true. For example, the presence of bats, bugs, or vandals very likely diminished the market value of the houses in *Jablonski*, *Weintraub*, and *Willen*, or would have resulted in cost to rectify the unpleasant features. In buying Kellogg products that it could not sell, Kaloti surely suffered loss of its anticipated profit, and may have been saddled with unsaleable goods. However, sometimes the precise economic injury is more difficult to ascertain. For example, say that the reputed presence of ghosts had no effect on the market price of the house in *Stambovski* or that Rozen did a decent job on the tax returns of Greenberg's clients and generated the expected profits. The fact that there may be no measurable economic loss in these cases does not inevitably mean that there is no injury. The injury could lie simply in the fact that the victim finds herself in a contract that is completely different from what she expected and wanted.

The alternative remedies available for fraud allow a court to give relief whether or not actual economic loss resulted from the fraud. Even if there is no economic loss, a victim who does not desire the contract because of the misrepresentation is entitled to **avoid** it — to claim **rescission**. Upon rescission, a claim for **restitution** arises in favor of a party who has performed in whole or in part. In the absence of a contract, there is no basis for retaining a benefit given under the contract, so principles of unjust enrichment require that benefit to be returned. Benefit is measured by the value of property, which could be different from its contract price. This principle applies whether it is the victim or the perpetrator who has been enriched. However, the law imposes limits on the restitutionary rights of the perpetrator. Any

---

3. I hope you are not reading this case while eating. Just in case you are, it is also worth mentioning that on one occasion the buyer heard the toilet flushing repeatedly while he was waiting at the front door of the house. The buyer discovered later that the realtor (who was also a defendant in the case) was busy scooping up bat droppings and flushing them.

doubts on the value of his performance are resolved against him. In addition, the victim is not obliged to return property or its value to the extent that it was worthless when received or deteriorated as a result of its own defects. (See Restatement, Second, §§164, 376, and 385).

As noted in section 13.3, a contract induced by fraud is voidable, not void. This means that the victim may elect to rescind it if she desires, but may choose to keep it in force. If she does so, she can claim **damages** to compensate for the difference between the actual value of the performance and the value that it would have had as represented. This damages claim includes such losses as reduction in market value or the costs of bringing the property into the condition as represented.

Traditionally, the remedy of rescission and restitution derives from **contract** law, but the remedy of damages has its roots in **tort** (fraud being a tort as well as a breach of contract). This could make a difference to remedy. For example, a court that applies the traditional distinction would allow a plaintiff who sues for damages to claim punitive damages as well, because the suit is based on tort. However, punitive damages are not available in contract, so a court following the traditional distinction would not award punitive damages if the plaintiff sued for rescission. This does not make a lot of sense, since the defendant's wrongful act is exactly the same, whichever form of relief is sought. Also, a rigorous focus on the tort-contract distinction would mean that if a plaintiff sues for rescission, she cannot claim any damages, even if the tort led to economic loss. This distinction between the contract and tort derivation of the alternative remedies has faded, and many modern courts do not apply it. Rather, they simply treat the remedies as available possibilities and provide the relief called for by the harm to the victim. This means that in appropriate circumstances, a court may award rescission together with damages for proven loss beyond restitution (offset by any restitution due to the perpetrator), or that it may permit punitive damages in a rescission suit.

§13.7 NEGLIGENT OR INNOCENT MISREPRESENTATION

A misrepresentation made without the deliberate intent to mislead is classified either as negligent or innocent. (As mentioned earlier, a grossly negligent misrepresentation may qualify as fraud, because knowledge of falsity could be inferred where an assertion is made without confidence in its truth or a known basis in fact.) The distinction between negligence and innocence is not always easy to make, and it depends on the circumstances of each case. A misrepresentation is negligent if the person making it failed to act with reasonable care in ascertaining and communicating the truth, but it is innocent if no such duty was breached.

Although negligent and innocent misrepresentations do not carry the same degree of disapprobation as a deliberate lie, they do permit avoidance if they are material and have induced justifiable reliance. Restatement Second §§162, 163, and 164 make only one significant distinction between fraudulent and non-fraudulent misrepresentations: When the misrepresentation is not fraudulent, it recognizes **materiality** as an element.[4] Thus, an innocent or negligent misrepresentation only gives grounds for relief if it relates to a fact central to the transaction, and the party making the misrepresentation knew or had reason to know of its importance. It follows from this that the **test of justifiable reliance** is correspondingly strengthened, because materiality to the victim is seen from the reasonable perspective of the other. This approach accords with the general idea that some balance must be struck between the fault of the misrepresenting party and the reasonable expectations of the victim. To the extent that the misrepresenter is less culpable, one would expect a stronger showing of the importance of the misrepresentation and the victim's reasonable reliance. It was also noted in section 13.5.2 that parol evidence of a non-fraudulent misrepresentation is excluded by the parol evidence rule if the writing is integrated or the term is inconsistent with a partially integrated writing.

It can be difficult to distinguish an innocent or negligent misrepresentation from a **contractual promise**. For example, the seller of a house, having inspected it and found no termites, informs the buyer that the house is termite-free. If termites are present this could qualify as a misrepresentation, or it could be a warranty — a contractual promise that the house does not have termites. If it is the former, the remedy of avoidance is appropriate, but if it is the latter, the failure of the house to comply with the warranty is a breach of contract, giving rise to the remedies discussed in Chapter 18. The distinction is largely factual and interpretational. It depends on whether the assertion was merely a statement inducing the contract or was actually incorporated into the contract to become one of the promises made as part of the seller's consideration for the price of the house.

§13.8 DURESS

§13.8.1 The Nature of Duress

In older contract law, duress was available as a ground of avoiding a contract only in extreme circumstances. A party claiming duress had to show that the other had induced the contract by using **actual force** or an **unlawful threat**

---

4. As noted in section 13.6.5, Restatement Second does not require materiality for fraud even though many courts do.

of death or bodily harm (not merely property damage). In addition, the test of inducement was objective: The threat must have been such as would overcome the resistance of a person of "ordinary firmness." The example in section 13.2, involving Lilly Livered's sale of her casino at gunpoint to Attila "The Animal" Axehacker is a classic case of duress in this sense. Even under these strict standards, Lilly should be able to avoid the contract by showing that Attila engaged in the threatening conduct, that it was unlawful and constituted a credible threat, and that she was not being unduly wimpy in giving in to it.

During the last several decades duress has moved beyond these narrow confines. It is generally accepted that a person's free will can be undermined by unfair pressure short of physical compulsion or a threat of looming personal injury. **"Economic duress"** — an illegitimate threat to proprietary or economic interests — is well-recognized in modern cases as a basis for relief. Also, the strongly objective test of "ordinary firmness" has been abandoned in favor of a less rigorous standard that combines objective and subjective factors: Did the victim have **no reasonable alternative** but to agree? Duress has thus become a much broader doctrine, better able to accommodate situations in which one party uses subtle threats or improper pressure to gain the other's acquiescence to a transaction. As with fraud, the basis of avoidance is consistent with, but an exception to, the general objective test of assent. The underlying rationale is that the victim should not be held accountable for her apparent assent when it is not genuine, and the other party, having improperly induced it, does not have a compelling reliance interest.

The contemporary approach to duress is set out in Restatement Second §§174, 175, and 176. Section 174 deals with the rare situation in which a person's manifestation of assent is **physically compelled,** so that the act of manifesting assent is completely lacking in free will. For example, instead of Attila placing his gun up Lilly's nostril, inducing her to sign, he actually clasps her fingers around a pen and forces her hand across the paper to make a signature. Because Lilly is rendered like an automaton by the physical compulsion, §174 treats such an apparent contract as **void.** We need not be further concerned with this unusual situation, and turn to the more common forms of duress, covered by §§175 and 176, in which an **improper threat** has the effect of making the contract **voidable.** In essence, these sections set out the following elements: one of the parties must make a threat; the threat must be improper; and it must induce the apparent assent, in that it leaves the victim no reasonable alternative but to agree.

§13.8.2 The Threat

Although the contemporary doctrine of duress still requires an improper threat, the modern concept of threat has expanded well beyond the confines of its original scope. Today, a threat may be defined as an indication of intent to do or refrain from doing something so as to inflict some harm, loss, injury, or other undesirable consequences that would have an adverse effect on the victim's person or personal or economic interests. This encompasses a wide range of behavior, including not only **explicit** intimidation, but also subtle or even unspoken threats. The presence of an **implied** threat is determined by interpretation in the usual way, taking into account the circumstances of the relationship between the parties. The transaction is examined in context to ascertain if the words or actions of the one party show a reasonable intent to make a threat, reasonably so understood by the other. The threat may either be to take positive **action** or to **refrain from acting**, and the **harm** may consist of any adverse consequences sufficient to overcome the victim's resistance to the contract. A threat could even be implicit in the transaction when one party knows that the other will suffer undesirable consequences if the contract is not made, and uses this knowledge to take unfair advantage of the other's need.

While this wider and more realistic scope allows courts to police less obvious forms of duress, it is less certain and stable than the earlier, more rigid approach. As a result, it presents the danger of undue judicial interference in borderline cases where the line blurs between **legitimate hard bargaining** and **improper coercion**. In this area it must be used cautiously, because duress doctrine should be used only when there has been wrongful bargaining conduct, and should not be misapplied to overturn a tough or burdensome contract simply because one of the parties has managed to use bargaining advantage effectively.

An example will illustrate how difficult it can be to distinguish legally acceptable market behavior from unfair pressure: Say that Lilly needs to sell her casino quickly because she urgently needs money to pay for an operation to cure a dangerous medical condition. Attila knows of her trouble and also knows that she will have difficulty finding a buyer quickly. He therefore offers her less than market price for her casino. Because her need for the money is desperate, she sees no alternative but to sell to Attila for that price. Clearly, Attila has taken advantage of her plight, but the only threat he has made is that unless she meets his terms, he will not contract with her. Such a threat is implicit in all contract negotiations, so it can hardly be viewed as duress. This could simply be treated as a case in which Attila has used his market position to obtain a favorable deal.[5] In this example, Lilly's bargaining weakness was caused by her need for an operation, so her case invokes easy sympathy. Some needs are less compelling and thus move away from the borderline of duress, more clearly falling into the realm of legally

---

5. Although these facts do not fit comfortably into the elements of duress, if Attila's bargaining strategy is unfair and it results in unfair contract terms, the doctrine of unconscionability may provide relief to Lilly.

acceptable market interaction. Say, for example, that Attila desperately craved to own Lilly's casino, but Lilly refused to sell it unless he paid an exorbitant price. If Attila succumbs to his desires and agrees to buy at that price, he cannot claim that he acted under duress.

Because relief for duress is premised on wrongful coercion by one of the contracting parties, that party must usually be responsible for the threat. If the threat is made by a non-party, the victim cannot normally avoid the contract unless the other party is implicated in the threat or knowingly took advantage of it. Outside pressure should not readily defeat the legitimate expectations of an innocent party who relied on the transaction in good faith and without knowledge of the threat. For example, Attila made several fair and increasingly generous offers to buy Lilly's casino but Lilly steadfastly rebuffed him every time until, one day, she received a visit from his godfather, Bull "The Butcher" Bloodbath, who threatened to smash her kneecaps unless she sold to Attila. Duress is clearly present if Attila is in some way implicated in his godfather's threat. However, if Attila's godfather acted entirely independently and without Attila's knowledge, application of the doctrine of duress would defeat Attila's honest reliance interest in the fair contract. This means that in most cases, the victim cannot raise the defense of duress. However, the protection of Attila's reliance is not absolute, and may be outweighed by the public policy of protecting people from violence. Therefore, where the conduct of the non-party amounts to actual physical force against the victim or the threat of such force, the duress may be serious enough to render the contract void, not just voidable. The effect of this is that the contract is a nullity and cannot be enforced, even though Attila was entirely innocent and did not instigate or have knowledge of the duress. (Restatement, Second §174 gives some recognition to this principle, but would invoke it only where the physical compulsion is so great as to render the victim a mere instrument of the perpetrator.)

§13.8.3 Impropriety

When is a threat improper? In addition to the obvious threats of criminal or tortious conduct, modern law tends to take a broad view of impropriety, so that it could include any threatened behavior that **goes beyond the legitimate rights** of the party applying the pressure, or that constitutes an abuse of those rights. This would include, for example, a threat to engage in vexatious litigation, to withhold a performance or property to which the victim is entitled, to disclose information that would embarrass the victim, or otherwise to do something spiteful or vexatious purely for the sake of hurting the victim. It is, of course, not duress to threaten consequences, even dire ones, that may lawfully and properly be pursued in the absence of agreement. For example, at the time for renewal of an employment contract, an employee who has become indispensable may legitimately threaten to quit unless the employer agrees to a substantial raise. Similarly, a person with a colorable tort claim may justifiably threaten to sue unless the tortfeasor agrees to a settlement. However, a threat to file criminal charges is regarded as improper, even if prosecution is warranted, because it is against public policy for a person to use the threat of criminal prosecution as a bargaining chip.

§13.8.4 Inducement

As noted earlier, the older test for inducement was objective. It required not only that the threat was credible, but also that it would have overcome the resistance of a person of "ordinary firmness." The contemporary test is not so rigorous. Although it has an objective element, it also takes the *subjective attributes of the victim* into account, recognizing that a bully should not be able to enforce a contract merely because his victim is easily intimidated. The inquiry is whether, under all the circumstances, the duress *substantially overcame the free will of this party*, leaving him *no reasonable alternative* but to acquiesce. Inducement is therefore considered not in the abstract, but in light of the victim's needs, personality, and circumstances.

An alternative is only reasonable if it is a feasible and practical means of evading the consequences of the threat. If it would be unduly burdensome or risky, or would not likely avoid the threatened consequences, the victim cannot be said to have had a reasonable alternative to manifesting assent. For example, say that Attila owes Lilly $1 million from a prior transaction. He threatens not to pay her unless she agrees to sell her casino to him. Lilly does have the alternative of refusing to sell and commencing suit against Attila for the debt. However, this alternative is not reasonable for Lilly if she needs the money immediately and cannot afford the cost and delay of litigating to enforce payment.

§13.8.5 Remedy

It is sometimes said that when a contract is induced by an extreme degree of duress, such as actual physical force or a threat of physical violence, the contract is void, because there has been no assent. However, because duress doctrine is designed to protect the victim, the more common and logical approach is to treat it as *voidable* at the victim's election. (The situation involving extreme physical violence by a third party, discussed in section 13.8.2, is a narrow exception.) The victim may choose to abide by the contract despite the duress, or may decide to avoid it, claim restitution of any benefit conferred, and tender restoration of any benefit received.

The remedy of avoidance and restitution is subject to the same general principles discussed in connection with misrepresentation.

Although in most cases the victim must choose between keeping the contract, subject to all its terms, or avoiding it entirely, there are circumstances in which courts allow a middle path — retention of the contract subject to an **adjustment** of its terms. For example, if a party desires to keep property purchased, but can show that she was forced to pay an excessive price for it, the court may enforce the contract, subject to a refund to the victim of the amount in excess of fair value. If the act of duress is a tort, the victim is able to obtain *damages in tort* in addition to any relief under contract law.

§13.9 DURESS IN THE MODIFICATION OF AN EXISTING CONTRACT

Section 7.5 deals with the **pre-existing duty rule**, a rule of consideration doctrine declaring that a party does not suffer a legal detriment by promising to do what he is already bound to do under an existing contract. It follows from this rule that the modification of one party's contractual performance is not binding unless it is supported by new consideration given by the other. The principal purpose of the rule is to invalidate a one-sided contractual modification extracted by a party who threatens not to perform unless his compensation is increased. This indirect approach to policing modifications is illustrated by *Alaska Packers Assn. v. Domenico*, 117 F. 99 (9th Cir. 1902). A cannery contracted with a group of fishermen to harvest salmon during the short Alaskan season. After the fishermen had been transported to Alaska and the season had begun, they refused to continue work unless their wages were increased. (Their demand was based on the pretext that working conditions were more burdensome than expected, but this contention was disputed by the employer and not accepted at trial.) The employer had to acquiesce because it would have been impossible to get a replacement crew to Alaska in time for the harvest, but when the fishermen claimed the extra wages at the end of the season, the employer refused to pay. The court found against the fishermen on the basis that they had incurred no new detriment in exchange for the promise of a wage increase. However, the opinion makes it clear that the true reason for nonenforcement was that the court considered the demand for more money to have been extortionate and unjustified.

It was pointed out in section 7.5.2 that consideration doctrine is a clumsy tool for policing coerced modifications. It does not allow for easy discrimination between legitimate and improper modifications, and it can be circumvented if the party demanding the modification undertakes some new detriment of relatively small value in relation to the gain to be received, or if the parties go through the ritual of terminating the original contract and executing a new one. It is more efficient to focus directly on the problem of coerced modification by evaluating it under the rules of duress. That is, the modification should be upheld if it was fairly bargained, but it should be avoided if the one party's assent to provide increased compensation was induced by the other's improper threat to otherwise withhold his promised performance.

This is the approach adopted in *Austin Instrument Co. v. Loral Corp.*, 272 N.E.2d 533 (N.Y. 1971), Loral had been awarded a Navy contract to supply radar equipment. It was subject to strict delivery terms and a substantial liability for late delivery. It subcontracted with Austin for the supply of components. After performance had begun, Austin realized that it had underbid. It threatened not to deliver the parts ordered unless Loral agreed to a price increase. (The extent of the extortion was aggravated by the additional demand that Loral agree to use Austin as the subcontractor in another contract Loral had just made with the Navy.) Loral tried to find another supplier, but it could not obtain the components elsewhere in time. Faced with inevitable delay, liability for damages to the Navy, and harm to its reputation as a reliable contractor, Loral unsuccessfully tried to negotiate with Austin and eventually, under protest, gave in to its demands. After the completion of performance Loral refused to pay the extra price and Austin sued. The majority of the court held that Loral's free will was undermined by the pressure induced by Austin's threat of breach, so the modification was voidable on grounds of duress. However, a dissent expressed the view that the demand for a higher price was commercially reasonable because there had been a genuine escalation of costs, and agreements for price increases were not uncommon under such circumstances.

This difference in view shows that the distinction between a fair modification and an extortionate one is not always self-evident, but involves a careful evaluation of the motivation and business justification of the demand, the commercial expectations and practices, the force with which the demand is asserted, and the pressures to which the acquiescing party is subject. A subtle line separates opportunism and abuse of power from a fair request for an adjustment of terms.

Although *Austin Instrument* involved a sale of goods, the court did not refer to Article 2 and resolved the case under principles of common law. This shows that duress (and other common law policing doctrines) enable a court to invalidate unfair contract modifications directly without struggling with consideration issues. However, policing doctrines are only of use in avoiding an unfair modification. They do not provide a basis for upholding a fairly bargained modification that lacks consideration.

UCC §2.209[6] does a cleaner job of removing the issue of consideration from contract modification and focusing instead on whether the

---

6. Section 2.209 has not been significantly changed in the 2003 revision of Article 2.

modification was in good faith. Although the duty of good faith has a broader scope than duress doctrine, Comment 2 to §2.209[7] makes it clear that the section covers extortion of a modification by duress. As is always true of the good faith standard, the question of what constitutes a lack of good faith can be difficult to decide where the party's conduct falls short of fraud, duress, or other clearly improper conduct. It involves an evaluation of the state of mind of the party who seeks to enforce the modification in light of the overall commercial circumstances and the business justifications or other factors motivating the parties' agreement to a change in the contract terms.

Even when consideration doctrine is applied to a modification in a common law case, there are two situations recognized by Restatement Second §89 in which the modification may be enforced despite the absence of consideration. The first is when the party benefitted by the promise of modification has acted to her detriment in reliance on it, under circumstances in which it would be unjust to refuse enforcement — in other words, in appropriate circumstances — the doctrine of **promissory estoppel** may be applied to enforce a modification fully or in part. The second is when the modification was motivated by unforeseen **supervening difficulties**. That is, where a change in circumstances so alters a basic assumption of the contract, that the performance of the party seeking the modification becomes more burdensome than originally expected. Say that the manufacturer in the prior example did not underbid at the time of contracting. However, after the contract is executed, the price of the metal from which the machine is to be made escalates beyond all expectation, making the machine considerably more expensive to build. If the manufacturer then persuades the buyer to modify the contract, a court may uphold the modification under this exception to consideration doctrine because the adjustment was a response to unforeseen supervening difficulties.[8] (If the contract was for the sale of goods, this situation would be analyzed in the same way as any other modification and the supervening event would be just one of the factors taken into account in deciding if the modification was fairly bargained.)

§13.10 UNDUE INFLUENCE

The doctrine of undue influence was developed by courts of equity to deal with situations in which duress was not present, but one of the parties had a

---

7. The comment is the same in the 2003 revision.
8. As you will see in section 15.7, there is an affinity between the supervening difficulties doctrine and the defense of impracticability of performance. The difference, however, is that impracticability applies when the party suffering from the changed circumstances has not obtained a modification of the contract, but seeks to be excused from performance.

particularly **strong influence** over the other and **abused this position of dominance** to persuade the subservient party to enter a disadvantageous contract. Thus, while duress provides relief to one whose apparent assent has been induced by an unlawful threat, undue influence is concerned with cases of abuse of trust. Like duress, undue influence makes the contract voidable at the instance of the victim. In most jurisdictions, the doctrine has not been extended beyond its original confines and is not available to redress unfair persuasion in arms-length transactions. Restatement Second §177 reflects this narrow scope by confining the doctrine to *relationships of dependence and trust*. Although it would have been possible for courts to enlarge the scope of undue influence, making it available in all cases of unfair persuasion, the expanded concept of duress and the growing use of unconscionability provide a sufficient basis for the general regulation of bargaining, eliminating the need for a broader application of undue influence. As a result, undue influence has retained its specific character in most states.

To obtain relief for undue influence, the victim must establish two elements:

1. He had a relationship of dependency and trust with the other party that gave the other party dominance over him and justified him in believing that the dominant party would not act contrary to the victim's interests.
2. The dominant party improperly abused this position of trust and psychological advantage by unfairly persuading the victim to enter the contract adverse to his interests.

For example, say that Lilly's father had established and built up the casino. Lilly had never been involved in the business. When her father died and left the casino to her, she had to keep this large and complex enterprise running. Because she had no clue about casino management or business in general, she turned to her father's longtime bookkeeper, Sel "The Skimmer" Short, for assistance in running it. Taking advantage of her inexperience and faith in him, Sel persuaded Lilly to sell him a large amount of stock at a bargain price.

The law does not absolutely bar contracts between a dominant party and the party who depends on him, and relief is available only if the weaker party can show that the dominant party abused his power by unfair persuasion. Unfair persuasion is an elastic concept. When the relationship of dependency is strong and the resulting contract is clearly disadvantageous to the weaker party, unfair bargaining may be inferred from those facts alone, and it may not be necessary to point to any specific underhanded bargaining strategy. However, if the degree of dependency is not as intense or the terms of the contract are not patently unfair, evidence of improper bargaining or oppressive circumstances may be needed to bolster the claim of undue influence. Unseemly bargaining can, as usual, take many forms, including the use of high-pressure tactics, the failure to disclose information, concealment of self-interest, or discouraging recourse to other advisers.

---

§13.11 UNCONSCIONABILITY

§13.11.1 The Role of Unconscionability

As noted earlier, duress does not cover situations in which there is no threat, express or implied. This means that it does not provide a mechanism for policing contracts that are not induced by threat, yet are the result of unfair pressure or abuse of power. Similarly, unless there is some relationship of trust between the parties, undue influence is not available in most jurisdictions to redress an imposition of terms on a weaker party. Even when imposition is accompanied by some degree of dishonesty, fraud cannot be claimed unless the misrepresentation and its consequent inducement are serious enough to satisfy the elements of fraud. Nevertheless, meaningful and genuine assent may be just as badly undermined when one party is able to impose an unfair contract on the other, using a strong bargaining position or unethical tactics to take advantage of the other's weakness, ignorance, or distress. The law therefore needs a more general doctrine under which courts may provide relief in cases that do not clearly fall within any of the more specific doctrines. The concept of unconscionability helps to cater to these situations.

Unconscionability is most commonly associated with consumer transactions in which a relatively large and powerful corporation supplies a standard form contract that is signed by a consumer with little or no opportunity to negotiate its terms. However, it is important to take note of two points. First, as the following discussion will show, a contract is not unconscionable merely because it is on standard terms drafted by an economically powerful party. Second, the doctrine is not confined to consumer transactions. It is equally applicable to commercial transactions between businesses. Bear in mind that many businesses are small, and some are operated by an individual, so there is sometimes not a clear dividing line between an individual who makes a contract as a consumer or as a business. However, the degree to which the party claiming unconscionability has economic power and business sophistication does have an impact on the finding of unconscionability. Therefore, it is often more difficult for a commercial entity to obtain relief under this doctrine.

§13.11.2 The Nature and Origins of Unconscionability

Unconscionability originated as a discretionary bar to **equitable** relief in a contract suit. It is the function of a court of equity[9] to do justice between the parties, and it would therefore decline relief to a plaintiff who had behaved inequitably. For example, if a party to a contract sued for equitable relief (such as specific performance) under a contract that was harsh or unfairly bargained, the court would refuse to enforce it on the ground that to do so would offend its conscience. Even after the courts of law and equity were combined, many courts did not recognize unconscionability as generally available and would only consider using the doctrine when the relief sought in the case was equitable in nature. Because most contract cases involve claims for damages or other relief at law, and claims in equity are less common, relief for unconscionability was often unavailable.

This changed dramatically when the UCC was enacted because §2.302 adopted the doctrine as a general rule, applicable to all contracts for the sale of goods. As a result of the strong influence of the UCC on the common law, courts have increasingly applied unconscionability doctrine in cases at law involving contracts other than sales of goods. This trend was recognized and bolstered by Restatement Second §208, which closely follows the wording of UCC §2.302.

Juries are not used in cases at equity, so unconscionability, being equitable in its origins, is *decided by the judge*. Of course, the UCC could have changed this when it codified the doctrine, but because a finding of unconscionability has such a strong discretionary content, the drafters of the UCC chose to keep it within the realm of the judge. Section 2.302 therefore characterizes it as a matter of law. The Restatement Second adopts the same approach.

§13.11.3 The Elements of Unconscionability

The UCC and Restatement Second simply acknowledge that the court has the power to refuse enforcement of an unconscionable contract or to adjust the contract by removing or modifying the unconscionable provision. Neither section attempts to say what constitutes unconscionability, but the comments to §2.302[10] largely echoed in those to §208 of Restatement Second,

---

9. The distinction between law and equity is explained in section 2.5.
10. The 2003 revision of Article 2 makes no significant changes to §2.302. The Comments have been made more succinct, but their substance has not been changed.

suggest a two-part test that has become widely accepted. For relief to be granted on grounds of unconscionability, the transaction must exhibit both bargaining unfairness (commonly called **procedural unconscionability**) and resulting unfair or oppressive terms (commonly called **substantive unconscionability**). *Williams v. Walker Thomas Furniture Co.*, 350 F.2d 445 (D.C. Cir. 1965), one of the earliest cases to deal with the modern approach to unconscionability, couched these two elements in similar terms as consisting of the absence of meaningful choice by the one party resulting in contract terms unreasonably favorable to the other.[11] Most courts require both procedural and substantive unconscionability to be present, but some courts are willing to give relief for unconscionability if either of the elements is established. Even courts that demand a showing of both elements tend to balance them. Therefore, if one of them is strongly apparent, the court is likely to accept a fairly minimal showing of the other. In some situations one of the elements is so powerful that the court may assume the other to have been present if the facts provide any basis for making that assumption. (This is explained further below.) The following diagram represents the elements of unconscionability:

It is one thing to identify the dual elements of procedural and substantive unconscionability, but quite another to describe them with any certainty. As a result, courts and writers continue to struggle with the scope and content of the doctrine. We will now look more closely at each of these elements.

---

11. Walker Thomas sold furniture and appliances on credit to low-income buyers. As security for payment of the balance of the price, Walker Thomas structured the transaction to include a "cross-collateralization" provision in the contract. This gave it a security interest in the goods bought under the new transaction as well as in all goods that the customer had ever bought from it in the past. The effect of this was that if the customer defaulted, Walker Thomas could repossess not just the goods sold in that transaction, but all other goods bought in previous transactions. Used furniture and household items do not have much value and were probably not worth enough to settle the debt. Therefore, the real purpose of the clause was to increase the stakes of default and to put pressure on the customer not to miss payments. The trial court had declined to find the cross-collateralization clause unconscionable because the UCC had not yet been enacted in the District of Columbia at that time. The court of appeals held that the doctrine did apply and it remanded the case to the district court to consider whether the contracts satisfied the test that it articulated.

§13.11.4 Procedural Unconscionability

This element focuses on the *bargaining behavior* of the party alleged to have acted unconscionably. While Comment 1 to UCC §2.302 does not provide much guidance on what constitutes unconscionable bargaining, it states that the aim is to prevent "**oppression and unfair surprise**," but not to disturb the "allocation of risks because of superior bargaining power." Restatement Second Comment d to §208 makes a similar observation and expands on it by noting that gross inequality of bargaining power may satisfy the requirement of unconscionability if combined with substantively unfair terms. The Restatement comment also lists some indicia of oppressive bargaining, such as some degree of deception or compulsion, or an awareness by a dominant party of infirmity, or ignorance or lack of understanding on the part of the other.

As noted earlier, unconscionability doctrine is most useful when there are some elements of pressure, deception, or unfair persuasion present in the formation process, but these are not sufficient to qualify as duress, fraud, or undue influence. It is difficult to be more concrete, because unconscionability, by its nature, is intended to be an open-ended doctrine, allowing the court discretion to examine each case on its facts and to decide if underhanded or oppressive conduct by one of the parties is severe enough under the circumstances to merit the avoidance or adjustment of the contract.

The comments emphasize that mere *disparity of bargaining power* is not enough to constitute unconscionability. It is not the purpose of the doctrine to place the parties on a level of equality by eliminating the advantages enjoyed by a more powerful or sophisticated party. If this were so, most contracts could be challenged by a dissatisfied party on the basis that the other was smarter, bigger, or had better lawyers or more money or power. But this does not mean that the relative strength of the parties is irrelevant to the issue of unconscionability. Often it is only because of a disparity in power that a dominant party is able to behave in an unfair or oppressive manner or to insist on unfair terms. Similarly, the weaker party's lack of sophistication could make it easier to take advantage of her. Thus the key is not whether one party was more powerful, sophisticated, or knowledgeable than the other, but whether it abused its power to impose its will on the other party.

Having said this, it must be acknowledged that there are situations in which the abuse of power is quite subtle. There is no obvious dishonesty or unfair persuasion, yet it is nevertheless clear that one of the parties used its position of dominance to impose the contract (or unfavorable contract terms) on the weaker. That is, one of the parties enters the transaction with such bargaining power relative to the other, that the stronger party has enough control over the transaction to leave the weaker with no choice but to enter it on the terms proposed by the dominant party. Contracts entered into under these circumstances have come to be known as **contracts of adhesion** because the weaker party is seen as adhering without choice to terms dictated by the stronger. Contracts of adhesion are examined more fully in section 13.13, but it is useful to anticipate and emphasize the point made in that discussion, that a contract does not become adhesive or unconscionable merely because one of the parties has greater bargaining power. Comment 1 to UCC §2.203 specifically states that the purpose of unconscionability doctrine is not to disturb the allocation of risks resulting from superior bargaining power. It contemplates that some procedural impropriety — an abuse of that power — should be present as well. Nevertheless, when substantively unfair terms are present and are attributable to the bargaining dominance of the party favored by the terms, it is relatively easy to conclude that the weaker party was deprived of free choice by a degree of dominance that, in itself, amounted to procedural unfairness.

§13.11.5 Substantive Unconscionability

It should be apparent from the discussion of procedural unconscionability that there is a close relationship of cause and effect between the procedural and substantive elements: By engaging in unconscionable conduct during formation, one of the parties has been able to impose a substantively unconscionable contract or contract term on the other. It is not usually enough to show merely that the contract is substantively unfair, because it is not proper for a court to adjust a contract simply because one of the parties overpaid, underbid, or otherwise made a disadvantageous or unwanted deal. Unless this unfortunate state of affairs was caused by the behavior that qualifies as procedurally unconscionable, the parties should both be held to their manifested agreement. Once again, this general rule must be qualified by the caveat that the substantive and procedural elements do not have to be present to an equal degree. When the contract terms are grossly oppressive, procedural unfairness may be found simply in the opportunistic use of a position of dominance.

Most commonly, a contract is substantively unconscionable when its terms are **harsh, unfair, or unduly favorable to one of the parties**. One could think of endless examples of unfair terms, such as an excessive price for goods or services; exorbitant interest rates; harsh penalties in the event of default; the waiver of legal protection or of the right to seek legal redress in a proper forum, and so on. The test suggested by Comment 1 to §2.302 calls on the court to decide whether, "in the light of the general commercial background and the commercial needs of the particular trade or case, the clauses involved are *so one-sided as to be unconscionable under the circumstances* existing at the time of the contract." This is a hopeless circumlocution, but it does at least suggest that a contract or term is unconscionable if it favors one of the parties more than should reasonably be expected, given the commercial context in which the contract was made. The comment goes on to identify one of the goals of the doctrine as the prevention of *oppression*, which, while also rather vague, gives some further hint of the direction of the inquiry.

Although the conclusion that a contract is substantively unconscionable is normally based on the presence of unfair terms, it is possible for this element to be present even when the contract appears fair and reasonable from an objective standpoint. The unfairness could lie in the fact that the weaker party did not desire the transaction but was unfairly persuaded to enter it. For example, say that the conduct of a door-to-door sales representative is procedurally unconscionable because high-pressure techniques and smooth talk are used to bamboozle a hapless householder into buying an unneeded home appliance. Even if the price of the appliance and the other terms are reasonable, the contract as a whole may nevertheless be unconscionable, because it was unwanted by and imposed on the buyer.[12] As you can see, we are again looking at that balance between the substantive and procedural aspects of unconscionability.

A number of unconscionability cases involve the substantive unfairness of *excessive price*, so that particular form of unfairness may be used to illustrate the difficulty in deciding on the proper balance between the substantive and procedural components. In many cases, although there is no clear showing of bargaining unfairness, the buyer of goods or services (typically a consumer) has agreed to pay an excessive price for the purchase. Excessive price, on its own, should not normally be a basis for finding unconscionability if the disparity in exchange cannot be attributed to bargaining misbehavior. As emphasized in the discussion of consideration in section 7.6, the courts do not normally inquire into the adequacy of the exchange, but leave it to the parties to make their own judgments on the relative value of the performances. However, in some cases the disparity in value is so gross that courts refuse to enforce the contract at the price on which agreement was manifested. This has led to some debate about whether courts should exercise regulatory power over excessive pricing, even in the absence of proof of unfair bargaining. However, in most of the cases in which courts have intervened on the grounds of excessive price, there is at least some indication from the evidence that the high price would not have been obtained without improper bargaining methods, or at least an exploitation of the buyer's weakness, ignorance, or lack of choice.

§13.11.6 The Remedy for Unconscionability

As noted already, both the UCC and the Restatement Second leave it to the discretion of the court to devise the most appropriate response to an

---

12. Home solicitation sales are legislatively regulated, so the buyer may have statutory grounds of avoidance as well.

unconscionable contract or term. In exercising its discretion, the court is influenced, but not bound, by what relief the victim requests.

In some cases, the unconscionability so profoundly affects the quality of the victim's assent that she no longer desires the contract and should not be held to it. This is what would happen in the example of the consumer who was cajoled into buying the unwanted appliance. Here, the most appropriate remedy is for the court to refuse enforcement of the contract as a whole. This is tantamount to **avoidance and restitution**.

In other cases (particularly where the victim would like to keep the contract with appropriate adjustments), the better remedy may be to enforce the basic bargain but to change its terms to eliminate its unconscionable aspects. This may involve either **severing** the unconscionable part of the contract (that is, eliminating the unconscionable provision entirely) or just **altering** the term to make it fair. For example, a standard form contract for the sale of goods between a large retailer and a consumer requires all disputes to be arbitrated. The court finds that although the contract as a whole is unobjectionable, the arbitration term provides for a procedure that unduly favors the retailer. The consumer does not wish to avoid the contract as a whole but would like to avoid the arbitration term. The court could sever the arbitration term in its entirety, so that there is no longer any requirement to arbitrate and the parties must litigate their dispute before a court. Alternatively, the court could remove the unfair aspects of the arbitration term, but otherwise enforce it. This would mean that the parties are still bound to arbitrate, but the terms governing the arbitration are less one-sided. In deciding whether it is appropriate to sever or alter a term, the court considers factors such as the degree to which the term was imposed without meaningful choice, the form of relief requested by the victim of unconscionability, and the impact that the change will have on the basis of the parties' bargain. Courts usually aim to interfere as little as possible with the contract's terms, and to correct the contract without fundamentally altering its purpose. Where a term cannot be severed without doing significant harm to the basis of the bargain, alteration of the term may be less intrusive. If neither severance nor alteration can cure the unconscionability, or the change in the terms fundamentally changes the nature of the agreement, avoidance of the contract is probably the only proper remedy.

The flexibility of the remedy for unconscionability often has an impact on the court's decision to find that a term is unconscionable. Because the court knows that a finding of unconscionability will not inevitably lead to avoidance of the contract, the court may more readily make that finding. That is, the availability of a narrow, surgical remedy reduces the stakes of holding a term to be unconscionable.

§13.11.7 A Final Note on the Temptation to Overuse Unconscionability Doctrine

Because unconscionability is such a vague and discretionary doctrine, a student may be tempted to argue it whenever the parties are not of equal bargaining power and the weaker party complains of an adverse term or contract. It therefore must be stressed that courts are careful in using the doctrine. Although we have seen that the doctrine is broad enough to make it very difficult to predict how a court might react to a claim of unconscionability, most courts do look seriously at the two elements that we have discussed and commonly require a showing of both. This is not to say that a notable discrepancy in bargaining power and sophistication is irrelevant — this often explains why the dominant party was able to take advantage of the weaker one. Bear this in mind as you read the section 12.12 on contracts of adhesion.

§13.12 UNCONSCIONABILITY ISSUES IN STANDARD FORM CONTRACTS: ADHESION AND STANDARD TERMS NOT REVEALED AT THE TIME OF CONTRACTING

§13.12.1 Adhesion and the Role of Unconscionability in Redressing Dominant Power

Standard form contracts are necessary in a modern economy, and are crucial to efficiency and control where an enterprise enters into many transactions of a similar kind. The drafter of the standard contract clearly benefits from the contract's terms, which are written to serve its interests. However, the impact on the other party or on society need not be negative. If the form's terms are fair and not unduly one-sided they can create a sensible basis for contracting and could save transaction costs that keep prices down.

It is therefore important to recognize that standard form contracts are pervasive and they are not necessarily improper. However, they do create a problem where the party that drafted the form is dominant enough to impose its terms, and selfish enough to create terms that unduly favor its own interests. If there is no adequate market mechanism to allow the other party to negotiate a change in terms or to seek an alternative, there is a strong danger of adhesion — the imposition of unfavorable terms on a take-it-or-leave-it basis. We have already noted that there is a difference between the legitimate use of market power to achieve a desired bargain, and its improper use for exploitation and imposition. This distinction is most strongly tested by contracts of adhesion.

The following example illustrates this situation. Megalomarketing, Inc., the largest retailer on earth, opened one of its "big box" stores in a town. Its aggressive competitive techniques put all the smaller stores in the area out of business, so it is the only seller of groceries, pharmaceuticals, clothing, household goods, and sporting equipment for 100 miles around. It makes all its sales subject to a standard form contract drafted at corporate head-quarters. Sales staff has been instructed not to sell any goods to a customer who refuses to sign the form, and no local employee has authority to nego-tiate any change in the form. The form contains an arbitration provision that requires all disputes relating to any goods purchased to be settled by arbi-tration. There is nothing unfair about the arbitration procedure set out in the form, and arbitration agreements are favored as a matter of public policy because they provide for an informal means of resolving disputes. Never-theless, the negative aspect of the transaction is self-evident. Unless a cus-tomer travels 100 miles to another store, he is stuck with the form contract and its arbitration provision. He has no meaningful choice but to agree to this adhesive contract.[13] True, there is nothing really wrong with the arbi-tration clause as a matter of substantive unfairness, and we cannot really point to any bargaining impropriety. There is no deception and no improper threat, and we have noted frequently that a party has the right to decline to contract except on its own terms. Nevertheless, the sense of imposition is strong and it does not feel right that Megalomarketing can effectively legislate that the citizens of the town have no recourse to litigation in any of the many transactions in which Megalomarketing is involved.

There are means of tackling this type of problem by statute outside of contract law. Statutes regulating anticompetitive behavior (such as antitrust laws) hamper the ability of a large corporation to control a market; sometimes direct regulation of an industry (such as utilities or insurance) allows the government to control the terms of mass contracts; sometimes consumer protection statutes invalidate predatory terms or practices. However, in the absence of such legislative intervention, it is the courts' role to manage contracts of adhesion. Although some commentators have suggested that we need a separate doctrine to deal with adhesion, uncon-scionability remains the doctrine that applies.

---

13. The Megalomarketing example is deliberately extreme. In most cases, customers who deal with a large enterprise are not so thoroughly deprived of choice, and the presence of competition may make even the most powerful party susceptible to negotiation. For example, although an auto dealership may be huge and may use a standard form sale contract, stiff competition in the industry gives even the smallest customer considerable bargaining leverage.

As much as one may dislike the situation described above, it is not obvious that Megalomarketing's contracts with its customers are unconscionable — there is no clear case of either procedural or substantive unconscionability. This does not mean that a court could not be persuaded that the elements of unconscionability are satisfied because Megalomarketing applied its market power oppressively to achieve the substantively unfair result of depriving all its customers of recourse to court. (Of course it would be easier to make this case if the arbitration clause had some nasty provisions in it.) However, unconscionability doctrine is not supposed to be used merely to redress an imbalance of bargaining power.

In short, adhesion on its own, unaccompanied by any specific improper bargaining conduct, could satisfy the procedural element of unconscionability where it deprives the weaker party of meaningful choice and leads to the conclusion that the stronger party used its market power illegitimately. However, the absence of specific bargaining misbehavior would make this a borderline case of procedural unconscionability. Because the procedural and substantive elements should be balanced against each other, a strong degree of substantive unfairness must be present to compensate for the weak form of procedural unconscionability.

§13.12.2 Adhesive Terms Not Made Available at the Time of Contracting

Section 4.13 on offer and acceptance discussed the problem of standard terms that are not readily apparent to or revealed to a contracting party at the time of purchasing goods or services. These terms are commonly in a contract of adhesion in which the customer has no meaningful opportunity to bargain for a change in the standard terms, but this issue goes one step beyond what we discussed in section 13.12.1. Not only are the terms standard and non-negotiable, but the customer does not even see them when he buys the goods or services. With goods, the standard terms might be included in a sealed package, and with services (such as an insurance policy or a travel ticket) the terms might be sent later when the policy or ticket is delivered.

Section 4.13 refers to *ProCD, Inc. v. Zeidenberg*, 86 F.3d 1447 (7th Cir. 1996), which dealt with the retail purchase of software with terms included in the box, and *Casavant v. Norwegian Cruise Line, Inc.*, 829 N.E.2d 1171 (Mass. App. 2005) which concerned the purchase of cruise tickets with terms delivered with the tickets. *ProCD* treated the supply of software as an offer, accepted by the buyer when he failed to return the product after he had the opportunity to open the box and read the terms. *Casavant* held a forum selection clause in the cruise ticket unenforceable because it came too soon before the date of the cruise and the passenger was not given enough time to reject it. Although both the cases were discussed in connection with the question of whether the terms became part of the contract, they are also concerned with the fairness of this method of contracting and of the resulting terms. They therefore have a direct link to the issue of unconscionability. *ProCD* emphasized the importance of standard form contracting and its benefits in streamlining contract formation in a modern economy. Furthermore, the court noted that it would be very cumbersome to insist that standard terms are made apparent when goods or services are ordered, so the law has to accommodate the practice of disseminating standard forms thereafter. Although *ProCD* upheld the standard terms and *Casavant* did not, both cases stand for the proposition that it is neither procedurally nor substantively unconscionable for a party to provide standard terms that are not revealed to the other party at the time the transaction is entered provided that the terms are accessible, they are not outside the reasonable expectations of the marketplace, and they are not unduly harsh or one-sided.

The U.S. Supreme Court focused directly on the issue of unconscionability under these circumstances in *Carnival Cruise Lines, Inc. v. Shute*, 499 U.S. 585 (1991). Like the Casavants, the Shutes booked a cruise and were not given a copy of the contract's standard terms until they received their cruise tickets, some time later. One of the standard terms was a forum selection clause designating the Florida courts as the agreed forum for resolving disputes. During the cruise, Ms. Shute slipped and was injured. She sued Carnival for damages in the federal district court in Washington, her home state. The district court dismissed her case on the ground that it should have been commenced in Florida. The Ninth Circuit reversed because it did not consider the provision to have been freely bargained. The Supreme Court reversed the court of appeals and reinstated the dismissal. The majority of the court agreed that a standard clause on a ticket should be carefully scrutinized for fairness, but it is not presumptively invalid merely because the passenger had no opportunity to (or power to) negotiate it. The court stressed the efficiency and value of standard contracting, which should be facilitated unless it is abused. In the present case, the forum selection clause was reasonable because it centralized litigation in the courts of Carnival's home state and reduced costs of litigation. The forum selected was natural, not alien and there was no indication that it was chosen to frustrate claims. The dissent disagreed that efficiency and the reduction of Carnival's litigation costs were a good enough justification for depriving the passenger of the right to litigate in the forum that was most convenient and least expensive for her. This unfair result, combined with the likelihood that a passenger would not even notice the clause (it was one of 25 paragraphs on the ticket, not drawn to the passenger's attention at the time of contracting) led the dissent to conclude that the clause should not be enforced.

§13.13 POLICING CONTRACTS FOR ILLEGALITY OR CONTRAVENTION OF PUBLIC POLICY

§13.13.1 Illegality, Public Policy, and Freedom of Contract

It was noted in the introduction that the assent and reliance policies of contract law are not the only policies that may be implicated in the enforcement of a contract. Even when the contract is a full and genuine exercise of both parties' freedom of contract, it may break the law or so offend public policy that the court refuses to enforce it. This distinguishes regulation on grounds of illegality and public policy from the other doctrines discussed in this chapter: The issue here is not that one of the parties dealt wrongly with the other or that one party's assent is deficient (even though this factor could also be present in some cases), but that the contract is forbidden or does some damage to the public good. Therefore, the goal of policing here is different from that in cases where the only issue is bargaining impropriety. The court's concern goes beyond doing justice between the parties, to the *protection of the public interest.*

It is a bit artificial and sometimes quite difficult to make a firm **distinction between illegality and violation of public policy.** Courts do not always articulate the distinction and sometimes even use the words interchangeably. For the most part, it is not crucial to make the distinction because in many cases it would not lead to a difference in the analysis or result of the case. However, there is a conceptual difference between a contract that is illegal and one that offends public policy, and this difference can affect the court's approach to and resolution of a case. (This is explained in section 13.13.4.) It is therefore useful to understand it. A contract is illegal if it contravenes a statute or a rule of common law. The confusing part is that a violation of law is inevitably also contrary to public policy because all laws are enacted to effectuate public policy. In this sense, it means much the same to call a contract illegal or against public policy.

However, there are some contracts that do not violate a law, but the court nevertheless concludes, despite the fact that the contract is not illegal, that it is contrary to public policy. This, properly speaking, is what is meant when a contract is described as contrary to public policy — it is not forbidden by a specific statute or rule of common law, but it so harms the public welfare that the court should not enforce it. Where a contract is proscribed by law, the court does not usually have to invoke its discretionary powers in refusing to enforce it — the statute or established rule of common law has already made the policy decision. However, where a contract is not illegal, the determination that it violates public policy could involve the exercise of a much greater degree of judicial discretion. Courts tend to be wary of exercising this level of discretion because they do not wish to be seen as legislating from the bench.

Although the focus here is on the public interest, it is not typically some outside agency or public body that challenges the contract. The **claim** of illegality or a violation of public policy is **made by one of the parties** who seeks to escape an obligation arising out of the contract. It is therefore important to understand that in adjudicating an issue of illegality or public policy, a court is commonly resolving a dispute between the parties. One of them is trying to enforce the contract (or sometimes trying to obtain restitution for performance under the contract) and the other is resisting. Although balancing the equities between the parties is not as dominant a consideration as the public interest, it does have an influence on the outcome.

The end result of a determination that a contract is illegal or contravenes public policy has some similarity to the **remedies** for improper bargaining and is in some ways analogous. (A court may decide to refuse enforcement of the improper contract in its entirety, which sounds like the equivalent to avoidance, or it may keep the contract in place and refuse enforcement of only the offending term, which approximates severance.) However, because protection of the public interest is the court's principal goal in dealing with a contract that is illegal or violates public policy, the case is conceptually different from a situation of improper bargaining. This calls for a different approach to the issue of remedy. Society is the principal victim of a contract that is illegal or in violation of public policy. Therefore, where a contract directly violates a rule of law, or its harm to society is serious enough, a court is most unlikely to enforce it under any circumstances. Such a contract is more correctly characterized as void rather than voidable. The same is often true where the parties are joint perpetrators of the offense and it cannot be said that one used the illegal contract to victimize the other. On the other hand, where one of the parties is more to blame for the transaction, the other is a member of a group which the law seeks to protect, and the contract does not involve serious illegality, the contract is more accurately described as voidable. In short, the treatment of a contract that is illegal or contrary to public policy depends on the **nature and gravity** of the **violation,** the **goals of the law or public policy,** and the extent to which the **impropriety permeates the contract**. Sometimes the best way to protect the public interest is to refuse enforcement of the contract altogether, but in other cases, enforcement of the contract, with or without the adjustment of its terms, may best serve the public good. Sometimes, as we will see in section 13.13.4, a contract's illegality or violation of public policy could even affect a restitutionary claim of one of the parties arising from non-enforcement of the contract.

§13.13.2 Illegal Contracts

Some illegal contracts are such a serious violation of the law that performance of the contract (or sometimes even making the contract) is a criminal act. This would be true, for example, of a contract under which one of the parties pays the other to murder someone. Such a contract is not enforceable and its making or performance would lead to criminal prosecution. However, there is a difference between illegality and criminality, and not all illegal contracts are criminal. A statute or the common law could forbid a contract, but provide no consequence for violation of the law other than the non-enforcement of the contract. For purposes of contract law, we are not concerned with whether the transaction attracts criminal penalties. (Although the criminal nature of the contract could affect the court's approach to the equities and the public interest when it decides on what remedy is appropriate.)

The basic rule is that a court will not enforce an illegal contract or term, even if it is clear that the parties entered the contract voluntarily and there was no improper bargaining. For example, in *Parente v. Pirozzoli*, 866 A.2d 629 (Conn. App. 2005), the defendant wished to buy a bar but would have had difficulty in taking transfer of the liquor license because he was a convicted felon. He therefore entered into an agreement with the plaintiff under which the plaintiff would apply for the license as a front man, and the parties would then run the bar as equal partners. The license was granted and the parties went into business. When the partnership was later dissolved, the defendant refused to pay the plaintiff his share of the profits and the plaintiff sued. The court refused to enforce the contract because it was based on the unlawful purpose of evading the liquor control laws. Similarly, in *Homani v. Iranzadi*, 211 Cal. App. 3d 1104 (1989), the court refused to enforce an agreement to pay interest on a loan where, for the purpose of evading tax on the interest, the parties had agreed orally to the payment of interest, but signed a promissory note showing the loan as interest-free.

§13.13.3 Contracts Contrary to Public Policy

If a contract is not actually illegal, but it nevertheless offends public policy, the consequence of nonenforcement is not as inevitable. A decision on whether or not to enforce the contract involves a **balancing of policy concerns** and of the **equities** between the parties. Assuming that the contract suffers from no deficiencies in assent, the regulation of contracts on the basis of broader public interest creates a **tension between the policy of enforcing contracts** and the **other public policy** that would be frustrated by enforcement. To resolve this dissonance, the countervailing policies must be balanced. If the harm to the public interest outweighs the benefit of enforcement to the public and the parties, enforcement must be refused.

How does the court identify the existence and force of a public policy affected by the contract? In the easiest case, the policy may be expressed by legislation or well-established common law precedent. Of course, if the statute or rule of common law clearly prohibits a contract in violation of a particular policy, we have a case of illegality, as discussed above. But sometimes the law does not actually forbid a particular contract, yet it is apparent that the law's policy goals are incompatible with the recognition and enforcement of a contract of this kind. Because this often amounts to *judicial policymaking*, most courts are cautious about identifying public policy that does not have a firm base in statute or precedent. A court may try to seek guidance in other governmental policy pronouncements and may entertain policy arguments by the parties. If it should conclude that such a policy exists, it must then weigh it against the policy of upholding contracts.

Disclaimers of liability for negligent or intentional injury (exculpatory clauses) feature frequently in the caselaw, and provide a good illustration of public policy analysis. A disclaimer of liability for wrongful conduct pits the policy of freedom of contract against the tort policy of holding a tortfeasor accountable for injury caused by his actions and of deterring wrongful conduct. The policy of freedom of contract calls for the enforcement of a freely bargained consensual agreement, but the tort policy of accountability disfavors an agreement that absolves a tortfeasor in advance from liability for future conduct. This means that the public policies of contract and tort pull in opposite directions must be balanced. It is relatively easy to decide in favor of the tort policy where there is some problem with the way in which the disclaimer was entered into. The policy of freedom of contract is not well served by enforcing the contract unless the disclaimer is voluntary, fairly bargained, and expressed clearly and conspicuously. Therefore, as an initial matter, the court examines the disclaimer itself to decide if its enforcement serves the policies of contract law. Adhesion is a relevant consideration here, and a court is less likely to uphold a disclaimer if it was imposed on the injured party. In addition, courts insist that the language of the disclaimer must be explicit and must clearly show the intent to exonerate the party from liability. Because exculpatory provisions are not favored as a matter of policy, any unclear language is interpreted restrictively to cut down the scope of or eliminate the disclaimer.

Where the provision is absolutely clear and the victim's agreement to it is not in question, the competing tort and contract policies are in the starkest opposition. To decide which policy should predominate, courts weigh all the circumstances and considerations. Courts have identified several factors that are relevant to this decision. The scope and extent of the disclaimer is important. Although it may be acceptable to exclude liability for negligence, a disclaimer will not be enforced to the extent that it exculpates gross negligence or intentional misconduct. Where only negligent injury is covered, the court considers the importance or necessity of the service to the public (for example, a disclaimer in a residential lease is potentially much more harmful than one in a skydiving contract); the kinds of people who are likely to execute the disclaimer (for example, whether the service is used by the public at large, or only by a specialized or qualified group); the extent to which the provider of the service has control over the person or property of the victim; and the impact that not permitting the disclaimer will have on the public's ability to obtain the service at all, or at reasonable cost. If factors such as these balance in favor of holding the service provider responsible for negligence, the court will not enforce the disclaimer, even if it is freely executed and not adhesive.

Hanks v. Power Ridge Restaurant Corp., 885 A.2d 734 (Conn. 2005) and *McCune v. Myrtle Beach Indoor Shooting Range, Inc.*, 612 S.E.2d 462 (S.C. App. 2005) show how a court might balance all these considerations. In *Hanks*, the plaintiff was injured while snowtubing and sued the operator of the ski resort for damages, claiming that it had been negligent in the way that it constructed and supervised the snowtube run. Prior to snowtubing, the plaintiff had signed a release that exculpated the operator from liability for negligent injury. The court found that the disclaimer expressed the exclusion of liability in conspicuous and unmistakable language that would alert a reasonable person to its import. The agreement was very clearly written and it unmistakably emphasized that negligent conduct was covered by the disclaimer by capitalizing the word "negligence" several times.[14] Notwithstanding this, the court avoided the disclaimer on grounds of public policy because it found that the contract was adhesive, the snowtube run was open to all members of the public who had a reasonable expectation of safety, the operator controlled the run and rented the equipment, and it would not be in the public interest to allow the operator to shift risk of liability to the customer.

By contrast, in *McCune*, the plaintiff's eye was injured while participating in a paintball game because her mask did not fit properly. Before she began the game she signed a release that emphasized the risks of injury, acknowledged that she assumed such risks, and absolved the defendant from all liability for injury, whether caused by negligence or otherwise. The release specifically did not cover injury resulting from gross negligence or wanton misconduct. The exculpatory provisions were printed in capital letters. The court affirmed the trial court's grant of summary judgment in favor of the defendant. The release was explicit and clear, it did not seek to exclude

---

14. The plaintiff testified that although he had read the release (and his 12-year-old son had urged him not to sign it), he did not take it seriously or believe that it would be enforceable. The court pointed out that the plaintiff's subjective opinion of the effect of the clause was irrelevant under the objective test.

liability for conduct more serious than negligence, and it was a voluntary assumption of risk by the plaintiff. The court pointed out that it would not serve the public good if a business could not exclude liability by a reasonable and explicit disclaimer. The risk of liability would preclude many activities and events.

§13.13.4 The Effect of Contracts that are Illegal or Contrary to Public Policy

a. Illegal Contracts

The basic rule is that where the parties share the guilt of having entered an illegal contract, the court will keep aloof from the dispute and will not intervene to help either party. This is known as the **in pari delicto** rule, an abbreviation of the maxim *in pari delicto potior est conditio defendentis.* (When the parties are in equal guilt, the defendant's position is stronger.) The rule is not as straightforward as it sounds. First, although it refers to equal guilt, it really means that the guilt of the party seeking relief must be equal to or greater than that of the other party. Second, although it is sometimes possible to assign greater fault to one of the parties, it is not always easy to do this. Third, and less obvious, the rule does not simply depend on an evaluation of the relative guilt of the parties. It also takes into account the equities between the parties and considers whether the public interest is best served by giving or declining relief. This means that weighing the relative guilt of the parties is just one aspect of a broader inquiry into the circumstances of the transaction, the relationship of the parties and their motivations, and the public interest served by the law.

The *in pari delicto* rule is therefore not an absolute bar to relief where the court finds that the party requesting relief bears equal or greater guilt. Rather, it is a starting premise from which the court may depart to the extent that it considers that the equities between the parties and the public interest so demand. The weighing of these factors is illustrated by the *Parente* and *Homani* cases discussed in section 13.3.2. In *Parente*, the plaintiff argued that if the court refused to award him his share of the partnership profits, the defendant, who instigated the scheme to evade the liquor control laws, would be rewarded by a windfall. Although the court recognized this, it felt that the public interest was best served by refusing enforcement. Not only should the court not sanction such a contract, but the refusal of enforcement would create a disincentive for others to act as front men in the future. This decision shows the difficulty of achieving the right balance. It could just as well have been argued that the plaintiff was guiltier than the defendant and allowing him to keep the defendant's share of the profits created an incentive to use a front man to deceive the liquor control authority.

In *Homani*, the court was unpersuaded by the lender's argument that the borrower received a windfall. The court considered that the public interest was best served by removing the lender's incentive to enter such a transaction. This result makes sense. After all, it was the lender who stood to benefit from the tax evasion, and he was most guilty of breaking the law.

The effect of applying the in *pari delicto* rule is that the court declines to award relief and leaves the parties as it finds them. This obvious effect of this is that the court will refuse to **enforce** the contract where one of the parties sues for enforcement. This is what happened in both *Parente* and *Homani*. Refusal of enforcement is a natural consequence of illegality because enforcement is an affirmative recognition of the contract, and a court is understandably reluctant to play any role in upholding the improper contract. However, the in *pari delicto* rule also has a less obvious impact. The court may also apply it where a party does not claim enforcement of the contract, but concedes it is illegal and asks for **restitution** of a benefit that he conferred on the other party under the contract. The refusal of restitution is not as easily justified as non-enforcement because the grant of the remedy would not require recognition of the contract. Quite the opposite, it is based on the premise that no contract exists. Nevertheless, once the contract is found to be illegal, the in *pari delicto* rule covers all claims associated with it, and even a restitutionary claim could be denied if the equities and the public interest make that appropriate.

To illustrate the considerations that a court weighs in deciding on whether to grant restitution, return to the sale of the casino by Lilly Livered to Attila "The Animal" Axehacker.

In contravention of a statute forbidding the ownership of casinos by mobsters, Lilly sold her casino to Attila, a gangster, for $10 million. Both parties knew about the prohibition. At the time of executing the agreement, Attila made a down payment of $100,000 to Lilly. A few days later she repudiated the contract. Clearly, the contract is unenforceable, and Attila cannot sue for relief on the contract, whether in the form of specific performance or damages for breach. Can he get the $100,000 back? There is no obvious answer: It could be argued that, as the mobster seeking to acquire the casino, he is more to blame than the seller. But the contrary argument could be made that people like Lilly, by deliberately violating the law, make possible the very harm that the statute seeks to avert. The determination of which of these alternatives best serves the public interest is also difficult to make: Is it better to allow her to keep a windfall profit from her deliberately wrongful transaction, or to allow the court's process to be used by a thug to recover the down payment made in an attempt to violate the law? Unless it is demonstrated that judicial intervention is the more appropriate alternative, the thrust of the in *pari delicto* rule is to leave the parties as they are.

As a second example, a liquor store sells a case of scotch to a 20-year-old minor, violating a statute (known to both parties) that prohibits the sale of alcohol to persons under the age of 21.[15] The buyer paid for the scotch in cash, but the seller now refuses delivery. Again, the buyer clearly cannot enforce the contract, but can he get his money back? One could argue that the buyer had no business trying to purchase the liquor and deserves no help from the court in recovering the payment. However, it seems intolerable to allow the seller to keep his money. If the whole idea of barring the sale of liquor to young people is that they do not have the maturity to use it responsibly, it would seem that this lack of maturity also diminishes blame vis-à-vis the adult seller. It is relevant that a central purpose of the law is to protect people like the buyer. The law sees him more as a victim and therefore less to blame for the illegal transaction.

b. Contracts that Violate Public Policy

When the contract is not illegal, but offends public policy, the same rules are generally applicable, but not with the same degree of force: Although such contracts are usually unenforceable, the fact that they are not actually illegal gives the court greater flexibility in tailoring relief. Therefore, in appropriate circumstances, **enforcement on adjusted terms** may be a better solution when the equities favor the party who seeks enforcement and the harm to the public interest can be averted or minimized by eliminating the offensive terms. If enforcement is refused, the in pari delicto rule may be applied to deny restitution, but because the wrongfulness is less grave, the equities are more likely to favor restoration of any benefit conferred.

An example based on a **covenant not to compete** illustrates the adjusted enforcement of a contract that offends public policy: A covenant not to compete is an undertaking by a person associated with a business that, upon leaving the business, he will not, for a specified period and in a specified area, engage in activity that competes with the business. Such covenants may be found in employment or partnership agreements or in contracts for the sale of a business. Say that a well-established pediatrician takes in a newly-qualified doctor into her practice as a junior partner. The established doctor is concerned that her new partner may work with her just long enough to get experience and a following among her patients, and that he will then terminate the partnership and set up practice on his own. To avoid this, she demands a provision in the partnership agreement in terms of which the junior partner undertakes that upon leaving the partnership, he will not practice medicine within a ten-mile radius of the partnership premises for a period of five years.

---

15. Although the general rule is that a person must be over 21 to buy liquor, in most states a person acquires contractual capacity at 18. The contract is therefore not avoidable for lack of capacity.

There is a long-established public policy against agreements that stifle competition or that restrict a person's freedom to earn a livelihood by full participation in the market. This policy underlies the antitrust laws, which prohibit various kinds of anticompetitive behavior. But even in situations not covered by the antitrust legislation (such as the present case) courts apply the policy when a contract unduly hampers competition. The covenant not to compete is not per se invalid, but the court will assess its impact on competition under all the circumstances of the case, taking into account factors including the legitimate interests (such as patient goodwill) of the established doctor, the mores of the medical profession, the hardship on the junior doctor, the patients' right to use a doctor of their choice, and the fairness of the bargaining process leading to agreement on the provision. If, on balance, the deleterious impact of the clause outweighs the interests of the established doctor, the court may refuse to enforce the clause altogether. Alteratively, it may cut down the restraint to a level that goes no further than necessary to protect those interests, reducing the time or geographic limit of the restraint or defining the prohibited activity more narrowly (for example, to cover pediatrics, rather than medical practice generally). In this case, therefore, a violation of public policy does not usually render the entire contract unenforceable, but more likely results in the elimination or adjustment of the offending provision.

Examples

1. Cookie Racha owns a house built in 1915. The house has been plagued with chronic cockroach infestation. Although Cookie fumigated it regularly, roaches reappeared in ever increasing numbers within a few weeks of treatment. Also, the house was slowly sinking into soft ground on one side. The sinking can only be corrected by an expensive process that requires the side of the house to be jacked up while a firm concrete foundation is laid. The sinking has caused deep cracks in the living room wall. Cookie has replastered the wall a few times, but the continuing movement reopened the cracks soon afterwards. Cookie had already become quite sick of the house when she recently read in the newspaper that the neighboring property had been bought by the state for use as a halfway house for paroled sex offenders. This was the final straw and she decided to sell.

   Acting on the advice of her realtor, Chic "The Snake" Canery, she fumigated the house, plastered the cracks, and repainted the wall just before the house was placed on the market. Each time that the house was shown, Chic ensured that all the lights were on. Not only did this present the house in a more attractive manner, but the brightness discouraged the regenerating population of roaches from venturing into full view. Chic brought Bugsy Crawley to see the house. Cookie happened to be present and saw that Bugsy seemed to be very interested in buying the house. During their brief conversation Bugsy said to Cookie, "Does the house have termites?" Cookie had never seen signs of termites in the house, so she simply answered, "No."

A week later, Cookie happened to notice signs of termite damage in the basement. On the very next day she received an offer from Bugsy to buy the house for the full asking price. She accepted immediately. The terms of the contract of sale were set out in Bugsy's offer, made on a standard form provided by the realtor. One of the standard terms was a merger clause that stated that no representations had been made save for those expressed in the writing. The writing simply set out the basic terms of the transaction and made no representations concerning the property. The transaction closed a short while later, and Bugsy moved into his new home. It did not take very long before the roaches reappeared, the wall cracked, the sex offenders moved in next door and the termites were discovered. Does Bugsy have grounds for avoiding the sale?

2. Tuttu Tango is a 65-year-old retired tax lawyer. Her life had become quite dull since retirement, and she was looking for excitement. One day she was invited to accompany a friend to a free introductory dance lesson at the Fraud Astaire Dance Studios. During the lesson, she fell into the clutches of Gig Aloe, a suave and unctuous dance instructor employed by Fraud Astaire. Gig subjected Tuttu to all the charm and flattery that he had perfected by taking Fraud Astaire's super sales course. After observing Tuttu's inept and clumsy cavortings on the dance floor, he pretended to be very impressed. He told her enthusiastically that she had a wonderful natural talent and ageless grace. He said that he was convinced that with proper training, she had the potential of becoming an elegant and alluring dancer. Tuttu had been around the block a few times, so she didn't really believe a word of this. But Gig was cute and he would be her instructor, so she agreed to sign up for a month's worth of lessons at a cost of $100. Gig produced a form and asked her to sign it. He cleverly positioned his hand over the top of the form so Tuttu could not see the top few lines. This little trick worked, because Tuttu did not pay much attention to the form and signed it without trying to read it. Had she been more astute, she would have seen that Gig had given her a life membership contract form to sign, in which she irrevocably purchased a lifetime of lessons for a fee of $10,000, payable within seven days of signing.

A few days later Tuttu went to the studio for her first lesson. She discovered that Gig had been fired and replaced by a decidedly uninteresting instructor — a beefy middle-aged man who wore a string tie. Tuttu went to the manager to tell him that she wanted to cancel her month's lessons. She was shocked when the manager corrected her, showing her the contract form in which she had signed up, not for a month, but a lifetime. He told her that it was studio policy never to release customers from their commitments, and pointed out that her payment was due within the next few days.

Does the common law give her the right to cancel? (Answer on common law principles only, and disregard any consumer protection legislation of which you may have heard.)

3. Sweaty Shoppe, Inc. is a retailer of sports and fitness clothing. It sells a wide variety of all brands of merchandise including goods marketed under its own "Du Resse" trademark. The Du Resse products are made by Sweaty Shoppe's manufacturing division that operates a factory in a small undeveloped country. Brute Force, Inc. makes very expensive weightlifting equipment. Sweaty Shoppe considers these products over-priced and has steadfastly refused to carry them despite several requests by Brute Force.

The president of Brute Force has a friend who works for an organization that monitors violations of human rights. This friend gave him a copy of a secret report that convincingly describes shocking conditions at Sweaty Shoppe's factory, including the virtual enslavement of child workers who are forced to labor in the cruelest conditions for pitifully low wages. If this information is made public, it would cause incalculable harm to Sweaty Shoppe's reputation and customer relations. Also, because a federal law makes it a criminal offense to import goods fabricated by child laborers, the publication of the report would attract a government investigation, possibly leading to prosecution. Realizing this, the president of Brute Force showed a copy of the report to Sweaty Shoppe and threatened to leak it to the press unless Sweaty Shoppe agreed to buy, maintain stocks of, and vigorously promote a full line of Brute Force's products.

Although Sweaty Shoppe knows the report is untrue, it is concerned that many customers would believe it. Also, the government would be bound to initiate an investigation that would be messy, intrusive, and burdensome. Sweaty Shoppe therefore decided to accede to Brute Force's demand and entered the purchase and promotion contract. A week later, the report surfaced anyway because the human rights organization released it.

(a) As Sweaty Shoppe no longer has an incentive to deal with Brute Force's goods, it would like to avoid the contract. Does it have grounds?

(b) Would your answer change if the report was in fact true?

4. D. Fense Contractors, Inc. was awarded a contract by the Air Force to manufacture an early warning system for detecting invasions of alien spacecraft. The system had been designed in an underground lab by a brilliant scientist, and the contract had very precise specifications.

D. Fense was obliged to give this endeavor absolute priority and was to deliver the completed machine in one year. The contract provided that if delivery was late, the Air Force would be entitled to claim liquidated damages in a horrendous amount for each day of delay. Also, it was well known in the defense industry that a contractor who has proved unreliable would have great difficulty in obtaining further government contracts in the future. D. Fense's plant was not sufficiently secure for work of a top secret nature, so it needed to find suitable premises. After some investigation, it discovered that an obscure company, Clandestine Industries of America, Inc. (CIA) had an idle plant that was ideal for the project. CIA agreed to let the premises to D. Fense for one year at an annual rent of $1 million. Six months later, after D. Fense had set up operations in the premises, CIA's auditors surveyed the market and discovered that it had undercharged for the use of the premises, which could have been let for $1.25 million a year. CIA approached D. Fense with these figures and requested an additional $250,000 rent. When D. Fense refused, CIA threatened to terminate the lease and evict D. Fense from the plant. D. Fense knew that even if it defended eviction proceedings, the litigation would be disruptive and the outcome uncertain. It could not seek new premises and begin operations elsewhere without considerable trouble and delay, and it faced real danger of being prevented from honoring its delivery commitments to the Air Force. D. Fense reluctantly decided not to fight CIA on the demand for a price increase and gave in, promising to pay the additional $250,000 at the end of the lease term.

When the lease term had run, D. Fense refused to pay any more than the originally agreed rent. Can CIA enforce the modification?

5. One afternoon, Hardy Ticker developed intense chest pains while digging in his garden. His neighbor, Sam Aritan, noticed his distress and came over to see if he was alright. On being told the problem, Sam put Hardy into his car and rushed him to the nearest hospital, The Sisters of Good Conscience. The receptionist insisted that admission forms be completed before Hardy could be sent to the emergency room. Sam was concerned that Hardy needed urgent attention and begged the receptionist to admit Hardy while he completed the forms. The receptionist agreed. Sam completed as much of Hardy's biographical information as he knew and handed the form to the receptionist. She told him that he had to sign it, which he did. He noticed that the form had about half a page of printed text above the signature blank, but he did not read it. Had he done so, he would have found that he had signed a standard form contract with a provision that obligated the signatory to pay all the hospital's charges for treatment administered to the patient.

Sadly, Hardy died despite the efforts of the emergency room doctors. It was then discovered that he was insolvent and there is nothing in his estate. The hospital therefore demands payment of its fees from Sam, based on his signature on the form contract. Must Sam pay?

6. Mary Maker, a resident of California, decided to go on a cruise. After studying the brochures of several cruise lines, she settled on a seven-day package from Los Angeles to Mexico on the ship S.S. Briny Binge, owned and operated by Party Lines, Inc. Party Lines has its headquarters in Miami, Florida, and operates cruises out of Miami and Los Angeles. Mary called her local travel agent and booked. A week later she received her ticket, printed on one side of a single sheet of paper. She checked to make sure that the dates and cabin booking were correct. She did not otherwise read the printed matter on the ticket, despite a warning, printed on the ticket in large red letters, that stated "PASSENGER: THIS DOCUMENT AFFECTS YOUR LEGAL RIGHTS. READ IT!" Had she read the document, she would have found the following provision:

"This ticket is issued subject to the following terms and conditions:
1. Party Lines, Inc. shall not be responsible for loss or harm suffered by the passenger while on board the ship, whether or not caused by the negligence of Party Lines, Inc. or any of its employees or agents.
2. In the event of any dispute between Party Lines, Inc. and the passenger arising out of this transaction, the courts of the State of Florida shall have exclusive jurisdiction to hear and resolve such dispute."

Mary embarked on the ship. Three days into the cruise, as she made her way to her cabin in the small hours of the morning, she did not notice a steep, poorly illuminated staircase. She tumbled down the stairs and injured herself. Upon returning home, Mary sued Party Lines in a California court, alleging that the company was negligent in failing to light the staircase. She claimed medical expenses and damages for pain and suffering. Party Lines requests summary judgment on the grounds that the California court has no jurisdiction in terms of the contract and that, in any event, Mary had contractually waived any claim that she may otherwise have had. Should summary judgment be granted?

7. Hi Rate Gems, Inc. operates a retail jewelry store in a less affluent neighborhood and draws most of its customers from the local area. They are typically quite poor and do not have the means to buy jewelry for cash, nor could they qualify for credit under the usual market standards. To make sales, Hi Rate has found it necessary to provide financing to its customers under a lenient credit policy. As a result, its losses from uncollectible debt are much higher than those of more conservative lending institutions. To compensate for this, it prices its jewelry about 20 percent higher than the prevailing market and charges interest five percent above the market rate. To obtain credit, a customer is obliged to sign a standard form contract under which Hi Rate retains a security interest in the items purchased. This means that if the customer should default in payments,

Hi Rate has the right to repossess the jewelry, to credit its value against the balance owing, and to institute collection action against the customer for any remaining deficiency.

Rock Sparkler bought a diamond nose stud with matching earrings from Hi Rate for $2,000. Rock did not have the $2,000, and his terrible credit record assured that no sensible lender would advance him a penny. He therefore applied for credit from Hi Rate. One of the questions on the form asked if any judgments had been granted against the applicant. Rock knew of at least five such unsatisfied judgments, but he feared that disclosing them would be fatal to the application. He did not wish to lie, so he simply ignored the question and left the space blank. Luckily, the credit clerk did not notice the omission because he did not look at the application very carefully before approving the financing. The sales assistant then filled out the details of the items purchased and the monthly payment rate on the standard form purchase agreement, and handed it to Rock for his signature. The assistant made no attempt to explain the form's printed terms to Rock, who did not read it before signing. He then took the jewelry and left.

A few weeks later, Hi Rate's credit manager was reviewing the applications and noticed that Rock had not answered the question about judgments. He checked the public record and discovered the unsatisfied judgments. Hi Rate wishes to rescind the contract and get the jewelry back. Has it the right to do so?

8. All the facts regarding the formation of the contract are the same as in Example 7. The only factual difference is as follows: Hi Rate did not check the public record. It is happy with the transaction and has no desire to avoid the contract. However, a short time after the purchase, Rock had misgivings about buying the jewelry. He would like to cancel the sale and return it. May he do so?

9. Rob Graves plundered a 3,000-year-old bronze figurine from the tomb of an ancient king. He smuggled it into the U.S. and used his contacts in the world of art collecting to find a buyer. He was put in touch with Ann Tiquity, a wealthy collector. Ann asked Rob how he acquired the figurine, and he told her that he had inherited it from his grandfather, who found it while participating in an archeological dig in the late nineteenth century. Ann knows a great deal about art and had little trouble identifying the bronze as genuine. However, she comes from a very wealthy family and has always associated with rich people. She is therefore quite used to the idea that art treasures and other valuables are inherited from relatives, and Rob's explanation seemed quite reasonable to her. She purchased the figurine from him for $5 million cash, a remarkably low price for so rare a piece. In fact, after buying it, Ann had it appraised at $7 million.

Assume that federal law forbids the smuggling and sale of plundered artifacts and permits their confiscation and return to the country of origin. The statute does not apply to artifacts imported before 1900. Both parties knew about the law at the time of the transaction. A few weeks after the sale, U.S. Customs agents traced the figurine to Ann, took it from her and returned it to the government of the country from which it was smuggled. Ann has sued Rob for the return of the $5 million. Assuming that the federal statute contains no provisions dealing with the rights between the parties to the forbidden sale, should she be given restitution of her payment?

Explanations

1. There are a number of statements, acts, or silences that could qualify as misrepresentations. Before examining them, we must address a preliminary issue raised by the **merger clause** in the written agreement: Even if the agreement is fully integrated, the parol evidence rule does not bar evidence of oral or prior written fraudulent misrepresentations. Hill v. Jones, discussed in section 13.6.2 in relation to nondisclosure also held that a party may not use a merger clause to exclude evidence of her fraudulent conduct. However, a completely integrated writing with an effective merger clause does bar parol evidence of innocent or negligent misrepresentations. The merger clause is on a standard form, which may make a court less likely to take it seriously in deciding the question of integration. Note, however, that it was not Cookie's form.

    Cookie did not make any statement asserting that the house was **free of cockroaches** or that it was **stable**. However, concealment of the truth by conduct is as much an affirmative misrepresentation as a verbal misstatement. When Cookie knew the truth and intended by the act of concealment to induce the contract, the requisite scienter was present and the misrepresentation is fraudulent. It seems clear that Cookie's motive in fumigating and performing the cosmetic repairs to the wall went beyond acceptable preparations for sale and were deliberate steps to conceal serious problems that would have made the house less marketable.

    The misrepresentation must have induced Bugsy to enter the contract on the agreed terms. When fraud is involved, the test for inducement is commonly based on a subjective standard. Bugsy must show that the misrepresented fact was influential to him and that, given his circumstances and personal attributes, he was justified in relying on the false words or appearance. Of course, it is easier to show subjective inducement if the misrepresentation concerns a fact that would have been regarded as material and would have been relied on by a reasonable person. Although we do not know what motivated Bugsy to make the offer, the concealed facts are important even if viewed objectively, so it should not be difficult for him to show that they influenced him to make the offer. Bugsy probably should have had the house inspected for structural soundness and pests, or should at least have asked about more than just termites. His reliance on appearances may not have been justified. His lack of vigilance could weaken his case, but a court is likely to weigh his neglect against Cookie's active dishonesty, and her deliberate concealment will likely outweigh Bugsy's omission. Finally, prejudice is obvious. Not only does the house have a chronic cockroach problem, but it requires expensive repairs. Bugsy probably overpaid by agreeing to the full asking price, which we can assume was at least equal to the market price of the home in the condition represented. In any event, he does not want a home with these problems at any price.

When asked by Bugsy if the house had **termites**, Cookie answered incorrectly that it did not. Because she did not know about the termites at the time that she made the misrepresentation, it was innocent or, at worst, negligent. In *Halpert v. Rosenthal*, 267 A.2d 730 (R.I. 1970), the seller made a similar representation without knowledge of a termite infestation, but the court pointed out that even an innocent misrepresentation is grounds for avoidance if it is material and justifiably relied on by the other party. This rule does not apply in the present case because the integrated writing with a merger clause precludes Bugsy from introducing parol evidence of a non-fraudulent misrepresentation.

However, this does not end the matter. Before the contract was concluded, Cookie discovered the termites and acquired information that showed her previous representation to be false. She had a duty to disclose this to Bugsy before accepting his offer. As she did not, her newfound knowledge removed the innocence from her misrepresentation and made it fraudulent. She is in no better a position than if she had deliberately lied at the time of being asked the question, and the fact that Bugsy asked is good evidence that he relied on the answer in deciding to enter the contract.

Cookie also failed to tell Bugsy that a **halfway house for sex offenders** was to be opened on the adjacent property. Although the nondisclosure of known information is not as obviously fraud as an affirmative act of lying or concealing the truth, it can be fraud if the duty of fair dealing imposes an obligation to speak. It can be difficult to decide when disclosure is required, because the law recognizes that fair dealing does not compel a party to bare all information pertinent to the transaction. Furthermore, even if there was a duty to speak, the omission may not be as culpable as a positive act. As a result, the prerequisites for relief are not as heavily weighted against the perpetrator, and the victim is more readily held accountable for failure to make diligent inquiry. As a general guide, a party is only required to disclose information if four conditions are satisfied: She knows that the other is unaware of it; the knowledge would be reasonably likely to influence the other's decision to enter the transaction; the information is not readily accessible to the other by diligent inquiry; and the information is not fairly regarded as the party's own property, having been acquired by special efforts or study.

Given the outcry when a released sex offender takes up residence in a neighborhood, a reasonable person would assume that this information would be material to a homebuyer. The information is not proprietary, so Cookie cannot claim that she had the right to keep it to herself. However, the proposed home is a public project that has already been reported in the press. The information is freely available and for all Cookie knows, Bugsy has also read the paper. If not, it would be easy enough for him to gain access to the information. On balance, if he did not know about the halfway house, his lack of inquiry should preclude relief on this ground despite Cookie's silence.

2. This example is a factual variation of a couple of infamous Arthur Murray cases decided in the 1960s. In *Vokes v. Arthur Murray, Inc.*, 212 So. 2d 906 (Fla. 1968), and *Syester v. Banta*, 133 N.W.2d 666 (Iowa 1965), Arthur Murray franchisees employed the deliberate tactic of ongoing and excessive flattery to induce untalented elderly women to sign up for astoundingly large quantities of dance lessons at grotesque total cost. In both cases the importuning, begun at first contact, was reinforced and accelerated during a long period of continuing lessons. The courts found that the fulsome praise, unremitting sweet talk, undeserved medals and awards, and untrue claims of progress were so extreme as to pass beyond good customer relations and become outright fraud.

The fraud in these cases was not the misrepresentation of an external objective fact, but of an opinion. By pretending that they believed the victims to have talent and potential, the studio employees lied about what they thought, inducing the victims to buy copious quantities of lessons. Although false opinions do not always qualify as factual misrepresentations, a deliberate misstatement of opinion can be fraud when the party expressing it claims to have the knowledge and expertise to form a judgment and should realize that the victim is relying on an honest assessment. As the brief description of the case suggests, the behavior of the Arthur Murray studios went far beyond the expression of a dishonest opinion. The transactions were thoroughly unsavory. Lonely and gullible elderly women were cruelly manipulated for a long period and induced to spend substantial amounts of their savings on extended courses of dance lessons that were unlikely to be used up in their lifetimes.

Fraud was the basis for relief in both cases, but the facts make an overwhelming case of unconscionability as well: As a result of the studios' slimy bargaining methods, their victims were induced to enter contracts for lessons well in excess of their needs at a ludicrous cost. Unconscionability doctrine is not needed when the elements of fraud are satisfied. However, if there is any doubt about establishing fraud, unconscionability serves as an alternative theory for avoidance. Tuttu's case may be an example of this.

Fraud Astaire's conduct was not as egregious as that of the Arthur Murray studios, and Tuttu, being a worldly former tax lawyer, is not as sympathetic a victim as the plaintiffs in those cases. Nevertheless, there were two instances of dishonesty by Gig, acting on behalf of Fraud Astaire, that could provide an argument for fraud. First, he deliberately misrepresented his opinion. However, this may not be a good basis for establishing fraud because his misrepresentation apparently did not induce Tuttu to enter the contract. Tuttu was not taken in by his flattery and was motivated by deeper urges. (Although he turned out not to be the instructor, there is no indication that he realized that this was an inducing factor or that he knew of and failed to disclose his impending dismissal.)

Second, he concealed the true nature of the form by placing his hands over it. If this is fraud, it would be in the factum, not in the inducement, because it relates to the document being signed rather than to a motivating fact. Note also that the misrepresentation is by concealment, not affirmative assertion. Although his intent is dishonest, Tuttu is probably damned by her sophistication and training. While an illiterate or naive person may be able to convince a factfinder of having been bamboozled into unwittingly signing a lifetime contract, Tuttu, a trained lawyer, should have known better than to sign something without reading it. The strategically placed hand adds no force to her case. Although the writing was concealed, it was easily discoverable (in fact, the attempt at concealment should have excited her suspicion). While inducement is based on a largely subjective standard, her attributes affect the credibility of any claim that she was actually induced to sign as a result of the clumsy deception. Having said this, it must be acknowledged that an argument of fraud is not entirely inconceivable if Tuttu can show an intent to defraud. Even extreme neglect may be outweighed by clear proof of the perpetrator's dishonesty.

If fraud is not a promising avenue for attack, unconscionability may be more successful. Bargaining unfairness short of actual fraud may be sufficient to show procedural unconscionability, and it should not be too difficult to demonstrate the substantive unfairness of a $10,000 contract for lifetime dance instruction. Unconscionability is less potent a weapon in the hands of a well-educated and commercially proficient party, but even former tax lawyers can be caught off guard by predators in the marketplace.

3(a). Sweaty Shoppe should be able to avoid the contract on grounds of duress because it has been induced to enter the contract by Brute Force's wrongful threat. The threatened action would lead to economic harm rather than physical injury, but it is well accepted in contemporary law that duress encompasses a wrongful threat of economic damage. There is nothing subtle about the threat in this case. It is blackmail pure and simple. Even if the disclosure had been motivated only by an honest desire to keep the public informed, the dissemination of false allegations could be wrongful in itself and may result in liability for defamation. When the threat of dissemination is meant to gain a private economic advantage, the wrongfulness is beyond debate.

The facts indicate that Sweaty Shoppe was in fact induced to enter the contract by the threat. Although modern law rejects the objective test of "ordinary firmness," the victim must still show justification for giving in to the threat. The test is whether, given all the circumstances, the victim had no reasonable alternative but to acquiesce. Sweaty Shoppe did have alternatives. The most obvious would have been to refuse to contract with Brute Force and to deal with the consequences of the disclosure by suing for defamation, mounting a publicity campaign to correct the public perception, and averting prosecution by convincing the government of its compliance with the law. However, this is not likely to be regarded as a reasonable alternative given the cost and expense as well as the strong likelihood that Sweaty Shoppe would probably never be able to fully redeem its public image. Another possible alternative may be to try to avert the harm by seeking an injunction against release of the information. However, even if a court could be persuaded to enjoin publication, the proceedings would inevitably engender the very publicity sought to be avoided. There are probably other alternatives that could be suggested, but the court is likely to be sympathetic to the victim's claim that they all seemed risky and harmful.

The compelling effect of potential harm to customer goodwill is illustrated by *S. P. Dunham & Co. v. Kudra*, 131 A.2d 306 (N.J. 1957).

Unknown to its customers, when a department store accepted their fur coats for cleaning and storage, the store did not keep the coats itself, but entrusted them to a concessionaire, who in turn stored the coats with a rival store. The concessionaire became bankrupt and did not pay storage charges due on these and other garments. The rival store wrongfully refused to release the coats unless the department store agreed to pay the concessionaire's debt. Although it was not legally responsible for the debt, the department store agreed to pay it to avoid the embarrassment of not being able to return its customers' coats and having to reveal that they were being stored with a competitor. The court held that although the store had the alternative of refusing to pay and suing for return of the wrongfully retained coats, this alternative was not reasonable because the publicity and delay of litigation would result in the very harm to customer relations that the department store was anxious to avoid.

3(b). Explanation 3(a) argues that the likely result under those facts is that Sweaty Shoppe would be able to avoid the contract. I think that the end result would be the same even if the allegations about the working conditions had been true. The truth of the allegations does not change the conclusion that the threat is wrongful. Because the facts are true, the act of publication is no longer wrongful in itself if motivated by the desire to serve the public interest. However, even a proper act loses its legitimacy if performed for the ulterior motive of blackmail for private advantage. Knowing the truth, Brute Force chose not to reveal the facts to the public, but rather to conceal it for a price, using the power of its knowledge to coerce Sweaty Shoppe into a contract.

In addition, as the importation of goods manufactured with child labor is a crime, Brute Force has done more than merely threaten adverse publicity. It is essentially agreeing not to report the criminal activity in exchange for the commitment to purchase its products. This is a dereliction of duty and a violation of public policy. Knowledge of criminal activity cannot be used as a bargaining chip in contract negotiations. This is illustrated by *Germantown Mortgage Co. v. Rawlinson*, 491 A.2d 138 (Pa. 1985). After discovering that its employee had been embezzling money, the employer persuaded the employee's wife to undertake repayment of the funds. In addition to other questionable bargaining tactics, it intimated that it would not press charges against the employee if she agreed to the commitment. Although the act of prosecuting the employee would have been justified, the court found a wrongful threat because the employer used its power to prosecute for the purpose of inducing the contract.

The element of inducement is, if anything, strengthened by the fact that the allegations are true. It weakens or eliminates the alternative of allowing the dissemination of the information and trying to counter it. As the court pointed out in *Germantown Mortgage*, the threat is improper, whether or not the party is guilty of the alleged action. But if the party is guilty, the threat is even more intimidating, and the apprehension of the threatened disclosure is more likely to cloud judgment and volition. These considerations suggest that Sweaty Shoppe should be able to avoid the contract on the grounds of duress.

Apart from satisfying the elements of duress, the contract implicates other public policies. A public policy analysis strengthens the conclusion that Brute Force should not be able to enforce the contract against Sweaty Shoppe. There are a number of public policies implicated in this case. Brute Force has offended two policies: Its attempt at blackmail violates the assent policy of contract law, and its illegitimate use of the threat of criminal prosecution harms the public interest in the proper investigation and punishment of criminal activity. Sweaty Shoppe has also violated policy by using child labor. This mutual misbehavior leads to the additional consideration of whether the public welfare is best served by refusing enforcement of the contract. The answer must be that it is. To refuse enforcement directly serves two of these policies and is at least consonant with the third. It upholds the assent policy by not binding Sweaty Shoppe to a coerced transaction. By refusing to recognize the binding effect of a commitment not to prosecute, it reduces the incentive to bargain over criminal prosecution. A contrary argument may be that a refusal of relief to Sweaty Shoppe would further the policy against child labor by punishing it for its nefarious foreign activity. However, this consideration is outweighed by those in favor of non-enforcement because the law provides other penalties for addressing this problem.

4. This contract does not involve a sale of goods, so the common law applies. In traditional common law analysis, the modification is unenforceable because CIA had a pre-existing duty to let the premises for the original rent, and it suffered no new detriment in exchange for D. Fense's promise to pay more money. (The undertaking not to breach does not qualify as a legal detriment because although CIA has the power to breach, it has no legal right to do so.) Therefore, while the real reason for refusing enforcement is that the modification was coerced, consideration doctrine achieves this purpose indirectly by focusing on the lack of exchange in the modification.

Although consideration doctrine can serve the purpose of policing for unfair modifications, it does not assure correct resolution, because it focuses on the exchange rather than on the justification for the modification. It could therefore lead to the enforcement of an unfair modification if some small detriment is given for it, or conversely, it could result in the nonenforcement of a fair modification simply because no new detriment was suffered by the party who was benefited by the change. Recognizing this, a court may decide to move away from consideration analysis in a common law case, and to adopt the approach of policing more directly on the basis of duress. This is what the court did in *Austin Instrument* discussed in section 13.9. In a sale of goods, §2.209 avoids the awkwardness that consideration doctrine creates in the policing of modifications by declaring that an agreement modifying a contract does not need consideration and by prescribing a good faith test.

5.   A similar situation occurred in *Phoenix Baptist Hospital v. Aiken*, 877 P.2d 1345 (Ariz. 1994). After rushing his wife to the hospital, a husband signed a form contract obliging him to pay the hospital's charges. In the absence of this undertaking he would not have been personally liable for his wife's medical expenses. The hospital sued him and applied for summary judgment on the basis of his signature on the form. The court refused summary judgment and held that the husband was entitled to go to trial on the question of whether the contract was unconscionable. The court said that the contract appeared adhesive, signed under traumatic and hurried circumstances in which the husband had little realistic opportunity to know what he was signing. Even if he did know, the emotional stress and the need for the hospital's immediate services would likely leave him without power to bargain, and give him no choice but to acquiesce in order to ensure that his wife received medical attention. The court considered that adhesion of this kind could make the contract procedurally unconscionable. In addition, substantive unconscionability could lie in the fact that he assumed liability for which he would not otherwise be responsible, and that he could not reasonably have expected to be provided for in the form that he signed. *Phoenix Baptist Hospital* did not involve a sale of goods, so unconscionability doctrine did not derive from UCC §2.302. This is one of the many modern cases that recognizes unconscionability as a doctrine applicable to contracts under common law.

    As discussed more fully in section 13.12 and Example 6, adhesion and procedural unconscionability are not present merely because the contract is a standard form drafted by the party with greater bargaining power, or because the choices of the weaker party are limited. However, when the services contracted for are desperately and urgently needed, and the party to perform the services presents a form without explanation or a reasonable opportunity to read, in circumstances that make bargaining burdensome or futile, it should not be very difficult to make a case for procedural unconscionability. It is not required that the hospital purposely used unfair bargaining methods to trick or coerce Sam into signing. The procurement of apparent assent under these circumstances should be enough. Sam's emotional stake in the rendition of the services to Hardy is not as strong as that of a spouse, but the stress and urgency of the situation is patent. Sam would not have to show that the terms were objectively unfair — for example, that the hospital charged an excessive price. The substantive unconscionability lies in the fact that Sam incurred an obligation that he would not otherwise have, for services from which he received no personal gain. In this respect, his case is stronger than that of a spouse. There is thus an adequate showing of substantive unconscionability — but even if a court may question this conclusion, the strong showing of procedural unfairness would seem to place beyond doubt the need to give Sam relief.

Unconscionability is the most appropriate basis for relief in this case. Could it also have been argued under a theory of duress? Duress doctrine has expanded enough to make this a possibility, in that the threat to withhold medical services for Hardy undermined Sam's free will and coerced him into signing. However, this strains the concept of improper threat because the hospital did nothing more than indicate intent not to enter a contract except on its own terms. This cannot be a threat unless it can be concluded that the hospital had a duty outside of contract law to render services to any patient brought in.

6. Obviously, Mary is not seeking avoidance of the contract. Rather, to assert her tort claim, she must persuade the court that she is not bound by the forum selection clause and liability disclaimer.

We must begin by considering a **contract formation** issue. Mary did not actually receive the terms until she got the tickets. As mentioned in section 13.12.2 and discussed more fully in section 4.13, there is some ambiguity as to when the contract was formed in a case like this. Offer and acceptance could have occurred when Mary booked the trip, or it could have happened only after Party Lines made an offer by sending the tickets to Mary and she accepted the offer by keeping the tickets without protest. This latter interpretation seems less likely because there seems to be no indication that the parties intended that Mary would not be bound until she received and had a chance to review the tickets. Let us therefore assume that the contract was formed at the time of booking. Mary may argue that Party Lines did not properly reveal the disputed terms at that time, and they therefore did not form part of the contract. A court may find this argument persuasive, especially if it is bothered by the adhesive nature of the contract and its orientation is toward the protection of the less powerful party. However, it may not. In *Carnival Cruise Lines* (discussed in section 13.12.2) the majority of the U.S. Supreme Court held that it is not per se invalid for a party to impose standard terms that are not articulated to the other party at the time of contracting, provided that there is a reasonable expectation that the contract is likely to be subject to standard terms and the terms themselves are not unusual or oppressive. Of course, the cruise line cannot conceal the terms and it must have been ready to make them available if asked. However, if Mary did not inquire, she failed to fulfill her duty to read and cannot later complain that she did not know about them. The facts do not reveal common practice in the travel industry, but we can probably agree, as reasonable consumers, that the usual expectation in that market is that tickets are subject to standard terms.

If we conclude that the standard terms are part of the contract, we have to decide whether they bar Mary's suit. This raises the policing doctrines of unconscionability and public policy. Before we turn to those, we should **examine the language** of the provisions to make sure that they mean what Party Lines contends. That is, if the forum selection clause and the disclaimer can be **interpreted** not to apply to this lawsuit, we do not need to invoke any policing doctrine to avoid them. The disclaimer's language creates some doubt about its scope. It exonerates Party Lines from "loss or harm." The provision does not expressly mention personal injury, and the juxtaposition of the words "loss" and "harm" could suggest that only economic damage is contemplated. The public policy of reading negligence disclaimers as narrowly as possible, combined with the *contra preferentum* rule could persuade a court that the clause does not cover personal injury at all. If the court accepts this interpretation, the disclaimer is simply inapplicable and we need not be concerned with avoiding it. The forum selection clause may also be subject to interpretational challenge. Mary could argue that "any dispute . . . arising out of [the] . . . transaction" is not broad enough to cover tort claims for personal injury and should be confined to disputes relating to the performance of services promised under the contract. If the court accepts this interpretation, the California suit can proceed without any determination of whether the clause is avoidable.

If the provisions are interpreted to mean what Party Lines says they mean, they are enforceable unless they can be avoided. There is no indication of fraud or duress, so **unconscionability** doctrine offers Mary the best hope of eliminating the provisions. This is a contract of adhesion with standard terms that Mary did not negotiate or even read. However, that is not enough to make the terms unconscionable. To establish procedural unconscionability, Mary must produce evidence of some form of underhand dealing, which she cannot do on these facts, or must at least show that the terms were imposed on her without any meaningful choice, under circumstances that make the imposition oppressive. The terms were not made available to her at the time of booking, so this is a point in her favor. However, she should have expected standard terms, but she did not ask about or negotiate over them, and subsequently failed to read them when she did receive them. In addition, there is no indication that she tried to shop around to see if better terms were available from a competitor. Her case for procedural unconscionability is weak. She may have a better chance of showing substantive unconscionability, but this is not an easy case either. To establish substantive unconscionability, Mary must do more than show that the terms served Party Line's interest and were adverse to hers. She must establish that they were not justified by business realities and were so one-sided as to be oppressive. *Carnival Cruise Lines*, discussed in section 13.12.2, upheld a forum selection clause under circumstances very similar to these because the clause was a reasonable cost-saving measure that selected an appropriate forum and was not designed to suppress suit. The liability disclaimer must be analyzed similarly. It is potentially unfair, but not per se unconscionable to disclaim liability for negligent injury. In evaluating the fairness of a disclaimer the court looks at factors such as the nature of the service, the parties who are likely to avail themselves of it, the degree to which a user of the service places herself under the control of the cruise line, the scope of the disclaimer, the conspicuousness of its disclosure, the business justification for including it, the reasonableness of the clause in light of accepted commercial practice, and whether the price of the cruise would have been higher in the absence of the exclusion of liability. In short, neither procedural nor substantive unconscionability is strongly shown on these facts, and Mary's prospects of avoiding the provisions do not look very promising.

Finally, although public policy considerations have already been raised in the discussion of unconscionability, it is worth noting that even if a provision is fairly bargained, it can still be attacked as violating **public policy**. Where public policy outside of the area of contract is implicated, the court must balance that public policy against the policy of freedom of contract. The forum selection clause affects Mary's right to sue in a court that would otherwise have jurisdiction. It thereby impairs a strong public interest in uninhibited access to justice. The majority in *Carnival Cruise Lines* held that this policy does not absolutely invalidate an agreement restricting this right of access provided that the agreement is genuine and freely made and the selected forum is reasonable. Of course, the strong public policy of access to justice means that the clause must be scrutinized carefully. As noted in section 13.12.2, the clause withstood the scrutiny of the majority of the Supreme Court, but not the dissent.

As discussed in section 13.13.3 disclaimers of liability are also scrutinized carefully because public policy requires that a person is held accountable for negligent injury. (A disclaimer of liability for deliberate injury would unquestionably violate public policy, but this is not in issue here. At worst, Party Lines was negligent and the disclaimer mentions only negligent injury.) The question of whether the disclaimer so offends public policy as to be unenforceable is very similar to the question of whether the disclaimer is substantively unconscionable and involves consideration of the same factors.

7. Rock's failure to disclose the judgments likely qualifies as a fraudulent misrepresentation. Even though he did not affirmatively lie, he declined to disclose known information when asked. In some situations it may be difficult to decide if a party has the duty to disclose facts pertinent to the transaction, but this is not such a case. It is generally accepted that a duty of honest response does arise if the other party asks a direct question, particularly when the information sought is not of a proprietary nature. By ignoring the question with knowledge that a true answer would imperil the credit application, Rock makes a deliberate misrepresentation of fact with knowledge of its falsity and intent to induce the contract.

It is more difficult to say whether the misrepresentation did in fact induce the contract. A debtor's unreliability in other transactions is generally a crucial factor in the decision to grant credit. However, Hi Rate's cursory look at the form suggests that its standard for granting credit is very low indeed. If it really cared about the applicant's credit history or was truly interested in the answers on the application, it would have taken more trouble to read the form. Furthermore, judgments are a matter of public record, easily accessible to the prospective creditor. A creditor who regards this information as crucial would not simply rely on the applicant's disclosure and would check. Normally, when fraud is involved, the serious malfeasance of the perpetrator outweighs any lapse of care by the victim in failing to check the facts. But actual inducement must still be shown, and where the victim is sophisticated enough to know better, careless gullibility may break the chain of justified reliance.

In addition, there is some suggestion in this case that Hi Rate is not being entirely responsible or socially conscious in selling expensive luxury items to people who cannot afford them, and that it has ameliorated its risk of loss by padding its prices and interest rates. Although this does not excuse Rock's dishonesty, Hi Rate cannot comfortably don the mantle of innocent dupe. It can fairly be expected to take care of its own interests. In short, without condoning Rock's deceitful silence, a court may be indisposed to allow Hi Rate out of the contract. As long as Rock continues to make his payments as promised, Hi Rate must live with the risk of his lack of creditworthiness.

8. There is nothing to suggest that Hi Rate made any misrepresentation to Rock, or that it applied any threat to make him enter the contract. Therefore, if Rock is to have any right of avoidance, it must be based on unconscionability.[16] Avoidance of the contract, as opposed to enforcement on adjusted terms, is within the range of relief available to Rock at the court's discretion.

Because Hi Rate seems to have a captive market and it imposes higher prices and adverse terms on its customers under standard form contracts, one may jump to the conclusion that Hi Rate is a predatory mass contractor subjecting a whole section of the community to its harsh contracts of adhesion. This conclusion is even more tempting if one perceives it as socially harmful to sell luxury items on credit to people who cannot afford them. However, one cannot conclude as a matter of law that the contract is unconscionable under these circumstances. The transaction must be evaluated to see if it satisfies the two elements of unconscionability.

Hi Rate did not employ high-pressure selling techniques or deceptive practices that could lead to a clear-cut case of **procedural unconscionability**. However, *Williams v. Walker Thomas Furniture*, discussed in section 13.11.3, suggests that the contract could be procedurally unconscionable if Rock had no meaningful choice — the contract is adhesive because Hi Rate, the dominant party, had the power to dictate the terms, and Rock, the weaker party had no choice but to accept those terms. Under some circumstances, the mere fact of adhesion, without a demonstration of specific bargaining impropriety, could satisfy the procedural element of unconscionability. (This conclusion could be strengthened slightly if the terms were not conspicuous and drawn to Rock's attention.)

---

16. As the following discussion shows, the public policy of consumer protection is inherent in the unconscionability analysis and is one of the motivations for unconscionability doctrine. One could therefore say that the right of avoidance is based on public policy, but this is always true because all contract doctrines have a policy basis.

However, the claim of lack of meaningful choice is tenuous in relation to a sale of luxury goods. True, this may have been the only means Rock had to acquire the jewelry, but he could have chosen not to buy it at all. In addition, there is no indication that Rock tried to buy the jewelry elsewhere or that he protested over or tried to negotiate the price or other terms. In some cases the weaker party's lack of sophistication can bolster the sense of imposition, but Rock does not appear to be particularly unsophisticated. Remember that he was sly enough to practice his own bit of deception.

Even if the basis for procedural unconscionability is shaky, a court may still find the contract to be unconscionable if the weaker party can show a strong degree of **substantive unconscionability**. This seems unlikely in this case. The contract terms are adverse to Rock, but the higher price and interest rate could be based on sound business practice and could conform to reasonable commercial practice in a high-risk credit market. Hi Rate's retention of a security interest to secure the price is a widely-accepted means of protecting a creditor from default, and the facts do not suggest that the security agreement has unusually harsh terms (for example, such as the cross-collateralization term in *Williams*).

9. This example involves issues of fraud and illegality. Rob made a fraudulent misrepresentation by lying about the way in which he acquired the figurine. Two elements of fraud, scienter and prejudice, are surely satisfied. Scienter is present because Rob knew the statement was false and must have realized that Ann, as a collector, probably knew the law, and would likely not have bought the figurine if she thought it had been illegally smuggled into the U.S. He therefore deliberately made a false statement with intent to induce the contract. Injury to Ann is obvious because she has paid for the piece that has been lost as a result of the flaw in title, concealed by Rob's lie.

The element that is in doubt is inducement. Normally, the test for inducement in a fraud case is largely subjective — it tries to glean the actual state of mind of the victim, and to determine whether the misrepresentation did in fact induce her to enter the contract. A subjective test would give Ann some hope of convincing the factfinder that she truly was as naive and unworldly as the facts suggest. However, even under a subjective test, her claimed innocence strains credulity. Given her knowledge of art dealings and law, a more likely explanation is that she deliberately avoided inquiry because the bargain was too good to miss, and she did not want to know the truth.

Therefore, even under the usual subjective standard, Ann could have trouble showing inducement. However, in this particular case, there is a strong argument for not using a subjective test of inducement, but of objectively evaluating her reliance on the misrepresentation. On an objective test, her chance of success is remote. Although we do not have evidence of acceptable market behavior, we can at least make the preliminary assumption that a reasonable collector, knowing the risk of confiscation, would not likely spend $5 million on an artifact without verifying the truth of Rob's assertion.

The reason for moving to an objective test in this case lies in the fact that reliance on Rob's fraudulent misrepresentation would lead Ann to violate the law, so we are no longer concerned only with the assent and reliance policies of contract law, but also with the policy reflected in the federal statute. If the only matter at stake was Ann's duty to herself, we could accept her genuine reliance, even if she had been sloppy in failing to probe further. Her fault in lack of vigilance pales before Rob's venality, and a subjective standard meets the need of balancing the assent and reliance policies of contract law. However, by making the purchase of smuggled artifacts unlawful, the statute imposes a public duty on Ann that goes beyond her responsibility to safeguard her own interests, and it demands a higher level of justification for her conduct. By buying the property, she makes its smuggling worthwhile and she frustrates the goals of the law. Her role is similar to that of a fence receiving stolen goods, and public policy may demand that she be held accountable for her (objective) reason to know of the figurine's origins. She may even have an affirmative duty to verify the seller's assertion. If this is so, she fails the test of inducement and is not entitled to relief.

Ann may therefore have difficulty establishing fraud and probably cannot base her claim for avoidance of the contract and restitution on that theory. However, illegality may provide an alternative ground on which to claim restitution. The federal statute, although it does not expressly declare the contract void, does have that effect by confiscating the artifact despite its sale by the smuggler. When illegality affects the contract, a party who has performed under it is normally granted restitution unless the court determines her conduct to have been so contrary to law and morality that it refuses to come to her aid and decides to leave the parties as it finds them. This principle is expressed in the *in pari delicto* rule, under which the court weighs the relative guilt of the parties and will refuse to order restitution if Ann is as much or more at fault than Rob. In applying the rule, the court does not look only at relative blame, but also considers whether restitution will advance or harm the policy goals of the law. As mentioned before, the allocation of blame between a thief and the buyer of the stolen property who makes the theft worthwhile is not self-evident. However, Rob seems to be the guiltier of the two. Not only did he steal and smuggle the figurine, but he then lied to Ann about the origin of his possession, leading her (even if not entirely innocently) into the illegal transaction.

On the question of policy, it is difficult to say if the statutory goal of discouraging these transactions is better served by leaving the buyer with the loss or by making the smuggler restore his ill-gotten gains. Unless the former situation clearly appears more helpful to the statutory purpose, the balance favors restitution. It is important to bear in mind that the decision on restitution takes the public interest into account and is not simply a matter of doing justice between the parties, so the mere fact that Rob was unjustly enriched at Ann's expense is not conclusive.

Incapacity

§14.1 THE SCOPE AND FOCUS OF THE DOCTRINES DISCUSSED IN THIS CHAPTER

The law generally assumes that all persons have the capacity to enter contracts. The two exceptions to this rule are minors and mentally incompetent adults. A minor's lack of contractual capacity is relatively easy to establish because it is largely based on the objective criterion of age. The determination that an adult lacks contractual capacity is more complex because it requires proof of mental illness or disturbance sufficiently serious to render the person incompetent. Although mental incapacity is necessarily based on the party's subjective state of mind, her mental condition is proved by objective evidence of her behavior observed by others, and by expert psychiatric evidence.

There are connections between incapacity and the doctrines discussed in Chapter 13, but there are also notable differences. The underlying rationale for permitting the avoidance of a contract entered into by a person who lacks mental capacity is the *protection of the incapacitated person*. This suggests analogies both to improper bargaining and public policy. However, there are important distinctions.

Although improper bargaining may sometimes be present in an incapacity case, especially where the other party has exploited the lack of capacity, there is *no requirement* that any *improper bargaining* be proved. Where the other party has taken advantage of the incapacitated party, this obviously has an influence on the court's decision on whether to permit avoidance of the contract on grounds of incapacity. However, the fundamental basis of incapacity is the *legal status* of the incapacitated party. This means that incapacity can be invoked even where there was no deception or illegitimate pressure in the formation of the contract and it is on fair terms.

Incapacity is based on the *public policy* of protecting an incapacitated person from assuming contractual duties to which she was not capable of assenting. However, incapacity usually does not create tension between the contract policy of freedom of contract and the more general, policy, external to contract law, of protecting mentally incapacitated people. Rather, the policies pull in the same direction because the incapacitated party's lack of mental competence means that her apparent assent to the contract is illusory. The policy of freedom of contract is not served by holding a person incapable of assent to a false manifestation of it.

Like improper bargaining, incapacity renders the contract voidable, not void. Usually, *avoidance* of the contract in its entirety is the only appropriate form of relief. Severance is not a proper solution because the incapacity affects the whole contract, not just a term of it. Because there has been no breach of a contract, damages are not called for unless the conduct of the other party gives rise to some other cause of action. As in other situations of avoidance, rescission of the contract is accompanied by *restitution* of any benefit conferred under the contract. However, in the case of a minor, there are exceptions to this.

§14.2 MINORITY

§14.2.1 The Basis and Nature of a Minor's Contractual Incapacity

A person attains majority at the age of 18 in most states. Before that time, the minor' does not have the legal capacity to be bound in contract, and the contract is **voidable** at the minor's instance. As explained in section 13.3. a voidable contract is not absolutely void, but may be annulled or affirmed at the instance of the party entitled to invoke that election. This means that the minor may **disaffirm** it at any time before reaching the age of majority, or within a reasonable time thereafter. Because a minor has no capacity to

---

1. The word "infant" is sometimes used in legal texts to refer to a person below the age of majority. The word sounds odd in contemporary usage, because we now take it to mean a baby.

contract, it follows that she does not have the capacity to affirm the contract while still a minor. This is why the right to make the election extends for a reasonable time past the attainment of majority. This right is not compromised or waived until majority, even though the minor never tried to disaffirm. Even a fully performed contract can be disaffirmed within a reasonable time after majority.

If the minor has not disaffirmed the contract by the time that he **reaches the age of majority**, he may **ratify** it as a major. Ratification can be express, or it could be by conduct if the minor takes a benefit under the contract after majority, or it could be implied if the minor fails to disaffirm the contract within a reasonable time after becoming a major. For example, in *In re The Score Board, Inc.*, 238 B.R. 585 (D.N.J. 1999) Kobe Bryant, the professional basketball player, entered into a contract at the age of 17 under which he granted rights to the use of his name and image on products. He turned 18 six weeks later. Shortly after his birthday, he deposited a check of $10,000, an initial payment under the contract, in his bank account. He continued to perform under the contract for the subsequent year and a half, and then became dissatisfied with the contract and sought to disaffirm it on the grounds that he was a minor when it was made. The court refused disaffirmance. It held that it did not have to decide if his failure to disaffirm the contract within a reasonable time constituted a ratification because he ratified the contract by affirmative conduct when he deposited the check.

The legal incapacity of a minor is based on the policy of protecting minors from their own immaturity and preventing their exploitation by adults. Of course, any law protecting a party from contractual liability also places that party under a *disability* because sensible and informed people will decline to contract with one who lacks capacity. Incapacity is therefore not always a desirable state, and the law should not impose it unless the duty to protect outweighs the liberty interests of the protected class. In the case of minors, society has long been satisfied that this is true, and the rule has beneficial effects in most cases. However, it inevitably has some negative impact on the autonomy of an older and more independent minor.

Although the basis of incapacity is the policy of protection from immaturity and exploitation, this does not mean that the minor has to prove bad judgment, predatory behavior by the adult party, or unfair terms to avoid the contract. A minor's incapacity is a purely *objective* fact, in the sense that it is based solely on the minor's age, and not on subjective attributes such as intelligence or sophistication, or on transactional circumstances such as the other party's unfair bargaining or the harshness of the contract's terms. Because minors typically look young enough to alert a prudent person to the possibility that they are under age, a person contracting with one of youthful appearance is deemed to be placed on inquiry. A party who does not bother to inquire therefore cannot argue that the minor looked older than her years. Similarly, it does not matter that the minor was close to majority at the time of contracting. It may be arbitrary to fix a particular birthday as the date on which a person comes of age, in that a person does not magically acquire full wisdom at the stroke of midnight. Nevertheless, the law generally prefers the certainty of treating majority as an objective fact, over the uncertainty of a more personalized inquiry into the minor's actual maturity and judgment. The objective test leads to a simple dichotomy, so that unless the official age of majority was reached before the contract, it is voidable. (These issues concerning a minor's contract were raised in the examples in Chapter 3 to illustrate the doctrine of precedent.)

§14.2.2 Situations in Which a Minor May Incur Legal Liability

There are some limited situations in which a minor can incur legal liability as a result of having entered a contract. However, this liability may not be equal to the minor's full contractual commitment and may be confined to restitution for benefits received.

The most common situation in which a minor can incur liability is if the contract is for **necessaries**. A necessary is not the same as a necessity, and it has a broader meaning. It includes not only the bare necessities of life, but whatever goods or services are needed for the minor's livelihood, or appropriate to his standard of living and position. However, it does not include luxuries. The question of what constitutes a necessary is factual and based on all the circumstances. As you may expect, what one court accepts as a necessary another could see as a luxury. For example, while some courts may agree with the average teenager that a car is a necessary, the court in *Bowling v. Sperry*, 184 N.E.2d 901 (Ind. 1962) did not consider it to be so, even though the minor would have found the car useful as a means of transport to his summer job. If the minor lives at home or is supported by her parents, even goods or services that would otherwise be required for subsistence are not likely to qualify as necessaries. For example, in *Webster St. Partnership v. Sheridan*, 368 N.W.2d 439 (Neb. 1985) the court held that an apartment leased by a minor was not a necessary. Although shelter is normally vital to an acceptable standard of living, the minor could have moved back to his parents' home whenever he wanted.

The concept of **emancipation** is important to the minor's liability for necessaries. *Webster St. Partnership* took the approach that unless a minor is emancipated, he has no liability for necessaries at all because his parents have a duty to support him. Other courts do not follow such a firm rule, even though they are more likely to classify goods or services as necessaries where the minor is emancipated. The exact meaning of "emancipated" is not entirely clear. Some courts define it narrowly to include only marriage or military enlistment. Other courts adopt a broader test, and find emancipation if the minor has established her own home and is independent of her parents and not supported by them.

There is also a difference of view on the **enforcement of a claim for necessaries**. Some courts see a contract for necessaries as an exception to the rule that the minor can avoid the contract. They therefore simply enforce it as if it was a major's contract. Other courts avoid the contract even though it involved necessaries, but hold the minor liable for restitution on the theory of unjust enrichment. This means that if the market value of the goods or services is less than the contract price, the minor is only liable for that lower value.

The minor's ability to escape liability under a contract is weakened if she deliberately **misrepresented her age** and the other party, acting reasonably, was misled by the misrepresentation and gave value to the minor or otherwise suffered a detriment in reasonable reliance on it. A court may fully enforce the contract by estopping the minor from asserting minority. (See section 8.4 for an explanation of estoppel.) Alternatively, the court may deny enforcement of the contract but hold the minor liable for the tort of fraud. (Accountability for tortious conduct typically begins at an earlier age than contractual capacity.) The remedy in tort is different from that in contract and aims at restoring the other party's loss rather than giving him the benefit of his bargain.

Apart from any recognition of liability under these principles of common law, a state or federal **statute** may confer contractual capacity on a minor with regard to certain types of contract. For example, minors are usually able to enter into insurance contracts or banking transactions, and a state may validate a minor's employment contract provided that it complies with the state's regulation of child labor.

§14.2.3 Restitution or Other Relief Following Disaffirmation

If the contract is purely executory — that is, neither party has performed — disaffirmance simply terminates it. However, if either party had given value to the other before disaffirmance, the effect of disaffirmance is more complicated. Where a contract between parties of full contractual capacity is avoided, each party must restore whatever she has received from the other under the avoided contract. When the avoidance concerns a minor's contract, this general rule is not as firmly followed. The major party must always restore in full the value of anything that he has received from the minor. However, the minor is generally only liable to return to the major party whatever she still has of the major's contract performance at the time of avoidance. As part of the goal of protecting the minor from an improvident contract, the minor is shielded from liability beyond the duty to return the present and existing economic advantage that he retains at the time of avoidance. She does not have to pay the major the value of services or of property that has been consumed or lost. For example, say that the minor bought a car for $10,000. The minor paid $2,000 down and agreed to pay the balance in installments. Six months later, the car was stolen, and the minor had never bought comprehensive insurance for it. The minor may disaffirm the contract and is entitled to restitution of the $2,000 downpayment as well as the installments that she paid during the six months. As she no longer has the car, she has no obligation to restore the value of the car to the seller. She is also not obliged to compensate the seller for the value of her six months' use of the car. Similarly, if the car was not stolen but damaged in an accident, the minor's only obligation on disaffirmance is to return the damaged car to the seller.

Some courts apply this rule absolutely, but others are concerned that it is too generous to the minor. A few courts do require the minor to restore the value of what she has received, whether or not she still has it. Others courts are willing, in limited circumstances, to impose some liability on a minor beyond the bare return of what she still has. For example, if the contract was fair and did not exploit the minor, and the major was not aware of the minority, a court may allow the major party to offset (deduct) the value received by the minor against what he is obliged to refund to the minor. (That is, if the minor has paid the major party, the restitution of that payment by the major party is reduced by the value of the benefit to the minor.) Some courts limit the value of the benefit to an offset against the major's restitution, but others have granted a judgment against the minor beyond the amount of the offset. *Dodson v. Schrader,* 824 S.W.2d 545 (Tenn. 1992) is an example of the former approach. The minor had paid cash for a truck and had then caused severe damage to its engine by neglect. The court permitted the minor to avoid the contract and to recover the cash paid for the truck, but it allowed the major party to offset against his restitutionary payment the value of the minor's use of the truck and its depreciation. By contrast, in *Valencia v. White,* 654 P.2d 287 (Ariz. 1982) the court imposed liability on a minor, beyond an offset against restitution, for the cost of repairing a truck that the minor had used in his trucking business. Instead of granting restitutionary relief to the major for the value of its performance, a court may allow the major to recover in tort where the minor's fault caused the deterioration in the property. (For example, if the car accident mentioned above was caused by the minor's negligence, the court may not allow the major to recover the value of the undamaged car or the value of the minor's use, but may hold the minor liable in tort for the damage to the car.)

§14.3 MENTAL INCAPACITY

§14.3.1 The Basis and Nature of Voidability Due to Mental Incapacity

In contrast to the objective incapacity of a minor, based on the fact of age alone irrespective of the minor's actual state of mind, the mental incapacity of a major is based purely on his **subjective attributes**. As has often been stressed, when a contracting party is of full age, the objective test of intent holds him accountable for manifested assent. The law does not excuse people from contractual obligations merely because they are of below average intelligence, misguided, or weird. However, the policy of protecting persons who are mentally disabled places limits on this emphasis on objectivity. If a party suffers from a mental disability so severe as to preclude formulation of the requisite contractual intent, he cannot be held to his apparent agreement. Mental incompetence is determined at the *time of contracting*. If it can be proved to have existed at that time, it is a basis for avoidance even if the condition was temporary or has since been cured.

The common law has long recognized mental incapacity as a basis for avoiding a contract, but the issue in contemporary law revolves around the standards for avoidance. The established test for incapacity is strict and narrow, covering only the most severe and debilitating forms of mental disability. But in more recent times, there has been a trend toward broadening the test to include a wider range of psychological disturbances that impair a person's ability to make rational decisions.

When a person has been declared incompetent by a court and a guardian has been appointed to administer his property, the fact of incapacity is clear. However, if there has been no adjudication of incapacity prior to the contract, the presumption is that adult parties were fully capable of contracting. The **burden** therefore lies on the allegedly incompetent party (or those representing his interests) to prove a disabling mental condition. This requires a demonstration both that the condition existed, and that it was in nature and extent severe enough to preclude an adequate degree of assent. To show this, it is usually necessary to produce expert psychiatric evidence as well as testimony by people who observed the behavior of the party at the time of the transaction. In *Gaddy v. Douglass*, 597 S.E.2d 12 (S.C. App. 2004) the dementia of the mentally incapacitated party, an elderly woman with advanced Alzheimer's disease, was convincingly established by the testimony of three neurologists who examined her and three lay people who observed her conduct and attested to her gradual mental deterioration, confusion, and forgetfulness. As a result of this testimony, the court avoided a power of attorney that the patient had executed in favor of some grasping

459

relatives who induced her to sign it after they knew that she was suffering from the disease.

As noted earlier, a person dealing with a youthful party is placed on inquiry and cannot claim that she believed the minor to be older. By contrast, when the mental capacity of an adult is concerned, the *presumption is in favor of capacity*, so the other party is entitled to rely on apparent capacity unless some behavior or other circumstances signal a problem. As a result, the *other party's knowledge or reason to know* of the incapacity is an important factor when mental incompetence is claimed. Some forms of mental disability produce behavioral symptoms that are readily observable, leading to an easy conclusion that the other party did know or should have realized that she was dealing with a mentally incompetent person. However, this is not invariably true. The effect of the illness may be subtle and not easily detected — especially when negotiation is brief, and the parties do not have a prior relationship.

The purpose of permitting avoidance is the protection of the disabled person and his estate, but the observation concerning minors' contracts applies even more strongly here: The benign motive of protection carries a risk of **paternalism and intrusion**. It could mean that a person diagnosed with or suspected of having a mental disease is deprived of his freedom to contract because others will not risk dealing with him. Even if that problem were overcome and a contract were made, a finding of incapacity might still undermine the party's autonomy. In many cases, it is not the contracting party himself who desires to escape the contract, but his friends or relatives who seek to have him declared incompetent so that the contract can be avoided. In situations like this, a court has to be particularly careful that it is truly serving his best interests and not unduly interfering with his contractual liberty.

§14.3.2 The Test for Mental Incapacity

As mentioned earlier, the established test for mental incapacity is strict. The contract can only be avoided if, at the time of contracting, the party was *unable to understand the nature and consequences of the transaction*. This standard, called the **cognitive** test, confines avoidance to cases in which the party was so profoundly disabled that he did not know what he was doing. Because the lack of capacity is so serious, it is usually likely to have been quite apparent to the other party, who should have realized that there was a problem. Therefore, the equities strongly favor avoidance because the other party cannot fairly claim to have reasonably relied on the genuineness of manifested intent. For this reason, and because a narrow test is easier to apply, some courts still prefer it.

However, other courts consider it to be outdated and too rigid. Growing insight into psychology over the last few decades has shown that there are many forms of mental incapacity that fall short of cognitive disability, but that nevertheless so affect a person's *judgment, self-control, and motivation*, that he is incapable of genuine assent. This has led to a broader test that recognizes not only cognitive disorders, but also an illness or defect that impairs the party's ability to transact in a reasonable manner. This test is described by different names, including the **motivational, affective**, or **volitional** test. Because this type of incapacity may be less apparent to the other party, it is only grounds for avoidance if the other had reason to know of the condition. Restatement Second §15(1) adopts the broader test.

Davis v. Davis, 89 P.3d 1206 (Or. App. 2004) is a good illustration of the difference in approach and result between the narrower and wider tests. The parties entered into a divorce settlement in which the wife gave the husband full ownership of some stock options and of their interest in a software company. About a month later, the wife moved to avoid the settlement on the grounds that she was not mentally competent when she made it. The couple had been married for about 17 years. The husband had physically abused the wife on numerous occasions during the marriage. A social worker who treated the wife after the dissolution testified that the wife loved and feared the husband enormously. The wife was diagnosed as suffering from depression, post-traumatic stress syndrome, and battered woman's syndrome. When the parties met to negotiate the settlement, the wife was emotionally distraught and also had hopes of reconciliation. When she expressed her desire to reconcile, the husband made it clear that he was not interested and he also verbally abused her at one point during the course of the meeting. At the end of this emotional meeting, the wife told her attorney that she did not want to fight any more and wanted to get the meeting over with. Contrary to her attorney's advice, she did not press for a half share in the stock options and interest in the software company, but insisted on signing the agreement that gave the husband full ownership. The majority of the court of appeals upheld the trial court's dismissal of the wife's motion to set aside the agreement. Both courts considered themselves bound by the cognitive test, which had been adopted by the state supreme court. A concurring judge regretfully accepted this legal conclusion, but expressed the view that the affective test is more in accord with psychological theory and reflects a better understanding of human behavior.

This description of the case shows two things. First, it demonstrates the truth of the concurring judge's view that there are many situations in which a strict cognitive test disregards what could be a real and serious impairment of the capacity to make a rational and voluntary decision. Second, it suggests the hazard of the broader test. If mental incapacity is wide enough to encompass severe emotional disturbance short of cognitive disability, the test becomes less predictable and harder to apply. At the borderline, it may be difficult to distinguish incapacity that merits avoidance from the various kinds of eccentric, strangely motivated, ill-advised, or irrational decision making that affects many transactions in the marketplace. It is important to remember that when the law speaks of mental incompetence it refers to clinically recognized illness, and not to incompetence in the general sense.

Courts that use the wider test seek to keep it under control by insisting on both psychiatric testimony, establishing a clinically recognized condition, and factual evidence, showing irrational or peculiar behavior during the period of and relevant to the transaction. As an added safeguard, the test emphasizes a balanced approach that takes into account not only the protection of the incompetent party, but also the rights and **reasonable expectations** of the **other party**. This means that even if the court finds some disturbance in the mind of the party seeking avoidance, it may conclude that the resulting disability is outweighed by the injustice of upsetting a fair contract entered into in good faith by the other party.

Neither test is premised on the requirement that the party seeking avoidance shows that the terms of the contract are unfair. The basis of avoidance is lack of meaningful assent, not harshness in the terms of the contract. Therefore, even a contract with perfectly reasonable terms can be avoided if the elements of the test are satisfied. Of course, if the terms are so unfair or so heavily in favor of the other party that they would not have been agreed to by a rational person in the position of the party seeking avoidance, this can be persuasive supporting evidence of incompetence. It also affects the equities in favor of avoidance, as mentioned earlier.

§14.3.3 Avoidance and Its Consequences

Like a minor's contract, the contract of a mentally incompetent person is voidable, not void. Unlike minority, however, mental disability does not disappear on a set and certain date, after which the fact of disaffirmance or ratification can be settled. The fate of a contract by a mentally incapacitated person may therefore hang in the balance until either it is disaffirmed or the incapacity abates, and the formerly incompetent party affirms it. (Or a guardian is ultimately appointed and does so.) In the interim, there may be performance or the other party may have otherwise changed his position in reliance on the contract. If that party had not taken unfair advantage of the other's mental incapacity — that is, he contracted on fair terms without awareness of the incapacity, Restatement Second §15(2) acknowledges his interests. It provides for termination of the power of avoidance to the extent that the contract has been so performed, or circumstances have so changed that avoidance would be unjust.

If the contract is avoided, the parties must be *restored to the status quo ante.* Both must return money or property received under the contract, or the value of property consumed or dissipated, or of services rendered. However, if the other party knew of and took advantage of the incompetence, the disabled party may be excused from paying to the extent that benefits received did not ultimately enrich him.

§14.3.4 Incapacity Induced by Alcohol or Drug Abuse

Incapacity caused by intoxication is viewed less sympathetically than that resulting from age, illness, or injury, because the incapacitated party is seen as having some blame for the problem. However, courts are aware of the compulsive nature of alcoholism and drug abuse. They therefore recognize that if intoxication is severe enough, its impairing effect can be just as profound as mental illness. Furthermore, that degree of inebriation is usually obvious enough to be apparent to the other party, so a strong inference can be drawn that he deliberately took advantage of it. Therefore, despite any moral reprobation that a court may feel about the conduct of the intoxicated party, courts do generally permit avoidance on the ground of incapacity if the level of intoxication is sufficient to deprive him of understanding or of the ability to act rationally, and the other party had reason to know of this. Restatement Second §16 follows this approach. The case for relief is even stronger if the terms of the resulting contract are unfair or unduly favorable to the other party.

Examples

1. Hardy Culturalist, age 19, was about to leave his hometown to attend college. Up to that time, he had operated a very successful part-time yard maintenance business on weekends. As he would no longer be able to service his customers, he wished to dispose of his lawnmower, trimmer, wheelbarrow, and other garden tools. Lon Mower, a 16-year-old high-school junior, who lived with his parents next door to Hardy, was interested in filling the gap that would be left by Hardy's departure. He wanted to buy the equipment and try to take over Hardy's customers. Hardy and Lon began negotiations, and eventually reached agreement on the sale of all the equipment for $800. This is a fair price, somewhat below its market value. Lon did not have that much money in his savings account, so he paid $300 to Hardy and undertook to pay the balance in installments of $50 per month, which he expected would be generated from his yardwork. Lon had just taken a business law course in high school, so he knew that a sale of goods over $500 had to be recorded in writing and signed. He therefore drew up a simple document reflecting their agreement, and they both signed it.

14. Incapacity

1(a). After taking delivery of the equipment and paying Hardy the $300, Lon began work. He successfully groomed about five yards in the first week, but did not enjoy the hard labor very much and began to regret having undertaken this new venture. In the second week, he had a disaster. He lost control of the lawnmower, which ran over the trimmer, completely mangling it, and then plunged off a steep embankment and exploded. This experience convinced Lon that yardwork was not for him. He wishes to cancel the sale, get his $300 back, and return all the surviving equipment to Hardy. May he do this?

1(b). Say that at the time he made the contract with Hardy, Lon was 17 years old and just two weeks short of his eighteenth birthday. Lon took delivery of the equipment and paid Hardy the $300. He used the garden equipment for five weeks and then decided that he no longer wished to do landscaping work. (The calamity involving the runaway lawnmower did not occur and Lon was able to return the equipment to Hardy in much the same condition as when he bought it.) Lon would like to avoid the contract, return the equipment to Hardy, and get his money back. Under state law, a person acquires contractual capacity at the age of 18. Does this change in the facts affect Lon's ability to disaffirm the contract?

2. Bonna Petite is a precocious 17-year-old with an appetite for *haute cuisine*. For a while she had been dying to eat lunch at Trés Cher, the most elegant and expensive restaurant in town. One day she put on her mother's best business suit and groomed herself meticulously, succeeding in making herself look like a young executive of around 25 years of age. She set off for the restaurant, where she was seated and served a magnificent lunch. At the end of the meal she summoned the waiter and said, "*Garçon*, this has been an excellent repast. It is therefore with some sadness that I must inform you that I am a minor. I hereby disaffirm my contract to purchase this lunch from you." (By the way, she did not leave a tip either.) The age of majority in Bonna's state is 18, so she is a minor. May she do this?

3. Price Slasher, a man of 82, had lived in his house for 45 years. During the last ten years of that period, following the death of his wife, he had lived alone. As he got older, it had become increasingly more burdensome for him to maintain the house and to take care of domestic chores. He therefore decided that the time had come for him to sell it and to move to an assisted living complex. Price had always been a stubborn, impatient, and difficult man, and this had become worse as he aged. He hated asking anyone for help, and he rarely sought or listened to advice. His insistence on self-reliance had become quite worrisome to his daughter lately, because he did not seem to manage

his affairs very well. He was constantly losing things, could not keep his bank account balanced, forgot to pay some bills, and double-paid others without realizing it.

When he told his daughter that he planned to sell the house, she offered to help him, but he declined her assistance. She then begged him to get it appraised and to list it with a reputable realtor. He refused, insisting that he was fully aware of the market, knew exactly how much the house was worth, and was perfectly capable of negotiating the sale himself. In this he was quite wrong. His information about the market was years out of date, and he had never been much of a negotiator.

Price advertised the house for sale at a figure that was about 25 percent lower than its true market value. Lowe Ball saw the advertisement and came to see the house. It did not take him long to make an offer at the full asking price, which Price accepted. Lowe's contact with Price during the transaction was quite minimal. The parties had a short conversation when Lowe inspected the house, and another when the written offer was submitted and accepted. Lowe did not attempt to negotiate the price because he realized that Price's price was good (although he did not realize that it was so far below the market value of the house). His only impression about Price was that he was an elderly man of few words who seemed to know exactly what he wanted.

After the contract of sale had been signed, Price told his daughter about it. She was appalled because she knew that he had let the house go for a patently inadequate price. A long family meeting took place that evening, at which his daughter and other relatives finally convinced Price that he had sold too cheaply. He now wishes to rescind the sale. Does he have grounds to do so?

4. Bourne Tushop, age 20, bought an expensive luxury car on credit. He negotiated effectively with the salesman, beating the price down by $1,500. He then spent over 30 minutes reading the sales contract before he signed it. After driving the car for two weeks he decided that he did not like it any more, and he wished to return it. Dr. Heddy Shrinker, prominent psychiatrist, has done some studies of young adults who have been raised by indulgent, status-conscious parents. She has identified a form of dysfunctional conduct in many of them that she calls Bipolar Reflexive Acquisition Trauma (BRAT). As part of this syndrome, the young people compulsively purchase fashionable, expensive, and unneeded consumer products. Very shortly afterwards, they realize the futility of what they have done and experience deep regret and depression. Dr. Shrinker has examined Bourne and has concluded that he suffers from the syndrome. He has had it since his

mid-teens and can only be cured by several years of therapy and counseling.

May Bourne rely on his disorder to avoid the contract?

Explanations

1(a). This is a sale of goods, but apart from the statute of frauds issue, which Lon has cleverly identified, there are no special rules applicable in this case. UCC Article 2 does not deal with minors' contracts, which are therefore governed in sales transactions by general principles of common law.

Because Lon is a minor, he may disaffirm the contract. It does not matter that he may have been smart and sophisticated enough to understand exactly what he was doing, that he was knowledgeable about the statute of frauds, or that he planned to use the equipment for a moneymaking venture. The protection from contractual commitment afforded a minor is based on the objective fact of age and does not take account of the subjective attributes of the minor. The objective criterion of minority also makes it irrelevant that Hardy was little over the age of minority himself, or that the contract was on fair terms. He does not fit the stereotype of the grasping, advantage-taking adult who should know better than to exploit a kid, but Lon's right to disaffirm does not depend on a showing of bargaining impropriety. There is also no basis for holding that the garden equipment was a necessary. Although tools used to earn a livelihood might qualify as a necessary where the minor is self-supporting, Lon was a high school student who lived with and was supported by his parents.

When the minor elects to disaffirm the contract, each party must restore what was received from the other. However, if the minor has lost, consumed, or damaged property obtained under the contract, the established rule is that he is responsible to restore only what he has at the time of disaffirmance and need not compensate the major for any shortfall. Under this rule, Lon is entitled to his $300 back and must return the surviving equipment to Hardy. Some courts have recognized that a rigid rule to this effect may not be fair in every case, and have been willing, in proper circumstances, to hold the minor liable for more than the mere return of existing enrichment.

There are two separate theories of liability. If the property was destroyed tortiously, the minor may be liable in tort for the loss in value, provided that the minor is old enough to be accountable for negligence under the state's tort law. If Lon was negligent in losing control of the mower, this approach would make Lon responsible to reimburse Hardy for the value of lost mower and trimmer, in addition to returning the other equipment.

As an alternative to tort liability, some courts have adopted the approach that if the minor has benefitted from the use of the property, the value of that benefit may be recoverable from the minor. Some courts confine recovery to an offset against any restitution due to the minor, but others are willing to grant a money judgment against the minor, imposing liability on him greater than any offset against restitution. Lon was not benefitted by the destruction of the mower and trimmer, so he cannot be held liable for their value. However, he did earn money by using the equipment for a week. He may therefore be responsible, in addition to restoring the remaining tools to Hardy, for payment of the rental value of all the equipment for a week

If the court does not apply either of the above principles to compensate Hardy for the loss, he may try the argument that the mower and trimmer were necessaries, because Lon used them to earn money. If this argument is accepted, Lon would, in addition to returning the remaining equipment, be liable to pay for the mower and trimmer, based on the lesser rate of the contract value or fair market value at the time of sale. In this case, fair value was apparently above the contract price, so the contract price of the destroyed mower and trimmer would be the proper measure of recovery. However, to avoid watering down the protection of minors, courts tend to be conservative in classifying property or services as necessaries. Lon was still in school and living with his parents and did the yardwork part-time. As this was not his livelihood, the equipment is unlikely to be regarded as a necessary.

1(b). The fact that Lon was almost 18, rather than 16, at the time of contracting does not affect Lon's right to avoid the contract. Minority is measured objectively, and the only question is whether or not Lon was a minor at the time of contracting, even if he was almost a major. However, once a minor reaches the age of majority, he may ratify the contract, thereby fully validating it and terminating the power to avoid it. Ratification may be express, or it could be implied where the minor fails to disaffirm the contract within a reasonable time of reaching majority or otherwise acts in a way that signifies an intent to ratify.

The measurement of a reasonable time for disaffirmance is a factual question, based on all the circumstances of the case. About three weeks have passed since Lon's eighteenth birthday and he has not yet disaffirmed. His failure to act for three weeks may in itself constitute a ratification. Even if this passive delay in disaffirming is not, in itself, enough to constitute ratification, Lon continued to use the equipment during the three-week period. This action is inconsistent with an intent to disaffirm, and likely constitutes conduct evidencing an intent to ratify.

2. A minor may disaffirm her contract at any time before or within a reasonable time after attaining majority. The general rule is that she must restore any benefits that she still retains at the time of disaffirmance, but is not accountable for the value of property that has been consumed or dissipated. (In a sense, she does still have Trés Cher's property and will retain it until the process of digestion is complete, but Trés Cher would probably not be too interested in the "disgorgement" of this benefit.)

   The general rule places the burden on Trés Cher to inquire about the age of its youthful-looking customers, and it bears the risk of failing to do so, even if she looked older than she was. On the other hand, Bonna has behaved very badly, and the law should not encourage our young citizens to do this kind of thing. The following arguments could be made to hold her accountable to pay for the meal, but they probably will not work:

(a) Trés Cher could invoke the rule that a minor is liable to pay the value of a necessary. Food required for sustenance surely qualifies as a necessary. But even a good meal, going beyond the minimum needed to sustain life, could be a necessary, because the concept goes beyond bare subsistence and takes into account the minor's reasonable and accustomed style of living. A fine meal in a top restaurant may be a little excessive unless Bonna is an actual member of the House of Windsor. Apart from this, goods are only deemed necessaries if the minor had no means of obtaining them unless she contracted for them herself. There is no indication that Bonna was in this position. She lived with her parents and had access to their refrigerator.

(b) A minor may be liable for deliberately misrepresenting her age. A misrepresentation could occur by conduct or concealment, but where minors are concerned, courts generally require an affirmative lie about age. Dressing up is not enough to constitute a deliberate misrepresentation.

(c) Although the established rule is that a minor is responsible to restore only the existing benefit received under the contract, some courts have moved away from that absolute rule and do permit restitution of the value of a consumed benefit provided that the contract was fair and the major party was unaware of the minority. There is a stronger incentive for adopting this approach where, as here, the minor was willful in causing the major party's loss. The court may limit the minor's obligation to restore the value of his benefit to an offset against the major party's restitutionary obligation to the minor. If the court adopts this limitation in the present case and so confines the major party's recovery against the minor, Trés Cher would receive nothing. Bonna did not pay cash for the meal and there is no restitution owed to her against which her obligation could be offset.

As a matter of policy, a rule that confines the major party's recovery to the minor's existing benefit most strongly advances the goal of protecting the minor against improvident conduct that creates liability. However, a rule that makes a minor fully accountable for the value of the benefit, even if consumed or lost, allows the court to sanction the minor's irresponsible or antisocial conduct. A rule that makes the minor accountable for a consumed or lost benefit, but only to the extent of an offset against the major party's restitutionary obligation, is a compromise solution that tries to accommodate both these goals.

Even if the court declines to deviate from the established rule and refuses to hold the minor liable for any restitution of a lost or consumed benefit, a 17-year-old could be liable in tort or criminal law for intentional wrongdoing. The ordering of a meal with intent not to pay for it is fraud.

3. The facts concerning Price's mental capacity are deliberately vague but suggestive. It appears that he has certain character traits, such as stubbornness, resistance to advice, weak negotiating skills, and impatience, that are likely to place him at risk of entering into a disadvantageous contract. These flaws in his nature may indicate that he probably lacks skill in contracting, but do not, on their own, constitute the kind of mental incompetence that would give rise to a claim for avoidance. However, there are indications that the effect of these shortcomings have been aggravated by mental infirmity, manifested in symptoms such as loss of memory and confusion. His family has noticed a deterioration in his mental capacity, but this is not necessarily something that was obvious to Lowe.

    A person is presumed to be competent to contract. If Price seeks to avoid the contract on the basis of incapacity, he must prove that he was mentally incompetent at the time of entering the contract. The degree of incompetence to be established depends on whether the jurisdiction follows the older cognitive test — that he could not understand the nature and consequences of the transaction; or has accepted the looser motivational standard — that his mental defect impaired his ability to transact in a reasonable manner. The motivational test is satisfied by a much less serious degree of infirmity, but for that reason it more strongly protects the reasonable reliance interest of the other party, and is not a basis for avoidance unless Lowe had reason to know of Price's inability to conduct the transaction rationally.

Evidence of Price's behavior during the transaction is the most probitive indication of his mental state, and is also relevant to the question of whether Lowe had reason to know of his incompetence. However, evidence of his conduct immediately before and after the transaction is also a pertinent indicator of his state of mind at the time of contracting. Price's daughter can testify about his confused and disoriented behavior during the period surrounding the transaction, but Lowe was the only person who observed Price during the transaction, and he claims to have found nothing amiss. Both of them could be telling the truth, because Price's condition seems to have manifested itself in lapses. The anecdotal evidence may therefore be quite inconclusive, and it may not be possible for Price to make a case for avoidance unless he can offer expert testimony by a psychiatrist who has examined him, diagnosed his condition, and can convince the factfinder that it is serious enough to have impaired his ability to contract under the applicable test.

Although evidence of Price's mental state is the most directly relevant to the decision on whether to permit avoidance on grounds of incapacity, courts are concerned with balancing the protection of the incapacitated party against the need to treat the other party fairly and to foster the security of transactions. Therefore, testimony about the transacting environment is often of great relevance, particularly when the mental incapacity falls short of a palpable cognitive disorder. Such factors as the adequacy of consideration given to the incompetent party, the fairness of the contract terms, any abuse of trust or confidence by the other party, and any other bargaining impropriety could influence the outcome of the case. In the present case, if Lowe is believed, he was guilty of no deliberate underhand dealing and had no reason to notice anything peculiar in Price's demeanor that may have alerted him to a problem. He offered what was asked for the property, and his only sin was that he made an attractive bargain. However, a 25 percent shortfall from the market price is quite extreme, and (even though Lowe may not have known how good a price it was) this could in itself be regarded as an indication to a reasonable buyer that something was wrong with Price. A person who makes a particularly favorable exchange with one who suffers from a mental disability is not in a particularly strong position.

In *Heights Realty Ltd. v. Phillips*, 749 P.2d 77 (N.M. 1988), an 84-year-old woman entered into an exclusive listing agreement with a realtor, and then refused to sell the property when the realtor found a willing and able buyer. Although there was nothing unfair or extraordinary about the contract terms, and the realtor testified that the seller was "sharp as a tack" during their negotiations, the seller had been in a gradual and subtle mental decline for some years. Her deteriorating mental condition was described by a number of family members, who had noticed erratic and confused behavior, memory lapses, and mismanagement of her affairs. A psychiatrist testified that although it could not be stated conclusively that she was mentally incompetent, this could be asserted as a matter of medical probability. He believed that she probably realized that she was contracting for the purpose of selling her property, but could not have understood the detailed terms of her contract. During the course of the suit, she was in fact adjudged incompetent and was represented by a conservator. The court, applying the stricter cognitive test followed in the jurisdiction, found that the combination of psychiatric and anecdotal evidence was sufficient to satisfy the seller's burden of establishing mental incompetence under that standard.

4. Bourne surely fails the cognitive test of mental incapacity because there is no indication that he could not understand and appreciate the nature and consequences of his acts when entering the transaction. A court that accepts the looser test of Restatement Second §15 would allow him to avoid the sale if he can show that a mental illness or defect affected his ability to act in a reasonable manner in the transaction and that the car dealer had reason to know of his condition.

    For the first element, a mental disease or defect must be established. Even under the more lenient test, a person cannot claim mental incapacity just because he made a quirky or unreasonable judgment, or because he was motivated by irrational desires. Dr. Shrinker has identified something that may be called a mental condition, but even if the conclusions of her research are correct, this may not be a profound enough problem to qualify as an incapacity. Of course, even if we accept Dr. Shrinker's opinion, the dealer will probably be able to find its own equally qualified expert to contradict everything that she says. In the end, the question of whether the disease exists, and if so, whether Bourne suffers from it so as to impair his rationality, will come down to a battle of the experts. One of the problems with the more open test is that conflicting psychiatric opinion evidence must be evaluated by lay people. This is ameliorated somewhat if the disease has any observable symptoms, because evidence of Bourne's behavior would be available to bolster the psychiatric evaluation. As Bourne bears the burden of proof, any uncertainty must be resolved against him.

Even if a mental condition is established, relief is still not granted unless the need to protect Bourne from his incapacity outweighs the dealer's right to enforcement of its reasonable expectations. Therefore, Bourne must also show that the dealer knew or had reason to know of his incapacity. Some mental conditions are made obvious by the patient's conduct, but others are more subtle. The brief facts given here do not suggest any observable conduct that may have put the dealer on notice that Bourne could not make rational judgments or exercise control over his actions. In the end, the court would have to strike a balance, based on all the circumstances of the transaction. It seems unlikely that avoidance would be permitted. Bourne's disease, if it exists at all, is rather self-indulgent, and the dealer's reliance interest appears to be strong and legitimate.

Of course, if Bourne succeeds in avoiding the contract, he must return the car to the dealer and is entitled to restitution of his payments. However, as discussed in Example 1, he may in addition be liable to the dealer for the value of his use of the car for the two weeks.

CHAPTER 15

Mistake, Impracticability, and Frustration of Purpose

§15.1 THE COMMON THEMES AND THE DIFFERENCES BETWEEN MISTAKE, IMPRACTICABILITY, AND FRUSTRATION OF PURPOSE

The three doctrines considered in this chapter have common themes that make it useful to consider them together. They are each concerned with a situation in which the exchange between the parties turns out to be very different from what was expected. In the case of mistake, this is caused by a serious factual error made by one or both parties at the time of contracting, so that the contract is premised on incorrect information. By contrast, impracticability and frustration arise when there is no false premise at the time of contracting, but events change drastically enough after formation to belie the original expectation of the parties. An issue of mistake, impracticability, or frustration may be raised at various stages after formation of the contract and for the purpose of achieving different ends. For example, before performance is due, it may be used to excuse the prospective performance. After performance has been rendered, it could be used as a defense to a claim that the performance fell short of that called for by the contract. Most commonly, its effect is termination of the contract, but sometimes adjustment of the contract terms is the more appropriate remedy.

Each of the doctrines pose two central questions that will be constant themes in our discussion:

1. *Materiality — How fundamental is the discrepancy between the expected and the actual exchange?* This question is concerned with the impact of the mistake or altered circumstances on the bargain reasonably anticipated by the parties. Relief is only available when the impact is so material that it changes the very basis of their bargain.
2. *Risk — Which party should be made to bear the consequences of this defeat of the original expectations?* The fact that original expectations have been fundamentally upset only justifies relief if the party seeking it does not bear the risk of this upset. The allocation of risk may be clear from the terms of the contract, or it may have to be established by interpretation from the circumstances of the transaction. The determination of risk allocation is a crucial aspect of the judicial inquiry in all these cases.

Having identified common themes, it is important to stress the difference between mistake, on the one hand, and impracticability and frustration on the other. As noted earlier, the doctrine of **mistake** applies when the contract is based on an **erroneous belief at the time of contracting** that certain facts are true. The error causes one or both parties to manifest assent that would not have been given had the true facts been known. When the error is later discovered the mistaken party — or one of them, if the parties shared the mistake — may have grounds to avoid (or in a special case, to claim adjustment of) the contract. In this sense, mistake causes a *defect in assent* similar to that resulting from fraud, duress, or unconscionability so that the basis for relief is that *apparent assent is not genuine.* Even under the objective test, a party is not held accountable for a manifestation of assent when the error is grave and justifiable enough. Because mistake has this commonality with the doctrines discussed in Chapter 13, it could have been dealt with there. However, it differs from them in that the defect in assent is *caused by misinformation, not by deception, improper pressure, or other bargaining misbehavior.* Of course, sometimes the error of one party may have been induced by or deliberately taken advantage of by the other. If so, this strengthens the case for mistake and it may also allow the party to invoke alternative grounds for relief based on fraud or unconscionability. Notwithstanding, bear in mind that the elements of mistake do not include a requirement of improper bargaining, so relief is possible even when the other party has not behaved wrongfully.

In contrast to mistake, **impracticability and frustration** are concerned with the impact of **supervening events** on the transaction. These doctrines are not based on any defect in assent at the time of contracting, but aim to provide relief when the basis of a **fully consensual transaction is**

profoundly altered by some external event that occurs **afterwards**. (In this discussion I adopt the position that impracticality and frustration are always concerned with supervening events, and that the distinction between these doctrines and mistake is primarily based on chronology. There are cases that have found impracticality or frustration where, unknown to the parties, the event had already occurred at the time of contracting. The cases could just as well have been handled under the rules of mistake, with no difference in the ultimate result. The notion of *contemporaneous impracticability* or frustration therefore seems to serve no purpose, except to duplicate and create confusion with mistake, and it is best disregarded in favor of the clarity of drawing a firm temporal line between a mistake and supervening impracticability or frustration.)

§15.2 THE MEANING OF MISTAKE AND THE DISTINCTION BETWEEN MUTUAL AND UNILATERAL MISTAKE

§15.2.1 The Legal Meaning of Mistake: An Error of Fact

In lay terms, "mistake" has quite a wide range of meaning. It could refer to a factual error, but it might also include a bad judgment, a rash decision, or simply a situation that did not work out well. For example, it may have been a real mistake to buy that ugly chair, to invest in your cousin's harebrained enterprise or to drive to town instead of taking the bus. The legal meaning of "mistake" is much narrower. It is confined to **errors of fact**, that is, to errors about some **thing or event that actually occurred or existed** and can be **ascertained by objective evidence**. This leads to a number of important observations on the scope of mistake doctrine:

a. An Error in Judgment Does Not Qualify as a Mistake

A party cannot escape a disadvantageous or regrettable contract resulting from poor judgment. Say, for example, that a buyer of a plot of land purchases it in the belief that it is worth more than the asking price, but then finds that this is untrue. Or a buyer of stock believes wrongly that the company is undervalued and the stock is considerably more valuable than its price. If these parties were to be allowed to avoid their obligations simply because they had judged wrongly, no transaction could be secure. Although this distinction can be drawn in principle, it is not always a simple matter to distinguish an error in judgment from a mistake of fact. Judgments are usually based on fact, and less obvious cases could require some unravelling.

A famous old case and a more modern one illustrate the subtle distinction between a mistake of fact and of judgment. In *Sherwood v. Walker*, 33 N.W. 919 (Mich. 1887) a cattle breeder, believing a highly pedigreed cow to be infertile, sold it as a beef cow for a fraction of its value. Before delivery, the seller discovered the cow to be pregnant and he refused to deliver it to the buyer. The buyer sued to compel delivery but the court allowed the seller to avoid the contract for mistake. The court's test for mistake is obsolete, but the important point of the case, for our purposes, is that the majority and dissenting opinions differ on whether the belief that the cow was infertile should be treated as a mistake. The majority thought that it was, but the dissent felt that the cow's ability to breed was really a question of judgment. Neither party knew for sure that the cow was infertile. The seller gambled that it was, and the buyer that it was not. The buyer's judgment was right and he should not be deprived of the fruits of his successful speculation.

Firestone & Parson, Inc. v. Union League of Philadelphia, 672 F. Supp. 819 (E.D. Pa. 1987) involved the sale of a painting attributed to Albert Bierstadt, the celebrated nineteenth-century landscape painter. At the time of the sale, art experts regarded the painting as Bierstadt's and the parties had no reason to believe otherwise. As a result, it was sold for $500,000. Several years after the sale, scholarly research revealed that the painting was not by Bierstadt. As a result, it was worth only a tenth of what was paid for it. The buyer sued for avoidance of the contract. The suit was dismissed because the statute of limitations had run. However, the court discussed the claim of mistake and suggested that even had the buyer sued in time, the contract would not have been avoidable. The value and authorship of a work of art, based on expert opinion, is more a matter of judgment than of fact.

b. An Incorrect Prediction of Future Events Is Not a Mistake

A future event may one day become a fact, but until it has happened, it cannot be thought of as a fact by anyone except Nostradamus. Therefore, as a rule, it is generally accurate to say that the mistake must relate to a fact in existence at the time of contracting. A party cannot claim relief for an erroneous prediction. This is often closely related to point *a* above, because most predictions at the time of contract are speculations concerning the future value of the transaction and are therefore in the nature of judgments. For example, if a buyer of oranges purchases them in the belief that the market will rise, he cannot complain if it later turns out that he was wrong. This is not a mistake in the legal sense, but simply an erroneous prediction (or misjudgment) of profitability. Again, although the distinction between fact and prediction is easy to draw in some cases, there are situations in which a contractual assumption may have both factual and speculative elements. When that happens, it can be difficult to decide if the error should be treated as a mistake.

c. Mistake of Fact Must Be Distinguished From Mistake as to Meaning (Misunderstanding)

When the parties dispute the meaning of a contract term, this could be characterized as a type of mistake — one of the parties is mistaken as to the intention of the other. We saw in Chapter 10 that the interpretation of meaning is regarded as a question of fact, but that does not mean that a misinterpretation of meaning is a mistake of fact. Mistake doctrine is not concerned with this type of error, which is not a mistake as to some external fact, but rather a mistake as to the meaning of a manifestation of assent. It is resolved by the process of interpretation, governed by the principles set out in Chapter 10. That is, the correct meaning of a manifestation is decided by determining the reasonable meaning of the words or conduct in context.

A court might miss this distinction, as shown by *Monarch Marketing System Co. v. Reed's Photo Mart*, 485 S.W.2d 905 (Tex. 1972). The photo store had meant to order 4,000 custom labels. The letter "M" was understood in trade usage to signify a quantity of 1,000. Instead of filling in a quantity of "4M" in its order form, the store erroneously wrote the order for "4MM" labels. When the 4 million labels were delivered, the store refused to accept them and the supplier sued for the price. The court resolved the case on the basis of mistake and found that the elements of unilateral mistake were not satisfied. (We will examine these elements shortly. In essence, the court found that the store's unilateral mistake did not merit avoidance because the store was responsible for the mistake, the supplier had no way of realizing that the order was wrong, and if the contract was not enforced, the supplier would suffer a loss which it could not recover by selling the customized labels to anyone else.) The result is doubtless correct, but the basis for reaching it is wrong. This was not a mistake as to an external fact, but an error in communication. Under the objective test, the store is held to the supplier's reasonable understanding of its manifestation of intent.

d. A Mistake of Law Could Qualify As a Fact

Older cases did not regard an error of law as a mistake of fact, and refused to apply mistake doctrine to a mistake of law. Modern cases are more likely to treat the legal rules applicable to a transaction as facts — to see those legal rules as constituting an existing state of affairs that can be objectively ascertained. The court did not take this approach in *Burggraff v. Baum*, 720 A.2d 1167 (Me. 1998) which involved a sale of seafront property. The buyers intended to build a house and a cabin on the property, and the cabin was to be sited close to the water. Prior to the sale, the buyers had discussed their plans in detail with the sellers, so the sellers understood that this was the buyers' intent. The buyers had also researched the zoning ordinance and had concluded that the zoning ordinance required a 75-foot setback from the water. After they bought the house, the buyers discovered that they had overlooked another statute that required a 250-foot setback. When the sellers refused to reduce the price, the buyers sued for rescission on grounds of mistake. The court refused to grant rescission because it held that this was a mistake of law, not fact. Parties are presumed to know the law and ignorance of the law is no excuse. The opinion made an interesting distinction. The court suggested that had the parties not known that any regulation existed this might have been a mistake of fact. But once they knew that that the setback was regulated and they erred as to the law's provisions, this was a mistake of law.

Even if a court does treat an error of law as a mistake of fact, the maxim "ignorance of the law is no excuse" could still have an impact on the right of avoidance. The court might deny avoidance because the party claiming avoidance should have known the law and therefore bore the risk of mistake. (Risk allocation is discussed in sections 15.3 and 15.4.)

e. Situations that Appear to Call for the Application of Mistake Doctrine May Be More Properly Treated as a Breach of a Contractual Commitment

This is not so much a new point as a reinforcement of two prior observations that merit strong emphasis: It has already been noted that many mistakes in the lay sense do not constitute mistakes in the legal sense, and that risk allocation is crucial consideration in deciding whether a mistake should be grounds for relief. A party's responsibility for her own judgments and the parties' understanding about risk allocation may mean that a mistake does not call for application of mistake doctrine, but should be treated as the breach of a contractual promise (that is, a warranty) or as a misrepresentation.

For example, a buyer purchases a painting for $5 million, based on the seller's claim that it is a genuine Van Gogh. It turns out to be a forgery. Only by carefully examining the facts of the transaction and weighing the closely related issues of judgment and risk allocation can we decide which party must be assigned responsibility for the problem. Some of the questions to consider would be: Did the seller knowingly or unwittingly give false information to the buyer or conceal facts? If so, there may be a misrepresentation. Did the seller promise that this was a genuine Van Gogh? If so, there may be a breach of warranty. Was this an uncertain fact on which both parties gambled? If so, the buyer may be stuck with the bad judgment. Was the genuineness a basic premise of the contract? If so, maybe an actionable mistake was made. The characterization is important, because the remedies are very different, ranging from no remedy at all to rescission for mistake or innocent misrepresentation, to expectation damages for breach of warranty, to expectation damages plus possible punitive damages for fraud.

§15.2.2 Mutual and Unilateral Mistake

Established doctrine draws a distinction between mutual mistake, in which the error is shared by both parties, and the unilateral mistake of only one of the parties. This sounds like a simple distinction, but it can be quite subtle and elusive. This is because a mistake is only **mutual** if it relates to a factual assumption so shared by the parties, that it is a **joint premise** of their bargain. A mistake is **unilateral**, not only in the obvious case where **one party knows the true facts and the other does not**, but also where both parties may be unaware of the truth, yet the fact in issue affects the decision of only one of the parties and is of no interest or relevance to the other. In other words, although neither knows the truth, the erroneous fact is a **basic assumption of only one of the parties** because the other is neutral on it. This means that the distinction between mutual and unilateral mistake is not necessarily merely a matter of deciding whether one or both parties had been misinformed. The contract must be interpreted in context to decide if it was built around the mutual assumption that a particular fact was true.

The relativity of the distinction may be illustrated by a couple of examples: A builder buys some land from a person claiming to be the owner of the land. The builder intends to build a house on it for resale. He makes a contract with an earthmover to clear and excavate the land. Immediately afterwards, and before any work is started, the builder discovers that the seller did not have title to the land. The builder therefore does not own it and cannot build on it. It could be said that the builder and earthmover entered their contract under the mutual mistake of fact that the builder owned the land. That is, the builder's ownership was a shared basic assumption of the contract. However, the better view is that the earthmover does not care who owns the property, and any mistake as to the existence of valid title is purely the builder's affair. This being so, the mistake is properly treated as unilateral on the builder's part.

Assume that the mistake does not relate to the ownership of the property. Instead, the earthmover made an arithmetical error in calculating the number of hours required to perform the excavation and accordingly submitted a bid 25 percent lower than its actual cost of doing the work. The builder, not realizing the error, accepts the earthmover's figure. Again, one could see this as a mutual erroneous assumption that the earthmover's calculations are correct. However, it is better treated as a unilateral error of the excavator. See also *Bert Allen Toyota, Inc. v. Grasz*, 909 So. 2d 763 (Miss. App. 2005) in which a car dealer's computer miscalculated the price of the car, resulting in a sale price $2,000 lower than it should have been. The dealer argued that this was a mutual mistake because both parties relied on the erroneous price calculated by the computer. The court disagreed. The buyer was interested only in the bottom line and the miscalculation that led to the final price was the dealer's unilateral mistake. These examples are not meant to suggest that there is a firm rule for distinguishing mutual and unilateral mistake. In each case the conclusion is based on assessing the relationship of the mistaken fact to the basis of the contract.

The decision on whether or not relief should be granted for the mistake is based on the considerations discussed in the following sections. When you read them you will find that unilateral and mutual mistake involve essentially the same basic inquiry — that is, their elements are the same in many respects. However, in addition to sharing the elements of mutual mistake, unilateral mistake has its own further prerequisites. This is because a party who has made a unilateral mistake must make a stronger case for relief by demonstrating that the unfairness of enforcing the contract outweighs the need to protect the reasonable reliance of the other party.

In other words, unilateral mistake calls for a stronger focus on the relative equities of enforcement or nonenforcement. In a sense, this is an additional element but, as you will see, it follows quite logically from and is really inherent in the elements held in common with mutual mistake. Thus, the difference between the elements of mutual and unilateral mistake are largely a matter of emphasis and focus. This is just as well, considering that it is sometimes difficult to decide if the error was a shared assumption or purely one-sided. Misclassification need not be fatally wrong if the elements are properly analyzed because, in the end, both types of mistake must be resolved by deciding who should suffer the consequences of the error, in light of the factual indications of contractual intent and the surrounding equities. UCC Article 2 does not deal with the doctrine of mistake, so a mistake in a contract for the sale of goods is governed by principles of common law.

§15.3 THE ELEMENTS OF MUTUAL MISTAKE

According to Restatement Second §152 (read with §§151 and 154), a mutual mistake is avoidable by the adversely affected party if the following prerequisites are satisfied:

1. *At the time of contracting, the parties must have shared an erroneous belief concerning a fact.* As noted already, a mistake in the legal sense is an error relating to a fact. The error must be made at the time of contracting and it must relate to a state of affairs existing at the time, rather than one predicted to occur in the future.
2. *The erroneous fact was a basic assumption on which the contract was made.* The mistaken fact must be so *fundamental to the shared intent and purpose of both parties* that it is reasonable to conclude that they would not have made the contract at all or on the present terms had they known the truth. For example, the seller sold a lakefront lot to the buyer for $500,000.

The price was that high because this is a prime waterfront location surrounded by expensive homes in a popular vacation area. The seller knew that the buyer intended to build a luxury home on the lot and both parties believed that the lot was suitable for building. Neither party knew at the time of contracting that the lot is on porous and unstable land and it cannot support a building. Given the parties' shared understanding of the purpose of the sale, the mistake is the basis of the bargain.

3. *The mistake must have a material effect on the agreed exchange of performances.* This sounds like a repetition of the prior element, because it would seem to follow that an erroneous basic assumption of the contract will inevitably have a material effect on the exchange. This is often true, but the focus of these elements is different. Sometimes, the materiality of the effect on the exchange is obvious. For example, if the land in the above illustration is worth only $25,000 because it cannot support a building, the contract price of $500,000 reflects the contrary erroneous belief. The mistake not only forms the basis of the bargain but it also has a material effect on the exchange. However, the interaction between the basis of the bargain and materiality could be more subtle. Say that the lakefront location is so desirable that the land can most likely be resold to a campground operator for $500,000 despite its unsuitability for building. The evaluation of materiality is more difficult. Although the mistake still forms the basis of the bargain, the seller could argue that it does not affect the market value of the property. Because the buyer can recoup the price by reselling it, the error is immaterial and should not be grounds for relief. This argument may work, but it is important to bear in mind that the buyer did not buy the property for the purpose of resale, and he does end up with something very different from what he bargained for. A court may find this to be material even though there is no identifiable economic loss.

Thus, the test of **basic assumption** examines the aggrieved party's **motivation**, as shared with the other party, but **materiality** calls for an assessment of the **mistake's impact on the balance of the exchange** to see if it substantially deprived the adversely affected party of the value expected. Restatement Second §152, Comment c, suggests that the test is whether the error creates an overall imbalance between the parties by making the exchange less desirable to the adversely affected party and more advantageous to the other. This element thus contains a component of equitable balancing, in which the court examines the effect of the mistake on both the parties to decide the fairness of enforcing the contract despite the mistake.

4. *The adversely affected party must not have borne the risk of the mistake.* Although this question is commonly phrased so as to focus on the assumption of

risk by the adversely affected party, the issue is to *allocate the risk of error to one party or the other.* There is no such thing as a neutral decision on risk because a determination that one party did not bear the risk inevitably means that the other did. (Although it is possible to find that the parties shared the risk, this does not seem to happen very often.) The allocation of risk is often the dispositive element in mistake cases. Despite everything that has been said up to now, and no matter how serious the error, if the adversely affected party bore the risk of mistake, there can be no avoidance of the contract.

How can one tell who assumed the risk of the mistake? The first place to turn for an answer to this question is the contract itself. The resolution is clearest if the *contract expressly addresses the risk.* Risk allocation is clear if the contract for the sale of the lakeside lot states, "While the seller believes that the lot is suitable for building, he neither represents nor warrants that this belief is correct. The buyer may not terminate this contract if this belief proves to be wrong." Even if the contract is not that clear, risk allocation may be *inferred from the contract terms* in context by the usual process of interpretation or construction. As always, **factual interpretation** is attempted first, but if no evidence of actual agreement can be found, the court must assign the risk in the way most reasonable under the circumstances, based on general expectations and practices in the market or community. That is, the court must resolve the question by **construction**, determining how the parties would reasonably have allocated the risk, had they thought of the issue.

Many different factors may come into play in the process of construing risk allocation. If a pertinent commercial practice exists, it is a strong indicator of the parties' reasonable expectation or risk. For example, it would be useful to know if buyers of land normally investigate its suitability for building. If so, this buyer's failure to investigate would be an assumption of the risk of error. Similarly, if loss or liability can be insured against in transactions of this type, it would be helpful to know which party normally takes out the policy. In some cases, there may be a legal rule that dictates or suggests risk allocation in the absence of contrary agreement. For example, the rule of *caveat emptor* (buyer beware) usually applies to a sale of real estate, so the buyer bears the risk of any defect in the property in the absence of an express warranty by the seller.

§15.4 THE ELEMENTS OF UNILATERAL MISTAKE

The elements of unilateral mistake are set out in Restatement Second §153. Relief for unilateral mistake has basically the same prerequisites as mutual mistake, but because the mistake is one-sided, the common elements are phrased somewhat differently and an additional concern must be taken into account: Because only one party has made a mistake, the expectations of the non-mistaken party must be protected insofar as they are reasonable and legitimate. Therefore, unilateral mistake is grounds for relief only if the equities favoring release of the mistaken party outweigh the need to uphold the rights of the non-mistaken party. As noted in section 15.2.2, this additional concern is really implicit in the other elements that unilateral mistake shares with mutual mistake.

The elements for unilateral mistake are:

1. *The error concerns a fact.* This requirement is no different from mutual mistake.

2. *The fact is a basic assumption on which the mistaken party made the contract.* Of course, we are concerned here not with a shared assumption, but with the individual motive of only one of the parties, which has not necessarily been communicated to the other. Nevertheless, the subjectivity of this requirement is not a threat to the reliance interest of the other party, which is taken care of by the other elements.

3. *The mistake has a material effect on the exchange, adverse to the mistaken party.* As with mutual mistake, this element concerns the mistake's objectively determinable impact on the exchange of values.

4. *The mistaken party must not bear the risk of the mistake.* The allocation of risk involves issues of interpretation and construction the same as those in mutual mistake, but this element has a particular twist in unilateral mistake cases because there is often some degree of *negligence* involved in a one-sided error. If negligence automatically placed the risk of error on the mistaken party, unilateral mistake would rarely permit avoidance. Courts recognize this and tolerate some degree of negligence, provided that the other elements are satisfied. However, negligence does have a significant impact on the decision on whether to grant relief. For example, in *Bert Allen Toyota, Inc. v. Grasz*, cited in section 15.2.2, the court refused the dealer's claim for avoidance of the contract where its computer miscalculated the price. The court found that the dealer failed to exercise reasonable care when it did not check the computer's calculations, especially because it was aware that the computer had made errors before. The more serious the degree of negligence — such as gross negligence, recklessness, or dereliction of a duty owed to the other party — the greater the likelihood that the court will find that the negligent party assumed the risk of mistake. Quite apart from its role in the element of risk allocation, the carelessness of the mistaken party could have an impact on the balance of the equities discussed below. That is, even if there has not been enough sloppiness or serious negligence to dispose of the

case on the question of risk allocation, the mistaken party's fault could tip the balance in favor of the other party.

5. *The equities must favor relief for the mistake.* While equitable balancing takes into account factors beyond the first four elements, it obviously cannot be performed in isolation from them. In other words, the degree to which the first four elements are satisfied forms a vital component in the overall balance. Beyond this, the court also balances the impact of avoidance on the parties. It weighs the hardship that enforcement would have on the mistaken party against the hardship of avoidance on the other party. These equitable considerations are therefore quite far ranging. They take into account not only relative innocence and fault, but also the economic consequences of avoidance on each of the parties.

Therefore, the balance weighs most heavily in favor of the non-mistaken party when the mistake involved a degree of negligence by the other, the non-mistaken party had no reason to realize the mistake, and took action in reliance on the contract. In such a situation, her good faith reliance on the apparent assent of the mistaken party has led her to incur some commitment or expense, so that avoidance would go beyond depriving her of the good bargain, but would actually cause her loss. The protection of good faith reliance is the central issue, but the principle may be articulated in different ways — for example, it is sometimes expressed as a rule to the effect that a contract cannot be avoided for unilateral mistake unless the innocent non-mistaken party can be restored to the status quo. It is sometimes stated that relief should be denied unless the mistaken party promptly notifies the other upon becoming aware of the error. This rule is aimed at ameliorating any prejudicial reliance on the mistake, and it also reflects another factor in the balance — the degree of diligence exercised by the mistaken party. At the other end of the scale, if the non-mistaken party realized the error and kept quiet in order to jump at the bargain, or worse, if the non-mistaken party actually caused the error, her reliance interest is at its weakest. Between these extremes, there are countless variations in relative fault and hardship, so that the balance may be harder to find.

To make this more concrete, refer back to the mistaken bid cases discussed in section 5.3 in relation to the application of promissory estoppel to create an option, particularly *Drennan v. Star Paving,* 333 P.2d 757 (Cal. 1958), *Deide Construction v. Monterey Mechanical Co.,* 22 Cal. Rptr. 3d 763 (Cal. App. 2005), and *I&R Mechanical, Inc. v. Hazelton Mfg. Co.,* 817 N.E.2d 799 (Mass. App. 2004). The cases all involved similar facts: A subcontractor made an error in its bid to the prime contractor, the prime contractor then used that bid in calculating its own bid to the owner. After the owner accepted the prime contactor's bid, and the prime contractor was committed to the owner, the subcontractor discovered the error and attempted to revoke its own bid. In section 5.3 we saw that under some circumstances promissory estoppel can be used to make the subcontractor's bid irrevocable even though it did not qualify as option with consideration and the prime contractor had not accepted it before attempted revocation. Where the court finds that the bid is irrevocable, acceptance by the prime contractor within a reasonable time creates a contract with the subcontractor.

When you look at these cases in the present context, you should see that they also present an issue of unilateral mistake. That is, even if the court finds that a contract came into being through the process of offer and acceptance, the subcontractor can seek to avoid that contract on the basis of unilateral mistake. *Drennan* specifically addressed this issue and found that the subcontractor's miscalculation of its costs were not grounds to avoid the contract for unilateral mistake. The error was caused by the subcontractor's negligence, and because there was a considerable variation in bids for the work, the prime contractor had no reason to suspect that the subcontractor's low bid was a result of error. The prime contractor had committed itself to the owner on the strength of the bid, and the equities favored leaving the loss with the subcontractor. In *Drennan*, the balance of the relative hardship on the parties was about even. However, the result could have been different if, say, the prime contractor had such a good profit margin in its contract with the owner that the extra cost of the subcontract could be absorbed without making the prime contract unprofitable, but the subcontractor is in such perilous financial circumstances that the loss on this job might put it out of business.

The other two cases did not discuss the issue of mistake, but both pointed out that the discrepancy between the subcontractor's bid and that of its competitors was relevant to promissory estoppel relief. If the subcontractor's bid was significantly lower than competing bids and the prime contractor should have realized the possibility of error, it should not be given promissory estoppel relief. The same consideration applies where the issue is not whether the bid should be treated as a binding offer, but whether, assuming a contract, the erroneous bid should be grounds for relief for mistake. The non-mistaken party cannot jump at a bargain by taking advantage of an apparent error. (Recall that these circumstances could give the subcontractor alternative grounds for relief on grounds of fraudulent nondisclosure. As discussed in section 13.6.2, silence can amount to fraud where a party keeps quite after becoming aware that the other party has made a mistake.)

§15.5 RELIEF FOR MISTAKE

The principal remedy for mistake is **avoidance** of the contract at the instance of the mistaken party. There is only one mistaken party when the mistake is unilateral, but if the mistake is mutual the parties share the error. If both wish to avoid the contract, it can simply be rescinded by agreement. However, if only one is hurt by the mistake and the other benefits from or is unaffected by it, it stands to reason that the claim for avoidance will be made by the adversely affected party. Avoidance brings the contract to an end and both parties must **restore any benefit** resulting from performance that was rendered prior to termination. If the benefit is property still in existence, the property itself must be returned, otherwise restitution must be made of the value of services or property consumed or incapable of return. Value is normally based on the market worth of the property or services (of which the contract value may be probitive evidence). However, the court has some discretion in determining the basis of valuation, and it may use some other measure appropriate under the circumstances. For example, if the party who conferred the benefit was more to blame for the mistake, the value of consumed goods or services could be confined to the actual ultimate economic benefit enjoyed by the other party.

Because relief for mistake derives from equity, the court has some flexibility in remedy and could provide relief other than avoidance and restitution if the equities so dictate. For example, avoidance on the grounds of unilateral mistake could be ordered subject to the payment of *reliance expenses* designed to restore the non-mistaken party to the status quo. In relatively rare cases, the court may keep the contract in force with an *adjustment to its terms* to counter the effect of the mistake. This is what the court did in *Aluminum Company of America v. Essex Group, Inc.*, 499 F. Supp. 53 (W.D. Pa. 1980). The court found that the parties had made a mutual mistake in adopting a particular pricing formula as an accurate predictor of Alcoa's costs. As a result, the cost of Alcoa's performance under the contract greatly exceeded the price payable under the contract. (The reason for the court's conclusion and the facts of the case are discussed more in sections 15.7.1 and 15.7.3a below.) The court felt that it would be unfair to allow Alcoa to avoid the contract as a whole because this would completely deprive Essex of its bargain and would give Alcoa the windfall of full release from its contractual commitment. It therefore adjusted the price term to give Alcoa a profit that accorded with the parties' reasonable expectations.

This alternative is not widely recognized in the caselaw, and even if a court is willing to allow it in principle, it is not appropriate if the mistake is so fundamental that the entire character of the transaction is altered, or its basic purpose is defeated. It is also seldom the best solution if the contract is entirely executory, and neither party performed or otherwise relied on it before the mistake was discovered. However, in some cases, if avoidance would be disruptive and the error relates to an aspect of the contract that can be adjusted (say to a price calculation), an alteration of terms may be a fair remedy. Even here, adjustment of terms must be approached with caution because the court should not readily remake the contract on terms that were not agreed to, especially if that subjects one of the parties to an unexpected and more burdensome obligation.

§15.6 MISTAKE IN TRANSCRIPTION: REFORMATION

Some mistakes may relate, not to a factual premise of the agreement, but to **the way in which the agreement is expressed in writing**. For example, a memorandum of agreement reflects the price of a piece of land as $280,000. The buyer contends that the parties had orally agreed to a price of $250,000, and that the written price is a typographical error not noticed by the buyer when signing the document.

Mistakes in transcription are completely different in nature from those discussed in the prior sections. The "fact" that is wrong is **not one that motivated the transaction**, but one **inherent in the written record** of the transaction. The problem is not that the manifestation is based on a faulty premise, but that it is false in itself. Nevertheless, an error in expression has one thing in common with a mistake of underlying fact: In both cases one of the parties seeks to avoid the apparent meaning of a manifestation of assent by showing that it was induced by error. In the case of mistake as to an underlying fact, the goal is to negate assent and avoid the contract. When the mistake is in transcription, the desired relief is to have the writing changed to reflect what was actually agreed. It must be stressed that the goal of reformation is to correct the contract to ensure that it reflects what was actually agreed, not to adjust or rewrite its terms. For example, in *Silsbe v. Houston Levee Industrial Park, LLC*, 165 S.W.3d 260 (Tenn. App. 2005) the holder of an option was not able to exercise it on the day before it expired because that day was a public holiday. After the grantor refused to recognize the exercise of the option after the expiry date, the holder sued, seeking reformation of the contract on the grounds that the parties had mistakenly selected a public holiday as the deadline for exercising the option. The court refused reformation. Although the parties may not have realized that the deadline fell on a public holiday, this was the date that they intended. The option therefore correctly reflected the parties' intent and reformation would have changed the contract rather than corrected an error in expression.

If both parties recognize that an error has occurred in transcription and they act honestly, the problem can be disposed of simply by amending the writing and initialling the change. But life is not always that simple because the party benefiting from the error may claim (whether genuinely or disingenuously) that the writing is correct. If so, the other party is able to seek the equity-based remedy of reformation to have the court correct the writing so that it accurately reflects what was agreed. This remedy involves both a declaration by the court that the contract is on terms other than reflected in the writing, and enforcement on those terms.

Because a signed writing is usually regarded as the most reliable evidence of what was agreed, a party seeking reformation has a difficult burden. He must convincingly show that an error was indeed made in recording the terms agreed, and must also plausibly explain why the error was made and why he failed to notice it when signing the document. Because the right to reformation cannot be shown except by recourse to evidence extrinsic to the writing, the **parol evidence rule** does not bar the introduction of evidence for the purpose of showing a mistake in transcription. If it did, the remedy of reformation could never be used.

A question of reformation could also be presented when the parties chose words in their writing that do not have the legal effect intended. For example, a written contract for the sale of a car states that it is sold "as is." This is a legal term of art that means that it is sold without any warranties. However, the buyer contends that the parties were unaware of that meaning and did not intend it at all. The seller had added a number of accessories to the car, and the words "as is" were used merely to reflect their agreement that these accessories were to be included. This kind of transcription error is more complicated than the error in the previous illustration involving the incorrect reflection of price, because it is more difficult to distinguish the problem of misrecording from an error in understanding that would need to be resolved by interpretation on the principles discussed in Chapter 10. If the dispute centers around what the parties meant by the term "as is," it is a question of interpretation. However, if the argument is that they agreed on what it was supposed to mean, but the objective appearance of the document, in employing this term, is different from intended, it is a case for reformation. In either event, the party who argues for the idiosyncratic meaning will probably have an evidentiary headache (including possible problems under the parol evidence rule because this is less obviously a simple matter of reformation) if the other now denies that the meaning was intended. Note also that there is a subtle difference between the erroneous expression of agreement by the incorrect use of a legal term and a mutual mistake of law. By using the phrase "as is" the parties do, in a sense, make a legal error — but that error relates not to what the law is, but to the legal meaning of the word-symbol used in the writing.

§15.7 IMPRACTICABILITY OF PERFORMANCE

§15.7.1 The Nature of Impracticability Doctrine, Contrasted with Mistake

Mistake concerns an error of fact in existence at the time of contracting, so fundamental to the premise of the contract that it precludes the formation of true assent. Impracticability applies when events following contract formation[1] are so different from the assumptions on which the contract was based, that it would be unfair to hold the adversely affected party to its commitments. Although there are close affinities between mistake and impracticability, as you will see when comparing their elements, they have an important difference in scope and purpose. A mistake causes a defect in contract formation, permitting a party to be excused from accountability for a manifestation of assent. Impracticability has nothing to do with any problem in formation and presupposes that a binding contract was made. Rather, it is concerned with whether a **post-formation change of circumstances** has such a **serious effect** on the **reasonable expectations** of the parties, that it should be allowed to **excuse performance**.

An example will illustrate this difference: The owner of a beachfront cabin makes a contract to sell it. Unknown to both parties at the time of contracting, a tidal wave swept the cabin into the sea just a few hours before the contract was executed. They are mutually mistaken that the cabin exists. However, if the tidal wave hits after the contract was made, but before the seller transfers and delivers the cabin to the buyer, there was no error about its existence at the time of contracting. Instead, the issue is whether this supervening event should permit the seller to escape liability for failure to deliver the cabin as promised in the otherwise valid and enforceable contract.

Although it is usually easy to distinguish mistake from impracticability, sometimes the facts are ambiguous enough to make this unclear. The case could be resolved either on grounds of mistake or impracticability, depending on the court's perspective. For example, in *Aluminum Company of America*, cited in section 15.5, the parties entered into a long-term contract under which Alcoa would smelt alumina for Essex. The parties based their pricing formula on the Wholesale Price Index-Industrial Commodities (WPI). They used the WPI because it had reliably corresponded to Alcoa's costs of production in prior years and they assumed that it would continue to do so. However, a few years after the contract had been executed, electricity prices

---

1. As noted in section 15.1, there are cases in which the circumstances causing the impracticality existed at the time of contracting. This situation is unusual, and impracticality is more commonly associated with supervening events. This discussion is therefore confined to supervening impracticability.

increased steeply because of the OPEC oil embargo and the higher cost of producing electricity in compliance with pollution regulations. As a result, the WPI ceased to be an accurate predictor of Alcoa's costs, which escalated to such an extent that its costs exceeded the contract price under the formula. The court treated this as a case of mistake because it held that the parties erroneously assumed at the time of the contract that the WPI index was an appropriate standard for achieving the goal of measuring Alcoa's future costs. This could just as well have been treated as an impracticability case because the oil embargo and tougher environmental regulations, which caused the WPI to be inaccurate, were supervening events. The court acknowledged this by discussing impracticability as an alternative basis for its decision. (We will discuss the resolution of the case in section 15.7.3a.)

The issue in an impracticability case is not whether the party can be forced to perform. Clearly, in the above example of the cabin, the seller cannot deliver it because it is flotsam on the ocean. The issue is whether, by failing to perform, he has breached the contract. If failure to perform is excused on grounds of impracticability, the seller of the cabin is not in breach and is therefore not liable to pay damages to the buyer. On the facts of this example, impracticability would completely excuse the seller's performance. It follows, of course, that the buyer would not be required to perform either, so the effect of impracticability is to terminate the contract. If either party has partly performed before this (say, for example, that the buyer made a down payment), the benefit of that performance must be restored.

§15.7.2 The Early Form of the Doctrine: Impossibility of Performance

In older common law, once a contract had been made, the parties were absolutely bound and remained committed even if a change in circumstances made it extremely difficult or even impossible for one of them to perform. (As just noted, the party was not expected to work a miracle by performing the impossible, but the failure to perform was not excused by the supervening event and was a breach giving rise to a damages claim.) By the mid-nineteenth century, the harshness of this rule was ameliorated by judicial recognition of the doctrine of impossibility of performance. In its original form, as articulated by the English case of *Taylor v. Caldwell*, 122 Eng. Rep. 309 (Queens Bench, 1863), the doctrine was quite narrow: If, when making the contract, the parties reasonably contemplated that its **performance was dependent** on the **continued existence of a person or thing**, the post-formation **death** of the person or **destruction** of the thing, **not caused by the fault** of the party seeking relief, would **excuse performance** by that party, and hence, also the return performance, resulting in termination of the contract without liability for breach.

In *Taylor*, the contract was for the hire of a music hall that burned down after the contract was made and before the time for performance. Although the obligation to provide the hall was not qualified by any express term of the contract, the court found the continuing existence of the hall to have been a basic assumption of the contract. This led to the legal implication of a term that the destruction of the hall excused performance. As originally formulated, the defense of impossibility was confined to situations in which the change of circumstances made the contract *objectively* impossible to perform. That is, the event must have completely defeated the ability to deliver the performance, not only by this party, but by a reasonable person in his position. Say, for example, that the fire merely damaged the music hall. If a reasonable owner could have restored it sufficiently in time for the performance, this owner could not claim the defense of impossibility merely because he did not have the resources or energy to do so.

§15.7.3 The Contemporary Doctrine of Impracticability of Performance

During the course of this century, the doctrine of impossibility has come to be perceived as too restricted. There are situations in which events do not make performance absolutely impossible, yet they place such a great and unexpected burden on the party that fairness demands relief. As a result, the scope of the doctrine has broadened and has been renamed "impracticability" to reflect this change. As in so many other areas of contract law, a strong impetus for change in the doctrine came from the UCC. Section 2.615[2] enacted the broader concept of impracticability as the standard for sales of goods, and this has been influential in reinforcing change in common law doctrine too. By embracing a formulation based on the UCC, Restatement Second §§261 to 272 reinforces the common law's movement away from the stricter impossibility standard. There are a number of differences between UCC §2.615 and the provisions of the Restatement Second, but the basic concepts are the same. This discussion focuses on general principles applicable to both.

If all of its elements are established, the excuse of impracticability is available to the party who is adversely affected by the change in circumstances. (UCC §2.615 assumes that it will always be the seller who claims impracticability, but this need not necessarily be so, and courts have recognized that a buyer can use the excuse in appropriate circumstances.) Although these elements are identified and discussed separately, the defense of impracticability is better understood if one recognizes that they are very

---

2. Section 2.615 is not significantly changed in the 2003 revision of Article 2.

much interwoven and that the facts affecting one are often relevant to the others. All the elements must be satisfied for the defense to be available. As in mistake, risk allocation is usually the predominant and pervasive consideration. We now examine each of the elements:

a. After the Contract Was Made, an Event Occurred, the Non-Occurrence of Which Was a Basic Assumption of the Contract

This concept is very much like its equivalent element in mistake doctrine, except that the basic assumption relates not to an existing but to a future state of affairs. The idea here is that when the parties entered the contract they expressly or impliedly made assumptions about the future course of events and these assumptions were a *central motivation of the contract*. Whether or not a basic assumption is articulated, it must be patent enough from the circumstances and the apparent purpose of the contract that it is reasonable to conclude that the parties must have shared it.

Having entered the contract on this basic assumption, the parties are then faced with an event so contrary to the assumption that it *changes the very basis of the exchange*. Comment 1 to UCC §2.615 describes this occurrence as an "unforeseen supervening circumstance not within the contemplation of the parties at the time of contracting." This suggests that the event must be so unexpected that the parties did not think of it at the time of contracting, or if they did, that they did not consider it to be a realistic likelihood.

The comment uses the word "unforeseen," which must be distinguished from "unforeseeable." An event is **unforeseen** by the parties if they themselves **did not contemplate it as a real likelihood**. That is, although it could be imagined, the parties did not expect it to happen and contracted on the assumption that it would not. It may be a possibility, but is not treated by the parties as a probability. An event is **unforeseeable** if it **could not have been conceived of by a reasonable person**. To require unforeseeability would impose too stringent a test, making the defense of impracticability available only when the supervening event is beyond human experience. For example, it is unforeseeable that a music hall could be demolished by a rampaging dinosaur or other large beast,[3] but its destruction by fire is certainly within the range of possibility. Therefore, fire was foreseeable at the time of contracting, but it was not foreseen by the parties if, under all the circumstances, it is shown that they did not think of it at all or, even if one or both may have realized the possibility, it was not considered a strong enough likelihood to be raised and dealt with as a contingency. Of course, the fact that the event was unforeseen does not, on its own, mean that the defense of impracticability will succeed. This is only the first of the elements that must be satisfied.

---

3. Of course, the fact that I (and several talented "B" movie creators) have contemplated this possibility may mean that it is indeed foreseeable.

Often, even though the non-occurrence of the event was a basic assumption of the contract, the risk of the occurrence may have been impliedly assumed by the party claiming impracticality. That is, if the parties foresaw the likelihood of the event, they probably allocated the risk of its happening (expressly or impliedly) in the contract. However, even if they did not foresee it, commercial practice or other surrounding circumstances may give rise to an implication of risk assumption.

Impracticability arises from the occurrence of an event, so we must identify **what types of happening might constitute an event**. Again, there is an analogy to mistake, in that an event is a factual situation, albeit one that arises after the contract. Most **occurrences external to the contract** qualify as events: war, a natural disaster, a strike, and so on. A **change in the law or government regulation** is also an event. Therefore, if the law changes to prohibit a performance that was lawful at the time of contracting, the change in the law defeats a basic assumption of the contract. UCC §2.615(a) and Restatement Second §264 expressly recognize this by providing that good faith compliance with governmental regulation excuses performance, even if the regulation is later found to be invalid. Say, for example, that the music hall did not burn down, but shortly after the contract was made, the city council strengthened its public safety regulations so that the hall no longer satisfied them and cannot be lawfully let for public performances. If the council's action was unexpected and was given no advance publicity, this would be an unforeseen contingency that defeats the basic assumption that the hall could be used. This example highlights the development of the law from impossibility to impracticability. It would still be possible for the lessor to make the hall available and for the buyer to pay the rent, but the contract is made impracticable because its basic assumption has been overturned.[4]

A **change in market conditions** is generally not regarded as a contingency beyond the contemplation of the parties because the very purpose of setting a price or committing to a future delivery of goods or services is based on the possibility that prices or demand may change. Therefore, the basic assumption of most contracts is not that the market will remain constant, but that it might change. However, the basic assumption of any particular contract is a factual question, so this general approach should not be treated as an invariable rule. It is possible that a constant market was assumed in a contract, or even if not, that the market variation results from a

---

4. In anticipation of the discussion in section 15.8, it is also worth pointing out that these facts would support an argument that the purpose of the contract has been frustrated: Although the lessor can still deliver possession of the hall and the lessee can still pay the rent, the purpose of the hiring — the use of the hall for a public concert — has been negated by the new regulations. This illustrates the observation in section 15.8 that impracticality is broad enough to cover most, if not all, situations that would have required a separate doctrine of frustration in earlier law.

disruption which causes changes way beyond reasonable expectations. This is particularly so if some unexpected calamity, such as a sudden war, embargo, or natural disaster is the cause of the market changes. This has happened a number of times, and there are cases arising from events such as the Suez crisis, the Vietnam War, and the OPEC oil embargo, in which the supplier of a commodity or service has claimed impracticability based on greatly added expense or burdens on performance caused by the crisis. In some of the cases, the international disturbance was found to render performance impracticable, but in others, the defense did not succeed, either because the disruption was foreseen by the parties or because one of the other elements of the defense (such as extreme hardship or risk allocation) was not satisfied.

Aluminum Company of America, discussed in sections 15.5 and 15.7.1, is an example of a case in which the court did recognize that severe market disruption made a contract impracticable. The parties entered into a long-term contract under which Alcoa smelted alumina for Essex. (The base period of the contract was 16 years with a five-year renewal option). They devised a pricing formula which used the WPI as the basis of determining Alcoa's projected costs over the life of the contract, intending that the price would escalate in relation to increases in the WPI. After the contract was executed, the WPI became an unrealistic predictor of Alcoa's costs because electricity charges, which were only a small part of the costs that made up the WPI, increased dramatically as a result of the OPEC oil embargo, combined with tougher environmental regulation. This caused the costs calculated under the WPI to be much lower than Alcoa's actual costs, and Alcoa suffered huge losses which would have amounted to about $60 million over the term of the contract. Although the court resolved the case in favor of Alcoa on the basis of mistake, it discussed impracticability as an alternative basis for relief. It concluded that the increase in electricity costs and the scale of the resulting loss were of such dramatic proportions that they were not foreseen by the parties and went beyond the level of risk that Alcoa had assumed.

b. The Effect of the Event Is to Render the Party's Performance "Impracticable," that Is, Unduly Burdensome

A loss in certainty is the price paid for the law's movement away from the more discernible standard of impossibility, toward the vaguer and more relative concept of impracticability. Once a party no longer has to establish that performance is objectively incapable of being rendered, we are left with the task of deciding how extensively the performance must have changed to qualify as impracticable. If impracticability merely required a showing of inconvenience, lack of profitability, or the loss of a better opportunity, it would be too easy for a party to escape a contract that turns out to be disadvantageous because of a change in the market or commercial environment.

Therefore, relief is only appropriate if the change is extreme or very burdensome. In a sense, this requirement is similar to the element of *materiality* in mistake. The event must have such a severe impact on the performance that it cannot be rendered without great loss, risk, or other hardship. Unfortunately, this is as vague as it sounds, but it necessarily must be so, because impracticality is relative and must be assessed on all the facts of the case.

In the easiest case, an event that creates objective impossibility also renders the performance impracticable, because the wider doctrine includes cases that would have satisfied the narrower standard. Therefore, if the parties contemplated the rental of a specific music hall, the destruction of the hall makes performance impossible and hence also impracticable. However, as the facts move beyond this clearer case, the determination becomes more difficult. Say that the music hall did not burn down, but after the contract is made, the premium payable by the lessor for liability insurance increases tenfold because of a large number of theater fires in the region over the last year. As a result, if the lessor is to permit use of the premises by the public, he must pay a huge insurance premium that will exceed the earnings he will make from renting the hall. Both parties can still perform — the lessor can make the hall available and the lessee can pay the rent — but the increase in insurance rates has imposed a financial burden (or a massive risk of liability, if the policy is not renewed) on the lessor that may make its performance impracticable.

Consider another example: The hall does burn down, but there is another hall in the same block owned by a competitor of the lessor. The hall is about the same size, is equally suitable for the performance, and it is available for the night of the concert. The lessee contends that the lessor's performance is therefore still possible, because the exact identity of the hall is immaterial, and the lessor can still provide appropriate premises by hiring the second hall and making it available to the lessee as a substitute for the destroyed hall. The problem is that the owner of the surviving hall demands a rental from the lessor far higher than that which the lessor is to be paid by the lessee under the contract, so the lessor will lose money by doing this (or by paying the rental difference to the lessee as damages if he refuses). If the lessee's contention is correct and the identity of the hall was not a central term of the contract, the lessor's performance is not impossible, so the question becomes whether the loss to be incurred in finding a substitute renders it sufficiently burdensome to constitute impracticability.

There is no definitive answer to the question in these cases. However, they point to the focus of the inquiry — the economic impact of the unforeseen supervening event. A prospective loss that is not negligible could satisfy this element. The magnitude and effect of the loss is obviously of crucial significance, and a huge loss that threatens the lessee's financial survival is more likely to be seen as making the performance impracticable, than a manageable smaller loss. This may make it sound as if the defense of impracticability can be easily invoked whenever a serious prospective loss is shown. But remember that this element is only one of several that must be satisfied, and proof of the most devastating loss is not enough to assure relief if the other elements are not also present.

c. The Party Seeking Relief Was Not at Fault in Causing the Occurrence

A person should not be able to take advantage of his own wrongful or negligent act, and a party who disables himself from performing, or makes performance more difficult, cannot expect to be excused from liability. Thus, the lessor of the music hall would have a nerve claiming impracticability if he deliberately set the fire. Similarly, a person cannot be excused from liability just because it turns out that he is incompetent and cannot perform as promised. However, the issue of fault could be more subtle. Should the lessor be denied relief if the fire was caused by an antiquated and improperly maintained electrical system in the music hall? In less obvious cases, the degree to which the party was in some way responsible for his troubles, or could have surmounted them with reasonable effort, is a relevant factor to be taken into account.

d. The Party Seeking Relief Must Not Have Borne the Risk of the Event Occurring

As with mistake, the risk allocation is often the dispositive issue in impracticability cases. In many ways, the other elements foreshadow the question of risk allocation and seem to be no more than components of it. (In fact, as you may have sensed, the issue of risk allocation was constantly lurking in the discussion of the other elements and had to be restrained from jumping out.) The analysis of risk allocation is basically the same as for mistake: If the party adversely affected by the event had *expressly or impliedly assumed the risk of its occurrence*, the non-performance cannot be excused even though all the other elements are satisfied.

The first place to look in determining risk allocation is the contract itself. If the parties realized that a particular future event could affect performance, the contract may have an express and specific term assigning risk. For example, a consignor of goods and a shipping company may contemplate the possibility that a war may break out along the route, requiring a diversion of the ship. If so, they may specifically state in the contract which party will bear the loss and expense of the diversion. Even if the parties do not have a particular contingency in mind, the contract may have a more general provision allocating the risk of disruptions or calamities. This is known as a **force majeure** clause. It may provide, for example, that the shipping company shall have the right to charge for the cost of any diversion or delay of the ship resulting from war, revolution, national disasters, governmental action, and so on.

Even in the absence of these more direct types of risk allocation clauses, the contract may impliedly place risk on a party by means of a provision such as a warranty, an undertaking to obtain insurance, or some other commitment from which the assumption of risk may be inferred. In fact, a term expressly allocating the risk of certain events to one party may give rise to the inference that the other assumed the risk of events not enumerated. For example, a clause states that the shipping company may charge for additional expenses caused by war, revolution, and governmental action. If the ship is seized by pirates and held hostage for ransom, the loss of this disruption is not apparently covered by the contract, so it could be inferred that the consignor of the freight was intended to bear it. It is good planning for the parties to consider potential risks and to provide for them clearly in the contract. This reduces the possibility of later disputes and litigation. Of course, as the last example suggests, no risk allocation provision is foolproof. It may fail to contemplate the actual event that occurs.

If the contract terms do not settle the issue, its *context*, including normal *commercial practices and expectations*, must be examined to decide where the risk should lie. On this basis, we can reconsider some of the prior examples, to show that risk allocation may preclude relief even though the other elements may be satisfied. The lessee of the music hall will probably not be able to claim impracticability on the basis of poor ticket sales. Unless the contract provides otherwise, commercial practice in the entertainment industry probably places this risk on the promoter of the concert and will not allow him to foist it on the lessor by cancelling the booking if sales are weak. Practices concerning insurance can often help to settle risk allocation where the contract does not deal with the issue. Therefore (contrary to the result in *Taylor*), the lessee may be able to argue that the fact that the owner has an insurable interest in the hall suggests that the burning of the hall was the owner's risk, and he cannot use this calamity as the basis for escaping liability to the lessee. Finally, it is worth reiterating a point made in the discussion of basic assumption, and to emphasize that the assumptions underlying the contract are closely intertwined with the question of risk allocation: For example, unless the contract provides otherwise, the usual commercial assumption is that a party takes the risk of market fluctuations unless the change is so dramatic and unexpected as to be beyond the normal range of risk.

§15.7.4 Relief for Impracticability

When impracticability fully defeats the feasibility of performance by a party, it is a **complete defense** to that party's failure to perform, **relieving** him of the **duty of performance** and liability for **damages**. Release of that party also discharges the contractual duties of the other. If any performance had been rendered by either party under the contract prior to the finding of impracticability, the benefit or its value must be returned, measured in accordance with the same restitutionary principles applicable to mistake.

If impracticability does not go to the entire basis of the contract, the court has the discretion to award **relief short of fully excusing performance**. This is recognized in general terms by Comments 6 and 7 to UCC §2.615, and in more detail by Restatement Second §§269 and 270. It may be more appropriate to adjust the terms of the contract, to excuse a portion of the performance (with a reciprocal reduction in counterperformance), or simply to permit a delay if this would enable the difficulties to be surmounted.

If performance rendered under the contract has not benefited the other party, there is normally no claim for **restitution**. However, if the equities so demand, a court may be willing to stretch the elements of unjust enrichment to afford relief. For example, in *Albre Marble & Tile Co. v. John Bowen Co.*, 155 N.E.2d 437 (Mass. 1959) a prime contract was declared invalid because of improper bidding procedures. Prior to this, the prime contractor and subcontractor had entered into a contract for tile and marble work. The termination of the prime contract made the subcontract impracticable. The subcontractor had done preliminary work which had not yet been incorporated into the building and had not benefited the contractor. Nevertheless, the court held that the equities required restitution of the market value of the subcontractor's work because the prime contractor was partially responsible for the invalidity of the prime contract.

§15.8 FRUSTRATION OF PURPOSE

The doctrine of frustration of purpose developed as an extension of impossibility. It was designed to provide relief when a party could not show that an unexpected supervening event rendered his performance impossible, yet it so destroyed the value of the transaction for him that the contract's underlying purpose was frustrated. Because contemporary doctrine has expanded beyond the confines of impossibility, there is probably no longer a need for a separate doctrine of frustration of purpose. Frustration could simply be treated as a class of impracticability and subsumed into that doctrine. Notwithstanding, these two closely-linked defenses continue to coexist and are treated by courts (and by Restatement Second §265) as separate but allied. It is therefore necessary to understand the difference between them. However, if you should find it difficult to decide whether a particular case involves impracticality or frustration, take comfort in the thought that misclassification probably will not make much difference in result. They involve essentially the same issues and lead to the same type of relief. The only difference between them lies in the sometimes subtle distinction between an event that makes a party's performance unduly burdensome, and one that makes it pointless. (UCC Article 2 doesn't provide for a separate doctrine of frustration.)

Like impracticability, frustration is concerned with a **post-formation event**, the **non-occurrence** of which was a **basic assumption** on which the contract was made. This event must not have been caused by the fault of the party whose purpose is frustrated, and that party must not have borne the risk of its occurrence. The essential difference lies in the effect of the event. It does not directly affect the performance of the adversely affected party by making it unduly burdensome. Rather, its impact is on the benefit reasonably expected by that party in exchange for the performance. The event so **seriously affects the value or usefulness** of that benefit that it **frustrates the contract's central purpose** for that party. This cannot be a secret or obscure purpose, because a party's private motivation is not relevant to the contract and cannot be the basis of disappointing the other party's reliance. Therefore, the purpose must be so patent and obvious to the other party that it can reasonably be regarded as the *shared basis* of the contract. The purpose of most commercial contracts is to make a profit. However, although it could be said that profit is the underlying purpose of a contract, this does not mean that a party can invoke the doctrine of frustration of purpose merely because the contract is no longer profitable to him as a result of events after contract formation. A party cannot so easily escape the performance of a contract that turns out to have been a bad deal. This distinction was made in *Karl Wendt Farm Equipment Co. v. International Harvester Co.*, 931 F.2d 1112 (6th Cir. 1991). Following losses resulting from a bad downturn in the farm equipment market, I.H. sold its farm equipment division and terminated a number of dealerships. The plaintiff, one of the terminated dealers, sued I.H. for breach of contract. I.H. raised the defense of frustration of purpose on the grounds that the loss of profit from adverse economic conditions frustrated the purpose of the contract. The court rejected the defense of frustration of purpose. It said the primary purpose of the contract was to sell farm equipment. This purpose could still be achieved, even if the desired goal of profitability could not be.[5]

The classic illustration of frustration is supplied by another beloved English case, *Krell v. Henry*, 2 K.B. 740 (1903). Krell owned a flat on the route to be taken by the coronation procession of Edward VII. Krell was out of the country and instructed his solicitor to attempt to let the premises while he was away. A sign was placed in the window stating that the flat was

---

5. I.H. also raised the defense of impracticability which the court also rejected. It held that the poor market conditions were not so severe as to pass beyond the range of the normal risk that I.H. bore, and the impact of the market downturn was not grave enough to constitute undue hardship to I.H. The fact that the circumstances of the case gave rise to alternative arguments of impracticability and frustration of purpose, and that both failed, shows the close connection between the doctrines.

available to be let for viewing the procession. Henry responded to the sign and contracted to hire the flat on the two days of the coronation celebrations. The King became ill before the coronation and it was postponed, so Henry was left with no need for the premises on the days in question and he did not use them. Krell sued him for the balance of the agreed rental. (Henry had made a down payment but apparently did not pursue a counterclaim for a refund of the deposit.) The court resolved the case by using an adaptation of the impossibility defense of *Taylor v. Caldwell*. Although the contract did not expressly state the purpose of the rental of the flat, both parties understood that Henry's sole purpose in making it was to view the coronation procession. This purpose was the very foundation of the contract. The postponement of the coronation was a supervening event that had not reasonably been contemplated by the parties at the time of contracting. Although it did not make either party's performance impossible (Henry could still pay the agreed rent and Krell could give him possession of the flat), it so defeated the purpose of the contract that it should excuse Henry's performance. A concurring opinion in the case agreed with this analysis but raised the question of whether Henry would have been the more appropriate party to bear the risk of the coronation's postponement. This is a fair question and it again raises the point that when the contract does not itself provide for risk allocation, it is not always easy to know who should suffer the loss caused by the frustration. It is by no means self-evident that the court was right in imposing it on the lessor rather than the lessee.

Examples

1. Tiffany De Canter owned an ornate silver jug. She bought it some years ago for a substantial amount of money, believing it to be the work of Maestro Da Silva, an important nineteenth-century silversmith. Since she acquired it, Tiffany has had it examined by several experts. Although some of them thought that it might have been made by Da Silva, the prevailing view among them is that it was the product of one of his pupils. It has therefore been appraised at $10,000. Had it been authenticated as the work of Da Silva, it would be worth $1 million. Based on its appraised value, Tiffany grossly overpaid for the jug. She hates it and gets irritated every time she sees it. She therefore decided to sell it.

   Sterling Silverman, an art collector, has seen the jug and is familiar with Da Silva's work. He has a hunch that the experts may be wrong in concluding that it was not made by Da Silva. Upon hearing that Tiffany wished to sell it, he immediately made an offer to buy it at her full asking price of $12,000. Tiffany accepted his offer and a written contract of sale was executed. The writing was a simple document that identified the parties, set out the physical description of the jug, and stated the price and delivery obligation. A few months after the sale was completed, a scholar unearthed some previously unknown notebooks and sketches by Da Silva that conclusively proved that he had made the jug.

Can Tiffany avoid the sale to Sterling?

2. Manny Lisa recently became wealthy through the exercise of his stock options. All his newfound rich friends owned portraits of themselves painted by the celebrated society portraitist Leonardo De Fancy. Although he is clueless about art, Manny decided to get hold of the divine Leonardo and commission a portrait. He looked in the yellow pages under "Painters, portrait" and found a listing for De Fancy, Leonardo. He called the number and spoke to Leonardo, who agreed to paint his portrait for $250. Manny was astounded at how reasonable this was, and he accepted. The parties arranged a date for a sitting at the end of the week.

    A couple of days later, Manny discovered from a more worldly friend that the person who is listed in the yellow pages is not the Leonardo, but his father, Leonardo De Fancy the Elder, a talentless hack who ekes out a meager living by painting the children of middle-class suburbanites. Being unschooled in the ways of the art world, Manny had not known that a famous celebrity portraitist like the real Leonardo does not advertise in the yellow pages and only accepts commissions on referral. Furthermore, his charge for a portrait would be about 40 times what Manny had agreed to pay Leonardo the Elder.

    Understandably, Manny no longer desires the portrait for which he contracted. Can he avoid the contract?

3. Reliabuild Contractors, Inc. was invited by the owner of property to submit a bid for the erection of a new building. Reliabuild planned to do all the work itself except for the excavation of the land. It needed to know the cost of excavation before it could complete its bid, so it sent the building plans to Bill Dozer, an earthmover whom it had used with satisfactory results on several prior projects. Bill studied the plans and calculated his own cost. Unfortunately, he did this while watching his favorite afternoon talk show, and he did not concentrate properly. As a result, he added wrongly and miscalculated his cost as $500,000 instead of $800,000. He then added a ten percent profit of $50,000 and submitted a written bid of $550,000 to Reliabuild. Reliabuild calculated its own bid on the basis of this figure and submitted it to the owner. Reliabuild's bid was about $400,000 less than the lowest competing bid, so the owner accepted it. Reliabuild then accepted Bill's bid.

    A few days before Bill was to begin his performance, he reviewed his bid and discovered his miscalculation. The error would not only deprive him of his expected profit, but would result in a loss of $250,000. He could not absorb such a loss, which would put him out of business. Bill called Reliabuild immediately, explained the error, and withdrew from the contract. Reliabuild told Bill that it regarded this as a repudiation and would hold him liable for damages. Reliabuild then sought other bids and accepted the lowest one of $900,000. As a result, Reliabuild had to pay $350,000 more than it originally expected and lost about 80 percent of the profit it had anticipated on the project.

Reliabuild claims the $350,000 from Bill as damages for breach of contract. Does Bill have a defense?

4. Change the facts of Example 3 as follows: Assume that when Bill explained the mistake, Reliabuild did not wish to drive him out of business by insisting that he perform at a great loss. It therefore took pity on him and agreed to release him from his obligation. Reliabuild does not itself wish to assume the extra cost of employing a more expensive subcontractor, so it in turn seeks to withdraw from its contract with the owner. The owner is not so kind and threatens suit if Reliabuild does not perform as agreed. Can Reliabuild escape its contract with the owner?

5. Merlin Magnifico, Master of the Impossible, is a magician. On July 1 he entered into a contract with Showstopper Promotions, Inc. under which he agreed, for a fee of $10,000, to perform a magical extravaganza at the Pyro Palace Theater on August 30. This contract forms the basis of the separate and distinct factual variations set out in the following questions.

(a) On July 20, Merlin tried to perform the most daring escape trick ever attempted. He jumped out of a plane all trussed up like a turkey, allowing himself two minutes to free himself and pull his parachute cord. He succeeded in loosening his bonds, but in his feverish unravelling, also mistakenly untied his parachute harness.

(i) Is the estate of the late Merlin Magnifico liable to Showstopper for the substantial profits it lost as a result of having to cancel the show and refund the price of tickets sold?

(ii) This sad event had an impact (no, I would not be so callous as to intend a pun) on a transaction between two other parties: By July 15, all the tickets to Merlin's show had been sold, and people were clamoring to buy tickets from those who had been lucky enough to get them. Buck Fast had managed to buy a ticket for $50 when they first went on sale. His friend Fanny De Voted adored Merlin and desperately wanted to see the show. She nagged Buck to sell the ticket to her, offering an increasingly higher price each time he refused. Eventually he gave in and sold it to her when her offer reached $150. When Merlin was killed, Showstopper cancelled the show and announced that ticketholders should return their tickets for a refund. Naturally, Showstopper will only refund the face value of the ticket, so Fanny demands that Buck repay her the excess of $100. Buck refuses. Is Fanny entitled to the return of her money?

(b) Change the facts so that Merlin did succeed in accomplishing the parachute trick. As a result, he became an instant worldwide sensation. He is now able to command a fee of $500,000 for a booking. He does not wish to perform for Showstopper at the measly rate of $10,000. Can he escape the contract?

(c) Merlin survived his parachute prank, only to be apprehended by grim-faced F.A.A. officials for failing to obtain the permits needed for exiting an aircraft in a state of physical restraint. To avoid prosecution and stern punishment, Merlin entered into a consent decree with the F.A.A. in which he undertook never again to perform magic tricks on land or sea, or in the air. When Merlin told Showstopper that he could no longer perform on August 30, Showstopper sued him for breach of contract. Does he have a defense?

(d) The trick of July 20 did not happen. (In fact, Merlin is terrified of heights and can only undertake air travel under deep sedation with his seatbelt firmly fastened.) Merlin was therefore willing and able to give his show at the end of August. On August 15 the Pyro Palace burned down. Showstopper had sold almost all the tickets to the extravaganza and did not wish to cancel or postpone it. It therefore hired a smelly but capacious high school gym for the performance. Merlin says that it is beneath his dignity to do his act in a school gym, and he wishes to cancel the contract. Does he have grounds for doing so?

(e) None of the above catastrophes happened. However, ticket sales for the show were appalling. Despite intensive promotion, Showstopper had filled only 30 percent of the house by August 20. It is clear that Showstopper will incur a substantial loss if the show goes on. Showstopper takes the position that, known to Merlin, its obvious purpose in entering the contract was to make a profit. The supervening lack of interest on the part of the public has frustrated this purpose, and Showstopper is therefore entitled to cancel the contract with Merlin. Is this a good argument?

6. Professor Goldbrick hates grading exams. One day he saw an advertisement by Slacker Software, Inc., in which it claimed that it could design computer programs to meet any educational need. Goldbrick

contacted Slacker and asked if they could devise a program that could grade essay exams. Slacker took full details of what Goldbrick would need and said it would consider the matter and get back to him. A few weeks later, Slacker sent him a written proposal in which it undertook to create a program of the kind he required. It was based on a complex system of identifying key words and phrases in electronically written essay answers. Because the program was so innovative, Slacker wanted the obscene price of $100,000 for producing it. Goldbrick hated grading so much that he decided it was worth it, even though it meant that he would have to sell all his assets to come up with the money. The parties entered a contract under which Slacker undertook to deliver the program within six months.

Slacker set to work on the program immediately. After struggling with it for four frustrating months, Slacker concluded that its original concept would not work. The program required considerable further research and refinement that would push Slacker's development costs to $150,000, which exceeds the contract price by $50,000. It therefore told Goldbrick that it could not produce the program and cancelled the contract. Goldbrick is deeply disappointed. He would like to contract with another programmer and hold Slacker liable for any difference in price. Would Slacker be liable?

7.   Crystal Springer owns land on which a pristine spring is located. The sweet water emerges from the earth in a completely pure state. Crystal bottles her water and sells it to health food shops. Because Crystal's water is so exquisite, it is regarded as the champagne of bottled water. Although it is more expensive than other brands, it is whisked away by customers as soon as stores place it on the shelf. Holy Foods, a preeminent organic grocery store, entered into a contract with Crystal under which it bought 20,000 bottles of her water a year for five years, to be specially bottled for Holy Foods under its own "Holy Water" label. The contract provides a stated price for the water, to be adjusted at the beginning of each year in accordance with the Consumer Price Index. The contract makes no provision for changing the quantity of water supplied or terminating the contract.

The contract was performed satisfactorily for two years. Just before the third year, Crystal's spring dried up. A hydrologist has determined that this was caused by an unusual phenomenon. A subterranean tremor had blocked the channel to the surface of the land and prevents the stream from reaching it. The problem can be rectified by an expensive excavation. Crystal can obtain a mortgage on the land to pay for the excavation, but the payments under the mortgage would be so high that Crystal could not expect to make a profit from sales of her bottled water for the next 15 years. Crystal therefore decided not to do the excavation. She notified her customers including Holy Foods, that she would not deliver the water promised for the remaining years of their contracts.

Holy Foods can obtain water of a quality equivalent to Crystal's but it has to import it from the foothills of the Himalayas at a much higher cost. Assume that Holy Foods can prove a loss of profits as a result of Crystal's failure to complete her performance under the contract. Is Crystal liable to Holy Foods for this loss?

8. Fast Fryers, a new fast-food chicken restaurant, ordered 1,000 chickens from Fairest Fowls, Inc., a poultry supplier. When the chickens were delivered, Fast Fryers found them to be tough and unusable for frying. Unknown to Fast Fryers (who is new to the chicken industry and unfamiliar with its customs) there is a well-established usage in the industry that the word "chicken" refers only to old, tough birds, suitable only for stewing or soup. A frying chicken is known in the industry as a "poulet." Can Fast Fryers avoid the contract on the basis of its mistake as to the meaning of "chicken"?

Explanations

1. Tiffany is a sophisticated seller who made her judgment without any reliance on a representation by Sterling or under any pressure from him. In the absence of deception or other improper bargaining, the only possible basis for avoidance is mistake. (It may be tempting to find unconscionability in the grossly inadequate price. Although there is some recognition that a gross disparity in exchange could, on its own, be grounds for unconscionability, the generally accepted view is that this substantive unfairness must have resulted from wrongful bargaining conduct or at least from an environment that would allow advantage to be taken of a vulnerable party. This is discussed in section 13.11.) This is a sale of goods, but mistake is not specifically dealt with in UCC Article 2, so it is governed by common law rules.

The error in this case does not concern the actual identity of the jug, but its authorship. The identity of its maker is a fact, and the low price reflects an erroneous shared basic assumption (that is, a mutual mistake) about it. However, both parties were aware of the possibility of incorrect attribution, and if they were wrong, this is more a question of incorrect judgment. Tiffany gambled that she was correct in believing it to be a work of Da Silva's pupil, in which case, she obtained a good price, somewhat above its true market value. Sterling speculated that the experts might be wrong, in which case he would make a killing. When parties deal with each other in an

505

arms-length market transaction, their respective reliance interests are entitled to protection. One of them cannot be deprived of his bargain because it later turns out that the other made a poor judgment.

Thus, the case can be disposed of quickly by treating it as a misjudgment on Tiffany's part and not an error of fact at all. However, even if, as an initial matter, it was to be conceded that there was a mistake of fact, the analysis of risk allocation leads to the same result: Tiffany must be held responsible for her own judgment. The written contract simply describes the jug without making any representation of authorship, and there is no other term that expressly allocates the risk of error. In the absence of guidance in the contract itself, risk must be allocated to the party who should most appropriately bear it under all the circumstances of the transaction. When the parties knowingly enter a contract for the sale of a work of art of uncertain attribution, the risk must lie with the party whose judgment proves to be wrong. This is the resolution suggested in *Firestone & Parson, Inc.* and the dissent in *Sherwood v. Walker* discussed in section 15.2.1a.

2. There are two possible arguments that Manny could make for avoidance, but both would be difficult to establish on these facts. He could claim that Leonardo the Elder made a fraudulent misrepresentation by nondisclosure when he advertised under the name shared with his celebrated son and failed to indicate that he was not *the* Leonardo. This argument seems tenuous. Although there is some chance of confusion, and maybe a possibility that Leonardo was consciously taking advantage of his son's name recognition, the two painters operate in different spheres. Leonardo the Elder has not misrepresented his name and he made no claim to be a society painter. His advertising in the yellow pages and the modesty of his fee suggest that he may not even have imagined that there would be any reasonable confusion. Furthermore, any duty that he may have had to alert potential customers to the fact that he was not *the* Leonardo seems to be outweighed by Manny's carelessness in not making proper enquiries to obtain easily ascertainable information, especially in light of the low price.

Manny's other possible argument is that the contract was induced by unilateral mistake. A mistake as to the identity of the other party is treated as a factual error. The mistake did relate to Manny's basic assumption in entering the contract. It is harder to say whether the error materially affected the exchange of values. Manny got what he paid for, but there could still be a material impact on the exchange because this was not the portrait that Manny bargained for. Unless Manny is gorgeous, he does not have much chance of recouping the price by selling the painting.

The resolution of this issue may not be crucial, because Manny is likely to lose on the allocation of risk and the equities. Manny may have been untutored in the ways of the art world, but he had ready access to information and advice and should have proceeded more carefully before committing himself to ordering a painting from the wrong artist. There do not seem to be strong equities for shifting the risk to Leonardo. There is nothing to suggest that Leonardo had reason to suspect an error and exploited it, and he has a legitimate reliance interest worthy of protection.

3.   This Example does not implicate the promissory estoppel issue in *Drennan v. Star Paving*, discussed in sections 5.3 and 15.4 because the offer was accepted before Bill tried to revoke it. We can therefore focus purely on the mistake analysis presented by these facts.

This mistake is not mutual, but unilateral on Bill's part. In a sense, Reliabuild has also been in error over the correct price for the earthmoving, but this does not make the mistake mutual. The calculation of Bill's price is solely within his realm and forms his individual basic assumption. Reliabuild was not involved in the determination of Bill's price. It simply reacts to the end result of Bill's calculations, which it will accept or reject. Are the requirements of unilateral mistake satisfied? Bill should not have much trouble with the first three: His cost in doing the work is a fact. It was a basic assumption on which he entered the contract. It materially effects the exchange, in that it causes him to undercharge so badly that his expected profit becomes an unbearable loss.

He is not likely to do as well with the issues of risk allocation and equitable balancing. His miscalculation is not simply a matter of conscientious error, but results from sloppy inattention to his work.[6] This, on its own, may be enough to preclude relief in that his degree of negligence amounted to an assumption of the risk of mistake. Even if this does not dispose of the matter, the cause and nature of the mistake will weigh against him in the balance of the equities. On the other side of the balance is the hardship he will suffer if the contract is enforced. The damages may put him out of business, but shifting the loss to Reliabuild will apparently have a less devastating effect because it has a bigger profit margin and may be able to better absorb it. When the potential impact of the mistake is so severe to the mistaken party as to threaten his livelihood, and only reduces the gains of the other party, a court may be swayed by the balance of hardship.

---

6. Of course, this will only come to light if he or one of his employees reveals that the TV was absorbing his attention while he was doing his calculations.

Nevertheless, the relative depth of the parties' pockets, while a relevant consideration, may not be weighty enough to be the overriding factor in the decision to foist the loss onto one of them. Relative blame and innocence must be considered as well. In this case, Bill's carelessness must be weighed against Reliabuild's justifiable reliance on his contractual commitment. It could be that Reliabuild, as an experienced prime contractor, should have realized that the bid was too low, but there are no facts to indicate this. If it had no reason to have suspected the mistake, it made its own commitment to the owner in reasonable reliance on Bill's manifestation of assent. Bill cannot be released from his obligation without subjecting Reliabuild to the substantial harm of either reneging on its obligation to the owner, with the probability of ensuing litigation, loss of reputation and loss of profit, or of having to pay the additional cost of a substitute. In other words, Reliabuild cannot be restored to the status quo if Bill is allowed to escape liability under their contract.

4.   If Reliabuild releases Bill from his subcontract, the question becomes whether Reliabuild itself could use mistake as the basis for seeking relief under the prime contract. That is, Reliabuild could argue that it made an error in its own cost calculations, based on having been given incorrect information by Bill. The argument would run as follows: Bill's charges are a fact forming Reliabuild's basic assumption in entering the prime contract, and the mistake has a material effect in the exchange of values. As Reliabuild had no reason to realize that Bill had made a mistake, and because it had used Bill before without trouble, it did not lack diligence in assuming that his bid was accurate. For this reason, it did not assume the risk of mistake, and there is no carelessness to be weighed against it in balancing the equities. Enforcement of the contract would have a harsh impact on Reliabuild, which would lose 80 percent of its profit, and the only impact on the owner is that it loses its bargain price. Finally, the fact that the lowest competing bid was $400,000 more means that the owner was unfairly benefitted by the mistake and may reasonably have been alerted to the possibility of error by the wide discrepancy.

There is a reasonable argument to the contrary: It may not be appropriate to allocate the risk of this error to the owner, who did not deal with Bill and had no means of evaluating his bid. Furthermore, the owner had no role in releasing Bill, and Reliabuild took it upon itself to forgive Bill's negligence and to abandon any recourse against him. Notwithstanding, Reliabuild's argument could succeed on all the equities of the case. It worked on similar facts in *Wil-Fred's Inc. v. Metropolitan Sanitary District*, 372 N.E.2d 946 (Ill. 1978).

The prime contractor released a subcontractor from a miscalculated bid and then sought to avoid the prime contract with the sanitary district on the ground of mistake. The court permitted avoidance because it found that the prime contractor had not been grossly negligent in relying on the subcontractor's bid and the sanitary district lost only an unduly cheap bargain. (There was an additional fact in the case that favored relief. The subcontractor's error could have been caused in part by the sanitary district's badly-drawn specifications.)

This example involves an error in the bid at the time of contracting, so it is best characterized as an issue of mistake. However, it could conceivably be treated under the doctrine of impracticability. Bill's withdrawal after formation of the contract could be seen as an unforeseen supervening event, the non-occurrence of which was a basic assumption of the contract between Reliabuild and the owner. As a result, Reliabuild's performance becomes unduly burdensome. However, even if the case is analyzed under impracticability, the result should not change, because fault and risk allocation are again the dispositive considerations and they should be resolved in the same way.

On the facts of this example, Reliabuild voluntarily released Bill and then sought to avoid its contract with the owner. If Reliabuild had refused to release Bill, and he had sued Reliabuild for avoidance on grounds of mistake, would the equities in favor of Bill's avoidance be strengthened by the possibility that Reliabuild could avoid liability to the owner by itself claiming mistake? Reliabuild's prospect of escaping liability for breach of the prime contract should not change the equities. It would have to suffer the cost and risk of litigation over that issue with the owner. In addition, even if it is successful in avoiding the prime contract, it would still suffer the serious consequences of losing the profit on the prime contract, alienating its customer, and harming its reputation.

5.   All the factual variations in this example involve supervening events — occurrences after contract formation that may be grounds for a claim of impracticability or frustration of purpose.

5(a)(i). Even under the original doctrine of impossibility, performance was excused by the death of a party whose continued existence was necessary for the performance. This may seem ridiculously obvious, but remember, as the question indicates, the issue is not whether Merlin's corpse can be made to do magic tricks, but whether his estate is liable for damages. The initial two elements of impracticability are satisfied: As the contract was for Merlin's personal services, it was clearly dependent on his continued vitality. His death is a supervening event contrary to the contract's basic assumption.

The more difficult question is who bore the risk of his death. The contract itself does not assign the risk, so the allocation must be made in light of the parties' reasonable expectations, determined from all the circumstances surrounding the transaction. These circumstances may include a particular practice in the entertainment industry that may help to determine the normal incidence of risk when an artist dies before a show. (For example, promoters may regularly insure the lives of performers who have been booked.) If not, general community expectations must be determined and any pertinent considerations of public policy must be taken into account. It is difficult to be sure what result would be reached. Many contracts do not terminate as a result of the death of a party, so that performance or damages becomes an obligation of his estate. As noted above, this may not be the reasonable expectation when the contract is for personal services. In this case, however, the risk allocation is also influenced by the circumstances of Merlin's death. Impossibility or impracticability cannot be used as a defense by a party who is at fault in causing the supervening event, and it could be argued that Merlin recklessly caused his own death. This may, in itself, be grounds for withholding relief from his estate. If not, it may tip the balance in the determination of risk.

5(a)(ii). Fanny's demand for refund of the $100 is, in effect, a claim of restitution based on the implicit contention that the cancellation of the magic show frustrated the purpose of her contract with Buck. (As you may recognize, these facts are a less regal adaptation of *Krell v. Henry*.) These facts show how difficult it can be to distinguish impracticality and frustration. The latter seems more appropriate here because the contractual performance — the exchange of a ticket for $150 — has not been altered by the supervening event. Rather, the goal and purpose of the exchange have been defeated. (However, it could just as plausibly be argued that the supervening event so devalued the exchange for Fanny that her performance was rendered unduly burdensome, and impracticality doctrine is applicable.)

The first three elements of frustration are clearly satisfied: Merlin's death and the ensuing cancellation of the show were supervening events that defeated a shared basic assumption of the parties entering the contract, and neither was at fault in causing the event. Therefore, once again, risk allocation becomes the determinative issue.

In the absence of any assignment of risk in the contract itself, the risk of the show's cancellation must be placed where the parties reasonably would have expected it. The show's promoter has readily undertaken to refund all amounts it has received for tickets, which suggests that it is common practice for the promoter of an event to assume the risk of cancellation. However, it does not follow that a consumer seller would similarly assume that risk. In a consumer-to-consumer sale, it may be more consonant with common practice to conclude (in the absence of a warranty) that the buyer assumes the risk that the item or service purchased will be worth less than its price, and the seller assumes the countervailing risk that it will be worth more.

Thus, although a contrary argument could be made, Fanny may be the more appropriate party to bear the risk of cancellation. If so, she cannot recover the $100 paid to Buck. (This is contrary to the result in *Krell v. Henry*, but the concurring opinion in that case questioned the issue of risk allocation.) If the opposite result is reached and Buck bears the risk, she can terminate the contract on grounds of frustration of purpose. In that case, any benefit conferred by either party on the other must be restored as unjust enrichment. Fanny still has the ticket worth $50 (the amount of the refund), so that value given by Buck must be offset against the $150 paid by Fanny, leaving her with a net recovery of $100.

5(b). The only basis on which Merlin could escape the contract is to contend that his new-found fame is a supervening event that defeats the basic assumption on which the parties contracted for his services at the relatively modest sum of $10,000. As a result, his loss of the opportunity to earn 50 times that amount is such a burden as to make his performance impracticable. He should not get away with this because he does not show either that performance has become unduly burdensome or that Showstopper bears the risk of the change in circumstances. Impracticability should not be permitted as an excuse when the change in market conditions merely has the effect of making the performance more valuable than anticipated, especially when the harm to Merlin is nothing more than the loss of an opportunity to sell his services at greater advantage. In addition, the argument made in Question 5(a)(ii) is applicable here too: Each party made a judgment in assenting to the price of $10,000, and neither can complain if that judgment turns out to have been wrong.

5(c). Compliance with a change in the law or government regulation or with a judicial or administrative order is generally regarded as a basis for excusing performance on grounds of impracticability. The F.A.A.'s prohibition on Merlin's further career as a magician could fall into this category, but because the bar on his performance resulted from his violation of the law, he should be denied relief. Even had he not entered a consent decree, the event precluding his performance arises from his own fault, and he must be held to have assumed the risk of its occurrence. This resolution is made more compelling by the fact that the F.A.A. may not unilaterally have imposed the prohibition, and Merlin acquiesced in it by entering a consent decree to avoid other punishment.

These are sufficient grounds to defeat a claim of impracticability, but one further issue should be noted: I have no idea if the F.A.A. has the authority to dispose of Merlin's case in this way. If it does not, the order may be invalid. This would not in itself prevent a claim of impracticability, provided that compliance with the order is in good faith. Therefore, if Merlin were able to overcome the problems of fault and risk allocation, he could still not claim impracticability without showing that the order was valid or, if not, that he acted in good faith in complying with it.

5(d). At last, we get to the fiery destruction of the Pyro Palace, but with a twist on *Taylor v. Caldwell* in that Showstopper, the impresario, is willing to provide a substitute but the star of the show objects and suggests that the fire has rendered performance impracticable. The key consideration on these facts is whether the destruction of the Pyro Palace defeats a basic assumption of the contract, rendering Merlin's performance unduly burdensome. (The other elements are not in issue because Merlin had no role in causing the fire and was not at fault, and Showstopper, as the promoter and renter of the hall, is more likely than Merlin to bear the risk of its destruction.)

The contract apparently contemplated the use of the Pyro Palace for the show, but this is not quite the same as saying that the theater's continued existence was a basic assumption of the contract. If an alternative venue is equally suitable and may be obtained without undue hardship, the destruction of the Pyro Palace does not defeat a basic assumption of the contract. Even if a substitute hall is permissible under the contract, it may have been a basic assumption that the hall would be of a particular quality or be equipped with special facilities. If this is so, the school gym may so badly fall short of the contemplated standard that performance in it would cause Merlin severe hardship or loss. This may be the consequence if the hall does not have the facilities he needs to stage his show, or if performance in it would damage his reputation or standing as an artiste. However, a mere claim of offense to his dignity does not suggest a problem of these proportions.

5(e). Most commercial contracts are motivated by the prospect of profit, so if Showstopper's argument was taken seriously, no party could ever be held to a contract once it becomes apparent that its expectation of profit will be disappointed. Therefore, although profitmaking may, in a sense, be the purpose of a contract, the doctrine of frustration does not simply focus on this underlying "bottom line" purpose, but calls for a more penetrating examination of the parties' mutual objective in entering the contract. This shared objective must be determined in light of the contract's allocation of risk. The facts do not make it clear who bore the risk of poor sales. However, if the contract did not specifically allocate this risk to Merlin, and there is no usage to the contrary, the reasonable inference from the structure of the contract is that Showstopper assumed this risk. Merlin agreed to perform for a fixed fee, and Showstopper would keep whatever proceeds were generated from ticket sales. If Showstopper bore the risk of poor ticket sales, it follows that it was not the common purpose of the contract that Showstopper would make a profit. Rather, the common purpose was to stage a public entertainment. The prospect of making a profit may have strongly motivated Showstopper to undertake the venture, but that was its purpose, not Merlin's. Viewed this way, we can see that the purpose of staging the show has not been frustrated.

Showstopper based its argument on frustration of purpose. It could equally have argued that the supervening event of poor ticket sales contract rendered the contract impracticable. (A similar alternative argument was made and rejected in *Karl Wendt Equipment* discussed in section 15.8.) Because the defenses of frustration of purpose and impracticability are so closely related, we should get the same answer, whichever one is used. Again, the key to resolving an impracticability defense is to determine who bore the risk of poor ticket sales. If Showstopper bore that risk, it cannot escape the contract on grounds of impracticability.

6. This is one of those ambiguous situations that sounds like a case of impracticability, but is better characterized as a unilateral mistake. The only supervening event is the discovery that the program is not capable of production for the price quoted. However, this is not really a supervening event at all, but rather Slacker's post-contractual realization that it underestimated the complexity and cost of production. Luckily, incorrect labelling should not have any practical consequence because risk allocation, the element common to both defenses, points to the same result.

Let us consider mistake first. Slacker, the expert, is approached by Gold-brick, a lay customer who desires an end product and has no idea about what may be involved in creating it. Slacker makes its own evaluation of what would need to be done to create the product and then makes an unqualified promise to deliver the program in six months. We may simply describe this as an error in judgment, or we could say that Slacker assumed the risk that it could not perform for the price quoted. However phrased, the point is that Goldbrick had no way of knowing that Slacker had misjudged the complexity of the project, and Slacker was foolishly overconfident in giving him an absolute promise. When a manufacturer undertakes to create an innovative custom-made product — a prototype — it cannot know for sure what may lie ahead in its development. To protect itself from unpleasant discoveries, it should draw the contract so as to articulate the experimental nature of the project and provide for a price increase, a delay in delivery, or a right to terminate if production difficulties are encountered. By not doing this, it assumes the risk of unforeseen problems. This being so, Slacker is liable for Goldbrick's expectation damages measured as the difference between its contract price and the higher price charged by the other programmer. It sounds as if this will be a horrendous figure, but the equities should not be balanced to take this hardship into account if risk assumption is clearly resolved against Slacker.

It was noted earlier that this is not properly viewed as an impracticability case, but that even if it was analyzed as such, the same result would apply because Slacker assumed the risk of post-contractual difficulties in production. An impracticability defense was raised unsuccessfully in *United States v. Wegematic Corp.*, 360 F.2d 674 (2d Cir. 1966), a case with facts analogous to those here. An electronics manufacturer made a contract with the Federal Reserve Board for the supply of a computer system (touted as "revolutionary") by a specified date. The manufacturer encountered numerous difficulties in building the system, and eventually notified the Board that it could not produce it. The Board ordered an equivalent system from another vendor and sued the manufacturer for damages. The court rejected the manufacturer's defense of impracticability on the grounds that it had assumed the risk of technical difficulties in the fabrication of the system. Although the system may have been an experimental prototype, the manufacturer's promise was simply to deliver a working computer by a specified time. (The court also found that performance was not impracticable because the element of undue hardship was not satisfied. Problems in the system could have been rectified by costly but not overwhelmingly burdensome redesign.)

7. Crystal has breached the contract and is liable for Holy Foods' damages unless she has the defense of impracticability. Bottled water satisfies the definition of "goods" under UCC article 2, so the issue of impracticability must be resolved under UCC §2.615. The analysis of

impracticability under §2.615 is substantially the same as under contemporary common law.

The blockage that diverted the stream was a supervening event. Section 2.615 requires that it must have been an event "the nonoccurrence of which was a basic assumption on which the contract was made." Comment 1 to §2.615 paraphrases this by stating that the contract must have become impracticable because of unforeseen supervening circumstances not within the parties contemplation at the time of contracting. The blockage is described as an unusual phenomenon. This suggests that the parties probably did not contemplate it as a possibility. There is no indication that they discussed or provided for it in the agreement.

The supply of water is not objectively impossible because there is a means of restoring the stream. However, §2.615 (like the common law) does not require impossibility, but impracticability. Mere increase in cost, lack of profit, or even some degree of loss, is not enough to make a performance impracticable. The scale of the problem must be large enough that it makes the performance so burdensome that it cannot be rendered without devastating loss, great risk, or serious hardship. The facts here have a good chance of meeting this standard. The high cost of curing the problem is disproportionate to the value of the water. It would take Crystal 15 years of sales to pay off the cost of the work. Although the excavation may pay for itself in the very long term, it would impose a significant burden on Crystal. She would not derive any income from her business for 15 years, even if we assume that the market for her water remains strong.

Crystal was not in any way at fault in causing the occurrence, so she is doing well so far in establishing the elements of impracticability. This leaves risk allocation as the crucial factor in deciding if she should be excused from performance. The contract makes no provision for reductions in quantity for any reason, so the parties' intent must be determined from interpretation of the contract as a whole in context. If no factual indicators of intent are available, the court must construe the parties' reasonable intent. We have no evidence of express terms or pertinent usage or custom, so are left with nothing more than the bare terms of the contract to decide if Crystal assumed this risk. The contract establishes a formula for fixing the price of the water over the five-year period. Where parties fix the price in the contract, the seller is usually assumed to undertake the risk of any increases in cost. In addition, the seller of goods assumes the risk that she may not be able to make or obtain the goods promised in the contract. However, the cost increase here was so unforeseen and so great that a court could conclude that it goes well beyond the normal level of risk assumed in a fixed price contract. If so, Crystal can escape the contract on grounds of impracticability.

It is worth making a final observation about this contract. Where parties enter into a long-term relationship, they run a greater risk of unforeseen future contingencies. Although it may be difficult to imagine all the things that could go wrong to make the contract unexpectedly burdensome to one of the parties, a generally-worded clause, excusing performance in case of a *force majeur* could help a party like Crystal in establishing grounds for excusing performance.

8. If this Example reminds you of *Frigaliment Importing*, the cherished chicken case in section 10.6.2, that should give you a clue to its answer. Your immediate reaction may be to resolve the case on the basis of unilateral mistake because the trade usage is, after all, a fact external to the contract. However, as we saw in section 10.6.2, a trade usage, although extrinsic to the written contract, is not treated as a fact external to the contract itself, but is part of the context used to give meaning to the terms used by the parties. Unless specifically included, a usage is an implied term of the contract. Therefore, this issue is properly resolved, not as a question of mistake, but as a question of interpretation: If the usage is proved to exist, the question is whether Fast Fryers, as a new entrant to the industry, had reason to know of it. If so, as a matter of interpretation, the word "chicken" means stewing chicken and Fast Fryers is bound to a contract for the purchase of 1,000 tough old birds.

CHAPTER 16

Conditions and Promises

§16.1 THE STRUCTURE OF A CONTRACT: AN INTRODUCTION TO PROMISES AND CONDITIONS

Most terms in a contract are promises or conditions — or both. The meaning, nature, and effect of a promise is very familiar by now. The concept of promise was introduced right at the beginning of this book, and its central role in all contractual relationships has been emphasized ever since. Although conditions are just as much a fundamental component of contracts, their presence and function have not been much discussed in previous chapters. It is the purpose of this chapter to introduce the concept of conditions and to examine their functions. In doing this, we will look more carefully at the structure of a contract and explore the way in which conditions and promises interact to form the basis of the contractual relationship. We will then proceed, in this chapter and the next, to consider the performance obligations created by the network of promises and conditions, and to address the problems that are created when those obligations are violated. You will encounter some unfamiliar terminology, but this does not mean that we are entering some new and alien field of contract law. Most, if not all, of the substantive principles discussed here have been covered already, and the breakdown of a contract into promises and conditions is simply the means by which its structure is studied. As is so often the case, you will find that the key to analysis is interpretation — the determination of the parties' intent, as expressed by them in their contract or as inferred from surrounding evidence and reasonable expectations.

16. Conditions and Promises

We begin with a set of definitions and some simple examples to introduce terminology and to provide an initial insight into the reason for differentiating promises and conditions.

A **promise** was defined in section 1.2.4 as an **undertaking to act or refrain from acting in a specified way at some future time**. As we have seen repeatedly since then, the exchange of promises (or of at least one promise for a performance) is what contracts are all about. Thus, for example, when parties make a contract for the sale of land, the buyer promises to pay the price in exchange for the seller's promise to convey title and possession of the land. This can be illustrated by a diagram similar to those used to explain the exchange element of consideration:

A **condition** is an **event** that is **not certain to occur**. A promised performance under a contract is subject to a condition if the **parties agree** that the **performance** is **contingent** on the **occurrence of the uncertain event**. That is, when making the contract, the parties agree that a particular promised performance or set of performances will not become due until and unless a particular uncertain event occurs. As this suggests, conditions commonly concern *future events* because, in most cases, the uncertainty no longer exists once the event has happened. However, there are situations in which a useful purpose is served by making performance conditional on a *past event*. Although the event in question may have occurred, the parties themselves may be uncertain about whether it took place, and it may be inconvenient or impossible for the parties to find this out at the time that they wish to execute their contract. To avoid the risk of having the agreement unravel while they delay to get the information, they could enter the contract immediately subject to the condition that their agreement — or the obligation of one of them — is contingent upon the event having occurred. (This is illustrated in section 16.2.)

The following example provides a simple illustration of the way in which conditions and promises may be combined to structure a contract in a way that binds the parties, yet allows them to deal with the risk of uncertainty: Buyer is interested in acquiring land to build a housing tract. At the time of negotiations, the land is zoned for agricultural use, but Seller has applied for rezoning for residential development. If the application succeeds, the land can be developed profitably. If not, it can be used only for farming. The parties do not know how the zoning authority will rule on the application, but neither wants to delay contracting until its outcome for fear that the other will lose interest in the transaction. Buyer does not wish to commit himself absolutely at this stage, because he does not wish to be stuck with farmland. To solve this problem, the parties can make a contract now for the sale of the land and include a provision in the contract stating: "Buyer's obligation to purchase this property is conditional upon the grant of the pending rezoning application within 60 days of the date of this agreement." The success of the rezoning application within the next 60 days — a future uncertain event — is therefore a condition of Buyer's promise to pay and take transfer of the land. (Or stated differently, Buyer's promise to pay and take transfer of the land is conditional upon the grant of the application.[1]) Until the condition occurs, Buyer's duty to perform is suspended. If it occurs, the duty becomes due and must be performed, but if the condition is not satisfied by the time that the 60 days has passed, the Buyer's obligation to perform never takes effect, and it falls away. This can be represented as follows:

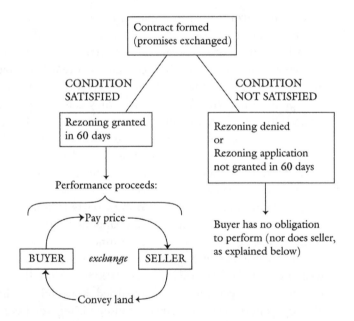

The parties' purpose in structuring the transaction in this way is to *allocate the risk* of the denial or inaction by the zoning authority. If Buyer had simply purchased the property unconditionally, he would have taken the risk of being saddled with an unwanted farm or a costly delay in the ability to

---

1. This variation in terminology can be confusing, so make a point of recognizing that these statements mean the same thing, whether made in the active voice (rezoning **is a condition of** Buyer's performance) or the passive voice (Buyer's performance **is conditional on** the rezoning).

develop it. Because Buyer does not wish to assume this risk, he uses a condition as an escape clause.

§16.2 THE MEANING AND SCOPE OF "UNCERTAIN EVENT"

As noted earlier, uncertainty most commonly relates to future events, but it is possible for parties to be unsure about an *event that has already happened* at the time of contracting. Although a past event is not uncertain in a general sense — someone probably knows that it did or did not occur and the parties themselves can find out about it — it may nevertheless be unknown to and not readily ascertainable by them at the time they are ready to form the contract. If they wish to avoid the inconvenience or risk of suspending formation until the information is obtained, they can enter the contract immediately, but make performance conditional on the event's currently unknown outcome. For example, say that Buyer and Seller know that the zoning authority made a decision late on Friday afternoon, but it is now Saturday, and the decision cannot be discovered until Monday morning. The parties would like to sign their contract before Seller leaves on vacation on Sunday morning. By making Buyer's obligation to purchase conditional on the application having been granted, they can execute the contract on Saturday without subjecting Buyer to the risk of having bought farmland incapable of development. Although this condition is based on a past event, there is still some element of futurity in that the knowledge cannot be obtained until Monday. The outcome therefore does qualify as uncertain as far as the parties are concerned.

Most conditions, however, do not relate to unknown past events, but are based on something that has not happened at the time of contracting. All future events may be thought of as uncertain to some degree, so in the broadest sense, everything that has not yet occurred must be a *future uncertain event*. But the law regards an event as uncertain if, in light of human experience, its occurrence is not regarded as strongly predictable. Therefore, although a pessimist may fear otherwise, it is regarded as certain that the sun will rise tomorrow morning, or that Friday will follow Thursday, or that January 1 of next year will arrive. A provision in a contract that calls for performance upon the occurrence of so certain an event is not thought of as a condition at all, but merely fixes the time for performance. The passage of time is not regarded as a condition. Or, if you prefer, it is a condition with such a strong probability of occurrence that its legal effect is insignificant. (We return to this distinction in section 16.10.) By contrast, the grant of the rezoning application is not so sure a thing. Even if it was carefully prepared, complies with the prescribed procedures, and makes a compelling case on the merits, we cannot say with the same degree of confidence that its success is inevitable. It therefore qualifies as uncertain.

Although uncertainty about the happening of the event is necessary to qualify the event as a condition, this does not invariably mean that a condition is intended merely because the contract links performance to some uncertain future event. It could be that the parties do not really contemplate the event as uncertain, assume that it will occur, and merely use it as a means of *setting the time for performance*. If, as a matter of interpretation, the parties do not intend the performance to be contingent upon the event, it should not be treated as a condition. This distinction is explained in section 16.10.

Although a condition is spoken of as an **event**, the contingency need not be an **affirmative happening**. It could also be a negative contingency — a **non-happening**. In the above example, the zoning authority's approval of the application is an affirmative event. But it would just as much be a condition if the buyer's performance was subject to something not taking place: Say that the zoning authority had approved the application at the time of contracting, but irate neighbors had threatened to appeal the decision. The contract of sale could provide that the buyer's obligation to purchase is conditional on the approval not being successfully appealed.

§16.3 THE INTENT TO CREATE A CONDITION: EXPRESS, IMPLIED, AND CONSTRUED CONDITIONS

Like all terms of a contract, a condition exists because the parties have agreed to it. Similarly, like all other contractual provisions, the mutual intent to create a condition and the condition's scope and meaning are matters of interpretation. Sometimes the language used by the parties to express this intent is clear, express, and unambiguous, but it could just as likely be obscure and uncertain. In some contracts, the intent to create a condition is not articulated at all, but such intent may be established by evidence extrinsic to the express words used by the parties, or it may be construed by the court. These issues are resolved by applying the general principles of interpretation discussed in Chapter 10.

§16.3.1 Express Conditions

We have already seen an example of an express condition in the land sale contract described above: The contract expressly stated that Buyer's obligation to purchase the land was contingent on approval of the zoning application within 60 days of the date of the agreement. A condition is express if the **language of the contract, on its face** and without reference to extrinsic evidence, **articulates** the **intent** to **make performance contingent on the event**. Commonly, conditions are expressly denoted by using conditional language such as "on condition that," "subject to," "provided that," or "if," but no special incantation is required as long as the intention of establishing a condition arises from the language itself. For a term to be an express condition, it is not enough that the term itself is expressed. Its *conditional nature* must also be *apparent from the language* used. Thus, if a contractual provision states "Seller shall transfer title to the land," this is an express term — an express promise by the seller — but as the obligation is not stated to be contingent on any event, it is not expressly conditional. (It is, however, likely to be subject to an implied condition, as discussed below.)

Because it is the function of courts to give effect to apparent contractual intent, the general approach to express conditions is to apply them strictly, even if this may have a harsh result on one of the parties. Provided that the meaning of the condition is clear, the fact that the parties have articulated it must mean that they intended it to be satisfied exactly as stated. This principle is reflected in the rule that there must be *strict compliance* with an express condition. For example, an insurance policy states that the insurer's duty to reimburse for loss is conditional upon the insured giving it written notice of the loss within ten days of the loss occurring. If the insured does not give notice until the morning of the eleventh day, the condition is not satisfied. Even if the few hours delay may seem insignificant, and enforcement of the condition means that the insured loses the right of reimbursement for which she has paid a hefty premium, the rule of strict enforcement precludes an argument that there was substantial compliance with the condition of notice.

Luttiger v. Rosen, 316 A.2d 757 (Conn. 1972) provides another example of strict construction of an express condition, which allowed a party to refuse to proceed with the contract on technical grounds. The buyers bought a home subject to the condition that they could obtain a mortgage for a stated amount, subject to interest up to a stated maximum rate. They applied for a loan and the lender was willing to grant the application, but only at an interest rate higher than specified as the maximum in the contract. The buyers notified the seller that the condition had not been fulfilled and terminated the contract. In response, the seller offered to compensate for the higher interest rate by making up the difference between the rate specified in the condition and the rate offered by the lender. The buyers declined and persisted in refusing to go ahead with the contract. The court said that the buyers had no obligation to buy the house because the condition was express and had not been exactly fulfilled. The seller's offer to compensate the buyers for the higher interest rate did not change the fact that the condition had not been satisfied. This result seems highly technical because the seller's offer would have entirely eliminated the cost of the higher interest rate, and the buyers would have received exactly what they bargained for.

As technical as the result of strict compliance may be, it is important to recognize that the parties did go to the trouble of making the condition express, thereby manifesting the intent that it be taken literally. We will see in section 16.9 that this principle of strict compliance with express conditions does not apply to conditions that are not express. We will also see in section 16.11 that there are some circumstances that allow the court to ameliorate the harsh result of strict compliance with an express condition.

§16.3.2 Conditions Implied in Fact

Even if there is **no express language** creating a condition, **contextual evidence** may **support the inference** that the **parties intended a performance** to be **conditional**. Like other terms in a contract, a condition can be implied in fact by interpreting the words used by the parties in light of the circumstances surrounding the formation of their contract. As with other terms, there is no difference in legal effect between an express and an implied condition. The difference lies in the nature of the evidence available to establish its existence. An express condition is apparent from the language of the contract itself—the actual words of the parties are the best evidence of what they intended. However, an implied condition is not ascertainable simply from the wording of the contract, but is established once contextual evidence is introduced to cast light on what was meant. Because this contextual evidence may be less firm and more equivocal that express language, a court may have some greater flexibility in interpreting an implied condition in a way that avoids the harsh results that would have been more inevitable had the condition been clearly expressed. That is, although strict compliance with the condition is still required, the less direct and absolute nature of contextual inference may permit an interpretation that the action or event did in fact satisfy the condition.

As with all terms implied in fact, if the agreement is recorded in writing, the parol evidence rule may preclude contextual evidence of a condition that varies an integrated term or conflicts with the writing. However, as noted in section 12.10, there is a traditionally recognized exception to the parol evidence rule when the evidence is offered to establish that the contract as a whole was subject to a condition precedent.

§16.3.3 Constructive Conditions

Although a condition may not be expressed or inferable from contextual evidence, it could be implied in law. The process of legal implication of conditions is the same as for any other contractual term, and is subject to the general principles discussed in Chapter 10: In essence, although there may be no evidence that the parties actually agreed to the condition, a court will imply it as a matter of law if the circumstances and nature of the contract compel the conclusion that the condition should exist as a matter of policy, or that if the parties had addressed the issue, they *reasonably would have intended* it to be part of their contract.

Construed conditions may be illustrated by returning to the example involving the sale of land subject to the express condition that the rezoning application would be granted. If you think about the exchange of performances contemplated in that contract, you will realize that while the express condition may be the only one visible, there are surely two more lurking under the surface of the express agreement: In promising to pay the price of the land, Buyer must reasonably have expected that his obligation to pay was conditional on Seller conveying the land, and Seller surely did not expect to transfer the land to Buyer without getting paid. Thus, each party's performance must reasonably be intended as a condition of the other's. Buyer's duty to pay is contingent on Seller's transfer and vice versa. (The respective performances do qualify as uncertain events, because the honoring of a contractual commitment is not inevitable and assured.)

These conditions are construed rather than implied in fact, because there is apparently no actual evidence that the parties discussed the question or expressed this intent to each other. But remember that the dividing line between factual interpretation and legal implication is not always easily discernable, and they tend to blur into each other at the edges. In other words, the conclusion that each performance is conditional upon the other could be reached as a question of fact if there is evidence (such as trade usage, prior dealings, or statements made during negotiations) to support it. But even in the absence of any such evidence, it may be possible to reach the same conclusion by implication of law from the nature of the exchange relationship. In an exchange transaction, unless the language of the contract or its surrounding circumstances clearly indicate a contrary intent, the parties must almost always be taken to have expected that the principal promises exchanged would be **dependent** on each other — that they would be what are known as **constructive conditions of exchange**. If they were not, this would lead to the bizarre situation in which a party could be forced to perform even when the other has failed or refused to do so.

The effect of this is that there is an initial condition that the rezoning must be approved. If it is not, Buyer has no obligation to pay and because Buyer's payment is a condition of Seller's obligation to convey, the non-fulfillment of the condition of payment releases Seller too. If the rezoning is approved, we are left with the two conditions relating to the performances, and each party must tender performance (that is, show a readiness, willingness, and ability to perform) in order to be entitled to performance by the other. We must therefore expand the previous diagram to look like this:

So far we have identified the mutual performances as conditions of each other, but as the diagram shows, we have not dealt with the sequence in which the conditions must be satisfied, or with some other important distinctions between these two conditions and the one that relates to the rezoning. These matters will be discussed in succeeding sections.

§16.4 A CONDITION OF ONE PARTY'S PERFORMANCE, AS DISTINCT FROM A CONDITION OF THE CONTRACT AS A WHOLE

In the prior section, the success of the rezoning application was described as a condition to Buyer's obligation. Because Buyer's performance is, in turn, a condition of Seller's obligation, it follows that if the rezoning is denied and Buyer does not perform, Seller is also relieved of her obligation to perform. As a result, the entire contract falls away. That is,

Why is this two-stage analysis necessary? Could it not simply be said that both parties' obligations are conditional on the grant of the application? That is,

Rezoning refused

↓

Contract falls away—neither party performs

This sounds like the same thing, with one less step in the analysis, but the situations are significantly different. If the *contract as a whole* was *conditional* on the rezoning approval, this would mean that if the application is denied, *neither party is bound* to the transaction. Even if Buyer decided that he wanted the land despite the failure of the application, he could not disregard the condition, tender his payment, and hold Seller to the contract. This is probably not what was intended. Rather, the purpose of the condition is to affect only Buyer's obligation — it is *included purely for Buyer's protection*, and not for Seller's benefit. If Buyer decides that he still wants the land with its present zoning, he should be able to waive the condition and proceed with the transaction.[2] Seller is not in any way deprived of her expected exchange and has no cause for complaint.

However, if the terms or circumstances of the transaction were otherwise, we may reach a different conclusion on the intent of the condition. Say that the sale price of the land was fixed at a base amount of $100,000 (being its current market value as farmland) plus ten percent of Buyer's profits upon selling off the subdivided lots. If the condition of rezoning is not satisfied, Buyer could not subdivide, and Seller would be deprived of her expected share of the profits. If Seller's incentive for selling the land was to share in the profit of development, and she would not have sold the property for its price as farmland, the condition can no longer be seen as merely for Buyer's benefit. It affects the contract's value to Seller as well. It must surely have been intended that neither Buyer nor Seller could unilaterally waive the condition and hold the other to the contract despite its non-fulfillment. This means that the condition was an event upon which the duties of *both* parties were *contingent* — the entire contract was subject to the condition.

In short, if a condition is intended to relate only to the performance of one of the parties, that party can chose to perform despite its non-occurrence and may fully enforce the contract against the other. But if the condition relates to the contract as a whole, its non-occurrence discharges the right of both parties to demand performance, and neither can unilaterally waive it. To decide the intended scope of the condition, its purpose must be ascertained by the usual process of interpreting the contract's wording in context.

---

2. Waiver of condition is discussed further in section 16.11.2.

§16.5 PURE CONDITIONS AND PROMISSORY CONDITIONS

It has already been stated that when the operative terms of a contract are analyzed, each can be classified as either a promise or a condition. Some terms may be classified as **pure promises** — they are not conditions at all, but merely undertakings.[3] Others may be **pure conditions** — they contain no promise but merely describe an event that must occur for a duty of performance to arise. However, some terms in a contract combine both these elements. They not only identify an event that must occur for performance to become due, but they also contain a promise by one of the parties that the event will take place. A term that is not only a condition, but is both a condition and a promise that the condition will occur, is called a **promissory condition**. This concept often confuses students on first exposure, but it is not as strange and esoteric as it sounds.

The usual process of interpretation and construction must be followed to decide if a term is a pure promise, a pure condition, or a promissory condition. If the express language of the contract does not clearly settle this question, it must be resolved with reference to any factual evidence of intent or, failing that, by construing the parties' reasonable intention. Our land sale example may be used to illustrate:

In agreeing to the sale of the land conditional upon the success of the rezoning application, the parties apparently intend to place the fate of the transaction on an event beyond their control. The application has been made, nothing more can be done by either to influence the result, and there is no indication in the contract that either of them guarantees the outcome of the application. From this it must be inferred that they intended the rezoning to be a pure condition. By contrast, the conditions that make the performance of each party contingent on that of the other are promissory conditions. Each party does have control over the satisfaction of the condition that he or she will perform, and each, by committing to perform, has promised that the condition will be satisfied. The payment and conveyance of the land are not simply conditions, but promises as well. This distinction may be portrayed as follows:

---

3. The role and effect of pure promises is explained in sections 16.6 and 16.8.4.

In the above example, the event constituting the condition of each party's performance is the actual performance of the other. When a party's own performance is the condition, that party has some ability to ensure that the promised condition will occur, and can make the commitment with some confidence that the condition will be satisfied. However, if the condition is some event that is beyond her control, she takes a greater risk in promising that it will occur. Therefore, in cases of doubt, it is generally assumed that a pure condition is intended when a party has no power to influence the happening of the event, but a promissory condition is intended if she can play a role in affecting the outcome. It must be stressed that this is merely an assumption — a rough guide. It is not a firm rule. The agreement could expressly or impliedly indicate that the parties intended otherwise. If she is willing to take the risk, there is no barrier to a party assuming responsibility for the happening of an event that she cannot control. For example, instead of simply making their land sale contract conditional on approval of the rezoning application, the parties could have included a warranty by Seller that the application would be granted. Although the disposition of the application is beyond her control, Seller promises that it will succeed. If it does not, there is both a failure of the condition and a breach of Seller's contractual promise.

The significance of the distinction between a pure and a promissory condition lies in the *different effect of promises and conditions.* If a condition is not satisfied, the performance contingent on that condition does not become due. If it is a **pure condition**, the **performance obligation falls away** and there is no basis for claiming breach of contract. However, if a contractual *promise is broken,* the promisor is liable for *breach* of contract. It follows that if a **promissory condition** is not fulfilled, the party whose performance was contingent on it is entitled **both** to **withhold counter performance** and to seek a **remedy for breach**. Therefore, in examining the language of a contract in context to interpret a term as a pure or promissory condition, it is helpful to ask two questions: First, did the parties intend a performance to be excused if the event does not occur? If the answer is "yes," the event is a condition of that performance. If the answer to Question 1 is yes, did the parties intend that one of them is responsible for the event's occurrence and would be liable for breach of contract if it does not occur? If the answer is "no," the event is a pure condition. If it is "yes," it is a promissory condition.

§16.6 THE TIME SEQUENCE: CONDITIONS PRECEDENT AND CONCURRENT CONDITIONS

Another difference between the conditions in the land sale example is that the condition relating to rezoning must occur before Buyer's (and consequently, Seller's) performance becomes due. Because its fulfillment must precede the performance contingent upon it, it is known as a **condition precedent**. However, the contract does not indicate a sequence for fulfillment of the conditions of paying and conveyance of the land. If no such order of performance is expressed, it must be determined by interpreting the parties' intent in light of any contextual evidence or, in the absence of such evidence, by construing what must reasonably have been intended. When a contract provides for counter-performances in exchange for each other, and the contract does not prescribe a sequence of performances, the general presumption is that if the performances are **capable of being rendered simultaneously**, they are due at the same time. They are **concurrent conditions**. Thus, the promissory conditions of payment and conveyance of the land, each being capable of exchange by a single act, are concurrent conditions. Each is a condition of the other and they must be performed at the same time. This means that the parties must get together at an appointed place and perform simultaneously. If this had been the sale of goods, there could have been a physical exchange of the goods and cash, but in a real estate transaction, the funds would be deposited in escrow and released to the seller upon recording of the transfer. Because the performances are concurrent conditions of each other, both parties must show up for the exchange ready, willing, and able to tender performance. If one of them is available to tender performance but the other can or will not, the tendering party is excused from delivering his performance and may sue for breach. Our diagram now looks like this:

If performances are **not capable of being rendered simultaneously** because one of them requires a period of time to perform and the other can be rendered instantly, the general presumption, unless the contract indicates a different sequence, is that the performance that takes time must go first and must be concluded before the instantaneous one is due. That is, the completion of the longer performance is a **condition precedent** to the instantaneous one. For example, when Seller originally decided to make application for the rezoning of her land, she hired an attorney to prepare and submit the rezoning application for her. Unless that contract provided otherwise, the attorney's fee would only have been due after the attorney had completed the work. Her performance in handling the application takes time to complete, and it is therefore deemed to be a condition precedent to Seller's instantaneous action of paying the fee.

When one party's performance is a condition precedent to the other's, their mutual promises are still dependent in a broad sense. They are exchanged for each other, and both parties are motivated to perform by the incentive of receiving the other's performance. However, they are not mutually dependent in the same way as concurrent promissory conditions in that one of the parties — the attorney — must go first. Therefore while the client's promise of later performance is fully dependent on the attorney's earlier performance, the attorney's performance is subject to no condition at all. Her duty to perform is absolute and not contingent on the happening of any prior event.

The effect of this is that the attorney's performance is a promissory condition precedent to the client's payment, but the client's payment is not a condition of anything. It is the last performance in the chain and no further contractual duties are contingent on it. It is therefore a **pure promise**. In short, although the promises may still be thought of as dependent in the exchange sense (and as we will see in section 17.7.2, the attorney would not have to perform if the client repudiated his obligation in advance), the nature of the performances has the effect of making the attorney's promise a condition.[4] This may be shown as follows:

---

4. This is expanded upon further in section 16.8.4.

§16.7 CONDITIONS PRECEDENT AND SUBSEQUENT

In our land sale example, the contract stated simply that Buyer's obligation to purchase the land was conditional on the grant of the rezoning application. This led us to the interpretation that the rezoning is a condition precedent to Buyer's obligation. However, our path to this conclusion is made a little more complicated as a result of a rather arcane and technical distinction in doctrine. Properly speaking, it is only correct to describe this as a condition precedent if the parties intend that Buyer's obligation to purchase does not become due until and unless the application is granted. However, if they intend that the obligation to purchase falls due immediately upon execution of the contract and is then discharged if the application is not granted, the condition is not precedent but subsequent. The difference is that a **condition precedent** is a **prerequisite to the duty arising**, while a **condition subsequent terminates a duty** that came into existence when the contract was formed. That is, when a performance is subject to a condition precedent, the duty to perform, although created at the time of contracting, exists in only potential or contingent form. If the condition occurs, it is converted from a potential to an actual duty. By contrast, if a performance is subject to a condition subsequent, the duty to perform arises immediately upon contracting but is discharged if the condition occurs. This can be portrayed diagrammatically as follows:

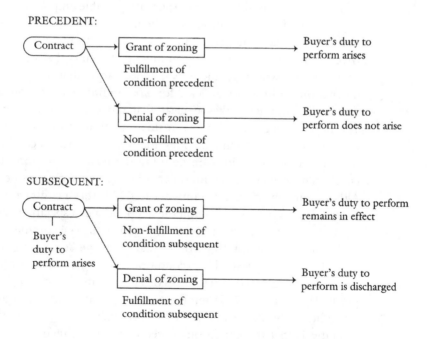

PRECEDENT:

Contract → Grant of zoning → Buyer's duty to perform arises
Fulfillment of condition precedent

→ Denial of zoning → Buyer's duty to perform does not arise
Non-fulfillment of condition precedent

SUBSEQUENT:

Contract → Grant of zoning → Buyer's duty to perform remains in effect
Buyer's duty to perform arises
Non-fulfillment of condition subsequent

→ Denial of zoning → Buyer's duty to perform is discharged
Fulfillment of condition subsequent

The distinction is frustrating because it is so much dependent upon the way in which the condition is phrased in the contract. It depends on the interpretation of often subtle nuances in the contract's wording that were probably not intended by the parties. (Indeed, even courts and writers often speak of a discharge of a duty by non-fulfillment of a condition precedent.) Luckily, the distinction can be disregarded for most purposes because it makes no difference to the substantive result. In the case of both types of condition, the ultimate effect is that the conditional duty need not be performed. That is, whether we treat the approval of the zoning application as a condition precedent, or its disapproval as a condition subsequent, the end result is that Buyer need not proceed with the purchase.

The principal significance of the distinction lies in its impact on the burden of proof. The fulfillment of a condition precedent is regarded as an element of the plaintiff's case in suing on the contract and must be proved by the party seeking to enforce it. Conversely, the occurrence of a condition subsequent is a defense to non-performance and must be proved by the party whose performance obligation has allegedly been discharged. (Therefore, if the grant of the rezoning application is a condition precedent, Seller would have to prove that rezoning was granted in order to enforce the contract, but if the failure of the application is a condition subsequent, Buyer would have to prove refusal of the application to escape the obligation to purchase the land.)

Although the distinction's principal significance relates to the burden of proof, one should not underplay its possible importance. When the happening of the condition is difficult to prove, the incidence of the burden can make the difference between winning or losing the case. Given the likely confusion and unintended results that could flow from subtleties in wording, there is a good argument for abolishing the distinction entirely, or at least for not finding a condition subsequent unless the contract makes it clear that the parties really did intend it. The Restatement Second tends in this direction. It disfavors the concept of conditions subsequent and does not even refer to such conditions in the text of any of its sections. In defining the term "condition" in §224, it confines it to an event that must occur before a performance becomes due. Although it concedes, in Comment e to §224, that a contract may provide for the discharge of a duty upon the happening of a specified event, it does not consider such a term to be a condition at all. The comment indicates a preference for interpreting contractual language as creating a condition precedent and suggests that a condition subsequent should not be found merely because the contract speaks of a duty being "discharged" or "extinguished." Section 227(3) reinforces this by stating that in cases of doubt, a condition should be interpreted as precedent. The overall effect of this thinking is that the condition subsequent has declined in importance in modern cases.

§16.8 THE PURPOSE OF USING CONDITIONS IN A CONTRACT

The preceding discussion has already provided several indications of the role played in the contract by conditions. In this section, attention is focused more directly on that subject. It is important to remember that conditions are contractual terms, available to be used or avoided by the parties in formulating their agreement. By properly using conditions, they can provide for contingencies, allocate risks, and generally control the way in which their bargain is to be performed. To the extent that they can do this clearly and expressly, they are less likely to have disputes later on. However, as we have already seen, in the absence of clear provisions, unexpressed conditions may still be found by applying principles of interpretation and construction to determine what the parties had or reasonably must have intended. The following are the most common purposes achieved by conditions.

§16.8.1 The Use of a Condition as a Complete or Partial "Escape Clause"

The land sale example demonstrated Buyer's purpose in making his commitment conditional upon the granting of the rezoning application — he did not wish to buy the land if it could not be developed. Used in this way, a non-promissory condition enables the parties to enter into a contract now, while permitting one (or both) of them to terminate the relationship and escape the commitment if a contemplated event does not occur. (In this example, as explained in section 16.4, the condition is interpreted as relating to Buyer's performance only, so it is his escape clause, not Seller's. The facts of the example were then varied to illustrate a condition intended to allow both parties to escape the transaction.)

In the land sale contract, the rezoning has been interpreted as a pure condition, so that Buyer escapes his obligation simply because the condition is not satisfied. He has no obligation to make any effort to bring about its fulfillment. However, some conditions create an escape that is less absolute, because they expressly or impliedly require the party to *take steps to try and make the event happen*. If so, the party is released from performance only if the condition is unfulfilled despite his efforts to make it come about. This can be illustrated by changing the facts of the example. Say that at the time of sale, the application for rezoning had not yet been made. Buyer is willing to submit an application, but does not wish to gamble on its success. The parties could enter a contract in which Buyer undertakes to make and conscientiously pursue the application, but is excused from

533

proceeding with the purchase if the application is declined. In this contract, Buyer makes an initial promise to apply for the rezoning, but the success of the application is a condition precedent to his obligation to buy the land. This is not completely a promissory condition, because Buyer does not promise that it will be satisfied. However, he does make a *promise to take all reasonable steps in good faith to try to get it fulfilled.* If he does this and fails, he escapes the contract, but if he does not make a conscientious effort to get the rezoning, he has broken his promise and will be liable for breach of contract.

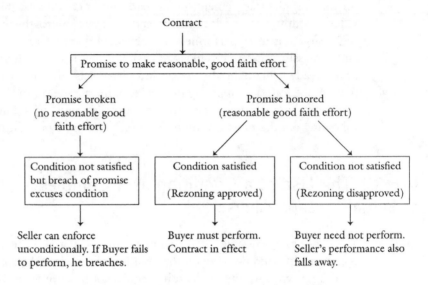

The same characteristics can be found in a common contract to buy a home, under which the buyer's obligation to proceed with the purchase is subject to his being able to obtain a mortgage or to sell his current home. The buyer undertakes to make reasonable efforts to satisfy the condition and cannot escape the promise to buy unless the condition is unfulfilled despite those efforts. In some cases, the promise to make reasonable or good faith efforts to satisfy the condition is expressed in the contract, but it may not be. If not, the contract must be interpreted to decide if such a commitment can be implied in fact or law.

Fry v. George Elkins Co., 327 P.2d 905 (Cal. 1958) and *Luttiger v. Rosen* (mentioned in section 16.3.1 in relation to strict compliance with an express condition) illustrate the operation of a financing contingency in a home purchase. In Fry, the seller advised the buyer to apply for financing to the holder of the existing mortgage on the property. The seller told the buyer that the mortgage holder would be likely to grant a mortgage to the buyer, and the mortgage holder itself indicated its willingness to deal with the buyer. The buyer disregarded this advice and instead applied to two other lenders, both of which declined to provide financing. The buyer terminated the contract on the grounds of non-fulfillment of the financing contingency. The court held that the buyer's two applications were not a diligent effort to secure financing because he failed to seek financing from the most promising source. (This conclusion was bolstered by evidence that the buyer had lost interest in the purchase and was looking for a way to get out of it.) In *Luttiger*, the buyers bought a home subject to the condition that they could obtain a mortgage on stated terms. They were reliably told that only one lender would accept their application for a home mortgage in the amount specified in the contract. They applied to that lender, which was willing to give them a loan, but at an interest rate higher than specified as the maximum in the contract. They declined the loan on those terms and notified the seller that they withdrew from the purchase because the condition had not been satisfied. The seller argued that the buyers had not made best efforts by applying to only one lender. The court conceded that a buyer would normally be expected to make more than just one application. However, the court found that on the facts of this case, it would have been futile to apply to other lenders because the buyers had been reliably told that this was the only lender who would entertain their application. Therefore, the buyers had adequately fulfilled their promise to make best efforts to try to have the condition fulfilled.

§16.8.2 The Use of a Condition to Permit the Exercise of Judgment by One of the Parties or a Third Party

One of the parties to a contract may wish to have some discretion in evaluating a future state of affairs (whether this relates to circumstances external to the contract or to the other party's performance) before rendering her own performance. To achieve this, the party could have a term included in the contract making her satisfaction (or her agent's satisfaction) with the specified state of affairs a condition precedent of her performance. This type of term, known as a **condition of satisfaction**, is useful to a party who does not wish to take the risk of performing until she is sure that circumstances are as desired or that the other party has properly done what the contract requires. A few examples will illustrate conditions of this kind and show how they may be employed:

A person contracts to have her portrait painted. In the contract, she undertakes to buy the portrait for $1,000 upon its completion, on condition that she likes it. The condition gives the buyer a means to escape the contract if she is not satisfied with the portrait, and places the risk of making her happy on the artist. In this illustration, the future state of affairs to be evaluated by the buyer is the adequacy of the painter's performance.

A buyer contracts to purchase an old building for the purpose of restoring it and making it into shops, but she is not sure if this kind of development would be successful. She therefore makes her promise to buy the building conditional on her determination, following a feasibility study, that it can be profitably renovated. The risk to be managed by the condition of satisfaction in this case is not related to the adequacy of the other party's performance, but to an external state of affairs — the economic environment — on which the buyer has inadequate information at the time of contracting.

In some cases, the evaluation is not to be done by the party herself, but by some expert third party. For example, a buyer may contract to buy a building subject to the condition that her engineer finds it to be structurally sound, or the owner of property may promise to pay a builder for construction work on condition that her architect certifies the work as competent.

In dealing with consideration doctrine in section 7.9.4, we saw that if a promisor reserves unrestrained discretion to perform, the apparent promise is **illusory** and cannot be consideration. Therefore, a promise conditional on the satisfaction of one of the parties could fail as consideration unless there is some limitation on that party's ability to claim dissatisfaction. The contract may itself express the *standard by which to measure satisfaction*, but if it does not, it is usually possible to imply such a standard, either as a matter of factual interpretation or legal implication. As a general rule, in the absence of the expression of a contrary intent, an *objective* test is used to limit discretion if, based on the underlying purpose and nature of the contract, the reason for the evaluation is to ensure that *commercial or technical standards* are satisfied. Under such an objective test, the question is whether the party is reasonable in being dissatisfied. In the above examples, it is a fair assumption that the market feasibility of the renovation, the soundness of the building, and the quality of the construction work would all fit into this category. Conversely, if the goal of the contract is to provide a performance that satisfies *personal preference involving matters of taste or aesthetics*, satisfaction is judged on a *subjective* standard: Is the party's dissatisfaction *honest and genuine?* The painting probably falls into this category, and the buyer may be able to show honest dissatisfaction with her portrait, even if art critics consider it to be a fine piece of work.

Two cases illustrate some of the considerations that a court takes into account in deciding whether to imply a subjective or objective standard of satisfaction. In *Hutton v. Monograms Plus, Inc.*, 604 N.E.2d 200 (Ohio App. 2000) a franchise agreement permitted the franchisee to terminate the franchise and get a refund of the franchise fee if he could not obtain "financing suitable to him." The trial court held that the term "to him" signified a subjective standard. The court of appeals disagreed. The use of that language was not enough to overturn the usual assumption that the parties intend an objective standard in the evaluation of matters of commercial utility. Because it would be unusual for the parties to agree to a subjective standard in a commercial contract, much clearer language must be used to express that intent. By contrast, in *Forman v. Benson*, 446 N.E.2d 535 (Ill. 1983) the court did find that the parties to a commercial contract intended satisfaction to be subjective. A contract of sale was conditional on the seller's satisfaction with the buyer's credit report. The seller rejected the report on the basis that it showed the buyer to be in shaky financial condition. The loan officer of a financial institution testified that his company would regard the buyer's credit as excellent on the basis of the report. The trial court applied an objective standard and held that the seller had been unreasonable in rejecting the report. The supreme court agreed that an objective test of satisfaction normally applies to matters of commercial quality and that the seller's dissatisfaction would not have met the reasonableness standard. However, it held that on the particular facts of the case, the parties intended a subjective standard. The seller was an individual, not in the business of lending money or familiar with commercial standards of evaluating credit, and the condition was included in the contract to allay his concerns about giving credit to the buyer and to induce his agreement. (Although the court decided in favor of the seller on the use of a subjective standard, it ultimately ruled against the seller on the issue of dissatisfaction because it found that the seller's dissatisfaction was not genuine and in good faith. The evidence showed that he was unhappy with the contract price and had used his claimed dissatisfaction as a pretext for terminating the agreement only after the buyer refused to renegotiate the price.)

The court's justification for applying a subjective standard was that the seller was not a commercial lender and should not be subject to industry standards of reasonableness. Note, however, that the court could have accommodated the seller's individual circumstances just as well by using an objective test: his satisfaction could have been measured by the standard of a reasonable non-professional lender in his position, taking into account his level of expertise and his economic circumstances.

In some cases, the choice of standard can completely change the result. As *Forman* shows, had the seller been honest in his dissatisfaction with the credit report, he would have been able to escape the contract even though a reasonable lender would have been satisfied with it. However, the case also reminds us of a point that has been made several times before in regard to the difference between objective reasonableness and subjective good faith: Where a party unreasonably rejects a performance or state of affairs as unsatisfactory to him, he will have to provide convincing evidence of his peculiar attitude or attributes to explain why his unreasonable dissatisfaction is honest and genuine. Notwithstanding, there is a difference in the focus of the two tests. The good faith test is more oriented to personal judgment, while reasonableness focuses more on market or mechanical factors. Restatement Second §228 expresses a preference for use of the objective standard in case of doubt, because it is obviously fairer and more predictable. A party should not be taken to have subjected herself to the risk of the other's purely subjective foibles unless this is made clear in the contract or is necessarily inferred from the nature of the transaction.

Like the conditions discussed at the end of section 16.7.1, the promise inherent in a condition of satisfaction is not a promise to ensure that the condition is fulfilled, but only a promise to act in good faith or reasonably to cooperate in achieving its fulfillment. It provides an escape from the contract, but only if the condition is unfulfilled despite the reasonable or honest evaluation of the party with the conditional obligation. Therefore, if a party refuses to perform on the basis of unreasonable or false dissatisfaction, the condition of satisfaction is deemed fulfilled, and the refusal of performance is a breach.

§16.8.3 The Use of a Condition to Provide for Alternative Performances

In the example involving the sale of land subject to rezoning, the denial of the application completely released Buyer from his promise to buy the land. However, a condition need not invariably result in the total termination of a party's performance obligation. Because a condition is a contractual term, the parties can agree that some other consequence will follow its non-fulfillment. To illustrate, reconsider the land sale example with slightly changed facts: As before, at the time of contracting, Seller's application for rezoning was pending. If it succeeds, the land can be used for a housing development, but if not, it can only be used for farming. Buyer wishes to have the land irrespective of the outcome, but the parties recognize that its value will be very much higher if the zoning is changed. To accommodate the uncertainty of the application's outcome, they may contract for the sale, but may provide in the contract that its purchase price is $100,000 (its market value as farmland), yet if the rezoning application is successful, the price will be $300,000 (its value as a tract capable of residential development). Here, as before, the parties agree to make Buyer's performance contingent on an uncertain future event — the change in zoning. However, the condition does not operate to release Buyer, but to commit him to an alternative promise that changes the extent of his performance. The condition is used as a *channeling device*, not as an escape clause.

§16.8.4 The Use of a Condition to Regulate the Sequence of Performance

In the land sale example, the two dependent promises — Buyer's promise to pay and the seller's to convey the land — were construed as concurrent. This meant that the performances were conditions of each other and had to be exchanged simultaneously. This conclusion was reached because the contract did not indicate a contrary intent, and concurrent performance was the most reasonable construction under the circumstances. As noted in section 16.6, when a *contract is silent on the sequence of performance,* the law recognizes two *default rules:* If the performances are capable of being rendered simultaneously, the presumption is that the parties intended concurrent performance. However, if one of the performances is capable of being rendered instantaneously and the other needs time to be accomplished, the completion of the longer performance is deemed to be a condition precedent of the instantaneous one. This means that the party with the longer performance must go first. Of course, these are only default rules, so the *parties can change them by providing differently* in their contract. They can set up any sequence of performances that they think fit, and can even split up one or both parties' performances to provide for portions of each to be rendered serially. Sometimes this intent is spelled out expressly, but it could also arise by factual implication from the nature and structure of the contract. Because the promises are dependent, it follows that the earlier performance to be rendered by one of the parties is a promissory condition precedent of the next performance in the sequence, to be rendered by the other.

We begin with the simplest illustration: Buyer and Seller contract for the sale of a piece of land on credit. The contract states that Seller will convey the land immediately, and Buyer will pay for it in six months. The promises are still dependent, in the sense that Seller would not have to convey the land if Buyer repudiated his promise before conveyance fell due. But it is clearly no longer true that performances must be simultaneous, so they are not, in that sense, conditions of each other. Instead, even though the parties have not said so expressly, the sequence prescribed for performance leads to the reasonable inference that conveyance of the land is a **condition precedent** to payment of the price in six months. (As noted in section 16.2, the passage of the six months after conveyance is not itself a condition because the mere affluxion of time is not regarded as an uncertain event.) Note that once Seller has performed, Buyer is committed to pay in six months. This is the last promise to be honored in the transaction, and as such it is a **pure promise**. It obviously cannot be a promissory condition because it is not a condition of anything — no further performance is contingent on it.

Seller's conveyance of the land   [Seller's promise]

↓

construed as a promissory condition precedent to

↓

Buyer's payment   [Buyer's promise]

This example illustrates the point made in section 16.3. Even though the promises are express, the conditional nature of the seller's promise is not articulated, so the condition itself is not express, but construed — it is inferred as being what the parties reasonably must have intended by providing for the order of performances. (For it to be both an express promise and an express condition, the contract would have to have contained language stating that the seller undertakes to convey the land, and that this conveyance is a condition of the buyer's payment.) It makes no difference to the ultimate legal effect of a condition whether it is express or construed. However, as a matter of planning, when parties intend to sequence their performances, it makes more sense to set this out clearly in the contract, rather than to argue about it before a court.

We now consider a second, more complex illustration (a further embellishment of the previous land sale example) to see how the parties are able to use sequential conditions to break up their performance obligations into stages and to provide for several consecutive performances as well as a set of simultaneous performances. The contract so structured has a combination of pure conditions, promissory conditions precedent, promissory concurrent conditions, and pure promises. Say that the contract commits Buyer to purchase the land for $300,000 on condition that the zoning application is granted. However, it does not simply provide, as before, for the simultaneous transfer of price for title. Instead, it specifies that if the application does succeed, Buyer will pay a down payment of $30,000 to Seller immediately upon the grant of the application; a further $250,000 will be paid concurrently with Seller's transfer of title to Buyer; and the remaining balance of $20,000 will be paid one month after the transfer. The purpose here is not simply to give Buyer an escape if the rezoning is refused, but also to distribute the risk of breach between the parties and to extend credit to Buyer for part of the price.

The initial condition that the rezoning must be approved is an **express condition precedent** to the buyer's promise to purchase the land. As before, this is likely to be interpreted as a **pure condition**. There is nothing from which to conclude that it was intended as promissory, because the fate of the application is out of the buyer's control, and the language of the contract does not indicate that he intended to guarantee that it would happen, or that he has to do anything to try to bring it about. Therefore, if the rezoning is refused, the buyer has the right to escape the contract, and the seller's dependent promise falls away too.

If the rezoning is approved, the contract requires Buyer immediately to pay a deposit of $30,000 to Seller. This payment is performance of part of Buyer's consideration and it is expressly promised. Although the parties have not expressly called this a condition of the subsequent transfer of the land, this is the reasonable construction of what was intended. The apparent purpose of the deposit is to show Buyer's earnest (that is, to indicate his commitment) and to alleviate Seller's risk that Buyer may breach, so it can reasonably be inferred that if payment is not made, Seller is relieved of her subsequent obligation to perform by tendering conveyance of the property. Furthermore, if Buyer should breach by not causing the condition to be satisfied, he would also be liable to Seller for breach of contract. The undertaking is therefore not only an **express promise**, but also a **construed promissory condition precedent** to Seller's performance.

If both the conditions of approval and payment of the deposit are satisfied, the next set of terms involve the simultaneous conveyance of title and payment of $250,000. As in the earlier example, these are **express promises**, construed as dependent on each other, to be performed simultaneously — that is, **construed promissory concurrent conditions**. If either party fails to tender performance at the time appointed for the exchange, the other has the right both to withhold the return performance and to treat the failure as a breach of contract.

If all the above conditions are satisfied, one promised performance remains following the transfer of the land against payment of the $250,000 — Buyer's payment of the final installment of $20,000. This is a **pure promise**. Although payment is an event, there is no later performance that is contingent on it, so it is not a condition. If Buyer fails to pay, Seller has nothing to withhold, but she can enforce the promise by suing for breach. A diagram of the contract's structure looks like this:

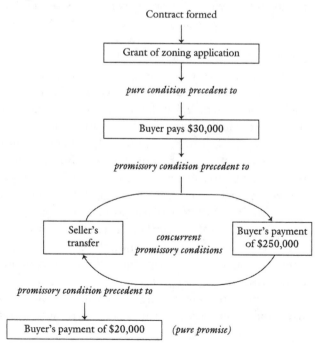

It is worth stressing again that the distinction made in the above example between promises, conditions, and promissory conditions was a matter of interpretation and construction, based on any express language used by the parties, or in the absence of such clear language, on their apparent intent as evidenced by any contextual evidence, or failing that, as reasonably inferred. In this case, there was no extrinsic evidence of negotiations, trade usage, or other facts, so reasonable meaning was construed from nothing more than the language and structure of the writing itself.

This analysis makes it clear why conditions are useful in establishing a particular sequence of performances, requiring obligations to be satisfied serially or concurrently. The party who performs first takes the risk of not receiving the return performance when it later becomes due. By using conditions, the parties can structure the contract so that risk goes to the party who is willing to bear it. If neither party wishes to assume the risk of relying on the other's credit, concurrent performances may be the answer. In the above example, the exchange of title and money could have been performed concurrently, but the parties chose to break up Buyer's performance obligation and to provide for it in stages.

In other contracts it may not be possible for parties to perform simultaneously because one party's performance will take time, while the other's can be rendered instantaneously. As noted above, unless the parties provide differently, the presumption in such a contract is that completion of the longer performance is a condition precedent of the instantaneous one. A final example, involving a construction contract, demonstrates how parties may use conditions to avoid this result and allocate risk more evenly. If the owner of property contracts with a builder to build a house on it, the builder's performance — constructing the house — will take several weeks or months, while the owner's performance — payment — could be accomplished in a single instant. In the absence of a different sequence set out in the contract, the completion of construction is construed as a promissory condition precedent to the payment. This places the entire risk of the owner's non-payment on the builder. If the builder does not wish for this result, she could ensure that the contract prescribes a different order of performance. The owner will probably not agree to pay in advance, because that shifts the whole risk of the builder's non-performance to him. But the parties may be able to agree on a sequence that shares the risk of default and ensures that neither party is exposed to the full burden of trusting the other. To do this, the parties may use promissory conditions to break the performance into stages. For example, the contract may require the owner to pay a ten percent deposit one week after the contract is signed; one week thereafter, the builder must begin to excavate and build the foundation; on completion the owner must pay a further ten percent of the price; the builder must then frame the house; when that is done the owner must pay another ten percent. This sequence of alternating performances goes on until the entire house is built and the builder has received periodic payments of 90 percent, upon which the owner must pay the final installment. Each of the incremental performances is a promise by the one party and also a condition precedent to the next stage of performance by the other, so that if any one stage of performance is not rendered, the party entitled to that performance can refuse to render the consequent return performance and claim breach. For instance, if the owner fails to pay after the excavation and foundation, the builder has the right to refuse to do the framing and may also sue the owner for breaching the contract. The sequence looks like this:

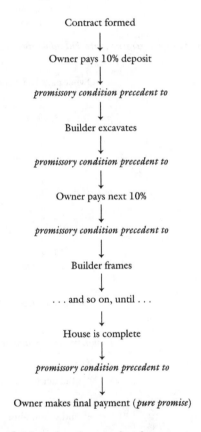

Contract formed
↓
Owner pays 10% deposit
↓
promissory condition precedent to
↓
Builder excavates
↓
promissory condition precedent to
↓
Owner pays next 10%
↓
promissory condition precedent to
↓
Builder frames
↓
. . . and so on, until . . .
↓
House is complete
↓
promissory condition precedent to
↓
Owner makes final payment (*pure promise*)

We could add a further detail to make this contract a little more complex: The parties agree further that the owner's obligation to make the deposit and to proceed with the construction is conditional on the owner obtaining a building permit. They also agree that before the owner has to pay for any stage of construction, his architect will inspect the work and certify it as in accordance with specifications and competently performed. By agreeing to these terms, the parties have added an initial condition precedent that allows the owner to escape the contract if the city refuses a permit, but impliedly requires the owner to make reasonable efforts to obtain the permit. They have also conditioned the owner's second and later payment obligations on his architect's satisfaction with the builder's performance. Because this involves a matter of technical judgment, the dissatisfaction must be reasonable. I am not sure if my sanity (or yours) can withstand another diagram, but here goes:

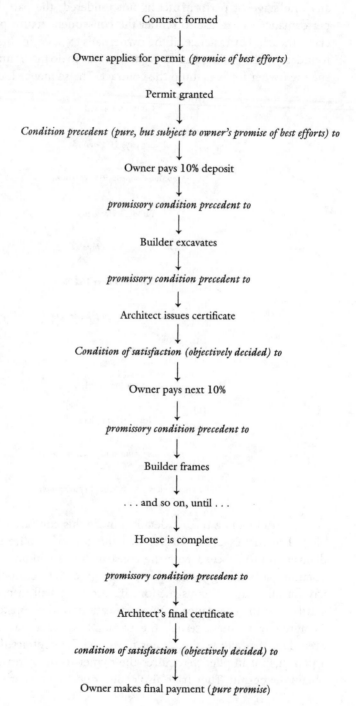

Contract formed

↓

Owner applies for permit *(promise of best efforts)*

↓

Permit granted

↓

Condition precedent (pure, but subject to owner's promise of best efforts) to

↓

Owner pays 10% deposit

↓

promissory condition precedent to

↓

Builder excavates

↓

promissory condition precedent to

↓

Architect issues certificate

↓

Condition of satisfaction (objectively decided) to

↓

Owner pays next 10%

↓

promissory condition precedent to

↓

Builder frames

↓

. . . and so on, until . . .

↓

House is complete

↓

promissory condition precedent to

↓

Architect's final certificate

↓

condition of satisfaction (objectively decided) to

↓

Owner makes final payment *(pure promise)*

§16.9 STRICT OR SUBSTANTIAL COMPLIANCE WITH A CONDITION: THE DIFFERENT RULES OF INTERPRETATION GOVERNING EXPRESS AND CONSTRUED CONDITIONS

As we have seen the fundamental rule is that when a performance is subject to a condition, the duty to perform does not arise unless the condition is fulfilled. Section 16.3.1 explained that if the parties have taken the trouble to create an express condition by clear language in the contract, this rule is regarded as absolute: Unless the *express condition* is exactly satisfied, the conditional duty does not become due. The justification for this doctrine of *strict compliance* is that the parties have clearly chosen to make performance subject to the stated event, and the court should honor this intention by upholding the beneficiary party's right to demand nothing less than exact fulfillment of the condition. Therefore, even if it seems that the condition is rather technical and apparently unimportant, or even if it has been substantially satisfied, so that the shortcoming in compliance is rather unimportant or trivial, the court should not second-guess the parties by treating the condition as having been met.

Luttiger v. Rosen has already been used in section 16.3.1 to illustrate this point. To reinforce *Luttiger*, apply this principle to the land sale example used earlier in this chapter. Recall that the land sale contract expressly made Buyer's obligation to purchase the property conditional upon the grant of the rezoning application within 60 days of the date of the agreement. If the rezoning has not yet been approved by the 60th day, but it is granted on the 61st, the condition has not been fulfilled. Because the condition is express, Buyer is entitled to demand that it is strictly complied with. Seller should not be able to claim its fulfillment by arguing that a one-day delay in the grant is unimportant and the short delay has no real impact on the value of the transaction to Buyer. This could be a harsh result for Seller, particularly if Buyer is using technical non-fulfillment as a pretext to avoid a contract that he no longer desires. Nevertheless, the rationale is that Seller agreed to a condition on these express terms, and if the event does not occur precisely as contemplated, she has no basis for complaint.

In some cases, the harsh results of this approach may be ameliorated by excusing the condition on one of the grounds discussed in section 16.11, but only if the facts fit into one of the recognized bases for excuse. It is also sometimes possible to avoid an unfair result by interpreting the condition so as to find that it was in fact satisfied, but this solution is only available if the language of the condition admits of such a meaning. It would not, for example, be easy to interpret the clear wording "within 60 days of the date of this agreement" to mean "within 61 days." However, if the condition was for approval of the rezoning "within a reasonable time," the less precise language of this express condition provides greater flexibility in interpretation and makes it easier for a court to conclude that the condition was in fact fulfilled.

A similar flexibility in interpretation occurs when a condition is not expressly stated, but it is **implied in fact**. Although the factually implied condition is, in legal effect, no different from an express one and just as much merits rigorous enforcement, the process of deciding on exactly what the condition was gives the court some leeway. If alternative interpretations are possible, the court may be able to avoid the one that would lead to a harsh result, and favor the one that supports the conclusion that the condition was in fact satisfied.

As we have seen, many conditions are neither express nor implied from factual evidence, but are **construed** as a matter of law, based on what the parties reasonably must have intended. A construed condition is found by the court, in the absence of clearly established actual intent, for the purpose of giving reasonable effect to the parties' agreement. For fairly obvious reasons, a *standard of strict compliance is not appropriate* where a condition is construed: Because the condition is not established by a clear manifestation of assent, the parties' intent to agree to strict compliance is not as certain. Furthermore, construction is a search for the apparent expectations of the parties, measured in light of what would be reasonable. The court is therefore unlikely to construe a condition so strictly that it would require exact compliance and admit of no flexibility.

The distinction between strict compliance with an express condition and substantial compliance with a construed condition may be illustrated by looking again at the example involving the building contract under which the owner undertook to make a ten percent down payment a week after execution of the contract, and the builder committed to begin construction a week thereafter. The owner has expressly promised to make the down payment. If the language of the contract clearly articulates that this is also a condition precedent to the builder's duty to commence performance, the owner's failure to pay the full amount of the deposit by due date constitutes non-fulfillment of the condition, so that the builder's obligation to perform does not arise. Because strict compliance is required, the owner will not be deemed to have satisfied the condition if, say, he pays the deposit one day late. However, if the promise's role as a condition is not expressly stated but is construed as a matter of reasonable intent from the way in which the contract has set out the sequence of performances, the court has more flexibility. It may employ the doctrine of substantial compliance and decide whether the delay in payment is good enough to constitute fulfillment of the condition.

Of course, we must not forget that the owner's down payment is not simply a condition, but *also a promise* (that is, a promissory condition).

Therefore, late payment of the deposit raises not only the question of whether strict compliance with the condition is required, but also whether the owner's breach of his promise to pay at the time specified is a serious or minor breach. This issue is deferred to Chapter 17, but it is useful to note at this stage that where a promissory condition is involved, the impact of the deficiency in performance must be evaluated from both perspectives. As Chapter 17 will show, there is usually a close coordination in the results of these two enquiries, so that a minor breach that qualifies as *substantial performance* of the *promise* is likely to be also a *substantial compliance* with the *condition*, and a material breach will likely be a non-fulfillment of the condition as well. The effect of this may be illustrated by returning to our example: If late payment is a serious violation of the contract, the builder would be entitled to withhold performance and also to rescind the contract and claim the full extent of relief necessary to compensate for the lost expectation. However, if the delay is trivial, substantial compliance with the condition does not discharge the builder's duty to perform, and the minor breach does not permit rescission. The builder must perform and is confined to claiming compensation, in the form of a monetary allowance, for any loss caused by the inadequacy of performance.

§16.10 DISTINGUISHING A CONDITION FROM AN EVENT THAT SETS THE TIME FOR PERFORMANCE

In requiring a down payment from the owner, the construction contract specified that the payment must be made one week following the execution of the contract. As stated in section 16.2, the passage of time is not a condition because this is not regarded in law as an uncertain future event. The purpose of the provision is merely to set a time for the owner's performance, not to impose a condition on it. However, sometimes it is trickier to differentiate between a time-setting event and a condition. Say, for example, that the contract required the owner to make the down payment on payday, which is at the end of the month. Two days after the contract was signed, the owner's employer filed bankruptcy. It is clear that the employer is so badly insolvent that its estate will not have enough funds to pay salaries due to employees — payday will never dawn.

If the parties intended simply to fix a time for payment, the owner is obliged to make the down payment at the end of the month, the day on which the employer's debt to him was due, whether or not he actually collects it. But if the parties intended the owner's obligation to be conditional on his receiving his salary, the non-occurrence of that event discharges his duty. Unless the contract makes it clear which of these alternatives was intended, the import of a term like this must be determined by interpretation or construction. In most cases, in the absence of evidence of a contrary intent, the most reasonable construction is that the promisor, not the promisee, bore the risk that the funds would not become available, so that the term merely postpones payment for a stated period and does not make performance conditional on the event occurring.[5]

Two cases involving construction subcontracts provide a further illustration. In *Thos. J. Dyer Co. v. Bishop International Engineering Co.*, 303 F.2d 655 (6th Cir. 1962) the contract stated that payment to a subcontractor would not be due "until five (5) days after Owner shall have paid Contractor therefor." The court concluded that this was merely a term setting the time for payment, and not a term that made the owner's payment of the contractor a condition of the contractor's obligation to pay the subcontractor. The court reasoned that the subcontractor had no contractual relationship with the owner, did not deal with it directly, and did not have the opportunity to evaluate its creditworthiness. Therefore, unless the parties use very clear language of condition, they cannot be taken to have placed the risk of the owner's non-payment on the subcontractor. The same approach was taken in *Peacock Construction Co., Inc. v. Modern Air Conditioning, Inc.*, 3534 So. 2d 840 (Fla. 1977), in which the contract stated that final payment would be made to the subcontractor "within 30 days after . . . full payment . . . by the Owner."

§16.11 THE EXCUSE OF CONDITIONS: WRONGFUL PREVENTION, WAIVER OR ESTOPPEL, AND FORFEITURE

If a performance is subject to a condition, it does not fall due unless that condition is satisfied. However, circumstances may change after the contract is entered into, making it unfair or unreasonable to require the condition to be satisfied, or the inequitable conduct of the beneficiary of the condition may preclude his assertion of its non-fulfillment, or the impact of the condition may otherwise be so harsh that its enforcement would be unjust. To take account of this, the law recognizes certain limited and defined situations in which the condition may be excused to prevent injustice. If grounds for excuse exist, the condition falls away and the contingent obligation becomes absolute. That is, it is no longer conditional and must be performed despite the non-occurrence of the event originally contemplated in the contract. In this section we look at three of the most common and important bases for excuse.

---

5. We will not consider here the question of whether the owner would be able to use the excuse of impracticability to avoid liability for failing to perform.

§16.11.1 The Party Favored by the Condition Wrongfully Prevents or Hinders Its Fulfillment

Some conditions are completely beyond the control of the promisor, and she has no power to do anything to facilitate or to hinder their occurrence. For example, if a lessor promises the lessee that she will install air conditioning in the premises next year if the average temperature for this August reaches 100 degrees, there is little that the lessor can do to manipulate the weather so as to influence the fulfillment of the condition. If a party has no capacity to influence the happening of the condition, she cannot, of course, wrongfully prevent its fulfillment. But some conditions are, to a greater or lesser extent, capable of being influenced by one or both parties.

a. When a Party Has a Duty to Take Active Steps to Facilitate Occurrence of the Condition

We have already seen that even if a party does not promise that the condition will be fulfilled, she may at least have some role to play in affecting it, and may expressly or impliedly promise to make a *reasonable or good faith effort* to attempt to bring it about. For example, the buyer of a home may undertake to purchase it on condition that she is able to obtain a mortgage loan for 90 percent of the purchase price. She does not promise that she will obtain the loan, but she does have the duty (even if this is not expressly stated) to make best efforts to get it. Although fulfillment of the condition is not entirely within her control, she does have a role to play in bringing it about. If she makes adequate efforts to obtain the financing, but fails, the condition is not fulfilled and she has no duty to proceed with the purchase. However, if she does not try to get the loan, or makes only a halfhearted or token attempt, she violates her duty to deal fairly with the seller. She is therefore taken to have hindered fulfillment of the condition. This allows the seller to claim that the condition is excused, so that he can enforce her promise to purchase the house as if the condition had not existed.

b. Obstructive Conduct

Even if a party has no duty to cooperate actively in the condition's fulfillment, the *obligation of fair dealing* may require her not to do anything to obstruct fulfillment of the condition. The example involving the sale of farmland subject to rezoning may be used again to illustrate this point. Because the rezoning application had already been submitted by Seller and was awaiting disposition by the zoning authority, Buyer had no duty to take any action to prosecute the application or to ensure the condition's occurrence. (That is, it is a pure condition, without any promissory elements.) Nevertheless,

Buyer's general obligation of fair dealing does create an implied promise not to act in bad faith to prevent its occurrence. Therefore, the condition may be excused if its non-occurrence resulted from some wrongful action by Buyer to negatively influence the local authority's decision. (For example, he persuaded a neighboring landowner to file an objection to the application, or he lobbied members of the board to vote against it.)

To be wrongful, the action need not break the law. It is enough that it *faithlessly undermines the contract*, betraying the other party's reasonable expectations. In the above example, the obligation not to obstruct fulfillment of the condition is an obvious implication because Buyer's actions would be inconsistent with the contract's purpose. However, one should not assume, as a matter of course, that every contract imposes an implied duty not to act in a way that obstructs fulfillment of a condition. This is a matter of interpretation, dependent on the apparent intent of the parties, and some contracts may contemplate that the promisor does have the right to try to avoid satisfaction of the condition. For example, if a buyer promises to purchase goods from the seller on condition that he cannot find them cheaper elsewhere, the buyer obviously has the right to try to avoid satisfaction of the condition by seeking cheaper goods, and these efforts would not be a wrongful obstruction of the condition.

c. The Link Between Conduct and Non-Fulfillment

When the promisor has wrongfully failed to make a good faith and reasonable effort to facilitate occurrence or has acted in an obstructive way, it may not be clear if that conduct was directly responsible for non-fulfillment of the condition. For example, the buyer of the house may not have obtained a mortgage, even had she made a genuine and conscientious effort, or the rezoning board may have refused the application even without Buyer's interference. Some courts have imposed a strict test of causation, excusing the condition only if it can be shown that the condition would have been fulfilled, but for the promisor's obstruction. A less rigorous test, favored by other courts, does not require the promisee to demonstrate as strong a causal link, but merely to show that the promisor's conduct played a significant role in the condition's non-fulfillment.

§16.11.2 Estoppel or Waiver

Estoppel and waiver are distinct doctrines, but they are quite muddled in the context of excuse of conditions because conduct is often ambiguous enough to be classified as giving rise to either of them. As a result, courts sometimes do not take the trouble to differentiate them, and Restatement Second §§84 and 230(3) combine them into a general principle of excuse.

The basic idea is that after the contract is entered into, the promisor whose duty is conditional indicates by *words or conduct* that he will perform even if the condition does not occur. This indication of *intent not to require compliance with the condition* may take place either before the time on which the condition is to occur, or after that time has passed and the condition has not been satisfied. Although there are some differences in legal analysis depending on whether the condition is dispensed with before or after it is due to occur, these will not be explored here. This discussion is confined to an explanation of the basic principles applicable in either case. Although the two doctrines of estoppel and waiver are intermingled in this area, they do give rise to distinct justifications for excusing a condition, so it is useful to describe them separately and to show why they are so easily mixed up.

a. Estoppel

Estoppel, an equitable doctrine, was introduced in section 8.4. Its purpose is to prevent the unfair assertion of rights by a person who has acted inconsistently with those rights. The basic effect of the doctrine is to preclude a person from asserting a right when, by *deliberate words or conduct*, and with *knowledge or reason to know* that the words or conduct will *likely be relied on* by another, the actor causes the other party *detriment by inducing the justifiable belief* that the *right does not exist* or that it *will not be asserted*. In the context of conditions, the party who is the beneficiary of the condition may be estopped from claiming its non-fulfillment if, by her words or conduct, she induces the other party to act to his detriment by causing him justifiably to believe that the condition has been satisfied, or that compliance with it will not be required. (If, instead of misrepresenting a fact, the beneficiary party promises that she will not require compliance with the condition, the basis for relief is promissory estoppel rather than equitable estoppel, but the elements for relief are so similar, that the analysis is the same.)

To illustrate, consider again the example involving the sale of land subject to the condition that the rezoning application is granted within 60 days of execution of the contract. Fifty-five days after execution of the contract, the zoning authority tells Seller that it will not be ready to make a decision for at least two weeks. When Seller informs Buyer of this, he responds by stating that he is willing to wait an additional two weeks. On the strength of this, Seller forgoes an opportunity to sell the land to someone else. If, on the 61st day, Buyer sought to escape the contract by asserting non-fulfillment of the condition, he would likely be estopped from doing so, because he deliberately indicated to Seller that he would not insist on compliance with the 60-day provision and Seller justifiably relied on that assertion to her detriment.

b. Waiver

A waiver occurs when, after the contract has been made, the beneficiary of a condition agrees to perform even if the condition is not satisfied. In essence, the waiver is a **voluntary abandonment of a contractual right**. (Naturally, a party can only waive a condition that is solely for his benefit. One party cannot waive rights belonging to the other.) For example, after the rezoning application is denied, Buyer informs Seller that he wishes to proceed with the transaction despite the denial. If Buyer then refuses to perform, Seller can claim that Buyer's performance obligation became unconditional because the condition was excused by the waiver. A waiver must be distinguished from a contract modification. A modification is a contract in itself—a mutual agreement under which one party agrees to relinquish rights in return for consideration given by the other. A waiver is one-sided—one of the parties *unilaterally* gives up a contractual right without asking for or receiving anything in exchange. Because consideration is required for a valid modification, the general rule is that if the right to be given up is an important part of the exchange under the contract (that is, it is a material right) it cannot be validly relinquished by a unilateral waiver. Its abandonment must be exchanged for consideration in a fully-fledged contractual modification. However, if the right relinquished is **non-material**— ancillary, and not a central part of the contractual exchange — the consideration requirement is dispensed with and it can be validly waived. To decide if the grant of the rezoning application was a material part of the exchange and therefore not validly waivable without consideration, the role of the condition and its significance in the exchange must be determined by interpretation. (This is, of course, the common law rule, because UCC §2.209 does not require consideration for a modification. Therefore, even the waiver of a material part of the exchange would be valid despite a lack of consideration.)

The issue of consideration for a waiver only arises when it is the party entitled to the conditional performance who seeks to excuse the condition and to enforce the performance against the beneficiary of the condition. It does not apply when it is the beneficiary of the condition who elects to abandon his right to protection of the condition. For example, it was mentioned in section 16.4 that if the grant of the rezoning application is solely for Buyer's benefit, he can decide to proceed with the sale of the property as farmland, even if the application is denied. In such a case, Buyer is not attempting to enforce rights arising out of the excuse of a condition, but is merely enforcing his original rights for which he gave consideration under the contract. Seller cannot resist this by arguing that she gave Buyer no consideration for his waiver.

c. Distinguishing Waiver from Estoppel

As noted earlier, it can be difficult to distinguish waiver from estoppel. The estoppel example given above can be used to show just how ambiguous the distinction can be. In that example, it was stated that Buyer's conduct in indicating that he would wait a further two weeks for approval estopped him from asserting non-fulfillment of the condition on the 61st day. It could just as well be said that Buyer waived his right to have the condition fulfilled within 60 days. If the time for approval is not a central component of the exchange (which it appears not to be, but that is a question of interpretation), the waiver without consideration is valid and binding. Thus, in most situations, conduct by the party benefitted by the condition could equally well support an estoppel or waiver argument, so they should generally be regarded as alternative bases for excuse. Selection of the theory to be used would be based on the issues of reliance and materiality. Estoppel is more appropriate if detrimental reliance can be shown and there is some question about whether the right relinquished is material enough to require consideration. Waiver is a better argument if no prejudicial reliance can be established, but there is an argument that the abandoned right is ancillary, not central to the exchange.

d. Retraction of a Waiver

Although, as stated earlier, we will not go into the details of the distinction between waivers prior to and after the due date for occurrence of the condition, there is one point on which it is useful to indicate a difference in approach. Because a waiver is not supported by consideration, a waiver made prior to the due date for the condition's fulfillment can be retracted. But here again, principles of estoppel and waiver intermingle, making the right to withdraw the waiver subject to protection of the other party's reliance. The ability to retract the waiver is lost if notice of the retraction is not received by the other party in time to allow him to take any action necessary to bring the condition about, or if he has taken detrimental action in reliance on the waiver. If the waiver is made after the time for occurrence of the condition has passed (so that it is clear that the condition has failed to occur), it cannot be retracted because the party benefitted by the condition is treated as having made a final election to proceed with the transaction despite non-occurrence of the condition.

§16.11.3 Forfeiture

In a sense, any finding of liability under a contract, or any conclusion that a party is not entitled to performance because of the non-fulfillment of a condition, results in some forfeiture of money or expected benefits. Therefore, when forfeiture is raised as a basis for excusing a condition, it must mean more than this. As a general matter, forfeiture is an appropriate basis for excusing a condition only if its enforcement would result in an **unfair, disproportionate, and harsh deprivation** of the rights or property of the party who expects performance, and a **windfall or unfair benefit** to the party whose performance is subject to the condition. Thus, in deciding forfeiture, the court *balances the relative hardships* between the parties. It weighs the burden on the party who would suffer if the condition was enforced against the harm that excuse would do to the beneficiary of the condition.

This ground for excusing a condition is really a safety valve that ameliorates the harsh results that may follow from the rule of strict compliance with express conditions. It is therefore most useful when the condition is express and unambiguous, and is not needed when the court has flexibility in construing the terms and scope of the condition, or when ambiguous language can be interpreted in a way that avoids an unfair result. (In setting out standards of interpretation, Restatement Second §227 expresses a general preference in favor of interpretation that will avoid forfeiture in cases when there is doubt about the existence, scope, or nature of a condition.)

The principal purpose of the forfeiture doctrine, set out in Restatement Second §229, is to allow the court to disregard an express condition of a *technical or procedural nature* where the *strict enforcement* of the condition would have the *unfair impact* described above. It should therefore not be used if the occurrence of the condition is a material part of the exchange. To illustrate, say that an insurance policy provides two express conditions to the insurer's liability. The first is that the insured must pay the annual premium, and the second is that the insured must notify the insurer of loss within five days of its occurrence. Payment of the premium is surely a material part of the exchange — it is the entire consideration bargained for by the insurer. Therefore, if the insured suffers a loss after failing to pay the premium, he cannot claim unfair forfeiture of his right to reimbursement and ask the court to excuse the condition of payment. However, if he has paid the premium, and he does give notice of loss, but is one day late in giving it, the court is more likely to be sympathetic to an argument that the insurer's insistence on strict fulfillment is a technicality, and the insured's deprivation of his right of reimbursement would be an unfair forfeiture.

Examples

1. This first example is an exercise in classification. Identify the promises, conditions, and promissory conditions in the following contracts. Having identified the conditions, consider whether they are express or construed and precedent or concurrent.

   1(a). A lessor and a lessee entered into a lease of real property for a two-year term at a rent of $1,200 a month, payable in advance by the first day of each month. The lease gave the lessee the right to renew the lease for a further two years provided that she delivered written notice of renewal to the lessor not later than 30 days prior to the end of the second year of the lease. The rent for the renewal period would be $1,500 per month, but if the lessee satisfactorily repainted the premises in the first month of the renewal period, the rent would be $1,400 per month.

1(b). An insurance policy provides that in consideration for an annual premium, payable in advance, the insurer will reimburse the insured for any loss by fire occurring on the insured premises, provided that the insured furnishes satisfactory proof of loss to the insurer within 30 days of the loss.

1(c). On June 1, the owner of land granted an option to purchase the land. The prospective buyer had until June 30 to exercise the option. On June 10, a second buyer expressed interest in purchasing the land, and the owner entered into a contract with him under which she agreed to sell it for $100,000 if the grantee of the option failed to exercise it by its expiration on June 30.

1(d). Following discussions on the possible sale of a car, the owner of the car writes to the prospective buyer, stating, "I will sell you my car for $5,000 on condition that you communicate your acceptance to me within five days of the date of this letter."

2. Wendy Vendee entered into a contract with Homer Sellar for the purchase of Homer's house for $200,000. The contract, recorded on a standard form, provided that Wendy would pay $50,000 in cash on closing and would pay the balance of the price in installments over 15 years. To secure payment of the balance, Homer would take a first mortgage in the property, to be recorded at the time of transfer. In a blank space at the end of the form, Homer wrote the sentence, "This contract is contingent on seller's approval of buyer's credit report." Both parties initialed this handwritten addition.

Shortly after the contract was signed, Homer obtained a credit report on Wendy. It showed that Wendy had gone on a credit-card spending binge five years ago and had to file a voluntary bankruptcy petition to discharge unmanageable debt. The report also showed that since obtaining her bankruptcy discharge, Wendy apparently no longer used credit cards and had not defaulted on any other debts. Homer considers bankruptcy to be shameful and thinks it immoral for a person to go on a spending spree and then file bankruptcy to get out of paying her debts in full. He no longer wished to deal with someone as unworthy as Wendy, and he certainly did not trust her enough to give her credit. Homer therefore disapproved the credit report and declared the sale to be terminated.

Wendy objected and said that Homer had no basis to reject her credit report. Wendy can show that Homer's attitude is tougher than that prevailing among financial institutions in the consumer credit industry, which would be likely to approve Wendy's credit under these circumstances. The reasoning in the industry is that a five-year-old abuse of credit and bankruptcy filing should not be held against a borrower who has behaved responsibly since then, particularly when the loan applied for is fully secured by a mortgage on real property. Did Homer have the right to disapprove the report and cancel the sale?

3. Assume that the contract between Wendy Vendee and Homer Sellar was on slightly different terms: Like the contract in Example 2, it provided for the sale of the home to Wendy for $200,000, of which $50,000 would be paid in cash on closing, and the balance would be paid over 15 years, secured by a mortgage on the property. The contract had no condition concerning a credit report. Instead, in the blank space at the end of the form contract, the parties had included the following handwritten term:

> This contract is subject to the buyer's sale of her present home for not less than $165,000 within 30 days hereof.

The reason for including this term was that at the time of the contract Wendy already owned a smaller house that she needed to sell, so that she could use the proceeds to pay the $50,000 cash due on closing. Wendy's old home was subject to a mortgage of $100,000, so she had to sell it for at least $165,000 to pay the mortgage, broker's fees, and other costs, leaving $50,000 clear for her cash payment to Homer.

Consider the following separate and distinct factual variations:

3(a). After signing the contract, Wendy decided that she would save having to pay realtor's commission by marketing the house herself. She bought one of those "for sale by owner" kits, erected "for sale" signs, and placed advertisements in the paper. Unfortunately, Wendy is overbearing and insensitive and has no skill in dealing with people. Although several prospective buyers responded to her advertising, she managed to scare all of them away by her rude and aggressive sales technique. As a result, she had not managed to sell her house by the end of the 30-day period. Wendy therefore claims that she is no longer obliged to buy Homer's house. Is she correct?

3(b). On the 25th day after signing the contract with Homer, Wendy received an offer to sell her house for $165,000. In terms of the offer, the offeror's commitment to proceed with the purchase was contingent on the offeror being able to obtain financing. Wendy accepted the offer on the next day. The offeror immediately submitted a loan application to a mortgage company, but no decision had been made on the application four days later, the expiry date of the 30-day period under the contract between Wendy and Homer. What is the status of Wendy's contract with Homer?

3(c). After signing the contract with Homer, Wendy decided that she would not sell her existing house as planned, but would keep it as rental property. To raise the down payment, she would instead borrow the $50,000 from her sister. She immediately called Homer, explained this, and told him that she waived the condition. Does Homer have any grounds for objection?

4. Consider a third variation of the contract between Wendy and Homer. As before, it provided for the sale of the house to Wendy for $200,000, of which $50,000 was to be paid in cash on closing. However, unlike the prior examples, the contract did not provide for Homer himself to extend credit for the sale on security of a mortgage (Wendy was to seek her own financing) and Wendy did not currently own a home. The contract was therefore not contingent on a satisfactory credit report or on the sale of existing property. Instead, it contained the following provision:

> This sale is subject to the buyer obtaining a loan from a bank or other lending institution, secured by a first mortgage on the property purchased hereunder, in an amount of not less than $150,000, extending for a term of at least 15 years, and at a rate of interest not exceeding eight percent per annum. If, after the exercise of due diligence, the buyer is unable to obtain financing on these terms, this contract shall terminate, and neither party shall have any liability to the other.

Immediately after Wendy signed the agreement, she consulted a mortgage broker. Upon reviewing Wendy's truthful and accurate financial statement, the broker told Wendy that her income was insufficient and her indebtedness too large to qualify her for a loan of $150,000 from any lender that he knew. This made Wendy realize that she had bought a house beyond her means, and she was relieved that the financing contingency had been included in the agreement of sale. She promptly notified Homer of termination of the sale on the ground that the condition had not been satisfied. On hearing that Wendy had given up after an interview with a single broker and had done nothing more to seek financing, Homer claimed that Wendy had not exercised due diligence in trying to satisfy the condition. Is he correct?

5.   Primo Contracting Co. is a general contractor. It was engaged in the construction of an office building under a contract with the owner of the property. Primo entered into a subcontract with President Conditioning, Inc. (PC) for the supply and installation of the building's air conditioning unit. The subcontract between Primo and PC required the unit to be installed by July 1, and further stated: "The price due to PC under this contract shall not be payable until the project's architect has certified that the air conditioning unit has been properly installed in working order and, following such certification, Primo has received payment for this work from the owner."

PC competently installed a fully operational air conditioning unit by June 15. On June 17, before the unit had been inspected by the architect, the owner of the property filed for bankruptcy. The owner's estate is hopelessly insolvent so no funds will be available to pay any of the debts arising from the construction. The project was abandoned and the architect resigned. Primo has not been paid for any work done during the last month, including the air conditioning.[6]

PC has demanded payment from Primo, but Primo has refused on the grounds that neither of the two conditions to its obligation to pay — the architect's certification and the owner's payment — have been fulfilled. Is this a good argument?

6.   Larson E. Grand owned an old vacant office building in a bad part of town. Because the building was unoccupied, he did not see the point of paying for burglary insurance, but he did need insurance for destruction to the building itself by fire, vandalism, and other disasters. He therefore bought an insurance policy covering these risks from Equity & Fidelity Indemnity Co., Inc. (E. & F.) The relevant terms of the policy stated:

(a) In consideration for the premium paid, Insurer undertakes to reimburse Insured for any loss resulting from damage to or destruction of the above-described premises caused by fire, storm, explosion, nuclear accident, civil commotion, or vandalism.

(b) For the purposes of this policy, "vandalism" is restricted to and includes only wilful and malicious physical injury to the premises and excludes any loss by pilferage, theft, or burglary.

(c) No claim shall be paid under this policy unless Insured notifies Insurer of loss within seven days thereof, and submits proof of

---

6. You may be aware that unpaid contractors and subcontractors are entitled to a statutory lien (called a construction lien or a mechanic's lien) for unpaid labor or materials used to improve real property. This lien attaches to the realty and it arises in favor of a subcontractor even though it had no contract with the owner. Disregard these lien rights for the purposes of this Example. (Assume, say, that the lien rights are worthless because the property is fully encumbered by a pre-existing mortgage.)

loss within a further 14 days. No action taken by Insurer to investigate such claim shall operate as a waiver of any of the terms of this policy.

The plumbing in the building was copper pipe that has some value as scrap. A few months after the policy was issued, someone broke into the building and removed all the copper pipe. To extract the pipe, the thief ripped open walls and floorboards, causing extensive damage to the building.

Larson discovered the break-in the next morning. He had to leave town on a trip that day, and did not report the loss to E. & F. until his return, eight days later. When he notified E. & F. of the loss, he told its representative that the break-in had occurred eight days previously. The E. & F. representative did not comment on this. E. & F. sent out a loss adjuster the next day. After inspecting the premises, the adjuster said "Get estimates for fixing this damage and get them to me as soon as you can. I must warn you, however, that this looks like burglary, not vandalism, and I don't think it is covered by your policy." Larson protested that it looked like vandalism of the worst kind, but the adjuster said that there was no point in their arguing about it. The claims department would make the decision, so Larson should submit the estimates and see what happens. Larson submitted the estimates a couple of days later. Shortly afterwards, he received a letter from E. & F. rejecting his claim on the basis that the loss resulted from burglary and was excluded from coverage. Should Larson accept this?

7.   Sue Burbanite owned a piece of land in a fast-growing suburb. Sprawl-ing Malls, Inc., a developer of shopping malls, had some interest in building a mall on Sue's land. However, it needed to study more carefully the economic feasibility of the project, and to raise adequate funds from investors. In 2005, Sprawling Malls entered into negotia-tions with Sue to acquire an option to purchase the land. Sprawling Malls believed that it could conduct a comprehensive feasibility study and attract investors within a year. It therefore proposed buying a year's option to purchase the property. Sue was amenable to this, and the parties ultimately entered into an option contract on December 1, 2005, under which Sprawling Malls was given the option to purchase the land for $1.5 million. The provisions of the contract concerning the option itself were as follows: Sprawling Malls agreed to pay Sue $10,000 for the year's option, payable on the sign-ing of the contract. If Sprawling Malls wished to exercise its option to purchase the property it was required ". . . by not later than November 30, 2006, to deliver to Sue Burbanite written notice of its intention to exercise the option."

After the contract was signed, Sprawling Malls paid Sue the $10,000 and began its feasibility study. By June 2006 the study had been completed at a cost of $300,000. It showed the shopping center development to be a viable project. Armed with the study, Sprawling Malls began to solicit investors. After some considerable effort, it finally managed to raise the necessary capital by late November 2006. On November 29, it mailed written notice to Sue, exercising its option to purchase the land. The letter was delayed in the mail and not received until December 1.

Sue had wanted to escape her contract with Sprawling Malls because the value of the property had increased since December 2005, and she would now be able to sell it for more than $1.5 million. She therefore rejected the attempted exercise of the option on the basis that it was received after the expiry of the option period. Does Sprawling Malls have a basis for challenging this?

Explanations

1(a). The lessee's payment of rent and the lessor's obligation to give the lessee use and occupation of the premises are dependent promises. That is, each party's performance is a promissory condition of the other's. Even if the conditional nature of the promises is not expressly stated in the lease, it is easily construed as being what the parties reasonably must have intended. The parties have structured the lease so that the performance of each is broken into monthly segments. The lessee's payment of the month's rent is a condition precedent to that month's tenancy, and the lessor's making the premises available for that month is in turn a condition precedent to the next rent payment. (So, if either party breaches his obligation, the other can withhold the next performance in the sequence in addition to suing for damages for breach of the lease.)

With regard to the lessee's renewal option, her delivery of notice of renewal within the prescribed time is an express condition precedent to the extension of the lease for another two years. (Its conditional nature is expressed in the language of the lease by use of the term "provided that.") It is not a promissory condition, nor even a condition subject to an implied promise to use best efforts, because the lessee has no obligation to renew and need not deliver the notice unless she wishes to extend the lease. If she does want to extend, she must comply exactly with the terms of the condition. As an express condition, it will be strictly enforced.

If the lessee does exercise the renewal option, the same set of promissory conditions — payment of rent and occupation of the premises — continue through the renewal period. In addition, the lease contains another condition intended to give the lessee a choice of alternative performances: If she paints the premises in the first month of the renewal period, her rent is reduced by $100 per month. Although this condition does not use clear language of condition such as "on condition that" or "provided that," its conditional nature is clear enough to qualify it as express. It is not a promissory condition, in that the lessee has no obligation to paint the premises if she would rather pay the extra rent.

Finally, if the lessee does elect to paint the premises, she implicitly promises to do so in a workmanlike manner. The rent reduction is contingent on the paint job being satisfactory to the lessor. This condition of satisfaction is subject to a promise (implied in law, if not expressed) that the lessor will act reasonably or in good faith in assessing whether the painting is satisfactory. The preference is for an objective standard to measure satisfaction, particularly if the work is commercial or technical in nature. However, a subjective good faith standard is used if it is clear from the wording of the contract or from the nature of the performance that the parties intended satisfaction to be measured by the individual taste of the party who is to make the judgment.

1(b). The insurer's obligation to indemnify the insured is subject to four conditions precedent. The first is that the insured has paid the premium due under the policy. The second is that a loss by fire on the premises occurs, the third is that the insured gives proof of loss within the time specified, and the fourth is that the insurer is satisfied with the proof.

Payment of the premium appears to be a condition precedent to coverage. The language of the payment term, as suggested by the question, simply denotes the premium as consideration and does not, in so many words, expressly call it a condition of coverage. However, this does appear to be the import of the wording. The insured may or may not have promised to pay the premium. If he committed himself to pay it, it is a promissory condition. However, the application for coverage may not have obliged him to pay, but may merely have provided that coverage would not be extended unless it was paid. In that case, it is a pure condition.

The condition of loss does not use expressly conditional terminology, but there can be no doubt that loss must be a condition precedent to indemnity. This is so obvious that the implication of a condition is inevitable. It is also obvious that this cannot be a promissory condition. It would be a bizarre policy indeed, under which the insured committed himself to suffer a loss.

The condition of notice is express. It is also a pure condition because the insured has no obligation to submit the proof if he does not wish to claim under the policy. That is, the insurer would have no claim for breach if the insured failed to notify of loss. It would simply have no duty to indemnify.

The condition of satisfactory proof, like the condition of satisfaction in Example 1(a), is subject to an implied promise that limits the insurer's discretion to be dissatisfied. Unquestionably, satisfaction must be measured here on an objective reasonableness standard.

1(c). The owner's obligation to sell the land to the buyer is subject to an express condition precedent that the option-holder does not exercise the option by June 30. This is not a promissory condition, because the seller makes no promise that the option will not be exercised. The purpose of the condition is to allow the parties to execute the sale agreement immediately, but to protect the seller from having committed to sell the property to two people. The condition enables the seller to escape the second contract if the grantee of the option (the first offeree) binds her by exercising the option. If the grantee of the option does not exercise it, the seller's obligation to convey the property becomes due, and accordingly, so does the buyer's obligation to pay for it. Even in the absence of expressly conditional language, these mutual promises of performances are construed as conditions of each other. Unless a different sequence is prescribed by the contract, they are deemed to be concurrent conditions because both are capable of instantaneous performance.

1(d). The letter is an offer, and one could say, broadly speaking, that the creation of the contract is conditional on acceptance within the time prescribed. However, despite the use of the word "condition" in the letter, the acceptance within five days is not a condition at all, in the sense used in this chapter. It is simply the time specified for acceptance. If the offer is accepted in time, a contract will be formed, under which the car is exchanged for $5,000. At that point, conditions in the contract will come into effect. The seller's promise to deliver the car and the buyer's promise to pay for it are dependent promises. Even if not expressly stated to be conditions of each other, they are construed promissory conditions. As in Example 1(c), they can be performed at the same time and are therefore deemed concurrent unless the contract specifies an order of performance.

2. This Example builds on *Foreman v. Benson* discussed in section 16.8.2, but provides detailed facts to allow you to apply the principles of the case. The provision concerning the credit report is a condition of

satisfaction. It is an express condition precedent to Homer's obligation to sell the property to Wendy on credit. The purpose of the condition is obvious: It is intended to protect Homer from having to extend credit to Wendy if she proves to be uncreditworthy. Of course, Homer could have checked Wendy's credit before making the contract, but this would have delayed execution of the contract and risked loss of the deal. Homer avoided this risk by entering the contract immediately, subject to a satisfactory credit report.

A condition of satisfaction is not fully a promissory condition because Homer does not promise that he will be satisfied. However, this does not mean that Homer has unfettered discretion in deciding whether to be satisfied. Even if nothing is expressed in the contract to restrict his discretion, the law implies an obligation on him to exercise judgment honestly or reasonably. Unless the contract indicates differently, the objective standard is preferred, especially if the judgment involves matters of technical or commercial quality. The subjective standard of good faith is confined to contracts in which it is clearly contemplated that the performance must appeal to the party's aesthetic sense or personal taste.

The satisfaction condition simply refers to Homer's approval of the credit report and gives no indication of how his satisfaction is to be judged. Creditworthiness is quintessentially a matter of commercial utility, capable of being judged by market standards. Therefore, unless the contract clearly calls for a subjective evaluation, a buyer who submits to a credit check is not likely to have assumed the risk of subjecting herself to the seller's idiosyncrasies. Therefore, the fact that Homer has atypically strong moral qualms about bankruptcy is probably not good enough a basis for his dissatisfaction. He must judge Wendy's credit history purely on the basis of whether a person with her credit history presents a risk of default beyond a reasonably acceptable level.

However, even if we hold Homer to an objective standard, that does not automatically mean that we should apply the industry standard suggested by Wendy. Homer is not a member of the consumer financing establishment, but a simple homeowner who is selling his home on credit. A large and wealthy institution, which can distribute risks of default among many customers, is likely to be less risk-averse than a private seller. For this reason, the question is not what would constitute a reasonable credit report for the consumer credit industry, but what would be an acceptable report for a self-financing private seller. In other words, the answer suggested here is that an objective test be used, but the reasonable person evaluating the report should not be a professional lender, but a lender in Homer's position.

3(a). Because Wendy cannot afford to buy Homer's property without first selling her existing home, she has sensibly made her obligation to Homer contingent on selling it. That is, to avert the risk of being committed to Homer without any prospect of raising the $50,000, Wendy has agreed with Homer that her obligation to purchase his property is subject to the express condition precedent that Wendy can sell her home in 30 days. Although this is not a fully promissory condition, in that Wendy does not absolutely commit to ensuring that the house will be sold, it is subject to the implied promise that Wendy will make a diligent effort to try to fulfill the condition. Diligence is not to be judged entirely subjectively, because Homer cannot be taken to have assumed the risk of idiosyncratic or irrational behavior.

Therefore, the test is whether Wendy made an honest and genuine effort, as may reasonably be expected from a person in her position. Wendy may have tried hard to sell her house, but that does not seem good enough. Quite apart from Wendy's unfortunate personality, she was apparently not an experienced dealer in real estate. Given the short time provided in the contract for the satisfaction of the condition, she should not have attempted to sell the house on her own. This conclusion is reinforced by the fact that the price to be realized to satisfy the condition took broker's commission into account, indicating that the parties' reasonable expectation was that a broker would be used.

If it is found that Wendy did not satisfy her implied obligation to use best efforts, this would be a ground for excusing the condition, so that the condition is deemed fulfilled. Homer can insist on her performance. If she fails to render it, she is in breach and Homer can sue for appropriate relief.

3(b). The condition is that Wendy must sell her house within 30 days of the date of her contract with Homer. Because the contract expressly requires the conditional event to occur within a stated time, exact compliance with the time period is required, and failure of occurrence within that time is non-fulfillment of the condition. However, the problem raised by this question centers on the meaning of the condition: What is meant by "sale"? The question serves as a reminder that even where a condition is express, it may be stated in ambiguous language that requires interpretation or construction. If the "sale" is accomplished upon execution of the sale agreement, the condition has been satisfied. But if the "sale" is regarded as suspended until the contingency of financing is met, it occurred beyond the 30-day period.

There is no evidence that the parties discussed or otherwise manifested what they intended by use of the word "sale," so there may be no factual basis for interpretation unless some pertinent and applicable market usage can be shown. In the absence of evidence of meaning, the court must construe the meaning of the term so as best to give effect to what the parties reasonably must have intended. Legally, when Wendy accepted the offer from her buyer, a complete and binding contract of sale was formed. Although that sale was itself subject to a condition precedent, it is an effective contract. A binding contract came into being upon execution, even though her buyer's duties of performance would not become due until the condition was satisfied. On this view, the sale did occur within the 30-day period. This means, of course, that Wendy took a risk by entering into a contingent sale of her existing house, because if her buyer cannot get financing, she is stuck. Wendy could argue that the financing contingency was included to guard against this very risk, so the word "sale" must apply only to a sale that is final and non-contingent. A court may accept this argument, but it stretches the plain meaning of the word "sale." We can infer that Wendy herself understood her conditional sale to qualify as a "sale." Why else would she have accepted the offer from the buyer?

Even if we are to accept that "sale" does not include a conditional sale, so the condition was not fulfilled, Homer has additional arguments to hold Wendy to the contract. Wendy's actions could constitute a waiver of the condition. Alternatively, Wendy may have failed to make best efforts by accepting this offer instead of spending the next few days trying to get a better one.

3(c). Although Wendy could have abandoned this condition had it been solely for her benefit, the condition was not necessarily intended for her protection alone, and she therefore should not be able to waive it unilaterally. In addition to allowing her an escape if she cannot sell her house, the condition ensures that upon buying Homer's house, Wendy will have discharged the mortgage debt on her prior home. As the person financing Wendy's purchase of his house, Homer has an obvious stake in the level of her debt and may reasonably have taken this into account in agreeing to extend credit to her for the balance of the price. If she keeps her existing house and borrows money for the down payment, she increases her debt load, which may heighten the risk that she will default on her mortgage payments to Homer. (Although his mortgage in the property does secure his right to payment, foreclosure is inconvenient and costly, and there is always a danger that the proceeds of a foreclosure sale will not fully cover the balance of the mortgage.)

4. Like the conditions in Examples 2 and 3, the financing contingency is not fully a promissory condition, but the beneficiary party (Wendy)

does commit to make best efforts to attempt its satisfaction. As long as she diligently applied for financing, she can escape the contract without liability for breach if she fails to obtain it. Unlike the previous example, Wendy's promise of due diligence is expressed in the contract and need not be construed. The sole question is whether her single discouraging interview with a mortgage broker was enough of an effort to qualify as due diligence.

The question of whether a buyer used best efforts to try to have the condition satisfied is factual, to be decided under all the circumstances. In *Luttiger v. Rosen*, discussed in section 16.8.1, the court found that although the buyer had applied to only one lender, this was enough to satisfy the best efforts standard because the buyer had reliable information that applications to other lenders would be futile. Notwithstanding, the buyer takes a high risk of breaching the promise of best efforts by making such a modest effort. Wendy's effort is even feebler than the buyer's in *Luttiger* because she gave up on the strength of what the broker told her and did not even try to get financing. Unless she can show that the broker was correct, so that loan applications would be a pointless waste of time, she had a duty to make applications. The fact that her prospects of financing are uncertain should not dissuade her. After all, if she was assured of a loan, she would not have needed the protection of the condition. Wendy's decision not to make any loan applications looks especially bad in light of the fact that her desire to buy the house cooled once she realized that the house was too expensive for her. That creates the suspicion that she lost the motivation to make any further effort at all.

5. The contract expressly makes payment conditional upon the *architect's certification* of proper completion of PC's performance. It necessarily follows from this express condition that the proper performance itself is also a condition precedent to payment. Although the architect has not given the certificate, it is clear that the condition of proper completion of the work has been satisfied. Primo does not contend otherwise. The certification is a condition of satisfaction under which the performance must meet a standard of competence to be evaluated by a third-party expert. Although the architect was employed by the owner of the property and is its agent, her role in this contract between Primo and PC is to act on behalf of Primo.

Obviously, Primo cannot evade fulfillment of the condition simply because the architect is no longer available to inspect the work. Although it is not Primo's fault that the architect resigned, its implied duty to cooperate in the fulfillment of the condition requires it to ensure that inspection takes place within a reasonable time of completion of PC's performance. Its failure to facilitate occurrence of the condition is a wrongful hindrance of fulfillment which excuses the condition. (Alternatively, excuse could also be based on the argument that Primo waived the condition by declining to have the work inspected within a reasonable time. Another alternative is to argue excuse on grounds of unfair forfeiture because PC would surely be grievously harmed if the technicality of non-certification could be allowed to deny payment for satisfactory work. However, forfeiture is a discretionary doctrine that is not needed if there are more concrete bases for excuse.)

Primo argues that its receipt of the *owner's payment* for the air conditioning is a condition precedent to its obligation to pay PC. If this is so, Primo would be justified in not paying, because it has not been (and will not be) paid for the air conditioning. The parties' intent on this matter is a question of interpretation. If there is extrinsic evidence that casts light on the meaning of the clause (such as evidence of trade usage or of discussions between the parties), this would help to determine the intent of the language. If no such evidence is available, the reasonable meaning of the wording of the contract must be sought in light of the purpose of the contract as a whole. As we are told of no usage or other contextual evidence, our interpretation will be based solely on the language used in the contract.

At first sight, the language seems relatively clear. Payment from the owner does sound like an express condition precedent. It follows the condition of certification in the same sentence. This suggests that both of these events must occur before Primo's payment obligation falls due. However, courts interpreting payment provisions like this one such as the courts in *Thos. J. Dyer Co.* and *Peacock Construction* cited in section 16.10, tend to be skeptical of the argument that they are intended to be conditions. Unless the language (read in light of any contextual evidence that might be available) makes it very clear that the owner's payment was intended as a condition precedent, the assumption is that a term like this is more likely to have been intended as merely fixing a time for payment. Therefore, even if the owner does not pay the contractor, the contractor must pay the subcontractor within a reasonable time. The reasoning behind this interpretation is that, unless the parties express such an intention unequivocally, they cannot be taken to have placed the risk of the owner's non-payment on the subcontractor, who has no contractual relationship with the owner but is employed by the prime contractor. Risk is more rationally left with the prime contractor, who has dealt with the owner and had the opportunity to evaluate its credit-worthiness. Therefore, although the language in the contract does admit of the interpretation that the owner's payment is a condition, it is not strong enough to overturn the usual assumption that the parties could not have intended to shift the risk of the owner's default to PC.

6. Two express conditions precedent are implicated in this dispute. The first is that a loss must occur of a kind covered by the policy. The second is that the insured must follow the prescribed claim procedure.

Has there been fulfillment of the condition precedent that a covered loss occurred? The policy covers loss by vandalism, which it defines as wilful and malicious damage to the premises. However, it specifically excludes coverage for pilferage, theft or burglary. Therefore, the first issue is one of interpreting the language of the policy to determine if the losses are encompassed within the risk that is insured. Because this is a standard form insurance policy drafted by the insurer, the contra proferentum rule is particularly applicable. Any doubt in the meaning of a provision in it will be resolved against the insurer.

There are two separate items of loss caused by the removal of the pipe: The loss of the pipe itself and the damage caused to walls and floors in removing it. Does this loss result from vandalism? Vandalism is commonly thought of as the deliberate harming or defacement of property, purely for its own sake. However, the concept is broad enough to include purposeful damage motivated by economic gain. It is beyond doubt that the thief acted wilfully (deliberately) and maliciously (with intent to violate the law and Larson's rights) in causing the loss. This applies not only to the taking of the pipe, but also to the concomitant destruction. The problem is that the policy draws a distinction between loss from vandalism and that from burglary, so when a wrongful act gives rise to injury of both kinds, the apparent conflict in terms must be reconciled.

In *United States Fidelity & Guaranty Co. v. Bimco Iron & Metal Corp.*, 464 S.W.2d 353 (Tex. 1971), an insurance policy similarly distinguished vandalism, which it covered, from burglary which it excluded. Burglars entered the insured premises and stole electrical transformers and wiring, causing damage to the building.

The court narrowly construed "burglary" to exclude from coverage only the theft of personal property from the premises. It correspondingly enlarged the meaning of "vandalism" to include any malicious damage to the building, even if motivated by theft of a component of the structure. The court held that the insurer was obliged to reimburse the insured not only for the damage to the structure, but also for the value of the electrical components that were removed. (A concurring judge would have confined reimbursement to damage to the structure because he felt that once property had been removed, this constituted a loss from burglary that was excluded by the policy.) If this interpretation is applied to Larson's policy, it covers both the damage to the building and the value of the pipe that was removed.

Has the insured followed the prescribed claim procedure? Even if the loss is covered by the policy, satisfying the first condition precedent, E. & F. is still not obliged to indemnify Larson for the loss unless the second condition — notice within seven days of loss and proof of loss 14 days thereafter — is also fulfilled. Because the condition is express, strict compliance is required. Larson's late notice failed to satisfy the condition exactly. This would preclude recovery under the policy unless there is a basis for excusing strict compliance.

Larson was about a day late in giving notice of his claim. However, E. & F. may have tacitly waived the condition of seven-day notice by not raising the delay during the phone call reporting the loss, and by sending an adjuster out to investigate the claim, knowing that the loss had occurred eight days before. In addition, both the adjuster and the letter rejecting the claim based the rejection on the coverage, not on the late notice. A waiver does not have to be by express words. It can be inferred from conduct if the party knows or has reason to know of non-compliance with a condition and yet acts as if the condition is satisfied. (Such conduct could also give rise to an estoppel, but waiver is a better theory because Larson has taken no detrimental action in reliance on the representation.) A waiver of rights without consideration is effective provided that the condition is ancillary and technical, rather than a material component of the exchange. Although prompt notice is important to an insurer, who needs the opportunity to investigate a claim while it is fresh, a relatively short delay in notice is likely to be interpreted as a waivable ancillary matter.

The policy states that the insurer does not waive rights under the policy by investigating a claim. Non-waiver clauses (or non-waiver agreements made after the loss has occurred) provide only limited protection to the insurer. They prevent an inference of waiver merely from the insurer's action in investigating or processing the claim, but they do not annul words or actions that more forcefully point to waiver. For example, in *Connecticut Fire Insurance Co. v. Fox*, 361 F.2d 1 (10th Cir. 1966), a fire damaged the aptly-named Firebird Motor Hotel. The insurer's agent had the insured sign a non-waiver agreement prior to investigating the loss, which stated that investigation would not constitute a waiver of any conditions of the policy, and also that no company representative had authority to waive conditions orally. Despite this clause, the court found that an adjuster had in fact waived timely proof of loss through an ongoing course of interaction with the insured and by settling a claim made by a motel guest. E. & F.'s actions do not as strongly point to waiver, but they did go beyond the narrow range of investigation covered by the non-waiver clause. Neither the adjuster nor the person who processed the claim raised the issue of delay, and the claim was rejected solely on the grounds that the loss was not covered by the policy.

In *Bimco*, the insured had also filed its proof of loss late, so the issue of waiver came up in that case as well. Although the court found that the insurer had waived the condition of timely proof of loss, the case has stronger facts than are present in Larson's claim. In *Bimco*, the insurer had conceded some liability for loss. While it rejected the claim for the stolen electrical equipment, it did accept a claim for damage to a door caused by the burglars. The court said that had the insurer completely denied liability on any grounds, even if it failed to mention the delay, this would not have constituted a waiver. But the fact that it accepted some liability must be taken as a waiver of the tardiness of the proof. Because the insurer had not merely investigated the claim but had sought to settle it by agreeing to pay for the door, the court found that it could not claim protection under a non-waiver agreement which stipulated that investigation of the claim would not operate as a waiver. In our case, E. & F. made no concession of liability at all. On the basis of *Bimco*, the mere fact that it denied liability on grounds other than a delay in notice, is not in itself sufficient as a waiver. However, it could be argued that the approach in *Bimco* is too restrictive, and that a failure to raise or rely on the issue of late notice in denying the claim should be enough to constitute a waiver. This argument is particularly attractive when there has been substantial compliance with the condition, the delay has caused no apparent harm to the insurer, and refusal of payment seems to be based on nothing more than a technicality.

7. The delivery of the notice by November 30, 2006, is an express condition precedent to Sue's obligation to sell the land to Sprawling Malls. It is not a promissory condition — Sprawling Malls has no commitment to ensure that it is satisfied. The purpose of the condition is to give it the discretion to send the notice if it wishes to exercise its option and purchase the land, but imposes no obligation on it to do so if it decides to allow the option to lapse.

Sprawling Malls did decide to exercise its option, but its notice of intent arrived a day late. Because the delivery of notice by November 30 is an express condition, it must be complied with strictly. If Sprawling Malls wanted the land, it had to deliver its notice to Sue within the time stated. Although the notice was mailed before November 30, the contract specified delivery — that is, receipt — by that date, and delivery occurred a day after the deadline. Although a day's delay may be a small deviation from the terms of the condition, this is not taken into account under the rule that requires strict compliance with express conditions. The rationale is that once the parties have taken the trouble to articulate and define the condition, the court should not tamper with their expressed intention. Of course, if the language used to describe the condition is unclear, the court may have some flexibility in interpreting what the condition required, but the language of this condition concerning the manner and time of exercising the option is unambiguous and provides no basis for an interpretation favorable to Sprawling Malls. Therefore, unless there is some ground for excusing exact compliance with the condition, the day's delay in delivery results in non-fulfillment of the condition, and Sprawling Malls has lost its right to buy the land.

The only possible ground for excuse presented by these facts is forfeiture. Courts have the discretion to excuse exact compliance with a condition (or to excuse the condition altogether, if appropriate) when strict enforcement of the condition would result in a disproportionate and unfair forfeiture by one of the parties and a windfall gain by the other. The policy of preventing unfair forfeiture acts as a counterweight to the rule of strict compliance, allowing courts some flexibility in averting particularly harsh and unfair results where there has been a minor or technical non-compliance with a condition. This does not mean, of course, that courts routinely excuse express conditions on the basis of forfeiture. To do so would eliminate the rule of strict compliance. For forfeiture to apply as a ground for excuse, the strict enforcement of the condition must result in undue hardship to the party seeking excuse and inappropriately extensive gain to the beneficiary of the condition. The balance of hardship against unfair gain must be evaluated in light of the relationship of the condition to the exchange as a whole.

In this case, the short delay in delivery of the notice certainly results in considerable hardship to Sprawling Malls: It loses its right to buy the land, gets no benefit from the $10,000 that it paid for the option, and no chance to recoup its substantial expense in conducting the study, or to enjoy the fruits of its efforts in securing financing for the project. True, it bought an option for a year, not a year and a day, so the effect of excusing exact compliance would be to give it a longer option than it purchased. Sprawling Malls was at fault in entrusting such an important communication to the vagaries of the mails, but this was not an egregious sin. It is more the result of poor judgment than of some deliberate attempt to prolong the option period for the purpose of speculating for an additional time at Sue's expense. Looking at the delay from Sue's perspective, we must recognize that she bargained on being bound to the option until no later than November 30. The exact duration of an option is generally regarded as material, and a day's extension should not be assumed to be a trivial matter. However, the equities do not strongly favor strict compliance: She received a substantial payment for the option; the price of the land itself is apparently fair, based on its market value at the time of contracting; she has not yet taken any action in reliance on the lapse; and her motivation in refusing to accept the notice is that she can do better reselling the land. There may be enough here to tilt the balance in favor of excusing the failure of exact compliance with the condition.

This was the conclusion reached on similar facts in *Holiday Inns of America v. Knight*, 450 P.2d 42 (Cal. 1969). Holiday Inns had purchased an option to buy land. The initial period of the option was one year, but it could be extended annually for a further four years. To extend it, Holiday Inns had to pay a renewal fee of $10,000 per year, to be made by July 1 of each year. Holiday Inns had renewed the option for two years and had developed adjacent land over this period, thereby increasing the value of the property subject to the option. It intended to renew the option for a third time, and mailed its check for the renewal fee just before due date. However, the grantor did not receive it until July 2 and refused to extend the option. Holiday Inns successfully sued for a declaratory judgment that the option had been validly extended. The court excused the failure of strict compliance on the ground that it would be an unfair forfeiture for Holiday Inns to lose its option because of a short delay. The court based this conclusion on the fact that the delay did not have a material impact on the exchange, Holiday Inns had not been attempting to take advantage of the grantor by extending the option beyond the period purchased, and it would be unfair to make it sacrifice the $30,000 in option fees that it had already spent for the first three years of the option. (Although the development on the adjacent land could be seen as further justification for excusing the condition, giving Holiday Inns a stronger case on the equities than Sprawling Malls, the court did not base its determination on this fact.)

Breach and Repudiation

§17.1 THE SCOPE OF THIS CHAPTER: NON-FULFILLMENT OF A PROMISE

The distinction was drawn in Chapter 16 between the non-fulfillment of a condition, which excuses the conditional performance, and the failure to honor a promise, which results in liability for breach of contract. If a term is a promissory condition — that is, one of the parties undertook that it would be satisfied — its non-fulfillment has the combined effect of entitling the other party both to withhold performance and to seek a remedy for breach. Chapter 16 concentrated on the effect of conditions and their non-fulfillment. This chapter considers the impact and consequences of the breach of a promise. Because promises are so often conditions as well (promissory conditions), a failure to perform often constitutes both a breach of the promise and non-fulfillment of a condition. Therefore, while we can make this distinction for the purpose of analysis, it is important to understand that in many cases a single default in performance raises the question of both breach and non-fulfillment.

An example will help to frame the issues and make the discussion less abstract: Violet Ultra decided to add a deck to the back of her home so that she could enjoy her favorite leisure activity — sunbathing. On July 1, Violet entered into a contract with Woody Sawyer, a carpenter, under which Woody undertook to build a $20' \times 15'$ deck onto Violet's home for $5,000. The contract, written on a sheet of paper and signed by the parties, states that Violet will make an initial cash payment of $2,000 to Woody by 5 P.M. on July 6. Woody will begin work on July 7 and will complete the deck by July 9, upon which Violet will pay him the balance of $3,000 in cash. Although no express language of condition has been used, it is easily inferable from the sequence set out in the contract that the parties intend Violet's down payment on July 6 to be a promissory condition precedent — the payment is not only expressly promised, but is also impliedly a condition precedent to Woody's performance. Woody expressly promises to begin the work one day later on July 7 and to complete it within three days, by July 9. The fact that final payment is to be made on completion gives rise to the inference that Woody's performance is not merely a promise, but also an implied condition precedent to Violet's final performance, the $3,000 payment. As there is no further performance contingent on this payment, it is a pure promise.

If both parties perform as undertaken, the promises are honored, the conditions fulfilled, and the transaction ends happily. As Restatement Second §235(1) says (maybe somewhat self-evidently), a contractual duty is discharged by full performance. However, all kinds of things could go wrong: At some point before performance is to commence on July 6, one of the parties may renege or indicate an intention to breach the contract; or Violet may not make the down payment at all, or in full, or on time; or Woody may not show up for work on July 7, or may not complete the deck by July 9; or Woody may begin and complete the deck on time, but may make it one foot too short. The purpose of this chapter is to discuss the legal effect of breaches like this relating both to pure promises and to promissory conditions. Sections 17.2-17.6 deal with breach proper (that is, a violation of a promise that occurs at or after performance is due) and section 17.7 examines the particular issues that arise when a party repudiates the contract in advance of the time of his performance. The importance and extent of the breach is a crucial factor throughout this chapter, so we begin by differentiating breaches of different degrees of gravity.

§17.2 THE NATURE OF BREACH

As intimated above, a party breaches a contract by failing, for whatever reason, to honor a promise of performance when that performance falls due. Four questions need to be resolved to establish that a breach of contract has occurred.

First, we must determine the existence and content of the contractual undertaking to ascertain the exact nature and extent of the promise that was made. This involves interpreting the contract through the process discussed in Chapter 10.

Second, we must establish the date that the promised performance fell due. Although a party can repudiate a contract before his performance is due (as discussed in section 17.1), a breach by failure to perform or improper performance cannot occur until the time arises for the party's duty to render it. If the contract does not clearly and expressly state the due date for the party's performance, this must be determined by interpretation or construction. Also, if the performance is subject to a condition precedent, it is not due until the condition is satisfied.

Third, we must decide if the performance complied with the promise. Any shortfall from the promised performance is a breach. If the party has not performed at all, non-compliance is easy to see. However, where a party has rendered a performance that is alleged to be inadequate or deficient, the question of whether it satisfies the contractual duty can be difficult to resolve.

Finally, having determined that a breach did occur, we must decide on the severity of the breach and on the promisee's rights in reacting to the breach. Some breaches are serious and fundamental enough to entitle the promisee to withhold any return performance, terminate the contract, and sue for full expectation relief. A breach of this kind is described as total and material. If the breach is less severe, or if the promisor should be given an opportunity to rectify it, the response of terminating the contract is extreme. The promisee is confined to a less drastic remedy that adjusts for the breach by allowing the promisor to cure it or to pay damages to compensate for the shortfall in performance. This final point is the subject of the following sections.

§17.3 THE SIGNIFICANCE OF A BREACH: MATERIAL BREACH OR SUBSTANTIAL PERFORMANCE, AND TOTAL OR PARTIAL BREACH

§17.3.1 Introduction to the Distinction

Any performance that falls short of that promised is a breach. However, some breaches are relatively trivial and others are serious, and not all breaches should be treated in the same way. This essential difference affects the promisee's permissible reaction to the breach. It is helpful to state the basic rule in short diagrammatic form at the outset, and to then expand on and explain it:

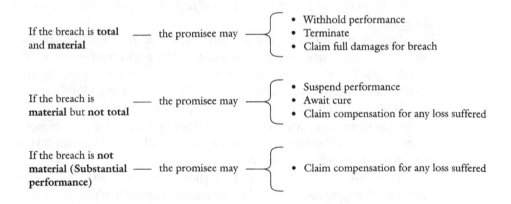

If the breach is **total** and **material**	— the promisee may —	• Withhold performance • Terminate • Claim full damages for breach
If the breach is **material** but **not total**	— the promisee may —	• Suspend performance • Await cure • Claim compensation for any loss suffered
If the breach is **not material (Substantial performance)**	— the promisee may —	• Claim compensation for any loss suffered

The basic point of the rules set out in the diagram is that when a breach is profound enough to qualify as *material and total*, the promisee's expectations under the contract have been completely dashed, and he should therefore have the right to **terminate the contract** — that is, to end the transaction and to sue the breacher for whatever relief is necessary to compensate him for **loss of his bargain**.[1] Because most promises exchanged in a contract are dependent, as explained in section 16.3.3, each party's performance is an express, implied, or construed condition of the other's duty to perform. Therefore, if one party materially breaches his performance obligation, this is not only a breach of the promise, but also *the non-fulfillment of the condition* to any performance that may not yet have been rendered by the other party. This is why a total and material breach permits the victim to *withhold* any

---

1. The nature and extent of these damages is considered in Chapter 18. They could include the extra cost of a substitute transaction, loss of profits, and reimbursement of costs or other losses arising as a consequence of the breach. The basic goal of the damages is to award a sum of money to place the victim in the position he would have been in had no breach occurred.

performance that he has not rendered. (Of course, if the victim of the breach has fully performed before the breach occurs, there is nothing left to suspend, so only termination and damages are in issue.) It should be noted that although the victim of a material and total breach has the right to terminate, withhold performance, and claim full damages for breach, he is not compelled to follow this course. If he wishes to do so, and he believes that the transaction can be saved, he may elect not to terminate and to treat the breach as partial, giving the breacher another chance to perform as promised.

If the breach is not so severe as to undermine the promisee's reasonable expectations, and the performance is substantially in compliance with what was promised, a less drastic reaction is called for. When such *substantial performance* has been rendered, it would be unfairly harsh on the breacher to allow the promisee to terminate, thereby depriving the breacher of all benefit of the bargain and making him liable for the whole range of damages. Of course, substantial performance is nevertheless a breach, because it does fall short of what was promised, so the promisee is not without remedy. However, the promisee is obliged to stick to the contract and perform his side of the bargain, but is entitled to a *monetary adjustment* to compensate for the deficiency in the performance received from the breacher. This measure of damages is usually based on the cost of rectifying the deficiency, or possibly on the actual loss in the value of the performance, as discussed in section 17.3.3. Such damages could be substantially less than what would be awarded for a total and material breach.

The words **"total" and "partial" breach** could be just another way of describing a material breach and a trivial one that results in substantial performance. That is, when a party has substantially performed, the deficiency in performance is said to be a partial breach. However, the reference to total and partial breach is also used to identify a somewhat different but allied issue: A breach is called partial when, even if it may become material in time, it is not yet important enough to so qualify, because there is a possibility of **cure**. That is, the deficiency may be rectified to prevent it from reaching the level of total and material breach. Thus, a partial breach could be one that is potentially serious enough to give rise to a right of termination, but that may be averted if the breacher remedies it in time. This is why the diagram shows that when a breach is partial, there is not yet a right to termination. The victim's recourse is to suspend his own performance while waiting to see if the breach will be cured. If it is, the breach is over (or, at worst, it is a trivial one, resulting in substantial performance) and the only remedy the victim has is to recover any loss that may have been occasioned by the delay in proper performance. However, if the potentially serious partial breach is not cured, it becomes a total, and because it is now material, it gives rise to all the rights and remedies available for such a breach. The concepts of partial breach and cure are discussed more fully in section 17.3.4.

Before leaving this topic, it may be helpful to make one more observation on the slippery semantics of the phrase "partial breach": It is also sometimes used to describe the situation mentioned earlier, in which a *material breach has occurred*, but the victim has elected not to terminate and to give the breacher a chance to remedy it. When that happens, it is often said that the *victim has treated the breach as partial*. In this sense, the breach may have been interpreted as total rather than partial, based on the manifested intent of the parties at the time of contracting, but the victim has decided to treat it as partial. He may therefore have committed himself to proceed as if it were partial, and will be entitled to termination only if there is no subsequent cure.

§17.3.2 What Makes a Breach Material?

The gravity and extent of a breach is a matter of interpretation that can only be resolved by examining the language of the contract in context and evaluating the shortfall in performance in light of the reasonable expectations of the parties. To decide if a breach is material, we use a test similar to that applied to determine the materiality of a term:[2] A breach is material if the failure or deficiency in performance is **so central to the contract** that it **substantially impairs its value** and deeply disappoints the reasonable expectations of the promisee. This is a rather broad and vague test, but it must be so, because materiality is a factual question that cannot be resolved in the abstract. In essence, one must consider the entirety of the exchange contemplated in the contract and decide if the defective or absent performance forms a *significant part of the consideration bargained for* by the promisee.

The extent of the performance affected by the breach — measured both by its value and its proportion to the performance as a whole — is obviously a crucial ingredient. Therefore, for example, a breach at the outset of performance that affects the value of the entire exchange is patently more material than one occurring near the end of the performance and having an impact on only a small aspect of what was promised. However, this is *not the only consideration*, and all the circumstances must be evaluated to judge the significance of a breach. Also, the equities between the parties are relevant here, as elsewhere, so a court may look not only at the deprivation suffered by the promisee as a result of the breach, but also at the degree of hardship (that is, forfeiture) that would be suffered by the breacher if termination were allowed. A breach does not need to be deliberate or willful to be material, and its importance is not diminished merely because it was unintended or undesired by the breacher. However, in balancing the equities, courts may give some weight to the *willfulness or innocence* of the breacher.

---

2. *See* sections 6.5.2, 6.5.3, and 10.2.

The importance of some breaches is so obvious that the resolution of their materiality requires no effort at probing contractual intent. In the contract between Violet and Woody for the construction of a deck for $5,000, one would not need deep analysis to conclude that it would be a material breach if Violet failed to make any down payment at all. Woody's complete failure to build the deck likewise would be unquestionably material. In each case, the party has broken a promise that goes to the very heart of the exchange. However, the issue of materiality would be less obvious if Violet tendered payment of only $1,000 (half the required down payment) on July 6, promising to have another $1,000 ready for Woody when he comes to begin the work on July 7. To decide if that is a material breach, we would have to determine the apparent intent of the parties and ascertain if Woody's contractual rights (including the security he is entitled to expect from advance payment) are seriously affected by having to wait until the next morning for the rest of his down payment. The express written terms of the contract do not indicate the purpose of the down payment. If the contextual evidence provides no explanation, we must assume that its purpose was simply to apportion the risk of giving credit, so it would seem that the short delay is not important as long as payment is made before work begins. But maybe it was understood by the parties that Woody needed the full $2,000 on the day before beginning work to purchase materials to be used in the construction. If so, the delay appears more serious because Woody may have to take time on July 7 to get the materials, causing him delay and possible lost productivity.

As noted earlier, if the breach is material, it so badly defeats the promisee's expectations that she is entitled to terminate the contract and sue for whatever relief is necessary to compensate for loss of the bargain. Although damages are discussed more fully in Chapter 18, a simple example concerning damages is helpful here to illustrate the impact of material breach. If Violet completely fails to pay the down payment, thereby breaching materially, Woody has the right to terminate the contract, not begin the deck, and to sue Violet for the profit that he expected to make on the job, calculated by deducting his costs from the contract price. Conversely, if Violet paid Woody the $2,000 on July 6, but Woody then materially breached by completely failing to build the deck, Violet could terminate, withhold the payment of $3,000 that would otherwise have been due on July 9, and sue for damages. If the reasonable price of having someone else build the deck is no more than Woody had charged under the contract, Violet could at least sue Woody for recovery of the $2,000 paid. But if the reasonable price of having another contractor build the deck is more than the contract price, say $5,500, Violet could sue Woody for $2,500 (the $2,000 paid to Woody plus the extra $500 paid to the new contractor for the equivalent performance). This is how much extra Violet ended up paying, so it must be awarded to her as damages to put her into the position equivalent to full contractual performance—a deck for $5,000.

§17.3.3 Substantial Performance

It is sometimes said that substantial performance is the opposite of material breach. This is not strictly correct because the true opposite of material breach is complete and compliant performance, and substantial performance is nevertheless a breach. However, it is a **non-material** breach. Therefore, once it is determined that a breach is not material, it is necessarily **partial**, and the performance that has been rendered is substantial. This means, of course, that the question of whether substantial performance has been rendered is gauged by the same interpretive process as that used to decide materiality, and the fundamental issue is to decide the relationship of the breach to the overall exchange in values.

For example, in the contract between Violet and Woody, say that it was established that the only reason for providing for the $2,000 down payment was that Woody and Violet wished to distribute the risk of default so that Woody would not have to begin work without the $2,000 in his pocket. If Violet tendered $1,000 in cash on July 6 and promised payment of the remainder of the deposit on the next morning before Woody begins work, the slight delay in performance could be interpreted as a trivial breach. The late payment would therefore qualify as substantial performance. If so, Woody has no basis for terminating. He must accept the deficient performance and be satisfied with whatever monetary adjustment is appropriate. In this case, his only apparent loss is one day's interest on $1,000. Consider a further example: Say that the contract required Woody to treat the finished deck with a clear sealant. Woody completed the deck on time, but he failed to apply the sealant. If, as is likely, this is found to be a relatively minor part of the exchange, his breach is partial and he has substantially performed. As a result, Violet cannot withhold her full payment of the balance of $3,000 and terminate. Rather, she must perform as promised by paying the $3,000, less any offset to which she is entitled as damages for partial breach, which probably would be measured by the reasonable cost of having someone else seal the deck.

The best-known case involving substantial performance is *Jacob & Youngs v. Kent*, 129 N.E. 889 (N.Y. 1921). A builder had completed the construction of a grand country home for a total price of $77,000, a considerable sum in 1914. The owner refused to pay the balance of the contract price (about $3,500) to the builder on the grounds that the builder had breached the contract by installing plumbing pipe of the wrong brand in the house. The builder had overlooked a specification in the contract that called for the pipe to be of Reading brand. As a result more than half the pipe was made by other manufacturers. There was no difference in quality between the Reading pipe and the other brands. However, the owner refused to pay the balance of the contract price on the grounds that the cost of remedying the breach far exceeded this amount. Because the pipe was already encased within the walls, the cost of removing and replacing the wrong pipe would have involved the demolition and rebuilding of a significant portion of the house. Judge Cardozo, writing for the majority of the court, found the breach to be both inadvertent[3] and trivial. Although the specification of the brand was an express promise in the contract, there was nothing in the contract to indicate that the parties considered the actual brand to be a significant term. They were more concerned about the quality of the pipe, and as the other brands were of equal quality, the breach was not material. The dissent disagreed that the breach should be treated as trivial. The owner had specified that Reading pipe be used, and the court should not deprive him of his bargain by assuming that the pipe brand was unimportant to him.

Plante v. Jacobs, 103 N.W.2d 296 (Wis. 1960) and *Lyon v. Belosky Construction*, 247 A.D.2d 730 (1998) further illustrate the considerations that a court takes into account in deciding if a breach is material. In *Plante*, the builder of a house misplaced the wall dividing the living room and kitchen, making the living room about a foot smaller than required by the plan. The court found the breach to be immaterial because the house was built to stock specifications, there was no indication that the buyers considered the exact size of the rooms important, and the placement of the wall did not affect the house's market value. In *Lyon*, the builder centered the roof of the house wrongly. This did not affect the structural utility or soundness of the roof, but it changed the appearance of the roof so that it looked different from how it was supposed to look. Because the house had been completed, the defect could only be rectified by demolishing and rebuilding the roof at a cost of about $73,000. The court found, nevertheless, that the breach was material because the owners had designed and built the house as their home and its aesthetic appearance was of great importance to them.

§17.3.4 Relief for Substantial Performance and Adjustment to Avoid Unfair Forfeiture

Although other remedial issues are deferred to Chapter 18, we have identified the basic principle of relief when a contract has been substantially performed, and it is opportune to pursue it further here. As the above examples show, the general rule is that when one party's performance falls short of that promised in the contract, but performance is sufficient to qualify as substantial, the other party is not entitled to withhold any return performance that is due but has the right to claim damages for the breach.

---

3. The fact that the court found the breach to have been inadvertent, not deliberate, was important to the court's ultimate decision on the appropriate measure of relief. (The remedial aspect of the case is discussed in section 17.3.4.) The dissent disagreed with the majority's finding that the breach was not deliberate.

These damages may be offset against any payment still due to the breacher or, if no such return performance is outstanding, they form the basis of a money judgment against the breacher. The **usual measure of damages** is the **cost** to place the promisee in the position he would have been in had the performance been in **full compliance** with the contract. In most cases, this is represented by an award of the amount of money necessary to *correct the shortfall in performance*. For example, if work was improperly done or property supplied was defective, compensation is measured by the cost to the promisee of rectifying the work or repairing the property. If the breach lies in a failure to complete performance, the completion cost is the proper measure. If the breach involves a delay in performance, compensation is appropriately measured by determining the loss caused by the delay.

In some cases, the cost of rectifying the performance may be *disproportionate* to any realistic loss actually suffered by the promisee. If the court feels that damages measured by the cost of rectification are not an accurate measure of actual harm, but would provide a windfall to the promisee and impose an **unfair forfeiture** on the breacher, the court may adjust the damages to better represent the true harm to the promisee. This measure of damages is based on the *difference in value* between what was promised and what was performed. Because a determination of unfair forfeiture is not simply a matter of arithmetic, and also takes into account the balance of the equities between the parties,[4] a court is more likely to make this adjustment if the non-compliance was inadvertent and is less likely to do so if the failure to perform in accordance with the contract was deliberate.

For example, recall that the contract between Violet and Woody specified that the dimensions of the deck must be $20' \times 15'$. Say that Woody constructed a beautiful deck by the contractual completion date of July 9, but on measuring it, Violet discovered that it was actually $19'8'' \times 14'7''$. Assume that the court finds that the construction of a deck with this slight deficiency in size constitutes substantial performance because it was not a material term of the contract that the deck conform precisely to the specified dimensions. It must then be decided what relief should be given to Violet to compensate for the breach. The cost to rectify the deficiency is likely to be immense, because one cannot add little wood chips to the end of the deck to get it to the right size. Correction would probably, at a minimum, entail some demolition, destruction of some of the materials, and the purchase and installation of new lumber. This would impose liability on Woody for a considerable amount of damages based on the cost of remedying a fault that the court has found to be trivial. (And indeed, as it has been concluded that the precise deck size was not a material part of what Violet reasonably expected, it must follow that she would be unlikely to waste the damage

---

4. The concept of balancing the equities in the context of forfeiture is discussed in sections 16.11.3 and 18.6.6.

award on rectifying so trivial a fault. She would more probably live with the slightly smaller deck and use the money for a more sensible purpose, such as to pay for a nice beach vacation.)

Therefore, on these facts, a court would be likely to find that damages based on the cost of rectification are so disproportionate to the actual harm suffered by Violet that they would be an unfair forfeiture to Woody. This concept is sometimes rather inaccurately described as the doctrine of **"economic waste."** That term derives from the notion that it would be a waste of money for Violet to tear down and rebuild the deck to rectify the minor defect. However, the term is a little misleading because, as already indicated, Violet would not be obliged to waste the money in this way. The award of damages simply involves money changing hands, and Violet could invest her damages award or spend it more productively. The real point is unfair forfeiture. When cost of rectification is not used, damages are based on loss in value. It may be that Violet can establish that a deck of $19'8'' \times 14'7''$ has a market value less than a deck of the size promised. If so, that is her loss. However, if there is no difference in value she is entitled to no damages at all.

Because the majority in *Jacob & Youngs* found that the contract had been substantially performed, Judge Cardozo went on to deal with the issue of unfair forfeiture. Although he recognized that the cost of rectifying the defect is the usual measure of damages, he found that a damages award calculated on the basis of the great cost of reconstruction would be grossly out of proportion to the actual loss suffered by the owner. It would confer an unfair benefit on the owner and unduly penalize the builder for a minor and inadvertent breach. (Cardozo made it clear that it was important that the breach was not willful. Had the breach been deliberate, the court would not have treated it as minor.) The court therefore limited the owner's damages to the difference in market value between a house fitted only with Reading pipe and a house fitted with pipe of the same quality made by different manufacturers. This market difference was zero. The same approach was adopted in *Plante*, in which the court found that the misplacement of the wall did not diminish the market value of the house. By contrast, in *Lyon*, the court rejected the builder's argument that loss in market value should be the basis of measuring damages. Because the appearance of the house was of great importance to the owners, who bought the house to live in, not to resell, the cost of replacement, not market value reduction, was the proper measure.

Khiterer v. Bell, 800 N.Y.S.2d 348 (2005), a small claims court decision, provides a clear and succinct recent application of the doctrine in *Jacob & Youngs*. A patient sued her dentist for fitting porcelain crowns instead of crowns made of porcelain on gold. The court accepted that this was a breach of contract. However, the dentist testified that all-porcelain crowns were no less expensive and were therapeutically superior. It was also apparent that the dentist's breach was inadvertent and not deliberate. The court held that the cost of replacement would be unfairly disproportionate and confined the patient to loss in value. As the patient could show no actual injury, she was awarded nominal damages.

§17.3.5 Partial Breach and Cure

Some breaches have such an immediate, irreparable, and significant impact on the promisee's rights that they are material as soon as they occur, and there is nothing that the promisor can do to rectify them. Other breaches are by nature so trivial that they could never result in a total breach of the contract, even if no attempt was made to remedy them. However, between these poles, there are breaches that are *potentially material* when they occur, but at that stage they are still regarded as partial because they are not yet serious enough to be total. The breacher can prevent such a breach from becoming total by *curing the deficiency* within a reasonable time.

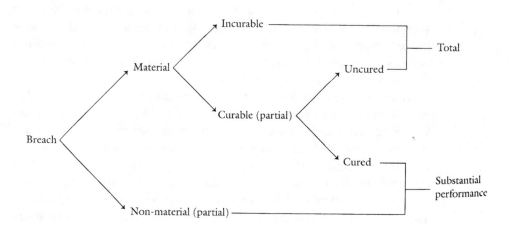

For example, say that the contract for the deck specified that the down payment of $2,000 was to be paid no later than 5 P.M. on July 6. Violet failed to pay by that time. If Woody called shortly afterwards to ask where the payment was, and Violet told him that she no longer wanted the deck and would not pay, the breach would be material and total. Non-performance is absolute and Violet indicates no intent to cure it. However, if Violet's response was that she was running late and would deliver the cash to Woody as soon as she could get out to his place, the issue is more difficult. Failure to pay on time is a breach, but unless payment by precisely 5 P.M. is a material term of the contract (or, to use the well-worn phrase, "time is of the essence"), a short delay in payment may be only a trivial breach. If so, Violet's failure to pay by 5 P.M. is a partial breach, and as there is a prospect of cure, it will only become total once a reasonable time has passed and she has still not paid.

Therefore, if Woody refuses to wait and terminates immediately, he must be able to show that the exact time for payment was such a material term of the contract that even a short delay in payment is a total breach. It cannot be cured because the clock cannot be turned back to eliminate the delay. However, if payment exactly on time was not a material term, Woody must give Violet the opportunity to cure by showing up with the money within a reasonable time. To decide materiality, the contract's language must be interpreted in context. The basic inquiry is whether a delay in payment would have a significant negative impact on Woody's reasonable contractual expectations by seriously affecting the transaction's value to him. Here again, the question of whether the delay is willful or caused by circumstances beyond the promisor's control is not directly relevant to the inquiry into the totality of the breach, but the promisor's state of mind has some bearing on the issue. If the breach was not deliberate, this may signal a greater likelihood of a genuine desire to cure it and could persuade a court in a close case to treat the breach as partial.

On the facts given in the present example, it seems unlikely that payment by exactly 5 P.M. was "of the essence," so Woody probably must afford Violet an opportunity to cure. If he does so, and Violet does attempt a cure, the next difficult question may be whether Violet's cure was *complete* and accomplished within a *reasonable time*. This, again, must be decided with reference to Woody's reasonable expectations under the contract. A few hours' delay may be a trivial breach. But if Violet is a day late, or she shows up a couple of hours later with a check instead of cash, the impact of the delay is more serious. A promisor who waits too long to cure, or whose performance is still not substantially compliant, loses the right to cure. The partial breach thereupon becomes total. It must be reiterated that the promisor does not invariably have the right to cure a breach. Some breaches are fundamental enough that they cannot be fixed at all, or even if they could be reversed, given time, the delay in performance would itself be a material breach.

§17.4 THE RELATIONSHIP BETWEEN THE MATERIALITY OF BREACH AND THE NON-FULFILLMENT OF A CONDITION

The above discussion has intimated how the analysis of conditions, set out in Chapter 16, ties into the issue of breach of promise. It is worth restating this succinctly to dispel any confusion:

Where a term of a contract is both a promise and a condition (a promissory condition), a material and total breach of the promise is also the non-fulfillment of the condition. This is why the promisor can not only sue for damages for the breach, but is also entitled to withhold her own performance, which is contingent on the promissory condition.

If the breach is material, but not total because it can be cured, the promisee cannot immediately sue for damages for breach or terminate the contract. However, the conditional nature of the breached promise allows the promisee to suspend her own performance until such time as the condition is fulfilled by cure.

If the breach is not material so that the promissory condition is substantially performed, the doctrine of substantial compliance with the condition will also apply. This means that the promisee cannot sue for total breach and cannot suspend her own contingent performance, but must perform and seek recourse for the breach through compensation for the shortfall in performance. In *Jacob & Youngs*, Judge Cardozo couched his discussion of substantial performance in the language of conditions. Because he found that the failure to use Reading pipe was a trivial breach, he described the brand specification as an "independent promise." By this he meant that although promises in a contract are normally dependent (that is, promissory conditions of each other) a non-material breach of one of those promises should not be treated as a complete failure of the condition. Therefore, the non-breaching party's remaining obligation of performance must not be treated as conditional on exact fulfillment of the breached promissory condition. As a result, he cannot claim total breach and withhold his return performance, but remains bound to perform, subject to the offset of any damages caused by the breach.

If the breached promise is an express condition so that the doctrine of substantial compliance does not apply, it would be hard to argue that the failure to render performance in exact compliance with the promise could be anything other than a material breach. Any shortfall in performance cannot be treated as substantial performance.

§17.5 SUBSTANTIAL PERFORMANCE UNDER UCC ARTICLE 2: PERFECT TENDER AND CURE

§17.5.1 Perfect Tender

Following the execution of a contract for the sale of goods, the seller is obliged to deliver the goods to the buyer at the time and place specified in the contract. Upon tender of delivery, the buyer has the right to inspect the goods to see if they conform to the contract, and if they do not, the buyer may reject them. Both the inspection and rejection must be within a reasonable time. It is beyond our scope to deal with Article 2's detailed rules concerning the tender and acceptance or rejection of goods. Our concern is with the Code's treatment of substantial performance and cure, which is notably different from the common law.

The rule was established, long before the enactment of the UCC, that the doctrine of *substantial performance is not applicable to a sale of goods*. The buyer is entitled to **"perfect tender"** of the goods ordered and has the **right to reject** goods that **fail to conform exactly** to what was called for by the contract. This rule has been retained in §2.601,[5] which permits the buyer to reject goods that "fail in any respect to conform to the contract." This is reinforced by §2.106(2), which provides for no qualification of substantial conformity, when it defines "conforming" as meaning "in accordance with the obligations under the contract."

Although the perfect tender rule provides little room for a court to recognize substantial performance, there is some scope for avoiding it under the right circumstances. For example, where the buyer's rejection of goods is clearly pretextual — that is, she rejects them on the basis of some minor nonconformity because she no longer wants them, a court may apply the general obligation of good faith and fair dealing to preclude rejection on a technicality.

Also, the rules relating to acceptance and rejection of goods sometimes give the court an opportunity to prevent a rejection of goods on trivial grounds. As noted above, it is beyond our scope to go into the intricacies of rejection, but we can note generally that the buyer must act promptly and follow the proper procedure to effectively reject goods. If the buyer delays beyond a reasonable time or slips up procedurally in rejecting, the rejection is ineffective and the buyer is deemed to have accepted the goods. If the buyer has accepted the goods, she can only thereafter revoke her acceptance if she satisfies a number of requirements, including the requirement that the non-conformity substantially impairs their value. (That is, although the rule of substantial performance does not apply where the buyer rejects the goods, it does apply where the buyer seeks to revoke its acceptance of the goods.) If the goods have been accepted and the acceptance cannot be revoked the buyer is confined by UCC §2.718 to damages based on the loss in value as a result of the nonconformity. The interaction between the perfect tender rule and the buyer's failure to reject the goods is illustrated by *Khiterer v. Bell*, the case discussed in section 17.3.4, in which a dentist fitted crowns made of porcelain instead of gold and porcelain. The court held that the dental services predominated over the sale aspect of the contract, so the common law rule of substantial performance applied. However, it went on to point out that even if this had been predominantly a sale of goods, the perfect tender rule would not have applied because the patient had accepted the

---

5. Section 2.601 is not significantly changed in the 2003 revision of Article 2. The revision makes no change to §2.106(2), and changes §2.508 as explained in footnotes 5 and 6.

crowns by not having them removed for two years after they were fitted. She could thereafter only revoke her acceptance if the nonconformity substantially impaired their value, which it did not.

§17.5.2 Cure

Under prescribed circumstances, UCC §2.508 permits the seller to avoid final rejection of nonconforming goods by curing the deficient tender. Where cure is possible, §2.508 mitigates the harsh effect of the perfect tender rule. The strength of the seller's right to cure depends on whether the seller would have time to affect the cure before the date due for the delivery of the goods under the contract. If the seller tenders delivery before due date, so that the buyer's rejection occurs before that date, the seller has a much greater right to cure than if the goods were delivered on or after due date. The reason for this is the perfect tender rule. Unlike the common law, which treats late performance as a material breach only if the date of performance is material, the perfect tender rule gives the buyer the right to reject late delivery even if time of delivery is not a material term. Section 2.508 takes this into account by imposing more stringent limitations on the seller's right to cure after the contractual delivery date. Section 2.508 operates as follows:

When the goods are delivered, the buyer has the right to inspect them within a reasonable time. If they are non-conforming, she has the right, within a further reasonable time, to reject them. If the seller delivered the goods in good time *before* the time required for delivery in the contract, the delivery date may still not have passed by the time that the buyer (having acted with the required reasonable promptness) exercises the right of rejection. If so, §2.508(1) gives the seller an *unconditional right to notify the buyer seasonably of intent to cure* and to affect the cure by *substituting a conforming delivery before that time expires.*[6]

If the *contractual delivery date has passed,* this unrestricted ability to cure is no longer available, but a qualified right to cure still exists for a reasonable time. Section 2.508(2) permits the seller to *notify the buyer seasonably of intent to cure* and to *affect the cure within a reasonable time,* provided that ". . . the seller had *reasonable grounds to believe* [that the tender of delivery] would be *acceptable with or without money allowance. . . .*"[7] This means that if the seller had no reason to know that the

---

6. Section 2.508(1) has been changed in the 2003 revision of Article 2 to make it clear that the seller's initial nonconforming performance must have been in good faith, the cure must be made at the seller's expense, the seller must compensate the buyer for reasonable expenses caused by the breach and cure, and the conforming tender must be made within the time for performance agreed to in the contract.

7. The 2003 revision of §2.508(2) eliminates the requirement that the seller had reasonable grounds to believe that the tender would be acceptable to the buyer. Instead, it imposes a more generalized standard. As in §2.508(1), the seller must have performed in good faith in making the nonconforming tender. In addition, the cure must be "appropriate and timely

goods were non-conforming, or realized that they were, but reasonably believed that the buyer would nevertheless take them if an appropriate price adjustment was made, the seller may be able to rectify the non-conformity even after the date for delivery had passed. However, the cure must be within a reasonable time, and the issue of what is reasonable depends on the nature and purpose of the sale. When delivery on the exact date specified is a material term of the contract (that is, it is clear from the contract that any delay in delivery would be a serious breach), there may be no reasonable time for cure. In other cases, the time for substituting a conforming delivery could range from a few hours to days, depending on the circumstances of the contract.

The question of whether goods conform to the contract is *factual*, based on an interpretation of what was called for under the contract, and an *evaluation* of the character of what was performed. Non-conformity may lie in the quality, quantity, or attributes of the goods themselves, or in the manner in which they are provided, such as the way in which they are packaged or delivered. It is not always easy to resolve a dispute concerning the fact and extent of an alleged non-conformity with the contract. Even if non-conformity is established or conceded, there could still be a controversy over what is appropriate to cure the deficiency.

For example, say that consumer buys a new dining room table from a furniture store. When it arrives on the date scheduled for delivery, the buyer notices a large scratch across the top and rejects the table. The seller concedes that this is a non-conformity and gives the buyer a couple of options: She can keep the scratched table at a discount of 10 percent off the price, or the seller will take the table back, refinish it, and redeliver it in a week. The buyer, a consumer of fierce disposition, refuses to accept either option and demands delivery of another table today, failing which she threatens to terminate the sale, purchase a substitute elsewhere, and hold the seller liable for any additional cost. She points out that she bought and paid for a new table, and she neither wants a scratched one for less money nor a refinished one. Furthermore, she was promised delivery today, not next week. This dispute relates to the sufficiency of the seller's offer to cure. The buyer adopts the position that nothing short of the immediate delivery of a new table would be an adequate cure, but the seller considers it appropriate to offer a monetary allowance or the delivery of a repaired table in a week.

Both parties take the risk of breaching the contract by insisting on their positions. If the buyer is wrong, her termination is based on partial breach, which the seller was not given a reasonable opportunity to cure. She thereby

---

under the circumstances." Official Comment 3 to revised §2.508 indicates that although the "reasonable grounds to believe" test has been abandoned, the good faith requirement prevents the seller from trying to save the contract by deliberately tendering goods that he knows the buyer cannot use, and then when the buyer rejects those goods, asserting a right to cure. As with cure under §2.508(1), the seller is responsible for the expense of cure and must compensate the buyer for the reasonable expenses caused by the breach and cure.

commits a breach herself. If the seller is wrong, it loses the chance to rectify the breach by an effective cure within the time for delivery and converts its partial breach into a total one. To decide who is right, the judgments called for by §2.508 must be made: Was the seller justified in believing that the tender was conforming or otherwise acceptable? Is delivery by the date specified in the contract of the essence, and if not, is a week's delay reasonable? Will the table, as refinished, conform to the contract? However you may be inclined to answer these questions, recognize that each of them requires an interpretation of the contract to determine the parties' reasonable expectations.

In the above example, the contract involves a single delivery of one item. When the contract calls for the delivery of a quantity of goods in installments, the perfect tender rule is further qualified. This issue is best deferred until after the discussion of repudiation and is covered in section 17.7.8.

---

§17.6 THE BREACHING PARTY'S RECOVERY FOLLOWING MATERIAL BREACH AND THE CONCEPT OF DIVISIBILITY

§17.6.1 The Forfeiture of Contractual Rights by a Party Who Breaches Materially

It was noted in sections 17.3.4 and 17.4 that a party who substantially performs is entitled to return performance under the contract, subject to an offset for damages caused by the partial breach. This means that if the other party fails to render the return performance, the breacher may sue for enforcement of the contract despite the partial breach. However, if the breach is material and total, the breacher has no right to sue for enforcement of the contract. A **material breach** operates as a **renunciation of the contract by the breacher**, who thereby **forfeits all rights under it** and has no contractual claim to enforce. This follows naturally from the principle that a material and total breach terminates the victim's obligation to render return performance. It would be very odd if, after Violet materially and totally breached by failing to pay her deposit at all, she could sue Woody for damages based on his failure to build the deck.

§17.6.2 Restitution in Favor of a Party Who Has Breached Materially

The above rule is concerned with suit on the contract and does not cover the breacher's right to claim restitution on the theory of unjust enrichment when she has performed part of her obligation before breaching, thereby giving some benefit to the other party. Once the contract has been terminated following her breach, the rationale for any benefit conferred on the other party under the contract falls away. To the extent that this benefit enriches the other party, he is unjustly enriched at her expense and should restore it. It must be stressed that a claim for restoration of the benefit is not based on the contract, *but on the separate and distinct theory of unjust enrichment*.

For example, say that Violet made her down payment of $2,000 to Woody on July 7. That evening, Violet happened to read a terrifying magazine article on the ghastly effects of suntanning, and she decided that she would never go outdoors again unless wrapped in a heavy shroud. No longer having any need of a deck, she dismissed Woody when he arrived to begin work on July 7. By repudiating her obligation to pay the remainder of the contract price and preventing him from performing, Violet has materially and totally breached the contract. Woody therefore has the right to terminate and (as we shall discuss further in Chapter 18) to recover damages from her to compensate him for his lost profit. His expected profit under the contract is the difference between what it would have cost him to build the deck (say this would have been $3,500) and the contract price of $5,000, which is $1,500. However, Violet has already partially performed under the contract by paying him $2,000. He no longer has a justification for keeping this payment because the premise under which it had been given to him — that he will build a deck — has fallen away. Under principles of unjust enrichment, the payment must be restored to Violet to the extent that it exceeds her debt to him for damages. Thus, Woody has a damages claim against Violet for $1,500, and she has a restitutionary claim against him for $2,000. Once these claims are set off against each other, Woody owes Violet $500. Stated differently, to the extent that the value of what Woody received from Violet under the breached contract exceeds his loss occasioned by the breach, he has received a windfall at her expense. Under principles of unjust enrichment, he has been unfairly benefitted and must restore the value of that benefit. This principle is adopted by Restatement Second §374, which recognizes a *right of restitution in favor of a material breacher* to the extent that the *benefit conferred on the other party exceeds his claim for damages*.

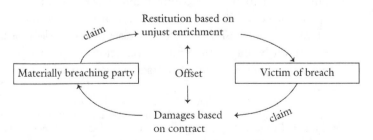

Although the Restatement's position is widely recognized by courts, there are cases that are less generous in allowing restitution to a party who has materially breached. Some courts consider it inappropriate to assist a material breacher at all, because to do so allows her to use her wrongful act as the basis of a claim. Others apply this thinking only when the breach was willful. This punitive stance disallows any restitutionary recovery to the breacher and can have very unfair results because it disproportionally punishes a party who has rendered considerable performance before breaching. That is, the greater the value of what was performed before the breach, the greater the forfeiture.

UCC Article 2 follows an approach similar to that of Restatement Second in that it permits restitution in favor of a breaching party, whether or not the breach was willful. But it does impose a modest penalty on a breaching buyer. Section 2.718(2)(b) allows a defaulting buyer to obtain restitution of payments to the seller to the extent that they exceed any amount of validly agreed damages,[8] or the smaller of $500 or 20 percent of the price. Apart from this penalty, any restitutionary recovery under §2.718(2) is offset under §2.718(3) by any damages to which the seller is entitled under Article 2.[9]

The example concerning Violet's restitutionary recovery from Woody involved restoration of a money payment. It therefore did not present any issue of *valuation of the benefit*. Recognize, however, that if the breacher's performance was not the payment of money, but the rendition of a service or the transfer of property, the value of the benefit could be a matter of dispute. The general approach, reflected in Restatement Second §371 and §374, Comment b is to give the breacher the **lesser of the market value** (quantum meruit or quantum valebant) of the service or property, or the other party's **ultimate economic enrichment** (the actual increase in his economic wealth). Although the contract price may be used as evidence of value, it is not dispositive.

§17.6.3 The Enforcement Rights of a Material Breacher When the Contract Is Divisible

Divisibility is a concept of limited application, only relevant when there is some reason to break a contract into discrete units, and the contract is capable of being divided up into a set of self-standing components. Most contracts are *not divisible* because they *contemplate the exchange of unitary performances* and cannot be fragmented into a collection of independent, self-contained exchanges. However, some contracts are structured in a way that allow them

---

8. Agreed damages are explained in section 18.11.

9. In the 2003 revision of Article 2, the buyer's restitutionary recovery is no longer subject to the offset of $500 or 20 percent of the price. The seller may offset only actual damages under §2.718(3) or agreed damages under §2.718(2).

to be broken up into *sets of matching performances*, each of which can be treated as a *self-sufficient "mini-contract"* within the larger contractual relationship. The determination of whether a contract is divisible is a matter of interpretation, and a court should not find a contract to be capable of division unless it is clear that this does not conflict with the apparent intent of the parties or damage the value of a performance reasonably expected by either of them.

Menorah Chapels at Millburn v. Needle, 899 A.2d 316 (N.J. Super. A.D. 2006) is a good illustration of the analysis used to determine divisibility. Needle contracted with Menorah, a funeral home, for the provision of funeral services for his father-in-law. The contract specified that the funeral services would comply with orthodox Jewish ritual. One of the requirements of orthodox ritual is that the body must be attended at all times prior to burial by watchers or *shomers* who take shifts in maintaining a constant vigil over it. Menorah's price list specifically included the provision of watchers on request and it was undisputed that Needle made such a request. In breach of this provision, Menorah provided a watcher for only three of the six shifts during the period prior to the burial. When Needle refused to pay Menorah, it sued for the contract price less a deduction of $390 for the three missed shifts. Menorah argued that the contract was divisible because each of its services was separately priced and could be ordered or declined by the customer. The trial court found the contract to be divisible, but the appellate court disagreed. The crucial question is whether it was the basis of the parties' bargain that the contract be performed in its entirety. The mere fact that the services were separately priced was not enough to make the contract divisible, especially in this case where itemization was required by state consumer protection laws. The underlying purpose of the contract was to provide a complete orthodox funeral, and Menorah could not simply fail to provide one of the services and sue under the contract for the price of what it did perform. The court remanded the case to the trial court to determine if the breach was material, and, if so, to calculate Menorah's recovery on the basis of *quantum meruit*.

As *Menorah Chapels* shows, division of a contract may be useful when there has been a breach or some other problem, such as illegality or impracticability, that affects only a portion of the contract, but does not taint the contract as a whole. In the context of material breach, if a contract is capable of division, splitting it into a set of relatively autonomous subparts may enable a party who has materially breached one part to isolate the breach and confine it to the affected part, so that the remainder of the contract is not sullied by the breach. This will enable him to treat the unaffected portion of the contract as if no breach had occurred and to enforce rights that have accrued in that portion. That is, if a contract is divisible, a material breach relating to only part of it is confined to that part, and the breacher can enforce the remainder without being subject to the general rule precluding action on the contract by the party who has materially breached it.

Sadly, the contract between Violet and Woody, no doubt a source of such intense fascination up to now, cannot be used to illustrate the concept of divisibility. The parties contemplate an exchange of two single, unitary performances — a deck for $5,000. Would the contract be divisible if it broke up performance into sequential stages (similar to the construction contracts discussed in section 16.8.4) and allocated payment of a specified portion of the price to each stage of work? That is:

Violet pays $1,000, and Woody then delivers the lumber
↓
Violet pays a further $1,000, and Woody then builds the supports
↓
Violet pays another $2,000, and Woody then lays the decking
↓
Violet pays the final $1,000, and Woody then completes the deck by installing the railing

We now have a series of matched sequential performances, in which the parties have broken down the price into installments, each of which is identified with a specific stage of the construction. However, this alone will not make the contract divisible unless the parties intended to enter into a group of four self-contained discrete exchanges. In seeking their true intention, we must ask if the contract manifests a reasonable expectation that each of the sequential exchanges could be treated as a complete performance of an independently valuable transaction. To answer yes, we would at least have to be satisfied that the payment provided for each piece of the construction was exactly equivalent to its proportional value under the contract, and we would have to be sure that if Woody ceased work after completing any one component, Violet would receive the full value contemplated by the contract for that component. If this is not so, the likely purpose of breaking performance into stages was simply to alternate the risk of credit between the parties.

A better argument for divisibility could be made if Violet was a home builder who had erected four new houses in a subdivision. She entered into a contract with Woody under which he agreed to build a deck onto each of the houses for $5,000 apiece. After completing two of them, he materially breached by abandoning the job. Because each of the four components of the contract are distinct, the payment provided is exactly equivalent to the contractual value of the performance, and the breach affects only the two uncompleted decks, in no way detracting from the value of the finished ones, this contract can be interpreted as divisible. Of course, this does not affect Violet's right to claim damages from Woody for losses resulting from his failure to build the two decks, but it does affect his ability to recover for the work that he has done. If Violet has not paid him for the completed decks, he can sue her on the contract for payment of the contract price. He is not simply relegated to a restitutionary claim for the work done, which would, at best, require him to prove the less certain (and possibly lower) value of the benefit. In those jurisdictions which deny restitutionary relief to a breacher, a finding of divisibility is even more important, because a claim on the contract may be the only basis of recovery.

§17.7 ANTICIPATORY REPUDIATION

§17.7.1 The Distinction Between Breach and Repudiation

It was stated in section 17.2 that a breach, properly speaking, can only occur when the promised performance falls due. However, it is possible for a party to breach in advance of performance — to repudiate her obligation in anticipation — if, before the time for performance, she **makes it clear by words or actions** that she **will breach when performance falls due**. A repudiation may occur between the time that the contract is made and the time due for its performance — that is, one of the parties repudiates before either party has begun performance under the contract. It may also occur after performance under the contract has begun, but before the due date of the repudiated performance.

To illustrate, recall that in the contract between Violet Ultra and Woody Sawyer, executed on July 1, Violet did not have to make her down payment of $2,000 before July 6, Woody did not have to begin work until July 7, and Violet did not have to pay the last installment of $3,000 until the deck was complete on July 9. It stands to reason that Violet cannot be in breach for not paying until July 6, and Woody cannot be in breach by failing to perform before July 7. However, if the conduct of a party goes beyond mere passive waiting for the due date, and he manifests the intent in advance that he will not perform when that date arrives, he repudiates the contract. For example, Woody would be guilty of repudiation if, on July 2, he tells Violet that he no longer intends to build the deck for her and will not show up to begin work July 7. In this case, Woody has repudiated in the period before performance was due by either party.

Say that Woody did not repudiate, Violet paid the deposit on July 6, and Woody began work on July 7. On the evening of July 7, Violet confesses to Woody that she is broke and cannot find the $3,000 that she is supposed to pay upon completion of the deck. Although the performance of the contract is already underway, Violet's statement is still a repudiation, not a breach, because she made it before her payment was due.

§17.7.2 The Purpose and Value of the Doctrine of Anticipatory Repudiation

Older common law did not recognize the concept of anticipatory repudiation, so the promisee had no right to react to such an advance indication of breach. He had to wait until the time of performance to see if breach would in fact occur. In the interim, he had to hold himself available to tender his return performance when it fell due. Under this rule, if Violet told Woody on July 2 that she no longer wished him to build the deck, he could not have responded to Violet's statement of intent on July 2, but would have been required to wait until July 6 to see if Violet would in fact not make the down payment. To hold himself available to do the work on July 7 in the event that Violet repents, Woody would be obliged to refuse any other offers of work for the period of July 7-July 9, thereby losing any opportunity to mitigate his loss. Under the old approach, the situation would be even worse if the victim of the repudiation had to perform first, because the law did not allow him to suspend his performance while waiting to see if the other party carried through with the threatened breach. So, if it had been Woody who repudiated on July 2 by telling Violet that he would not show up on July 7 to begin work, Violet would not have been allowed to react to this by withholding the payment of $2,000 due on July 6. On the facts of these examples, the victim of the repudiation only had to wait a few days to know if a breach would occur, but the harm could be even worse if the period before the due date of performance had been longer.

During the nineteenth century, courts came to recognize that this approach was both unfair to the promisee and inefficient. The English case of *Hoechster v. De La Tour*, 118 Eng. Rep. 922 (Q.B. 1853), is generally regarded as the preeminent judicial pronouncement that when one of the parties clearly repudiates a material promise in advance, the other may treat this as a breach immediately and may seek relief for breach without delay. The doctrine of anticipatory repudiation is now well established in common law and under the UCC. Although the UCC does not define what constitutes a repudiation (thus leaving this issue to the common law, even in sales of goods), it does codify and make some refinements to the doctrine in UCC §§2.609-2.612.[10] As in other areas, the changes brought about by the UCC have been influential in developing common law rules, and their spirit is reflected in the treatment of repudiation in Restatement Second §§243 and 250-257.

The basic approach is that a *clear, unequivocal, and voluntary repudiation* by one of the parties is recognized as the equivalent of a material and total breach, provided that the threatened action or failure to act *would be a material and total breach* if it happened at the time due for performance. As the non-breaching party's promise of performance is dependent on the repudiator's promised performance (whether expressly or impliedly), the advance indication of prospective breach also amounts to an *advance failure of the condition.* This is so, whether or not the repudiated performance would, in the normal course, have been due before and thus a condition precedent to, the return performance.

For example, Woody's promise to build the deck is a dependent promise — a construed condition of Violet's performance. But because it is required to be performed only after Violet has paid the $2,000 deposit, it is not a condition precedent to Violet's payment of the deposit. In fact, the opposite is true: The payment is a condition precedent to the work. However, if Woody repudiates the contract on July 2, it would be absurd to argue that Violet is nevertheless compelled to pay on July 6, because the contract does not make her payment conditional on Woody performing first. It must necessarily be implicit in the contract that Violet's obligation to render the first performance is contingent on Woody not repudiating

---

10. The 2003 revision of Article 2 adds a new subsection to §2.610 that does provide guidance on when a party can be treated as having repudiated. Official Comment 5 to revised §2.610 indicates that it is based on Restatement, Second §250. (The language is quite different, but the basic concept is similar.) Revised §2.610(2) reads: "Repudiation includes language that a reasonable person would interpret to mean that the other party will not or cannot make a performance still due under the contract or voluntary, affirmative conduct that would appear to a reasonable person to make future performance by the other party impossible."

before her performance falls due. In other words, a repudiation has the effect of accelerating the due date of the breacher's promissory condition for the purpose of allowing the victim of the repudiation to withhold any return performance that would otherwise have been due first.

§17.7.3 The Response to a Repudiation

When a repudiation has occurred, the other party has a choice between two alternatives. Her one option is to *accept the repudiation by treating it as an immediate breach*. This entitles her to refuse to render her own performance, to terminate the contract, and to sue for relief for total breach. Her other alternative is to *delay responding* to the repudiation to see if the repudiating party repents. She may even take affirmative steps to encourage retraction of the repudiation by notifying the promisor that he has a specified time to recant, failing which the repudiation will be accepted. If she does this, she *may change her mind at any time before retraction* and accept the repudiation.

Whichever choice the victim of an apparent repudiation makes, she incurs some risk. If she responds by terminating, she takes the chance that the other party will deny that he repudiated, and declare her termination to be a breach. The more equivocal or unclear the alleged repudiation, the greater this risk becomes. If her response is to delay accepting the repudiation, she runs the risk of a court ultimately finding that she aggravated her damages by not terminating immediately and taking action to mitigate her loss. The clearer and firmer the repudiation, the greater this risk becomes. For example, *Oloffson v. Coomer*, 296 N.E.2d 871 (Ill. 1973) involved a contract between a farmer and a grain dealer for the sale of corn to be planted by the farmer. About three months before the first delivery was due, the farmer told the dealer that he did not intend to plant the corn. This was an unequivocal repudiation, but the dealer refused to accept it and insisted that the farmer perform. The dealer persisted in this response even though the farmer reaffirmed his intent not to deliver the corn on several other occasions in the succeeding months. Because he had not accepted the repudiation and continued to demand performance, the dealer delayed making a substitute purchase until the due date for delivery under the contract. By then, the market price of corn had increased above the market price on the date of the repudiation. The court refused to award damages to the dealer because it found that he had not acted reasonably in refusing to accept the unequivocal repudiation and buying a substitute immediately. The dealer's unreasonableness in hoping for a retraction of the repudiation is particularly clear in this case because the farmer's repudiation was so express and he did not plant the corn. In other cases, the repudiation may be less certain, and the judgment more difficult to make. This issue is taken up again in section 17.7.5.

§17.7.4 The Elements of Repudiation

As stated already, for a prospective non-performance to constitute a material and total repudiation of the contract, the promisor must clearly, unequivocally, and voluntarily communicate an intention not to render the promised performance when it falls due. This intention could be communicated by words or conduct. This definition indicates that words or conduct must satisfy a number of prerequisites to qualify as a repudiation:

a. The Prospective Action or Inaction Indicated by the Promisor Must Be Serious Enough to Qualify as a Material and Total Breach of the Contract

An advance repudiation cannot itself give rise to a right of termination, with-holding of performance, and damages unless the threatened deviation from what was promised would constitute a material and total breach if it occurred at the time performance falls due. It is obviously a material repudiation if the promisor manifests the intent by words or conduct of not performing at all, but it would also constitute a material repudiation if the promisor communicates the intent to render a substantially deficient performance, or to refuse performance unless the promisee agrees to do or pay more than the contract requires. But an indication of intent to deviate in some minor way from the promised performance, while it may ultimately lead to a claim for damages for substantial performance, cannot be grounds for the extreme reaction of termination.

b. The Promisor's Statement or Conduct Must Clearly Indicate to the Reasonable Promisee that the Promisor Intends to Breach Materially When the Time for Performance Arrives

The question of whether words or action indicate a clear and unequivocal intent to breach is one of interpretation. The meaning of the words and actions must be ascertained. As is true in other matters of interpretation, an *objective test* is used. The law is not so much concerned with the promisor's actual intent or the promisee's subjective interpretation of the statement or action, but with the way in which the promisee should reasonably have understood it.

As we have often seen, verbal expressions of intent can be obscure or ambiguous, presenting difficulties in interpretation. But the meaning of conduct can be even more difficult to divine. For this reason, a court is unlikely to find a repudiation by conduct unless it is unquestionably so inconsistent with an intent to perform as promised, that the promisor's purpose of abandoning the contract is beyond doubt. It is sometimes said that the promisor's conduct must be such as to make her future performance impossible. This is something of an overstatement, but it does convey the need for very unambiguous behavior. For example, if, on July 2, Violet has the deck built by another contractor, her conduct clearly indicates an intent to repudiate. However, if, on July 2, she puts her house on the market, her intent is not as clear. It is possible that she has changed her mind and will fail to perform on July 6, but it could also be that she still intends to build the deck to make the house more saleable. Although faced with this uncertainty, Woody would be taking a risk in declaring a repudiation. However, he may be able to clarify Violet's intentions by asking for an assurance of performance, as discussed in section 17.7.7.

c. The Promisor's Statement or Conduct in Repudiating Must Be Voluntary, That Is, It Must Have Been Deliberate and Purposeful Rather than Inadvertent or Beyond the Promisor's Control

This may seem to contradict what was said in the immediately preceding point, which focuses on the objective meaning of the manifestation of the promisor's intent rather than on his state of mind. However, even under an objective test, there must be an adequate degree of volition underlying the manifestation. The requirement that the promisor's words or conduct must be deliberate and voluntary means only that he makes the statement or takes the action purposefully. It does not mean that the promisor must have acted in bad faith, or must have realized that the threatened course of conduct or the assertion of rights would constitute a breach. It is thus possible for a promisor to repudiate purposefully in the belief that he is acting fully within his rights. For example, Woody may firmly believe that he is entitled by trade usage to begin work, not on July 7, but within a reasonable time after the promised date of performance. He therefore tells Violet on July 3 that he is running behind schedule and expects to start her deck on July 14. If Woody is wrong in his understanding of the contract, and a week's delay is a material breach, his statement is a deliberate expression of intent to deliver a materially deficient performance and a repudiation. His innocent state of mind does not justify it.

A **statement of intent** not to perform does not usually raise a question of voluntariness because a verbal expression of intent is usually deliberate unless it was coerced. Therefore, when a statement is made, the primary issue is one of interpreting its meaning: Is the promisor saying that she will not perform, or is she merely expressing a lack of confidence in her ability to perform, or complaining about the terms of the contract?

It can be considerably more difficult to establish deliberateness when prospective breach is indicated by **conduct** because action is sometimes inadvertent or compelled by circumstances beyond the promisor's control. For this reason, it is only when the conduct demonstrates an unwillingness to perform that it is regarded as a repudiation. If the action does not lead to the conclusion of willful abandonment of the contract, it is premature for the promisee to declare a repudiation, but again, there may be grounds to demand an assurance of performance.

This principle applies even more strongly when the promisor has taken no action and made no statement at all, but a change of circumstances makes it likely that a breach will occur when the time for performance arrives. For example, if a large judgment is recorded against Violet on July 2, this creates the possibility that she may not be able to pay the deposit on July 6. Similarly, if Woody has to finish another project before beginning Violet's job, and his other work is considerably behind schedule on July 2, this may indicate that he will not be able to begin performance as promised anytime close to July 7. Even though these circumstances may indicate the possibility of breach, there has not been any statement or conduct indicating an unwillingness to perform, and the promisee cannot treat the contract as repudiated. This is because the promisor should be given the opportunity of trying to overcome the obstacles to performance. After all, the performance is not yet due and there is no indication of a lack of desire to proceed with the contract, despite the adversity. There are not yet grounds to hold the promisor to an advance breach. Again, if it appears that the obstacles to performance may be insurmountable, the promisee's remedy is to demand an assurance of performance.

§17.7.5 The Dangers of Dealing with Possible Repudiation

The three rules explained above inhibit the promisee's ability to react to a prospect of future breach. This is an appropriate control because a repudiation, by definition, occurs before performance is due, and there must be some restraint on the promisee's ability to declare breach in advance. If this could be too easily asserted, the promisor would be vulnerable to an unjustified or premature claim of prospective breach whenever any uncertainty arose about his future performance. This protection is not so crucial when the repudiation is conscious and knowledgeable: The repudiating party knows that he no longer wishes to or is able to perform, and he makes it clear that he is abandoning the contract, with full awareness that he will be liable for breach. But risks arise, both to the promisor and the promisee, when there is any degree of uncertainty about the existence and extent of the right claimed to have been repudiated, or when it is unclear if the conduct amounts to a repudiation, or when there is doubt about the appropriate level of response. It may take litigation to resolve whether the promisor's indication of intent really was a repudiation of an important contractual duty, and if the promisee overreacts in response, this could itself amount to a repudiation.

For example, the contract between Woody and Violet said nothing about the wood to be used for the deck. On July 5, the day before Violet was to make her down payment, Woody mentioned to her that he intended to use a pressure-treated fir. She objected and told him that she had assumed that he would use cedar, which is reputed to be the best material for decking and is the wood most commonly chosen. Woody said that pressure-treated fir is less expensive than cedar and is just as good in appearance and durability. He was willing to use cedar if she wished, but that would add $750 onto the price. Violet insisted on cedar but refused to pay more. A dispute followed that resulted in the termination of the transaction amidst mutual recrimination. At this point both parties believe that they are in the right, but one is wrong and is going to be found to have repudiated the contract. It may take litigation to finally resolve the uncertainty.

In the above example, it was at least clear what Woody planned to provide as his performance (Violet knew he was going to use fir), so the uncertainty was confined to the question of whether the use of fir would be a material breach of the contract. However, the uncertainty could be even worse, because it could happen that there is not even clarity about the promisor's intentions. Say that Violet discovered on July 3 that Woody left town to interview for a job in another city and is expected back on the morning of July 8, the day after he is supposed to begin the deck. This makes her dilemma more difficult. She must make a judgment on whether the information is correct. If it is, does Woody's conduct reasonably mean that he has abandoned the job entirely, or will he just be late? If delay seems more likely than abandonment, is a day's delay a material breach? Even if the breach would be total, his performance is not due for a few days, so should she find another contractor or should she give Woody a chance to repent? If the latter, should she put him on terms or just wait? If she follows that course and it turns out that Woody has in fact repudiated, would her delay in arranging a substitute increase her loss and if so, would a court refuse to compensate her for this increased loss on the basis that her delay aggravated her damages?[11] She may be able to resolve some of these problems by calling for an assurance of performance as discussed in section 17.7.7, but even that procedure carries some risk.

§17.7.6 Retraction of Repudiation

It was stated in section 17.7.3 that (subject to the duty to mitigate damages) a promisee is not obliged to accept a repudiation when it occurs, and can wait to see if the promisor repents. She is entitled, but not obliged, to give notice to the promisor demanding retraction of the repudiation within a specified time. It follows from this that the promisor has the ability to retract a repudiation. This should not be too startling a proposition, because, after

---

11. Mitigation of damages is discussed in section 18.6.3.

all, a repudiation is by definition a prospective breach that occurs before the due date of performance. However, repudiation is a wrongful act, and the ability to recant is not absolute. As the promisee does have the option of not waiting for a retraction, the promisor's ability to retract is lost as soon as the promisee *notifies the promisor that the repudiation has been accepted*. Even in the absence of such notification, the promisor cannot take back the repudiation if the promisee has treated it as final and has taken *action in reliance* on it, resulting in a significant change in her position. This principle recognizes that once the promisor has committed the wrongful act of repudiation, he does not deserve an express response to it. The promisee is entitled to act on the strength of the repudiation without further communication, and this reliance interest is protected, whether or not the promisor is aware that the opportunity for repentance has passed.

§17.7.7 Prospective Non-Performance and Assurance of Performance

It has already been stressed that a prospective inability or apparent reluctance to perform may not be strong enough to constitute a repudiation, so that the promisee takes a considerable risk in treating it as such. Yet if the uncertain prospect of repudiation does ultimately ripen into an actual repudiation or breach, inaction may result in inconvenience or even in loss that may have been preventable by an early response. The promisee who does not wish to remain passive, but would like to try to avoid overreaction, has one further option — to demand an assurance of performance. Both UCC §2.609 and Restatement Second §251 give some power to a promisee to try and safeguard his rights by taking a median response to words, conduct, or circumstances that suggest, but do not firmly establish, a likelihood of future breach. Although such a response ameliorates the risk of passivity or an inappropriately aggressive reaction to possible repudiation, it does not entirely eliminate it.

UCC §2.609[12] provides that if a party has *reasonable grounds for insecurity* regarding the other's performance, she may make a *written demand* for an *adequate assurance of due performance*. Until that assurance is received, the party requesting it may, *if commercially reasonable, suspend* any of her *own performance* for which she has *not already received the agreed return*. *The party receiving a justified demand for assurance must provide an adequate assurance within a reasonable time, not exceeding 30 days*. If he fails to do so, he has repudiated the contract. Restatement Second §251 differs in its wording to some extent, but is largely to similar effect. As is always true of rights codified in the UCC, the ability to demand an assurance in appropriate circumstances is more certain where a sale of

---

12. The 2003 revision of Article 2 makes no significant changes to §2.609.

goods is concerned because the right has a statutory base and is not dependent upon judicial adoption. That is, while many courts have recognized this right under common law, one cannot assume that the courts of every state have done so.

Although UCC §2.609 and Restatement §251 set out the broad rules under which a party who feels insecure about the prospect of receiving performance may demand an assurance of adequate and due performance, they leave many questions to the judgment of both the party demanding the assurance and the party responding to the demand. An error in judgment by either party could lead to serious consequences for that party. To begin with, the party requesting the assurance must be satisfied that her grounds for insecurity are reasonable. In making the demand, she must decide what assurance would solve the insecurity and whether it is reasonable to ask for it. When she receives the response, she must decide whether it cures the problem. If she misjudged and asked for too little, the assurance may be meaningless. If her misjudgment was to make a demand that was unjustified or went beyond her rights, she would herself commit a breach by insisting on the assurance and in suspending her own performance. This happened in *Pittsburgh-Des Moines Steel Co. v. Brookhaven Manor Water Co.*, 532 F.2d 572 (7th Cir. 1976). The parties entered into a contract for the manufacture and installation of a water tank. (Although this was a large item and the contract involved installation, it was a sale of goods.) The contract required the buyer to pay for the tank only after completion of the installation. Before the seller had begun to make the tank (and therefore some considerable time before payment would have been due) the seller heard that the buyer was experiencing difficulty in securing a loan to pay for the tank. The seller had already begun to regret extending credit to the buyer, and its misgivings grew when it heard that the buyer may have trouble financing the purchase. It therefore reacted to this information by demanding that the buyer deposit funds in escrow to cover payment for the tank and that the buyer's president guarantee the debt until the escrow was established. The seller stated that it would suspend its own performance until its demands were met. The buyer refused and the transaction collapsed. Both parties claimed that the other had repudiated. Applying UCC §2.609, the court found that the seller had repudiated. Its demand was premature because the time for payment was a long way off and it was not clear that the buyer would ultimately fail to get financing. The seller therefore did not have reasonable grounds for insecurity. Even if such reasonable grounds had been established, the court found the demand for assurance to be excessive. The seller's refusal to perform unless there was a payment into escrow and a guarantee by the president amounted to a unilateral revocation of the credit term of the contract, and constituted a repudiation.

The facts of *Pittsburgh-Des Moines Steel Co.* also illustrate the hazard to the party from whom the assurance is demanded. When faced with a demand for an assurance, the party has to decide how to react and runs the risk of responding wrongly. If it accedes to the demand, it avoids the danger of repudiation. However, if the assurance demanded is burdensome, it incurs the cost or disadvantage of giving it. If it refuses the demand or offers less than what is demanded, it takes the chance that the court will ultimately approve of its response on the basis that the demand was unjustified or excessive. If the court decides otherwise and finds the demand to have been justified and appropriate, refusal to give the demanded assurance converts the formerly equivocal situation into a clear repudiation.

As a further illustration, consider again the contract under which Woody agreed to build a deck for Violet for $5,000. Violet was to pay Woody $2,000 in advance of the work on July 6, and the balance on completion. After receiving the down payment on July 6, Woody begins work on July 7. While he is working at the house on that day, the sheriff arrives with a writ of execution and levies on Violet's living room furniture. A couple of hours later, a repossessor from a finance company shows up and takes away Violet's car. This is very disconcerting to Woody, who begins to wonder if Violet will be able to pay the $3,000 due upon completion of the deck. He cannot treat the execution and repossession as a repudiation of Violet's promise to pay him, because Violet herself has not said or done anything to indicate an intent not to perform, but he hates the idea of continuing work in the face of a serious possibility of non-payment.

If the activity at Violet's home on July 7 gives Woody reasonable grounds to believe that Violet will breach when her performance falls due, he may demand an adequate assurance of performance from Violet.[13] Violet must respond satisfactorily within a reasonable time. While Woody is waiting for her response, he may stop work on the deck, and if he does not get an adequate assurance in time, he may treat the contract as breached. This is all very well, but you can probably see immediately that there could be serious issues for dispute, some of which may be: Does Woody really have reasonable grounds for feeling insecure? If not, his suspension of performance is itself a breach. If he is justified in demanding assurance, what should he ask for? Merely asking Violet to reaffirm that she will pay is not very helpful, because the assurance could just be a hollow promise and Violet may not admit that she is in financial trouble. It would be much more reassuring if Violet would pay right now, but is Woody entitled to demand that? In effect, this would be a revocation of the credit that he agreed to give her, and such a stringent demand could be a violation of his duties under the

---

13. This contract is a hybrid because Woody is both selling goods (the materials) and performing services, so there may be a question of whether the transaction falls within UCC Article 2. However, unless the jurisdiction does not follow Restatement Second §251, the broad principles are not notably different under the UCC and common law.

contract. Maybe Woody could ask Violet to deposit the payment in escrow, or for a financial statement showing that the funds are available, but this first alternative may ask too much, and the second too little. Once Woody settles on his demand, Violet has to decide how to respond. If she feels that he is not justified in feeling insecure, she could refuse the assurance. If she feels that it is excessive, she could offer a more modest assurance. But if she is wrong, her refusal to comply with the demand crystalizes the uncertainty into a repudiation.

There are no easy answers to these fact-based questions, but this example highlights the kinds of concerns that may arise when a prospective breach is perceived. Of course, not all cases end up in a morass of uncertainty, and the ability to demand assurances does often enable a party either to obtain adequate security or to establish a repudiation.

§17.7.8 Transactions Involving Installments

Issues of repudiation and total breach are highlighted in contracts that call for performance in installments. When a breach occurs in the performance of an earlier installment, it can be difficult to know if the breach *affects only the defective installment* or is *so serious as to undermine the contract in its entirety*, operating as *a repudiation of all remaining installments.*

For example, Seller, a manufacturer of machinery, contracts with Buyer for the sale of three of its machines to be used by Buyer in its factory. Under the contract, the machines are to be delivered a month apart from each other. Because Buyer is depending on prompt delivery to avoid disruption of its business, the contract requires delivery of the machines on the exact dates specified. The first machine is delivered on time and is installed. After two days of operation it breaks down as a result of a defect that cannot be repaired without removal of the machine. Because timely delivery is important in the transaction, the defect in the first machine is likely to be a material and total breach of Seller's performance obligation with respect to the first installment, but does this also constitute a material and total repudiation of the future installments and hence a breach of the contract as a whole? That is, does the delivery of a defective first installment so seriously impair Buyer's expectations concerning the remaining machines that it is a repudiation of the performance promised in the future? If so, Buyer may use the present breach as the basis for terminating the entire contract. If not, the breach does not impact future performance, so that Buyer continues to be obliged to accept and pay for the later two machines, and is confined to a remedy for breach of the current installment.

As this is a sale of goods, the principles governing these questions are set out in UCC §2.612, which qualifies the perfect tender rule of §2.601 in contracts providing for delivery in installments. Section 2.612(2) states that a nonconformity in an installment permits the buyer to reject that installment only if the nonconformity substantially impairs the value of the installment, and the nonconformity cannot be cured.[14] For the nonconformity to impair, not just that installment, but the contract as a whole, §2.612(3) requires that the deficiency in the installment "*substantially impairs the value of the whole*" contract. This means that when a breach occurs in an earlier installment, it must be determined whether this is a breach so fundamental to the whole contract as to constitute not merely a partial breach, but a total and material breach of the contract as a whole. If it does, the breach operates not only as a breach of the current installment, but also as an advance breach (that is, repudiation) of the performance obligations due in the future. The question is whether it is pervasive and irreparable enough to make it clear that the promisor is incapable of rendering, or unwilling to render, substantially compliant performance in the future.

An express rule governing installment sales is particularly necessary when a sale of goods is involved because the perfect tender rule does not permit application of the doctrine of substantial performance. At common law there is less need for having a special rule for installment contracts because the result of §2.612 can be achieved by applying the general principles of substantial performance, under which the breach relating to one installment will only be a total breach if it results in an incurable material violation of the contract as a whole. This is reflected in Restatement Second §243(4), which, in dealing generally with total breach (and not with specific reference to installment transactions), adopts language similar to that used in UCC §2.612.

Examples

1. Sue Burbanite had just bought a newly built home on a small suburban lot. The builder had not landscaped the lot, which was uneven, bare, and muddy. Sue therefore hired Holmes Wrecker, a landscaping contractor, to level and shape the ground and to form contours and beds so that Sue could later plant trees, shrubs, and grass. Holmes drew up a landscaping plan that was incorporated into a written contract. In terms of the contract, Holmes undertook to begin the work on May 1 and to complete it

---

14. The 2003 revision of §2.612(2) removes the language "and cannot be cured." However, revised §2.508 makes it clear that its cure provisions apply to installment contracts under §2.612. The effect of this is to reinforce that the seller has the right to cure a nonconforming tender of an installment, provided that the cure satisfies the standards set out in §2.508. Under the current §2.612, there is some question about whether the seller's cure right in an installment contract is the same as or distinct from (and subject to different standards from) the general right to cure under §2.508.

by May 5. Sue promised to pay the price of $5,000 in two equal install-ments due on May 3 and 5.

Holmes began work on May 1. The earthmoving proceeded well until the afternoon of May 2, when Holmes lost control of his bulldozer as he was trying to negotiate a narrow section of the lot at the corner of the house. The machine smashed into a pillar supporting an upper-floor deck, causing the entire deck to collapse. Sue, who happened to be sitting on the deck at the time, was thrown to the ground and would have been seriously injured had her fall not been cushioned by a pile of mud. Enraged, Sue chased Holmes off the premises, hurling abuse and mud clods at him.

On the morning of May 3, Holmes arrived at Sue's property. He apologized for ruining her deck and explained that he misjudged the space available for maneuvering. He told her that he was insured, and that his insurer would pay for the rebuilding of the deck. In the interim, he said he was willing to resume work. Sue had calmed down by this time, and she agreed to let him continue. He then reminded her that her first installment was due on that day. Sue was astounded at the man's nerve. She pointed out that he had a large and unpaid liability to her for the damage to the deck, and until that was settled, he had no right to expect any money from her. He responded that his insurer would handle the deck, and that payment under the contract was a separate matter altogether. As the parties could not resolve this impasse, Holmes left without doing any further work.

Holmes's insurer did eventually pay to have the deck rebuilt and Sue had the landscaping completed by another contractor. The second con-tractor charged more than she would have paid Holmes under the con-tract, so she sued Holmes for the difference. Holmes contested liability and counter-claimed for the cost of the work performed prior to termi-nation, plus the profit that he lost by being denied the opportunity to complete his performance. Who should prevail?

2. Standard Home Construction, Inc. builds houses for individual home-owners. It usually works from one of its stock plans, which may be modified to suit the needs or desires of a particular customer. Standard entered into a contract with Lofty Lanky to build a ranch-style house on a lot owned by Lofty. The price of the completed house was $300,000. The contract called for the house to be built in accordance with a stock plan and specifications, a copy of which was annexed to the signed memo-randum of agreement. However, one change was made in the specifica-tions, increasing the ceiling height from the standard 8' to 9'. This change was recorded in the contract itself and in the specifications, and it was reflected in the price of the house, which was $20,000 more than normal. Lofty desired this change because he is 7'2" tall and feels uncomfortable in a house with low ceilings.

Standard began work and building proceeded on schedule. It was not until the house was fully framed and work had begun on the roof trusses that Lofty first noticed that the base of the roof seemed lower than it should be. On taking some measurements he realized that when the ceilings were installed, they would be only 8' from the floor. He immediately contacted Standard and a meeting was held on site. Standard conceded that the house was a foot too low. Apparently the foreman was very familiar with the stock plan, having built many houses like this one. He therefore failed to consult the plan carefully and had simply not noticed the change in the specifications.

The only way to correct the error is to demolish and rebuild a significant part of the existing work. This would entail considerable additional labor and the destruction and waste of materials, which would increase Standard's cost of building the house to $360,000. Although this would mean that Standard would lose $60,000 on the contract, it accepts responsibility for fixing its mistake and is willing to take the loss. Because there is plenty of time left before the date specified in the contract for completion of the house, the demolition and rebuilding will not cause Standard to exceed the deadline for completing its performance. However, Lofty has lost faith in Standard. He is appalled by the foreman's inattentiveness to the plan and the lack of proper supervision. He wonders what other mistakes Standard will make. He is also concerned that Standard has the incentive to cut corners in completing the house to try to reduce the size of its loss.

Lofty therefore terminated the contract with Standard. He plans to have another contractor correct the error and complete the house. He intends to claim damages from Standard for the additional cost of completing the house in accordance with the contract specifications.[15] Was Lofty entitled to fire Standard and to hold it liable for the additional cost?

3. All the facts are the same as in Example 2, except for Standard's reaction upon discovering the foreman's oversight. Although Standard is apologetic for the error, it considers it a ridiculous waste and a great hardship to dismantle the completed work and rebuild it. Standard can prove that although higher ceilings may be an attractive feature to some buyers, others would consider them a drawback. As a result, the higher ceilings would not make the house more saleable and would not increase

---

15. The facts show that Standard has no prospect of making any profit on this contract. In fact it stands to lose $60,000. You may therefore wonder why it would make any difference to Standard whether it did the work itself or paid compensation to Lofty so that he can have the work done by someone else. The answer is that if another contractor does the work, the cost is likely to be much higher than the $60,000 that Standard would lose by completing the contract itself. While Standard would do the work at cost, the claim of another contractor would include its profit on the transaction. In addition, if Standard did the work itself, it would be better able to keep the costs to a minimum by carefully managing the work.

its market value. Standard also feels that Lofty is making a big fuss for nothing — after all, there will still be several inches of clearance between his head and the ceiling. It therefore refuses to rebuild the house and insists that Lofty allow it to complete the house with the lower ceilings. It would, of course, deduct the extra charge of $20,000 from the price. Lofty does not find this solution attractive. He demands that Standard rectify the error itself, and if it refuses to do so, he threatens to terminate the contract, hire someone else to bring the house into conformity, and hold Standard liable for his damages.

(a) Is Lofty entitled to make this demand?

(b) Would your answer change if Lofty did not plan to live in the house, but was building it on speculation for immediate resale? He specified the 9′ ceilings because he thinks that they give the house an airy feel that makes it more attractive to buyers.

4. Sandy Shaw owns a small motel (called "Sandy Shaw's Motel"), a few blocks off the main strip of a seaside town. Sandy entered into a contract with Bill Board, a signwriter, under which Bill undertook to paint four signs for Sandy. Two of the signs, measuring 6′ long and 4′ high, were to read, "Sandy Shaw's Motel — elegance and comfort by the sea. Turn just three blocks ahead." The price of these signs was $500 each. Sandy planned to erect them facing incoming traffic at either end of the town's main road. The third and fourth signs were to be arrow-shaped, measuring 5′ long and 2′ high, bearing the legend, "This way to Sandy Shaw's Motel." The price of these signs was $400 each. Sandy planned to place them facing opposite directions on the main road at its intersection with the street leading to the motel. The contract required all four signs to be delivered together two weeks after execution of the contract, and payment was due on delivery.

Bill delivered all four signs as promised. On inspecting them, Sandy finds that the two signs meant for erection at the ends of the main road are only 5′ high and 3′ wide. She demands that Bill must either redo these signs or pay her the cost of having them redone by someone else. Is this demand tenable?

5. Change the facts of Example 4 to the following extent: Bill made the two signs for erection at each end of the main road and delivered them on time. These signs fully conformed to the contract and Sandy has put them up. Bill failed to deliver the other two signs on time, but Sandy was willing to forgive this on the strength of Bill's promise that they would be delivered shortly. Despite several weeks of constant nagging by Sandy, Bill never got around to doing the other two signs. Eventually, Sandy lost patience with him, terminated the contract, and had those signs painted by another sign-writer. She had not paid Bill for the first two signs and when he asked for his money, Sandy told him that he was

not entitled to payment because he never finished the job. Is Sandy right? Although this is a sale of goods, consider the question under both the common law and UCC Article 2.

6. Consider another variation of the contract between Sandy Shaw and Bill Board. The terms of the contract concerning the goods and the price are the same as before. However, it has a different delivery term. It calls for Bill to deliver the four signs in installments. The first is to be delivered within a week of the contract, and the remaining three at weekly intervals thereafter. Sandy is to pay for each sign on delivery. Following formation, Bill made the first sign and delivered it to Sandy exactly on time. Sandy was unimpressed. It read:

Sandy Shors   Motel eligence and cumfert by thesea. Just three   bloks ahed.

Furthermore, the lettering was uneven and not placed symmetrically on the board. The paintwork was sloppy and there were runs and dribbles all over the sign.

Sandy pointed out these faults with some forcefulness. Bill apologized and admitted that he had trouble with spelling. He told Sandy that if she wrote out the message for him, he would redo the sign properly and deliver it within a day. Sandy cannot imagine that Bill could do a decent sign, even if she helped him with his spelling. She sees nothing but aggravation and conflict as she battles with him over this and the other three signs, and she is sure that if she allows him to try again, she will end up with unusable garbage and will have to hire someone else to redo the job. Does she have the right to cancel her contract with Bill?

7. Here is another factual variation of the contract between Sandy Shaw and Bill Board: As before, Bill agreed to make four signs for the prices stated earlier. However, Bill did not simply undertake to deliver them, but also agreed to erect them in position. In addition, because the town requires a permit to be obtained before any new signs are placed next to the roadway, Bill promised to obtain the necessary permit from the town council before erecting the signs. Bill was obliged to have the signs completed, authorized, and installed within four weeks of signing the contract. Sandy agreed to pay 25 percent of the price of the signs within a week of signing the contract, and the balance after erection of the signs.

Two days after the contract was entered into (and therefore 26 days before the date specified for the completion of Bill's performance), Sandy read in the local newspaper that the town council had just refused a permit application made by Bill for another customer. The refusal was based not only on the fact that the application was sloppily handled and full of errors and omissions, but also on the ground that the design of the proposed sign violated the town's ordinance. Apparently Bill responded to this denial by ranting and making threatening gestures at the councilors. As a result, he was forcibly ejected from the hearing and told not to return.

On the day that she read this, Sandy wrote to Bill, expressing alarm at the report of his behavior, and voicing concern that his prior conduct would make it impossible for him to secure a permit for her signs. The letter concluded that unless Bill could allay her fears by getting a permit within the next week, she would consider the contract at an end. In the interim, she would withhold her 25 percent payment until she received notice that the application had been granted. Bill wrote her a reply on the very same day, saying that it was neither convenient nor necessary for him to get the permit so quickly, but assuring her that it would be in hand by the time that the signs are due for erection. He reminded her that he was expecting her payment of 25 percent of the price in five days, as agreed. What should she do now?

8. In May, Cleaver Carnage, a famous chef, entered into a contract with Televicious, Inc., the owner and operator of a television network, to produce and star in a weekly cooking show, to be called "Cleaver's Critter Cookout." The show was to run for a trial season from September 1-October 30. Each weekly installment was to begin with live video footage showing Cleaver hunting and slaughtering various woodland creatures. The scene would then change to Cleaver's well-equipped studio kitchen, in which he would prepare a delectable dish from the day's catch.

In July, Televicious came under great pressure from various consumer groups and government agencies to reduce the level of violence in its broad-casts. In attempting to respond to community concerns, it reviewed its fall programming and decided to cancel several shows that seemed unnecessarily gruesome. Cleaver's cooking show was one of them. Televicious proposed to replace it with a program entitled "Longevity with Legumes," to be hosted by Lena Lofatt, a widely published author of health-conscious recipe books. Televicious wrote to Cleaver on July 30, informing him that his services were no longer required. Cleaver responded immediately by writing a letter to Televicious, pointing out correctly that the contract gave Televicious no right to cancel unilaterally, and notifying it that he continued to hold it to the contract.

By August 10, Cleaver had heard nothing more from Televicious. On that day he received an offer to work during September as camp chef for a culinary safari of central Africa. Although he was quite attracted by the invitation, he decided that it was not nearly as beneficial to his career as a television program would be. Because he still hoped that Televicious would repent if given some time, he declined the offer of the safari and waited for its response to his letter. His optimism was in vain. A week later, he received a terse note from Televicious, stating that the decision was final. By now, it is too late for Cleaver to find anything else to replace his aborted television venture. What are his rights?

Explanations

1. Holmes's commencement of work is an express promise and a construed condition precedent to Sue's payment of the $2,500 on May 3. Sue's performance of this promise is, in turn, a construed condition precedent to Holmes's continued performance. If Holmes materially breached his promissory condition precedent, Sue would have been entitled to refuse the payment, but if he did not, her refusal to pay would have been a material breach of her promise and also a non-fulfillment of the condition to Holmes's further work. Therefore, if Holmes breached materially, Sue's non-payment was justified, Holmes had no right to leave the job, and Sue can terminate and claim damages for total breach. Conversely, if he did not breach materially, Sue's refusal of payment was a material and total breach, giving Holmes the right to terminate his own performance, to end the contract, and to claim full expectation damages from Sue.

    Was Sue entitled to refuse payment? Although the contract does not say so expressly, it is implied that Holmes would not simply begin work on May 1, but that he would continue to perform in a satisfactory and workmanlike manner in the period before payment fell due. This performance was a construed condition precedent to Sue's payment, so that if he materially and totally breached his promise, Sue had the right to withhold her performance, terminate, and claim expectation damages. Apart from demolishing the deck, there is no suggestion that Holmes did anything wrong, so our determination of the respective rights of the parties must begin by deciding how that unfortunate incident ties into his contractual obligations. In the absence of a more specific yardstick set out in the contract, the question of whether the quality of the work is sufficient to be reasonably workmanlike is judged by prevailing commercial standards — it must be so regarded by reasonable participants in the market. A small deviation from this standard would be a minor breach, resulting in substantial performance, but a significant departure would be material, and if not curable, total.

    One does not need extensive evidence of commercial expectations to accept the proposition that a landscaper's duty of workmanlike performance includes an obligation to exercise reasonable care in the use of heavy equipment and to avoid demolition of the structures erected on the land. Holmes apparently failed in this duty, with grave consequences. The materiality of a breach is a factual question, to be determined with reference to the terms of the contract in context. Given the extent of the damage caused by the breach and Holmes's apparent inability to manage his equipment properly, the deviation from his contractual duty should qualify as material.

But even if the breach was material, Sue elected not to treat it as total. She was willing to allow Holmes back on the job. However, she refused to render her own performance until her claim against him for the damage to the deck had been paid. If a party chooses to treat a breach as partial, she must normally render her own performance when it becomes due. By electing not to pursue her right to declare total breach, she forgoes the remedies for total breach, including the right to withhold her own performance. However, she is entitled to an offset for the damages caused by the breach, so when, as in this case, those damages for partial breach are likely to be extensive, and may well equal or exceed her obligation to Holmes, it would be unfair to expect her to pay Holmes first and later struggle to recover for her loss. Under these circumstances, it is makes sense to allow her to hold back her payment for the purpose of set off. As she was justified in not paying, Holmes's abandonment of the job converted his partial breach into a total breach and entitled Sue to terminate and claim damages.

This example is based on *K & G Construction Co. v. Harris*, 164 A.2d 451 (Md. 1960), in which an excavator damaged the owner's house by driving a bulldozer too close to it. The owner allowed the excavator to continue work, but refused to pay the next installment due for the work on the grounds that the damage to the house exceeded the amount owing to the excavator. (Unlike Holmes, the excavator did not admit liability for the damage.) When the owner refused to pay, the excavator abandoned the work. The court held that by damaging the house, the excavator breached his promise (which was express in that case, not implied) to perform in a workmanlike manner. This was a material breach as well as the nonfulfillment of a construed condition of the owner's payment. Although the owner initially treated the breach as partial by allowing the excavator to continue work, nonfulfillment of the condition justified her refusal to pay the installment. By abandoning the work, the excavator turned the partial breach into a total one, entitling the owner to terminate the contract and claim damages.

2.   Standard has breached the contract by failing to comply with the specifications. If the breach is material and total, Lofty has the right to respond as he intends, seeking termination of the contract

and compensation for any expectation damages that may be suffered.[16]

Standard does not claim that it has substantially performed, and it has undertaken to demolish and rebuild. It, in effect, concedes that the breach is material. We therefore do not have to consider this question on the present facts. (It is raised by the facts of Example 3.) The only issue is whether the breach is total — that is, whether Lofty can terminate immediately without giving Standard the opportunity to perform the tendered cure. Standard proposes to give Lofty his exact contractual expectations.[17] Lofty rejects this because he claims to have lost faith in Standard and does not believe that he will ultimately get a house of the quality contemplated by the contract.

When the contract involves a sale of goods, the right to cure a defective performance has a clear statutory basis under UCC §2.508. However, the common law concept of partial breach also envisages the possibility of cure when the breach is not so immediately and irrevocably material as to be incapable of reversal, and the breaching party shows a desire to remedy the defective performance within a reasonable time. The efforts at cure must produce a performance in compliance with the contract. If the finished product remains significantly deficient, the failure to cure properly will itself be a material breach. (Conversely, if the cure falls short of the promised performance in only a minor respect, it will constitute substantial performance.) However, Lofty does not wish to give Standard any opportunity to attempt a cure. He claims the right to terminate immediately on the basis that the proposed cure will not give him the benefit of his bargain. He bases this assertion on the conviction that Standard's pre-existing incompetence and sloppiness could continue in its efforts to cure and could be exacerbated by its incentive to compromise the quality of its performance, leaving him with a patchwork job.

Although Lofty's concerns may be genuine, if he rejects the offer of cure, he may later have some trouble establishing that they were realistic and reasonable. There is no indication that Standard is incapable of

---

16. We focus here on the breach issue and defer detailed discussion of damages for total breach to Chapter 18. For the present, it is enough to note that the basic measurement of damages would be the difference between the contract price and the reasonable cost to have another contractor complete the house as specified in the contract. This would include the cost of demolishing the nonconforming work and completing the house. Because Lofty has no doubt already made some periodic payments to Standard for the work done before its breach, these payments would also have to be taken into account in calculating damages.

17. The facts make it clear that Standard's proposed cure will not delay completion of the house beyond the contract's completion date. This removes the complication that would arise if the cure cannot be effected in time. If cure causes a delay beyond the date specified for performance, the delay itself could be a material breach if time is of the essence.

following a plan, or that it would approach the rectification of performance grudgingly. If cure is feasible and the will to cure is apparent, the promisee takes a risk that a court may later disagree with his prediction of inadequate performance, and may find him to have acted unreasonably in preventing rectification of the breach.

3(a). Lofty has not yet terminated the contract. Instead, he treated the breach as partial and offered Standard an opportunity to cure it by rectifying the construction to bring the house into conformity with the contract. Standard refuses to effect this cure and offers instead to cure by reducing the price of the house. Standard's response is based on its view that construction of a house with $8'$ ceilings would be substantial performance of its contract obligations. If Standard is wrong, Lofty may respond to its refusal to cure by declaring total breach. He may then terminate the contract and hire another contractor to complete the house in accordance with the contract specifications. If Standard is correct, Lofty has no right to terminate the contract and must accept the defective performance. He would then have a claim for damages to compensate for the breach. Standard says he can be compensated adequately by a $20,000 price reduction. (Assume for now that this would be the proper recovery if Standard had substantially performed. We will discuss the remedy for substantial performance in Explanation 3(b).)

Is construction of a house with $8'$ ceilings substantial performance of Standard's contract obligations? This is a factual question, to be determined by interpreting the contract to decide on the parties' reasonable expectations. The term must have been so central to the bargain that its breach would deprive Lofty of the value reasonably anticipated. There are several indications that the specification of $9'$ ceilings was a material term. It was not simply part of the standard specifications, but was deliberately inserted into the contract. Lofty's height, one of the reasons why he wanted higher ceilings, was apparent to Standard. Lofty built the house for his own use and occupation, not for resale. The defect detracts from the comfort and enjoyment that Lofty reasonably expected from the house, so the fact that the lower ceilings would not affect the market price should not be a significant consideration. (The question of how the analysis of materiality might change if Lofty had bought the house for resale is discussed in Explanation 3(b).)

The facts of Lofty's case invoke *Jacob & Youngs v. Kent*, *Plante v. Jacobs*, and *Lyon v. Belosky Construction*, discussed in section 17.3.3. As those cases show, the court's task in deciding on the materiality of a breach is to differentiate those deviations that go to the heart of the contract from those that do not. This distinction is made by measuring the gravity of the breach in light of the contract's language, circumstances, and purpose. The circumstances of this case make the breach akin to the material breach found in *Lyon* and distinguish it from the minor breaches found in *Jacob & Youngs* and *Plante*. Lofty is therefore entitled to refuse the cure of a price reduction. If Standard persists in its refusal to rectify the error, Lofty may declare total breach, terminate the contract, and claim damages from Standard based on the difference between the contract price and the cost of completing the house to contract specifications.

3(b). The facts are now that Lofty is in the business of building houses for resale and the parties understood that he would market the house on completion. If Standard can prove that the lower ceilings have no impact on the market price and saleability of the house, it has a much stronger chance of establishing that the breach is not material — that it has no impact on the value of the contract to Lofty. In addition, as the breach was inadvertent rather than deliberate, a court is likely to be more sympathetic to Standard's assertion that the breach was immaterial so as to shield it from the severe consequences of total breach. However, although the facts suggest a better case for arguing substantial performance, this is not a foregone conclusion. As the dissent in *Jacob & Youngs* pointed out, once the parties go to the trouble of specifying a term in clear and express language, the court should be slow to second-guess them and to declare the term immaterial merely because it seems unimportant to the court. This applies even more so in Lofty's case than in *Jacob & Youngs* because the parties deliberately changed the ceiling height in the specifications and increased the contract price accordingly. Therefore, even though Lofty will not live in the house, and even if Standard can prove that the lower ceilings will not alter the market value or saleability of the house, a court could still find that the parties intended the specification of 9' ceilings to be a material term of the contract.

Although it is by no means certain that a court will find that Standard substantially performed, we will assume that it does find substantial performance so that we can discuss the remedy for partial breach. The normal measure of damages for partial breach is the cost of rectifying the defective work. This would include the cost of the partial demolition of the structure and its rebuilding — a significant amount of liability, not much different from what Standard would have incurred had the court found a total breach. The fact that the damages would be so high if measured by the cost to complete suggests that this may be a case to consider using a different measure. This is particularly so because such a large award of damages would be disproportionate to the actual harm that Lofty is likely to suffer because he will make no loss on resale of the house. Given the economics of the situation, Lofty is not likely to use the award of damages to change the ceiling height of the house, so he will receive a windfall that imposes a hardship on Standard beyond what is merited by a non-material breach. In *Jacob & Youngs* and *Plante*, the courts resolved this problem by limiting damages to the reduction in market value resulting from the breach. In both those cases, as in this case, the diminution in market value was zero.

4. This question again raises the issue of substantial performance. If the common law applied to this contract, the analysis of this question would be very much like that in prior examples: We would have to decide if the size of the signs was a material term of the contract. If it was, Bill has materially breached. A breach of that magnitude[18] would give Sandy the right to demand compliant performance or, failing that, to claim expectation damages measured by the cost of placing her in the position that she would have been in, had the breach not occurred. One cannot reach a definitive conclusion about the materiality of the sign's dimensions on the facts available, but as the purpose of the sign is to advertise the motel to passing motorists, size may well be material. However, if the size of the sign is not material, the otherwise competent performance may be substantial, in which case the cost of rectification may not be an appropriate remedy, because it will presumably require nothing less than scrapping the signs and making new ones. This may constitute an unfair forfeiture to Bill, so Sandy may be confined to a claim for the difference in value (if any) between what she contracted for and what she received.

However, this contract cannot simply be analyzed under common law. Bill's undertaking to make the sign is not a contract to perform a service for Sandy, but a sale of goods. The transaction involves the exchange of an end product — the completed signs — for money. (It is, of course, common for a manufacturer to sell goods that it has fabricated, and this is no less a sale because the goods are custom-made.) As this is a sale, the doctrine of substantial performance does not apply. Under §2.601, the buyer may reject the goods if they fail in any respect to conform to the contract. This right of rejection is mitigated by the seller's right to cure under §2.508, but this does not help Bill very much because Sandy is willing to allow him to cure. Bill's problem is that cure cannot be accomplished without completely redoing the signs, which is likely to be quite burdensome and could lead to a loss on the contract. The perfect tender rule

---

18. This sounds like a subtly clever pun, but it's not.

therefore takes a very different direction from the common law. If the tender of the goods is nonconforming, the buyer has the right to reject it and there is no room to consider whether Bill has substantially performed or to take unfair forfeiture into account. (As noted in section 17.5.1, the circumstances may allow the court some flexibility if the buyer did not reject properly or in time or there are clear grounds for finding that the buyer acted in bad faith in rejecting the goods, but no circumstances of this kind seem to be present here.)

5. There is no issue here of perfect tender, substantial performance, or rejection with regard to the two signs delivered. They are apparently satisfactory and in use. Nor is there any doubt that Bill has totally breached his outstanding performance obligations, giving Sandy the right to terminate that portion of the contract relating to the remaining performance. We are spared the issue of Sandy's damages because she claims none. She apparently incurred no demonstrable loss as a result of the delay in getting the signs up, or on account of having to pay more for a substitute. Therefore, the only issue is whether Bill's breach permits Sandy to keep his signs without paying for them.

Although this is a sale of goods, the question asks for an analysis under the **common law** for comparison purposes. The common law requires a determination of whether failure to deliver half the signs was a material and total breach. This would most likely be answered in the affirmative, especially after the failure persisted beyond a reasonable cure period. As a material breacher, Bill has no right to sue on the contract unless it is divisible. If it is divisible, he may enforce those portions of the contract that he has fully performed (subject to an offset for any damages suffered by Sandy, had she incurred loss or expense relating to the breached portion). If it is not divisible, he has no claim in contract. In some jurisdictions, he may obtain relief on the theory of unjust enrichment (again, subject to any offset for Sandy's damages), but there are courts that refuse even restitutionary relief to a breaching party. Others permit it only when the breach is not willful. Even in those jurisdictions that permit restitutionary recovery, it is likely to be a more difficult and less attractive claim than contractual relief, because the breacher must prove the value of the ultimate economic enrichment actually conferred on the non-breaching party, which could well be lower than the contract price.

Is this contract divisible? Divisibility is a question of fact, to be decided by interpreting the contract in context. The contract is not divisible if the parties intended the exchange as an integrated whole, so that their reasonable expectations are defeated if any portion of it is eliminated. However, the contract is divisible if it can be separated into component parts, each with a distinct consideration, and the value of the components that were performed is not diminished by removing those that were not performed. This contract called for four signs. Bill supplied the two at the entrances of the town, but failed to supply the two that actually pointed to the motel. The argument in favor of divisibility is that the price of each sign is provided for separately in the contract, and the delivered signs have value as self-standing advertisements for the motel. The argument against divisibility is that the signs were intended to work in conjunction with each other, and the pointers were intended to follow up on the other signs by directing guests to the motel.

In *John v. United Advertising, Inc.*, 439 P.2d 53 (Colo. 1968), the owner of a motel contracted with an advertising agency for the installation and upkeep of seven signs. The contract (structured as a lease and maintenance agreement, not a sale) provided separate rent for each sign. Five of the signs were properly erected but two were not. The motel owner argued that the signs should be seen as a unit, designed to lead tourists to the motel. The advertising agency argued that each sign was self-sufficient and was charged for separately. In addition, the contract actually stated that each of the items in the contract could be terminated or modified without affecting others. (This contractual provision makes the case for division in *John* even stronger than in our case.) The court agreed with the advertising agency that the contract was divisible.

If the contract is divisible, Bill can enforce it with regard to the signs that were delivered and recover their contract price. Sandy would be able to offset her damages against this recovery if her reasonable cost of having the remaining two signs done by another painter exceeded the contract price for those signs. If the contract is not divisible, Bill's recovery is confined to a claim for unjust enrichment, subject to the qualifications mentioned above.

Does this analysis change because this is a **sale of goods**? No section of UCC Article 2 speaks directly to this question, so the above principles of common law are applicable. To the extent that Article 2 deals indirectly with the issue of severability, its approach is consistent with these principles. There are several provisions that recognize the concept of divisibility where the language and purpose of the contract, viewed in its commercial context, indicate that division of the goods into separate units would not impair the value of performance. Section 2.601 suggests that contracts for the sale of goods are normally divisible if the goods can be broken down into "commercial units." It contemplates that a buyer has the right to accept a "commercial unit" of goods that comply, and to reject the rest. To constitute a "commercial unit," an item or collection of goods must be regarded as a unit in commercial usage and must be capable of being traded as a unit without any impairment of value on the market. (*See* §2.105(6).[19]) This approach is also reflected in the general remedy provisions in §§2.702 and 2.711; in §2.709, which allows the seller to recover the price of accepted goods; and in Comment 2 to §2.612,[20] in which the drafters make it clear that when the parties apparently intended delivery in installments, a commercially reasonable fact-based interpretation must be used to apportion price to deliveries, and to break the contract into a set of self-standing exchanges.

6.   Because the contract ". . . authorizes the delivery of goods in separate lots to be separately accepted . . ." it satisfies the definition of an installment contract in §2.612. That section allows the buyer to reject any installment that has a non-conformity that substantially impairs its value. If cure is possible and permissible, the buyer may not reject the installment if the seller gives an adequate assurance of cure. In other words, to be able to reject this installment, Sandy must show three things: First, that the goods are non-conforming; second, that the non-conformity is serious enough that it substantially reduces the value of that installment; and third, that the non-conformity cannot be cured. That is, where an installment sale is concerned, the perfect tender rule does not apply and the test for rejection is more equivalent to the common law substantial performance standard.

There can be little doubt that the sign is materially deficient, so the determinative issue is whether the defect is curable. Although the standards of §2.508 may be applicable to the cure of an installment sale, there is some question about whether its specific requirements have been replaced by a more general and looser test set out in Comment 5 to §2.612.[21] That comment indicates that an installment delivery must be accepted if the nonconformity is curable by a price adjustment or later delivery and the seller gives adequate assurance of cure. It could be, therefore, that in an installment sale, we need not be concerned with the rule in §2.508(2) that only permits cure after the time for delivery if the seller had reasonable grounds to believe that the non-conforming tender would be acceptable. (This rule would otherwise apply here because the sign was delivered on its due date, and the time for Bill's performance had expired before he could attempt to redo it.) In any event, under both §2.508 and

---

19. Section 2.105(6) is renumbered §2.105(5) in the 2003 revision of Article 2.
20. These sections and the Comment continue to adopt this approach in the 2003 revision of Article 2.
21. As noted in footnote 14, the 2003 revision of §2.508 makes it clear that its standards do apply to installment contracts.

Comment 5 to §2.612, cure is only permitted if effective remediation is assured and is affected within a reasonable time.

Is Bill's assurance of cure adequate? Although Bill, in his incompetent fog, may have thought that his sloppy work would have been acceptable to Sandy, it is unlikely that he was reasonable in this belief. Furthermore, even if he earnestly intends to make a better sign, bad spelling is not his only shortcoming. Given the atrocious quality of the work tendered, Sandy has no reasonable expectation that cure will be adequate. She should therefore be entitled to reject this installment.

But Sandy does not wish simply to reject this sign. She would like to end the entire contract. Even if a non-conformity allows rejection of the installment under §2.612(2), the breach does not give Sandy the right to cancel the entire contract unless a further element, required by §2.612(3) is satisfied: To terminate the entire contract on the basis of a non-conformity in one or more installments, the buyer must show that the breach "substantially impairs" the value of the contract as a whole. That is, the breach relating to an installment is usually regarded as a partial breach, giving rise only to relief for that non-conformity. The buyer cannot use it as a basis of terminating the entire contract unless it so fundamentally undermines the exchange of values that it defeats the buyer's reasonable expectations concerning the remaining performance.

Therefore, even a serious defect in the sign delivered would not entitle Sandy to terminate the contract relating to the remaining signs unless the defective sign was so interlinked with the others that the defect substantially diminished their value too. This could happen, for example, when the goods in the deficient installment are such a major component of the sale that the other installments have little purpose without it, or when the goods delivered in each installment must be combined to provide the benefit bargained for, and have little use to the buyer on their own. A situation like this does not seem to be involved here. It was already suggested in Example 5 that the contract is probably divisible.

However, the whole contract could also be substantially impaired if the defect is due to such incompetence that the buyer has no reason to expect that the seller is capable of proper performance in future. Comment 6 to §2.612 indicates that the reasonable perception of failure of performance must go beyond insecurity. If the buyer merely has doubts about future installments, the proper course is to demand an assurance of performance under §2.609. However, if the defect in the installment strongly demonstrates that the seller will never be able to deliver what was promised, so that the prospect of adequate future performance is so remote as to be tantamount to a repudiation, the buyer should be able to declare a breach of the entire contract based on the defective installment. Bill's amateurish attempt at signwriting and his apparent obliviousness to its deficiencies should entitle Sandy to use this breach as the basis for termination of the entire contract.

7.   Because this contract involves the performance of services in connection with the sale of the signs, it is no longer as obviously subject to the UCC. In a mixed transaction, some courts decide this scope issue by looking at the dominant purpose of the contract. Others apply Article 2 to the sales component, but not to the service aspect. (See Example 1 of Chapter 2.) On the dominant purpose test, this probably still qualifies as a sale of goods, because the services are ancillary to the sale and do not appear to have increased the price. For the purpose of discussion, assume that Article 2 is applicable to the transaction. However, it would not make any substantive difference in many jurisdictions if this conclusion is wrong, because the relevant UCC section, 2.609, is mirrored in Restatement Second §251.

    Bill's performance is not due for 26 days, so he cannot yet be in breach of his obligations. Furthermore, his actions before the council cannot be treated as a repudiation, because he has not made an unequivocal statement or taken clear action to indicate an intention not to perform this contract when the time comes. Notwithstanding, his conduct in an unrelated contract of a similar kind has made Sandy feel insecure about his ability to perform his obligations to her in the near future. This has caused her to write to him, making a demand that goes beyond what she is entitled to under the contract, and threatens suspension of her own performance unless the demand is met. If she is unjustified in this demand, then either her failure to pay in five days or her termination at the end of a week would itself be a repudiation of her contractual obligations. Indeed, the very act of making the demand could constitute an unequivocal repudiation, if the demand states the intention to withhold performance unless its unjustified terms are met.

    When one party has reasonable grounds to feel insecure about the other's performance, §2.609 permits the insecure party to suspend her own performance and to make a written demand for an adequate assurance of due performance. Upon receiving a justified demand, the other party must provide an adequate assurance within a reasonable time, not exceeding 30 days, failing which, he has repudiated. Both the demand and the response must be reasonable, so this process imposes a duty of careful judgment on each of the parties: The party making the demand must not overreact to the possible threat of breach and must decide not only if the circumstances warrant a demand, but also what assurance is needed. If she is unreasonable in her perception of potential breach, the act of making the demand could itself indicate intent to repudiate. Even if not, repudiation could occur if she follows up by withholding a due performance. In addition, the demand must be carefully aimed. If she asks for too little, the assurance may be useless, but if she asks too much, she could be taken to have repudiated the contract herself by refusing to perform unless the other party agrees to a forced modification. Upon receiving the demand, the other party must react to it within the time prescribed by §2.609. If it is unjustified, he has the right to refuse it altogether. If it is justified but excessive, he may offer a more modest assurance. But if it is justified, failure to give the demanded assurance is a repudiation.

It seems likely that Sandy was acting reasonably in her concern about Bill's likelihood of obtaining a permit. His conduct in a similar transaction for another customer suggests not only that he has some difficulty in complying with the permit requirements, but also that he lacks self-control and the political finesse to deal with public officials. In addition, he has no doubt alienated the very people who must decide his next application. If we accept that Sandy had the right to demand an assurance, did she go too far in requiring the permit to be obtained in a week? Sometimes, particularly when the other party has said or done something to cast doubt on the desire to perform, it may be enough to ask for verbal reassurance. In a case like this, a mere reaffirmation is not likely to be very helpful. Bill really cannot alleviate her concerns simply by stating that he is still committed to perform, because he may be incapable of doing so. However, by insisting on an immediate successful application, Sandy seeks to force a modification of the contract by accelerating Bill's performance (and possibly doing so at a rate that makes it difficult or impossible for him to comply with the demand). A demand that requires the other party to assume more onerous performance obligations is seldom permissible. To justify it, the prospect of breach must be particularly strong, and there must be no less intrusive way of eliminating the insecurity. In this case, performance is still some time off and Bill has given no indication that he will not make the application. A more appropriate demand may have called on Bill to give a prompt and explicit account of how he plans to avoid a similar outcome in Sandy's application.

If the demand was appropriate, Bill's refusal to honor it would be a repudiation, and Sandy could immediately terminate. Conversely, if as suggested above, the demand was excessive, Sandy may have repudiated simply by making it. However, we do not have to resolve that issue, because Bill has not treated it as a repudiation.

He has given a response that he sees as adequate and reminded Sandy about her payment due in a few days. This requires a further judgment by Sandy. She could simply back down and pay on due date, hoping that Bill will perform as required. Alternatively, she could try a different and less stringent demand, suspending payment until Bill responds, or she could press her original demand and withhold her payment. If she takes either of these latter courses, she goes out on a limb and can only hope that if the matter is litigated, the court shares her view that the response was inadequate and the demanded assurance was no more than she needed to remove her insecurity.

8.   On July 30, Televicious unequivocally repudiated the contract. This gave Cleaver the option either of accepting the repudiation and immediately pursuing his remedy for total breach, or of declining to act on the repudiation and giving Televicious the opportunity to repent within a reasonable time. He chose the latter course. After about ten days had passed without any sign of retraction from Televicious, Cleaver was given the chance to recoup some of his potential loss by agreeing to join the African safari during September. Despite his initial decision, Cleaver has the right to change his mind and accept the repudiation at any time before retraction is communicated to him. He therefore could have accepted the offer to be a chef on the safari. He would have had no obligation to notify Televicious of this, because the repudiation cannot be retracted once Cleaver has made another commitment on the strength of it. Having accepted the repudiation, Cleaver would no longer have had to hold himself available to perform for Televicious, and could have sued immediately for damages based on the difference between what he would have received under the contract with Televicious, and what he would have earned from the substitute employment. (We leave to Chapter 18 the question of whether someone in Cleaver's position could also have claimed any damages resulting from the loss of potential fame and fortune as a TV celebrity.)

However, Cleaver decided to pass up the opportunity in the hope that Televicious would have a change of heart. When he is eventually left with nothing to do in September, his decision to wait may be held against him. If, when he ultimately sues Televicious for damages, he is found to have acted unreasonably in continuing to await a retraction, his recovery from Televicious will be reduced to the extent that he should have acted to avoid the loss. That is, under the principle of mitigation of damages, he will not be able to hold Televicious liable for the amount that he could have recouped had he resigned himself to the repudiation and gone on the safari.

The crucial question is therefore whether Cleaver was reasonable in continuing to hold out hope for a retraction on August 10. Reasonableness is always a factual issue, to be decided in light of the nature and clarity of the repudiation and the likelihood of repentance under all the circumstances of the case. Televicious clearly and unconditionally expressed its intention to breach and completely ignored Cleaver's invitation to reconsider. He was given no reason to believe that Televicious would change its mind and was unduly optimistic in waiting further. He did not even attempt another communication before refusing the substitute employment. Under these circumstances, he would have quite a difficult task in convincing a court that he reasonably acted to cut down his loss. (Let us assume for now that the safari was indeed an appropriate substitute contract. This question will be discussed further in Chapter 18.)

Remedies for Breach of Contract

§18.1 THE SCOPE OF THIS CHAPTER

Because a contract creates obligations enforceable in law, its breach by one of the parties entitles the other to commence suit to enforce it. This does not mean, of course, that the victim of a breach will inevitably sue. Breaches are often settled by negotiation or by methods of resolution other than litigation, such as mediation or arbitration. Even if not, the victim may decide not to sue because the amount at stake is too small to justify the expense of litigation, or because of the difficulty of proving economic injury, or because it seems clear that the breaching party has no funds or other assets available to pay any judgment that may be obtained. Although the possibilities of informal or non-judicial enforcement, the economic feasibility of litigation, and the problem of actually collecting on the judgment should always be borne in mind, they are not addressed here. It is the concern of this chapter to set out the policies, general principles, and rules that govern the choice of remedy for breach and the measurement of compensation. We therefore focus on the judicial enforcement of the contract following its breach. (This does not mean that the principles discussed here are applicable only in litigation. The rules governing the nature and extent of judicial relief are obviously also relevant to, and form the basis of, any alternative method of resolving liability for breach.)

This is not the only part of the book in which judicial remedies are covered. There are many examples in prior chapters of remedies available to a party to redress a wrong that arises in the context of a transaction.

For example, the remedy of avoidance has been discussed repeatedly in connection with topics such as duress, fraud, and mistake. This chapter is distinct in that it deals only with remedies for breach of contract. The discussion here *presupposes* that a *valid and enforceable contract* has been entered into and that one of the parties has *materially breached* that contract. We are not concerned at this point with the issue of what is required for the creation of a valid and enforceable contract, nor with what constitutes a breach, whether a breach occurred, or if that breach is material or trivial. Those matters are considered in prior chapters. For present purposes, the fact of material breach of a binding contract is treated as a given.[1] Therefore, whether you are reading this chapter at the end of the course, after having dealt with the issue of breach, or your contracts course deals with damages at or near the beginning of the year, just accept as a premise that the question of material breach must be settled as a precursor to the determination of damages.

Once these initial issues concerning the formation and breach of a contract have been disposed of, and it is established that the plaintiff does have a claim against the defendant, the remedial issues fall into three distinct but interrelated inquiries: First we must determine the nature and extent of the plaintiff's compensable loss, including both the harm suffered and the availability and form of the legal remedy or remedies to redress it. Second, if there is more than one means of remedying the loss, we must decide which of the available remedies most efficiently and comprehensively compensates for it. Finally, we must take into account any policies or principles that may limit the defendant's liability for the loss.

§18.2 THE BASIC GOAL OF REMEDIES FOR BREACH: ENFORCEMENT OF THE EXPECTATION INTEREST

§18.2.1 The Nature of the Expectation Interest

A valid and enforceable contract justifies a *future expectation* by each of the parties. They are both entitled to expect that the other will honor the contractual promise made and will perform as undertaken. If one of the parties fails to do so, thereby breaching the contract, the expectations of the other have been disappointed. Therefore, the fundamental goal of the remedy for breach is to cure that disappointment by giving the victim of the breach exactly what was promised and justifiably expected under the contract. This starkly contrasts contract damages from those for tort: While tort damages

---

1. Damages for non-material breach are discussed in section 17.3.

seek to compensate for something lost—to restore the victim to the pre-injury position, contract damages aim at compensating for something that was not gained—what the plaintiff should have had. This goal of enforcing contractual expectations is the beacon that guides contract remedies. The principle is described in a number of alternative ways, all of which have essentially the same meaning: Sometimes it is said that the goal is to protect the plaintiff's **expectation interest**; sometimes it is described as giving the plaintiff the **benefit of her bargain**; and sometimes it is said that the purpose of contract remedies is to place the victim of breach in the **position** that she **would have been in had no breach occurred**. This goal of damages applies both at the common law and under the UCC, which codifies it in §1.106.[2]

A party's expectation interest is the value of the performance to her, based on the purpose of the contract, as gleaned from its wording and the circumstances surrounding the contract's formation. However, even though the expectation interest is based on the contractual expectations of the particular party aggrieved by the breach, it is not determined on the purely subjective criterion of her privately held, subjective belief about what she would derive from the contract. Contracts are interpreted *objectively*, so her expectations must be in accordance with what a reasonable person in her position would have expected as the benefit of the transaction, given the language used by the parties to express their agreement, and the circumstances surrounding it.

§18.2.2 An Introduction to the Means of Enforcement: The Primacy of Monetary Compensation over Specific Relief

The most direct and accurate way of enforcing the plaintiff's reasonable expectations under the contract would be for the court to grant an order of **specific performance** of the contract. This is an order to the defendant requiring him to perform as promised. For example, Harpo C. Cord owns the only extant piano known to have been used by Chopin. He entered into a contract with Nick L. Odeon under which he agreed to sell it to Nick for $25 million. Harpo breached the contract by refusing to go through with the sale. Nick's expectation is to gain the piano in exchange for depleting his bank account by $25 million, so the most accurate means for the court to ensure that he achieves that expectation is to compel Harpo to deliver the instrument against payment of its price. This seems like the most obvious solution, and on these facts—because the piano is unique—the court may

---

2. Section 1.106 is renumbered §1.305 in revised Article 1, with no significant changes.

see this as the most effective and desirable resolution. However, specific performance is not the norm. It is reserved for unusual cases where damages are shown to be incapable of adequately compensating the plaintiff. More commonly, the plaintiff's disappointed expectations are compensated for by an award of money.

Why does the law prefer a *money equivalent of expectation* over the real thing? The answer lies partly in considerations of *practicality and policy*, and partly in the *traditional dichotomy between law and equity.* The practical and policy issues may be illustrated by the following example: Sara Nade, an aspiring singer, had entered a singing competition in the hope of winning first prize, the chance to sing the national anthem at an important sports event. To give herself the best chance of winning, she contracted with Harmony R. Peggio, a voice coach, to receive an intensive period of voice training in the week before the competition. Under their contract Harmony undertook, for a fee of $1,500, to give Sara four hours of coaching every day in that week. A few days before the course of instruction was to begin, Harmony notified Sara that she would be leaving town to do a last-minute concert tour, so she could not give the lessons as promised. Sara's expectation interest is to have the lessons for $1,500, and therefore the most accurate way of ensuring that Sara gets exactly what she expected would be for a court to compel Harmony to decline the tour and to give the promised lessons. However, in this situation the remedy of specific performance presents a number of problems: It would be difficult for the court to ensure that Harmony put her best efforts into a job that she is forced to do; the compulsion takes on the aspect of involuntary servitude; and the solution is not very efficient if another teacher could be found instead. For these reasons, it makes sense to allow Harmony to go on her tour, but if her breach results in a loss to Sara, to hold her liable to compensate for that loss.

As noted earlier, the preference for monetary relief is not based only on concerns of practicality, forced labor, and efficiency. Even if none of these problems exists, our legal tradition emphasizes damages as the standard remedy for breach of contract and disfavors specific relief in all but the most compelling circumstances. This is because the award of money *damages* was a remedy that could be granted by courts of *law,* whereas *specific performance* was granted only by a court of *equity.* (The distinction between law and equity is explained in section 2.5 and is discussed further in section 18.10.1.) Courts of equity were intended to intervene only when the available remedies at law were inadequate, and therefore a plaintiff who sought the equitable relief of specific performance was required to show that the nature of the expectation interest was such that the only means of achieving adequate relief was by the specific enforcement of the contract. Although courts of law and equity were merged some time ago, this ancient distinction still haunts our decisionmaking. As a result, even if it is practicable to give the plaintiff precisely what she expected, a money substitute is used in the great majority of cases: The plaintiff is awarded a sum of money that aims, as closely as possible, to put her into the economic position she would have been in had the contract been performed.

What is the basic principle on which this monetary award is calculated? To illustrate it, let us add some facts to the case of Harmony's breach of the voice-training contract: After Harmony's breach, Sara was able to find another voice coach, who was available to give her equivalent lessons for the same amount of time, but who charged $1,800 for the course. By hiring him, she got the lessons expected for $300 more, so to place her in her expected position, damages of $300 must be awarded against Harmony. Of course, this is not exactly Sara's expectation, because the teacher was different. However, we can seldom achieve the plaintiff's exact position by paying her money. The aim is to get as close possible. It should also be apparent that the concern here is only with economic loss, so if Sara could obtain the equivalent lessons at exactly the same price as Harmony charged under the contract, she has suffered no financial loss at all and is entitled to no damages for the breach.

§18.2.3 Fundamental Principles of Expectation Relief

The above examples suggest a number of important basic principles which will be recurring themes of the discussion that follows.

a. The Achievement of the Plaintiff's Expectation is an Aspiration Seldom Precisely Realized

Contractual remedies aim to place the plaintiff in the position she would have been in had there been no breach, but because specific performance is available in only limited circumstances, the precise attainment of that expectation is seldom achieved. The best a court can do, in most cases, is to try to determine, as closely as possible, what monetary award will approximate that result.

This is already clear from the discussion of Sara's employment of a substitute trainer. The monetary award provides her with the compensation of getting the same hours of instruction for the same price, but it does not give her the less tangible benefit of being instructed by the teacher that she bargained for. The facts of the example, having been drawn with deliberate simplicity, do not illustrate some of the additional difficulties that may get in the way of an accurate measure of the value of the expectation. We will consider these later. For the present just bear in mind that the more complex the facts become, and the more uncertain the consequences of breach are, the harder it is to determine the amount of damages necessary to approximate the plaintiff's rightful position. Sometimes the amount awarded may undercompensate the plaintiff, and sometimes it may overcompensate her. It is important to remember that the burden of proving damages is on the plaintiff, who bears the ultimate risk of failing to persuade the factfinder about the fact or extent of loss. This burden is alleviated in some situations by evidentiary presumptions or inferences.

b. The Economic Nature of Contract Remedies

In the discussion of Harmony's breach, no mention was made of any award for Sara's aggravation, inconvenience, or emotional distress in trying to cope with this last-minute letdown and in finding a replacement for Harmony. Unlike tort law, which is very solicitous of emotional trauma, contract law is dry-eyed and coldly commercial. It does not, except in the most unusual cases, take any account of non-economic injury.

It is implicit in the principle that contract law compensates only for economic injury; that there is usually no sanction for a breach that causes no economic loss.[3] This may be disturbing to one who approaches this chapter after having spent so much effort learning that contractual obligations are binding and legally enforceable. Nevertheless, this is a basic truth of contractual remedies. If the contract is not one of the few that qualifies for specific enforcement, and no economic loss can be established, a breach normally results in no legal liability. (Of course, a breach may nevertheless carry some adverse non-legal consequences, such as loss of goodwill or reputation.) It follows naturally from this that damages measured purely by the extent of the plaintiff's loss do not generally distinguish between breaches that are inadvertent and those that are willful and purposeful. Because the focus is on rectifying harm and not on sanctioning improper conduct, punitive damages are not typically available for a breach of contract (except in unusually egregious cases), even when the violation of the contractual duty was deliberate.

c. The Moral Dimension of Contract Remedies

The strong emphasis on the compensatory nature of contract remedies suggests that contract law approaches breach quite amorally: The law does not care if a party fails to honor her contract, provided that she compensates the other for any loss resulting from her faithlessness. A contractual promise means nothing more than a **commitment either to perform or to pay compensation** for not doing so — a party may usually feel free to renege on her obligations and "buy out" the other party's rights by paying

---

3. There are limited exceptions to this rule — discussed in section 18.3 — when the defendant's conduct in breaching is particularly outrageous or the contract is especially aimed at giving the plaintiff a non-economic benefit.

damages. Although this is largely true, there are some rules of contract law that have particular or stricter application where a breach is wilful or has an immoral dimension. In addition, there are various ways in which the court's or jury's disapprobation of the breacher's conduct might be more subtly reflected in the disposition of the case. For example, a court may use flexible rules to shift the burden of proof or otherwise give a plaintiff some advantage where the breach was purposeful, and a jury usually has enough leeway to be more generous to the plaintiff in awarding damages against a defendant whose breach was calculated and unethical.

d. The Economic Justification for Confining Damages to Financial Loss: The Concept of Efficient Breach

Although the principle of confining damages to financial loss predates the widespread resort to economics to explain, criticize, or justify legal rules, in recent times it has become popular to analyze the rule in economic terms. It is now commonly rationalized by the concept of efficient breach. A breach of contract is said to be *efficient* if the *defendant's cost to perform* would *exceed the benefit that performance* would give to *both parties*. Where this is so, the defendant saves enough money by breaching to enable her to pay compensatory damages to the plaintiff and still come out ahead. Provided that one looks only at the *economic impact* of the breach, one can say in such a case that the defendant's breach does not harm the plaintiff, who receives the financial benefit of his bargain, and yet it improves the defendant's position. In this sense, it satisfies the criterion of economic efficiency in that it makes the defendant better off without making the plaintiff worse off. If this is true, it could be argued that a *rational contracting party* with *full information* will choose to breach where circumstances make the breach efficient. This leads to the argument that the law should not discourage this because a legal rule that permits efficient breach — such as the rule that a plaintiff is entitled only to damages for economic loss — is itself efficient and thus best serves the interests of society.

Although analysis of this type is of some help in understanding and justifying the approach to contract damages, it has many limitations. The most significant is, of course, that it takes into account neither important non-economic values (such as reliability, fair dealing, or faithfulness), nor those consequences of breach that are not measurable in economic terms (such as inconvenience, disappointment, or frustration). As a result, a conclusion that a breach imposes no harm on the plaintiff or on society may be misguided if based purely on quantifiable financial considerations.

Furthermore, economically efficient decisionmaking can only be achieved if all the conditions are right: The market must be competitive and stable, so that the relative costs and benefits of performing and breaching can be gauged. The party contemplating breach must be capable of acting voluntarily and rationally, and must have sufficiently full and reliable information to enable her to make a prediction of likely losses and gains. In addition, the **transaction costs** involved in terminating this contract and making substitutes must be small enough so as not to eliminate any advantage achieved by the breach. (Transaction costs are those costs incurred by both parties in dealing with the breach and any substitute transactions. They would include such expenses as the cost to the breaching party of entering into the other transaction perceived as more profitable, the aggrieved party's costs in finding and making a substitute contract, and the costs of litigating or otherwise resolving the breach issue between the parties.) Such ideal conditions are seldom likely to exist, which means that it will often be difficult to know at the time of breach whether it will turn out to have been economically efficient. Even if the party predicts an advantageous outcome at the time of the breach, economic conditions and subsequent circumstances may render it otherwise. To the extent that a theory of efficient breach is predicated on an unrealistic assumption of rational, voluntary, and informed behavior in a perfect market, with negligible transaction costs, it is likely to be unreliable, and more an academic model than a reflection of reality.

§18.2.4 The Enforcement of a Damage Award

The illustrations in section 18.2.2 do not indicate what happens after Sara gets her judgment of $300 against Harmony. The means of collecting payment on a judgment is beyond our scope, but it is useful to describe it briefly to provide an overall picture of the enforcement process. After the judgment is obtained (or if appealed, once it is affirmed on appeal),[4] Harmony may pay it voluntarily, thereby ending the matter. If she does not, Sara's only means of enforcing the judgment is to have a **writ of execution** issued by the clerk of the court to the sheriff (or equivalent official), calling on that official to find, seize, and sell property owned by Harmony to satisfy the judgment. The sheriff tries to execute the writ by finding property sufficient to satisfy the amount of the judgment, taking custody of it (known as levying upon it), and selling it at public auction. The proceeds of the sale are then paid to Sara, less the costs of execution. There are variations of this procedure that need not concern us here.

The point is that a **judgment** itself is **merely a finding of liability**. It does not guarantee that the plaintiff will get paid. If the defendant fails to

---

4. The claim in the example is for $300. Although it is used here for the purposes of illustrating the process of collection, it should be noted that when the amount in issue is that small (or indeed, even considerably larger), very few plaintiffs would incur the legal expense of pursuing it. It would not take long for legal costs to exceed it.

satisfy it, and no assets can be found to execute upon, the plaintiff may see her money. This sobering reality must be taken into account by any who decides to initiate litigation, and it means that being able to establish breach and damages are only part of the problem of enforcement. A judgment in law for damages is said to be *in rem* — it is enforceable only against the property of the defendant, and if the defendant has no property, the plaintiff loses in the end, having incurred substantial legal costs in the process.

§18.3 THE CALCULATION OF EXPECTATION DAMAGES

It is essential to bear in mind that the aim of expectation damages is to *simulate as closely as possible the plaintiff's economic situation in the absence of breach.* To determine the amount of money needed to approximate that position, a comparison must be made between what the plaintiff had the *right to expect and what she actually got.* Although the facts needed to calculate these two points of comparison can be very complicated and sometimes immensely difficult to prove, the basic concept of the comparison is straightforward. If one does not keep it in sight and use it constantly as a yardstick, one risks getting lost and confused.

Different formulas have been devised for use in making the comparison. These formulas are really just checklists to remind one of the factors to be taken into account, and they are only helpful to the extent that they do reliably cover every component of the calculation and signal clearly what figures go into each of them. A particular formula may be specific to certain kinds of cases and may not work well in others. In general, there are two essential elements to any formula, no matter how it structures the calculation: One part of it will *count up the plaintiff's losses* caused by the breach, and the other will *take into account any gains or recoupments* that she has made as a result of termination of the contract. Damages consist of the losses less the gains. The Restatement Second §347 suggests the following general formula:

Damages =
Plaintiff's loss in value caused by the defendant's non-performance
> (This is determined by deducting the contractual value of what the plaintiff received from what she was promised)

Plus
Any **other loss**
> (This includes consequential and incidental damages)

Less
Any **cost or loss** the plaintiff **avoided** by not having to perform

The principles and method of calculation are best explained by some concrete illustrations that describe some different types of situations and the various considerations that must be taken into account under each of them. Note that the actual ingredients of the calculation shift in accordance with the nature of the contract in question, but that the basic inquiry is always the same — the determination of damages always revolves around a comparison between the plaintiff's rightful position under the contract and her actual situation as a result of the breach.

a. Cases Involving a Substitute Transaction Made by the Plaintiff: Damages are Based on the Loss Incurred as a Result of Having to Make the Substitute Contract

We have already seen that in her simple contract for the purchase of voice training services, Sara's damages could be calculated by measuring the difference between what it would have cost her to receive the services under the contract, and what it ultimately cost her to obtain equivalent services elsewhere. That is, had the contract not been breached by Harmony, she would have had 28 hours of voice training for $1,500. As a result of the breach, she had 28 hours of training for $1,800, so damages of $300 puts her in the position she would have been in had the contract been performed.

Exactly the same calculation and result would occur if, instead of purchasing lessons for $1,500, Sara had bought a car from Harmony for that price, Harmony breached by refusing to deliver, and Sara managed to find an equivalent substitute on the market for $1,800. UCC §2.712[5] codifies this by expressing the buyer's damages as the difference between the cover (i.e., repurchase) price and the contract price.

Change the facts: It is Sara who breached by canceling the lessons, and Harmony entered a substitute transaction by taking on a new student to fill the slot left open by Sara's breach. The same principle applies, but because the plaintiff is the provider of services, damage results only if the gains from the substitute transaction are less than those expected from the breached

---

5. Section 2.712 is not significantly changed in the 2003 revision of Article 2.

contract. For example, assume that Harmony could not find a replacement student at Sara's advanced level, and so she accepted a more junior student at the lower rate of $700 for the 28 hours. Harmony would be entitled to damages of $800, calculated by deducting the $700 earnings under the substitute contract from the $1,500 she expected to earn under her contract with Harmony. Similarly, a seller of goods who reasonably resells the goods at a lower price following the buyer's breach is entitled under UCC §2.706[6] to the difference between the contract price and the lower resale price.

b. Cases in which the Plaintiff could have Made a Substitute Transaction, but Did Not Do So or Failed to Do So Reasonably: Damages are Measured by a Comparison Between the Contract Price and the Market Value of a Substitute

Under both the common law and the UCC, if the aggrieved party did not enter into a substitute transaction, she is entitled to sue for loss based on a *hypothetical substitute*, valued at the market rate (which would have to be established by testimony, typically of an expert witness). Therefore, if, after Harmony's breach, Sara decided not to find a replacement teacher, and if the market value of the lessons is higher than what Harmony charged her, she could still sue Harmony for the difference between the market value of 28 hours of equivalent instruction and the contract price. Similarly, following Sara's breach, Harmony could have decided not to book the other student and could have claimed the difference between the contract price and the market rate she would have earned had she taken the substitute student. The same principle applies under the UCC. Section 2.713[7] allows the buyer the market-contract difference as damages, and §2.708(1)[8] provides for contract-market damages for the seller.

The market price may also be used as the basis for calculating damages when the plaintiff did enter a substitute transaction, but the principle of mitigation, discussed in section 18.6.2, makes it inappropriate to award damages based on the actual cost of the substitute because the cost of the substitute transaction was higher than it needed to have been. This may happen when the market was rising and the plaintiff waited too long before making the substitute contract, or she chose an unreasonably expensive substitute. For example, following Harmony's breach, Sara hired a substitute teacher for $1,800, but that teacher charges more than the market rate of $1,600. If Sara could reasonably have found a teacher at the market rate, her damages will be confined to $100. This principle applies under the UCC as well and is reflected in UCC §§2.706 and 2.712, which require resale or cover to be without unreasonable delay and on reasonable terms.

---

6. Section 2.706 is not substantially changed in the 2003 revision of Article 2.
7. Section 2.713 is not changed in this respect in the 2003 revision of Article 2.
8. Section 2.708(1) is not substantially changed in the 2003 revision of Article 2.

When market value is used as the basis of determining damages, it must be decided at which *place and time* the value must be determined. If the parties reside in the same place and the performance was to occur in that place, there is no problem in deciding on the locality of the market, but if more than one location is connected to the contract, it must be decided which one should be used to measure market value. In addition, a market may fluctuate, so it is necessary to decide the date on which value is to be measured. There are different views on the most appropriate choice of market, and some inconsistency on this issue between the common law, the treatment of the seller under UCC §2.708, and the treatment of the buyer under UCC §2.713.[9] Without getting into that complexity, it may simply be observed that the most sensible approach is to use the time and place that most closely approximates the market that the aggrieved party would reasonably have entered to obtain the substitute.

c. Cases Involving a Contract for Services, in which Breach Results in Lost Income that Cannot be Recouped: Damages May be Equivalent to the Full Value of the Expected Performance

Sometimes it may not be possible for the victim of a breach to find a substitute transaction. If the contract is for services, such as an employment contract in which the employee's only performance is her labor, and if the employee cannot find another job, a breach by the employer results in the employee's loss of her entire expectation under the contract. In such circumstances, the only way to compensate for the employee's disappointed expectation is to award damages equivalent to the full consideration due to her under the contract. For example, a few days before the voice training lessons are to begin, Sara reneges on her contract with Harmony because she decides that she does not need voice training. At this late date, Harmony cannot find another pupil to substitute for Sara, so she loses 28 hours of gainful employment. Sara would have come to Harmony's home for the lessons, and Harmony would not have incurred any costs in performing the service. That is, the full $1,500 would have been profit to her. Had the contract been performed she would have spent nothing and gained $1,500; now she still spends nothing, but gains nothing. Therefore, a payment of $1,500 is needed to give her the benefit of her bargain. Of course, this award really puts her in a better position than the contract would have done, because she does not have to work for it. But this is not taken into account when her savings — avoiding the act of working — have no monetary significance.

---

9. The 2003 revision of Article 2 eliminates this difference in the treatment of the seller and buyer. In both §2.708 and §2.713 the market price is measured at the time and place at which the goods were to be tendered under the contract.

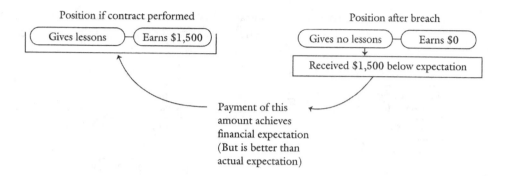

d. Cases in which the Breach of a Contract Results in the Plaintiff's Losing Income but also Saving Costs: Damages are Measured by Deducting Savings from Expected Returns

The result in the above example would be different if Harmony would have had to incur costs to perform. Say that she would have needed to hire an accompanist for $600 to play the piano during the lessons and she is able to avoid doing so as a result of the breach. This cost, which is incurred solely in the process of and for the purpose of performing, is known as a **direct or variable cost**. It must be distinguished from **fixed cost or overhead**, such as Harmony's rent or utilities, which would have to be paid whether or not she performed this contract, and is hence not saved by the breach. Because direct costs would have reduced her expected profit had the contract been performed, it stands to reason that as they are actually saved as a result of the breach (or could have been saved if the plaintiff acted reasonably), they must be deducted from gains to achieve true expectation.

Of course, she *must have been able to save the costs* by reasonable action. The above example assumed that Harmony had the right to cancel her contract with the accompanist, thereby avoiding that direct cost. However, if she could not cancel without incurring liability to him for his fee (that is, she

639

had made an irrevocable contractual commitment to him) she would not save these costs as a result of Sara's breach, and they would not be deducted.

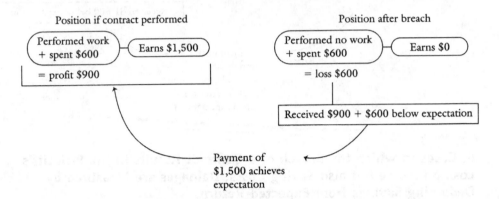

The same result would be reached if, instead of a contract for the provision of services, we were dealing with a sale of goods to be manufactured by the seller. If the buyer breached before the fabrication has begun, so that the seller avoids the direct costs of making the goods, the seller's damages are its lost profits on the sale, calculated by deducting the costs saved from the contract price.

As noted earlier, fixed costs (overhead expenses) are not saved by the breach and are not therefore deducted from damages. The above calculations therefore do not take into account costs such as the rent that Harmony paid for her studio or any other expenses that she had to incur in the course of her business, whether or not she taught Sara. Therefore, when we talk of the recovery of profit in a case like this, we mean gross, not net, profit.

In the first of the above illustrations, Harmony could avoid the direct cost of hiring the accompanist, so her damages are pure profit. But in the second, because she could not save this direct cost, her recovery includes both her *expected profit* and the *reimbursement* of the *wasted expenditure* that she incurred (or was committed to pay) in *reliance* on the contract. In a situation like this, when the plaintiff has incurred the expense of partial performance before the breach, a convenient formula for calculating expectation damages is therefore:

If the plaintiff has received any *part payment* under the contract or has managed to salvage any of the expenditure, that would be *offset* against recovery, and any *consequential or incidental losses* would be *added* to the recovery. Thus the full formula is:

Gross profit
+ reliance
− payments or proceeds
+ other loss (consequential or incidental damages)

Discussion of consequential and incidental damages is deferred for later, but the other three elements of the formula may be illustrated by the following further examples involving a construction contract and a sale of goods:

Some months before the singing competition, and in anticipation of winning it and becoming an internationally renowned star, Sara decided to build a fully-equipped recording studio onto the back of her house. She had the plans drawn, and entered into a contract with Ken Tractor to construct it for a total price of $75,000. The contract required Sara to make a down payment of $5,000 and to pay the remainder of the price in installments as the construction proceeded. Sara made the down payment, and Ken began work about two weeks before the competition. On the eve of the competition, he had reached the stage of completing the foundation and the framing of the new studio. Sara did not win the competition, and she immediately terminated the contract for construction of the studio. As she had no right to do this, she has breached. At that point, Ken had received only his initial payment of $5,000. His costs in material, laborer's wages, and subcontractor charges to date were $10,000. He can show that had he completed the studio, his total direct cost would have been $60,000. The above formula leads us to a damage recovery of $20,000:

Gross profit	Contract price	$75,000
	− total direct cost	$60,000
	=	$15,000
Plus reliance expenditure	+	$10,000
Total (profit + reliance)	=	$25,000
Less payments received	−	$5,000
Recovery	=	$20,000

If you make the comparison between Ken's expected position and his position following breach, as we have done in prior illustrations, you will find that the payment of $20,000 achieves his expectation.

Consider a different case: Sara decided to have a special evening gown made for her appearance at the competition. She contracted with Cadenza La Scala, a dressmaker, for the manufacture of the dress for $1,500. Sara paid a

641

deposit of $150 to Cadenza. After Cadenza had begun work, Sara decided that she had been profligate in ordering such an expensive outfit and decided to use an old prom dress instead. She immediately told Cadenza to stop work, thereby breaching the contract. At that stage, Cadenza had spent $200 on fabric that she had cut according to the pattern designed for Sara. In its present form, the cut fabric could be sold as scrap for $5. If Cadenza completes the dress, she will have to spend a further $50 on materials, but it would be very hard to sell the completed product because it was cut to fit Sara and it reflects her peculiar and rather eccentric fashion sense. This contract is a sale of goods, and UCC §2.708(2) codifies the formula set out above. Before looking at §2.708(2), we should note that as a manufacturer of the goods, Cadenza has the option under §2.704(2)[10] of either scrapping the dress or of completing it and selling it to someone else. In making this choice, she must exercise commercially reasonable judgment. She would be justified in completing and attempting to resell the dress if she reasonably believed that by doing so, she could recoup all or most of the profit lost by Sara's breach, thereby reducing or eliminating her damages. As there is unlikely to be a ready market for such an idiosyncratic piece of clothing, the more reasonable judgment would be to scrap it and to seek damages under our formula, which is adopted in §2.708(2).[11] Her recovery would be:

Gross profit {	Contract price	$1,500
	− total direct cost	−$250
		=$1,250
Plus reliance expenditure		+$200
Total (profit + reliance)		=$1,450
Less payments made ($150)		
and salvage ($5)		−$155
Recovery		=$1,295

Sara's down payment is of course an offset, as it was in the prior example, but the salvage must also be included in the deduction because it is, in a

---

10. Section 2.704(2) has not been changed in the 2003 revision of Article 2.

11. Currently, §2.708(2) states that in calculating the seller's lost profit, due allowance must be made for costs reasonably incurred, and due credit must be given for payments or proceeds of resale. The 2003 revision of §2.708(2) eliminates this language. However, Official Comment 1(e) to revised §2.708 indicates that this is not intended to change the general principle in most cases that payments and proceeds of resale must be deducted from damages. The removal of the language is intended to remove confusion in situations in which the price received by the plaintiff on resale does not really recoup its loss because the breach has resulted in a decrease in the plaintiff's volume of sales. Recovery in a lost volume situation is explained in section 18.6.3.d.

sense, a substitute transaction. Cadenza gains the $5 because she was able to sell the fabric—something she would not have been entitled to do in the absence of breach.

Having labored through this rather exhausting set of illustrations, you should by now be quite convinced of the basic point of this section: There are different ways of expressing the formula for measuring expectation damages. To be helpful, any formula employed must be geared to the facts of the particular type of case, and it must enable you to deal with the fundamental task of calculating the shortfall between what was reasonably expected under the contract and what was received.

§18.4 AN OVERVIEW OF EXPECTATION DAMAGES UNDER UCC ARTICLE 2

§18.4.1 The Basic Principles

The discussion of expectation damages in section 18.3 covers both the common law and UCC Article 2, and includes illustrations concerning sales of goods. You are therefore already familiar with the pertinent Code provisions. Notwithstanding, it may be helpful to review the Article 2 provisions on expectation damages as a whole to show their organization, the symmetry between buyer's and seller's remedies, and their basis in common law principles.

The concept of expectation relief under Article 2 is essentially the same as that under the common law. Like the common law, it reserves the remedy of specific performance for special cases and treats damages as the primary remedy for breach. The award of damages is meant to achieve, as closely as possible, the economic position the plaintiff would have been in had there been no breach. This principle is strongly articulated in §1.106(1),[12] which declares that UCC remedies ". . . shall be liberally administered to the end that the aggrieved party may be put in as good a position as if the other party had fully performed. . . ." Article 2 provides statutory formulas for calculating compensation. It organizes them into seller's remedies for the buyer's breach (§§2.703-2.710) and buyer's remedies for the seller's breach (§§2.711-2.717). Although there is necessarily some variation between these two sets of remedies, they are largely mirror images of each other, providing approximately equivalent rights to buyers and sellers, but taking into account the somewhat different remedial needs of each.

---

12. Section 1.106(1) is renumbered §1.305 in revised Article 1.

§18.4.2 The Seller's Remedies

Sections 2.706, 2.708, and 2.709[13] contain the core of the seller's expectation remedies. Section 2.709 is the seller's specific performance remedy for payment of the price of the goods. Like the common law, Article 2 sees specific enforcement of the contract as a limited and secondary remedy, available only when damages are inappropriate. Section 2.709 therefore allows the seller to claim the price of the goods only when the goods have been accepted by the buyer or they are incapable of being resold because they have been lost or damaged or are just not resalable.

The other two sections contain the primary remedies of the seller's expectation damages where the buyer breaches by failing to accept conforming goods tendered by the seller. Section 2.706 permits an aggrieved seller to enter a *substitute transaction* by reselling the goods and, provided that the resale is made in good faith and in a commercially reasonable manner, to recover the shortfall between the contract price and the resale price. Section 2.708(1) recognizes that damages may be based on a *hypothetical resale* as an alternative to actual resale. It allows the seller to calculate damages based on the difference between the contract price and the market price of the goods at the time and place at which delivery was to have been tendered under the contract. This may be used, for example, when the seller elects not to resell, or when the resale was not conducted reasonably, resulting in too low a resale price. Some, but not all, courts even allow it as an alternative when the seller has resold above the market price, so that the contract-market difference provides a more advantageous recovery.

When the remedy of contract-market damages does not give an adequate recovery[14] so that it is inappropriate to use the contract-market difference as a basis for measuring damages (such as cases in which the seller decides not to manufacture the goods following breach, or suffers a loss in volume of sales as explained in section 18.6.3), §2.708(2) permits recovery of the seller's *gross profit plus reliance expenses, less allowance for payments or salvage received.*

---

13. Sections 2.706, 2.708, and 2.709 are not changed significantly in the 2003 revision except that they all expressly recognize that a seller may obtain consequential damages in an appropriate case. By doing this, they clarify a longstanding disagreement under the current UCC, which does not mention consequential damages for a seller at all. Under current law, a few courts have found that sellers are entitled to consequential damages despite the UCC's failure to provide for them, but most courts have declined to award them. Consequential damages are explained in section 18.5.

14. The 2003 revision of §2.708(2) makes it clear that lost profits can also be claimed under that section when the resale remedy under §2.706 is inadequate. This is more a clarification than a change in the law.

§18.4.3 The Buyer's Remedies

The buyer's specific performance remedy is set out in §2.716.[15] It, too, is a secondary remedy, available only when damages cannot adequately compensate because the goods are fairly regarded as unique under the circumstances of the case. In other situations in which the buyer has rejected nonconforming goods or the seller has failed to deliver any goods at all, the buyer is confined to substitutionary damages, based on an actual good faith and reasonable **repurchase** of the goods (**cover**) under §2.712 or a **hypothetical repurchase** under 2.713,[16] calculated as the difference between the market price at the time the buyer learned of the breach and the contract price. (Note that the language identifying the buyer's hypothetical market is different from that set out for the seller in §2.708(1). This provision has caused interpretational difficulties that are not considered here.)[17] Article 2 prefers the cover-contract difference as the more realistic measure, but the buyer is permitted not to cover, and instead use the market price of the goods as a basis of recovery. The market standard is also used if the buyer did not act reasonably in covering, so that the cover price is excessive. As in the case of sellers, there is some controversy over whether a buyer who has covered at a price lower than the market may nevertheless elect to sue for damages based on the more advantageous market-contract difference.

In some cases, a buyer may not be able to make a substitute transaction and may suffer **consequential damages** as a result of the breach. If so, §§2.714 and 2.715 permit their recovery. (The nature of consequential damages and the prerequisites for their recovery is discussed below.)

---

15. In the 2003 revision of Article 2, language has been added to §2.716 that upholds the specific performance remedy where the parties have agreed to it, and the transaction is not a consumer contract. In addition, under revised Article 2, it will no longer be correct to classify the remedy solely as a buyer's remedy. The section's heading has been changed by deleting the words "buyer's right," so that the heading refers to specific performance generally. This means that §2.716 will not longer be merely a buyer's remedy, but could be available to a seller as well. Official Comment 1(a) to revised §2.716 states that the change is intended to make it clear that either a seller or a buyer is entitled to specific performance in the proper case. As noted in section 18.4.2, the seller's usual equivalent of specific performance is the remedy for the price under §2.709. The seller does therefore not need to use §2.716 to claim specific performance in that sense. However, a buyer may have undertaken other commitments in the contract, which could be specifically enforced under §2.716 if they meet the qualifications of the section.

16. Sections 2.712 and 2.713 are not significantly changed in the 2003 revision of Article 2, except as noted in footnote 17.

17. Briefly stated, the seller's market price is measured in §2.708(1) at the time and place of tender, whereas §2.713 requires the buyer's damages to be measured at the place of tender, or in some cases, at the place to which goods are to be shipped. The time for measuring the buyer's damages is the time that the buyer learned of the breach. This has led to some difference in interpreting the proper time and place for determining market price where the buyer claims market-contract damages. The 2003 revision of §2.713 should eliminate this confusion because it uses the same standard — the time and place for tender — for both buyers and sellers.

Finally, when the seller has breached by delivering goods that are defective or not in conformity with what was promised under the contract, but the goods have been *accepted* by the buyer, damages based on an actual or hypothetical repurchase are not appropriate. Section 2.714[18] therefore measures damages for accepted goods based on the loss suffered by the buyer as a result of the *deficiency* in the goods. This principle ties in with the discussion of partial breach in Chapter 17.

§18.5 THE DISTINCTION BETWEEN DIRECT AND CONSEQUENTIAL DAMAGES

In all the examples used up to now, we have been concerned only with damages that are a direct result of the breach. That is, they can be readily and easily attributed to the breach and are designed to compensate for the very performance that has been promised. Thus, for example, after Harmony breached her promise to coach Sara, Sara's cost of hiring a substitute trainer does no more than substitute for the performance of the contract itself. The same is true when Ken Tractor or Cadenza La Scala seek their outlay and expected profit in their construction or manufacturing contracts. These cases are all characterized by the fact that the award of damages goes no further than the confines of the contract itself to compensate for the breach. The payment of money is designed to give nothing more than the benefit of performance, whether in the form of the costs of a substitute or the lost gains under the contract. The payment of damages thus acts as a **direct equivalent** for the **expected performance** and thereby fully cures the disappointed expectation. For this reason, the compensation paid is called **direct damages**.

In some cases, however, it is not enough to award only these direct damages, because the breach has had more far-ranging consequences. Not only has it disappointed the direct expectations under the contract, but it has *caused further losses in other transactions or endeavors that were dependent upon the contract.* For example, recall that Harmony had undertaken to give Sara a series of voice training lessons in the week before the competition. In our first illustration, she reneged just a few days before the lessons were to begin, but Sara was able to find another teacher. What if no other teacher was available, so that Sara could not obtain the training? As a result of being deprived of coaching in the crucial period before the competition, she was not adequately prepared for it. A whole horde of voice experts are available to testify, based on meticulous scientific tests, that Sara has talent of almost superhuman dimensions, and she would have been able to sing circles

---

18. Section 2.714 has not been significantly changed in the 2003 revision of Article 2.

around the other competitors had she received the week's intensive training. If this can indeed be shown, a mere award of the cost of a substitute teacher comes nowhere near to compensating for her contractual expectations. Her loss consequent upon the breach is far more serious and must take account of all the opportunities for fame and fortune that would have flowed from her success in the competition. These losses, consequent on the breach, are called **consequential damages**.

This example graphically portrays the difference between direct and consequential damages, but it also suggests some of the particular problems that a plaintiff must deal with to obtain consequential damages. Even if she has a bevy of experts to attest to her genius and the certainty of victory that would have followed proper training, Harmony can probably summon an equivalent phalanx of experts who will conclude differently. Even if Sara succeeds in convincing the factfinder of the important role that training would have played in her success, she must also establish the probability that Harmony's breach was the only reason why she did not win, that Harmony should reasonably have understood that this consequence was likely, and that Sara could not herself have taken some reasonable action to prevent it. Finally, Sara would also have to make a credible showing of the actual harm she suffered — that is, the opportunities that she lost, and would have to be able to place a plausible money value on her injury. All these considerations are commonly referred to as limitations on her recovery, and they are discussed more fully in the next section.

The above illustration involves a common law contract. As indicated in section 18.4.3, the buyer of goods may also suffer consequential damages as a result of the seller's breach. Sections 2.712, 2.713, and 2.714 all recognize that a buyer may suffer consequential damages apart from the direct damages covered by those sections, and §2.715(2) describes consequential damages as including "any loss resulting from general or particular requirements and needs of which the seller at the time of contracting had reason to know and which could not reasonably have been prevented by cover or otherwise." For example, say that the buyer operates a store that sells gift wrap, cards, and other such items. In July, she orders her annual stock of Christmas paper, boxes, ornaments, and cards from the seller, her major supplier, for delivery on November 1. On October 30, the seller repudiates that contract by notifying the buyer that it will not deliver the goods. The buyer tries to order substitute goods from other suppliers, but at that time all seasonal products have been sold to other stores so the buyer cannot cover. Direct damages, in the form of the difference between the cover price and the contract price, are therefore not available. The other form of direct damages — the market-contract difference — does not adequately compensate the buyer, who has lost profits as a result of the seller's breach. These lost profits are consequential damages that the buyer can claim under §2.715. Like Sara, the buyer must establish the amount of these damages and must prove that the seller reasonably should have contemplated that she .ld incur a loss of this kind as a result of the breach and that she was able to prevent the loss.

Although Article 2 expressly provides for a buyer's consequential amages, it says nothing of a seller's right to claim them. In addition, ;1.106(1) (renumbered §1.305(a) in revised Article 1) states that consequential damages are not available unless provided for in the UCC or another rule of law. It is possible that the drafters of the UCC did not mention sellers' consequential damages simply because they did not think that a seller would ever be likely to have consequential damages. Although sellers do not commonly suffer consequential damages, there have been cases in which a seller has been able to show that it suffered damages as a consequence of a buyer's breach. However many courts have declined to allow those damages on the basis that a seller is not entitled to them under Article 2.[19]

§18.6 LIMITATIONS ON EXPECTATION RECOVERY

§18.6.1 The Nature and Goals of the Limitations

As just intimated, a number of factors, often referred to as limitations on expectation damages, must be taken into account in reaching a final decision on the extent of the proper monetary award. Although called limitations, these factors are not, for the most part, external checks on damages, but are simply an expression of principles inherent in the goal of compensating for the loss of reasonable expectations. They represent the following specific values and practical considerations that are listed briefly before being examined in detail:

1. In determining damages for the breach of a contract, we must be careful to remember that the extent and scope of damages should be consistent with what was reasonably contemplated by the parties at the time of contracting. This gives rise to the concept of **foreseeability**.

2. Although the law sympathizes with the victim of a breach, it does not allow her to hold the breacher responsible for increased losses resulting from her own irrational or unfair behavior. Therefore, if the

19. As mentioned in footnote 13, §2.706, 2.708, and 2.709 are changed in the 2003 revision of Article 2 so that they all expressly recognize that a seller may obtain consequential damages in an appropriate case. The revision also adds a new subsection (2) to §2.710, which defines a seller's consequential damages in similar terms to those for a buyer in §2.715. Revised §2.710(2) confines a seller's claim for consequential damages to commercial transactions and precludes their recovery against a consumer buyer.

plaintiff unreasonably or dishonestly worsens the loss following breach, the damages will not include compensation for such aggravated loss. This is the principle of **mitigation**.

3. Because damages are intended to compensate for losses resulting from the breach, it follows that the plaintiff can claim only those damages caused by the breach. She must therefore show a causal link between the breach and the loss. This is the principle of **causation**.

4. As contract remedies are concerned with economic loss, it is not enough for the plaintiff to prove that a breach occurred. She must also show that the breach resulted in financial loss, and must provide adequate evidence of the monetary extent of the loss. This is the principle of **reasonable certainty**.

5. We have already seen in several different areas of contract law (for example, in sections 9.6.5, 14.2.3, 16.11.1, and 17.3.4) that courts exercise a general discretion to temper the enforcement of contract rights when rigid enforcement would have an unjustifiably harsh effect on the party against whom those rights are asserted. This general concept of **unfair forfeiture** is also applied when damages, otherwise available on a strict application of the rules, would unfairly harm the defendant and result in a windfall to the plaintiff.

§18.6.2 Foreseeability

An event or consequence is foreseeable when a reasonable person would realize the likelihood of its occurrence. Foreseeability is thus an *objective* concept, concerned not with what a particular person actually did foresee, but what she would have foreseen had she reasonably contemplated the course of likely future events. Applied in the context of liability for breach of contract, damages are foreseeable when, at the **time of making the contract**, the party who ultimately breached **reasonably should have realized** that those damages would be a **likely consequence of the breach**. Because contractual liability is based on the breach of a consensual relationship, it is a firm principle of our law that a breaching party should not be held accountable for losses unless, at the time of making the contract, she reasonably should have conceived of those losses as a *probable result of her breach*. The reasonable foresight of probable consequences depends on the extent of information available to a party, and it is not fair to impose liability on a breaching party if she could not reasonably have anticipated the loss when making the contract, because she did not have access to information at that time that would have alerted her to the probable result of her breach. The time of contracting, and not the time of breach, must necessarily be the point at which foreseeability is gauged if the crucial issue is whether the breaching party should be taken to have predicted and risked liability of the kind suffered.

Foreseeability is not likely to be an issue when direct damages are concerned. When parties enter a contract, they do or should understand that if one of them breaches, the other may lose a profit that would have been earned under the contract, or may suffer a loss or added expense in entering a substitute transaction. This does not mean that a party actually has to foresee the amount or exact nature of the loss or the precise way in which the other party would elect to attain his expectation, but merely that she reasonably understands that if she breaches, she will be responsible for lost profits or the cost of a reasonable substitute.

However, the breach could have consequences beyond the actual deprivation of the contracted performance because other transactions or ventures are dependent upon it. Unless the other party has some reason to know that her breach will have an impact beyond the simple deprivation of the immediate contract performance, it is not fair to hold her accountable for such **consequential losses**. This is the focus of the principle of foreseeability. It confines liability for consequential damages to those losses that a party reasonably should have contemplated, based on information to which she had access at the time of contracting, as a probable result of her breach.

The foreseeability principle is regarded as having been firmly established in the common law by the English case, *Hadley v. Baxendale*, 156 Eng. Rep. 145 (Exchequer 1864). The owners of a mill delivered a broken mill-shaft to a carrier for shipment to the manufacturer so that it could be used as a model for a new one. There was a delay in the shipment. Because this was the mill's only shaft, the delay idled the mill for longer than necessary. The owners sued the carrier for damages based on the profit that they lost when the mill could not operate during the period of delay. Although the court acknowledged that the delay did in fact directly result in the loss of profits, it declined to award those lost profits as damages. The court found the carrier not to be accountable for that loss because it was not told that this was the only shaft and had no way of knowing that a delay would cause the mill to lie idle.[20] The court enunciated the rule of foreseeability that is still current today and is reflected in modern formulations in language that deviates little from that used in the case: It held that damages for breach may only be recoverable if one of two conditions is satisfied: Either the loss must be one that may fairly and reasonably be considered to arise naturally — in the ordinary course of things — from the breach, or it must be one that may reasonably be supposed to have been contemplated by the parties at the time of

---

20. The headnote in the case always confounds students because it clearly states that the clerk was told that the mill was stopped. This has been explained by commentators on the basis that the headnote does not accurately reflect the facts, or that communication to the clerk was not sufficient to bind his employer.

contract as a *reasonable consequence* of breach. (Although *Hadley* refers to the parties' contemplation, we are, of course, principally interested in the reasonable contemplation of the party who breached. By referring to the common contemplation, the court merely denotes the objective standard — not what the breaching party actually knew and realized, but what he should reasonably have contemplated.)

The rule in *Hadley* may be found in both Restatement Second §351 and UCC §2.715.[21] In essence, it breaks damages into two categories:

a. General Damages

Damages that arise naturally, in the ordinary course, are called "general damages." They include not only all easily imaginable direct damages, but also those consequential damages that should be *obvious* to the breacher *without any special or particular knowledge* of the other party's circumstances or affairs, because such a loss would be a *normal and well-accepted likelihood* of the breach of a contract of this kind. Of course what is generally understood as a likely consequence of breach is not decided in the abstract, but in light of the market in which the parties are dealing.

For example, the roof of a home is damaged by a falling branch. The homeowner contracts with a roofer to repair the roof without delay, and the roofer promises to make the repair on the very day of the damage. If the roofer breaches the contract by not showing up, he must surely contemplate the probability of direct damages — that the owner may try to engage another roofer and to hold him liable for damages if the reasonable substitute is higher-priced. However, the breaching roofer must also reasonably realize that the owner may not be able to get someone else out immediately and that if it rains, there could be water damage to the interior of the house under the broken roof section. Any damage to the interior is consequential — it is not a cost of achieving the promised performance, but a loss resulting as a consequence of (I could have said "flowing from," but that sounds too much like a pun) the breach. This consequential damage would fall into the first category identified in *Hadley* because the possibility of rain damage is something that may reasonably be considered as arising naturally in the normal course of human experience. One needs no special information about the homeowner's affairs to recognize this risk of breach. (Of course, if the owner could have taken temporary measures to prevent water damage but did not do so, the owner's failure to mitigate could be a different basis for the denial of consequential damages.)

Prutch v. Ford Motor Co., 618 P.2d 657 (Colo. 1980) provides another example of consequential damages that arise naturally and in the ordinary course from the breach. A farmer could not fully harvest his crop because his

---

21. Section 2.715 is unchanged in the 2003 revision of Article 2.

Ford farming equipment did not function properly. The court held that the farmer's resulting lost profits were foreseeable by Ford because it understood that its equipment would be used in commercial farming, and should reasonably have contemplated that the failure of the equipment could cause such a loss.

b. Special Damages

The second category, called "special damages," can be illustrated by embellishing the facts of the last example. Say that the area beneath the broken roof happened to contain an expensive piece of electronic equipment that is affixed to the floor and cannot be moved or otherwise protected.[22] Unless the roofer was told or otherwise had reason to know about the equipment at the time that he made the contract, it would not be fair to hold him liable for damage to it because he had *no basis for expecting this loss.* Had he known about it, he may well have declined the contract or he may have decided to undertake it only if the owner paid a higher price to cover the cost of extra precautions or as a premium for the assumption of the greater risk of liability. By not giving the roofer the information, the homeowner deprives him of the means to make a rational decision on risk or to take additional steps to minimize the chance of breach. He therefore should not be able to hold him accountable for the unusual loss. Not only does the rule protect the roofer from surprise liability, but the fact that the rule exists is likely to be an incentive to a party in the owner's position to provide adequate information, which is likely to increase the *efficiency of transacting* and may even lessen the chance of breach. The foreseeability principle can therefore be justified as economically efficient as well as fair.

The concept of **reasonable contemplation** is central to the foreseeability of special damages, but its scope and meaning are elusive. To begin with, recognize that it does not require that a reasonable person in the breacher's position would have foreseen the exact loss with great precision and specificity. All that is required is that a loss of that **nature and approximate extent** could be conceived of as a **probability**. In requiring the contemplated loss to be probable, **rather than just possible**, the law does not cover every possibly imagined serendipitous or outlandish consequence, but it does cover more than those outcomes that are obvious inevitabilities. This means that it can be a subtle exercise to decide on the strength of the link between the information available to the breacher and her reasonable accountability for the ultimate consequences of her breach.

There is also some obscurity in the question of the relationship between the *nature of the exchange* under the contract and the *loss* — the extent to which

---

22. Again, if it could be moved, protected, or sheltered by a makeshift covering, the owner's failure to take action to safeguard it would raise the issue of mitigation of damages in addition to the foreseeability question.

the test of reasonable contemplation should take into account the type and value of the contractual exchange. There was a time, earlier this century, when courts described the test as one of *tacit agreement*: The circumstances of the contract must justify the conclusion, not merely that the breaching party should have foreseen the probability of loss, but must have tacitly accepted liability for it. That is, had the likely consequences of the breach been brought to her attention at the time of contracting, she would have agreed that she had assumed liability for them. The tacit agreement test would go beyond an evaluation of the information available to the breaching party at the time of contracting, and would also examine the question of whether the consideration given to her reflected the extent of risk assumed. The tacit agreement test is generally regarded as *too restrictive by modern courts*, and it is expressly rejected by Restatement Second §351, Comment *a* and UCC §2.715, Comment 2. In contemporary law, the focus of reasonable contemplation is therefore more on the relationship between the information available to the breacher and the loss, and less on the relationship of the loss to the extent of risk and the consideration received. In other words, it is possible that a party could be held to have contemplated great liability despite the modest value of what she was to gain from the contract. This does not mean that the value of the consideration given to the breacher is invariably irrelevant. A court may always take the equities into account (as expressly recognized by Restatement Second §351(3)) and if the consequential losses are greatly disproportionate to the value of the consideration paid to the breacher, a court may exercise its equitable discretion to curtail liability for them.

§18.6.3 Mitigation

a. The Purpose and Policy of Mitigation

In most cases, a rational party, faced with a breach by the other, will naturally take whatever action is necessary to avoid or minimize loss. Unless the victim of a breach is particularly stupid, litigious, or spiteful, her self-interest will propel her in the direction of keeping her loss as small as possible, rather than aggravating it in the hope that she will ultimately be able to recover it from the breaching party. This means that it happens only rarely that the plaintiff deliberately and maliciously sets out to increase her damages, just for the satisfaction of punishing the defendant with a large claim. More commonly, the defendant's allegation that the plaintiff failed to mitigate is likely to turn on the question of whether the plaintiff's response to the breach was an unreasonable or poor judgment that aggravated damages.

The basic principle of mitigation is that if the **plaintiff** has, through **bad faith** or **unreasonable** action (or inaction) **aggravated** her **damages**, the

defendant is not held responsible for the increase in loss caused by the plaintiff. This is often described as the plaintiff's *duty to mitigate damages*. Of course, this is not a duty in the normal sense, because the plaintiff owes it to no one but herself to keep her losses down. But if she fails in that duty to safeguard her own economic welfare, fairness dictates that she must be left with the added loss and the defendant should not be called on to pay it. It may be obvious from what has just been said that a failure to mitigate damages does not deprive the plaintiff of all relief, but affects recovery only to the extent that the damages were increased as a result of the plaintiff's conduct. The plaintiff is therefore still entitled to recover those damages that she could not have avoided by good faith or reasonable conduct.

It must be stressed that the question is not merely whether the plaintiff's response to the breach turned out, with hindsight, to be a wrong judgment that worsened the harm. Nor is it enough that a different response would have been preferable. The words "bad faith" and "unreasonable" indicate that there must be some element of fault on the plaintiff's part. It must be apparent that the plaintiff's behavior in reacting to the breach was dishonest, opportunistic, or vindictive, or that it so deviated from what would be expected, that it failed to conform to community standards of rationality. The law recognizes that the defendant has breached the contract, leaving the plaintiff in the unhappy position of having to salvage the benefit of her bargain. For this reason, the plaintiff, herself the victim of the defendant's wrong, should be given some leeway when her response is judged. It must be clear, under all the circumstances, that the plaintiff's reaction to the breach is sufficiently improper that it would be wrong to make the defendant bear the increased loss. Restatement Second §350 expresses this approach by stating that losses are not recoverable if the plaintiff could have avoided them without "undue risk, burden or humiliation," but the plaintiff should not be precluded from recovery to the extent that she made "reasonable but unsuccessful efforts to avoid harm."

The general principles of mitigation recognized in common law are applicable to UCC Article 2. Although there is no section specifically devoted to the principle, it is inherent in the Code by virtue of §1.103,[23] which incorporates consistent common law principles, and in the general remedial principle expressed in §1.106.[24] In addition, it is reflected throughout the remedies provisions of Article 2. Sections 2.706 and 2.712 require an aggrieved seller or buyer to act reasonably, in good faith, and within a reasonable time when making a substitute transaction; §2.715 bars a buyer from obtaining consequential damages that could have been prevented by cover or otherwise; §2.704(2) reflects the seller's duty to mitigate in deciding whether to complete the manufacture of specially ordered

---

23. Section 1.103(b) in revised Article 1.
24. Section 1.305 in revised Article 1.

goods; and §2.709 requires the seller to make reasonable attempts at resale before claiming the price of the goods from the buyer.

The principle of mitigation makes perfect sense on its own merits because the defendant should not be accountable to the extent that the consequences of breach are exaggerated by the plaintiff's fault, and because a rule that encourages the plaintiff to control loss is efficient and sensible. In addition, however, it is congruent with two other limitation principles: A loss caused by the plaintiff's improper actions is not reasonably foreseeable, and the plaintiff's conduct breaks the chain of causation between the breach and the loss.

b. The Reasonableness Test for Determining whether the Plaintiff Violated the Duty to Mitigate

As stated earlier, unless bad faith is evident, the plaintiff's accountability for aggravated loss depends upon the reasonableness of her response to breach. As always, reasonableness is a factual matter. The plaintiff's action (or failure to act) must be evaluated by an *objective standard* under all the circumstances of the case: Was it reasonable for a person in the plaintiff's position to have acted as she did? This inquiry takes into account a whole range of factual questions such as: what the plaintiff did or did not do; what choices were available to her; what risks, hardships, or inconveniences were involved in each choice; what her motivation was in choosing as she did; how much time she had available to respond; and how quickly she took action. All of these facts are looked at with a sympathetic eye on the plaintiff. As the breach compelled her to take action to safeguard her interests, courts are inclined to respect her judgment if it had an honest and rational basis, even if the defendant can point to a different response that may have been more effective in fully or partially preventing the loss. Because the plaintiff is the wronged party, she is not expected to take heroic or exhaustive action to keep damages at a minimum. The defendant cannot complain of a failure to mitigate if the action required to reduce loss would have been unduly burdensome, humiliating, or risky to the plaintiff. Similarly, the plaintiff cannot be expected to explore every conceivable possibility of avoiding loss or to try methods that reasonably appear to be futile.

The sympathetic approach to the plaintiff is reflected in the way in which the burden of proof is typically allocated when mitigation is in issue. The plaintiff bears the overall burden of proving her damages. But if she establishes loss and the defendant raises the issue of mitigation, the defendant must show that there was a reasonable means available to the plaintiff to curtail her loss and that if she had followed that course, a reduction in the loss would have been likely.

Once it is established that the plaintiff's reaction to the breach unjustifiably increased her loss, the next task is to calculate what the damages would have been had the proper response been made. This is also a factual issue, involving an inquiry into the causal link between the plaintiff's conduct and the loss.[25]

c. The Substitute Transaction as Mitigation

The most obvious form of mitigation is the substitute transaction. We saw an example of this right at the beginning of this chapter when, a few days before the voice training was to begin, Harmony repudiated her contract with Sara to provide the lessons for a fee of $1,500. Sara hired another voice coach for $1,800 and claimed the $300 difference as expectation damages. The decision to hire another coach is itself an act of mitigation in that it prevented any consequential loss that Sara may have suffered by entering the competition without the training. (The fact that such a consequential loss may have been speculative and very difficult to prove increases Sara's incentive to avoid it.)

Although the hiring of the substitute coach prevented more serious consequential losses, the choice of the new coach is still subject to a standard of reasonableness. Sara must make reasonable and good faith efforts to find an equivalent coach at the most economic price. This does not mean that she has to use the cheapest substitute, or that she has to make exhaustive enquiries to find the best bargain available. However she will not recover the full cost of the substitute if, by the exercise of reasonable diligence, she would have been able to find an adequate substitute at a lower price. Sometimes, even with conscientious effort, the only substitute a victim can find is better than the contract performance. If this is the closest reasonable replacement for the performance, the court is likely to award the cost of it to the victim, even though it might give her more than her expectation under the contract. This may be the fairest resolution given that the breacher caused the problem and the victim has no choice but to take the more valuable substitute to approximate the performance promised by the breacher. For example, in *Handicapped Children's Education Board v. Lukaszewski,* 332 N.W.2d 774 (Wis. 1983) the defendant, a speech and language therapist, breached her employment contract by resigning. The Board sought to replace her. The only applicant for the position was more senior and had to be paid a higher salary in accordance with union rates. The Board hired that applicant and sued the defendant for the difference between what it would have paid the defendant under the contract and what it had to pay her replacement. The defendant argued that she should not be liable for this additional cost because the Board received the benefit of a more experienced therapist for the higher salary.

---

25. *See also* section 17.7.3 in which the issue of mitigation is discussed in relation to the decision by the victim of a repudiation on whether to accept and act on the repudiation immediately, or to await the possibility of retraction.

The court rejected this argument. The Board did not need or desire a more experienced therapist, but the defendant's breach left it with no choice but to take the only available substitute.

In Sara's case, the issue of a reasonable substitute comes up in connection with her claim for damages for its added cost. However, the issue also arises when the breach releases a plaintiff from performance, so that a *substitute transaction* becomes available to *reduce the plaintiff's loss.* For example, say that a few days before the voice training lessons were to begin, Sara repudiated the contract. Harmony now finds that she has 28 hours of free time in which she will not be gainfully employed. If she does nothing about this, she will lose her full profit from the transaction — the contract price of $1,500 less any costs. However, if she is able to take another student or otherwise use this time to generate income, she will reduce or possibly eliminate completely her loss from Sara's breach. It therefore stands to reason that if Harmony sues Sara for her lost profit, she will have to deduct whatever she earned in the time freed by Sara's breach. If she failed to use the time gainfully at all, she would have to show that, despite reasonable efforts, she was not able to mitigate damages by productively redeploying this time. If she used some or all of it but did not fully reduce her loss, she would have to show that she was not reasonably able to reduce her loss to a greater extent.

Assume that as soon as Sara repudiated, Harmony put up notices at local schools and colleges advertising her availability, and she also called all the people she knew who may have referrals. However, no one expressed interest in lessons for the week in question. Harmony also noticed a sign in the neighborhood hamburger joint that they were looking for part-time help. When she sues Sara for her full profit under the contract, two issues are likely to be raised: First, were her efforts in seeking other students reasonable under the circumstances? It sounds as if she did everything reasonably possible considering the short time available to fill the slot left empty by Sara's breach. Second, should she have tried to recoup her loss by taking a part-time job at the hamburger joint? It may be that by doing this work in the times set aside for Sara's lessons, she could have earned back part of her loss. However, as the victim of a breach, she is not expected to take every conceivable step to avoid loss. She is allowed *reasonable discretion in declining* to pursue *alternatives that are unsuitable*, and should not be deprived of recovery as a result. As a music teacher, she surely should not have to moonlight at a greasy fast-food place.

Parker v. Twentieth Century-Fox Film Corp., 474 P.2d 689 (Cal. 1970) involved the issue of whether the victim of a breach acted reasonably in refusing to mitigate her loss by entering into an available substitute transaction. The actress Shirley MacLaine (Parker) entered into a contract with the studio to star in a musical called *Bloomer Girl* for a fee of $750,000. The studio cancelled the production, thereby breaching the contract. As a substitute, the studio offered MacLaine the leading role in another movie, a western to be filmed in Australia. MacLaine rejected the substitute and sued for the full amount of the fee for *Bloomer Girl*. The studio argued that she was not entitled to any damages because she could have avoided all loss by taking the other role offered. The court disagreed and granted summary judgment to MacLaine for her full fee. The court found that the role in the western was both different from and inferior to the lead in *Bloomer Girl* because it was a poorer vehicle for her talents and the substitute contract eliminated her rights to approve personnel and screenplay. Although the victim of a breach must take reasonable steps to mitigate her loss, she is not required to suffer undue burden or prejudice. In the employment context, the court must be particularly solicitous of the impact that the offered substitute might have on the plaintiff's career goals, professional development, and dignity. (A dissenting justice was not persuaded that the role in the western was inferior. He felt that the case should go to trial, and should not be disposed of by summary judgment.) By contrast, in *Fair v. Red Lion Inn*, 943 P.2d 431 (Colo. 1997) an employee refused her ex-employer's offer to reinstate her after she had been wrongfully dismissed. The employee sued for damages for breach of the employment contract and claimed that she was not obliged to mitigate her loss by accepting reinstatement because she feared that the employer was not sincere and would just terminate her again later. The court conceded that it was natural for her to mistrust the employer, but she could not offer any evidence to support her concerns. She therefore could not claim damages that would have been avoided had she accepted the employer's offer of mitigation. (Note that in both these cases, the plaintiff's best prospect of mitigation was to enter into a substitute transaction with the breaching party. As *Fair* suggests, the victim may find it quite unpalatable to accept mitigation from the very person who breached the contract, but this on its own is not grounds enough to refuse the substitute transaction.)

Although the victim of the breach is not required to mitigate by entering into a substitute contract that is unduly burdensome, humiliating, or harmful to her long-term interests, if she does in fact take the substitute, her earnings must be deducted from her damages. For example, in *Marshall School District v. Hill*, 939 S.W.2d 319 (Ark. App. 1997) the school district wrongfully dismissed Hill, a teacher and football coach. He found work in a shirt factory for a while before he secured employment as a teacher in another school district. The court held that because these earnings, including the earnings from his factory work, were from substitute transactions that he actually entered following his dismissal, they should be offset against his damages.

d. Post-Breach Transactions that are not Appropriately Treated as Substitutes: The "Lost Volume" Situation

In the last example, it was assumed that any lessons given by Harmony would take place in the hours allocated to Sara under the contract. If this

is so, and if Harmony was otherwise fully booked, the new stu
truly be a substitute for the contractual performance becau
could not have taken on an additional student in the absence of a breac.
by Sara. That is, the only time available to take on extra work was time that
would have been committed to Sara had she not broken the contract.
However, if Harmony was not fully booked, she could have taken on
new students even if Sara had not breached. Therefore, a new student
accepted after Sara's breach does not substitute for Sara. It would make
no difference if Harmony schedules the new student for the time formerly
devoted to Sara because Harmony would have simply booked the student at
a different time had Sara not breached. Therefore, one should not automatically assume that a similar transaction after the breach must be a substitute
for the broken contract. It should only be so treated if it is clear that the
plaintiff *would not or could not have entered it in the absence of breach.* Failure to
maintain this distinction carefully could lead to an unfair and unwarranted
reduction of the plaintiff's recovery by offsetting the proceeds of an entirely
independent transaction.

Consider a second illustration, based on a sale of goods: A homeowner
sells her used fridge for $200, but the buyer breaches the contract by failing
to take delivery and pay for it. The seller then sells it to someone else for the
same price. Obviously, the second sale is a substitute because the seller had
only that one fridge to sell. However, if the seller was not a homeowner
trying to sell a single fridge, but a huge appliance store with a whole
warehouse of fridges of this exact make and model, the resale of the
fridge to the second buyer is not so clearly a substitute transaction. Because
the seller has a stock of identical products, it had another one to sell to the
second buyer even had the first buyer not breached. It could therefore have
sold two fridges instead of one, and the breach has the effect of *reducing its
volume of sales.* If the seller can establish such a lost volume situation, the
second sale is *not a substitute,* its proceeds should not be treated as reducing
the loss from the breach, and the seller is entitled to recover its full profit
expected under the breached transaction. In a sale of goods, §2.708(2)
caters for lost volume. It provides in essence that when the usual measure
of damages — the difference between the contract price and the market
price on resale — is inadequate to fully compensate the seller, the seller's
lost profit on the sale is the appropriate measure.

Rodriguez v. Learjet, Inc., 24 Kan. App. 2d 461 (1997) illustrates the application of §2.708(2). After the buyer repudiated a contract for the purchase
of a jet the seller sold it to someone else. The court identified three elements
that a seller must establish to be treated as a lost-volume seller and found that
the seller had satisfied all three: It had shown that its plant was operating at
60 percent capacity, so it could have made and sold more planes; it proved
that the additional sale would have been profitable; and it established that it
probably would have made the subsequent sale even if the buyer had not

breached the contract. One of the elements specified in *Rodriguez* is that the seller can show that the additional sale would have been profitable. Some commentators have argued that this should be a crucial element because additional sales may not continue to generate profits equivalent to the profit on the sale in issue. Factors such as increases in the seller's marginal costs and competition in the market from used goods may reduce and ultimately eliminate profits from successive sales. Notwithstanding, many courts do not place such a rigorous burden on the seller, who is, after all, the injured party, and who is only required to prove loss on a preponderance of the evidence. In *National Controls, Inc. v. Commodore Business Machines, Inc.*, 163 Cal. App. 3d 688 (1985) the court noted that profits might diminish as more sales are made. However, it observed that most courts do not require the seller to produce economic analysis to refute this possibility. It held that the seller had made out a sufficient case by showing merely that it had unused capacity and could have produced more units than it was able to sell.

The language of current §2.708(2) is confusing because it provides that in calculating damages for lost profit, "due credit" must be given for "proceeds of resale." Taken literally, this language would eliminate the possibility of ever claiming lost profits if the seller resells the goods, even where the seller can show that the breach reduced its volume of sales. *National Controls*, adopting the approach of most courts, held that this part of the formula does not apply in a lost volume situation where the resale of the goods should not be seen as a substitute transaction and proceeds of the sale should not therefore be credited. The 2003 revision of Article 2 eliminates this reference to credit for proceeds of resale from §2.708(2). Official Comment 1(e) to revised §2.708 explains that the change is meant to clarify that proceeds of resale should not be taken into account in a lost volume situation.

§18.6.4 Causation

The concept of causation is not as prominent in contract law as it is in tort because it is usually more self-evident and its function can largely be accommodated within the principles of foreseeability, mitigation, and certainty. It is therefore not given much separate attention by courts and commentators. Nevertheless, it is worth articulating as a distinct limitation on relief. A breaching party cannot be accountable for loss that was not caused by her breach. There must be a **link between the breach and the loss**. Causation is not usually an issue when direct damages are concerned. Unless the plaintiff has broken the chain of causation by aggravating damages, there is invariably a clear causal link between the breach and the loss of the contractual bargain. However, consequential damages are by definition more remotely connected to the breach, and when they are claimed, it must be established that they were indeed a consequence of the breach.

To illustrate, consider again one of the variations of the example concerning Harmony's breach of her contract to give voice training lessons to Sara: Harmony reneged on the contract just before the lessons were to begin, and Sara could not find a replacement teacher, so she had no choice but to sing in the competition without having had any coaching in the prior week. She loses the competition and sues Harmony for a huge amount of damages to compensate her for the loss of a career as a singing star. Her theory is that Harmony's breach prevented her from winning and deprived her of the career opportunities that would have resulted. It does not take much imagination to realize that she has serious difficulties in establishing a cause and effect between the breach and her alleged loss. She may not be able to show a probable link between her failure to win and the lack of coaching because there are too many variables that could have intervened: She may not have been as talented as her competitors, she may have had a bad night, or the judges may have been wrong. Even if she could show a strong likelihood of success in the competition, she cannot go on to show that she would have had opportunities as a result, or that she would have acted successfully in pursuing them.

As you will readily recognize, some of the problems that Sara faces in proving her case may be described in terms of mitigation (did she make reasonable efforts to prevent or staunch the negative consequences of the breach?), or foreseeability (could Harmony have reasonably contemplated this huge loss?), or reasonable certainty (can Sara establish the fact and extent of loss?). Nevertheless, the question of causation is also present in the inquiry, and it is a useful adjunct to the other limitations in analyzing the issue of liability and justifying the result.

§18.6.5 Reasonable Certainty

As the party seeking to enforce the contract, the plaintiff bears the burden of proving her loss. If she is unable to show on the *preponderance of the evidence* the fact and extent of her loss, she will not be able to recover damages. The limitation of reasonable certainty is really nothing more than the embodiment of this principle — the evidence must be sufficient to persuade the factfinder that the loss is more likely to have occurred than not, and must give the factfinder enough basis for calculating a monetary award. As this suggests, reasonable certainty involves two inquiries: The threshold question is whether the plaintiff has proved injury. If injury is shown, the next question is whether the plaintiff has provided sufficient evidence to enable the factfinder to determine the amount of the loss.

As a general rule, the *more clearly the plaintiff can demonstrate* the first element (the fact that some injury was suffered), the *greater effort the court (or jury) will make* to come up with some kind of *compensation figure*. This is because it has now

661

become clear that the plaintiff has indeed suffered as a result of the defendant's wrongful violation of her rights, and the court should strive, insofar as possible, to come up with a figure to compensate for the loss. This does not mean that the plaintiff will receive damages even if no relevant and plausible evidence is presented on the amount of her loss, but the court will try to do the best it can to fix damages with reference to whatever evidence is available.

This means that the second element is not a matter of all or nothing. Even if the evidence does not establish loss in the full amount claimed, it may be sufficient to justify an award of some lesser amount of compensation. This approach is reflected in Restatement Second §352, Comment a, which notes that although damages cannot be recovered for loss beyond the amount established with reasonable certainty, the policy of holding the breacher accountable for her wrongful act requires that doubts should generally be resolved against her once it is established that a significant injury has occurred. Therefore, the determination of damages is an approximation, not an exercise in mathematical precision. UCC §1.106, Comment 1,[26] expresses a similar sentiment.

Problems of certainty often affect direct damages, but they are even more likely to arise when the plaintiff seeks consequential damages. **Direct damages** may be difficult to prove, for example, when the plaintiff seeks his expected profit from the contract, but cannot prove what that profit would have been. Say that an engineering firm enters a contract with a paper mill to design and manufacture an innovative system for the safe disposal of chemical wastes. The contract price for the system is $2 million. Before work begins, the mill reneges on the contract. The engineering firm's direct damages are its lost profits on the job, which must be established by deducting its expected costs from the contract price. However, the system would have been so revolutionary that the engineering firm has no reliable evidence of what its costs would have been. If it cannot establish those prospective costs with reasonable certainty, it will not be able to show that it expected a profit from the contract and will not recover any direct damages. Of course, if the engineering firm had done its planning properly before quoting a price for the work, it would have made a cost projection that, if it appears reasonably accurate and reliable, will be sufficient evidence to establish loss on the preponderance of the evidence. *Benchmark Health Care Center, Inc. v. Cain*, 912 So. 2d 175 (Miss. App. 2005) illustrates a common judicial approach to the proof of direct lost profit damages. Benchmark wrongfully terminated a contract under which Cain was to provide rehabilitation therapy services for Benchmark for one year. Cain sued Benchmark for unpaid amounts due for services that had been rendered prior to termination and also claimed the profit that it would have made for the remainder

---

26. Section 1.305, Comment 1 in revised Article 1.

of the term of the contract had Benchmark not cancelled it. Benchmark challenged the jury's award of lost profit damages on the grounds that Cain had not proved lost profits on the preponderance of the evidence. The court upheld the jury award. The court noted that once the fact of loss has been shown, the plaintiff need not prove the amount of loss exactly or accurately. It is enough that the evidence allows the fact finder to make a fair and reasonable estimate of loss. The amount of probable lost profits over the remainder of the contract term was estimated by Cain's accountant, based on a projection from profits that Cain had made in the months prior to termination. The court said that while a future estimate necessarily involves some degree of speculation, the accountant documented and explained his methodology and his estimate was realistic.

Although direct damages can present problems of reasonable certainty, difficulty of proof is most commonly encountered when **consequential damages** are in issue. Sara's alleged loss of career opportunities, raised in the context of causation, is an extreme example of this. She would not only have trouble showing a causal link between her claimed loss and Harmony's breach of the voice training contract, but she would also have great difficulty in establishing the fact and amount of that loss. Some courts may regard those difficulties as insuperable. Others may be willing, upon being satisfied that the breach did remove all chance of her winning the competition, to allow the jury to place a value on her chance of winning.

Sara's claim is plagued with particularly troublesome issues of uncertainty. So was the claim of the baseball commissioner in *ESPN v. Office of the Commissioner of Baseball*, 76 F. Supp. 2d 416 (S.D.N.Y. 1999). ESPN breached its contract with major league baseball when it preempted games scheduled for Sunday night broadcast in favor of NFL games. The baseball commissioner claimed that as a result of this breach, the league had suffered the loss of television exposure and the associated prestige as well as opportunities for promotions and sponsorships. The problem was that the commissioner could not offer any evidence of how much the league lost. The court said that where it is clear that a breach victim has suffered damages, the court will do what it can to make an award. However, it must have some foundation for making a reasonable estimate of the loss and cannot construct a figure out of the air to compensate for speculative or intangible loss.

Many cases do not present such insurmountable difficulties of proof, and the plaintiff is able to provide enough evidence of the fact and quantum of loss to enable the trier of fact to make a consequential damages award. For example, in *Marvin Lumber and Cedar Co. v. PPG Industries, Inc.*, 401 F.3d 901 (8th Cir. 2005) PPG, a seller of wood preservative, breached its contract with Marvin by delivering preservative that did not work properly. As a result of the defective preservative, Marvin's products rotted, causing it problems with its customers and damaging its business. Marvin sued PPG for damages, including lost profits, and the jury awarded damages for lost profits.

663

The court of appeals upheld the award. The court stated the general principle that although purely speculative and conjectural damages will not be awarded, the plaintiff does not have to prove loss with exactitude. The evidence of lost profits in this case was the testimony of Marvin executives, based on its financial records, which showed that its profits had suffered since the problems with the wood preservative and that they would likely remain flat. The court held that this was sufficient evidence to support the jury award. Marvin had also claimed damages for loss of goodwill, which relates to the diminished value of the business and is distinct from lost profits. The court overturned the jury award of these damages because it found that the evidence of lost goodwill was conjectural and the loss was incapable of being quantified. In *Bollea v. World Championship Wrestling, Inc.*, 610 S.E.2d 92 (Ga. App. 2005), Bollea, professionally known as Hulk Hogan, sued WCW for damages for breach of contract. He claimed that WCW violated the terms of their contract by not making him the featured wrestler at a pay-per-view event entitled "Bash at the Beach." He alleged that as a result he had suffered significant consequential damages arising from lost bookings and reduced income from merchandising and promotions. WCW applied for summary judgment, denying that it breached the contract and arguing that any lost profits were too speculative. The court refused summary judgment and allowed Bollea to proceed to trial. It noted that he was an established wrestler with a long history of past earnings and profits. He therefore could succeed in showing lost profits with sufficient certainty to permit a jury to calculate his damages.

Both *Marvin* and *Bollea* involved plaintiffs with established businesses and a track record of past earnings that would allow them to make projections of loss as a result of the breach. Where the defendant's breach precludes the plaintiff from making expected profits from a **new business**, this track record is absent and the plaintiff's prospect of proving lost profit is weaker. Some courts (particularly in older cases) are hostile to a claim of lost profits where a business is new and untested, and treat evidence of potential profit as too speculative. However, the better view, more commonly found in modern cases, is to evaluate each claim on its facts to decide if there is enough information to provide a reasonable basis for determining the fact and extent of likely loss. For example, a young entrepreneur decides to open a gym in a neighborhood that does not have one. This is his first business venture, but he tackles it carefully by conducting a thorough market analysis, including an evaluation of the demand for a gym in the area, the profitability of existing businesses of that type in other neighborhoods, and projections of his expenses and receipts. After deciding that the business is viable, he enters into a lease with a shopping mall in the neighborhood. Just before he opens the business, the mall repudiates the lease. It takes him a few months to find other premises nearby, so he opens the gym six months later than he would have had the mall not repudiated. He sues the mall for the six months of profit that he lost as a result of opening late. His lost profit for the six months is inevitably somewhat speculative, but if his study and projections were properly done, he can show what profit equivalent businesses make, and he can prove what profit he made once he opened his gym, he should have a reasonable chance of being able to establish his loss on the preponderance of the evidence. This does not mean that he is assured of success. Many arguments can be made against awarding him his lost profits, especially if his projections are questionable, the other gyms are not comparable, and the economic environment at the time that he eventually opened the gym is different from that during the six months before he opened it. (If he did not find alternative premises and never set up the new business, his case would be weaker because he would then have no post-breach evidence of his capacity to run the business at a profit.)

§18.6.6 Unfair Forfeiture & sub.perform

The principle of unfair forfeiture was discussed in section 17.3.3 in relation to damages for substantial performance. Recall that the general principle, as reflected in *Jacob & Youngs v. Kent*, 129 N.E. 889 (N.Y. 1921) is that when a contract has been substantially performed and the cost of rectifying the non-material and non-willful breach is disproportionately large in relation to the value of the benefit that full performance will confer on the plaintiff, diminution of the ultimate value of the performance may be a more appropriate measure of damages. However, *Jacob & Youngs* confined this principle to situations in which there had been substantial performance. Where the breach is material, there is seldom a justification to limit damages merely because the amount needed to achieve the plaintiff's contractual expectations exceeds the enhancement of the ultimate objective market value of the promised performance. For example, in *American Standard, Inc. v. Schechman*, 427 N.E.2d 512 (N.Y. 1981), the owner of an industrial site sold the buildings and other movable property in exchange for $275,000 plus a promise to grade the property and to remove foundations and other structures from the property to a foot below grade level, leaving the vacant site in a reasonably attractive condition for resale. The buyer removed the property it had bought but did none of the grading and restoration work. The seller sued the buyer for $110,000, the cost of doing the work. The buyer sought to prove that its failure to restore the land reduced its market value by only $3,000, but the court refused to admit this evidence on the ground that the restoration of the land was a significant part of the consideration exchanged for the property sold and the parties intended the restoration of the property to be a material term of the contract. (Apart from this, *American Standard* is distinguishable from *Jacob & Youngs* because the breach was deliberate, not inadvertent.)

Peevyhouse v. Garland Coal & Mining Co., 382 P.2d 109 (Okla. 1963) is a famously controversial case that applied these principles where a mining company breached its contract with a landowner by failing to restore the land on completion of its strip-mining operations. The court refused to award damages to the owner based on the cost of restoring the land because that cost was greatly disproportionate to the amount by which the restoration would increase the land's market value. The court justified its decision by finding, probably incorrectly, that the restoration of the land was not a central obligation of the contract, but merely incidental to the contract's purpose of extracting coal for mutual profit. Some years later, the Tenth Circuit Court of appeals had to resolve a similar dispute arising in Oklahoma. In *Rock Island Improvement Co. v. Helmerich & Payne, Inc.*, 698 F.2d 1078 (10th Cir. 1983) the court refused to apply *Peevyhouse* on the grounds that it did not believe that the Oklahoma Supreme Court would follow it any longer. In the intervening years, state policy had changed to require mine operators to rehabilitate the land, so the reclamation obligation in the contract could no longer be regarded as immaterial and incidental to the main purpose of the contract.

§18.7 RELIANCE AND RESTITUTION AS ALTERNATIVES TO EXPECTATION

Although expectation damages are the primary remedy for breach of contract, they can only be recovered to the extent that the plaintiff can prove that the breach deprived her of an economic gain that would have resulted from the performance promised by the defendant in the contract. She must be able to show that she received less than her entitlement under the contract or was otherwise precluded from realizing an expected gain. It can happen that *a breach causes no economic loss* because, say, a substitute transaction can be found at the same or a lower cost, or because the contract was not profitable. If no loss can be shown, the plaintiff has no recourse for the defendant's wrongful act because there is no need for monetary compensation and contract remedies are not aimed at penalizing breaches. For example, if the seller of a house breaches the contract, but the buyer can purchase an equivalent house for the same or less money, the seller suffers no legal sanction for the breach.

However, the plaintiff's inability to prove expectation damages does not always end the matter of relief, because she *may be able to show that she has suffered losses other than her defeated expectation*. For example, even if a replacement house costs the same or less, the buyer may have partly performed before the breach by, say, paying a deposit to the seller. The buyer may also have incurred expenses in anticipation of receiving the benefits of the contract, say, by paying an architect to plan an alteration to the house. Damages of this kind may be recoverable under one or both of the alternative remedies of reliance and restitution.

The basic difference between reliance and restitution is that **reliance**, like expectation, is conceived of as a remedy based on **affirmation** of the contract — it is an enforcement of the contract, but **restitution** is premised on the theory of **disaffirmance** — it treats the breach as having caused the contract to fall away. This distinction, which will be made clearer as the remedies are discussed below, affects the aim and focus of the remedies. While the goal of expectation damages is to place the plaintiff in the position she would have been in had the contract been performed, reliance and restitutionary damages have more limited goals. **Reliance** damages aim to **refund expenses wasted or equivalent losses** by the plaintiff in reliance on the contract, thereby restoring her to the **status quo ante** — the position she would have been in had no contract been entered. **Restitution** seeks to return to the plaintiff the **value** of any **benefit conferred** on the defendant under the breached contract. It focuses not on the plaintiff's expectation or expenditure, but on the extent of the defendant's **enrichment** at her expense.

You should recognize, from the above description, that there is a close similarity between the reliance or restitutionary damages described here in connection with damages for breach of contract and the equivalent remedies discussed in relation to promissory estoppel (section 8.7) and unjust enrichment (section 9.6). Although the remedies are much the same, the cause of action that creates them is different. We deal with them here as possible bases of recovery for breach of contract rather than as remedies where no contract was created, but the law recognizes liability based on other grounds.

To illustrate the availability of and distinction between expectation, restitution, and reliance damages following a breach or contract, let us slightly embellish the above example of the house sale: The seller contracted to sell the house to the buyer for $150,000. After the contract was signed, the buyer paid $5,000 to the seller as a deposit. She also hired an architect to draw a plan to enlarge the living room and paid him a fee of $1,000. If, after the seller breaches, the buyer finds a reasonable replacement house for $155,000, she will claim and be entitled to expectation damages in the total amount of $11,000 because this is what she must receive to be in the position of having a house for $150,000. She gets not only the $5,000 extra cost of a substitute, but also reimbursement of her costs of $6,000 expended in reliance on the contract. Part of that reliance is the $5,000 she actually paid to the defendant — called **"essential"** (or sometimes **"direct"**) reliance, and part is the $1,000 wasted in having plans drawn that are now useless to her — called **"incidental"** (or sometimes **"consequential"**) reliance.[27]

---

27. These terms are expanded upon below with qualifications that are not raised at this stage.

However, assume that the buyer is able to purchase a replacement house for the same or less than the contract price, so she has suffered no loss in expectation. She would still be able to obtain reliance damages of $6,000 that would restore her to the status quo ante. If she chose to, she could instead recover restitutionary damages, but the benefit conferred on the seller is only $5,000. (Although the plans relate to the seller's house, she is not enriched by them because she did not ask for them to be drawn and presumably does not even have them.) Therefore, the buyer has no incentive to chose restitution in preference over reliance.

Notice that some items of damage are recoverable no matter which form of relief is sought. In this case: The $5,000 deposit is both a reliance expense (and consequently also part of expectation damages) and a benefit subject to restitution. Others may be consistent with only two (here, the wasted architect's fee is counted in both expectation and reliance) or available only under one (the cost of a substitute is claimable only under expectation). Naturally, the plaintiff will select as her first choice whichever of the alternative remedies provides the widest relief. The basic distinction can be represented as follows:

We will now proceed to a more detailed examination of reliance and restitution as alternatives to expectation and to each other.

§18.8 RELIANCE DAMAGES

§18.8.1 The Distinction Between Essential and Incidental Reliance

It was noted earlier that when a loss or expense is incurred in performing an obligation under the contract, the reliance motivating it is called "direct" or "essential" because it is directly based on the contract and essential to fulfilling the party's contractual commitment. However, if a loss or expense is incurred as a consequence of and incidentally to the contract, for the purpose of enjoying or taking advantage of the benefit expected from the contract, it is called "consequential" or "incidental." Sometimes this distinction is easy to draw, as in the case of the deposit and of the architect's plan in the prior illustration. However, the question of whether something is essential or incidental to a party's contractual performances requires an *interpretation* of the party's obligations under the contract. In some cases the distinction may be harder to draw.

For example, the owner of a store hires a signmaker to execute a large neon sign and to install it on a pylon to be erected by the owner in front of the building. In the contract, the signmaker guarantees that it will obtain approval for the sign from the city. The owner erects the pylon, but the signwriter is unable to obtain approval for the sign. Because he promised to do this, he has breached the contract. If we interpret the owner's erection of the pylon as necessary to enable the signmaker to perform, the expenses incurred in building it are essential reliance. However, if we interpret the purpose of the pylon merely as a means for the owner to obtain the benefit of the signmaker's performance, then the erection costs are incidental reliance. In some cases, the distinction may not have any significant effect on the result, but as discussed below, different rules apply to these different types of reliance, and the characterization could be significant.

There is one important point to bear in mind no matter how reliance expenses are classified. The basis of awarding reliance damages is **waste**. The expense or loss must cause prejudice to the plaintiff in that something of value has been wasted and cannot be salvaged. Thus, in the above example, it is indicated that the pylon is useless because the city will not approve the sign. If, following the breach, the owner finds another signmaker who is able to get the sign approved, the expense of constructing the pylon will not be wasted and cannot be recovered. (If the second signmaker charged more than the first, the owner would be able to recover the reasonable extra cost of the substitute as expectation damages.)

§18.8.2 Essential Reliance Damages

We have already seen in section 18.3 that in many types of contracts (especially when the aggrieved party's performance consisted of the supply of work or work and materials), expectation damages are made up of expected profit on the whole contract plus expenditure already incurred in reliance on the contract. In cases like this, essential reliance expenses are therefore a *component of expectation recovery*. For example, a builder contracts to build a house for $150,000. After the builder has performed about half of the work and spent $60,000, the property owner breaches by terminating the project. The builder can prove that his total cost to build the house would have been $120,000. His expectation damages are $90,000, consisting of his lost profit of $30,000 as well as the reimbursement of the expenses of $60,000 already incurred. Both these components must be included to give him the benefit of his bargain — a net gain of the $30,000 profit.

On the above facts, the builder could prove that his total cost would have been less than the contract price, so he can show that he expected a profit. However, this is not always the case. A plaintiff may have no reliable evidence from which to project his total expected costs, or he may have underbid so that projected total cost exceeds the contract. If the *plaintiff cannot prove that he would have made a profit on the contract had it been fully performed, he cannot claim a loss of profit.* He is nevertheless *still entitled* to recover the *essential reliance component* of his damages — the $60,000 actually spent in performing. (As these examples show, a plaintiff who can prove profit has no reason to confine his claim to reliance damages.)

When the plaintiff **would have made a loss** in full performance of the contract — that is, he had a **negative expectation** — the defendant's breach is a lucky break. It allows him to cease performance and curtail his loss. This means that if he is awarded his full reliance damages, he actually does *better than he expected.* For example, say that the builder agreed to build the house for $100,000, but his total cost to complete it would have been $120,000 so that he has an expected loss of $20,000. The owner breaches about halfway through the construction. At that point the builder has spent $60,000. If he is given the full amount of his reliance damages, he fully recovers his cost. Yet he only expected to recover five-sixths of his cost. A convincing argument could be made that this should not be the basis of any adjustment. The defendant breached and cannot be heard to complain if the breach enabled the plaintiff to avoid expected losses. However, because the law is concerned with trying to give the plaintiff true expectation, many courts consider it appropriate to take negative expectation into account when reliance damages are claimed. However, they qualify this rule by shifting the burden of proving negative expectation to the defendant so that in cases of doubt, the plaintiff does end up with full reimbursement.

Therefore, the general rule is that when the *defendant can prove* that the *plaintiff would have suffered a loss* in the event of complete performance, the plaintiff's reliance damages should cut back to bring his recovery into line with his expectations. Although some courts speak merely of the deduction of expected loss from the award of expenses, the better approach is to reduce the recovery *proportionally.* That is, to *prorate* the loss and to reduce the recovery of expenses by a percentage of the total loss equal to the ratio of expenses incurred to total expenses. Thus, on our facts, the builder has incurred half the costs, so his recovery should be reduced by half the loss, $10,000. This means that he recovers only $50,000 of the $60,000 spent. This is justified as being *consistent with his expectation*. Of course, it is still better than he expected, because he really anticipated being not $10,000 but $20,000 out of pocket. However, as he is the victim of the breach, we don't want to be too zealous in placing him in exactly his correct position, because that rewards the breacher by giving her full credit for the plaintiff's prospective loss.

It was mentioned earlier that to get reliance damages reduced, the defendant must prove that the plaintiff would have suffered a loss. The allocation of this burden of proof to the defendant is an accommodation to the plaintiff in recognition of the fact that the defendant was in the wrong for breaching the contract. Therefore, a plaintiff seeking recovery of reliance damages need only prove his expenditure and need not show that he would not have made a loss on the contract. If the defendant seeks a pro rata reduction, it is she who must show that it would have been a losing contract. This means that when projected costs are uncertain and the fact of loss unclear, the plaintiff will obtain full reimbursement of expenses.

A *pro rata reduction* of reliance is *not appropriate in every case*. Even if the defendant can prove that the plaintiff will ultimately have lost money on the contract, reliance expenses should not be reduced if the *purpose of the contract was not to make a profit*. For example, a homeowner contracts with an artist to execute a large and colorful mosaic at the entrance to his property. A vertical concrete slab must be built so that the artist can do the mosaic on it, and the owner undertakes to have the slab erected a month after execution of the contract so that the artist can begin work by that time. A couple of weeks after entering the contract, when the owner has half finished the slab, the artist repudiates the contract. The owner particularly wanted the work of this artist and does not wish for a substitute, so the hunk of concrete is now useless. Having no expectation damages, the owner claims his wasted expenses from the artist. Even if the artist can produce testimony from a bevy of realtors that the mosaic would have been so flashy that it would have reduced the market value of the property, this is not a proper case for reducing reliance recovery. Enhancement of the property value was not the purpose of the contract, and the possibility of economic loss is not relevant to the reimbursement of the wasted costs.

§18.8.3 Incidental Reliance Damages

As stated earlier, incidental reliance expenditure or loss is **incurred in consequence** of having made the **contract** and for the purpose of **using or enjoying the benefits expected** under it. Because these damages are premised on the plaintiff's reliance on the contract, they must necessarily have been induced by the contract and incurred after it was entered into. A loss or expense incurred in anticipation of the contract, but before it is actually formed, is therefore not included in incidental reliance damages. (Whether it may be recovered under the independent theory of promissory estoppel is discussed in Chapter 5.)

Incidental reliance may be illustrated and distinguished from essential reliance by using a variation of the example in section 18.6.5 of the young entrepreneur who entered into a lease of business premises for the purpose of opening a gym. At the time of signing the contract, he paid a deposit of $5,000 to the lessor as required under the contract. In addition, a short time before the business was due to open he spent $1,000 on flyers which he planned to distribute to advertise the opening of his gym. A few days after he had incurred this expense the lessor breached the lease by letting the premises to someone else. Say that no other suitable premises are available, so the lessee is forced to abandon his attempt to open the gym. Because he is entering a new business and has scant evidence to show what his profit would have been, the lessee decides not to try claiming his lost expectation, but instead confines himself to reliance damages. He has suffered both essential reliance damages — the deposit paid to the lessor as required by the contract, and incidental reliance damages — the **wasted expense** of the useless flyers. The former expense qualifies as essential reliance because it was incurred as part of his performance obligation. However, he had no contractual duty to have the flyers printed. He did this solely for his own purpose of attracting business. Even so, the expense was incurred in reliance on the contract, and the breach has defeated that reliance and made the expenditure useless.

Most commonly, incidental reliance takes the form illustrated above — an expenditure or outlay that is wasted as a result of the breach. But sometimes it is in the nature of a *lost opportunity or other gain sacrificed*. For example, after executing the lease of the premises, the lessee had given up his job so that he could operate his new gym, or he had declined an offer of other premises on the strength of this lease. Lost gains and opportunities are, of course, harder to prove and quantify than wasted expenditure, but they are recoverable if properly established, subject to the qualifications discussed below.

Because incidental reliance is ancillary to the contract, there must be a limit on it to protect the breaching party from liability for expenses that it could not fairly have expected, or that were not incurred reasonably. Therefore, incidental reliance is only recoverable if the defendant *foresaw or reasonably should have foreseen* the possibility of the loss or expenditure being incurred, and both the amount and nature of the loss or expenditure were *reasonable*. The mitigation principle applies here too, but it need not be stated as a separate requirement because it is inherent in the concept of reasonable reliance. As with all other types of damage, the loss or expense must be proved with reasonable certainty. As noted before, incidental reliance is only compensable to the extent that it had been **wasted**. Therefore the lessee could not claim wasted expenditures for the flyers if the breach occurred before they were printed and he had the ability to cancel the order. Similarly, if the loss can be salvaged or the items reused, any recoupment of the waste will limit the claim. (Again, this is consonant with the mitigation principle.) For example, say that in addition to flyers, the lessee had bought some gym equipment. Unlike the flyers, the equipment can be resold and the proceeds of resale will curtail the loss.

Where the incidental loss or expense would not be deducted from earnings to determine profit, the fact that the plaintiff would have made a loss upon fully performing the contract is not relevant to the reimbursement of reliance. Therefore, the incidental reliance damages are not subject to the *rule of proportionate reduction*. However, if the contract involves a money-making enterprise and the defendant can show that the venture as a whole would have resulted in a loss to the plaintiff, this reasonable expectation of loss could be taken into account and incidental reliance recovery could be reduced proportionately.

§18.9 RESTITUTIONARY DAMAGES

Restitutionary damages were explained in section 9.6, in which the basic premise of the remedy and measurement of relief were introduced. While the pertinent aspects of that discussion will be restated briefly in the course of this section, you should refer back to it if you want more detail. The purpose of restitutionary damages is to **restore to the plaintiff** the **value** of a **benefit unjustly conferred** on the defendant.[28] Section 9.6 focused on unjust enrichment as a theory of liability alternative to contract and dealt with situations in which the remedy of restitution is granted when a benefit was conferred on the defendant in the absence of contract. However, restitution is also available when a valid contract has been entered into and breached, because the plaintiff has the option of either suing on the contract for expectation or reliance, or of **disaffirming** the contract (that is, operating under the legal fiction that it does not exist) and suing in restitution for the recovery of benefits conferred under the now-defunct contract.

Stated differently, when the defendant commits a material breach, the plaintiff will, when possible, usually seek full enforcement of the contract to

---

28. This section discusses only restitution in favor of the victim of the breach. It does not consider restitution in favor of a breaching party, which is discussed in section 17.6.2. That section explains that, as a general rule, when a contract is rescinded for breach, the breaching party is also entitled to the restitution of any benefits that she conferred on the other party prior to her breach. However, the breaching party's restitution is subject to limitations and is offset by any damages due to the victim.

recover the value of her expectation. However, if the plaintiff cannot recover expectation damages either because she cannot prove them or because she has a negative expectation (that is, she would have lost money on the contract), she will be able to chose to recover in either reliance or restitution. If she claims reliance damages, she is still suing on the contract because, as explained above, reliance expense is a component of expectation damages. However, if she claims restitution, she proceeds on the theory that the breach ended the life of the contract, so that the defendant is no longer justified in retaining the benefit of any performance that the plaintiff rendered to her under it, and the value of that performance unjustly enriches her.

To understand why restitution often provides a different measure of recovery from reliance, one needs to remember their different goals, as mentioned in section 18.7: Reliance is aimed at the recovery of wasted expenses, while restitution is designed to restore the value of a benefit that the defendant has unjustly retained. Sometimes the plaintiff's expenditure may be exactly equal to the defendants's enrichment, so it would make no difference which basis of recovery was used. This is true, for example, when the benefit to the defendant is simply the payment of money. Therefore, if the seller of a house breaches the contract of sale after the buyer has paid a deposit of $5,000, the value of the benefit conferred is precisely equivalent to the plaintiff's expenditure (and interest on the money would be claimable in both restitution and reliance). However, in other situations the plaintiff's outlay could be considerably different from the value of what it produced. Say that a painter entered into a contract to paint a house, and the owner breached after the painter had stripped and primed the walls. If the painter had incurred expenses of $100 in doing this preparatory work, that is all he can recover in reliance. However, restitution based on the value of what has been done for the owner — commonly measured by the market value (quantum meruit) of the service — is likely to be more than what was actually spent. This is because it includes not only the cost of performance, but also the value of the plaintiff's labor or a reasonable profit. Conversely, restitution could be lower than reliance where the expenditure, although justifiable and reasonable, does not result in a benefit to the owner. This is particularly likely when the reliance is incidental so that nothing is actually given to the breacher.

Although market value is the preferred measure of value, the recipient's net gain is sometimes more appropriate. The factors that are taken into account in selecting the means of measurement are discussed in section 9.6 and are not repeated here. However, when restitution is based on the disaffirmance of a breached contract, there is one further question concerning the measurement of the benefit: If the market value of the benefit exceeds the value placed on it in the contract (that is, its contract price), should the contract price be an upper limit on recovery? For example, in the above contract to paint a house, say that the portion of the contract price attributable to stripping and priming the walls is $500, but the painter underbid and this price is lower than the market value of the work, which is $600.

The issue here is not quite the same as that of prorating reliance recovery where the plaintiff would have sustained a loss had the contract not been breached. However, depending on one's view, it can be seen either as analogous or distinguishable. If one emphasizes the difference in the underlying theories of reliance and restitution, disparate treatment is justified. Unlike reliance damages, restitution is not based on enforcement of the contract, but on the assumption that the contract no longer exists. There is no reason to give the defendant any right to rely on the breached contract for the purpose of curtailing the extent of the plaintiff's restitution. Conversely, if one sees the distinction between affirmance and disaffirmance as artificial — a contract does exist after all, and restitution is based on a legal fiction — consistency demands that the plaintiff's expectation should limit restitution in the same way as it does reliance.

§18.10 EQUITABLE REMEDIES: SPECIFIC PERFORMANCE AND INJUNCTIONS

§18.10.1 Specific Performance

It was noted in section 18.2.2 that the remedy of specific performance — a court order commanding the defendant to perform the contract as promised — would seem to be the most precise means of achieving the plaintiff's expectation. Yet, for a number of reasons, some historical and some based on practicality and principle, damages are the primary form of relief for breach of contract, and specific performance is reserved as an extraordinary remedy. The historical basis for the primacy of the damages remedy lies in the *dichotomy between law and equity*. As it was originally formed, the court of equity was a court of special resort, presided over by the Lord Chancellor, acting under the sovereign's prerogative power. The Lord Chancellor would intervene to do justice when the regular courts of law had no power to provide an adequate remedy to the plaintiff.[29] In the context of contract, the law courts were confined to awarding damages for breach and had no power to order the defendant to perform the contract. If damages were not an adequate remedy, the plaintiff had to approach the court of equity to request it to use its discretionary power to compel the defendant's performance. As one of the prerequisites for obtaining this equitable relief, the plaintiff had to show that the *normal legal remedy of damages would not provide*

---

29. *See* section 2.5 for a fuller explanation of the distinction between law and equity.

adequate relief. The most common examples of such situations are contracts for the sale of unique property that cannot be substituted for on the market; cases in which damages would be very difficult to prove with reasonable certainty; and cases in which the defendant is financially incapable of satisfying a money judgment.

Although courts of law and equity have long been combined, and the same judge decides on the alternative remedies of damages and specific performance, the requirement of establishing the inadequacy of the damage remedy still exists in our law. It is, of course, not as firm or rigid as it may once have been, and courts tend to focus more on the relative efficiency or effectiveness of the remedies. Nevertheless, the rule is still widely followed and is reflected in both Restatement Second §359 and UCC §§2.709 (the seller's action for the price) and 2.716 (the buyer's[30] remedy for specific performance).

The primacy of the damages remedy is not based purely on tradition, and there are often good practical and policy reasons for preferring damages over specific performance. Because specific performance is an equitable remedy, a court will only grant it if, on balancing the equities between the plaintiff and the defendant, and taking into account the societal interests at stake, the justification of affording the plaintiff this relief outweighs its drawbacks. This requires the court to evaluate a number of different factors, including the following issues and concerns:

1. In many cases it is simply more **efficient** to award damages. If the plaintiff is able to purchase substitute property or services on the market, it is just easier to award a sum of money to her to enable her to do that, rather than ordering the defendant to perform. It is only when there is no reasonable possibility of acquiring a substitute or no reasonable prospect of being able to establish or collect a monetary award that specific performance becomes a preferable remedy.

   The common law has long assumed that land is unique, so that damages are not an adequate remedy for the breach of a contract to *sell or lease real property.* Modern courts generally follow this traditional approach, and it is still relatively easy to obtain specific performance where the contract involves the sale or lease of real property. However, the rule is not absolute and a court may decline to follow it where the land does not in fact have special qualities and it is possible to calculate damages with reasonable certainty. In such a case **damages are an adequate remedy**. For example, in *Van Wagner Advertising Corp. v. S&M Enterprises*, 492 N.E.2d 756 (N.Y. App. 1986) the

---

30. As noted in footnote 15, the 2003 revision of Article 2 no longer treats specific performance solely as a buyer's remedy. However, the buyer will be the party that most commonly uses it.

owner of a building leased space on the building's exterior wall to an advertising agency for a term of several years. The wall faced an exit ramp of the Midtown Tunnel and was therefore visible to traffic using the ramp. The lessor breached the contract by terminating the lease and the advertising agency sued for specific performance on the grounds that the exposure of the wall to the busy offramp made it unique. The trial court refused summary judgment and awarded damages to the agency. The court of appeals affirmed. Although it accepted that the building wall offered advertising exposure that was, in a sense unique, the court said that this was not enough to support the remedy of specific performance. Uniqueness must be judged in light of the difficulty or ease of measuring the cost of a substitute having the special qualities of the leased property. There is a much stronger argument for awarding specific performance if the information available to assess the financial loss resulting from the breach is scanty or unreliable, leading to a high risk of the inaccurate measure of compensation. However, in this case, the agency's loss could be calculated quite reliably because it had subleased the space for part of the time and its loss on that lease was reliably quantifiable. As to the remainder of the lease term, there was a well-established market for commercial billboard space from which the value lost by the agency could be readily calculated.

Where *goods* are sold, the assumption is contrary to that usually applied to real property — except in special circumstances, goods are not considered unique and damages are therefore normally the most appropriate form of relief.

Under UCC §2.716, a buyer is relegated to a claim for damages and cannot get an order compelling the seller to perform unless she can show that the goods are unique or that the circumstances otherwise justify the order.[31] Comment 2 to that section explains that to be unique, an item does not necessarily have to be the only one of its kind in existence. The concept is broader than that and covers any situation in which it is not commercially feasible to obtain a substitute.

2. It could be unnecessarily **intrusive and harsh** to force the defendant to perform as promised. Unlike an award of damages, which operates in *rem* (as explained in section 18.2.4, it is simply a money judgment enforceable against the defendant's property), an order of specific performance operates in *personam*. This means that it is a command of the court directed at the person of the defendant. If she

---

31. The 2003 revision of Article 2 also permits specific performance in a non-consumer contract where the parties have agreed to that remedy.

disobeys it, she can be sanctioned for contempt of court and jailed or fined.

3. Concerns of **involuntary servitude** are raised where the performance involves personal services. Even if damages are not an adequate remedy, the constitutional bar on involuntary servitude precludes a court from ordering specific performance of a contract for personal services.

4. As in any equitable remedy, the court considers the impact on the parties of granting or denying the remedy. That is, one of the factors that it takes into account is the **balance of the equities and hardships** between the parties. Some of the factors that go into this balance are already taken into account in the other considerations listed here, but the equitable nature of the remedy gives the court the discretion to go beyond them to take account of special circumstances. For example, in *Kilarjian v. Vastola*, 877 A.2d 372 (N.J. Super. 2004) the Kilarjians bought the Vastolas' house. The Vastolas breached the contract by refusing to proceed with the transfer and the Kilarjians sued for specific performance. The court noted that under ordinary circumstances, specific performance would be an appropriate remedy because real property is presumed to be unique. However, the reason why the Vastolas breached was because Mrs. Vastola was suffering from a serious progressive neurological condition which disabled her and made it very difficult for the Vastolas to move. The court recognized that this was a hard case because the Kilarjians were entitled to the benefit of their bargain. However, it exercised its equitable discretion and refused specific performance on the grounds that it would be heartless and unjust to evict an ill woman from her home. Instead, the court remanded the case to the trial court to determine the Kilarjian's damages based on their wasted expenditures plus any amount by which their financing costs may have increased as a result of the breach.

5. In considering whether to grant an order of specific performance, the court must be mindful of the practicality of **enforcement**. Even if an order compelling performance does not amount to involuntary servitude, if the performance involves something more than the mere delivery or conveyance of property or documents, *problems of supervision* may arise. That is, the performance may require judicial monitoring to ensure that a reluctant defendant does not provide a grudging performance that falls below the reasonable standards required under the contract. The problem of supervision of performance is one of the factors that a court weighs in deciding whether it should grant specific performance, but it is not dispositive. If the court otherwise feels that specific performance is the best remedy, it

will undertake to supervise the performance if necessary. This can be accomplished by appointing a special master or some other person accountable to the court who will evaluate performance and possibly mediate any disputes that might arise in the course of carrying it out.

6. It is a general principle of equity that a court will not make a **vague** order. Its command most clearly tells the defendant what he must do to obey and avoid sanctions for contempt. This principle, combined with the courts' reluctance to invent contract terms for the parties, leads to the rule that specific performance will not be decreed unless the *contract is definite enough to form the basis of a clear order.* In Chapter 10 it was noted that if the parties are too vague or indefinite in their agreement, their arrangement may fail to qualify as a contract at all. However, even if the uncertainty is not so severe as to defeat a claim that a contract was made, it could render the contract sufficiently unclear to support an order of specific performance.

7. Specific performance can be a **partial remedy.** In the proper circumstances, a court has the discretion to order *performance of part of the contract in combination with an award of monetary damages* for the remainder. In many cases, specific performance is obviously an alternative to damages, so the plaintiff cannot get both remedies. However, when the breach has already caused a loss that will not be recouped by the specific performance, it is appropriate for the court to award damages to compensate for that irretrievable loss in addition to granting specific performance. For example, if the defendant refuses to convey business premises purchased by the plaintiff, the court could decree specific performance and also award the plaintiff whatever loss in profits she can show to have been suffered for the period of delay between the date for delivery under the contract and the date on which the order is finally complied with.

8. It probably goes without saying that a plaintiff who seeks specific performance must **render the return performance** to the defendant, and the court may grant its order conditional on the plaintiff doing so.

§18.10.2 Injunctions

An injunction is a court order that either compels the defendant to perform a specified act — called a mandatory injunction — or prohibits the defendant from performing a specified act — called a prohibitory injunction. An order of specific performance is really just a form of **mandatory injunction** — a court order compelling the defendant to render the performance that he promised in the contract. However, sometimes a **prohibitory injunction** may afford effective and appropriate relief to the victim of a breach. This may occur where the order directs the breaching party not to take action that violates the terms of the contract. (In such a case one could characterize the prohibitory injunction as a negative form of specific performance.) For example, in *Walgreen Co. v. Sara Creek Property Co.*, 966 F.2d 273 (7th Cir. 1992) Walgreen had a long-term lease of premises in a shopping mall owned by Sara Creek. The lease provided that Sara creek would not lease premises in the mall to another pharmacy. Sara Creek breached this term by entering into a lease with a discount store that had a pharmacy department. Walgreen sued Sara Creek, seeking an injunction prohibiting it from letting the premises to Walgreen's competitor. The court of appeals affirmed the trial court's grant of the injunction. The court noted that damages are the norm in a breach of contract case, and are usually the most efficient remedy. Therefore, the court will not grant an injunction unless the plaintiff can justify it by showing extraordinary circumstances and a balance of the equities in favor of granting it. Walgreen had demonstrated that an injunction was the most appropriate remedy in this case because the lease term was for many years and Walgreen would have great difficulty in accurately proving its loss of profits and goodwill over the term of the lease. The injunction was a simple prohibition and would not require court supervision, and neither Sara Creek nor the competing pharmacy would be unduly harmed by it.

A prohibitory injunction may also be helpful to a plaintiff where it is not aimed directly at conduct in violation of the contract, but instead strikes at the defendant's motivation to breach. That is, if the defendant's purpose in wrongfully terminating a contract was to enter into a more advantageous contract with someone else, an injunction prohibiting the defendant from performing the other contract could eliminate the advantage of breaching and encourage the defendant to relent. For example, say that Sara Nade contracted with Smalltime, Inc. to perform a concert. Sara repudiated the contract a short time afterwards because she received a much more lucrative offer from Worldwide Promotions, Inc. to perform on the same night. The court will not grant an order of specific performance to compel Sara to perform this personal service for Smalltime, but it may be willing to enjoin Sara from performing for Worldwide. This does not help Smalltime directly, but it removes Sara's motive for breaching and encourages her to retract her repudiation.

A prohibitory injunction is just as much an equitable remedy as an order for specific performance and is subject to the same equitable considerations. A court will not enjoin the defendant's conduct unless the plaintiff can show that the less intrusive legal remedy of damages is inadequate and that the need to protect the plaintiff's rights under the contract outweighs any hardship that the injunction might impose on the defendant, any problems of supervising the order, and any harm to the rights of innocent third parties or the public interest.

§18.11 LIQUIDATED (AGREED) DAMAGES

A liquidated damages (also called "agreed damages") provision is a term in a contract under which the parties agree that in the event of a breach by one of them, the breacher will pay damages in a specified sum or in accordance with a prescribed formula. If such a clause is valid, it has the effect of **settling in advance** what **damages** will be **due in the event of a breach.** The contract could liquidate damages for the breach of either party or for only for one of them. (If the liquidated damages clause covers breach by only one party, a breach by the other will require proof of damages in the usual way.) The exact meaning and effect of a liquidated damages provision is a matter of *interpretation,* but unless the language or context indicates otherwise, it is generally assumed that when damages have been validly liquidated in the contract, the fixing of the amount binds not only the defendant who is responsible for it, but also the plaintiff. That is, even if the breach causes the plaintiff greater loss than that provided, the plaintiff's *recovery is limited to the amount agreed.* However, unless the provision makes it clear that the liquidated damages are the plaintiff's *exclusive remedy,* Restatement Second §361 assumes that it does not prevent the plaintiff from electing to claim specific performance instead of damages.

There are a number of reasons why the parties may agree to commit themselves in advance to a set amount of damages in the event of breach: The principal one is that if damages are stipulated in the contract, it is *easier and more efficient to obtain relief* if a breach occurs, particularly if the transaction involves a venture that is speculative. The plaintiff avoids the problem of establishing foreseeability, mitigation, and certainty, and the defendant has a predetermined liability so that she can better predict the cost of breaching. In fact, if one of the parties is particularly concerned about protecting itself from the problem of establishing damages in the event of breach, the ability to stipulate damages in the contract may be a significant incentive to entering the contract.

However, liquidated damages have an obvious negative aspect. They are nothing more than *a forecast of probable loss.* Even if the parties try hard to make as precise and thoughtful a prognostication as possible, they can never prophesy exactly what the actual losses will be. If the outcome of the transaction is uncertain or speculative, reasonably accurate prediction of the impact of breach becomes more unlikely. The problem of unreliable prediction is, of course, increased to the extent that the parties are less careful in their projections. It may therefore turn out that the forecast of damage is very different from the loss that ultimately results from a breach, and that the agreed damages greatly overcompensate or undercompensate the plaintiff.

Liquidated damages have enough problems of accuracy, even when they are intended to be a reasonable forecast of harm. But sometimes their purpose is not to approximate anticipated harm, but to *discourage breach* by imposing a *penalty* designed to make breach too costly. That is, although the term is set out in the form of a pre-estimate of damages, its real goal is to make breaching so unattractive that the promisee will try to avoid it. Because the remedial system of contract law is based on the premise of compensation, courts have long followed the practice of refusing to enforce a provision that purports to liquidate damages, but in reality imposes a penalty for breach. While this approach is well-established, it continues to be controversial because it tries to accommodate two countervailing policies. The policy of *freedom of contract* pulls in the direction of enforcing the parties' agreement on damages, even if it provides for relief that goes beyond actual loss. However, the policy of confining contractual relief to *economic compensation* dictates that a provision that goes beyond that should not be enforced. To one who places stronger emphasis on freedom of contract, there is little justification for a court to interfere with fairly bargained liquidated damages provisions, and policing should be confined to fraud, duress, or other bargaining impropriety.[32] To one who more highly values the compensation policy, the goal of achieving an accurate expectation award demands a more rigorous examination of the purpose and effect of such clauses. The issue of *fairness* also comes into the question of whether or not agreed damages should be enforced despite their penal effect, but this issue tends to be resolved based on one's view of the relative primacy of the contract freedom or compensation principle. One could say that it is fair to hold the defendant to her commitment, even if this results in overcompensation of the plaintiff, but one could also say the opposite. Arguments based on the economic impact of agreed damages can be used to support either side of this debate: If such clauses overcompensate, they discourage efficient breach and should therefore be overturned. Conversely, the refusal to enforce agreed damages may deter and interfere with transactions by making it more difficult for parties to effectively allocate risk in their contract.

Despite the controversy, courts do continue to draw a distinction between enforceable liquidated damages provisions and unenforceable penalties. Given the uncertainty inherent in any prediction, the most difficult

---

32. Note that the issue of whether to enforce a liquidated damages provision is independent of questions such as duress, fraud, unconscionability, adhesion, or other bargaining unfairness discussed in Chapter 13. Of course, if assent to a liquidated damages clause is obtained by one of these improper means, that would in itself provide grounds for invalidating it.

practical problem created by the distinction is to devise standards for deciding when to treat the provision as legitimate and when to refuse enforcement. Because it is well known that courts will not enforce penalties, few contracts openly admit that the purpose of the clause is to penalize and discourage breach. When most such clauses routinely profess to be a true liquidation of damages, the express language of the contract must be regarded with some skepticism. Instead, courts have developed a policing mechanism in the form of a set of guidelines that look at the circumstances existing both at the time of executing the contract and at the time of breach. The purpose is, first, to evaluate whether, at the time of contracting, the parties intended to make a genuine pre-estimate of loss, and second, to compare the agreed damages to any actual damages that were in fact suffered.

Restatement Second §356 and UCC §2.718 reflect this bipartite test in almost identical language: Damages for breach by either party may be liquidated in the contract, but the provision will not be enforced and will be void as a penalty unless the amount it fixes as damages is *reasonable in light of anticipated or actual harm* caused by the breach.

§18.11.1 Anticipated Harm — Evaluation of the Liquidated Damages as at the Time of Contracting

To decide the reasonableness of the anticipation of harm, the court must consider two factors: the *expected difficulty of proving loss* and the degree to which the estimate of harm was a *reasonable advance estimate of that loss* — a principled and genuine attempt to predict likely loss.[33] On their face, these two factors *appear contradictory* because the more difficult it is to prove loss, the harder it must be to make any kind of reasonable pre-estimate of damages. However, the factors are not treated as rigid co-equal requirements, but as flexible

---

33. The 2003 revision of §2.718 confines to consumer contracts the requirement that the loss must be difficult to prove (or the likelihood that an adequate remedy might otherwise not be available). Therefore, under revised §2.718, the sole question in a non-consumer contract is whether the pre-estimate of harm was a reasonable advance estimate of the loss. In most sales of goods, it is not difficult to prove direct damages based on the difference between the contract price and an actual or hypothetical substitute transaction. For that reason, there is a good chance that a liquidated damages provision in a sale of goods will not satisfy the test that damages would have been difficult to prove. By eliminating this requirement, except in consumer contracts, the change should make it easier to enforce a liquidated damages clause in a commercial contract for the sale of goods. The 2003 revision of §2.718 also removes the language stating that an unreasonably large liquidated damages provision is void as a penalty. Official Comment 3 to revised §2.718 indicates that the reason for the change is that this language is redundant and misleading — the section already makes it clear that a liquidated damages provision should be enforced if it is reasonable.

considerations to be balanced against each other. Therefore, the more uncertain and speculative the damages, the less rigorous the court will be in examining the reliability of the pre-estimate. However, if anticipated damages would be relatively mechanical and routine, the parties are held to a stricter standard in trying to estimate them.

For example, if the contract relates to an innovative new business venture, it will likely be difficult to prove damages for breach with reasonable certainty, so the court should be rather accepting of the amount of agreed damages settled on by the parties, even if it is quite speculative. However, if the contract involves the sale of property for which there is an active market, substitutionary damages should be quite easy to prove, so the parties' means of determining the amount of agreed damages is more rigorously examined.

The general approach is to *place the greatest emphasis on this first stage* of the evaluation, so that if the clause was really not intended as a penalty and the parties were truly concerned about avoiding the uncertainty of a later dispute over loss, their genuine and principled attempt at estimation is worthy of respect. It may therefore be appropriate for the court to uphold the clause even if it appears that the actual loss suffered is smaller than predicted. This is reflected in both Restatement Second §356 and UCC §2.718, which call for reasonableness of the liquidated damages to be assessed in light of anticipated or actual harm. That is, it is not always necessary for the provision to satisfy both the test of reasonable prediction and the test of proportionality to actual loss.

§18.11.2 Actual Harm — Comparison Between Anticipated and Actual Loss

Although the comparison between anticipated and actual loss may be of secondary importance when evidence of genuine estimation is strong, courts are not likely to be oblivious to a substantial discrepancy between damages as agreed and as actually suffered. Of course, if, after breach, it turns out that damages are truly difficult to prove, this second stage of the inquiry becomes marginal or falls away. The uncertain and speculative nature of the loss vindicates the parties' judgment in trying to settle it in advance, provided that they made enough effort to satisfy the test of reasonable estimation. However, when it is possible to prove actual damages, courts balk at enforcing agreed damages that clearly and substantially exceed the plaintiff's loss. In fact, a gross disproportionality may in itself be evidence that the estimate was not a reasonable forecast of harm.

It may be helpful to represent these guidelines diagrammatically:

TIME OF CONTRACTING
The issue: Was this intended as a genuine liquidation of damages?

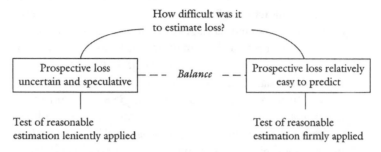

TIME OF BREACH
The issue: How does the estimate compare to the actual loss suffered?

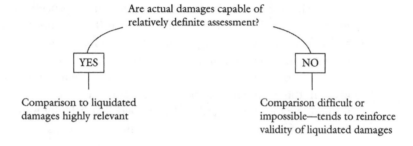

§18.11.3 Damage Limitation Provisions

A term limiting damages must be distinguished from an agreed damages provision. The purpose of a damage limitation is not to forecast harm and settle the amount of the loss in advance, but to place a limit on the relief that a party may claim in the event of breach. A common example of a damage limitation is a term stating that a party will not be liable for any consequential damages arising from the breach. This provision does not anticipate the amount of damages, but rather precludes a claim for any consequential damages and confines liability to direct damages.

A provision in a contract that fixes agreed damages in an unreasonably small amount is, strictly speaking, a liquidation of damages rather than a damage limitation, and should be analyzed as described in sections 18.11.1 and 18.11.2. However both Restatement, Second §356 and current UCC §2.718 focus on the penal nature of unreasonably large liquidated damages and do not seem to encompass unreasonably small liquidated damages.

(In fact, Comment *d* to §356 states that the section is not applicable to a term that fixes damages in an unreasonably small amount.) Revised UCC §2.718 is clearer on the distinction between damage limitations and liquidated damages and it covers both unreasonably large and unreasonably small liquidated damages. (The revised section eliminates reference to unreasonably large liquidated damages and Official Comment 3 makes it clear that a term fixing unreasonably small liquidated damages is also unenforceable.)

If a term is classified as a damage limitation, it is treated differently from a liquidated damages provision and it is not subject to the tests discussed above. Instead, Restatement Second §356, Comment *a*, UCC §2.718, Comment 1, and UCC §2.719[34] indicate that damage limitation provisions are enforceable unless they are *unconscionable*. A limitation of remedy that grossly undercompensates the victim of a breach and deprives her of meaningful relief could, of course, be substantively unconscionable. However, as the discussion of unconscionability in section 13.11 explains, a finding of unconscionability requires more than a harsh result. There must also be some evidence that the unfair term resulted from procedural unconscionability — that it was imposed on the plaintiff by improper bargaining. In addition to avoidance on grounds of unconscionability, §2.719 permits the non-enforcement of a limitation of damages where circumstances have caused the limited remedy to fail of its essential purpose. Therefore, even if the elements of unconscionability are not satisfied, a damage limitation can be disregarded if it is clear that it badly under-compensates the plaintiff or provides for a remedy that is valueless.

§18.12 INCIDENTAL DAMAGES, ATTORNEY'S FEES, AND INTEREST

In addition to the principal remedies discussed above, there are ancillary monetary awards that are often needed to fully compensate the plaintiff for a breach of contract. They are noted briefly here.

§18.12.1 Interest

When a *contract itself provides for the payment of interest* on an amount due by a party, the claim of interest is simply part of the plaintiff's damage recovery and is included in the claim. For example, if a lender makes a loan and the borrower breaches the contract by failing to repay it, the lender is entitled to sue for

---

34. The 2003 revision of §2.718 expressly states that the enforceability of a limitation of damages provision is governed by §2.719. Section 2.719 is not changed in the 2003 revision.

both the principal and for the full amount of accumulated interest at the rate provided in the contract. Interest continues to accrue until the debt is paid.

Even when the contract does not provide for the payment of interest, the general rule is that a plaintiff may recover interest on a *performance with a fixed or ascertainable money value* from the time that the performance became due to the time that payment is ultimately made. Such an award of interest may be seen as a form of consequential damages — because the plaintiff has lost the benefit of investing the money during the period between breach and recovery, or as a form of restitution — because the defendant has benefitted by its retention.

Even when damages are *uncertain until finally fixed in the judgment*, interest is commonly awarded to the plaintiff from the time between rendering of the judgment and its ultimate payment.

§18.12.2 Incidental Damages

Incidental damages are those expenses **reasonably incurred** by the plaintiff after the breach **in attempting to deal with the breach.** They are essentially the administrative costs of coping with the breach and taking whatever action is necessary to **protect and enforce the plaintiff's rights under the contract.** They include such items as the costs incurred in making arrangements to obtain substitute performance and to mitigate damages. For example, say that the buyer of goods breaches the contract by refusing to accept the goods when the seller tenders delivery. As a result, the seller has to transport them back to a warehouse, store them, and negotiate for their resale. All the additional costs of transport, storage, and negotiation are incidental damages and may be recovered by the seller, provided that they were incurred reasonably. (As this example involves a sale of goods, incidental damages are defined in UCC §§2.710 and 2.715,[35] but they are also available under common law.)

Although incidental damages do, in a sense, follow as a consequence of the breach, they are distinguishable from and should not be confused with consequential damages: They do not arise as a result of the impact of the breach on some other transaction or activity dependent on the contract, but are expenses directly related to the plaintiff's attempt to manage the effects of the breach.

§18.12.3 Attorney's Fees

Based on the above definition of incidental damages, one might assume that the plaintiff should be able to recover her attorney's fees incurred in suing to

---

35. The provisions relating to incidental damages are unchanged in the 2003 revision.

enforce the contract after breach. They are, after all, expenses that the plaintiff was forced to undertake in dealing with the breach and seeking to enforce her rights under the contract. Despite this, attorney's fees are not usually recoverable by the winner of a lawsuit unless the contract specifically allows them, they are authorized by statute, or the case falls within one of a few narrow categories of exception recognized at common law. The common law exceptions apply to bad faith and vexatious litigation and to other specific situations that need not concern us here. There is no statute that generally provides for the recovery of attorney's fees in contract cases (but individual states may have statutes that allow fees in certain types of contract suit). Therefore, the general rule is that attorney's fees are not recoverable by the winner of a suit on contract unless the contract itself makes provision for this.

The United States is one of the few countries in the world in which the prevailing party in litigation is not routinely entitled to recover attorney's fees from the loser. The debate over the merits of this approach is complex and beyond our scope. It is important to recognize, however, that unless one of the exceptions to the general rule applies, our system, by not reimbursing the plaintiff for the considerable expenses of litigation, does not really achieve its goal of placing the plaintiff in the position she would have been in had the contract been performed.

In tort cases, where a jury has a fairly wide discretion in deciding on the amount of non-economic damages (such as those awarded for mental distress or pain and suffering), it has some ability to increase the plaintiff's compensatory damages to take account of attorney's fees. If the case merits punitive damages, overcompensation may go far beyond this. By contrast, because contract damages are focused on provable economic loss, the jury has much less flexibility to inflate the award to cover the plaintiff's attorney's fees. This difference in approach between contract and tort can be justified on the basis that, unlike a tort victim, a contracting party is capable of providing in the contract for the award of attorney's fees (if she has the bargaining power to do so).

§18.13 NON-ECONOMIC DAMAGES AND PUNITIVES

§18.13.1 Mental Distress Damages

Because contract damages are geared to economic loss, they do not typically take account of any mental distress, inconvenience, humiliation, or other psychic harm caused by the breach. This principle is applied firmly, whether the aggrieved party is a corporation without heart or soul, or some poor individual who really is traumatized and distressed by the breach. For example, in Chrum v. Charles

Heating & Cooling, Inc., 327 N.W.2d 568 (Mich. 1982) a furnace bought from the defendant caught fire and destroyed the plaintiff's home. The court refused to award damages for mental distress because the contract was simply a commercial transaction, the breach of which led to property loss. *Valentine v. General American Credit*, 362 N.W.2d 628 (Mich. 1984) took the same approach where an employee claimed mental distress damages for wrongful discharge. The court recognized that the breach of an employment contract has a negative emotional effect on the employee, but the contract is commercial in nature, and compensation must be confined to any provable economic loss.

There are two situations in which courts have recognized exceptions to this rule. First, if the **breach of contract is also a tort**, the tortious nature of the breach permits compensation for whatever non-economic damages that the plaintiff suffered. However, this is not really much of an exception at all, because the true basis of recovery is tort, not contract, since a tort was in fact committed. For example, if a surgeon negligently performs an operation, thereby both breaching a contractual duty of competent performance and committing the tort of battery, the patient can recover not only any economic losses, but also damages for pain and suffering and emotional harm. Similarly, in *Chrum*, after concluding that the contract did not involve the kind of personal interests that merited mental distress damages, the court recognized that the plaintiff would be able to sue in tort for mental distress if the furnace had been installed negligently. It remanded the case to allow the plaintiff to pursue a tort claim.

The second exception concerns contracts whose **clear and principal purpose** is not to satisfy any economic or commercial goal of the plaintiff, but to give her an **emotional, sentimental, or psychic benefit**. It is the nature of the contract, not the nature of the breach that is crucial.[36] Courts that recognize this exception usually apply it very narrowly to contracts that so deeply involve matters of personal concern to the plaintiff that her non-economic purpose is clear and the defendant must reasonably have realized that a breach would likely inflict serious emotional distress on her. In refusing relief for the breach of the commercial contract in *Chrum*, the court cited cases in which breach appropriately gave rise to mental distress damages — a nursing home's breach of a caregiving contract by failure to notify the plaintiff of her mother's pending death, and a funeral home's breach of a burial contract by mutilating the body of the plaintiff's daughter. Breaches of contracts for funeral services feature quite regularly as the basis for awarding mental distress damages. For example, in *Menorah Chapels at Millburn v. Needle*, 899 A.2d 316 (N.J. Super. A.D. 2006) (discussed in section 17.6.3 in relation

---

36. Restatement, Second §353 describes this exception as applicable to a *contract or breach* of a kind that makes serious emotional disturbance particularly likely. Although the text of the section appears to contemplate either a contract or a breach that is likely to cause emotional distress, the comments and caselaw indicate that the nature of the contract is the key factor.

to divisibility) the court held that the plaintiff was entitled to mental distress damages where the funeral home breached the contract to perform funeral services by failing to ensure a proper vigil over the body in accordance with orthodox Jewish ritual. Breaches of contracts for wedding services are also usually good candidates for an award of mental distress damages. In *Dietsch v. Music Co.*, 543 N.E.2d 1302 (Ohio 1983) a band that failed to show up for a wedding was held liable for emotional distress damages.

When courts consider the propriety of awarding mental distress damages, they usually couch the discussion in terms of **foreseeability** and ask whether the nature of the contract such that the parties reasonably contemplated that its breach would lead to mental distress. For example, in *Menorah Chapels*, the court pointed out that because a contract for funeral services is designed to bring comfort to the bereaved, the chapel could readily foresee that its breach would cause emotional distress. However, while foreseeability of the emotional damage is an important factor in deciding whether to award mental distress damages, it must be stressed that the contemplation of possible mental distress is not enough. The sentimental or emotional character of the contract performance is crucial. In *Valentine*, the court recognized that an employer can readily foresee that wrongful dismissal will cause an employee mental distress. However, because the contract is commercial in nature, that foresight is not enough to entitle the employee to mental distress damages.

§18.13.2 Punitive Damages

As their name suggests, the purpose of punitive damages is to **punish** the defendant for particularly egregious conduct and to **deter** her from similar conduct in the future. Because the fate of the defendant is also likely to make an example of her and thereby have a deterrent effect on others, punitives are also sometimes called **exemplary.** Punitive damages are principally available in *tort* law. They are not appropriate when the tort involves ordinary negligence and are confined to cases in which the defendant *deliberately and maliciously injured* the plaintiff, or sometimes when the defendant acted in *callous and conscious disregard* of the plaintiff's rights. Although punitive damages are aimed at punishing the defendant, they are not in the form of a fine payable to the public treasury, but are awarded to the plaintiff in addition to whatever she is entitled to as compensatory damages. They are therefore a windfall that have the effect of overcompensating her. Because punitive damage awards can be large, the degree of overcompensation can be astounding.[37] Even in the area of tort law, where the jury's

---

37. The degree of overcompensation is reduced by the fact that a portion of the award will be used to pay attorney's fees and the costs of preparing for and conducting the litigation.

discretion to award punitive damages in appropriate cases is well-established, their scope and appropriateness is a matter of continuing controversy, and courts regularly reduce jury awards.

As emphasized many times in the preceding pages, the orientation of contract law is to the *compensation* of the plaintiff's economic loss, *not to the punishment and deterrence of breach*. As a result, it has long been seen as inappropriate to augment any compensatory award by punitive damages, even when the breach was deliberate and faithless. Restatement Second §355 reflects this attitude by taking the position that punitive damages are not recoverable for a breach of contract unless the breach consists of tortious conduct for which punitives would be available under tort law.

Where punitive damages are awarded for breach of contract, it is almost always because the defendant's conduct constitutes both a breach of contract and a **deliberate, independent tort**. This is illustrated by *America's Directories, Inc. v. Stellhorn One-Hour Photo, Inc.*, 833 N.E.2d 1059 (Ind. App. 2006), a fraud case discussed in sections 12.2 (the fraud exception to the parol evidence rule) and 13.6.2 (fraudulent promise). Recall that the seller of advertising in a phone directory made a fraudulent promise that it would permit the buyer to cancel the advertising after the first year of the three-year contract. The court upheld the jury's award to the buyer of both compensatory damages (for work and time lost in trying to deal with the fraud) and punitive damages. The court noted that in addition to violating the plaintiff's contract rights, fraud is independently recognized as a tort, and there was sufficient evidence for the jury to conclude that the seller committed the tort willfully and wantonly by intentionally misleading the buyer.

In a narrow range of cases, particularly involving an insurer's willful breach by unjustifiably failing to indemnify the insured promptly, adequately, or at all for loss covered by the policy, courts have been willing to award punitive damages even though tort law has not traditionally recognized the breach as an independent tort. (Some courts have overcome this barrier by creating a new tort, so that an egregious violation of the **duty of good faith and fair dealing** is recognized as a tort in itself.) Insurance policies are contracts of adhesion,[38] and the failure to indemnify the insured can have disastrous consequences for him. If an unscrupulous insurer deliberately fails to indemnify the insured until it is sued, the ultimate award of nothing more than compensatory damages is not likely to be much of a deterrent to future conduct of this kind. Therefore, punitive damages serve the purpose of increasing the risk of such behavior and may better dissuade the insurer from trying to evade its obligations. Although there are other types of contracts in which it may be appropriate to award punitive damages for bad faith breach, courts have not readily expanded this doctrine beyond the field of insurance.

---

38. Contracts of adhesion are discussed in section 13.12.

Examples

1. In January, the city council of Barbarian Bluffs decided to erect a monument to Barb Aryan, its founder. It commissioned Percy Vere, a local sculptor, to carve a giant bust of Barb into the granite bluff overlooking the town. In terms of his contract with the city, Percy undertook to begin work on the massive carving project in February and to complete it in time for the dedication in March of the following year. The town agreed to a fee of $250,000 for his work, to be paid upon completion of the carving. In February, Percy spent $50,000 to buy dynamite and other materials needed for his performance, and he hired two assistants at a monthly wage of $2,000 each. He began work immediately, and by April he had completed the blasting, erected scaffolding, and had begun the carving with jackhammers.

   The project had been controversial from the beginning, but as it proceeded, hostility to it intensified. A growing number of citizens became persuaded that Barb Aryan did not deserve a monument at all because she had been fierce and ruthless in the way that she had forced the aboriginal inhabitants to vacate the area. Many others felt that it was a sacrilege to despoil the natural contours of the bluff. By the end of April, the outrage of the townfolk had reached such a pitch that the council members realized that it would be politically unwise to proceed any further with the monument. They therefore voted to abandon it and in early May they told Percy to stop work. This was a material and total breach because the town had no right to cancel the contract. Percy refused to accept the town's cancellation and continued work for another two weeks, until forcibly ejected from the site by the sheriff.

   Had Percy stopped work when he was told to, he would already have paid $2,000 each to his assistants for wages earned to that stage and would have been required to pay them an additional $1,000 each as severance pay. As he had not used up all the materials bought for the job, he could have recouped $20,000 of the $50,000 spent by selling what remained of them. Because he refused to stop, he incurred an additional wage expense of $2,000 and used up a further amount of the materials, reducing their resale value by $5,000. Had the council not breached its contract, and had Percy been permitted to complete his performance, his total cost for the job would have been $150,000. What are his damages?

2. Buddy Beautiful is a celebrated supermodel, best known for his extremely seductive advertisements for men's fragrances and designer denim jeans. He decided to capitalize on his fame by becoming a movie star. Following intensive negotiations, his agent managed to

secure a contract for him with Medea Mogul, an important movie producer. In terms of the contract, Buddy would be paid $10 million for taking the lead role in a movie to be called *Buddy's Big Budget Adventure*, an expensive and riotous new comedy, full of cute jokes and romantic scenes in which Buddy would have the opportunity to remove some or all of his clothing. Production of the film was to begin two months after the contract was signed, and would last for six months.

About a month after entering the contract, Medea decided not to produce the film. She wrote to Buddy, informing him of the film's cancellation and offering him the leading role in another movie called *Hamlet* that would be produced instead during the same period. Although Medea assured him that this film would do his career far more good than *Buddy's Big Budget Adventure*, Buddy was unconvinced. He read the script, which was written in strange, complicated, old-fashioned language. It was difficult to follow and would be even harder to learn. From what he understood of it, it also seemed very sleazy and definitely "R" rated. It was about this dysfunctional Danish family who are rather lacking in traditional family values and are heavily into sex and violence. The character to be played by Buddy talks too much, never has any fun, and does not conform to the sexy, but cute and wholesome image Buddy wanted to project. Furthermore, in her letter Medea described *Hamlet* as an "art film," which apparently meant that its box office draw would be small. As a result, the letter regretted to inform him, his fee for starring in it would be only $5 million.

Despite his misgivings, Buddy decided that *Hamlet* was better than nothing, so he accepted the offer. Does he have any claim for damages against Medea? If so, how much?

3. Change the facts of Example 2 as follows: Buddy did not feel that playing Hamlet offered a suitable role, so he declined Medea's offer and insisted that she make the original movie as promised. Medea refused and their relationship broke down. Buddy put his agent to work seeking other movie opportunities. Despite a year's conscientious and persistent effort, the agent was unable to secure any film roles for Buddy. In the interim, Buddy had done no other work because he felt that he should hold himself available to perform whatever new film contract his agent should find. What damages, if any, should Buddy receive?

4. How would your answer to Example 3 change if two weeks after Medea's repudiation, Buddy entered into a contract with Dee Ziner, a designer of men's fashions, to model her new line of summer clothing? Buddy's performance under the modeling contract began immediately after execution of the contract and lasted one month. Buddy earned a fee of $1 million.

5. Because Buddy's agent could not find another film contract for him, his hopes for a movie career ended in failure. Buddy is convinced that had he made the comedy for Medea, he would have established himself as a star and enjoyed unlimited opportunities for further movies. He has now sued Medea for the $10 million payable under their contract, as well as $200 million in damages for the destruction of his movie career. Should he be awarded these damages?

6. Harpo C. Chord is a young and ambitious pianist. After struggling for many months to find work, he finally received an offer to play dinner music at Trés Trendi, a fancy restaurant. This was not quite what he had in mind as a career opportunity, but his financial reserves were much depleted and he was becoming desperate. He also realized that because the restaurant was in the theater district, many of its patrons were influential in the arts, so there was a good chance that someone important might notice his talent and offer him something better. He therefore accepted the offer and on January 15 he entered into a contract with Trés Trendi under which he would play the piano during dinner from 8 P.M. to midnight every night for a month. His performances would begin on February 1, and he would be paid "the going rate" for his services. Because neither party knew at the time of contracting what the current market rate was for a dinner pianist, Trés Trendi said that it would make inquiries and tell Harpo as soon as it found out.

   Having heard nothing from Trés Trendi for a week, Harpo called the manager to find out what rate of compensation had been established by the promised market survey. He was stunned when the manager told him that inquiries had shown that the market rate for a pianist was much higher than she had anticipated, so she had decided to scrap the idea of having live music in the restaurant. This is a clear breach of contract, and despite Harpo's fervent pleas, the manager refuses to relent.

   Having just gone through the agonizing process of looking for work, Harpo realizes that he has little chance of finding other employment for February. Besides, he wants to work for Trés Trendi so that he can showcase his talents to any useful diners that may be present. What recourse does he have?

7. Barney Sellers owned an acre of land in the suburbs. The land was once part of a farm that has long since been subdivided into smaller lots for housing. However, the original barn is still located on Barney's acre, which is otherwise vacant. When Barney retired last year, he decided to move from his home in the city to his suburban acre. He had plans drawn for a new house to be constructed on the eastern portion of his lot. The existing barn was on the western side of the lot,

so it did not interfere with his building plans, but it was quite an unsightly structure and would occupy space that Barney wished to use as a garden. The barn was in reasonably good condition and was easily removable, so he decided to sell it instead of demolishing it. He advertised it for sale and ultimately sold it to Penny Pincher for $5,000. In terms of the contract, Penny agreed to pay all the costs of removing the barn and also to break up its concrete foundation and remove the debris.

A few weeks later, Penny removed the barn. She was going to hire someone to break up and remove the concrete foundation, but when she discovered that the cheapest quote for the job was $7,000, she decided that it was a waste of money and refused to do it. The existence of the concrete slab will spoil Barney's landscaping plans and leave him with an eyesore in his backyard. However, because suburban land is scarce and of prime value, the presence of the slab would apparently not dissuade a typical buyer from purchasing the property at its full worth. As a result, the removal of the slab would not enhance the property's market value. What damages, if any, can Barney recover for Penny's breach?

8. To satisfy the demand for its required course on professional ethics, a law school offers a summer school ethics course every year. The course is usually in great demand and attracts about 50 students each summer. Last November, the law school contracted with Bill A. Billhours, a prominent local attorney, to teach the summer ethics course for a fee of $8,000. The contract obliged him to teach four evenings a week for eight weeks, beginning on June 1. On May 15, Bill was given the opportunity of advising a new client in connection with a huge international transaction. Participation in the proposed transaction promised to be both stimulating and lucrative, so Bill grabbed the chance of working on it. Unfortunately, the work required him to be out of the country for much of June and July, so it was no longer possible for him to teach. He called the dean of the law school on May 17 and told him that he could not teach summer school as planned.

8(a). Not wishing to disappoint the students who were relying on taking the course that summer, the dean immediately set to work finding a replacement. After making several unsuccessful calls, she was finally put in touch with Professor Wise, a world-famous expert on legal ethics and the author of several definitive books on the subject. Professor Wise had just retired, so he had no plans for the summer, but he was unwilling to teach for less than $10,000, plus his traveling and living expenses, which amount to a further $4,000. Desperate, the dean agreed to his terms. Can the law school recover all or any of the $14,000 from Bill?

8(b). Assume that the dean was unable to find anyone to teach the course because it is too late to find a teacher on such short notice. The dean cannot bear to let down all those students who are relying on taking the course during the summer. Is there anything she can do to force Bill into teaching?

8(c). Assume that the dean can neither find a substitute teacher nor compel Bill to teach. As a result, the summer ethics course has to be canceled. Based on enrollment before cancellation, the law school can show that it would have made $75,000 in tuition from the course. In addition, the law school was sued by one of the students who had enrolled in the course. The student had been relying on the course to complete his requirements for graduation in the summer so that he could graduate in August. He had a job beginning in August, but now he cannot begin work until after he graduates at the end of December. He therefore claimed three months' salary from the law school. To avoid adverse publicity and a negative impact on alumni relations, the law school paid the student's claim. What recourse, if any, does the school have against Bill?

9. Nat Atorium hired La Goon Pool Co. to build a swimming pool in his backyard. As the yard was small, the pool had to be placed not more than five feet from the rear wall of the house. La Goon brought its excavating equipment into the yard and one of its workers began to dig the hole. After spending some hours on the job and having excavated to a depth of about six feet, the operator started to become weary and careless. As a result, he dug too close to the house, undermining its foundation and causing the rear of the house to collapse. At the time, Nat was in one of the rear rooms and he could have been severely injured or killed had he not had the presence of mind to dive out of a door just as the room began to cave in. Although he escaped physical injury, he was badly traumatized by the close call and the destruction of half his house.

This experience has removed Nat's desire for a swimming pool. La Goon concedes that it is liable for the cost of repairing Nat's house, the fair market value of all personal property lost in the collapse, and the cost of filling in the hole and restoring the yard. However, Nat says this is not enough. He demands in addition:

(a) Compensation of $150,000 for the shock and distress that he suffered as a result of La Goon's incompetence.

(b) Compensation of $50,000 for the loss of irreplaceable family records and photographs that were among the personal property destroyed. Although they have no economic worth, they were of immense sentimental value to Nat.

(c) Punitive damages of $1 million.

Is Nat likely to succeed on any of these further claims?

10. Chic Canery has managed to train a troupe of chickens to perform amazing tricks. She has appeared on several TV shows with them and has attracted a lot of public attention. Asi-9 Productions, Inc., a show promoter, decided the market was ready for a live show featuring Chic and her chickens. It approached Chic with a proposal to produce such a show. Following negotiations, in January Chic and Asi-9 entered into a contract for the production of a show on July 4. The show was to be staged in a sports stadium with a capacity of 100,000 seats. Asi-9 would make all arrangements for the show and would be entitled to all proceeds from the event, save for a fee of $1 million to be paid to Chic. An advance of $100,000 on this fee would be paid to Chic on the signing of the contract, and the balance would be paid a week before the show.

Immediately after the contract was signed, Asi-9 paid the $100,000 to Chic and it began preparations for the show. It booked the stadium, hired a special staff to work exclusively on publicity and sales, and committed itself to the purchase of television advertising. On March 1, Chic changed her mind about doing the show and she repudiated the contract. After trying unsuccessfully to convince her to recant, Asi-9 had no choice but to accept the fact that Chic would not perform. As the theme and concept of the entire show were built on Chic's unique chicken act, it was too late to begin afresh by changing the theme and trying to find a new starring attraction. Asi-9 stopped all further work on the show and laid off its special staff. It exercised its cancellation right under the contract with the stadium and terminated its booking, forfeiting a $50,000 deposit. It had no right to cancel the television advertising slots. At the time of Chic's repudiation, Asi-9 had incurred the following expenses and commitments:

(a) Before making a final decision to enter the contract with Chic, it had spent $30,000 on a market analysis and profit projection for the show.

(b) It paid the $100,000 advance to Chic.

(c) It paid $25,000 in salary and severance pay to its special staff.

(d) It forfeited its $50,000 deposit on the stadium.

(e) It committed itself to pay $500,000 for television advertising.

According to the market analysis and projections made by Asi-9 before it entered the contract with Chic, it expected the show tickets to be sold out, generating income of $5 million. It expected further earnings of $3.5 million from the sale of T-shirts, souvenirs, and food. Its projected costs, including Chic's fee, were $5.5 million, so it expected a profit of $3 million. What damages is it likely to recover from Chic?

11. Benny Fishery Co. entered into a contract with Reliant Renovations, Inc. under which Reliant agreed to build an addition to Benny Fishery's processing plant. The contract required Reliant to excavate the site, build a foundation, and erect an aluminum structure on it. The total price for the project was $230,000. Reliant began work and encountered trouble immediately because the ground was much rockier than expected. As a result, it had to hire a subcontractor to blast the rock and had to use much heavier equipment than anticipated. This greatly increased its costs of excavation from an expected $50,000 to $100,000, and its total projected cost from $200,000 to $250,000. This meant that it now projected a loss of $20,000 on the contract. (Had Reliant conducted a proper inspection of the lot, it would have discovered this problem before bidding, so the underbidding is its own error in judgment. It acknowledges this and has not tried to use it as a basis for avoiding the contract for mistake or requesting a price modification.)

Soon after the excavation had been completed and before Reliant could proceed any further, Benny Fishery decided that it no longer needed the addition to its plant. It terminated the contract. As it had no right to do this, the termination was a total breach. The excavation work constitutes exactly one-quarter of Reliant's performance under the contract, and Benny Fishery has therefore offered to pay Reliant $57,500, which is exactly one-quarter of the contract price. Should Reliant accept this payment or demand more?

12. Gracie Spooner owns a busy hamburger joint. She recently decided to replace her grungy ketchup pumps with little plastic sachets of ketchup. To ensure a ready and stable supply of this vital ingredient in her cuisine, she entered into a one-year contract with Sauce Source, Inc., a wholesaler. Under the contract, Gracie committed herself to buy a minimum of ten boxes of sachets a month, at a price of $25 a box. The contract contained the following provision:

> The parties record that the pricing of the product sold under this contract is based on Buyer's commitment to take the minimum quantities specified above. Therefore if Buyer should breach this contract by failing to take the prescribed minimum quantity, Seller shall be entitled to damages based on the difference between the amount actually paid by Buyer for purchases of the product and the total minimum price payable for the full period of this contract. The parties expressly agree that this provision does not constitute a penalty, but is a genuine attempt to estimate damages and to avoid the uncertainty and difficulties of proof.

Gracie bought and paid for the minimum quantities required by the contract for seven months, but she found that she had grossly overestimated the amount of ketchup that she needed. Unopened boxes of sachets were beginning to pile up in her small storeroom, and it was clear to her that she already had enough ketchup to last her for more than a couple of years. She therefore declined to order or accept delivery of any more ketchup from Sauce Source. When the year-long contract period ended, Sauce Source sent an invoice to Gracie for $1,250, based on the price of the minimum quantity that she had failed to take during the last five months of the contract. Gracie protested to the manager of Sauce Source. She pointed out that ketchup had gone up in price since they made their contract, and she suggested that Sauce Source simply sell the remaining boxes at a better price to someone else. The manager told her that they had enough ketchup to keep all their customers supplied, with plenty over, so her breach actually reduced their volume of sales for the year. In any event, he reminded her that she did agree to this payment in the contract. Gracie feels that the invoice is ridiculous. Should she pay it?

Explanations

1. Had the town not breached the contract, Percy would have spent $150,000 and earned $250,000, leaving him with a profit of $100,000. This is his expectation interest. Had he incurred no costs, an award of $100,000 would fully compensate for the loss of this expectation, but as he has already made expenditures and commitments in reliance on the contract, these must be returned to him as well. Thus, his full expectation recovery is his reliance losses plus his expected profit.

    Had Percy stopped work immediately upon the town's breach, his outlay in reliance on the contract would have been $56,000. (The $50,000 spent on materials, the $4,000 paid in wages, and the $2,000 severance pay for which he was committed.) However, not all his reliance expenditure is wasted, because he can recover $20,000 as salvage for the unused materials; therefore this amount must not be included in his reliance loss, which is reduced to $36,000. This, added to his expected profit, leaves him with expectation damages of $136,000.

    We get the same answer if we use the formula of awarding him full contract recovery ($250,000) less costs saved as a result of the breach. By not completing the work, he saved $94,000 (total cost of $150,000 less costs already incurred, $56,000) and then recouped a further $20,000 of what he would have spent, making his total savings $114,000. This amount, deducted from $250,000, leaves $136,000.

Although $136,000 would have fully compensated Percy had he ceased work when told, it does not in fact give him his full expectation because he continued performing for an extra two weeks, incurring additional losses of $7,000 by using up more material and paying more wages to his assistants. He was not justified in obstinately persisting in his performance following the town's clear and unequivocal breach. In doing so, he unnecessarily increased his loss, and the mitigation principle precludes him from holding the town responsible for the resulting aggravation of his damages. In *Rockingham County v. Luten Bridge Co.*, 35 F.2d 301 (4th Cir. 1929), the county breached its contract for the construction of a bridge by terminating the project and telling the contractor to stop work. The contractor disregarded the instruction and continued to build the bridge. It was held entitled to recover its anticipated profit as well as those losses incurred up to the date of breach, but was denied any compensation for expenditures made after the breach.

2.   Buddy's acceptance of the offer to star in *Hamlet* could be seen as a modification of the contract. If it was, there is no issue of breach or damages — the parties have simply changed their terms. However, when one party seeks to substitute a performance different from that originally agreed, the circumstances are also consistent with breach and offer of mitigation. It is important to distinguish these situations by interpreting the words and conduct of the parties in context; otherwise a party accepting an offer of a mitigating substitute from the breacher could lose his claim for damages to compensate for the difference in value of the original and substitute performances.

In Buddy's case, the facts indicate that Medea breached and then offered a substitute in mitigation. This seems a more appropriate conclusion given Medea's attitude (she informed Buddy of her decision rather than seeking to negotiate a change) and Buddy's reluctant acquiescence. Since Medea terminated the contract before performance was due, this is an anticipatory repudiation. It is unequivocal, material, and total. (This issue is discussed in section 17.7.2.) Upon Medea's total breach, Buddy is entitled to sue for his lost profit under the contract, less any amount recovered in mitigation. (In an employment contract, lost profits are commonly equal to the full salary because employees usually do not have to incur costs to perform, but any earnings from substitute employment must be deducted from damages as mitigation.)

Hamlet is surely a substitute contract, because Buddy would not have been able to do both films, since the production dates are the same. (In fact, Medea's decision to produce the second was apparently based on her decision to cancel the first.) When, as a result of the breach, the plaintiff is released from his performance so that he can undertake other work that could not have been done in the absence of breach, any earnings from that other work must be treated as a gain from the breach and offset against damages. Therefore, his earnings from *Hamlet* ($5 million) must be deducted from his damages for the breach of the initial contract.

3.   Buddy has rejected the opportunity to reduce his damages by starring in *Hamlet* for $5 million. Because he could find no other substitute film contract, he has been idle for a year. It must therefore be decided if Buddy's refusal of Medea's offer and his failure to perform other work was a violation of his duty to mitigate, resulting in aggravated loss for which Medea should not be held accountable. If so, there must be an offset against his damages of the $5 million that he could have earned from *Hamlet*, or of whatever other amount he should have earned by other substitute work in the period that would have been occupied by filming *Buddy's Big Budget Adventure*.

Buddy may have failed to mitigate by **refusing the Hamlet role**. It may seem outrageous to expect the victim of a breach to accept mitigation by dealing with the very person who breached the contract and caused the loss. However courts generally take the attitude that mitigation opportunities offered by the breacher should be evaluated under the same standards as other available means to reduce damages: If this means of mitigation is not unduly risky, burdensome, or humiliating, it does not call on the victim to waive any right to relief under the breached contract, and it provides the most reasonable means of reducing the loss, the victim must pursue it, or risk losing the right to claim any damages that could have been prevented by taking it. Because the breacher has already shown herself to be untrustworthy, the victim may have justifiable concerns about whether she will prove similarly unreliable in the substitute contract. However, the victim needs to show more than a general apprehension that the breacher might again renege.

Parker v. Twentieth Century-Fox Film Corp., discussed in section 18.6.3b, held that an employee's duty of reasonable mitigation does not require her to accept work that is different and inferior to that provided for in the contract. Medea's offer of the role in *Hamlet* is clearly very different from that promised to Buddy under the contract, but is it inferior? Although *Hamlet* may be a finer piece of work than *Buddy's Big Budget Adventure*, the role of Hamlet could be inferior for Buddy's purposes. It does not have the same potential to showcase his talents, to reach his targeted audience, or to further his career goals. Note that inferiority is judged on the basis of the quality of the substitute work, and not by the mere fact that Buddy would be paid less for playing Hamlet. The difference in earnings can be compensated for by a damages award.

If Buddy's refusal of the role in Hamlet violated his duty to mitigate, he aggravated his damages by $5 million and his damages must be reduced accordingly. However, if he was justified in refusing the role, we still need to determine if he should have taken **other action to reduce his loss**. He did make considerable efforts to find another film role, but he may not have been reasonable in failing to seek modeling jobs. Although modeling is different from acting in a movie, this line of work is not necessarily inferior because it is a field in which he has achieved success and doing more modeling would likely not have a negative effect on his career goals. If Medea can show that Buddy could have found modeling work that would have curtailed his losses, his damages should be reduced by what he reasonably could have earned during the six-month period that became free as a result of the film's cancellation.

4. If Buddy should have accepted the Hamlet role, the answer does not change — the full $5 million that he should have earned, not just $1 million he actually earned, must be deducted from his damages. However, if his refusal of *Hamlet* was justified, the fee earned from the modeling job must be offset against the $10 million loss. The performance of Dee's modeling job took place during the period reserved for the filming, and Buddy could not have accepted it and earned the modeling fee had Medea not breached the movie contract. It is therefore a substitute transaction and the $1 million fee is a gain that would not have been made but for the breach. (If Buddy incurred any direct costs to perform for Dee, those would be subtracted before his earnings are offset. But in the typical employment contract it is the employee's time and labor that are being contracted for, and he does not usually have to spend much in rendering that performance. As a result, the employee's direct costs are likely to be small or even nonexistent.)

    Buddy can therefore claim damages for breach in the amount of $9 million — his full contract salary of $10 million less the $1 million earned in mitigation. This has the effect of overcompensating him because he receives his full contract fee even though he worked only for a month. However, Medea cannot complain because the benefit of not having to work so hard for his money does not reduce Buddy's financial loss. As in Example 2, the issue of whether the modeling job is different or inferior does not come up where Buddy accepted the substitute work. It is only relevant if he declines a substitute transaction.

5.   Buddy's claim for consequential damages is based on the theory that by losing his opportunity to star in *Buddy's Big Budget Adventure*, he was deprived of a successful movie career and lost $200 million. The mitigation issue would arise here again, because his failure to accept the Hamlet role may have precluded an opportunity to prevent this consequence. However, Buddy may argue that this consequential loss would have occurred whether or not he had accepted the Hamlet role, because *Hamlet* would not have advanced his career at all and may even have ruined it.

It is arguable that a movie producer should reasonably foresee that her failure to produce an actor's first film — especially if it is planned as an expensive blockbuster — could have an adverse impact on his career and deprive him of future opportunities. However, even if this is so, the overwhelming barrier to recovery is the highly speculative nature of the claim. It is unlikely that Buddy could prove with any degree of plausibility that the proposed movie would have been successful and would have advanced his career. There are just too many imponderables: Would he have performed well? Would good judgments have been made about publicity and promotion? Would the public have been attracted to the film and to him? Would it have made enough money to make him desirable to other producers? More uncertainties could be listed, but the point is made. Even if he could overcome this burden of showing a probability that opportunities would have been created, a further level of uncertainty would be encountered in trying to decide if he would have been lucky and clever enough to use them to advantage. In short, he cannot even prove what would have happened had the film been made, let alone establish a monetary value of the loss. The consequential damages claim must fail under the principles of certainty and causation.

The difficulty in establishing quantifiable loss when the breach results in a lost opportunity for publicity and its consequent career advancement is shown by another case springing from the entertainment industry: *Ericson v. Playgirl, Inc.*, 140 Cal. Rptr. 921 (Ct. App. 1977). *Playgirl* contracted with Ericson, one of its centerfold models and an aspiring actor, to rerun his pictures in its "*Best of Playgirl*" annual and to include him as one of the models on the annual's cover. When *Playgirl* failed to include Ericson on the cover, he sued it for consequential damages for breach of contract. He produced witnesses who testified generally on the benefits of publicity to an acting career and on the economic value of appearing on a magazine cover. The court found that *Playgirl* had breached the contract, but it awarded Ericson only nominal damages. The court accepted that as an abstract matter, exposure (forgive the double entendre) is valuable to an actor, but his evidence of loss was too generalized and non-specific. Any economically adverse consequences of the breach were pure conjecture.

6. Although Harpo's remuneration has not been settled, this should not affect the validity of the contract, because the parties have agreed on a market standard for determining it. A contract for a reasonable fee, to be based on an objectively ascertainable standard, is sufficiently definite for enforcement.[39] If Harpo has no reasonable opportunity to mitigate his loss by finding appropriate substitute employment, he will at a minimum be able to sue for what he would have earned under the contract (less direct costs saved, if any). To establish what this amount would have been, he would have to produce evidence of the market rate paid to a pianist of his experience for equivalent work in a restaurant of similar standing. Such evidence is apparently available. However, Harpo was expecting more than a mere month's employment. He was hoping to make contacts and to open opportunities by playing in the restaurant. Although unlike Mr. Ericson, whose case is discussed in Example 5, Harpo plans to keep his clothes on during performance, that example shows that it is difficult to establish measurable injury as a result of the loss of publicity. Therefore, an award of money damages would most likely cover only his direct damages and would fail to compensate him for speculative consequential damages.

When a plaintiff can show that a monetary award cannot adequately achieve his expectation, he establishes one of the essential grounds for the remedy of specific performance.[40] To get the order, Harpo must satisfy the court, in addition to showing the inadequacy of the damages remedy, that the court's burden of supervision is outweighed by the need for the remedy and that the balance of the equities favor granting the order. In addition, when there is some indefiniteness in the contract terms, even if the indefiniteness is not serious enough to invalidate the contract, the court may confine the plaintiff to damages unless the terms can be clearly established to support a precise and comprehensible order.

The indefiniteness in the fee to be paid to Harpo should not be a bar to relief because the court can establish the fee by reference to the market. There may also be some lack of detail with regard to Harpo's working conditions, which would have to be resolved, possibly also

---

39. This issue is discussed in section 10.10.1.
40. Of course, had Harpo breached, Trés Trendi would not have been able to obtain an order of specific performance to compel his personal services because of the strong policy against forcing an individual to work against his will. However, this policy is not implicated where the employee sues the employer for specific performance, and orders of reinstatement are common.

by reference to customary or reasonable standards. The primary focus of the definiteness principle in this context is to ensure that the order specifies Trés Trendi's duties precisely so that it knows what it must do to comply with the order to avoid contempt of court. By fixing the payment due to Harpo and detailing his working conditions, the court should be able to formulate a clear order. An order compelling Harpo's employment by a possibly begrudging employer does entail some burden of supervision to ensure that he is paid and that he is not mistreated or subjected to harassment. However, this supervisory task is not particularly onerous or exceptional. In a case like this the court is not likely to appoint an official to oversee the employment. It would be up to Harpo, if he alleges a breach of the order, to move for an order calling on Trés Trendi to show cause why it should not be held in contempt of court. The court would then conduct a hearing to determine if Trés Trendi violated the order and to impose a sanction if it did.

The equities of granting relief favor Harpo, not only because a damages award cannot adequately compensate him for his uncertain consequential damages, but also because Trés Trendi committed a willful breach and it suffers no undue hardship by allowing Harpo to play the piano in its restaurant for a fee that it would have to pay in any event as direct damages.

7. It is easy to identify the measure of damages required to place Barney in the position he would have been in had Penny not breached. It is the reasonable cost of demolishing the slab and removing the concrete debris, apparently $7,000. However, the facts show that although damages of $7,000 would give Barney the equivalent of performance in compliance with the contract, the breach did not actually cause him economic harm if his loss is instead measured by the diminution in the value of the property on which the work was to have been done. This raises the issue of whether the proper basis for recovery is the cost of giving him what was promised (which is $7,000) or the actual reduction in his wealth (which is zero). Stated differently, when the cost of giving the plaintiff his contractual expectation exceeds his actual ultimate financial loss, should his damages be confined to reimbursement of that ultimate loss?

As discussed in sections 17.3.3 and 18.6.6, Barney is normally entitled to the full measure of his expectation damages. However, if Penny's breach was not material or willful and the cost of giving Barney his contractual expectation would be an unfair forfeiture, the court may confine relief to Barney's ultimate economic loss, measured by the diminution in market value resulting from the breach. Penny's breach was deliberate, and that on its own is enough to preclude application of the unfair forfeiture doctrine. In addition, the breach was likely material. Materiality is a question of interpretation, to be decided by assessing the importance of the breach in light of the purpose of the contract, determined by its terms and context. Had Barney intended to resell the property, Penny's failure to remove the slab may have been immaterial because it had no impact on the market value of the property. (Even under these circumstances, this outcome is not assured because the parties did stipulate for the slab's removal as part of the consideration for the barn.) However, Barney plans to live on the property, and it therefore cannot be said that the removal of the slab was merely incidental to the sale.

8(a). When, following a total breach, the plaintiff obtains a reasonable substitute performance, expectation damages are the difference between what the plaintiff had to pay for the substitute and what it would have had to pay under the contract for the equivalent performance. When the substitute is not only more expensive in itself, but also involves the plaintiff in the extra expense of having to go outside the local market, the additional cost of transportation or (as in this case, travel and living expenses) is also included in determining the replacement cost. Therefore if Professor Wise is a reasonable substitute for Bill, the law school will be able to recover from Bill the $6,000 difference between what it paid to Wise, $14,000, and what it would have paid him, $8,000.

Although it is seldom likely that a substitute performance will exactly match that promised under the contract, both the compensation and the mitigation principle require that the replacement be as close as possible. If the plaintiff is awarded the added cost of a more valuable or better-quality replacement, it is overcompensated, and its damages must be reduced to reflect the lower cost of a nearer substitute. However, this principle is not rigidly applied so that the plaintiff is invariably precluded from receiving reimbursement of the full cost of a superior replacement. As the victim of breach, the plaintiff has the burden foisted on it of finding a substitute to effectively counter the ill effects of the breach, sometimes within a very short time. When the only reasonable option open to the plaintiff under all the circumstances is to select a better replacement, it may be appropriate to hold the defendant accountable for the full cost, even if this means that the plaintiff profits somewhat by a performance superior to that expected. This is particularly so when the better substitute gives the plaintiff no realizable economic advantage.

In this case, Bill breached about two weeks before classes were to begin, and the dean had little time to find a substitute. She did make immediate efforts and only hired Professor Wise when it was apparent that she would be unlikely to find anyone else. She has no duty of exhaustive inquiry, but need only make such good faith and reasonable efforts called for by the circumstances. Even if Professor Wise is more experienced, has greater prestige, and may possibly be a better teacher, he may be the most reasonable substitute.

8(b). A court will not decree specific performance of personal services. Quite apart from the obvious difficulty in supervising the performance of teaching duties, the compulsion of personal services is rather too much like involuntary servitude. Therefore, even though the plaintiff may have no adequate remedy at law, the considerations disfavoring specific enforcement outweigh the plaintiff's interest in performance.

If specific performance is not available, a court may be willing to grant the plaintiff a prohibitory injunction, restraining the defendant from entering into the transaction that motivated the breach. The concerns about involuntary servitude and difficulty of supervision are not present in such a negative order. Of course, preventing Bill from participating in the international transaction does not, in itself, achieve the school's expectation, but the idea is that by removing the motivation for the breach, the order will induce Bill to perform as promised. However, even when a prohibitory injunction is sought, courts are very wary about using their power of compulsion to prevent an individual from selling his labor and earning his livelihood as he sees fit. It is therefore in only the most compelling cases that a court will issue such an order.

Like specific performance, an injunction is an equitable remedy, subject to the same general prerequisites: The plaintiff must show that the legal remedy of damages is inadequate, and that the balance of equities favor the grant of the order. In this case, given the fact that no substitute is available, the possibility of substitutionary damages does not exist. This would lead to lost profits and consequential damages that (as Question 8(c) discusses) could be very speculative and difficult to prove. Furthermore, no monetary award can compensate for the immeasurable harm caused by the disruption of the law school's program, its inability to provide planned educational services, and the disappointment or even hostility of its students. Overall, a good argument can be made that the school has no adequate remedy at law. If this is so, the equities of trying to protect the law school's expectation weigh heavily in the balance. They are given further weight by the fact that Bill's breach is deliberate and motivated by ambition and financial reward. Nevertheless, Bill's primary professional pursuit is legal practice and the service of his clients' needs. It may simply be too harsh on Bill to restrain him. Also, there is a strong public interest in allowing people access to an attorney of their choice, so an injunction may improperly interfere with the attorney-client relationship. This would be particularly so if Bill has already agreed to represent the client. In short, without reaching a definitive conclusion, we can recognize that an injunction may be feasible, but there may not be enough here to overcome the court's disinclination to issue such an order.

8(c). Because the law school is unable, after reasonable effort, to replace Bill and avert the loss resulting from cancellation of the class, its net loss is claimable as direct damages. Of course, it cannot claim the full lost earnings of $75,000. First, it must establish that its forecast of tuition income is reasonably reliable and takes into account what likely proportion of enrolled students may exercise any available right to drop the course and be excused from paying tuition. Thereafter, it must deduct its savings from the breach and any recoupment of that loss. The most obvious saving is Bill's salary of $8,000. Although the facts do not indicate them, there may be some other variable (direct) costs that are saved, such as the cost of stationery supplies, which likely do not amount to much. Overhead expenses such as maintaining the buildings and paying support staff are likely not reduced at all by the breach and are not deducted as costs saved. In addition, there may be some recoupment of the lost earnings if some of the students decide to switch to another summer school class instead, or if the law school's fee structure is such that the students end up paying more tuition in the semester for having to take the ethics course then. Once all these savings and recoupments are calculated, the law school is entitled to claim its lost profit — expected earnings less savings and recoupment — from Bill.

The payment to the student who sued for lost salary is a consequential loss. When a breach of contract causes the plaintiff to breach a dependent contract with a third person, the plaintiff's liability to the third person could be recoverable provided that the requirements of causation, reasonable certainty, foreseeability, and mitigation are satisfied. Certainty could have been a problem had there been unresolved potential claims for lost employment opportunities, but as we are concerned with only one claim of a defined amount, the loss is quantifiable and defined. However, many questions are raised by the other prerequisites.

For the loss to be foreseeable, Bill must have known enough to reasonably realize that his breach could cause a loss of the kind claimed. It is a matter of some subtlety to determine how much information a reasonable party must have to make the consequential loss reasonably foreseeable. Modern courts do not favor the older "tacit agreement" test that required the defendant to have enough knowledge of the plaintiff's affairs so as to lead to the conclusion that he specifically contemplated the damages and must tacitly have assumed the risk to pay them if he breached. The contemporary test finds foreseeability if a reasonable person in the position of the defendant, under the circumstances of the transaction, should have foreseen the likelihood of damages of this kind if he breached the contract.

It is not clear if Bill specifically contemplated that a student who is deprived of taking a summer school class may fail to graduate as expected, lose salary, and hold the law school liable. However, as a member of the legal profession and a former law student, he could be taken to have reasonably understood that his breach could result in cancellation of the class, that most law students pursue legal studies for the purpose of securing gainful employment, that some may be using summer school to complete their degree requirements, and that ethics is a required course for graduation. This may be enough to create the reasonable foresight that his breach could lead to the damages that resulted.

Even if the loss is reasonably foreseeable, it is not clear from the facts that the law school would have been responsible for any losses suffered by students as a result of cancellation. If the law school, expressly or by common practice, reserved the right to cancel the course, the cancellation would not have been the breach of a contractual commitment to the enrolled students, and any payment would have been a purely voluntary act, for which Bill could not be held accountable. If the law school had made a firm contractual commitment to the students, Bill would either have needed to be told this, or it must have been so generally known to be the practice that he should have been aware of it.

Finally, even if the law school was liable for losses suffered by its students, it would still have to show that its action in paying the claim in full, instead of contesting it, was reasonable. Given the cost, uncertainty, and harm to goodwill that would have resulted from litigation, this may have been reasonable action provided that the student did in fact have a colorable claim. In short, an argument can be made for the recovery of this consequential loss, but the law school's success is dependent upon a number of uncertain questions.

9(a) & (b). *The claims for shock, distress, and sentimental loss.* The focus of contract damages is on economic loss, so the general rule is that no compensation is claimable for emotional distress or sentimental loss resulting from the breach. In some cases, losses of this nature could be excluded simply on the basis that they were not reasonably foreseeable. But even when there may have been some basis for contemplating them as a probable consequence of breach, the policy of confining contract damages to economic loss usually outweighs any sympathy for the plaintiff's suffering. There are, however, two situations in which courts have been willing to countenance a claim for emotional or sentimental damages:

The first occurs where the purpose of the contract is clearly and purely to enhance the plaintiff's emotional well-being. It may seem, at first thought, that the construction of a swimming pool in Nat's backyard, for his own personal use and enjoyment, is such a contract. However, courts constrict this exception more narrowly. As explained in section 18.13.1, the very basis and nature of the contract must be to provide sentimental or emotional benefit to the plaintiff. It is not enough, to remove the contract from the commercial realm, that the plaintiff's desire for the performance was motivated by personal pleasure rather than profit. The reason for this rather cold-hearted approach is probably quite obvious: If the exception were extended to cases like this, it could cover almost every consumer transaction in which it is clear that the primary motivation is the use of the property or services purchased to enhance quality or enjoyment of life.

The second situation in which a court may grant the plaintiff emotional distress damages is where the breach of contract is also a tort. This is not so much an exception to the rule barring emotional distress damages in contract, as a recognition that some breaches of contract may involve conduct that is also a violation of duty under the law of torts. The non-economic damages are therefore not really awarded for the breach of contract, but are independently compensable in tort. The damage to Nat's house was apparently caused by negligent operation of the earthmoving equipment. If this is so, the negligent performance is likely to constitute not only a breach of contract, but also a tort, allowing Nat to go forward with his claim for mental distress damages. (Whether he satisfies the requirements of tort law for award of these damages is beyond our scope.)

9(c). *Punitive damages.* The compensation principle also precludes punitive damages in most contract suits unless the breach is also a tort for which such damages are appropriate. Punitives are not generally available in tort law unless the injury was deliberate and malicious, or was at least the result of reckless and callous disregard for the plaintiff's rights. Therefore, even if LaGoon's employee did commit a tort by damaging Nat's house, this sounds more like a case of common negligence than the kind of conduct that warrants punitive relief.

10. If Asi-9's projections are credible, its expectation damages are its anticipated profit of $3 million plus the reliance expenses that it has already spent or committed for which it would have been reimbursed out of its earnings under the contract. (These expenses are discussed below.) It is not clear how convincing these projections may be. To recover lost profits, a plaintiff must be able to prove the fact and amount of those profits with reasonable certainty. Asi-9's projections may have been made by people with great expertise and experience and based on careful and thorough research. However, it is generally very difficult to establish prospective lost profits from a canceled entertainment event. Public taste can be unpredictable and often surprises even the most seasoned promoter. The prospect of profit is even less certain when the show centers on something as odd as a performing chicken act. Given the substantial projected costs of mounting the show, Asi-9 would have to do remarkably well in selling both its tickets and its associated knick-knacks. Its prediction that it could sell out a stadium of 100,000 seats shows laudable, but possibly misplaced, faith in the artistic sensibilities of the American public.

   If Asi-9 cannot prove lost profits, what other alternatives does it have? Restitutionary relief would be available to reclaim Chic's unjust enrichment, but that would cover only the $100,000 down payment. None of the other expenditure enriched her in any way. However, a plaintiff who cannot prove lost profit may nevertheless still recover as reliance damages the expense component of its expectation claim. A claim of reliance damages would permit the recovery of not only the $100,000 down payment, which qualifies as essential reliance, but also some of the other losses incurred in reliance on the contract. Provided that they were reasonably necessary to Asi-9's performance under the contract and were not profligate, the forfeited stadium deposit and the staff salaries are recoverable in reliance. (They are probably best classified as essential reliance, in that they were expended in furtherance of Asi-9's contractual obligation to arrange and promote the show.)

   The debt for television advertising would also fall into this category, but only to the extent that the expenditure is wasted and not salvageable. Although the advertising slots cannot be canceled, they may be assignable or diverted to use for other purposes. Therefore, to the extent that Asi-9 can recoup its expenditure by selling the slots or using them for another show, it is not claimable as a reliance loss.

   The cost of the market survey and profit projection were incurred before the contract was entered into, so even though these expenses were a waste in the end, they cannot, by definition, be treated as having been incurred in reliance on the contract. This seems to be the general approach to precontractual expenses, notwithstanding that the breach cut off any prospect of earning income that may have reimbursed them.[41]

As noted above, Asi-9 would claim reliance only if it could not prove its larger claim of lost profit. The plaintiff does not have to prove that the contract would have made a profit to recover reliance damages. However, when the purpose of the contract was profit, and the defendant is able to prove that the plaintiff would have made a loss in the event of complete performance, the court will reduce the reliance recovery pro rata to take account of this expectation of loss. In a case like this one, where profit is highly speculative, the risk of uncertainty therefore falls on the defendant. Chic probably has about as much chance of proving loss as Asi-9 has of proving profit, so she probably cannot satisfy her burden, and Asi-9's recovery is not likely to be subject to reduction.

There have been several cases in which a plaintiff who could not prove lost profits was held entitled to recover reliance expenses incurred pursuant to a contract to stage an entertainment event. For example, in *Chicago Coliseum Club v. Dempsey*, 265 Ill. App. 542 (1932) Jack Dempsey, the world-champion heavyweight boxer, repudiated a contract with the club to participate in a boxing match. The club was not able to prove its lost profit, but the court recognized its right to claim reliance damages for its post-contractual expenses reasonably and necessarily incurred in the course of organizing the match. (The club had also incurred expenses prior to the execution of the contract, but the court did not allow the recovery of these expenses, which predated and therefore could not have been incurred in reliance on the contract.) *Wartzman v. Hightower Productions, Ltd.*, 456 A.2d 82 (Md. 1983) involves an entertainment event almost as culturally significant as Chic's. A group of bright entrepreneurs embarked on an elaborate venture designed to make money out of breaking the world flag-pole-sitting record. They planned to lodge an entertainer in a specially-constructed perch atop a hydraulic lift mounted on a flatbed trailer, and to exhibit him around the country for about nine months, culminating in his descent from the perch in Times Square on New

---

41. There have been some situations in which courts have been willing to include precontractual expenses in reliance recovery. For example, if the defendant knew that the plaintiff was incurring the expenses in anticipation of the contract and had strongly indicated an intention to enter the contract, promissory estoppel relief may be available for the precontractual expenses. Also, the expenses take on the character of lost opportunity reliance if the plaintiff could have recouped them by entering a similar contract with a third party but gave up that chance by entering the contract with the defendant.

Year's Eve. They needed capital for this, so they contracted with an attorney to form a corporation that could solicit investments. The attorney was incompetent and failed to create an entity in compliance with securities law. This was only discovered after the promoters had incurred expenses in setting up the project. They could not proceed further without engaging in a complex and expensive procedure to remedy the violation of the securities law. The promoters could not afford the expense or the delay of the cure and the venture collapsed. The corporation was unable to prove that it would have made a profit from the venture, but the court awarded it reliance damages to compensate for the wasted expenditures incurred in reliance on the attorney's contractual commitment to incorporate the enterprise properly.

11. Had Reliant's cost been as it had estimated, it would have had a reasonable expectation of profit. Benny Fishery's material breach would have entitled it to full expectation damages, calculated by adding its reliance expenditure, which would have been $50,000, to its anticipated profit of $30,000. However, Reliant's miscalculation of its cost has defeated its expectation of profit and its claim for expectation damages. Its only reasonable expectation from full performance is a loss of $20,000. As a result, its claim is confined to reliance or restitutionary damages. Its reliance damages are its cost of $100,000, but they may be even less than this if the defendant can make a case for prorating them, as discussed below. Restitution is measured by the market value of the work performed (quantum meruit). Unless Reliant performed inefficiently, incurring costs in excess of what would be normal on the market, the value of its performance is likely to be higher than its cost, because it would include a reasonable profit. For the sake of illustration, if the costs are indeed efficient and the industry norm is to have a 10 percent profit margin on excavation work, the market value of the performance is $110,000. This being so, Reliant would elect to sue for the higher restitutionary relief. However, the question of whether restitution turns out to be the more advantageous measure of relief depends on whether the court allows unrestricted restitutionary recovery or imposes a limit on it based on the contract value of the performance.

When the defendant can prove that the plaintiff's reasonable expectation under the contract was to lose money, the plaintiff's reliance recovery may be reduced proportionately to adjust it for that expectation of loss. Note that the burden of proving the losing expectation is placed on the breaching defendant, and the plaintiff's reliance recovery is unaffected if the defendant cannot sustain the burden. It would unfairly undercompensate the plaintiff to deduct the full amount of the expected loss from a reliance recovery that constitutes only a portion of its performance. The deduction must therefore be pro rated so that it is no more than a share of the loss proportionate to the performance rendered. The most rational way of allocating the loss to completed performance is to determine its proportion of the total contractual performance based on the relationship of the cost incurred to the total cost of performance. In the present case, Reliant had incurred costs of $100,000 out of a total anticipated cost of $250,000—that is, two-fifths of the total. Therefore (provided that Benny Fishery can prove this anticipated loss), the $100,000 reliance expenses must be reduced by two-fifths of the total expected loss of $20,000, that is $8,000, leaving a recovery of $92,000.

The possibility of prorating makes reliance damages an even less attractive alternative to restitution if no equivalent principle applies to restitutionary recovery. Some courts feel that it should not, based on the theory that if the plaintiff elects to disaffirm the contract and sue for unjust enrichment, it should not be limited to the value placed on the performance in the contract. In the present case, it would mean that by choosing restitution, Reliant could recover the full market value of its work, which we have assumed to be around $110,000. A much more advantageous choice than reliance, which would, at best, yield $100,000 and, at worst, $92,000.

Some courts, uncomfortable with the anomaly of achieving different results in reliance and restitution for exactly the same breach, do treat the contract value of the performance as a limit on restitution. In the present case, as two-fifths in value of the work was done, a court following this rule would confine Reliant to two-fifths of the contract price of $230,000. This works out to a recovery of $92,000.

12. We will first deal with the question of whether Sauce Source should be awarded agreed damages, and will then consider what relief it should receive if the agreed damages provision is held invalid.

Should Sauce Source be awarded **agreed damages?** Sauce Source is attempting to enforce what purports to be an agreed damages provision.[42] We should note briefly, as an initial matter, that the term sounds rather like boilerplate, so it may be a standard term

---

42. When a party promises to take a specified quantity of goods or to pay for that quantity even if it is not taken, the term is sometimes characterized not as an attempt to liquidate damages, but as a "take or pay" provision. As such, it is seen as a promise of the alternative performances of either taking the goods or paying for them. If so interpreted, the provision is not subject to regulation as agreed damages and is upheld even if it does not satisfy the prerequisites for a valid agreed damages provision. "Take or pay" clauses are typically found in long-term supply contracts where the supplier incurs the bulk of its costs at the outset. The buyer's commitment to pay for a minimum quantity is justified because it is needed to enable the supplier to recoup that cost. Such facts are not present in our case, and we need not concern ourselves with this ethereal distinction. The clause is both described in the contract as, and functions as, a liquidation of damages.

printed on all Sauce Source's supply agreements. There is nothing wrong, per se, with a standard-form liquidated damages clause, but the fact that it is standardized may raise two issues for inquiry. First, it may create the suspicion that the apparent agreement to pay liquidated damages was not freely bargained. Second, the very fact of standardization may cast some doubt on whether the term could be a genuine estimate of the likely harm that would result from a breach of any particular transaction.

Although the first point is more fully discussed in section 13.12, and it is not given any detailed attention here, it is worth noting that if assent to the term was tainted by adhesion, unfair imposition, or other bargaining impropriety, that may furnish a separate and distinct basis for challenging it. However, the facts here do not suggest any claim of improper bargaining.

Even if there is no issue arising out of the legitimacy of the means by which assent was obtained, the compensation principle requires study of an agreed damages provision to ensure that it is a genuine attempt to liquidate damages and not an unenforceable penalty. Because this is a sale of goods, the validity of the provision is tested under UCC §2.718(1), which employs a two-point test, later adopted for the common law by Restatement Second §356. The agreed damages are examined in light of both the anticipated harm at the time of contracting, and the actual loss following breach. (Both §§2.718 and 356 speak of "anticipated or actual" loss, which makes it sound as if one looks at either one or the other. However, both are relevant, as discussed below.)

The first point of the test requires that the liquidation of damages must be a genuine attempt to reasonably estimate loss at the time of contracting. The more difficult the prospect of proving loss appeared at that time,[43] the greater leeway the parties should be given in coming up with a figure. However, if the basis of determining loss would reasonably have seemed relatively straightforward at the time of contracting, the parties are held to a higher standard in calculating a figure that approximates expected loss. Because the court must give substantial deference to the expressed will of the parties, it should be loath to avoid the clause if it was a genuine attempt to estimate damages in advance and to save the uncertainty and burden of establishing actual loss. Therefore, the first point of the test, focusing on the time of contracting, should be given greater weight.

In addition to evaluating the clause in the context existing at the time of contracting, the court must also take into account the

---

43. As noted in footnote 34, the 2003 revision of §2.718 eliminates the test of difficulty of proof of loss where the contract is not a consumer contract.

relationship between the agreed damages and the actual loss that was caused by the breach. When actual loss is apparent following breach, this second point of the test serves as a safety valve to prevent unfair overcompensation. If the plaintiff's true loss is disproportionately lower than the agreed damages, the policy of providing no more than compensation may call for a reduction of the defendant's liability to a more realistic level.

In the present contract, we are given no facts about how the agreed damages were calculated. In fact, as noted earlier, it may be that the clause does not in any way represent any attempt to estimate loss in this particular transaction, but may be no more than a piece of boilerplate inserted routinely into all Sauce Source's supply contracts. Although it is conceivable that a standardized estimate of loss may be valid for multiple transactions of the same kind, it is more likely that the use of a standard clause strongly suggests an absence of meaningful estimation.

In any event, even if it was not a standard form, the basis of determining damages under the clause cannot be justified as being a realistic prognostication of harm. In most sales of goods, the seller's damages are relatively easy to predict and calculate. If the goods are resold after breach, the difference between the contract and resale price is quite easily ascertainable. If they are not resold or the resale is unreasonable, the contract-market difference can be established. If there is no substitute sale (for example, because the seller loses volume of sales), the seller's lost profit can be proved without too much difficulty. Finally, if the goods are perishable and they cannot be resold, the seller is able to sue the buyer for their price. Although there could be uncertainties and disagreement on a number of issues, such as the reasonableness of resale, the market price, or the issue of lost volume, these difficulties are not comparable to, say, the problems of proving lost profits for a speculative venture. There is enough predictability to require the plaintiff to show a sensible basis for coming up with an estimate that bears some relationship to reality. Instead, Sauce Source has used a formula that assures it of full recovery of the sale price, no matter how much it actually delivers to Gracie. If there ever was a term designed as a disincentive to breach — that is, a penalty — this is it.

Furthermore, the amount of damages is quite random in its relationship to loss and ensures that Sauce Source is always overcompensated. To demonstrate, consider the following calculations based upon arbitrarily selected, but generous, actual damage figures: Gracie breached after taking her minimum requirements for seven months, so she is liable for agreed damages of $5 \times \$250 = \$1,250$, representing her failure to take 50 boxes of sachets.

If the ketchup can be readily resold at full price, the damages may over-compensate Sauce Source by a full $1,250 (less any incidental damages). But even if it resells at a huge loss, say at $5 a box, its actual damages would still be considerably less than what was agreed: They would be $1,000, the difference between the contract price of the 50 boxes ($1,250) and their resale price of $250.

Even if we assume that it makes no substitute transaction because it has more ketchup than it can sell, so it loses volume of sales, the agreed damages must still exceed its lost profit, no matter how big its profit margin may be. To illustrate, let's say that its total cost of selling each box is only $2, so that makes a generous profit of $23 per box. Its lost profit is still only $50 \times 23 = \$1,150 - \$100$ below the agreed damages.

In fact, there seem to be only two situations in which it could have anticipated a loss equal to the damages provided. Both are highly unlikely. First, if its costs are zero and it has suffered loss of volume, its lost profit would be equal to the agreed damages. Second, if it could not resell at all and the ketchup would spoil and have to be discarded, it would lose the entire contract price. Although this could occur where perishables are sold, the life expectancy of ketchup in sealed packages exceeds that of the average human.

This set of calculations is based on Gracie's breach in the seventh month of the contract. If you care to do some further arithmetic, you will see that the earlier the breach, the greater the discrepancy between the damages fixed and the reasonably likely harm. However, at no point, not even in the last month, does this disproportion entirely disappear. Having decided that the agreement on damages was not a reasonable forecast of harm, it is not necessary to proceed to the second stage by examining the discrepancy between actual and anticipated harm.

A somewhat similar analysis was undertaken by the court in *Lake River Corp. v. Carborundum Co.*, 769 F.2d 1284 (7th Cir. 1985), to demonstrate the penal nature of agreed damages in a more complex, but roughly analogous, case. Carborundum, a manufacturer of ferro-carbo (an abrasive powder used in steelmaking) entered into a contract with Lake River under which Lake River would provide distribution services to Carborundum by bagging the ferro-carbo and shipping it to Carborundum's customers. Lake River had to install a new bagging system to perform this work, so it insisted that the contract contain a specified minimum tonnage, and a three-year term. The contract provided that Carborundum would ship to Lake River, and even if not, would pay for a specified minimum tonnage. A downturn in steel production led to a reduced demand for ferro-carbo, and by the end of the contract term, Carborundum had shipped just over half of the minimum quantity to Lake River. Lake River sued for damages under the agreement, equal to about half the total amount that would have been due had the full minimum performance taken place.

The court (while expressing reservations over the wisdom of interfering with contract provisions fairly negotiated by sophisticated commercial entities, but considering itself bound by precedent on the issue) invalidated the clause as a penalty. This contract involved the rendering of a service, not a sale of goods, so common law applied. As it was a service contract, Lake River's damages would normally be its lost profit. Therefore, because the formulation of agreed damages did not take into account any costs saved by the breach, it would inevitably exceed Lake River's lost profit and its actual loss. The earlier in the period that the breach occurred, the greater the cost savings would be, and the higher the disproportion between realistic and agreed damages.

If **agreed damages** are **invalid** what are Sauce Source's **actual damages**? When an agreed damages provision is invalidated, the plaintiff does not lose all remedy. It may still recover whatever actual damages it suffered. If Gracie is correct in saying that the market value of ketchup rose since the contract was entered into, Sauce Source would not be able to claim contract-market damages. Further, if it did enter a substitute transaction by reselling in a commercially reasonable way, it probably sold at the higher price and cannot claim damages based on resale. It does make the argument, however, that even if it did make a subsequent sale, this was not a substitute because it has enough ketchup in stock to satisfy all demand. As discussed in section 18.6.3d, if Sauce Source can show that the breach caused a reduction in its volume of sales and that it had unused capacity to supply all of the demand for ketchup, it should be able to claim its lost profit under §2.708(2). Despite the language in §2.708(2) that "due credit" must be given for "proceeds of resale", most courts accept that this does not apply in a lost volume situation. (Revised §2.708(2) codifies this approach by eliminating the language from the section.)

19

Assignment, Delegation, and Third-Party Beneficiaries

---

§19.1 INTRODUCTION

During the entire course of this book, it has been emphasized that contract is a consensual relationship created by agreement between the parties. In dealing with the enforcement of contracts, it has been taken for granted that contractual rights and duties arise only between the parties and that the power of enforcement resides in each against the other. In the great majority of contracts, this assumption is accurate. A person who is not a party to a contract cannot be bound by it and acquires no rights under it. However, this chapter deals with two situations in which this rule is qualified. Although these situations have in common the fact that a non-party to the contract obtains the right to enforce a promise under it, they are otherwise quite distinct and are based on very different premises:

1. A contract may create rights in a third party when the parties to the contract expressly or impliedly agree, at the time of making it, that the performance of one of them will be rendered to or for the benefit of a person who is not a party to the contract, and that the non-party will have the right to enforce that commitment. The creation of the third-party rights is contemplated by the parties and occurs at the time of contract formation.
2. The assignment of contractual rights and the delegation of contractual duties does not involve any conferral of rights on a non-party at the time of contracting. Rather, it is the transfer of rights or

obligations by one of the parties at some time after the contract has been executed. Each party's right to performance under the contract is an asset belonging to that party. As a property interest, it is generally capable (with exceptions to be noted later) of being transferred (assigned) by sale, donation, or other means of disposition. When a party assigns rights under a contract (thereby becoming the assignor), ownership of those rights passes to the recipient (assignee) who is substituted for the assignor as the person entitled to performance. Instead of, or in addition to, assigning rights under a contract, a party may wish to transfer (delegate) all or some of her obligations under the contract. Unlike assignment, delegation is not based on any concept of ownership — one cannot own a duty. Nevertheless, it is also generally permissible provided that it does not impair the reasonable expectations of the party to whom the performance is due.

§19.2 THIRD-PARTY BENEFICIARIES

§19.2.1 The Distinction Between Intended and Incidental Beneficiaries

Contracts routinely benefit people who are not parties. For example, neighbors are benefitted by the aesthetic enjoyment of a well-groomed yard, resulting from a landscape maintenance contract between a homeowner and a gardener; nearby hotels are benefitted by a contract between a property owner and builder to erect a new convention center. In fact, in a complex interactive economy, vast numbers of contracts between strangers allow people to enjoy facilities and services that would otherwise not be available. However, even though these bystanders may derive some advantage from the contract, and even have an important stake in its performance, they have no legal rights under the contract. Therefore, if the landscaper or builder breaches the contract by failing to perform, the adjacent property owners have no cause of action to enforce it. They are known as **incidental beneficiaries** — the benefit they anticipated was purely a fortuitous and incidental result of a transaction between others. The contracting parties may have been pleased, indifferent, or resentful to see someone else derive benefits from their contract, but they did not make the contract for the purpose of conferring those benefits.

However, in contrast to these more commonplace situations in which the positive effects of the contract on a third party occur merely by happenstance, a contract may be entered for the *deliberate purpose of bestowing a benefit* — and more importantly, *a power to enforce that benefit* — on a third party. That is, a contract is properly described as for the benefit of a third party only if it manifests the intent to give a benefit to a third party, directly enforceable by that third party against the contracting party who undertakes to perform it. It is the creation of this directly enforceable right that is the hallmark of a contract for the benefit of a third party. For example, Debbie Tor owes $20,000 to Len Der. Debbie enters into a contract with Wendy Vendee under which Debbie sells a plot of land to Wendy for $20,000, and the contract stipulates that Wendy will pay the $20,000 to Len. Debbie's purpose, of course, is to have the proceeds of the property transmitted directly to Len to settle the debt. In this case, the payment to Len does not occur as a fortuitous result of the contract but is specifically called for by it. Len's benefit is not merely incidental, but is clearly contemplated and deliberately conferred. If it is expressed or can be reasonably inferred that the parties, in contracting for the performance to be rendered to Len, also intended to give Len the right to enforce Wendy's promise of performance directly and independently of Debbie, Len acquires the status of **intended beneficiary**.

When a contract is intended to confer a benefit on and create enforcement rights in a third-party beneficiary, the contracting party who is to render the performance to the beneficiary (in the example above, Wendy) is usually referred to as the **promisor**, and the contracting party whose right to performance has been conferred on the beneficiary (in the above example, Debbie) is usually called the **promisee**. This nomenclature could be confusing because in a bilateral contract the terms "promisor" and "promisee" are relative — each party is both a promisor with regard to his own performance and a promisee with regard to the performance promised by the other. However, as we look at the contracting parties from the perspective of the third-party beneficiary, "promisor" means the party who has committed to perform in favor of the beneficiary. The following diagram illustrates the basic relationship and the terminology:

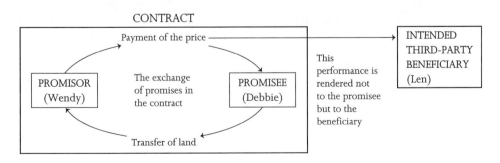

MJR
Diff

**

Normally, if the parties intend to confer the status of intended beneficiary on someone, that person is likely to be specifically named or identified in the contract. If this is not so, the strong inference is that the benefit is merely incidental. However, this conclusion is not inevitable. Intent to benefit is a matter of interpretation. Provided that the beneficiary will be *identifiable* when the *time for performance falls due*, it could be apparent that the parties did intend to create rights in his favor, despite the lack of specific identification at the time of contracting.

§19.2.2 The Essence of Intended Beneficiary Status: The Right of Independent Enforcement

As indicated above, when a contract confers the status of intended beneficiary on a third party, this does not mean only that performance must be rendered to or for the third party's benefit. It also means, as Restatement Second §304 provides, that the contract manifests the intent to grant the beneficiary an independent cause of action to enforce the promise. The grant of this enforcement right in the beneficiary is the central point of the third-party beneficiary doctrine and the distinguishing feature of a contract for the benefit of a third party. The beneficiary's direct cause of action against the promisor can be of great importance in making the benefit meaningful. He can pursue the right to performance on his own and does not have to depend on the promisee to take action on his behalf.

In the above example, if Len had no independent right of enforcement, he would not be able to sue Wendy, the promisor, if she failed to perform in his favor as promised. Debbie, the promisee, would be the only person who could sue Wendy for the payment, and Len's only claim would be against Debbie, his debtor under the loan contract. However, as an intended beneficiary, Len can sue Wendy directly if she fails to pay. He has this right of direct enforcement in addition to his right to sue Debbie under the loan contract, so he has two people against whom he can seek recourse for the unpaid loan. (Of course, he can only obtain a single satisfaction of his claim, so one of them is released from liability to him to the extent that the other pays). This may be represented as follows:

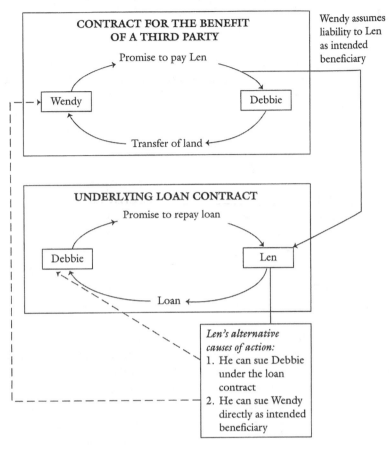

CONTRACT FOR THE BENEFIT OF A THIRD PARTY

Promise to pay Len

Wendy → Debbie

Transfer of land

Wendy assumes liability to Len as intended beneficiary

UNDERLYING LOAN CONTRACT

Promise to repay loan

Debbie · Len

Loan

Len's alternative causes of action:
1. He can sue Debbie under the loan contract
2. He can sue Wendy directly as intended beneficiary

English common law did not recognize such a direct cause of action in the beneficiary unless the beneficiary could establish either that the promisee was acting as his agent, or that the contract created a trust. However, in the mid-nineteenth century, the concept of direct enforcement by the beneficiary developed in American law. *Lawrence v. Fox*, 220 N.Y. 268 (1859), is recognized as the groundbreaking case. A man named Holly lent $300 to Fox. Holly was indebted to Lawrence for the same amount, and so Holly and Fox agreed that Fox would repay the loan amount to Lawrence. When he failed to pay, Lawrence sued Fox, who defended the suit on the basis that Lawrence had no standing to sue because he was not a party to the contract—there was no privity between them. The court rejected this defense and articulated the principle that even where no agency or trust is established, the parties to a contract do have the power to create rights enforceable by a person who is not a party to a contract, and that person can sue the promisor to enforce the performance undertaken to the promisee for his benefit.

§19.2.3 The Intent to Confer an Independent Right of Enforcement

The recognition of enforcement rights in a non-party may seem like a radical departure from the general concept of contract as a private consensual arrangement that creates rights only between those who have bound themselves to each other. However, the third-party beneficiary doctrine is consistent with that concept because the third party only acquires the right to enforce the benefit if it is apparent that the parties intended to give him that right — they have elected to create the beneficiary status as part of their agreement. As stressed already, it is not enough that the contract calls for performance to be rendered to the third party. It must also manifest the intention to give the third party the right to enforce the performance if it is not rendered. This is reflected in Restatement Second §302(1), which recognizes a "right to performance" (which means the right to enforce the performance) in the beneficiary only when it is *appropriate to effectuate the intention of the parties.*

Like all other contract terms, the intent to establish third-party enforcement rights is a matter of interpretation. If the contract expressly articulates the intent to confer or not to confer enforcement rights on a third party, the resolution of this question is relatively easy. *Sovereign Bank v. BJ's Wholesale Club, Inc.,* 395 F. Supp. 2d 183 (M.D. Pa. 2005) illustrates a situation in which a contract expressly precluded the enforcement of rights by a third party. Sovereign, a bank that issued credit cards, suffered losses when BJ's computer system was hacked into and its customers' credit card information was stolen. The theft of the information would not have been possible had BJ's complied with its contract for the processing of credit card payments with another bank, Fifth Third Bank, under which BJ's undertook not to store cardholder information in its system beyond the few minutes needed to process it. Sovereign sued BJ's on the theory that Sovereign was a third party beneficiary of BJ's contract with Fifth Third, but the court dismissed the claim because the contract specifically stated that it was not intended to be for the benefit of any third party and could be enforced only by the parties.

Where, as happens often, the contract does not clearly articulate the parties' intent, it must be gleaned by the normal process of interpreting the factual evidence of intent, and if that is inconclusive, by construing what the parties must reasonably have intended. As usual, an objective test is used. Because we are concerned with the rights of a third party, the objective test focuses on the parties' manifested intent, viewed from the perspective of a reasonable person in the position of the third party. Again, as usual, it is the mutual intent of the parties that is relevant, not the uncommunicated subjective intent of just one of them. It is not enough that the promisee intends to confer the benefit on the beneficiary. The promisor must reasonably have understood that she was agreeing to assume an obligation to the beneficiary. A second contract in *Sovereign Bank* illustrates this process of interpretation. In addition to its unsuccessful claim against BJ's based on BJ's contract with Fifth Third, Sovereign also sued Fifth Third, claiming to be an intended beneficiary of a contract between Fifth Third and Visa. Under that contract, Fifth Third undertook to Visa that it would ensure that its merchants would comply with Visa's operating regulations. These regulations forbad a merchant from retaining customers' credit card information. The contract between Fifth Third and Visa had no express language either precluding or recognizing enforcement rights by third parties. The court found that Sovereign was a third party beneficiary of the contract because the purpose of the contract provision was to benefit banks that issued credit cards by guaranteeing to them that the Visa network would function properly and could be participated in safely.

By contrast, the court found no intent to confer enforcement rights on a beneficiary in *Alaniz v. Schal Associates*, 529 N.E.2d 832 (Ill. 1988). A construction company had entered into a subcontract for roofing. In the contract, the construction company assumed the duty to maintain scaffolding in a safe condition. A worker employed by the roofing subcontractor was injured when scaffolding collapsed and he sued the construction company on the theory that he was an intended third party beneficiary of its contract with his employer. The court held that he was not. In addition to the provision relating to the scaffolding, the contract also provided that the roofing company would indemnify the construction company for any injury resulting from the use of the scaffolding. This showed that the purpose of the provision was simply to allocate responsibility for the scaffolding, and was purely for the benefit of the contracting parties. It was not intended to confer any rights on a non-party.

§19.2.4 The Relevance of the Relationship Between the Promisee and the Beneficiary: Creditor and Donee Beneficiaries

As just mentioned, Restatement Second §302(1) sets forth a broad standard to guide the determination of whether a non-party to the contract should be treated as an intended beneficiary: The recognition of the beneficiary's right to enforce performance must be appropriate to give effect to the parties' intent. The intent to confer the benefit is the central criterion and the focus of the inquiry. This is possibly all that needed to be said. However, motivated by a long tradition that it neither wishes to follow nor to abandon, §302(1) goes on to suggest what appears to be a second requirement: There must in addition be some *relationship* between the *promisee and the* beneficiary from which it can be inferred that the parties had the beneficiary's interests in mind when entering the contract. Although this seems to be set out as a prerequisite in addition to intent, it is really just a subset of the general inquiry into what the parties intended. If a relationship between the promisee and beneficiary can be identified to explain the motivation for conferring the benefit, the conclusion of intent to benefit is reinforced.

This bipartite inquiry originates from the established conception, reflected in the first Restatement, that a beneficiary can be regarded as intended, rather than incidental, only if one of two conditions is satisfied. Either the beneficiary must be a creditor of the promisee, or it must be clear that the promisee intended to make a gift of the benefit to the beneficiary. The situation involving a **creditor beneficiary** has already been illustrated by both *Lawrence v. Fox* and our example involving Debbie, who made a contract with Wendy under which Wendy would render performance to Debbie's creditor, Len. This set of relationships may be represented as follows:

[handwritten margin note: Test for finding an intended 3rd party]
[handwritten circled: 1]
[handwritten circled: 2]

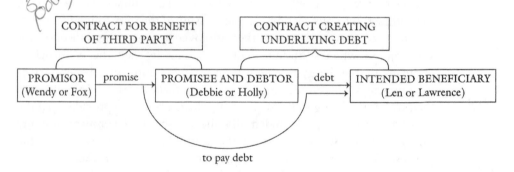

to pay debt

By contrast, if the promisee owes no debt to the third party, but intends to make a gift of the performance, the third party is a **donee beneficiary**. Although *Lawrence v. Fox* expressly dealt only with a creditor beneficiary, its basic principle was broad enough to be extended to cases in which the promisee was not indebted to the beneficiary. As a result, later cases recognized that a person could qualify as an intended beneficiary when the purpose of conferring the benefit was not to pay any debt, but to give her a gift. *Seaver v. Ransom*, 120 N.E. 639 (N.Y. 1918), is the most famous of these cases. A dying woman intended to bequeath a house to her niece. Upon being presented with a will that omitted this bequest, she agreed to sign on the strength of a promise by her husband, the residual legatee, that he would cure the omission by making provision in his own will for a bequest to the niece of equivalent value. When the husband eventually died, it was discovered that he had not made the bequest as he had promised his late wife. The niece sued his estate. The trial court gave judgment in favor of the niece on the theory that her uncle had held the house from his wife in constructive trust. Although it affirmed the judgment in favor of the niece, the court of appeals rejected the trust theory. Instead, basing its decision on *Lawrence* and subsequent cases, it found that there was no reason in principle to confine the third-party beneficiary doctrine to cases involving creditor beneficiaries. The uncle and aunt had made a contract under which the niece was an intended beneficiary, and she could enforce the promise against the uncle's estate.

As another illustration, say that Don Nation entered into a contract with Wendy Vendee under which he sold a plot of land to her for $20,000. His purpose in selling the land was not to pay a debt, as in the example involving Debbie, but to realize funds to be donated to his niece, Charity. Don therefore stipulates in the contract with Wendy that the sale price be paid directly to Charity. (Although the fact that Charity gave no consideration to Don for the benefit would preclude her from enforcing the promise against Don, the lack of consideration from Charity does not bar her suit against Wendy. The contract being enforced by Charity as an intended beneficiary is that between Don and Wendy, and consideration was exchanged between the parties to that contract.) This set of relationships may be shown as follows:

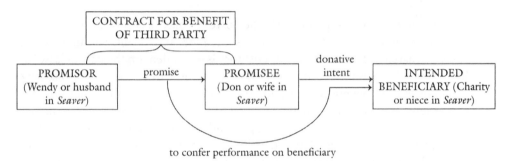

to confer performance on beneficiary

Section 302(1) attempts to move away from the creditor-donee dichotomy, which it finds too rigid and restrictive. However, it recognizes that the distinction is well-ingrained in the case law and cannot be ignored. It therefore acknowledges the distinction but alters it to make it more flexible. Many courts have followed its lead. Section 302(1) identifies two types of situations in which it recognizes a relationship sufficient to bolster the conclusion that the beneficiary was intended: The first, set out in §302(1)(a), approximates the concept of creditor beneficiary by covering cases in which performance of the promise will satisfy a monetary obligation due by the promisee to the beneficiary. This is somewhat narrower than the original category, which included not only monetary obligations, but also situations in which performance of the promise would satisfy an actual, supposed, or asserted duty of the promisee to the beneficiary. The narrowing of this category is more than compensated for by the widening of the second. The second, set out in §302(1)(b) is based on, but more expansive than, the older category of donee beneficiaries. It encompasses not only

727

situations in which gratuitous motives are apparent, but any case in which the circumstances indicate that the promisee intends to give the benefit of performance to the beneficiary. As just noted, this would include cases in which there is some supposed or asserted duty that is not clear enough to fall into §302(1)(a) as an actual liquidated monetary obligation. This sounds very vague and open-ended, but that is what is intended. The idea is to let courts decide case by case, with a strong focus on the parties' intent, as bolstered by some relationship between the promisee and the beneficiary that plausibly points to a motive for conferring the benefit. In *Sovereign Bank*, discussed in section 19.2.3, the court applied this broad ground of §302(1)(b) to find that the circumstances indicated intent to give the benefit of the performance to the beneficiary, who was neither a creditor nor a donee of the promise.

§19.2.5 Vesting of the Benefit and the Parties' Power to Modify or Terminate It

In the same way as parties have the power to make a contract, they have the power to modify or terminate it by subsequent agreement. The alteration or discharge of a contract, like its creation, is dependent on the parties' assent.[1] It would therefore seem to follow that as the parties to the contract have created the beneficiary's rights, they could agree to change them or take them away entirely. However, if they had the unrestricted power to do this, the status of intended beneficiary would be very uncertain and unreliable. To protect the beneficiary's actual or potential reliance on the contract, the rule has been developed that at some point after the contract is made, the benefit **vests** in the beneficiary — it becomes **irrevocably settled** on her so that it cannot be changed or withdrawn by the contracting parties without her consent. If the parties do agree to modify or discharge the contract after the benefit has vested, this agreement binds the parties between themselves, but it binds only them. It does not affect the rights of the beneficiary, who can enforce the performance as it vested under the original agreement. It is therefore possible that the promisee could agree to give up her own rights of enforcement or to change them so that they are less extensive than those that have vested in the beneficiary.

Over the years, different courts have adopted various approaches to the question of when the benefit vests. Some have treated it as vesting immediately upon formation of the contract, but others have required some manifestation of acceptance or some act of reliance on it by the beneficiary. The original Restatement had different rules for vesting depending on whether

---

1. Of course, consideration is generally required too, as discussed in sections 7.5.2 and 13.9.

the beneficiary was a donee or a creditor. Restatement Second §311(makes no such distinction. It seeks to clarify and standardize the rule for vesting, irrespective of the nature of the underlying relationship between the promisee and the beneficiary. It provides that the benefit vests in the beneficiary when she *manifests assent* to it at the request of one of the parties, or she *sues on it*, or she materially changes her position by acting in *justifiable reliance* on it. This formulation clearly shows the analogy between vesting and the formation of other promissory obligations. Its basis is quite akin to that for offer and acceptance or promissory estoppel: The right vests in the beneficiary either when she "accepts" it by manifesting assent to it, or when she has detrimentally relied on it. Once that has occurred, the contracting parties are committed to the conferral of rights, and the beneficiary's independent cause of action on the promise is secure.

This rule is subject to a qualification: As creators of the benefit, the contracting parties can confer it subject to whatever limitations and conditions they see fit. By so stipulating in the contract, they *can retain the power to modify it or take it away* even after it has vested in the beneficiary. These limitations will inhere in the right created in favor of the beneficiary, and it will vest subject to them. However, unless the parties clearly reserve the power to alter the rights conferred on the beneficiary after vesting, they lose it as against the beneficiary as soon as vesting occurs.

§19.2.6 The Promisee's Parallel Rights of Enforcement Against the Promisor

Notwithstanding the conferral and vesting of rights in the beneficiary, the promisee continues to be a party to the contract. As such, except to the extent that the beneficiary has enforced and obtained satisfaction of the performance, the promisee has the right to enforce the promise just as she would have had in an ordinary bilateral contract. (As explained below, the promise to be enforced is the promise to render performance to the beneficiary, not to the promisee.) Restatement Second §305(1) reflects this by stating that the promisor has a duty of performance to the promisee, even though he has a similar duty to the beneficiary. This does not mean that promisor has to perform the obligation twice. The promisee's right against the promisor is discharged to the extent that the promisor performs in favor of the beneficiary. If full performance is not rendered to the beneficiary, the promisee may enforce the obligation to perform any remaining balance.

The nature of the relief available to the promisee depends on the circumstances. When a claim for damages is not an adequate remedy, she may request specific performance — an order compelling the promisor to render the performance to the beneficiary. Alternatively, the promisee may

n for damages based on her contractual expectation. This will at least
her direct damages, measured by the loss in value of the promised
ice. In addition, if the failure to perform results in a foreseeable and
ble increase in the promisee's liability to the beneficiary or other
ntial loss, consequential damages may also be claimed.

§19.2.7 The Promisor's Ability to Raise Defenses Against the Beneficiary

The beneficiary's rights derive from the contract, so it stands to reason that
they are limited by any defense arising out of the contract. Therefore, the
basic rule, as reflected in Restatement Second §309, is that unless the contract makes it clear that it confers rights on the beneficiary free of defenses,
the beneficiary's rights are *subject to any limitations inherent in the contract*. The
promisor may raise against the beneficiary any defense that would have been
available against the promisee, arising out of a defect in the formation of the
contract (such as invalidity due to lack of consideration, voidability on
grounds of fraud, duress or some other bargaining defect, or unenforceability for failure to comply with the statute of frauds); or based on the
promisee's breach of contract; or arising out of post-formation occurrences
that affect the very basis of the contract, such as supervening impracticability
and the nonoccurrence of a condition. (The beneficiary's position is very
much like that of an assignee, discussed in section 19.3.3.)

Although a wrongful act of the promisee (such as breach or fraud) can
be raised by the promisor as a defense against the beneficiary, it does not impose
any liability on the beneficiary. He does not, by accepting the benefit, assume
any responsibility for proper behavior or performance by the promisee. Any
recourse that the promisor has must be pursued against the promisee.

Unless the contract expresses a contrary intent, the promisor cannot
raise against the beneficiary any *defense that is purely personal against the promisee*,
such as a defense that the promisee owes money to the promisor in another
transaction. Similarly, as we saw in section 19.2.5, if the promisee and
promisor make an agreement to modify or discharge the performance
after vesting, this agreement would be a defense to enforcement by the
promisee, but it would not avail against the beneficiary.

§19.2.8 The Beneficiary's Rights Against the Promisee in the Event of the Promisor's Non-Performance

As has been stated already, once the benefit has vested in the beneficiary, he
has a direct claim against the promisor and may proceed to enforce it if the

Hammer ✓
Sidway

promisor fails to perform. However, it may occur that the beneficiary is unsuccessful in obtaining satisfaction of his claim against the promisor either because the promisor has no money or assets to satisfy the claim, or because she is able to raise a defense available against the beneficiary. When that happens, the question is whether the beneficiary may then proceed against the promisee. The answer depends on whether the beneficiary is a creditor or donee.

key
Q/
When beneficiary is unsuccessful in obtaining claim

If the beneficiary is a donee, his relationship with the promisee is not supported by consideration. Therefore, the beneficiary has no enforceable claim against the promisee in the event that he is unable to recover from the promisor. However, if the beneficiary is a creditor of the promisee, he may, upon being unsuccessful in pursuing his claim against the promisor, proceed against the promisee to enforce the promisee's debt.

Some courts have not allowed the creditor beneficiary to sue the promisee after unsuccessfully trying to enforce rights against promisor. They have held that once the beneficiary elects to proceed against the promisor, the right of action against the promisor is substituted for and eliminates the cause of action on the original debt due by the promisee. (This is called **novation**.) However, the more common contemporary view, as expressed in Restatement Second §310, is that the beneficiary *surrenders no rights against the promisee* by seeking to enforce the benefit against the promisor. Instead, the promisee becomes a **surety** for the promisor, so that to the extent that the promisor fails to perform, the promisee remains liable for the outstanding amount of her undischarged debt to the beneficiary. (And, of course, the promisee may then attempt to recover from the promisor, based on the promisor's breach of her contract with the promisee.) This may be shown as follows:

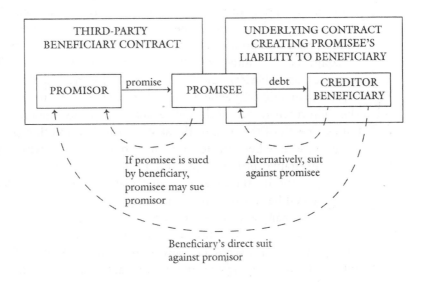

THIRD-PARTY BENEFICIARY CONTRACT

UNDERLYING CONTRACT CREATING PROMISEE'S LIABILITY TO BENEFICIARY

PROMISOR → promise → PROMISEE → debt → CREDITOR BENEFICIARY

If promisee is sued by beneficiary, promisee may sue promisor

Alternatively, suit against promisee

Beneficiary's direct suit against promisor

§19.2.9 Citizens' Claims as Intended Beneficiaries of Government Contracts

The government represents the public. In a broad sense, it can therefore be said that whenever the government enters a contract, it has the intention of conferring a benefit on the citizenry at large, or on a group of citizens whose interests are furthered by the contract. However, this does not mean that an individual citizen can sue to enforce the performance promised to the government. As with other contracts that result in a benefit to a non-party, the crucial question is not simply whether there was an intent to provide the benefit, but whether there was an intent to create an independent right of enforcement in the non-party. Therefore, as Restatement Second §313(1) makes clear, government contracts are to be *treated the same as contracts by private parties* in deciding whether a third party was an intended beneficiary: The terms of the contract must be interpreted in context to determine if it manifests the intent to confer a direct cause of action on the beneficiary.

For example, in *Klamath Water Users Protective Ass'n. v. Patterson*, 204 F.3d 1206 (9th Cir. 1999) irrigators claimed that they were the intended beneficiaries of a government agency's contract with a power company for the management of a dam. They argued that they therefore had the independent right to enforce the power company's obligation to maintain flow levels required by the contract. Although the court recognized that one of the goals of the contract was to satisfy the government's duty to water users, it had other aims as well, and there was nothing in the contract to rebut the usual presumption that citizens who benefit from a government contract are incidental beneficiaries with no private enforcement rights. In *Zigas v. Superior Court*, 174 Cal. Rptr. 806 (Cal. App. 1981) the court did find that citizens had an independent right of action to enforce a government contract. The owner of an apartment building violated its contract with HUD to keep rentals within prescribed limits. The court decided that the sole purpose of both the contract and its authorizing legislation was to benefit tenants by keeping rents at a reasonable level and that the parties must reasonably have intended to give tenants an independent cause of action to enforce the rent limitation. The court reached this conclusion because the tenants, not the government, lost as a result of the breach, the statute provided no other procedure for tenants to seek redress, the tenants' suit did not interfere with any remedial or administrative proceedings prescribed by the statute, and there was nothing in the contract that indicated that the parties expected that the owner would be shielded from tenant suits.

Because many government contracts are made in pursuance of a specific statutory policy, the question of whether a private right of action was intended is often answered not only by examining the terms of the contract, but also by interpreting the *legislation* that authorizes the contract, and the underlying public policy. In fact, the question of whether citizen enforcement is an appropriate means of effectuating government policy is often the dominant consideration in deciding if the plaintiff is an intended beneficiary.

Q asked for priv. rt of action

Because of concern that bedlam would result if courts too readily recognized private suits to enforce government contracts, the general assumption is that citizens are merely incidental beneficiaries of government contracts unless a private right of enforcement is clearly conferred by the contract or the authorizing statute, or the government has a specific legal obligation to provide the performance to the citizen (making the citizen, in effect, a creditor beneficiary). Comment *a* to §313 reflects this approach by suggesting that in cases of doubt, the contract should be interpreted as not making citizens intended beneficiaries.

Why citizens are incidental gov. ben

§19.2.10 The Claim of a Non-Client as the Third-Party Beneficiary of a Contract Between an Attorney and Client

Where an attorney breaches his contract with a client by negligent advice or representation, the client has a cause of action for malpractice. However, sometimes the attorney's negligence has a negative impact on the rights of a third party. An attorney's duty to act with reasonable competence runs only to his client, and courts generally do not recognize a cause of action for negligence in favor of a third party who suffered economic loss as a result of the attorney's negligence in handling the client's affairs. (All three of the cases discussed below refused to find an attorney liable to a non-client for malpractice.) This is based on the policy that potential malpractice liability to a non-client could distract an attorney from focusing on the client's best interests, could undermine the attorney's loyalty to his client, and could create a conflict of interest as the attorney tries to balance his duty to his client against the need to safeguard the non-client's interests.

However, under the right circumstances, courts have recognized that a non-client could acquire a cause of action against an attorney as an intended beneficiary of the contract between the attorney and client. The recognition of such a right can be very important where the client does not wish to sue the attorney, or, as often happens, the malpractice relates to the drafting of a will and only comes to light after the client is deceased. For example, in *Hale v. Groce*, 744 P.2d 1289 (Or. 1987) an attorney breached his contract with his client by failing to draw the client's will as instructed. As a result, a legatee was deprived of a legacy that the client had intended for him. The court found that the legatee was an intended beneficiary of the contract between the client and the attorney and therefore had an independent cause of action against the attorney for the breach. Similarly, in *Guy v. Liederbach*, 459 A.2d 744 (Pa. 1983)

733

the attorney had the named beneficiary of a will sign it as a witness, thereby voiding her legacy. Although the court noted that a legatee does not become a third-party beneficiary merely because she is named in the will, it found that she was an intended beneficiary of the attorney-client contract because unless she was given a right to enforce it, there would be no one to hold the attorney accountable for his breach. The testator was dead and the estate had no incentive to sue. *Noble v. Bruce,* 349 Md. 730 (1998) took a less sympathetic approach to testamentary beneficiaries. It found no express or implied intent in the contract between the testators and their attorney to confer a direct right of enforcement on the beneficiaries, and would not imply such a right merely because they were the only persons with an incentive to enforce the contract. The court's reluctance to find a right of independent enforcement was motivated by its concern that ready recognition of third-party beneficiary rights is just as harmful to the attorney-client relationship, and raises the same policy concerns, as allowing a non-client to sue the attorney for malpractice. The policy issue was emphasized in *Macht v. Estate of Dobkin,* 19 Mass. Rptr. 318 (Mass. Super. 2005), in which the client died before the attorney had complied with her instructions to draft a new will for her in which she would have left her estate to the plaintiff. The court stressed that the policy of protecting the attorney-client relationship is predominant, and there can be no finding that a non-client is an intended beneficiary if that would compromise the attorney's duty of undivided loyalty to the client. The court felt that the very existence of a dispute between the plaintiff and the testamentary heirs over disposition of the estate points to the possibility that the attorney could be faced with a conflict of interest in trying to accommodate the interests of the non-client.

§19.2.11 Construction Subcontractors as Third-Party Beneficiaries

Third-party beneficiary doctrine is sometimes invoked by a subcontractor who tries to obtain payment for its work from the owner of the property. To understand how the doctrine might arise in the construction setting, you need some background on the structure of a common construction transaction. The owner of a property decides to erect a building on it. The owner could take on the task of managing the project itself and could enter into many separate contracts with different specialists to perform components of the work such as excavation, carpentry, plumbing, and so on. However, if the owner does not have the time or the expertise to manage the construction itself, it makes a single contract with a prime or general contractor for the construction of the entire project. The general contractor is then responsible to employ subcontractors to perform specialized aspects of the job that it does not perform itself. The subcontract is solely between the general contractor and the subcontractor. The owner is not a party to it and has no contractual relationship with the subcontractor. When the work is done, the owner pays general contractor in terms of their contract. It is then up to the general contractor to pay the subcontractor.

This arrangement works well provided that the general contractor actually pays the subcontractor or has assets that could satisfy the subcontractor's claim if it is not paid. However, if the general contractor fails to pay the subcontractor and becomes insolvent, the unpaid subcontractor may try to recover from the owner. The subcontractor is not in contractual privity with the owner, so it cannot sue the owner on the basis of a direct contractual relationship. The subcontractor also has no restitutionary claim against the owner if the owner has already paid the general contractor for the work and therefore has not been unjustly enriched. To protect subcontractors from non-payment by the general contractor, state statutes give subcontractors a construction lien (also called a mechanics lien) on the real property of the owner[2] to secure the value of labor or materials furnished. If the subcontractor follows the prescribed procedure and files a claim of lien in time, it gets a lien on the owner's property to secure the value of its materials or labor. The subcontractor is entitled to this lien even if the owner has already paid the subcontractor (so the owner could be liable for double payment). If the owner does not satisfy the lien claim, the subcontractor can enforce the lien by foreclosing on the property.

A subcontractor who properly files a lien in time has no need to resort to third-party beneficiary doctrine. However, if he has lost his statutory lien right by failing to comply with the statutory procedure, his only chance of recovering from the owner is as an intended third-party beneficiary of the contract between the owner and the general contractor —that is, he must show that the owner's promise to pay for the work was intended to benefit any third-party subcontractor who was not paid by the general contractor. This is a difficult case to make where the owner had no interest in or control over what aspects of the work would be subcontracted or which subcontractors would be hired by the general contractor. Furthermore, the subcontractor's failure to secure his statutory lien right weakens his claim to be an intended beneficiary. The statutory filing procedures and time limits are controls that give the owner some degree of protection. If the subcontractor does not comply with them, he should not be able to use the doctrine to extend his right of recovery.

The situation is different if the contract between the owner and general contractor obliges the general contractor to obtain a payment bond. This is a form of insurance policy under which an insurer undertakes to the owner that it will pay any debts due by the general contractor to subcontractors.

---

2. Mechanics and construction liens are available only against owners who are private parties, and not against governmental entities.

(Although the general contractor procures the bond, it is a form of suretyship contract between the insurer and the owner intended to protect the owner from lien claims by subcontractors.) An unpaid subcontractor might claim that he is a third-party beneficiary of the bond. Where the owner is a government entity, it is usually easy for the subcontractor to assert rights as an intended beneficiary of the bond because most statutes or regulations authorizing the construction require a payment bond and specify that the bond is for the benefit of subcontractors. Where the owner is not a government entity, the determination of whether the bond was intended for the benefit of third-party subcontractors is decided by the usual process of interpretation. It could be found that the sole purpose of the bond is to protect the owner from lien claims. Any benefit to a subcontractor is purely incidental, and not intended to protect a subcontractor who failed to file a valid lien claim. However, courts tend to be sympathetic to subcontractors where a payment bond has been executed, and do commonly find the subcontractor to be an intended beneficiary of the bond.

§19.3 ASSIGNMENT AND DELEGATION

§19.3.1 The Basic Concept and Terminology

Section 19.2 is concerned with cases in which the parties to a contract intend, at the time of entering it, to confer an enforceable benefit on someone who is not a party to the contract. Although assignment and delegation also involve the introduction of a third party into the contract, the circumstances under which that happens and the legal relationship that arises is very different from that of a third party beneficiary. We are concerned here with the transfer by one party of his rights or obligations under an existing contract, and the rules and limitations governing that transfer. It is useful to begin with the terminology used to describe such a transfer and its participants: The **transfer of rights** is called an **assignment**, and the **transfer of duties** is a **delegation**. The person who **assigns a contractual right** is the **obligee** under the contract and becomes the **assignor**. The person to whom it is assigned is the **assignee**. The other party to the contract, whose duty is transferred to the assignee by the assignment, is referred to as the **obligor**. A person who **delegates her contractual duty** is the **obligor** under the contract and becomes the **delegator** of the duty. The person who assumes the duty is called the **delegate** (not delegatee). The other party to the contract, whose right to performance has been delegated, is called the **obligee**. In the following set of diagrams, assume that Party 2 is the person who decides to assign her obligations or delegate her duties. The relationships may be drawn like this:

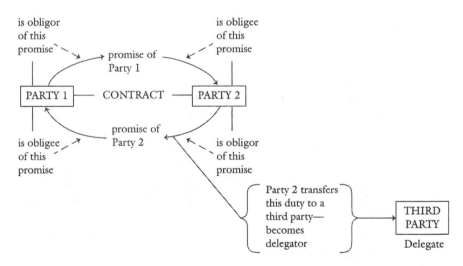

The transfer of contractual rights and duties may arise in all kinds of transactions and the rules described here could apply to any ordinary contract. We are no longer considering situations in which, as with the third-party beneficiary doctrine, a particular type of contract was created by the parties, designed from the outset to confer enforceable rights on a non-party. There are a number of reasons why a party may wish to transfer his rights, duties, or both rights and duties. Some of these motives will become apparent in the following discussion.

The law favors the free transferability of contractual rights and obligations and inclines to uphold the right of a party to make such a transfer. Therefore the general rule is that *unless a contract specifically prohibits* a party from *transferring her rights acquired* and *duties assumed* under it, or the *nature of the contract* is such that the transfer would *impair the other party's reasonable expectations* or would *offend public policy*, a party has the *power to transfer* contractual rights and obligations. This principle is well-established under common law, and is reflected in Restatement Second §317(2). It is also recognized in relation to sales of goods by UCC §2.210(2).[3]

It is probably self-evident that because we are dealing with the transfer of contractual rights and obligations, the issue of whether transfer is permitted can only arise *subsequent to the formation of the contract* that created those rights and obligations. That is, assignment and delegation are only possible once a contract has been made and those rights and obligations have come into existence. This must be distinguished from the rule that applies in the pre-contract period. As it was noted in section 4.7, the power to accept an offer is personal to the offeree and cannot be transferred unless the offer so authorizes.[4]

§19.3.2 The Nature of an Assignment

An assignment may be defined as a voluntary manifestation of intention by the holder of an existing right to make an immediate transfer of that right to another person. This definition breaks down into two essential components: First, the assignor must voluntarily manifest intent to assign the right; second, the right must be in existence at the time of assignment, and its transfer must take effect immediately.

Although a right can be transferred without the consent of the rightholder (for example, where a judgment creditor executes on the right by the process of garnishment, or the rightholder becomes bankrupt and the right passes to the trustee of his estate), we consider here only the **voluntary assignment** of rights. In most cases, assignment is effected through a contract between the assignor and the assignee, but the transaction does not have to qualify as a contract. For example, a right may be transferred gratuitously so that the transfer is a gift rather than under a contract with

---

3. Section 2.210 has been redrafted in the 2003 revision of Article 2. However, the changes are beyond our scope. The basic principle set out in current §2.210(2) is incorporated into revised §2.210(1)(a).

4. This rule does not apply to a valid option — a promise exchanged for consideration not to revoke the offer. As explained in section 5.4, the option is a contract in itself and the right to accept the offer in the option period is a binding contractual right. It can therefore be assigned.

consideration. Unless the contract creating the right forbids its assignment without the assent of the obligor, he need not be involved in the assignment.

There are some specialized types of assignment involving rights evidenced by commercial paper (such as negotiable instruments or documents) for which prescribed formalities must be satisfied. Apart from these transactions, which are beyond our scope, there are no particular formalities needed for an assignment of ordinary contract rights, but the transaction may be subject to the statute of frauds.

As section 19.3.4 explains, the effect of an assignment is to extinguish the assignor's right to performance from the obligee and to transfer it to the assignee. For such a complete transfer to occur, the right must be **in existence** and **transferred immediately.** Furthermore, the transfer must be a complete relinquishment of the right by the assignor in favor of the assignee, so that the assignor retains no control over it and no power to revoke it. This absolute and unequivocal transfer is necessary for the protection of the obligor, who must be able to rely on the fact that performance in favor of the assignee will discharge her obligation.

The effect of an assign. [handwritten marginal note]

A right comes into existence and can be assigned as soon as the contract creating it has been formed. The right can be conditional or not yet due at the time of assignment as long as it has been created already. For example, *Speelman v. Pascal*, 10 N.Y. 2d 313 (1961) involved the assignment of rights to a percentage of profits from the hit musical *My Fair Lady*. In 1952, Pascal acquired the rights from the estate of the late George Bernard Shaw to produce a musical based on his play *Pygmalion*. Before he even wrote the musical, he assigned a share of his profits to his secretary. He died soon thereafter, and the musical was not produced and staged until after his death. The court held the assignment to be effective. Although the musical was not yet in existence at the time of the assignment, the rights to future profits did exist and could be assigned. The assignee is bound by any conditions of performance and cannot enforce the right until such conditions have been satisfied and the maturity date of the right has arrived.

The assignment of a conditional or unmatured right must be distinguished from the transfer of a right that has not yet been created, but is *expected to arise in the future.* This does not qualify as an assignment. It may be a valid contract between the transferor and transferee, but it lacks the hallmark of an assignment — enforceability against the obligor. Similarly, a promise to assign an existing right in the future does not constitute an assignment. To constitute an assignment effective against the obligor, the transfer of the right must actually be accomplished, so that the transferee acquires it immediately.

§19.3.3 Restrictions on Assignment

As noted earlier, the general approach of the law is that contract rights should be freely assignable. The obligee's right to performance under the contract is one of his assets—an item of property with some value. It is property of a nature different from, say, his car or his house, in that it has no tangible physical existence. (It is called a "chose in action.") Nevertheless, it is his property all the same, and he should be able to dispose of it if he so desires. However, this right of disposition is subject to a qualification that arises from the nature of this particular kind of property. Unlike a car or house, a contract right represents a relationship with the obligor, who also has rights under it. Therefore, the obligee's power to deal with this property is tempered by the need to assure the obligor of her contractual expectation. Accordingly, the right cannot be assigned if doing so would violate the terms of the contract or otherwise materially impair the obligor's rights under it.

This means that an assignment cannot be validly made if the **contract prohibits** it. Because the law generally favors assignment, the contractual bar must be clearly expressed. Restatement Second §322 and UCC §2.210(3)[5] call for a restrictive interpretation of contract provisions that appear to preclude assignment. Any doubt or ambiguity should be resolved in favor of transferability, and a clause that prohibits "assignment of the contract" should, if possible, be taken to forbid only the delegation of duties. Even if a provision of the contract definitely does prohibit assignment, a court should assume, unless the contrary intent is clear, that although the assignment would be a breach (giving the obligor grounds for seeking a remedy for breach), the transfer of rights is itself effective. *Allhausen v. Caristo Construction Corp.*, 103 N.E.2d 891 (N.Y. 1952) involved an anti-assignment provision that expressly stipulated that rights could not be assigned and that any assignment was void. The provision was so clear that the court concluded that it did prohibit assignment of rights under the contract and the assignment was ineffective. The court did observe, however, that had the contract merely prohibited assignment and had not stated that an assignment would be void, the court would have upheld the assignment, but would have treated it as a breach of contract which would have entitled the obligor to any damages suffered as a result of the breach. (Because the assignment of rights to the obligor's performance is not usually likely to cause him economic loss, the breach of an anti-assignment provision would typically not result in any damages.)

A contract may not absolutely forbid assignment, but may **prohibit it without** the **consent** of the party whose rights are being assigned. (The anti-assignment clause in *Allhausen* did allow for assignment with permission, but the assignor did not try to get the obligor's permission before assigning its rights.) The general approach to a provision that requires permission to assign is reflected in *Julian v. Christopher*, 575

---

5. Section 2.210(3) is renumbered §2.210(4) in the 2003 revision of Article 2.

A.2d 735 (Md. 1990). Unless the contract makes it clear that the party has complete discretion to refuse permission, he is obliged to act reasonably in refusing it. This usually means, in effect, that he cannot legitimately refuse permission unless he can show that the assignment would be unduly burdensome or risky to him or would materially affect his contract rights.

This general presumption in favor of transferability does not apply to all situations, and there are some **types of contract** for which the opposite presumption holds — that is, they **may not be assigned** without specific authorization. Even in the absence of a clear prohibition, Restatement Second §317(2) and UCC §2.210(2) recognize that unless the contract specifically authorizes assignment, rights may not be assigned if this would *materially change the obligor's duty, increase the burden or risk* imposed by the contract, *impair her prospects of getting return performance,* or otherwise *substantially reduce its value to her.* Every assignment is likely to have some effect on the obligor's duty, even if that is nothing more than having to make a payment to someone other than the person she contracted with. The requirement of material impact prevents the obligor from resisting an assignment on the basis of some trivial change in her performance obligation.

To decide whether an assignment may have any of these materially adverse consequences, the contract must be interpreted in context. In many cases, especially when the performance in question is nothing more than the payment of money or the delivery of property, an assignment of rights is unlikely to have any negative impact on the obligor. It is a matter of indifference to her whether she pays or delivers to the original person with whom she contracted or to someone else designated by that person. However, in some contracts, the identity of the party who is to receive performance is important, and the obligor does have a *stake in performing only for the original obligee.* This may be true, for example, when performance is subject to a condition of satisfaction involving personal taste, or when the obligor reasonably expected to get some special advantage or credit by being associated with the obligee. (Cases like this may alternatively be viewed not as pure assignments, but as also involving a delegation of duty, on the ground that the obligee has a contractual duty to evaluate performance in good faith or to receive performance personally.)

Apart from any contractual barrier to assignment, the transfer of certain types of contract rights are *contrary to the public interest,* and therefore **prohibited** by **statute** or **public policy**. A common example is the statutory prohibition on the assignment of a claim for wages, intended to protect workers from disposing of earnings in advance of receiving them. Another example is a claim against an attorney for malpractice. Many courts have held the assignment of a legal malpractice claim to be contrary to public policy because of the uniquely personal nature of the attorney-client

Handwritten: Hand it to courts view mal pratice

relationship, which implicates confidentiality, loyalty, and trust. Some courts consider that public policy absolutely bars assignment of a malpractice claim, while others, such as *Gursky v. Rosenblum & Filan LLC*, 885 A.2d 163 (Conn. 2005) adopt a case-by-case approach that takes into account the nature of the breach and the circumstances of the assignment. In *Gursky*, the court held the assignment to be invalid because the assignee was the adversary of the client in the very action in which the malpractice was committed. That is, to settle the action in which the attorney had committed the malpractice, the client assigned his malpractice claim to the other party to the suit.

The assignment of claims that do not arise from contract are beyond our scope. However, it is worth noting that public policy forbids the assignment of certain kinds of non-contractual claims. For example, **a tort claim for personal injury** cannot be assigned because the trafficking in claims harms the public interest by enabling a litigious person to purchase and aggressively prosecute personal injury claims and by encouraging a tort victim to give up a potentially more valuable claim for advance payment.[6]

§19.3.4 The Effect of Assignment

After a valid assignment is made, the assignee substitutes for the assignor as the person to whom performance must be rendered. It therefore follows that although the obligor need not be a party to or assent to the assignment to make it effective, she must be *notified* of it so that she knows the person to whom performance is now due. There is no particular formality required for the notice, provided that it coherently indicates what right has been assigned, and to whom. The notice must be *received by the obligor* — that is, it must either come to her attention, or be delivered so that she reasonably should be aware of it. Either the assignor or the assignee may give the notice, but if it comes from the assignee, the obligor is entitled to adequate proof of the assignment.

If the obligor performs in favor of the assignor before receiving this notification, her obligation is discharged and she has no responsibility to the assignee. However, after receiving clear and adequate notification, the obligor, in effect, *holds the performance in trust for the assignee* and is obliged to ensure that he receives it. If the obligor disregards the assignment and performs for

---

6. This prohibition against the assignment of tort claims for personal injury has ties to the age-old common law policy against maintenance and champerty — the promotion of litigation for profit by persons who finance it in exchange for receiving part of the proceeds.

the assignor, she incurs *personal liability to the assignee* and will be obliged either to perform again or pay damages.[7] If the obligor pays the assignor after notice of assignment, he cannot defend against liability to the assignee merely on the ground that the assignor unilaterally countermanded his prior instruction to pay the assignee. For example, in *Herzog v. Irace*, 594 A.2d 1106 (Me. 1991) a client instructed his attorney to make payment of settlement proceeds to a creditor of the client — a doctor to whom the client owed fees for medical treatment. The client later changed his mind and told the attorney to pay the settlement to him, which the attorney did. When the doctor sued the attorney, the attorney argued that he had an ethical obligation to honor his client's instructions. The court disagreed. The attorney was aware that the client had assigned his payment right to the doctor, so the client no longer had a right to the settlement proceeds and could not validly revoke his instruction to pay the doctor.

The following simple example illustrates the basic effect and purpose of an assignment: Lender lends $10,000 to Borrower, who undertakes to repay the loan with interest in six months. After the loan is advanced, Lender no longer wishes to wait six months to get her money back. She therefore sells her contractual right of repayment to Finance Co. In this case, Lender is simply treating her contract right as a saleable asset and seeks to realize its economic worth.[8] Unless there is a term in the contract that forbids assignment, the transfer will surely be permissible, because it is not likely to have any materially adverse effect on Borrower's contractual burdens or expectations. Borrower has already received the performance of Lender's promise (advance of the loan funds) and his remaining duty is clear and not subject to any discretion or cooperation by the obligee. Borrower must simply pay a specified sum of money on a stated date. Lender falls out of the transaction and Finance Co. is substituted as the obligee. When the time for repayment comes, Borrower will pay Finance Co. Of course, Borrower must be notified of the assignment so that he knows (or reasonably should know) this. If he is not, his payment to Lender will discharge his duty. This transaction may be represented as follows:

---

7. Here again, there are special rules concerning the transfer of negotiable instruments and documents, for which notification alone is not enough.

8. Of course, as it is an intangible right, its value is dependent on Borrower's creditworthiness. Unless Lender can satisfy a prospective buyer that there is a strong likelihood that the loan will be repaid, she will not be able to sell it. Even if the right is saleable, it will not likely be sold for its face value of $10,000 but will be discounted to take account of the risk of default. This discount, together with the prospect of earning the interest payable by Borrower under the contract, may make this an attractive purchase for a buyer like Finance Co. that is willing to take the risk of default in the hope of gaining more than it paid.

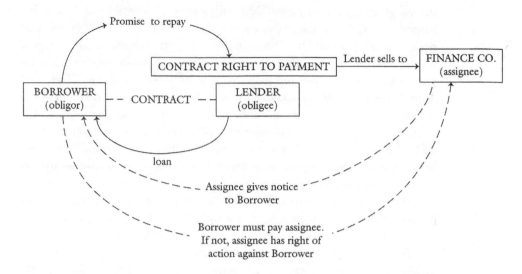

In this example, Lender assigned her contract right by sale, but sale is not the only reason for transferring rights. They may also be transferred for security — that is, used as collateral to secure a loan,[9] used to settle a pre-existing debt, or simply donated as a gift. Also, Lender assigned her entire right in the example, but she could have assigned just a portion of the performance, provided that a partial assignment would not materially burden Borrower.

§19.3.5 Defenses Against the Assignee

As a general rule, when rights are assigned, the assignee can get no greater right against the obligor than the assignor had. This is in accordance with the rather obvious proposition that when a person disposes of property, he *cannot validly transfer more than what he owns.* (Again, there are some important exceptions to this rule in the case of negotiable instruments and documents, but these are beyond our scope.) This means that the assignee takes the rights *subject to any conditions and defenses* that the obligor may have against the assignor *arising out of the contract.* For example, if the contract is avoidable

---

9. Assignment is commonly used for the purpose of securing a loan. While an important aspect of commercial transacting, the transfer of intangible rights as security is subject to complex and detailed rules that are beyond our scope. However, a brief description of the basic structure of such a transaction may be helpful: The owner of the contract right does not sell it outright, but instead borrows the needed funds and transfers the right to the lender as security for his promise to repay the money. In such a case, the transfer is not absolute. The secured creditor retains an interest in the contract right until such time as the loan is repaid, but has the right to foreclose on the security and collect payment of the contract performance in the event that its debtor defaults. There are variations on this format that need not concern us here.

by the obligor or unenforceable because of a defect in
contract, or the obligor's duty is subject to an unsatis
the assignor breached the contract, or the obligor's perfo
impracticable, these defenses can be raised against the assignee
way as they could have been against the assignor.

As in the case of a third-party beneficiary, the obligor may only use the
assignor's breach *defensively* against the assignee. That is, the assignor's breach
operates as a defense to the assignee's claim, and damages due to the obligor
by the assignor may be offset against the assignee's claim. However, the
assignee has no liability for the obligor's damages to the extent that they
exceed the amount of the offset.

The obligor's right to assert *defenses arising out of the contract is not cut off by the
notice of assignment*, so the defense is available against the assignee whether the
basis for it (for example, the assignor's breach) arose before or after
the obligor received notice. However, the notice does affect any *claim of
set off* that the obligor may have against the assignor, *arising out of a different
transaction.* The rule is that the assignee's rights are subject to any such right of
set off that arose before a notice of assignment, but cannot be defeated by
one that arose afterwards. For example, say that Lender lent $10,000 to
Borrower. In a completely separate contract, entered into a short while
later, Borrower sold her car to Lender for $5,000. Lender took delivery
of the car but failed to pay Borrower. When the time comes for Borrower
to repay the loan, she has the right to deduct the $5,000 owed to her by
Lender — she may set off the debt due to her under the car sale transaction
against the debt that she owes Lender. If Lender has assigned his rights under
the loan contract, Borrower's right of set off may be asserted against the
assignee provided that the right had not been assigned and notice of assignment received by her before the set off right arose. However, if she received
notice of assignment before the set off right was created, the claim of set off
may not be raised against the assignee.

Unless the assignment indicates an intent to the contrary, the *assignor
impliedly warrants* to the assignee that the rights assigned are *valid and not subject to
any defenses.* Therefore, if the obligor successfully raises a defense against the
assignee, the assignee usually has a cause of action against the assignor for
breach of this warranty.

§19.3.6 Delegation

Restatement Second §318 and UCC §2.210(1)[10] set out the basic principles
of delegation: An obligor is *entitled to delegate* his contractual duties unless this
violates the contract or public policy. As this suggests, the law's general approach to

---

10. Section 2.210(1) is renumbered §2.210(2)(a) in the 2003 revision Article 2.

delegation is much like that toward assignment. A party should be given the freedom to engage someone else to perform his contractual duties unless the contract prohibits this or the delegation otherwise impairs the obligee's reasonable expectations. However, it stands to reason that while a mere assignment of rights will often make little difference to the other party's contractual expectations, a delegation of duty could quite likely have a direct impact on them. This is particularly true if the contract is founded on the personal attributes or skills of the obligor.

Irrespective of whether the performance involves special skill or attributes, if the *contract makes it clear* that delegation is *forbidden*, this expressed intent will be given effect. A party is entitled, by so stipulating in the contract, to absolutely preclude the delegation of any duty owed to her. In the absence of a clear prohibition, delegation is allowed unless the obligee has a *substantial interest in* having the *obligor himself perform or control the duty*. This would be the case where the contract contemplates personal performance by the obligor or the obligor was chosen because of some particular attribute, skill, or talent relevant to performance. An impermissible delegation may in itself be a *repudiation* of the contract by the delegator, which may allow the obligee to declare advance breach and claim damages. If the obligee gives the delegator an opportunity to retract the delegation and he fails to do so in time and to render personal performance, this becomes a breach.

The effect of a permissible and effective delegation is that the delegator commits no breach of the contract by having his duty performed by the delegate, and the delegate's conforming performance discharges the delegator's contractual obligation. If a performance is properly delegated but the obligee refuses to accept it, this will be a breach by the obligee in the same way as it would have been to refuse the delegator's own performance.

Unlike assignment, *delegation does not result in a complete substitution* of the *delegate for the delegator*. Unless the obligee agrees (either in the contract or subsequently) to release the delegator from any further responsibility, he *remains obligated* under the contract. He cannot unilaterally release himself from his commitment to the obligee. Therefore, if the delegate fails to perform or renders a defective performance, this is as much a breach by the delegator as his own deficient performance would have been.

The delegate's nonperformance or defective performance could also render the delegate himself liable to the obligee but this is not inevitably so. It depends on whether the delegate has assumed the duty to the obligee by promising to perform it. Such a promise could be made directly to the obligee, or it could arise where the delegate has promised the delegator to perform, and this can be interpreted as a contract for the benefit of the obligee, as an intended third-party beneficiary. It is possible, therefore, that both the delegator and the delegate will be liable to the obligee in the event of the delegate's breach.

The following example illustrates how delegation may operate: Owner enters into a contract with Painter under which Painter undertakes to repaint the exterior of Owner's home for $5,000. Just before the work is due to begin, Painter decides that he does not wish to do the painting himself, so he hires Friend to do it. (There is no assignment here because Painter does not transfer his payment right to Friend, but makes a separate contract to pay him an hourly wage.) The delegation is established by a separate contract between Painter and Friend — Painter, in effect, subcontracts with Friend to do the job. (Painter may keep a profit from the transaction by paying Friend less than the price to be paid by Owner.) Assuming that Owner's contract with Painter does not expressly prohibit delegation or contemplate that Painter does the work personally, Painter's delegation of the performance is permissible. If Painter had been engaged to paint a mural on the side of the house, or if the house is one of those intricately detailed, multicolored Victorian "painted ladies," there would be a strong argument that the contract is based on his individual craftsmanship. But if it is just a routine housepainting job, the importance of Painter's personal attention to the job is less clear, and his performance is likely delegable unless the circumstances indicate that the contrary was intended.

§19.3.7 "Assignment" of the Contract: The Assignment of Rights and Delegation of Duties

In the immediately preceding example involving the housepainting contract, Painter did not assign his rights against Owner. He retained his right to her contractual performance (payment of the $5,000) and made a separate arrangement to remunerate Friend. However, Painter could have decided to transfer his entire package of rights and duties under the contract. This is sometimes referred to loosely as an assignment of Painter's contract. Restatement Second §328(1) more properly characterizes it as both an assignment of Painter's rights under the contract and a delegation of his duties. (UCC §2.210(4)[11] provides similarly for the assignment of a contract for the sale of goods.) Painter is an obligor who delegates *and* an obligee who assigns. Friend is the assignee of his rights *and* the delegate of his duties, and Owner is both the obligee as regards the delegated duty *and* the obligor as regards the assigned rights.

The transaction is subject to the rules governing both assignment and delegation. Where a contract is assigned as a whole, the assignment of rights may be unobjectionable, but the delegation of duties may reduce the value of the return performance reasonably expected by the original party. If so, the contract may not be assigned. This occurred in *Sally Beauty Co., Inc. v. Nexxus Products Co., Inc.*, 801 F.2d 1001 (7th Cir. 1986). Best Barber and Beauty Supply Co. was an exclusive distributor of Nexxus products. It sought to assign the exclusive distributorship to Sally which was owned by a competitor of Nexxus. Nexxus objected to the assignment of the contract on the grounds that the contract was for personal services and was based on a relationship of trust and confidence between the officers of Nexxus and Best. The court found the assignment of the contract rights was permissible. The contract did not involve services of a special or unique nature and the relationship between the management of Nexxus and Best was irrelevant. Even in the absence of assignment, corporate officers can change and neither party had the guarantee that they would be able to deal with the same officers throughout the term of the contract. The court did find, however, that the delegation of Best's duties under the distributorship deprived Nexxus of the benefit of its bargain because the distribution of its products would be in the hands of its competitor. (The dissent felt that this was not a good reason to preclude delegation because Sally would be obliged to use best efforts in selling Nexxus products.)

§19.3.8 Grounds for Insecurity Following Assignment or Delegation

When the assignment of a right or the delegation of a duty does not clearly impair the obligee's expectation of performance, but it gives the obligee reasonable grounds for insecurity, Restatement Second §317, Comment d, and UCC §2.210(5)[12] recognize the obligee's right to demand adequate

---

11. Section 2.210(4) is renumbered §2.210(3) in the 2003 revision of Article 2.
12. Section 2.210(5) is renumbered §2.210(2)(c) in the 2003 revision of Article 2.

assurances of performance. In an assignment, the assignor could be called upon to assure the obligor that the transfer of rights will not impair the obligor's prospect of return performance. In a delegation, the obligee may demand the assurance of proper performance, as appropriate, either from the delegator or the delegate. This process is equivalent to the demand for assurances discussed in section 17.7.7, when a promisee is concerned about the possibility of repudiation. If, following a justifiable demand, the person to whom it is addressed gives an adequate assurance that the performance will be rendered in accordance with the contract, the reasonable concern about impairment is resolved. If adequate assurances are not given, the assignment or delegation may be objected to. In some circumstances, the lack of assurance of performance may go beyond precluding effective transfer. It could amount to a repudiation by the assignor or delegator, permitting the other party to seek relief for anticipatory breach.

Examples

1. Tess Tatrix decided to leave her entire estate to Patty Third, her lifelong friend. She consulted Mel Practice, an attorney, for the purpose of making a will and instructed Mel to make Patty her heir. Mel was overworked and never got around to drafting the will even though Tess called him on several occasions to nag him about getting it done. Tess was about to fire Mel and use another attorney but she was killed in an accident before she could do so. She died intestate and her estate will go to her estranged brother. Does Patty have any cause of action against Mel?

2. Every year, Fair City holds a week-long celebration to commemorate its founding. This year it decided to set up a funfair in one of the city parks. It contracted with Meandering Merriment Co., to erect and operate the funfair for the week. Carr Parker owns a plot of vacant land a couple of blocks away from the park. When he heard that the fair was to be held so close to his property, he realized that parking would be at a premium in the area and that he could make a considerable amount of money by using his land as a parking lot. A month before the fair was due to open, he cleared the weeds and debris off the lot and leveled it so that cars could drive onto it. He painted signs and built a little booth to erect at the entrance. Two weeks before the fair was to begin, Meandering Merriment notified Fair City that it had double-booked for the week in question and could not set up the fair as agreed. It thereby repudiated its contract with Fair City. It was too late for the city to be able to make alternative arrangements, so it canceled the funfair.

   Carr has made careful projections of his expected profits for the week of the fair, based on the anticipated attendance at the fair and the number of cars that could be accommodated on the lot on each day. Assuming that he can establish his lost profits with reasonable certainty, should he be able to recover them from Meandering Merriment?

3. After Rock Sparkler and Di Amond had been dating for about a year, they decided to become engaged. They visited the showrooms of Belle Bijoux, a jewelry dealer, to pick out a ring. After examining the selection for some time and receiving solicitous guidance from Belle, Di and Rock agreed on a diamond ring priced at $4,500. Rock purchased the ring, took delivery of it, and placed it on Di's finger.

   About six months later, Rock fell in love with another woman and broke off his engagement to Di. To assuage his guilt at abandoning her, Rock told Di that he did not want the ring back. Di no longer wished to keep the ring, and she decided to sell it. She took it to an appraiser to get an accurate assessment of its value. On examining the stone, the appraiser told her that it was not a diamond at all, but merely a piece of cut glass.

   Di is very bitter about the breakup of her engagement to Rock, and she does not want to ask for his help in making a claim against Belle. Does Di have any basis for proceeding directly against Belle?

4. Ben Derfender's car was damaged by a hit-and-run driver. He claimed the $10,000 cost of repair from his insurer, but the insurer rejected his claim because he failed to report the collision in time. Ben retained Connie Flicted to represent him in challenging the insurer's denial of liability. The merits of Ben's claim were good, but the case was proceeding slowly and Ben needed some cash immediately. He therefore entered into a contract with Lon Shark under which Lon lent him §5,000. Ben undertook to repay the loan and interest to Lon as soon as he received payment of his pending claim against his insurer. Lon had Ben sign a letter in which he acknowledged his debt to Lon and agreed to pay the loan with interest from the proceeds of his claim. The letter ended by stating that Ben authorized his attorney, Connie Flicted, to pay Lon directly out of the proceeds. Ben gave the letter to Connie.

   About a month later, Connie settled Ben's claim against the insurer for §10,000. She had forgotten about Lon's letter and Ben did not remind her that §5,000 of the proceeds plus interest had to be paid to Lon. Connie retained her fee of §3,000 and paid the balance of §7,000 to Ben. Ben immediately spent the money and cannot repay Lon. Does Lon have grounds to recover the debt from Connie?

5. Gator Deli sells kosher food to the local orthodox Jewish community. For many years it had bought all its sausages from Frumme Mentsch, a devout member of the congregation and a strictly observant kosher butcher. Frumme decided to retire and sold his business to Chazzer Food

Corp., a large corporation that supplies food to the general market. As part of the sale of his business, Frumme assigned to Chazzer his two-year contract to supply sausages to Gator. Chazzer makes all its sausages in a huge plant in which it processes meat from a variety of animals. Neither the plant itself nor the meat used by Chazzer to make sausages is kosher. The contract says nothing about assignment. Can Gator object to the assignment of the contract?

6. Manny Quinn sells high-quality leather products. His store is well known for its exquisite alligator-skin purses. He buys the cured skins and gives them to his old friend Dell. E. Gator, who makes them into the purses of his own design. Dell is a talented designer and is obsessively exacting in his craftsmanship. Manny has had a warm friendship with Dell for years and has relied on him for a long time to produce exceptionally fine purses. Last year, Manny and Dell entered into a five-year contract under which Dell undertook to make a stated quantity of purses for Manny each year.

   A year after the contract was executed, Dell decided to retire to his cabin in the Everglades. He sold his business to Ann Phibian, his sulky and sullen apprentice. As part of the sale, Dell assigned Manny's contract to Ann. Ann has been well trained by Dell. Her designs are not as imaginative as Dell's but her craftsmanship is impeccable. However, Ann has an unpleasant nature and Manny finds her intimidating. He cannot face the thought of dealing with her over the next four years. He would prefer to terminate the contract and find someone else to make the purses. May he do so?

7. Percy Nality is a celebrity by profession. He entered into a contract with Hall Carnegie, an entertainment promoter, under which Percy would be paid $100,000 to deliver a speech as part of a special "Celebrity Lecture Series" that Hall intended to organize in the grand ballroom of a plush big-city hotel. Percy was paid his fee in advance upon signing of the contract. A few weeks before the speech was to be given, Hall decided that Percy had probably been a bad choice for his series because he was quite a boring person and had very little of consequence to say. He therefore booked another speaker for the event.

   To recover some of what he had paid Percy, Hall sold his contract with Percy to Rich X. Centric, who notified Percy that he had bought the right to Percy's performance. Rich informed Percy that instead of speaking in the "Celebrity Lecture Series," Percy was to come to Rich's home on the night set for the lecture, so that he could deliver his remarks to Rich and his wife in their living room. Percy refused and demanded that Hall allow him to speak at the event originally agreed upon. Hall declined this demand and warned Percy that if he did not deliver the speech to Rich, he would be in breach of contract. Percy did not show up at Rich's house on the evening set for delivery of the speech. What are the parties' respective rights and liabilities?

8. A lessee entered into a five-year lease of premises. The lease had a clause that provided, "The lessee may not assign this lease or any rights or interest in it without the express written permission of the lessor. Any such unauthorized assignment shall be void and shall give the lessor the right to terminate this lease immediately." A year after entering the lease, the lessee wishes to sublet the premises, but the lessor refuses to give permission. Is there anything that the lessee can do?

Explanations

1. Tess was not indebted to Patty, so Patty has no claim against the estate as a creditor and no basis for claiming testamentary rights. Her only recourse is against Mel. Assuming that Mel's delay in drafting the will was malpractice, Patty has no cause of action against him either in contract or for negligence. An attorney's duty of reasonably competent representation runs only to his client. This is founded on the policy that potential malpractice liability to a non-client could distract the attorney from focusing on his client's best interests, could undermine his loyalty to his client, and could create a conflict of interest as the attorney tires to fulfill his duty to his client while trying to protect himself from liability to the non-client.

Although she has no cause of action against Mel for malpractice, Patty may claim that she was the intended beneficiary of Mel's contract with Tess. Clearly, in contracting with Mel to draw a will appointing Patty as her sole heir, Tess intended to confer a benefit on Patty. However, that is not enough to make Patty the intended beneficiary of the contract. Patty must show that the contracting parties contemplated conferring an independent right of enforcement on her. If the parties have not expressed this intention expressly and clearly, the court must interpret the contract in context to determine it can be reasonably inferred. Where, as here, the sole purpose of the contract is to serve the interests of the third party, a court may find that it is reasonable to infer such an intent. However, some courts consider that the policy of protecting the attorney-client relationship is so strong, that any possibility of potential conflict of interest should weigh against the recognition of enforcement rights in a non-client.

2. Carr has no contract to provide parking for the fair, either with Fair City or with Meandering Merriment. His only basis for recovery against Meandering Merriment is as an intended beneficiary of its contract

with Fair City. Unquestionably, Fair City's intent in organizing the fair was to benefit the public generally as well as the local economy, including nearby entrepreneurs like Carr who were in a position to reap profits from the event. Actions by government bodies are usually intended to benefit citizens, but that does not mean that they are intended to confer a private right on any individual citizen to enforce the contract. In fact the usual assumption is that a private enforcement right was not intended unless the contract or any legislation authorizing it indicates otherwise or the public interest requires recognition of private enforcement rights to give effect to the governmental purpose. In the absence of such circumstances, it is solely up to the government body to decide whether to enforce its contracts. Too ready a recognition of private enforcement rights would harm the public interest by increasing the volume of litigation and making it difficult for government to function. In Carr's case there is nothing to show that the contract, its authorizing statute, or public policy conferred the right on Carr to sue Meandering Merriment. The city had given him no commitment to hold the fair, there is no evidence that the contract contemplated any benefit to him specifically, and there is no strong public interest at stake that can only be protected by allowing Carr a right of action.

3. If Belle knew that the diamond was fake, she is guilty of fraud. Even if she honestly believed the diamond to be genuine, the delivery of a piece of cut glass was a breach of her warranty that it was a diamond — whether such a warranty was given in so many words or arose by necessary inference from the price and description of the ring. (It would qualify as an express warranty under UCC §2.313(1)(b).[13]) There is no doubt that Rock would have a cause of action against her for breach of contract, but the issue is whether Di can proceed against her directly without relying on Rock to assert the claim. Although Di visited the showroom with Rock and helped select the ring, she was not a party to the contract for its sale. Her only basis for a direct claim against Belle (in the absence of some consumer protection statute that may extend rights to her) is as an intended beneficiary of Belle's contract with Rock.

It is clear that Rock intended Di to have the ring. This was obviously apparent to Belle at the time of contracting because she knew Rock was buying an engagement ring and saw Di participate in its selection. Of course, this is not enough on its own, because there must also have been an understanding between the parties that Di would acquire an independent right to enforce Belle's contractual warranty. Although it is unlikely that the parties would have discussed this, or even though of it at the time, intent to confer a right of action on the beneficiary need not be

---

13. Section 2.313(1)(b) is renumbered §2.313(2)(b) in the 2003 revision of Article 2.

articulated if, under all the circumstances, it is, in the words of Restatement Second §302(1), "appropriate to effectuate the intention of the parties." In this case, given Di's close involvement in the selection of the ring and the fact that she was to receive and own it, the recognition of her right to enforce Belle's warranty does seem consistent with the parties' intent.

The facts of this example are adapted from those in *Warren v. Monahan Beaches Jewelry Center, Inc.*, 548 So. 2d 870 (Fla. 1989). In that case, the plaintiff did not participate in the selection of the ring and was not known to the seller at the time of its purchase. However, the seller did know that its customer, the plaintiff's fiancée, was buying it as an engagement ring. After her fiancée gave her the ring, the plaintiff noticed a chip in it and took it back to the seller, who undertook to replace it as soon as new inventory came in. While she was waiting for the new stock, the plaintiff decided to have the ring appraised and discovered that the diamond was not genuine, but was cubic zirconia. The plaintiff then sued the seller directly. The seller responded by moving to dismiss her complaint on the basis that it did not allege sufficient facts to show that she was an intended beneficiary of the seller's contract with her fiancée. The appellate court found that the complaint did set out a cause of action. By alleging both the seller's pre-contractual discussions with the plaintiff's fiancée and its post-contractual dealings with the plaintiff herself, it adequately pleaded an intent to confer an enforceable benefit on the plaintiff. (The post-contractual dealings in *Warren* were useful bolstering evidence because they constituted a course of performance that helped to establish that the contracting parties intended to confer a right of enforcement on the beneficiary. Although no such evidence exists in Di's case, her evidence of the pre-contractual dealings is stronger than in *Warren*, and should be enough, on its own, to establish intent.)

4. Lon is clearly not an intended beneficiary of the contract in which Connie agreed to represent Ben because he was not contemplated as a beneficiary at the time that the contract was made. Also, Ben's mere sending of the letter to Connie does not give rise to a contract between Lon and Connie, and Lon has no promissory estoppel claim against Connie because he did not take action in reliance on any promise by her to transmit the proceeds to him. Although Connie was negligent in disregarding the letter, Lon is not her client and has no claim against her for malpractice. His only basis for recovering from her is as an assignee of Ben's claim against her.

An assignment is a voluntary manifestation of intent by the owner of the right to transfer it immediately and irrevocably to another. Unless the right is embodied in a negotiable instrument or document, the assignment does not need to comply with any formalities. Nor does it need to use any particular form of words, provided that intent to assign is apparent. Ben's letter acknowledges his debt to Lon and authorizes payment to him from the fund. Its reasonable import is that Ben intends irrevocably to assign his right to the funds to the extent stated. There is nothing in Ben's contract with Connie, or in the nature of the transaction, or as a matter of policy, that would rebut the usual presumption in favor of the free assignability of Ben's contract rights.

This is the assignment of a present right, not the transfer of a future right. The contracts giving rise to the claim against the insurer and Connie were both in existence at the time of the assignment, even though the claim against the insurer was not yet liquidated at that stage and the claim against Connie was conditional on her receiving the proceeds of the claim against the insurer. An unliquidated, contingent claim can be assigned.

Ben had anticipated that his right against the insurer would exceed the amount due to Lon for principal and interest, so he contemplated a partial assignment of his right. This is permissible provided that the splitting of the right does not impose a substantial risk or burden on Connie, the obligor. Where the right simply involves payment from a fund, a partial assignment is not likely to be burdensome or risky to the obligor.

A valid assignment is binding on the obligor as soon as she receives notice of it. (If she so requests, she is also entitled to receive adequate proof of it.) At that point, the assignee is substituted for the assignor as the party entitled to performance and the obligee can only discharge her contractual duty by rendering performance to the assignee. Connie's payment to Ben was improper and does not discharge her obligation to pay Lon.

5. Upon selling his business to Chazzer Food Corp., Frumme assigned to it his entire contract with Gator Deli — he both assigned his right to payment and delegated his duty to supply sausages. Because this is a sale of goods, the rules governing the assignment of rights and the delegation of duties are set out in UCC §2.210. The contract does not mention assignment, so §2.210 allows Gator to resist the assignment and delegation only if it would materially affect its rights and obligations under the contract, or the contract gives it a substantial interest in having Frumme personally render or control the performance. Frumme is a strictly kosher butcher, and had the contract been assigned to another strictly kosher butcher, Gator would probably have had no grounds to complain. There is nothing to suggest that Frumme's skills and attributes makes it crucial that he personally performs under the contract. However, the contract was assigned to a corporation that supplies food to the general market with a centralized butchery that

neither uses kosher meat nor processes it in accordance with Jewish law. It is surely a material term of the contract that the sausages are kosher, and the delegation of the duty to supply them fundamentally affects Gator's rights under the contract.

However, this does not mean that Gator has the immediate right to refuse the delegation and to declare Frumme to be in breach. The law's presumption in favor of assignability seeks to balance the rights of Frumme to sell his assets against Gator's right to achieve its contractual expectations. Therefore, as Chazzer has not stated that it will not comply with Frumme's contractual obligation to supply sausages that are kosher, Gator has to give it the opportunity to declare its intentions with regard to performance. Under §2.210(5) (renumbered §2.210(2)(c) in the 2003 revision of Article 2) Gator should treat the delegation as creating reasonable grounds for insecurity, and should clarify Chazzer's intentions by demanding an adequate assurance of performance. If Chazzer fails to provide an adequate assurance of performance, Gator has the right to refuse the delegation. In addition, because Frumme repudiates the contract by improperly delegating his duties, Gator can declare a material breach and can claim damages from him for any loss that it suffers. However, if Chazzer responds by giving the assurance that the sausages to be supplied under the contract will be processed separately from non-kosher meat in a plant and under a process that complies with Jewish law, Gator must accept the assignment and is remains bound by the contract. (Remember that even if the delegation is effective, it does not release Frumme from his obligations, and he remains responsible if Chazzer fails to perform properly.)

6. Dell's contract with Manny is for services, not the sale of goods. It is therefore subject to the common law. However, the common law principles are no different from those set out for a sale of goods in Example 5. Like the contract for the sale of sausages, this contract is assigned in its entirety and constitutes both an assignment of Dell's right to payment and his duty to make the purses. The contract is silent on assignment, so the rights are presumed to be assignable and the duties delegable unless this would violate public policy (which is not implicated here) or the nature and purpose of the contract is such that assignment would place an undue burden on Manny, would impair his prospects of return performance, or would defeat his substantial interest in having the obligor render or control the performance.

Manny's contract with Dell is highly personal in two respects. First, it is based on Dell's exceptional talent in design and craftsmanship. Second, it is grounded in a long and congenial relationship. The quality of Ann's work is equivalent to Dell's but she does not quite have his design flair. Dell's identity is clearly a significant factor in the contract, as would be true of any artist. This could be an important enough a feature of the contract to make Dell's personal performance the basis of the bargain. However, we cannot be sure of this without knowing more about the extent of the differences between his and Ann's work. The significance of the personal relationship is even more difficult to evaluate. Manny may not have entered into a long-term contract with someone with whom he did not have a good personal relationship. However, this is a commercial contract for the purpose of producing marketable products. Provided that purses of suitable quality can be produced, the parties do not have to be buddies, and their happy personal relationship may be incidental to the central purpose of the contract.[14]

In short, there is a chance that Manny could resist assignment of the contract, but this result is not assured. When the court balances Manny's reasonable contractual expectations against Dell's right to profit from the sale of his business, it could well find that Manny has not met the burden of showing this contract to be non-assignable.

7. If Hall's obligation under the contract is interpreted to be nothing more than the payment of the speaking fee, then Hall has fully performed and his sale of the contract is merely an assignment of his right to have Percy blabber for an hour or so. If this is the correct interpretation, then the performance due to Percy in return for the speech is not jeopardized because it has been paid, and unless Rich's house is substantially less accessible than the plush hotel, there seems to be little burden imposed on his ability to render his performance. The assignment of the right would therefore be unobjectionable.

However, it is more than likely that Percy did not bargain only for the fee, but also had a reasonable expectation of enjoying the prestige and exposure of participating in the lecture series. This right may or may not have demonstrable economic value, but its economic worth is not the issue. Even intangible or speculative benefits can be a material part of the bargain if they are reasonably contemplated by the parties. On this interpretation, the sale of Percy's performance also entails the delegation of Hall's duty to stage the speech as contemplated by the contract. (Or, to put it differently, Hall's assignment of his right to receive the speech materially reduces the value of the return performance due to Percy or impairs his chance of receiving it.)

If this is so, it follows that the assignment of the contract was a repudiation, and when Hall refused to retract before the due date for

---

14. It was noted in section 19.3.7 that a contracting party has no right to expect that he will continue to deal with corporate officers with whom he has a special relationship because officers can change even in the absence of assignment. This consideration is inapplicable where the contracting parties are individuals. However, the personal relationship of the parties is still likely to be incidental in most contracts.

performance, he materially violated his contractual promise. This gave Percy the right to withhold his own performance and to sue Hall for damages. Presumably at that late date Percy had no opportunity to mitigate by finding another lucrative engagement, so he can at least keep the $100,000 as direct damages. It may be possible for him to establish some economic loss for being deprived of the ability to speak in the lecture series, but such a loss is probably too uncertain and speculative, so consequential damages are unlikely to be provable. In addition, Hall is liable to Rich for failure to perform that contract. In transferring his right to Rich, Hall impliedly warranted the existence and validity of the right assigned. Therefore, if it was non-assignable, Rich can sue Hall for breach of this warranty. As he is unlikely to have suffered any consequential loss, his claim is probably confined to restitution of what he paid for the right.

By contrast to Percy's case, a right to the performance of personal services was held to be assignable in *Evening News Assn. v. Peterson*, 477 F. Supp. 77 (D.D.C. 1979). Peterson was employed as a news anchor at a television station. When the television station was sold, the seller assigned Peterson's employment contract to the buyer. Peterson objected to the assignment but the court upheld it. The assignment of the contract did not materially alter his working conditions, increase his burden of performance, or endanger his prospects of return performance.

8. Because the law has a general preference in favor of the assignability of rights and the delegation of duties, courts interpret anti-assignment clauses as narrowly as possible. The provision in the lease is clearly worded and it therefore must be taken to preclude effective transfer without the lessor's permission. As the lessee needs permission to sublet, we must now consider if there is anything that can be done to compel the lessor to give its permission or to override its refusal. Unless the lease makes it clear that the lessor reserves absolute discretion to refuse permission, the law implies an obligation on the lessor to act reasonably in refusing it. This accords with the normal marketplace expectation of commercially reasonable conduct and is consistent with the law's general policy of requiring parties to deal with each other fairly and in good faith. Therefore, to legitimately refuse permission to sublet, the lessor must show that it has reasonable grounds for objecting to the subtenant. For example, that it is financially unstable, would use the premises improperly, or would otherwise be an unsuitable occupant.

Glossary

Accord and satisfaction. A settlement of an existing claim under which the parties agree that one of them (the debtor) will give, and the other (the creditor) will accept a lesser performance than that originally claimed by the creditor. The agreement of settlement is the **accord**, and its execution by rendition of the settled performance is the **satisfaction.** Until the settlement is satisfied by performance, it is known as an executory accord.

Actions of Assumpsit, Covenant, and Debt. *See* Assumpsit; Covenant; Debt.

Agreed damages. *See* Liquidated.

Agreement to agree. Negotiating parties may have reached agreement in principle, but may not have settled all the terms of their proposed contract. They may decide to postpone resolution of those terms for later, agreeing to address them at a future date. This situation is sometimes described as an "agreement to agree." If the unresolved terms are material, no contract can come into existence until they are settled, so an "agreement to agree" is not a contract. However, the parties may have promised expressly or impliedly to continue to negotiate in good faith.

Anticipatory repudiation. A contract cannot be breached before the time of performance falls due. However, if, before his performance is due, a party makes it clear by unequivocal words or unambiguous voluntary conduct that he will not perform as promised, or will materially breach the contract when the time for performance arrives, he repudiates in anticipation of performance. The other party may react to this repudiation immediately and pursue relief for breach.

Assignment. The transfer of a contractual right, sometimes used more loosely to mean the transfer of both rights and duties under a contract.

Assumpsit. (Latin: "He undertook.") One of the common law forms of action under which suit was brought for damages for the breach of a contractual promise. Assumpsit, an extension of the tort action of trespass, was originally only available where the defendant performed improperly, causing harm to the plaintiff (misfeasance). It was later extended to cover situations in which the defendant broke his promise by failing to perform at all (nonfeasance). As assumpsit developed, it became the most flexible, efficient and comprehensive form of action for contract. It eventually overtook the other contractual writs of Covenant and Debt, emerging as the forebear of modern contract law.

Assurance of performance. *See* Prospective non-performance.

Balance of the equities. *See* Equitable balancing.

Bargain theory. *See* Consideration.

Battle of the forms. A nickname given to the situation in which the buyer and seller of goods attempt to form a contract by exchanging writings with mismatching terms. Often these terms are preprinted standard provisions, designed to protect the interests of the sender.

Bilateral contract. All contracts have two or more parties, so every contract is at least bilateral (or, if not, multilateral) in the lay sense. However, in contract law, the word "bilateral" is a term of art, meaning that at the instant of contract formation, there are promises outstanding by both parties. This is in contrast to a **unilateral contract**, under which the offeree's act of acceptance is also her act of performance, so that at the instant of formation, the offeree has already performed, and only the offeror's promise is outstanding. Unilateral contracts are relatively rare, and most contracts are bilateral in this sense. *See also* Unilateral contract.

Boilerplate. Standard provisions employed commonly in contracts of a particular kind, and often set out in preprinted standard form contract blanks.

Breach of contract. *See* Materiality; Partial breach; Substantial performance; Total breach.

Chancery. The Chancellor's Court. That is, the court of Equity.

Classical contract law. The name used to describe the law of contracts as it existed in the period running from the late nineteenth to early twentieth century, in which modern contract law was developed and systematized.

Common law. A term with three related but distinct meanings. It denotes:

1. The basic legal system of countries whose law derives from the common law of England.

2. The judge-made (as opposed to statutory) component of our law.

3. The process of legal analysis under which judges interpret, develop, and embellish rules of law.

Concurrent conditions. Where mutual performances under a contract are dependent on each other and the contract does not expressly or impliedly set out a sequence for performance, they must be rendered at the same time, and each performance is deemed in law to be a condition of the other. Therefore, if one of the parties fails to perform, the other is excused from doing so.

Condition. An event, not certain to occur, that must occur for the performance of a party to become due. If the parties agree that a particular performance under the contract (or the entire contract) is to be contingent on the happening of a future uncertain event, the performance (or the contract as a whole) is conditional. A condition may be **express** (that is, articulated in the agreement), **implied in fact**

(inferable from interpreting the agreement in context), or **construed** (deemed as a matter of legal implication to be what the parties must reasonably have intended). Conditions are also categorized as pure or promissory. A **pure condition** is simply an event specified as a contingency on which performance is dependent, and nothing more. If the event fails to occur, the performance dependent upon it need not be rendered, and neither party incurs any liability for the nonoccurrence. However, a **promissory condition** is both a condition and a promise. That is, one of the parties promises expressly or impliedly that the condition will occur, and becomes liable for breach of contract if it does not.

Conditions precedent or subsequent. A **condition precedent** is one that must be fulfilled before a duty to perform comes into effect. A **condition subsequent** is one that discharges a duty of performance. That is, the duty to perform arises immediately upon formation of the contract, but if the condition occurs, it falls away. A condition subsequent differs from a condition precedent in that it extinguishes an existing duty, while a condition precedent is a precondition to a duty arising. As a practical matter, it is almost always impossible to tell from the language of an agreement which of these two conditions was intended by the parties, and the law's general assumption is in favor of a condition precedent. There is little practical difference between them.

Consequential damages. Losses suffered by the victim of a breach going beyond the mere loss in value of the promised performance (direct damages), and resulting from the impact of the breach on other transactions or endeavors dependent on the contract.

Consideration. In its earliest formulation, "consideration" probably meant no more than that the contract was deliberately considered — that it was seriously contemplated and intended to be binding. As it has developed, it has come to mean that something of legal value (but not necessarily economic value) must be given by each party in exchange for what was promised or given by the other. Under the **bargain theory**, which prevails in modern law, a promise or performance qualifies as consideration only if it has been given in exchange for and induced the return promise or performance.

Construction/construed term. *See* Implied in law term.

Constructive conditions of exchange. Unless the contract expressly or impliedly indicates a different intent, the law generally presumes that the performances of the parties are interdependent. That is, each party's duty to perform is conditional on the other performing. Another way of stating this is to say contractual **promises are dependent** — that the promise made by one party is dependent on that made by the other.

Contra proferentum rule. A default rule of interpretation that where the meaning of language is unclear and cannot be resolved by contextual evidence, an interpretation is preferred that goes against the interests of the drafter, and in favor of the non-drafter.

Course of dealing/performance. Where contracting parties have entered into a number of successive transactions of a similar kind, the transactions that occurred before the contract in question are referred to as a **course of dealing.** Where there is some uncertainty in the meaning of a term in the current contract, evidence of the parties' course of dealing can be helpful in resolving it. The conduct of the parties in performing a contract after its execution is called a **course of performance.** Evidence of how the parties actually performed following the formation of the contract can likewise be useful in interpreting what they must have intended.

Covenant. In general terms, a covenant is simply an agreement. At early common law, Covenent was a form of action available to recover damages for breach of a promise under seal. Under the formalistic system of pleading in early common law, the action was not available for a contract that was not executed under seal.

Cure. A breaching party's rectification of the deficiency in performance.

Debt. In its contemporary meaning, a debt is an obligation to pay money. (Sometimes "debt" is used even more broadly — and somewhat inaccurately — to denote any obligation of performance.) At early common law, the **Action of Debt** was a form of action that lay for recovery of a sum certain in money arising out of a contract under which money had been lent to the defendant or goods or services had been delivered to him.

Delegation. The transfer of contractual duties.

Dependent promises. See Constructive conditions of exchange.

Deposited acceptance rule. See Mailbox rule.

Detriment. In law, "detriment" is sometimes used in its ordinary sense, to mean actual harm, prejudice, or injury. (Many courts require detriment in this sense before giving relief for promissory estoppel.) However, in consideration doctrine, "detriment" is used as a legal term of art. To suffer a **legal detriment**, a party must merely give up some legal right — do something that he is not obliged to do, or refrain from something that he is entitled to do. It does not matter if this legal detriment is of little or no economic value, or that it is not in fact harmful or injurious to the party suffering it.

Direct costs. See Fixed costs.

Direct damages. Losses incurred by the victim of a breach in acquiring the equivalent of the performance promised under the contract, so as to substitute for the performance that should have been rendered by the breacher.

Direct reliance. See Reliance damages.

Disaffirmance. Upon breach, the victim may either sue on the contract for expectation or reliance damages, or may elect to act as if no contract exists, and to sue for restitution under a theory of unjust enrichment. Disaffirmance is the plaintiff's formal abandonment of the contract in order to ground the unjust enrichment claim.

Divisibility. A contract is divisible if the mutual performances promised by the parties can be split up into a number of smaller, self sufficient exchanges. That is, the contract can be divided into independent and self-contained sets of matching performances.

Economic waste. If damages for rectifying a breach are disproportionate to the victim's true loss, the court has the discretion to adjust them downwards to more accurately reflect the actual loss. It is sometimes said that the basis for this adjustment is that it would be economically wasteful to spend a large sum on curing a relatively less valuable breach, but as the plaintiff would not be obliged to waste the damages award on rectifying the breach, the true basis for the rule is that it would be an unfair forfeiture to compel the breacher to pay damages disproportionate to actual loss.

Efficient breach. A breach is efficient if it makes the defendant better off without making the plaintiff worse off. If the defendant's cost to perform the contract (including the cost of lost opportunity for a more lucrative transaction) would exceed the benefit that performance would give both parties, the defendant may save (or earn) enough money by breaching to pay expectation damages to the plaintiff and still come out ahead. In purely economic terms, a breach in such circumstances does not harm the plaintiff, who is compensated by the payment of damages, while it increases the defendant's wealth. A breach can only be efficient if the transaction costs of each party in making substitute transactions and of settling or litigating the plaintiff's claim do not exceed the gains to be made from the breach. Also, it must be remembered that costs of breach are often not capable of accurate calculation, and breach has implications beyond economics.

Ejusdem generis. (Latin: "of the same kind.") A rule of interpretation under which specific words limit the meaning of general words with which they are associated.

Enforcement. A general word that denotes judicial recognition of a right. When it is said that a court enforces a contract, this means that the court will render judgment for relief upon breach of the contract. Enforcement does not necessarily take the form of a court order compelling the breaching party to perform his obligations under the contract — in fact such an order of **specific performance** is the exception rather than the rule. In most cases, the enforcement of a contract takes the form of a money judgment for **damages.** If the breaching party fails to pay the damages voluntarily, the means of compelling payment is by **execution.** *See also* Execution; Specific performance.

Equitable balancing. In judicial decisionmaking, the process under which the court takes into account the likely impact of countervailing resolutions, and attempts to reach a fair and balanced result by weighing the potential hardship to each party as well as their respective rights and the relative justice of their positions.

Equity. Apart from meaning "fairness" in a general sense, this word has a more technical meaning in the common law. It refers to the jurisdiction originally exercised by the Lord Chancellor, representing the monarch, for the purpose of granting discretionary relief when the more inflexible law courts were unable to provide an adequate remedy. Courts of law and equity have been combined for some time, but the distinction between suits of equitable and legal origin is still maintained.

Essential reliance. *See* Reliance damages.

Estoppel. (Also called **equitable estoppel** or **estoppel in pais.**) A doctrine derived from equity under which a person is precluded from asserting a right where she has, by deliberate words or conduct, misled the party against whom the rights are asserted into the justifiable belief that the right does not exist or will not be asserted.

Execution. The process of enforcing a money judgment, such as a judgment of contract damages, against the **judgment debtor** (the party against whom the judgment has been rendered.) The **judgment creditor** (the party in whose favor judgment was granted) has a **writ** issued and delivered to the appropriate official (usually called the **sheriff**), who then attempts to find property belonging to the judgment debtor. If such property is found, the sheriff **levies** on it — that is, takes legal custody of it, and after advertising it, sells it at public auction. The proceeds of the sale are then paid over to the judgment creditor.

Executory/executed. Until a **contract** has been fully performed, it is executory. Once it has been fully performed on both sides, it is executed. In the case of a **gift**, where the gift is merely promised, but not yet given, it is executory (and hence unenforceable under consideration doctrine), but once the gift has been transferred to the donee, it is executed, and no longer subject to invalidation under consideration doctrine.

Executory accord. *See* Accord and satisfaction.

Exemplary damages. *See* Punitive damages.

Express. Articulated or stated in words, rather than inferred from indirect language or circumstances.

Expressio unius est exclusio alterius. (Latin: "the expression of one thing excludes another.") A rule of interpretation under which the listing of a string of specific things, not followed by a general term, is taken to exclude unlisted things of the same kind.

Extrinsic evidence. *See* Four corners rule.

Fiction. *See* Legal fiction.

Firm offer. An offer that the offeror undertakes not to revoke for a stated or reasonable time. At common law, such an undertaking is not binding on the offeror unless the offer qualifies as a valid option, but under UCC Article 2, a firm offer is binding under defined circumstances.

Fixed costs (overhead). Costs that must be paid by a party whether or not she ceases performance under a contract. These overhead costs are distinguished from **variable (direct) costs**, which are costs incurred solely in the process of performance, and are saved when the party ceases performance. When the plaintiff's performance has ceased as a result of the defendant's breach, fixed costs, not being saved, are included in the plaintiff's damages, but variable costs, being saved, are not included in calculating the plaintiff's loss.

F.O.B. (Free on board.) A term in a sale of goods that identifies the seller's delivery commitment and risk of loss. The initials F.O.B. are followed by a specified place (for example, F.O.B. New York). The seller is responsible for the cost and risk of getting the goods to that place, and the buyer must accept delivery there. Upon taking delivery, the buyer assumes responsibility for the freight and risk of loss from that point.

Force majeure. (French: "superior force.") A force beyond the control of the parties, such as a natural disaster or war. A force majeure clause in a contract is one that releases a party from performance if that performance is rendered impracticable as a result of such an uncontrollable event.

Foreseen/foreseeable. An event is **foreseen** if the party in question recognizes the possibility of its occurrence and contemplates it as a real likelihood. However, foreseeability is based on a more objective standard: Whether or not the party in question does actually foresee the event, it is **foreseeable** if it can be conceived of by a reasonable person.

Forfeiture. *See* Unfair forfeiture.

Form of action. In older common law, different actions (for example, the contract actions of assumpsit, convenant, or debt, or the tort action of trespass) each covered a specific type of transaction or set of facts and had a particular form that had distinct features in its pleadings and in the manner in which evidence was presented and evaluated. This formalistic system no longer applies in modern law.

Four corners rule. A rule of interpretation that requires the meaning of a document to be ascertained with reference only to the language used in the document itself (that is, to be found within its "four corners"), without recourse to any extrinsic evidence. **Extrinsic evidence** is evidence of the context in which the document was executed. These facts outside the document, such as evidence of discussions, negotiations or dealings between the parties or trade usage, may help to cast light on what the parties meant by the language used in the document.

Fraud. A misrepresentation of fact, opinion, or intention, made with knowledge of its falsity and intent to mislead. Most fraudulent misrepresentations are **in the inducement** — they misrepresent something that underlies and induces the contract. In rarer cases, fraud may be **in the factum** — a misrepresentation of the nature and effect of the document signed.

Frustration of purpose. A contract's purpose is frustrated where, after it is made, an unforeseen event occurs, which so changes the circumstances surrounding it, that the contract's underlying purpose — as reasonably understood by both parties — is defeated. Although it is still possible to perform as originally intended, the point of the contract has disappeared. Under proper circumstances, the frustration of a contract's purpose is grounds for its termination.

Gap filler. A standard term recognized by law, implied as a matter of law into a contract to fill a gap in the parties' agreement.

Garnishment. A form of execution under which a writ is delivered to a person who holds property of the judgment debtor or owes money or another obligation to the judgment debtor, ordering that person to turn over the property or money to the court in satisfaction of the judgment. *See also* Execution; Writ.

General damages. In contract, damages that arise in the normal course of breach, including readily foreseeable direct damages, as well as those consequential damages that were reasonably foreseeable by the breacher at the time of contracting as a natural and probable consequence of the breach. (If the breacher could not reasonably have foreseen the damages without special information or knowledge of the victim's particular circumstances, the damages are special.)

Good faith. Actual honesty and fair dealing, with an absence of intent to act wrongfully. Despite the prevalence of an objective reasonableness standard in contract law, there are many situations in which the honesty of a party, measured subjectively by attempting to ascertain his actual state of mind, is relevant to the case.

Illusory promise. An apparent promise that is so qualified, or in respect of which such wide discretion is reserved, that the apparent promisor actually makes no binding commitment at all.

Implied in fact. A contract, term, or promise is implied in fact if it is not expressly stated, but it can be deduced as a matter of factual conclusion from other language used by the parties, or from conduct or the circumstances surrounding the transaction.

Implied in law contract, also known as **quasi-contract**, is not a contract at all, but a legal fiction originally created for procedural reasons — to allow the formalistic common law courts of a bygone era to use the contractual form of action as a basis for giving relief for unjust enrichment. In modern law, "quasi-contract" or "contract implied in law" is simply a term to describe one of the forms of an action for unjust enrichment.

Implied in law term, also known as a **construed** term, is a term found by the court to exist in a contract, even though the language of the contract does not state it, and it cannot be inferred as a matter of fact from contextual evidence. Legal implication is based on a policy judgment by the court (or by a statute or common law rule) that the term should be in the contract, even though the parties may not actually have agreed to it. The importation of the term into the contract is typically justified on the basis that the parties, as reasonable people, would have intended the term to apply had they thought about the issue.

Impracticability/impossibility. Under the older, narrower doctrine of **impossibility**, performance under a contract may be excused as impossible if the contract contemplated that performance to be dependent on the continued existence of a person or thing, and, without fault of the person claiming excuse, the person died or thing was destroyed after the contract's execution. The doctrine of **impracticability** is a modern expansion of the older impossibility doctrine. A party may be excused from performance if an unforeseen supervening event, occurring after formation of the contract, and not caused by the fault of the party claiming excuse, defeats a basic assumption on which the contract was made. To establish excuse on the basis of impracticability, the party must also show that the unforeseen event imposes a significant burden on him, beyond any risk that he expressly or impliedly assumed.

Incidental/intended beneficiary. *See* Third-party beneficiary.

Incidental damages. Costs and expenses incurred by the victim of a breach in attempting to deal with it and in taking action to seek a substitute transaction or to curtail losses.

Incidental reliance. *See* Reliance damages.

Indebitatus assumpsit. *See* Assumpsit.

Indefiniteness. Vagueness, ambiguity, or other uncertainty in an agreement.

Injunction. An order of court compelling the performance of a specified act (called a **mandatory** injunction) or prohibiting specific action (called a **prohibitory** injunction).

In pari delicto rule. (In pari delicto potior est conditio defendantis. Latin: "where the parties are in equal guilt, the defendant's position is the stronger.") An illegal contract is not enforceable, but if one of the parties has performed under the contract, he does have a restitutionary claim for the return of what was given to the other. However, if the party claiming restitution is as much or more to blame in breaking the law as the party who received the performance, the court has the discretion to leave the parties as it finds them, and to refuse to grant restitution.

In personam/in rem. An order or command of the court directed at the defendant and compelling him to do or refrain from doing something is an **in personam** order, and its disobedience will result in contempt of court. By contrast, a judgment of the court that the defendant owes monetary damages is not directed against the person of the defendant, but at his property — it is **in rem.** If the defendant fails to pay the judgment, it can only be enforced to the extent that the sheriff can find property of the defendant on which to levy execution.

Integration/integrated writing. A written record of agreement is said to be **totally integrated** if it clearly and unambiguously expresses all the terms agreed to by the parties, and is intended by them to be a complete and final expression of all the terms of their contract. If the written record does not fully and finally incorporate all of the agreed terms, but it does set out some of them completely, clearly, and unambiguously, it is said to be **partially integrated.** That is, the writing is a final expression of agreement with regard to those terms that are fully set out.

Interpretation. The process of inferring meaning from language or from factual evidence of the context in which the language was used.

Judgment creditor/debtor. *See* Execution.

Knockout rule. A rule applied by some courts in resolving the battle of the forms under UCC §2.207, under which conflicting terms in correspondence between the parties cancel each other out, leaving an open term to be filled by the gap fillers provided by the UCC.

Last shot rule. A rule at common law applicable where the process of negotiation takes place through correspondence. If the final communication in the series of correspondence contains new or different terms, and following receipt, the recipient renders performance without objecting to them, he is taken to have agreed to them.

Legal detriment. *See* Detriment.

Legal fiction. A factual assumption, deemed to be true in law, even though the "fact" is not established by evidence to be true, or, in some cases, is even contrary to the actual facts. Legal fictions are used to effectuate a public policy. For example, a thief steals $1,000, which he deposits in a bank account that contains $500 of his own money. He then withdraws $400 with which he buys lottery tickets. If his lottery tickets win no prize, the law assumes that he withdrew his own money, permitting the victim to recover the full amount of the stolen funds from the account. However, if he wins the lottery, the law assumes that he used the stolen funds to buy the ticket so that the victim can recover the prize as the fruits of the stolen money.

Legal realism. A philosophy of law that rejects the concept of law as a set of certain, neutral legal rules, and views it in a multidisciplinary context, in which legal doctrine is part of a larger process of decisionmaking and policymaking. The Realist school moved away from the formalism of Legal Positivism, to examine not only the rules of law, but also the operation of legal rules in the broader context of the legal process, society, and social policy.

Levy. *See* Execution.

Liquidated. A debt is liquidated when its monetary value is certain and fixed. In the context of damages for breach of contract, damages normally become liquidated once the breach has occurred and the damages can be calculated by arithmetical means. If the determination of damages cannot be made purely by arithmetical calculation (for example, because issues such as uncertainty, foreseeability, and mitigation have to be resolved), the damages only become liquidated once the factfinder has assessed them. At the time of contracting, the parties may wish to avoid disputes and uncertainty over damages if a breach should occur in the future, and they may therefore include a term in the contract itself that seeks to fix in advance the amount of damages to be paid if a breach occurs. Such a provision has the effect of liquidating anticipated damages in the event of a possible breach, and is known as a **"liquidated damages"** or **"agreed damages"** clause. It is enforceable provided that it was fairly bargained, was a genuine attempt to forecast probable loss, and is not disproportionate to the actual loss ultimately suffered. If it fails to meet these standards, it is treated as a penalty and is unenforceable. *See also* Penalty.

Lost volume. If a seller of goods or services has the capacity to supply the full demand for those goods or services, a breach by one buyer is not substituted for by a subsequent sale of the goods or services to another customer who would have bought the goods or services in any event. The breach has caused a loss in the volume of the plaintiff's sales and can only be compensated for by an award of lost profits.

Mailbox rule. (Also known as **"deposited acceptance rule."**) Where an offer expressly or impliedly authorizes acceptance through the mail or another non-instantaneous means of communication, the acceptance takes effect as soon as it is properly dispatched by the offeree.

Manifested intent. The apparent state of mind of a party, as demonstrated by her observable conduct or spoken or written words. *See also* Objective.

Material benefit rule. A doctrine that permits enforcement of a promise without present consideration where the promise is made in recognition of a benefit previously conferred on the promisor by the promisee, and enforcement is needed to prevent injustice. Because this doctrine is grounded in the idea that the promisor is morally obliged to honor a promise to pay for the prior benefit, it is sometimes called **"moral obligation."** This is an ambiguous term, and can easily be confused with the different usage of "moral obligation," which means simply that the obligation in question is binding only in conscience and is not capable of being legally enforced.

Materiality/material term/material breach. A term of a contract is material if it is an important component of the contract, so central to the values exchanged that it is a fundamental basis of the bargain between the parties. A material breach is a violation of a party's obligations under the contract, so serious that it defeats the other party's reasonable expectations under the contract by substantially depriving her of the value of the transaction. Materiality cannot be decided in the abstract, but must be determined by interpreting the contract.

Merchantable. Goods are merchantable if they meet minimum acceptable trade standards, and would be regarded as of adequate quality by a reasonable member of the trade.

Merger clause. A provision in a written agreement declaring that the writing contains all the terms agreed upon by the parties, and that no terms, other than those expressed in the writing have been agreed to. Such a provision is called a "merger clause" because its purpose is to "merge" all the agreed terms into the writing, so that the writing becomes the full and complete record of what was agreed, and neither party can later allege that terms exist beyond those expressed in the writing.

Mirror image rule. (Also known as **"ribbon matching rule."**) A rule that requires an acceptance to match the offer exactly, with no alteration or qualification. If the acceptance deviates from the offer in any way (or, in some courts, in a material way) it does not qualify as an acceptance, but is a rejection and possibly a counteroffer.

Misrepresentation. An assertion not in accordance with the truth. If the misrepresentation is made with **scienter** — knowledge of its falsity and intent to mislead, it is **fraudulent.** If it is made without scienter, it may be either **negligent** (the party making it would have known of its falsity had she taken reasonable care in ascertaining the truth) or **innocent** (the party did not breach a duty of care by failing to ascertain the truth).

Mistake. An error concerning a fact (including a rule of law) existing at the time of contracting. If the mistake is a common, shared assumption of the parties it is **mutual**, but if the error concerns a fact for which only one of the parties is responsible, it is **unilateral.**

Mitigation of damages. The avoidance or reduction of loss following a breach of contract.

Moral obligation. *See* Material benefit rule.

Mutual mistake. *See* Mistake.

Mutuality of obligation. When consideration consists of the exchange of promises, the commitment on both sides must be real and meaningful. If the apparent promise of one of the parties is illusory — so qualified or discretionary as to be no commitment at all — that party's apparent promise does not bind him. Because only the other is bound, the transaction lacks mutuality of obligation. This is just another way of saying that the person who made the illusory promise has given no consideration, and no valid contract was formed.

Noscitur a sociis. (Latin: "known from its associates.") A rule of interpretation under which the meaning of each individual word in a series is affected by and affects the meaning of the other words in that series.

Novation. A contract under which an existing contractual duty is discharged and a completely new one is substituted. The new contract may add a party who was not a party to the original contract.

Objective. Something is objective if it is presented to the consciousness, rather than **subjective** — within the consciousness itself. That is, it is external to the mind rather than within it. In contract law, the word is most commonly applied to describe the legal standard for gauging the state of mind — the intent or understanding — of a party. Therefore, the **objective test** of intent is concerned, not with the party's subjective state of mind — what that party actually thinks or believes, but with what the observable, external evidence of her words or conduct indicate her intention to be. In interpreting the manifest and external **objective evidence** of intent, the law does not attempt to enter the mind of the observer, to take his **subjective evidence** of what he actually understood the intention to be, but **evaluates it objectively** by asking what a reasonable person in the position of the observer would understand it to be. *See also* Reasonableness standard; Subjective standard.

Objective value. *See* Subjective value.

Obligor/obligee. An obligor is one who owes an obligation or debt, and an obligee is one to whom it is owed.

Officious intermeddler. In the context of unjust enrichment, a person who imposes an unsolicited benefit on another in the absence of emergency circumstances that would have justified the conferral of an unrequested benefit.

Option. A promise, legally binding on the offeror, to keep an offer open for a period of time. A valid option eliminates the offeror's usual power to disregard her commitment to keep the offer open and to revoke it at any time before it is accepted.

Output contract. *See* Requirements and output contracts.

Overhead. *See* Fixed costs.

Pacta sunt servanda. (Latin: "agreements must be kept.") This phrase asserts the moral imperative that the law should enforce contractual promises.

Parol evidence. Evidence of alleged terms not included in the written record of agreement, but claimed by one of the parties to have been agreed to orally before or at the time of execution of the written contract, or in a prior writing.

Partial breach. A breach that is not, or has not yet become significant enough to qualify as a total and material breach. A party who has substantially performed commits a partial breach, but even where performance is not substantial and the breach is potentially material, it remains a partial breach as long as there is a prospect that the breach will be cured.

Penalty. A provision in a contract that is designed to impose, or has the effect of imposing, a burden or punishment on a party for breaching, beyond any actual or expected loss that may be suffered by the victim of the breach.

Positivism. A legal philosophy that stresses the primacy of legal rules and considers the courts' principal role as the application of settled rules to the facts of individual cases.

Precedent. *See* Stare decisis.

Pre-existing duty rule. A rule of consideration doctrine that a the performance of or promise to perform an existing duty cannot qualify as consideration. Consideration consists of an exchange of legal detriments—each party must relinquish a legal right in exchange for the promise or performance received from the other. Therefore if a party already has a legal duty to do or refrain from doing something, his promise to do or refrain from that very act is no relinquishment of a right and cannot be a detriment.

Primary authority. *See* Secondary authority.

Promise. An undertaking to act or refrain from acting in a specified way at some future time.

Promisor/promisee. A promisor is one who makes a promise, and a promisee is one to whom a promise is made. In a bilateral contract, each party is both a promisor of the performance she has promised to the other party, and a promisee of the return performance promised to her by the other party. When consideration is in issue, the person whose promise is sought to be enforced (and whose consideration is not in doubt) is referred to as the promisor, and the promisee is the party whose consideration is in question. In the context of a contract for the benefit of a third party, the promisor is the party who is to perform in favor of the beneficiary, and the promisee is the other party to the contract who has called for the performance to be rendered to the beneficiary.

Promissory condition. *See* Condition.

Promissory estoppel. A doctrine, derived from equitable estoppel, under which a court has the discretion to enforce a non-contractual promise made with the intention of inducing reliance, and justifiably relied on by the promisee to her detriment. Depending on the needs of justice, The promise may be enforced fully, or only to the extent necessary to reimburse wasted costs and expenses.

Prospective non-performance. Words or conduct by a party prior to the due date of performance, or other circumstances arising before that due date, suggesting the likelihood or possibility of breach when the time for performance arrives. Although the signs of possible future breach are not clear and strong enough to be a repudiation, they may suggest the prospect of material breach, and may give the other party reasonable grounds for feeling insecure about receiving the promised performance. If such insecurity is justified, the insecure party may demand an **adequate assurance of performance**, and if none is given, may treat the failure to furnish adequate assurance as a repudiation.

Punitive or exemplary damages. Damages awarded, not to compensate the plaintiff for established loss, but to punish the defendant and to make an example of him.

Quantum meruit/quantum valebant. Quantum meruit (Latin: "as much as deserved") is the term used to denote the market value of services. **Quantum valebant** ("as much as they are worth") signifies the market value of goods. Market value is the common means of measuring the value of goods or services either in restitutionary claims or where a contract is based on a reasonable, rather than a specified price.

Quasi. A Latin word meaning "as if." This word, when used to qualify another (such as "quasi-contract") signifies that a legal fiction is being used. Although the doctrine or fact so qualified is not the same as that represented by the qualified word, it is deemed in law to be treated the same for some purposes. (For example, although a quasi-contract is not the same as an actual contract, it is treated like a contract for some purposes.)

Quasi-contract (quasi ex contractu). *See* Implied in law contract.

Realism. *See* Legal realism.

Reasonable expectations. A party's expectations about the performance and benefit of a contract, evaluated not on the basis of what the party claims to have actually expected, but on the basis of what she should have expected as a reasonable person. *See also* Reasonableness standard.

Reasonableness standard. A widely used standard of contract law, under which a party is held accountable for the reasonable import of her words and actions. The meaning of a party's words, or her intention, understanding, or conduct is evaluated on the basis of what a reasonable person in her position would have meant, understood or done. The **reasonable person** is a hypothetical construct, based on a community standard, typically represented by the jury. *See also* Objective.

Reliance damages. Reliance damages are those costs and expenses incurred in reliance on the contract (or, in promissory estoppel, in reliance on the promise), and wasted once the contract (or promise) is breached. If the cost or expense is incurred in performing duties required by the contract, it is **direct or essential reliance.** If the cost or expense is incurred for the purpose of enjoying or using a benefit reasonably expected from the contract, it is **incidental reliance.**

Repudiation. *See* Anticipatory repudiation.

Requirements and output contracts. A **requirements contract** is one in which the quantity of goods to be supplied is left flexible, and will be based on the buyer's requirements for the goods during the contract period. That is, the buyer agrees to buy all its requirements for the goods from the seller during the term of the contract, and the seller agrees to supply whatever the buyer orders. The buyer's discretion to fix quantities may be limited by a stated range of demand, or if not, by an obligation to act reasonably and in good faith. An **output contract** is similar, but the flexible quantity is based on the seller's production rather than the buyer's requirements. That is, the seller agrees to sell and the buyer agrees to buy the seller's entire output of the goods during the contract period. Again, the seller's discretion to fix production levels may be limited by a stated range, or by an obligation to act reasonably and in good faith.

Rescission. Broadly speaking, rescission is the cancellation of a contract. In its narrowest meaning, the word is confined to the cancellation of a contract by mutual consent. However, it may also be found in reference to the nullification of a contract (that is, avoidance) on grounds such as fraud or mistake. In its broadest usage, "rescission" could be meant as a synonym for "termination" where the victim of a material and total breach ends the contractual relationship, withholds further performance, and sues for damages.

Restitution. A judicial remedy under which the court grants judgment for the restoration of property (**specific restitution**) or its value (**monetary restitution**) to a party from whom the property was unjustly taken or has been unjustly retained.

Ribbon matching rule. *See* Mirror image rule.

Scienter. A central element of fraud, consisting of knowledge of the falsity of an assertion combined with an intent to mislead.

Seal. A wax impression or other insignia placed on paper by a person for the purpose of authenticating the document. In earlier law, a contract executed under seal did not require consideration, but this formal means of dispensing with the need for consideration has fallen away in most jurisdictions.

Secondary authority. A law review, textbook, or other scholarly commentary on the law that is not a binding source of law, but that may be persuasive to a court. Secondary authority is distinguished from **primary authority**, such as a statute or binding judicial precedent, which must be followed by a court.

Security interest. In interest in property (such as a mortgage), granted by a debtor to a creditor to secure payment of the debt. If the debtor defaults in payment, the creditor is entitled to foreclose on the property and sell it to satisfy the debt.

Security of transactions. The concept that the enforcement of individual contracts — and hence the protection of reliance in individual transactions — creates a broad sense of reliance throughout the economy, which facilitates market activity by promoting general confidence in the reliability of contractual undertakings.

Sheriff. *See* Execution.

Signature. Any mark or symbol executed or adopted by a party with the intention of authenticating a writing.

Special damages. In contract, special damages are consequential losses that derive from the plaintiff's special circumstances. Because they would not flow as an obvious and natural consequence of the breach, the defendant cannot reasonably foresee them at the time of contracting, and is therefore not liable for them, unless he is informed of the special circumstances at the time of contracting.

Specific performance. An order by the court directing the defendant to render the contractual performance as promised. Specific performance is an equitable remedy, and is the exception rather than the rule, available only where damages are not an adequate remedy.

Stare decisis. (Latin: "The decision stands.") The doctrine of precedent, under which a later court is bound by the earlier decisions of a court of equal or senior rank in the same judicial hierarchy.

Subjective standard. A test of intent based on what the parties actually understood, rather than on their objectively demonstrated intent — what their words or conduct reasonably indicate their intent to have been. The subjective standard is not used as a general test of intent, which has long been gauged objectively. However, the subjective standard is applied in discrete areas of contract law when a party's good faith is in issue, or her state of mind is otherwise relevant to the resolution of the case. *See also* Objective.

Subjective value. The value of property or services to the recipient personally, as opposed to **objective value**, which is measured by market worth.

Substantial performance. A performance under a contract that, while not fully in compliance with the contract (and therefore a breach), is nevertheless deficient in only a trivial way. Because the breach is not material, the plaintiff may not use it as a ground for rescinding the contract, but is confined to claiming monetary compensation for the shortfall in performance.

Take-or-pay provision. A term in a contract under which the buyer of goods or services commits himself to take a specified minimum quantity, and promises to pay for that minimum quantity whether or not he actually orders it.

Tender. An offer of payment or performance by a party who is ready, willing, and able to render it.

Termination of contract. Where a contract has been materially and totally breached, the victim of the breach may terminate the contract, bringing the relationship to an end for purposes of any outstanding future performance, and sue for damages for breach. Although "termination" may also be used to denote the end of a contract under other circumstances (such as by agreement between the parties, or following mistake, fraud, or other grounds of avoidance), the word "rescission" is more commonly used in that context.

Third-party beneficiary. A person who is not a party to a contract, but upon whom the parties intend to confer the benefit of performance together with an independent right to enforce that performance. A party on whom this independent right of enforcement is conferred is called an **intended beneficiary.** If a stranger to the contract fortuitously acquires an incidental benefit from the contract, without any intent of the parties to confer an enforcement right on him, he is merely an **incidental beneficiary** and has no right to sue on the contract.

"Time is of the essence." A boilerplate phrase that means that performance within the time specified is a material term of the contract, and that any delay will be a total and material breach of contract.

Total breach. A breach of contract that is both material and incurable, entitling the victim to rescind the contract and claim full expectation relief.

Trade usage. *See* Usage.

Transaction costs. The costs incurred in entering a transaction, which must be taken into account in determining if the transaction is economically efficient. When a contract has been breached, the transaction costs resulting from the breach include expenses such as the plaintiff's costs in finding a substitute, the breacher's costs in entering the other transaction perceived as more desirable, and the costs to both parties in negotiating a settlement of the plaintiff's claim or in litigating it. To decide if the breach is efficient, these costs must be deducted from the potential gains flowing from the breach.

Unconscionable. A concept, derived from equity, under which a court may use its discretion to refuse enforcement of a term or contract that shocks its conscience. In its modern formulation, unconscionability normally consists of both a **procedural** element (unfair bargaining) and a **substantive** element (resulting unfair terms).

Unfair forfeiture. A general principle of justice under which the court has the discretion to temper the enforcement of the injured party's legal rights to avoid a disproportionately harsh impact on the party against whom enforcement is sought.

Unforeseeable/unforeseen. *See* Foreseen/foreseeable.

Unilateral contract. A unilateral contract is one in which only one of the parties has a promise outstanding at the time that the contract is formed. It is distinct from a **bilateral contract**, in which there are promises due by both parties at the instant of formation. There can be no such thing as a "unilateral" contract as that word may be understood in a lay sense — a person cannot contract with himself, and a one-sided promise to another person does not qualify as a contract because it lacks consideration. In contract law "unilateral contract" is a term of art, used to describe a situation in which an offer prescribes that the only way it may be accepted is by the offeree rendering the very performance that will constitute the offeree's consideration under the contract. In this way, the act of signifying acceptance is at the same time the act of performance. The effect of this is that at the instance of acceptance, the offeree has completed the performance of his side of the transaction, and the only thing remaining is the offeror's promise of return performance. For example, an offeror offers to sell her car to the offeree for $5,000, and specifies that the offer may be accepted only by the offeree handing $5,000 in cash to the offeror. The payment is both the act of acceptance and the offeree's performance under the contract, so upon acceptance, the offeree has fully performed and the only thing remaining to be done under the contract is the performance of the offeror's promise to deliver the car. *See also* Bilateral contract.

Unilateral mistake. *See* Mistake.

Usage. The customs and established practices in a particular trade, industry, or market.

Ut res magis valeat quam pereat. (Latin: "The thing should rather have effect than be destroyed.") A rule of interpretation under which a court resolves uncertainty in favor of a meaning that is lawful, reasonable, and congruent with public policy.

Variable costs. *See* Fixed costs.

Vesting. The irrevocable settling of rights on a person.

Volunteer. In the context of unjust enrichment, a person who confers a benefit with gratuitous intent.

Waiver. A voluntary abandonment of a legal right.

Windfall. An unexpected and undeserved benefit. In the context of damages, an amount that exceeds what the plaintiff needs to be fully compensated for her loss.

Writ. A written order by a court, requiring or authorizing an act to be performed. A writ of execution or garnishment is an order to the sheriff or equivalent official, requiring her to seize property of the judgment debtor. (*See also* Execution.) In older common law, "writ" was also used to denote the document that commenced an action.

Index

Index